FROM
PEOPLE'S
WAR
TO
PEOPLE'S
RULE

Insurgency,
Intervention,
and the
Lessons
of Vietnam

FROM PEOPLE'S WAI

Insurgency,
Intervention,
and the
Lessons of
Vietnam

The

University

of North

Carolina

Press

Chapel Hill

and

London

PEOPLE'S RULE

TIMOTHY J. LOMPERIS

The paper in this book meets the guidelines for
permanence and durability of the Committee on
Production Guidelines for Book Longevity of the
Council on Library Resources.

Library of Congress Cataloging-in-Publication Data
Lomperis, Timothy J., 1947–
    From people's war to people's rule: insurgency,
intervention, and the lessons of Vietnam / Timothy J.
Lomperis.
    p.   cm.
    Includes bibliographical references and index.
    ISBN 0-8078-2273-6 (cloth: alk. paper).—
    ISBN 0-8078-4577-9 (pbk.: alk. paper)
    1. Vietnamese Conflict, 1961–1975—United States.
2. Vietnam—History—1945–1975.   3. Asia, Southeastern—
Politics and government—1945-   4. Insurgency—Asia,
Southeastern.   5. United States—Foreign relations, 1963–
1969.   I. Title.
DS558.L64   1996
959.704'3373—dc20   95-36667
                    CIP

00   99   98   97   96   5   4   3   2   1

Publication of this book was supported by
generous grants from the Earhart Foundation
and the John M. Olin Foundation, Inc.

To

Ana Maria

for her steadfast faith and abundant love

and to

Kristi and John Scott

for their therapeutic cheerfulness

CONTENTS

Preface, xi

Part I. Theory and Context
Introduction. From Ghost to Lesson, 3
1 On the Business of Lessons, 9
2 Legitimacy, Insurgency, and the International Context
of the Vietnam War, 30
3 Analytical Framework of Legitimacy, Insurgency, and Intervention, 49

Part II. Vietnam, the Deviant Case
4 Historical Setting: The Earthly Struggle for Heaven's Mandate, 85
5 Framework Analysis: The War without a Lesson?, 111

Part III. The Comparative Prism
6 China, 1920–1949: The Long March to Liberation, 133
7 Greece, 1941–1949: Three Rounds to Albania, 152
8 The Philippines, 1946–1956: Liberation Deflected, 173
9 Malaya, 1948–1960: The Unmaking of an Insurgency, 198
10 Cambodia's "Autogenocide" and the Disappearance of Laos,
1949–1975, 222

Part IV. Lessons
11 Findings from the Prism and an Application:
Sendero Luminoso of Peru, 265
Conclusion. The New Era: Wilson's Triumph over Lenin, 314

Appendix 1. Literatures of the Framework, 323
Appendix 2. A Tale of Two Strategies: An Alternative Explanation, 329
Appendix 3. Assumptions, Thematic Questions, and Propositions, 347

Notes, 351
Index, 415

TABLES AND FIGURES

Tables

1.1. Insurgencies and Intervention, 12

3.1. Domestic Legitimacy, 56

11.1. Comparative Legitimacy, 275

11.2. Comparative Intervention, 276

11.3. Alternative Explanation: Leadership/Strategy (L/S), 285

11.4. Candidate Lessons, 310

Figures

1.1. Balance of Intervention in Vietnam I: Franco-Viet Minh War, 1946–1954, 17

1.2. Balance of Intervention in Vietnam II: American Phase, 1960–1975, 18

1.3. Balance of Intervention in China, 1927–1949, 19

1.4. Balance of Intervention in Greece, 1941–1949, 20

1.5. Balance of Intervention in the Philippines, 1946–1956, 21

1.6. Balance of Intervention in Malaya, 1948–1960, 22

1.7. Balance of Intervention in Cambodia, 1970–1975, 23

1.8. Balance of Intervention in Laos, 1955–1975, 24

3.1. Transition from Traditional to Modern Society, 55

3.2. External Legitimacy Effects, 72

3.3. Insurgency: Exogenous and Independent Variables, 75

11.1. Benchmarks of Insurgent Success: Vietnam I, 267

11.2. Benchmarks of Insurgent Success: Vietnam II, 268

11.3. Benchmarks of Insurgent Success: China, 269

11.4. Benchmarks of Insurgent Success: Greece, 270

11.5. Benchmarks of Insurgent Success: Philippines, 271

11.6. Benchmarks of Insurgent Success: Malaya, 272

11.7. Benchmarks of Insurgent Success: Cambodia, 273

11.8. Benchmarks of Insurgent Success: Laos, 274

11.9. Benchmarks of Insurgent Success: Prognosis on Peru, 305

This book is inspired by the fact that the Vietnam War is not a good source for the lessons of Vietnam. Indeed, whenever it is placed in a group for comparison, it is always the different one, the one that doesn't fit. It was a conventional war like Korea at times, but it was more often a guerrilla war. Although it was a guerrilla war like Malaya or Greece, it was the conventional war that carried the day for the communist guerrillas. Vietnam is a hard war to define. Taken from a group to stand by itself, its legs go rubbery. Was it a single war whose single society was convulsed by revolution, or was it two wars involving two states in which one state was caught up in a guerrilla war within its boundaries while it was simultaneously the victim of "aggression" from the other? Beyond troubling boundaries, people and ideas within them are hard to separate. In Vietnam, nationalists could also be communists and vice versa. One of South Vietnam's presidents, the Roman Catholic Ngo Dinh Diem, was also called the "last Confucian." Though every war is complicated, few can lay claim to so much confusion. For that reason, lessons can be found for Vietnam only if they come from somewhere else.

In this "elsewhere" quest, this book is a blend of theory, policy, and history. Theoretically, the usual way to account for something like Vietnam is to propose two or three candidates for explaining the war and, through a book's many pages, conduct an intellectual shoot-out to declare one of them the winner in the conclusion's explanatory power awards ceremony. This book does not do that. Rather, it takes a fundamental belief about the war — that the Vietnam War was centrally a crisis in political legitimacy — and sees how far such a single explanation carries through a typology of eight cases. Hence, through a comparison of cases, it is a test of a single paradigmatic presupposition by means of a special analytical framework. As such an explanation, legitimacy works well for five of them but not so well for the remaining three.

Indeed, it works the poorest for the Vietnam War. This has prompted an appendix that provides an alternative explanation, one based on strategy. However neatly this appendix charts the strategic twists and turns of the Vietnam War to a communist victory, as an explanation it is surprised by an ambush. That is, as a demonstration of the efficacy of the revolutionary strategy of people's war, the communists, for purposes of explanation, helpfully followed this strategy to their defeat in the Tet offensive but then muddied this explanation by abandoning people's war and opportunistically seizing on an American conventional war strategy to gain their victory. As a people's war, then, the communist victory was a fraud. This strategic "resolution" creates a philosophic impasse. For some, a victory is a victory, however it is achieved. For others, more concerned about the conformity of ends to means, a victory can be claimed only if there is such a relationship. Thus the effect of this strategic explanation is only to revisit the murkiness of the war itself.

Any single explanation carries the risk of becoming a tautology. This book avoids that problem by differentiating the concept of legitimacy into three levels of intensifying commitment: legitimacy of interest, legitimacy of opportunity, and legitimacy of belief. An analytical framework based on these levels of legitimation is employed comparatively to diagnose the achievements of the two sides to an insurgency in their competitive struggle for the prize of legitimacy. There are some challenges to the use of this framework. First, the levels have an apples-and-oranges quality. Interest and opportunity levels of legitimacy can be defined deductively according to ready-made concepts of individual response (interest level) and group interactions (opportunity level). But beliefs about political legitimacy can be defined only by inductive historical discovery. This, second, imposes the responsibility of tracing the historical context in which these definitions emerged. They emerged in two intertwining strands: a general one of systemic transferral whereby European states (both democratic and Marxist) bequeathed their standards of legitimate governance to the developing societies of the Third World under the rubric of nation-building or revolutionary transformation, and a specific one whereby this traditional to modern transition was defined in terms of the historical set of political principles unique to individual societies. Indeed, it is my thesis that insurgencies in the Third World arose out of the stresses of these definitional transitions. Finally, there is the limitation for some scholars that this is macro-theory. That is, in treating legitimacy as a general, countrywide phenomenon, the opportunity for fine-grained micro-theory is lost.

Indeed, in a personal letter to the author, Chalmers Johnson, a prominent scholar on revolution, warned against basing a study of insurgency on legitimacy because the concept is too "intellectually traumatic." He also conceded that it is too important to ignore. Despite this warning, for theory, the focus of this book is on legitimacy, and on showing that even such a traumatic concept can be rendered analytically useful.

Policymakers, in reading books like this, will be looking for lessons. This work cannot provide a set of general lessons on insurgency and intervention because it is based on a specific set of cases, defined by their own limiting and group-selecting conditions. Nor can it predict the future of either an insurgency or an intervention. For these phenomena, leadership as a variable (whether brilliant, dull, or mercurial) is still too much of a rogue elephant for analytical control and prediction. In further recognition of this, each case has a section on contingencies in which asymmetries, errors, and reversibilities are surfaced to show that the results of each case might have been different. For lessons, then, the particular history of a case contains no general certainty.

What this book does offer is an analytical framework that permits the very general phenomenon of legitimacy to be differentiated so that the relative achievements of two competing claimants can be assessed. Further, through the "benchmarks of insurgent success," progress, both positive and negative, can be charted. Finally, a set of concepts is introduced that at least allows leadership to be categorized for comparative purposes, to wit, the illegitimacy lock, Bonapartism, Hannibalism, and bridge leadership. These three contributions of differentiations, benchmarks, and concepts do offer general diagnostic tools for assessing the efficacy of an intervention in an insurgency. In fact, an analysis of the ongoing Maoist insurgency in Peru is included in Chapter 11 to illustrate these diagnostic capabilities for at least qualified prediction. For policy, then, the focus of this book is on intervention, and how an intervention's success will be critically affected by its impact on the legitimacy struggle within the target society.

There is a lot of history in this book, at least for one written by a political scientist. The role of history here is to remind social scientists that most of their key concepts have been developed from the rich histories that went into their conceptualizations. Sovereignty, for example, owes its conceptualization to the histories that built both to the Treaty of Westphalia (1648) and to the French Revolution. What is lost too often in the models deductively abstracted from empirical phenomena and events is the historical context from which they should never be separated. For history, then, the focus of this book is on the definitional context out of which individual definitions of legitimacy arose.

This book has taken a long time, and throughout its preparation I was nurtured by warm personal support. Neil Sheehan took so long to write his *A Bright Shining Lie* (1988) that the two small daughters to whom he dedicated his book had grown up and left home by the time he finished. This book, fortunately, took only half the time, and our toddlers at the start are now only beginning their teens. They are still with us, and they can have something of their father back. During the work, the good cheer of Kristi and John Scott was a therapeutic tonic.

I dedicate this book to Ana Maria, my wife, because it could not have happened without her. Her love for me and faith in this project sustained me. Two disruptive moves for fellowships made this book, even as it nearly unmade her own career. Constant conversations, difficult editing, and being a sounding board for ideas, designs, and agonies are just a few of the many ways she was essential to this book's finishing. I cannot thank her enough.

My parents, Clarence and Marjorie Lomperis, also encouraged me throughout the project. As lifelong missionaries to India, they read many of the chapters and insisted that my Asian history be thoroughly grounded. As the earliest and most enduring of my teachers, they joined my wife in resuscitating my syntax.

I also received invaluable professional help. Four mentors in particular helped shape whatever scholarly virtue there is to this work. As my prize-winning dissertation director, Ole Holsti, at Duke University, first started me on my life of research and has been a constant advocate, supporter, and friend during the years of this project. Samuel Huntington added his voice of support when I was awarded a postdoctoral fellowship at Harvard's Center for International Affairs in 1985–86. His continued belief in this work has been important to my confidence in it. An unexpected bonus to this Harvard year was the friendships I made with two other "fellows," Doug Macdonald (now at Colgate) and Jim Wirtz (at the Naval Postgraduate School). My book completes what the three of us call the Huntington Trilogy on American Intervention in Asia, namely, *The Tet Offensive* (1991) by Jim and *Adventures in Chaos* (1992) by Doug. Back home at Duke, Allan Kornberg, as my department chairman, has been the ardent champion of my career and firm taskmaster in helping me revise the theoretical portions of the book. While in Cambridge, I also met Lucian Pye. As fellow missionary kids, we talked much, to my great profit, on the pitfalls and presciences that expatriate observers bring to the Asian scene. And we talked of the human dimensions to our respective guerrilla wars. Finally, though not a personal mentor, James C. Scott of Yale University gave generous amounts of his time to read early drafts of this work and to support this project through to its publication.

I would be remiss if I did not also acknowledge the valuable improvements I was able to make in response to sharp reactions from more critical readers. The most useful were my Duke colleagues Bob Bates, Peter Lange, and Don Horowitz. Among these colleagues Meg McKean is in a special category. An initial critic, my working her comprehensive comments into the work gradually earned her endorsement. I appreciated the time they all gave because I was the beneficiary of their headaches.

In addition to this general help, I wish to acknowledge the help I received from several people for specific parts of the manuscript. For the theoretical part, I am grateful for the reactions I collected from three presentations of it: before the International Political Economy Workshop at Duke, the Olin Security Seminar at Harvard, and a panel at the meeting of the American

Political Science Association in Atlanta in 1989. Richard Betts of Columbia helped sharpen many of my definitions in my presentation of Chapter 2 at a colloquium at the Wilson Center. The reactions of Allan Goodman at Georgetown and George Herring at Kentucky to my Vietnam chapters, as always, were invaluable. Finally, my comparative cases were substantially improved by the following: Steve Levine on China, Doug Macdonald and Jim Wirtz on Greece, Benedict Anderson on the Philippines, Lucian Pye and Don Horowitz on Malaya, and Joseph Zasloff on Laos and Cambodia.

This book also benefited mightily from some high-stepping legwork by wonderful people. There are a lot of footnotes on these pages, and many of them come from the tireless work of research assistants: Elizabeth Rogers, Stanley Ridgely, David Strom, and Tracy Haley from Duke as well as Jan Liam Wasley while I was at the Wilson Center. Johanna Scherrer, the head reference librarian at Duke, also deserves special recognition. There are also a lot of printed words here. Susan Emery, the chief administrative assistant in the political science department, supervised and organized the generous clerical support I received. It was Carla St. John, my secretary, however, who delivered this product. She "processed" the whole manuscript at least twice, rescued me from all manners of chaos, and cheerfully saw this project through to the finish. For all this from all these people, I can only say thank you.

Parts of this book are derived from previous publications of mine. The cooperation of these publishers in letting this material appear in this book has been a great help, and I wish to express my thanks. Parts of the introduction and conclusion are based on the prologue and epilogue to the revised edition of *The War Everyone Lost—and Won* (Washington, D.C.: Congressional Quarterly Press, 1993). Chapter 4 is a compression of Part One of the original *The War Everyone Lost—and Won* (Baton Rouge: Louisiana State University Press, 1984). The core of the much-expanded theoretical framework of Chapter 3 was published as "Vietnam's Offspring: The Lesson of Legitimacy" in the Winter 1986 issue of *Conflict Quarterly*. Similarly, the appendix on strategy is an expansion of an article, "Giap's Dream; Westmoreland's Nightmare," that appeared in the Summer 1988 issue of *Parameters*.

Books cost money, both to write and to produce. The help I have received to write this one has been generous. The Earhart Foundation provided me a handsome fellowship to supplement my fellowship at Harvard. Along the way, I received further supplemental help from Duke as well as a summer fellowship from the University Research Council. The Olin Postdoctoral fellowship I received at Harvard in 1985–86 was instrumental in giving me a year off to get this project started. When the Woodrow Wilson Center for International Scholars of the Smithsonian Institution made me one of its fellows in 1988–89, I not only had a wonderful experience in a true community of scholars, but I also finally began writing the book. This work continued at a feverish pace when I was a visiting scholar in the spring of 1989 at the Sino-Soviet Institute of George Washington University. For all this facilitation, I am deeply grateful.

To get to the main point, what I am most grateful for is the publication of this book by the University of North Carolina Press. I thank director Kate Douglas Torrey for being officially responsible: she signed my contract. The credit for bringing this book to press, however, belongs to Lewis Bateman, the executive editor. We first met at an academic conference in 1989, and, to my surprise and pleasure, he has been interested in this work ever since. When he finally received the completed manuscript in the fall of 1994, he handled it with a care and dispatch that have earned my undying gratitude. The ringing endorsements from the two anonymous reviewers have, in themselves, made the whole endeavor worthwhile. For managing this project to completion, I would be remiss not to acknowledge the tactful prodding of Pamela Upton. Not to be forgotten, of course, is the diligent forbearance of Trudie Calvert, my copyeditor, who polished my prose to a finesse utterly beyond my reach.

Though perhaps I am entitled to some remaining credit for surviving, everyone listed above must share the blame for letting this happen. I, at least, am grateful and will, in turn, accept the blame for any errors surviving their scrutiny.

PART I
Theory and
Context

Introduction

FROM GHOST TO LESSON

On the morning of April 30, 1975, three North Vietnamese tanks slammed through the gates of Saigon's Presidential Palace. The exultant troopers hoisted Hanoi's flag atop the courtyard flagpole. Hours earlier, in the predawn darkness, "Huey" helicopters plucked the final line of Americans from the rooftop of the U.S. Embassy in Operation Frequent Wind. Viewing newsclips of these jarring last images of the Vietnam War, President Gerald Ford remarked to an aide, "It's over. Let's put it behind us."[1]

Whatever else Americans have done with Vietnam, they have certainly not put it behind them. It is the living ghost that haunts them whenever the prospect looms for an American intervention in a "remote" Third World conflict. As killings, headlines, and pressures on the United States mount, the inexorable invocation follows: El Salvador, Nicaragua, Honduras, Peru, Afghanistan, Angola, or the Philippines is "another Vietnam." So, America, beware! Indeed, in 1984 former defense secretary Casper Weinberger, in outlining six tests for the commitment of U.S. military force, specifically invoked the lessons of Vietnam to reassure the nation that it would not be "dragged into a quagmire in Central America."[2]

The meaning of this dreaded invocation, nevertheless, remains problematic. As just one example, in taking up the issue in the fall of 1983 as to whether to grant President Ronald Reagan a resolution permitting the continued presence of U.S. Marines in Lebanon, senator after senator invoked the memory of Vietnam to justify opposite votes. Senator Charles Percy (R, Ill.) said he favored such an explicit resolution because he didn't want to "stumble into another Vietnam." Senator Joseph Biden (D, Del.), on the other hand, said he opposed the resolution because he didn't want the current generation "to suffer another Vietnam like my generation did." Further, the fractious congressional disputes over funding for the *contra* rebels in Nicaragua throughout the Reagan presidency were a postwar replay of the Great Vietnam War Debate.

George Bush ascended to the presidency in 1989 vowing, in his inaugural address, to slay the dragon of Vietnam. Though the Persian Gulf War of 1991 was not about Vietnam, it intruded itself everywhere. In the eleventh-hour congressional debate to grant President Bush the authorization to use force against Saddam Hussein, Vietnam was the favorite monster metaphor of the nay-sayers. Indeed, Saddam Hussein himself frequently conjured up apparitions of Vietnam, most graphically of its Stygian river of body bags, to scare away the Americans. When the Americans and their coalition partners entered the mouth of the Gulf anyway and blitzed the Iraqis out of Kuwait with their AirLand battle strategy and Sword Excalibur of technological wizardry, George Bush's exultations were more about Vietnam than Iraq: "By God, we've kicked the Vietnam syndrome once and for all," [3] and "The specter of Vietnam has been buried forever in the desert sands of the Arabian Peninsula." [4] And yet, as American forces pushed north into Iraq to the Euphrates River, Bush ordered a halt. To him, at the banks of these ancient waters, lay a Rubicon River leading to Baghdad—and another Saigon. Plainly, for Americans, pronouncements that the Vietnam War is "over" and "buried forever" do not mean much.

But Vietnam is a better ghost than a lesson. Though haunting as a memory and a metaphor, a ghost is not held down by any definition or bounded by an earthly context. Thus unfettered, it can be summoned for any lesson a conjurer wants. Ronald Reagan remembered Vietnam as a "noble crusade" and summoned it as a lesson to support his efforts to roll back communism in Central America. Antiwar activist Daniel Ellsberg, on the other hand, continues to relive Vietnam as a heinous "crime" and brandishes it as a weapon to slay America's "interventionist impulse." [5]

As a more serviceable lesson, the Vietnam War needs both a definition and a context. This book seeks to do both by providing a definitional perspective from which the war can be viewed, and then building on this perspective a context of similar cases from which the war's lessons can be derived. It involves several steps: the formulation of a pair of research questions that drive the investigation, the articulation of a paradigmatic presupposition about the Vietnam War that spells out a context for comparing it to similar cases, and, finally, the delineation of a conceptual framework for the actual task of comparing Vietnam to these other cases both to test and to temper whatever lessons may emerge from an examination of the single case of Vietnam. Pinned to the ground in this way, the ghost of Vietnam can become a lesson.

The definitional assumption that marks the perspective of this book is that the war in Vietnam reflected a society in the throes of a revolutionary insurgency struggling to form and consolidate an independent and modernizing state. The United States intervened in this struggle to support the incumbent regime in its bid to defeat the insurgents, who, in turn, received ideological and material help from the outside as well. The Vietnam War, then, was *both* an internal and an international war, one of both *insurgency* and *intervention*. Thus the "lessons of Vietnam" lie in answering two fundamental questions. First, what are the ingredients of a successful insurgency (and, conversely, of a successful counterinsurgency)? Second, what is the optimal level of a Western intervention, if any, in thwarting such a revolutionary insurgency? The first is an empirical question, the second a policy one flowing from it. These two agenda-setting questions form the boundaries of this book's perspective on the Vietnam War—and on insurgency and intervention.

As for these boundaries, the phenomenon bounded by these two questions is an insurgency. Answering these questions, then, depends on a theoretical presupposition about a revolutionary insurgency itself. It is my presupposition, then, that insurgencies, as part of a larger process of modernization, are best understood as crises in national political legitimacy and that the struggle between the two sides (the incumbents and the insurgents) is over competitive claims to, and definitions of, this legitimacy. Raising the concept of legitimacy inevitably brings up its companion concepts of power and authority. Indeed, William Connolly has referred to these three together as a "cluster concept." By this he means that power, authority, and legitimacy are discrete phenomena that nevertheless cannot be fully or practically separated from each other. That is, their individual definitions involve aspects of their cluster companions so that operational indicators or pieces of evidence for one concept can never be free of this definitional contamination.[6]

Accepting this ineluctable contamination, for this book, power is rule; authority, the right to rule; and legitimacy, the justification upon which authority is based and rule rendered "rightful." Thus, in Eqbal Ahmad's words, legitimacy is "that crucial and ubiquitous factor in politics which invests power with authority."[7] In a revolutionary insurgency, the incumbents and insurgents unquestionably struggle for power and for the authority to make their rule fully sovereign over their people. It is the peculiar property of an insurgency, however, that the struggle is protracted. Thus both sides are obligated to justify themselves and their cause to the society being subjected to the hardship of this conflict. In other words, their claims must be legitimated, or justified, for both power and authority to be realized and the struggle won. Thus insurgencies are won—or lost—by the relative amounts of legitimacy the two competing sides achieve and by the impact of foreign interventions on these amounts.

One can certainly argue that the Vietnam War (and insurgencies more generally) was centrally something else, but I do not. Different voices have claimed, for example, that the war was primarily a manifestation of the East-West struggle; that it was no more than a police or military problem that got a little out of hand; that the war hinged more on leadership and organization than anything else; or even that at root the war was a struggle over economic issues. Why I am not persuaded by these alternative presuppositions is explained in Chapter 2. If the war, more fundamentally, were any of these "something elses," then, of course, the lessons would be different. Thus understanding this paradigmatic presupposition of the Vietnam War as a crisis of political legitimacy is an absolute prerequisite to following the entire line of reasoning in this book.

As a society caught up in an insurgent struggle between incumbents and insurgents for the mantle of rule, and whose struggle had attracted substantial foreign intervention, Vietnam was not alone. In fact, in the post–World War II period there were six other cases in which societies were caught up in an insurgency similar to that in Vietnam (a Marxist people's war) that also attracted substantial Western intervention in support of the incumbent regimes. Thus this book first probes the Vietnam War for its results and compares them with the results of these other cases through the use of the conceptual framework explained in Chapter 3. Despite the uniqueness of all historical events, such a framework provides a common context for, in the words of the historian Edward H. Carr, discerning "what is general in the unique."[8]

What is interesting about this particular set of cases is that in three of them (Greece, the Philippines, and Malaya) the interventions were successful in beating back the insurgent challenges, and in five (counting Vietnam twice—once against the French and once against the Americans—as well as China, Cambodia, and Laos) they were not. More than just the lessons of Vietnam, then, this book is about the intersection of insurgency and intervention and eight cases in search of a theory about the conditions under which they intersect and what may be learned from the consequences.

The book divides into four parts. Part I sets out the theory and context.

Chapter 1 provides a general overview. Chapter 2 examines the historical development of legitimacy and the international context of the Vietnam conflict. Chapter 3 develops the conceptual framework employed in this study. Next, the two chapters in Part II evaluate the central case of Vietnam within this conceptual framework. Then, each of the five chapters in Part III is devoted to a similar analysis of each of the other cases (though Cambodia and Laos are combined into one chapter). Finally, Part IV sets out the general lessons that emerge from this analysis and discusses their contemporary implications for American foreign policy.

I make three major points. First, by itself, the Vietnam War has no lessons. As a ghost, Vietnam has been treated by policymakers as a crucial case for any decision to intervene in the Third World. Constrained, however, by an analytic definition and a comparative context, the Vietnam War stands as a deviant case, an outlier from the very set of cases used as the comparative prism from which its lessons should be drawn.

Second, lessons *do* emerge when the Vietnam War is passed through the analytic prism of companion cases. Looking at these insurgencies as struggles for national political legitimacy, claiming this legitimacy depends on which side makes good on key reforms that justify political rule for a more inclusive and equitably based polity. Empirically, two emerge as pivotal: land reform and, even more important, free, fair, and competitive elections—the true Achilles' heel of a revolutionary strategy of Marxist people's war and the chief lesson of this study. This is what is general in the unique histories of the eight insurgencies.

The latter's salience is owing to the fact that both people's war by revolutionary insurgency and nation-building by evolutionary democracy are common searches for an Aristotelian middle ground for a political community. Communists call this mobilization; democrats, participation. The difference is that the mobilization of people's war is exclusive in its drive for a monopolistic seizure of power, whereas the full participation called for by modernizing democrats requires compromise and power sharing. If incumbents can steel themselves to the risks of including insurgents in their polity and, specifically, their electoral rolls, elections leave people's war as a strategy either preempted, co-opted, or out in the cold.

Finally, this book concludes with a pronouncement of its own. Following Theda Skocpol's contention that the international environment is one of the major conditioning factors to the success or failure of revolutions,[9] it should be pointed out that the eight cases of this study occurred during an international period of decolonization which favored the success of revolutionary insurgencies. This period, from the end of World War II to the fall of Saigon, I term the Era of People's War. Since then, the international environment has shifted from a drive to seize power to a focus on governance and on managing power once it has been seized. Thus the agenda has switched from people's war to people's rule. The twentieth century's long detour of seduction by Vladimir Lenin's siren revolutionary call has faded, and Woodrow Wilson's steadier voice of democracy, self-determination, and national legitimacy can be heard once more.

Chapter 1

ON THE BUSINESS OF LESSONS

On the business of drawing lessons from historical events such as the Vietnam War, two principles are important. First, historical lessons are properly drawn only by comparing one component of an event to a similar component in another event, not by applying an entire event wholesale.[1] In other words, lessons come not from the outcomes of events themselves but from the components (factors or variables) that made them. With respect to the Vietnam War, this means that its lessons do not derive from the general outcome of victory or defeat but from the war's constitutive components. The blitzkrieg, for example, was not the cause of the German defeat in World War II, nor was people's war the strategy by which the Vietnamese communists came to power in 1975. Second, general lessons can rarely stand on a single case. In politics, lessons like Munich come around even less frequently than Halley's Comet. Thus a candidate lesson from a single historical case can be confirmed only by passing it through an array of comparable but competing cases — a figurative comparative prism — to see if it still holds.[2]

Accordingly, this chapter first presents the historical context out of which revolutionary insurgencies like the Vietnam War emerged. From this context, it explains the two phenomenon-setting criteria from which the eight core cases were chosen — the presence of Western intervention and the use of a Marxist people's war strategy by the insurgents — and defends this latter criterion against other strategies. It then discusses the two major research questions that are drawn from these criteria: what are the ingredients of a successful insurgency and what is the optimal level of intervention, if any, in one, as well as why the nature of their impact on the societal crisis of political legitimacy is central to answering both questions. It concludes with an explanation of the theory used in this book, the driving assumptions about these insurgencies and interventions, and the set of six thematic questions and attendant propositions that bind the eight cases together.

As a legitimacy crisis, the Vietnam War took place in both a general and a specific historical context. The general context emerged from a broad historical march that led to a global crisis after World War II. This crisis provoked the eruption of numerous insurgencies in the Third World (including the eight discussed in this book). In this march, the Vietnam War and its companion cases were part of a larger historical process of at least two centuries in which traditional and "backward" societies, under the shock of Western colonialism, were groping for modern states of their own definition and creation. For most of these countries, the nineteenth century was a period of dramatic change. Politically, the colonial powers regularized and strengthened the institutional hold of their rule. At the same time, the globalization of international trade and the establishment of a Western economic sector in colonial societies brought both economic growth and social dislocation. By the 1930s, continued social ferment and the decline in economic growth produced in all these cases some political impasse, serious social and economic turmoil, or both. During World War II, Axis armies of occupation sheared off the incumbent regimes of conquered countries and replaced them with pliant governments of collaboration. Revolutionary groups that sprouted from this prewar ferment gained unique political opportunities. As a consequence, when peace was restored, each returning regime faced a vastly different political equation: of waxing revolutionary groups poised for a bid for power in the face of a waning colonial order, and, with these changing tides, an imperative for a new basis for the justification of political rule — a new legitimacy.

In this post–World War II period, emerging countries in the rapidly decolonizing Third World launched programs of nation-building under the watchful eyes of the two competing power blocs: the "Socialist Commonwealth" led by the Soviet Union (and, to a lesser extent, China) and the liberal Western democracies led by the United States. Periodically, the communists intervened in these countries to support a revolutionary process of modernization (whether by coup d'état, insurrection, or insurgency) and

Western powers intervened either to preempt or to thwart such revolutionary threats so as to preserve programs of nation-building that might eventually embrace the features of a liberal democratic state. These interventions were part of the external international struggle between the two blocs, whereas the insurgencies themselves posed bottlenecks to the internal development of these modernizing states. This period of competition from 1945 to 1975 that intertwined the global balance of power with internal struggles in the Third World for nation-building and political legitimacy I term the Era of People's War.

The specific historical context was the particular crisis of political legitimacy in each of these societies. This context was the setting from which each society defined the principles upon which competitive claims to legitimacy had to be based. Legitimacy, as a basis upon which political authority is justified, is a general concept embedded in any political structure (in varying degrees), but it is also a particular one whose country-specific definition emerges from historical principles or beliefs unique to each society's political culture and institutional framework. Political legitimacy, then, is a concept of "universal particularism." [3] In social science terms, it is both nominal and essential in nature. That is, it consists of both general descriptive and deductive principles and a set of unique societal precepts drawn from an inductive process of historical discovery elicited from each national context. [4] As for insurgencies, and interventions in them, this means that the question of whether a specific intervention will enhance or debilitate the "client's" legitimacy will depend on the way rule and authority are particularly justified in that country.

During this thirty-year period, there were eight discrete cases of Western intervention in insurgencies in which the insurgents followed precepts of Marxist people's war laid down either by Mao Zedong of China or by the leading strategists of the Indochinese Communist party. Five of these insurgencies were successful, and three were not. The first success was Mao Zedong's Long March to liberation in China (1920–49). Mao's triumph was followed by the victory of Ho Chi Minh over the French in Vietnam (1946–54). This revolutionary tide, however, was checked by three dramatic failures: the three rounds of civil war in Greece (1941–49) that ultimately sent the communist insurgents fleeing into Albania; the unsuccessful bid for power by the communist Huks in the Philippines (1946–56); and the Emergency in Malaya (1948–60) in which the British and the Malayan government defeated the insurgency mounted by the Malayan Communist party. The tide surged anew, however, with a set of triple revolutionary victories in 1975 against regimes supported by the United States: the rout of the South Vietnamese army and engulfing of Saigon by the North Vietnamese army in April; the bloody siege and terrorizing of Phnom Penh by the Khmer Rouge

Table 1.1. Insurgencies and Intervention

Insurgency	Western Intervention	Eastern Bloc Intervention	*Specific* Marxist People's War
Vietnam I (Fr.)	●	●	●
Vietnam II (U.S.)	●	●	●
China	●	○	●
Greece	●	●	○
Philippines (Huk)	●		●
Malaya	●		●
Cambodia	●	●	●
Laos	●	●	●
El Salvador	●	●	
Nicaragua	●	●	
Peru (Sendero)	○		●
Bolivia	○	●(Cuba)	
Angola (+Moz.+Guin. Biss.)	○	●	
Eritrea (Eth.)		●	
Polisario (Morr.)	○		
Zimbabwe	○	●	
Algeria	●		
Afghanistan	●	●	
Dhofar	●		
Philippines (HPA)	○		●
Thailand	○	●(N.Vietnam)	●
Sri Lanka	●(India)		
Burma			
Timor			
Naxalites (India)			○

Key

☐ Core cases
○ Minimal or controversial

also in April; and the strikes, riots, and demonstrations that forced the government of Laos from power in December.

As Table 1.1 shows, there have been other insurgencies and many more interventions than those discussed in this book, but only these eight core cases meet the twin phenomenon-setting criteria of a Western intervention in a Marxist people's war (whether Chinese or Vietnamese). Substantial

Single Polity Outcome Sought	General People's War	Insurrection	Separatist or Ethnic Outcome Sought
●			
●			
●			
●	○	○	
●			
●			
●			
●			
●	●	○	
●	○	●	
○			○
●	●		
●	●		
	●		●
	●		●
●	●		
●	●	●	
●	●		
●	●		
●			
●			
	●		●
	●		●
	●		●
○			○

Western intervention occurred in all eight cases. Indeed, all but two of them (the Philippines and Malaya) garnered Eastern bloc intervention as well. This sets up the international side of this investigation, a study of competitive intervention.

Internally, why a specific Marxist people's war strategy is the other criterion requires explanation. Other strategies of revolutionary insurgency certainly abound. They include general people's or protracted war strategies used by insurgents in the Middle East and in the former Portuguese colonies of Angola, Mozambique, and Guinea-Bissau, the urban strategy of the Tupamaros in Uruguay; the more military "focalist" strategy of Fidel Castro in Cuba and Ché Guevara in Bolivia; and the separatist ethnic insurgencies in such widely scattered places as Northern Ireland, the Basque province of Spain, the Polisario in Morocco, and the Elam Tigers in Sri Lanka. For various reasons, these other strategies placed less emphasis on the mobilization of comprehensive popular support, and, as a result, the role of national legitimacy as a grounding presupposition fades somewhat in comparison to a Marxist people's war strategy which makes such mobilization a hallmark. Thus the findings of a study like this are less trustworthy in these different strategic terrains.

General people's wars amount to little more than struggles that become protracted out of necessity and rarely proceed from an articulate strategy of distinct phases as is the case with Marxist people's war. In these insurgencies, the legitimacy crisis contends with other issues such as factional, regional, and religious rivalries that detract from the centrality of this overarching crisis. Focalist strategies bypass the issue of mobilization altogether by assuming that a military spark will automatically trigger popular support. This is similar to an insurrection that seeks to overthrow the existing order in one fell swoop in which patient strategies of mobilization based on exploiting a legitimacy crisis are irrelevant. Finally, separatist insurgencies have no interest in resolving the legitimacy crisis of the society to which they are unhappily joined. The last thing separatists want are elections creating a binding government of national union. If anything, they seek referendums legitimating a societal divorce. Hence it is only a Marxist people's war that shares with its incumbent adversary the goal of an expanded political community, whether by mobilization or participation, based on the creation of a single Aristotelian middle ground. The tenets of this strategy are set forth in the next chapter.

In this work, the common factors of Western intervention, Eastern intervention, an insurgent strategy of Marxist people's war, and the seeking of a single polity bind the core cases to the intersection of insurgency and intervention in a political legitimacy crisis whose relative resolution spells out the terms for victory and defeat. With respect to comparative methods of similarities and differences, then, this book takes up eight cases of insurgency joined together by a similar set of conditions and seeks to explain their different outcomes.

The murkiness of the cases omitted from this study can be illustrated by brief discussion of a few of them. Fidel Castro's overthrow of the Batista regime in Cuba in 1959, as glorious as it was, provoked no special Western aid to shore up the Batista regime, and Castro himself did not become a confessed communist until after the success of his revolution. Similarly, Ché Guevara's romantic but fatal campaign in Bolivia in the mid-1960s was a classic case of an insurgency mounted entirely from external sources. To be sure, it involved an intervention, but because it had no support from the local population it hardly met the requirements of a "people's" war.

The defeat of France in 1962 in Algeria was at the hands of Muslim nationalists, not communists, as well as a weary French populace, and the French were maintaining a colonial order with little identifiable support from other Western powers. Also, the 1975 defeat of the Portuguese in their colonies of Angola, Mozambique, and Guinea-Bissau was the result of forces within Portuguese society as well as African liberation groups who professed a general socialist ideology but who again did not have to contend with demonstrable Western intervention.[5] The success of guerrilla leaders Joshua Nkomo and Robert Mugabe in Zimbabwe in 1980 rested more on an internationally brokered agreement and an electoral victory that was part of it than on a culmination of people's war. Interestingly, though, their victory at the polls illustrates that elections do not necessarily favor incumbent power structures and can put both sides at risk. Nonetheless, the white regime of Ian Smith could hardly qualify as a recipient of significant official Western assistance, although the white South African regime was certainly helpful. In addition, upheavals in Iran and Nicaragua in 1979 were more akin to revolutionary insurrections than to people's wars, were not communist-led (at least in the case of Iran), and were not actively opposed by Western powers.

Finally, the insurgencies in Peru and Ethiopia represent confusing combinations of strategy that make them difficult candidates for any comparative analysis. In Peru the Sendero Luminoso (Shining Path) insurgents follow a Maoist people's war strategy in pursuit of an irredentist revival of a preconquest Inca order for the Indians against the dominant Spanish and mestizo political culture. The ongoing Peruvian insurgency, nevertheless, will be analyzed in Chapter 11 to demonstrate the diagnostic capabilities of my framework. The seizure of the Ethiopian capital of Addis Ababa by insurgents in 1991 was done by one group seeking to unite the country under an Albanian model of revolution and another fighting for the secession of the northern province of Eritrea. The regime they overthrew was a Marxist one supported at one time by both the Cubans and the Soviets. Legitimacy, in Ethiopia, is a long way off for everyone.

From this general context of Western interventions in revolutionary insurgencies, viewed as manifestations of legitimacy crises, this book seeks to draw the lessons of one of them, the war in Vietnam, by answering two fundamental questions. First, what is the optimal level of Western intervention, if any, in Marxist people's war? By *level*, I refer to the increasing range of intervening activities that, put on a continuum of intensification, can start from rhetorical expressions of support and move on to a package of foreign aid that provides general development assistance (material support) not specific to the insurgency; to military aid and training missions perhaps accompanied by programmatic support to agencies of the host government such as the police, land reform agencies, and electoral commissions, all of whose specific purpose is to beat back the insurgency; to a massive level of political and economic support marking a commitment to the survival of the regime; to direct naval and air support; to the fielding of ground combat units either for the defense of installations and enclaves or for deployment on offensive operations; and, finally, to an assumption of "temporary" control over a certain range of host government activities.

The impact of Western interventions on our core insurgencies is illustrated by Figures 1.1 through 1.8, which chart the balances of intervention the two sides received. That the intervention at the different levels could be in various amounts is indicated by the relative thickness of the lines. A broken line indicates either a negligible amount or a controversial call as to the purpose of an activity. In all eight cases the incumbent regimes did receive various levels of Western intervention. Similarly, with the exceptions of the Philippines and Malaya, Eastern bloc countries intervened in support of most of the insurgents.

Intervention, therefore, does loom as an important factor, but by itself it cannot account for all the outcomes. Indeed, on the basis of intervention as an explanation, the cases break up into three groups. A favorable balance of intervention does correlate positively with the outcomes in Greece, the Philippines, and Malaya. That is, the incumbent regimes in these countries received more external assistance than their insurgent adversaries and won. In the cases of Cambodia and Laos, however, the level of intervention in support of both sides was approximately even, yet the insurgents won. Finally, in China and both the Vietnam cases, the incumbents received considerably more external assistance than the insurgents, but the insurgents won anyway. Thus in three of the cases an explanation on the basis of intervention adds up, but in five of them it does not.

A central thesis of this book is that the reason these balances of intervention do not add up is that the interventions were not free-floating. All eight cases involved interventions in support of a side caught up in a struggle for political legitimacy. The usefulness of each intervention, then, was determined not only by the general capabilities it added to its client but also by its impact on its client's claim to legitimacy as specifically defined or discovered in that society. The point is that the effect of the intervention could be either positive or negative, depending on the country-specific definition of legitimacy. In China and Vietnam, Western intervention had a negative

Figure 1.1. Balance of Intervention in Vietnam I: Franco–Viet Minh War, 1946–1954

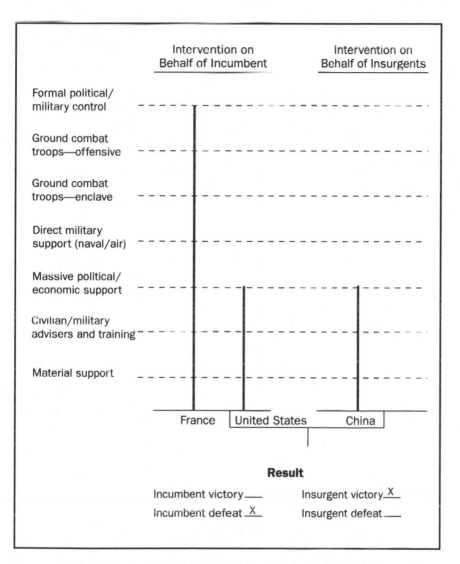

impact on legitimacy as defined in those countries, and, despite its massive scale, was to no avail. In Cambodia and Laos, the situation was more ambiguous in that the impact of Western intervention was negative, but less clearly so than in China and Vietnam, and the scale of Western aid was either insufficient (Cambodia) or lacking in constancy (Laos). In Greece, the Philippines, and Malaya, however, the Western interventions actually enhanced the legitimacy of the incumbent regimes.

In deciding whether to embark upon an intervention, a potential intervenor will need first to determine if a particular insurgency poses a suffi-

Figure 1.2. Balance of Intervention in Vietnam II: American Phase, 1960–1975

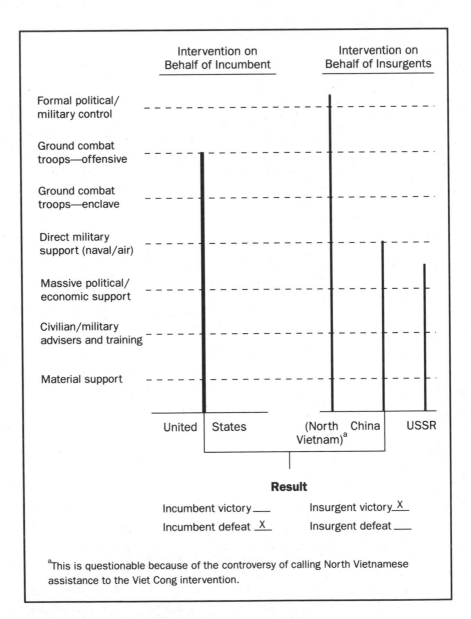

cient threat to his overall foreign policy interests to warrant such a step. This evaluation will derive from the foreign policy a country has fashioned to meet the dictates of a given global era. In the Era of People's War, the operative American foreign policy was containment. The dictates of this policy are considered in the next two chapters. (The conclusion discusses the implica-

Figure 1.3. Balance of Intervention in China, 1927–1949

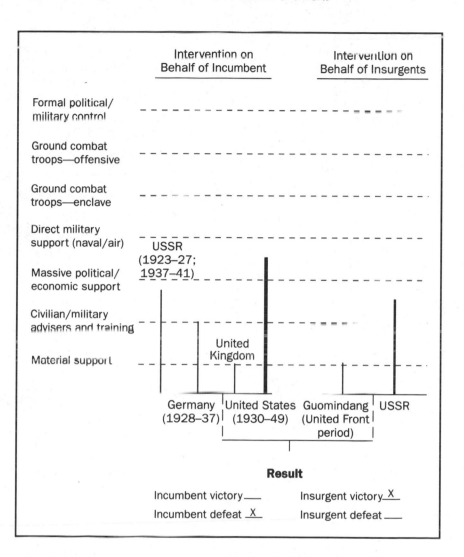

	Intervention on Behalf of Incumbent	Intervention on Behalf of Insurgents
Formal political/ military control		
Ground combat troops—offensive		
Ground combat troops—enclave		
Direct military support (naval/air)	USSR (1923–27; 1937–41)	
Massive political/ economic support		
Civilian/military advisers and training		
Material support	United Kingdom	

Germany (1928–37) — United States (1930–49) — Guomindang (United Front period) — USSR

Result

| Incumbent victory ___ | Insurgent victory _X_ |
| Incumbent defeat _X_ | Insurgent defeat ___ |

tions for foreign policy of a new era of people's rule.) If, on the basis of this foreign policy, the intervenor determines that an insurgency does warrant an intervention, he will then want to know what chances the insurgency has for success. This, of course, raises my second fundamental question: what are the components of a successful insurgency? Determining this will permit the intervenor to gauge the level and timing of his intervening moves.

The quick answer is that a successful insurgency is one that displaces an incumbent regime by mounting a successful challenge to its political legitimacy. But even though there are both general definitions and society-specific precepts, legitimacy is not something any ruling or challenging

Figure 1.4. Balance of Intervention in Greece, 1941–1949

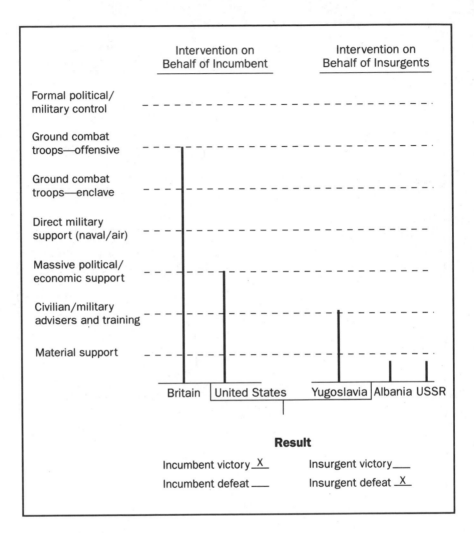

group possesses in an absolute sense. Like justice, power, authority, and other fundamental political concepts, legitimacy exists empirically only in relative amounts. In a struggle between contending sides for a superior claim to legitimacy, these claims have varying degrees of potency. The analytical framework of Chapter 3 will trace an ascent of legitimacy claims based on calculations of interest, commitments of opportunity, and professions of belief. In this struggle, there are three rising benchmarks for measuring the progress of an insurgency, which roughly correspond to the levels of this ascent: establishing a critical mass, building crossover points, and reaching a position for a strategic breakout. These concepts are also explained in Chapter 3. Together they establish the rules of evidence for this study.

Figure 1.5. Balance of Intervention in the Philippines, 1946–1956

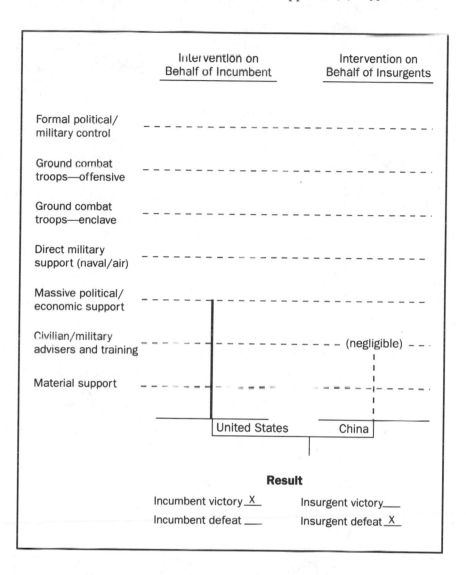

For determining a policy of intervention, this book confronts Mark Twain's classic dilemma of the cat on the stove. Does having been roasted on a burner once in Vietnam mean that all burners are forever hot? From the perspective of legitimacy, this book will present a thermometer for gauging the local political temperature for the probing cat paws of intervention.

Theoretically, this book makes the paradigmatic assumption that insurgencies come from outbreaks of crises in national legitimacy. Thus this study self-consciously analyzes such "internal wars" between incumbents and insurgents as struggles for claims to intensifying levels of legitimacy spelled

Figure 1.6. Balance of Intervention in Malaya, 1948–1960

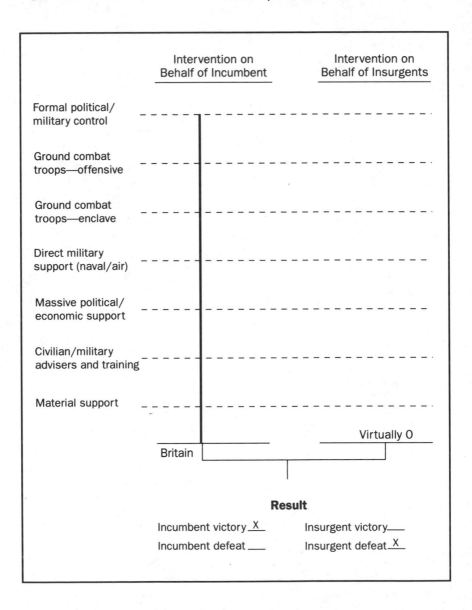

	Intervention on Behalf of Incumbent	Intervention on Behalf of Insurgents
Formal political/ military control		
Ground combat troops—offensive		
Ground combat troops—enclave		
Direct military support (naval/air)		
Massive political/ economic support		
Civilian/military advisers and training		
Material support		
	Britain	Virtually 0

Result

Incumbent victory _X_   Insurgent victory___

Incumbent defeat ___   Insurgent defeat _X_

out as a historical phenomenon in Chapter 2 and as an analytic construct in Chapter 3. In Harry Eckstein's terms, this book is a paradigmatic case study in that it is a comparative analysis by means of a single analytical framework based on a key presupposition about the phenomenon under study.[6]

Delimited as it is to eight main cases, for the purposes of building social science theory, this book is an exercise in typological rather than general theory. Its conclusions, therefore, can strictly stand for only the eight cases

Figure 1.7. Balance of Intervention in Cambodia, 1970–1975

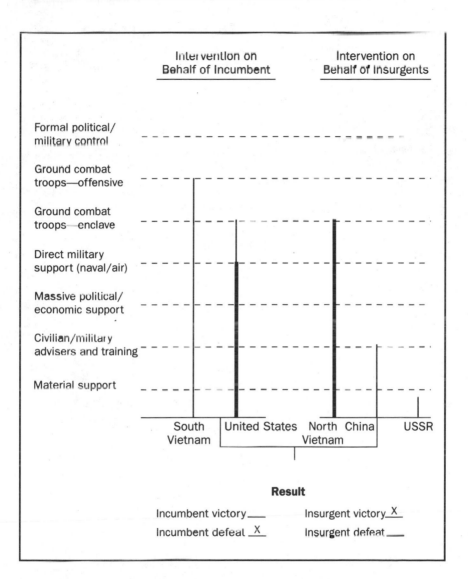

in question. The advantage of such inductive theory-building lies in the policy and historiographical realm of settling some of the unresolved questions of the Vietnam War inasmuch as it has been such a potent symbol for any policy debate over American intervention in the Third World. The larger goal is to generate spillover effects from the core cases to the general intersection of insurgency and intervention. To start this process, Chapter 11 discusses the relevance of this book's analytical findings to a diagnosis of the ongoing Maoist insurgency in Peru.

For this theoretical task, each core case will be discussed in terms of a set

Figure 1.8. Balance of Intervention in Laos, 1955–1975

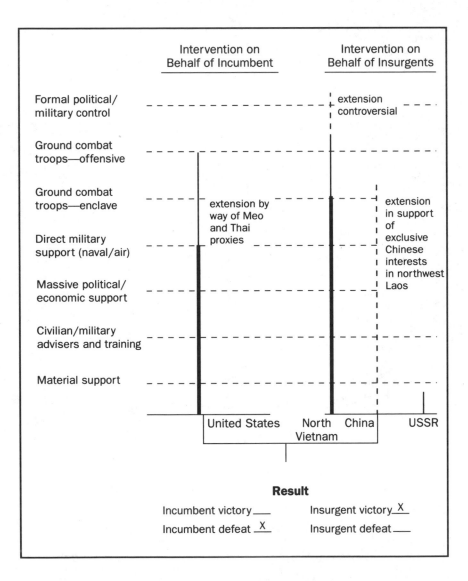

of six thematic questions and accompanying propositions so that the comparative analysis is one of structured, focused comparison.[7] These questions are "unpacked" from six assumptions that form a background of constants to this book. First, the war in Vietnam was wrapped up in the broader historical context of societies in the throes of revolutionary insurgency as they struggled to form and consolidate independent and modernizing states. Second, such a definitional struggle represented a general crisis of individual national political legitimacy. Third, in these insurgencies, Western powers were more inclined to intervene in the particular insurgent variant of the Marxist people's war than in others because its universal ideological claims were seen as threatening to the global balance of power in the East-West struggle of the Cold War. Fourth, the outcome of even this type of insurgency with its international intervention and universal ideological claims, nevertheless, turned on the relative success earned by the two sides in resolving this local crisis. Fifth, there was nothing inevitable or predetermined about any of the outcomes to these insurgencies. Finally, the true basis for a comparison of the Vietnam War with its companion cases for lessons is on the resolution of their respective legitimacy crises rather than on the general or immediate outcome of the insurgencies themselves. All of these assumptions are certainly contestable, but they do map out the vantage point from which the fundamental investigation, thematic questions, and theoretical framework of this book are drawn. These assumptions are explained further in the next two chapters.

Turning to these six thematic questions, the first is, *What is the historical setting out of which the insurgency developed and from which the country's specific definition of political legitimacy arose?* For the sake of both lesson making and comparative analysis, the answer to this question provides the specific context of each case and preserves its historical uniqueness as well as allowing what Max Weber called a *Verstehen* or empathy to develop for each of these struggles.[8] With this in mind, the cumulative comparisons of the cases with each other will be deferred until Chapter 11 so that an independent understanding of each case can develop before the comparative analysis is undertaken. Further, the historical setting provides the inductive "data base" from which the deductive generalizations of the framework analysis are derived.

With respect to this setting, as part of a process of political development from traditional to modern sources of legitimacy, my proposition (1.1) is to assert a historical flow. That is, in all core cases, the traditional definition of legitimacy was coming under attack in the interwar years (1920–40). This growing definitional crisis, out of which revolutionary groups emerged, received a foreign shock from World War II which touched off insurgencies both during and after the war because this shock overcame the asymmetric difficulties associated with starting an insurgency. Given this, my second proposition (1.2), or prediction, in this case, is that since such a "beneficial" future shock is unlikely, at least on a global scale, the chances are dim for any new surge of insurgencies such as occurred after World War II.

Second, *Within my analytical framework of legitimacy, how did the incumbents and insurgents fare competitively?* This framework analysis is the heart of each case and is built on a common set of factors that is derived from the literatures on legitimacy, modernization, and peasant mobilization, as well as on revolution, insurgency, and counterinsurgency. These literatures are given a fuller discussion in Appendix 1. The framework is superimposed on the historical setting of each case and provides the analytical context for comparison across cases. In this framework, legitimacy is depicted as being achieved at three levels of appeal or support: interest, opportunity, and belief. It is my proposition (2.1) that though most activity in an insurgency takes place at the opportunity level and its institutional contest for reforms of societal access (land reform) and political participation (elections), the resolution of an insurgency more critically lies at the level of belief.

Third, *How closely did the revolutionary insurgents follow a Marxist people's war strategy and what was the effect of this strategy on their claims to this legitimacy?* Though other strategies of insurgency have been mentioned, in confronting a classic insurgent condition in which the oppressed classes may want a new way, but the ruling class is still desirous of continuing in the old way (to paraphrase Lenin), it is my first proposition (3.1) that a Marxist people's war strategy is the most promising of these strategies because it has as its key fount of power the popular mobilization of previously apolitical segments of society, most often the peasantry. Thus the very adoption of this strategy should be a cause for serious concern by both the incumbent regime and potential intervenors. For this mobilization to be successful, however, my second proposition (3.2) is that the campaign shall have to be couched in terms of the society's particular precepts of political legitimacy. Mao called this discovering the "mass line." Another critical requirement for insurgent success is unity, and my third proposition (3.3) is that though this will be forged or frayed at the opportunity level of cadre organization, this achievement can be surely achieved only at the belief level of "revolutionary" legitimacy.

The fourth question is, *What was the impact of the Western intervention on this legitimacy crisis in creating a positive or negative effect on its client's claim to legitimacy?* Though this effect is key, each case will also briefly consider the impact of this intervention "offstage": on the intervening power's international position and on its own domestic legitimacy. For this question, I have two propositions. Following the propositions in the two previous questions about levels of legitimacy, first (4.1), though the main visible efforts of an intervention will be at the interest and opportunity levels, the primary effect will be at the belief level. Thus a well-designed and fully financed American program of land reform at the opportunity level may founder because the very presence of so many "foreign devils" in the government will undermine the belief-level legitimacy of the regime. In our cases, this is precisely what happened in Vietnam, whereas the British resettlement program of Chinese squatters in Malaya buttressed the English reputation for communal fairness.

The second proposition (4.2) here is that the critical level of intervention, with respect to this impact on legitimacy, is the dispatching of ground combat troops. As a symbol, this directly identifies the intervening state with the client regime and therefore requires that this foreign presence be justified by the basic principles of legitimacy of that society. Foreign troops in Vietnam humiliated the national belief that political rule came from a direct Mandate of Heaven rather than any mediation from American troop transport "freedom birds." In the Philippines, massive American assistance did not undermine the legitimacy of the Magsaysay regime. This assistance, however, did not include ground combat troops, and it is quite clear that had there been any, the regime would have run into trouble. In Greece, however, foreign troops on their soil flattered the Hellenic sense of global importance embodied in their Megali Idea. The Greek case, nevertheless, introduces a corollary to this proposition (4.2a). An intervening state may be reluctant to intervene with ground combat troops precisely because of this identification. Indeed, though the British sent troops to Greece, the Americans never did for this very reason.

The fifth question is, *What are the contingencies to these cases?* In the real world, it is by no means clear that a given historical event had to end the way it did, nor that in analyses of the balances of social forces do insurgents and incumbents confront each other as equals or as analytically homogeneous entities. For this question, the contingencies of these apples-against-oranges asymmetries as well as of the might-have-beens of errors and reversibilities are explored for each case.[9] Regarding asymmetries, I have three propositions. First (5.1a), both because it is illegal and because it requires killing, an insurgency is difficult to get off the ground. Second (5.1b), however, once an insurgency becomes a going concern, most of the advantage switches to the insurgents. Despite the superior material resources of the incumbents (augmented by foreign assistance), the insurgents have the easier task of destroying while the incumbents have to preserve the normal functioning of the society. Further, as the ruling regime, the incumbents are held to standards of performance (which are not stellar anywhere in the Third World), whereas insurgents, up to a point, can get away with mere promises of a better tomorrow. Third (5.1c), once an insurgency reaches the point at which belief-level appeals are important to its future, the Marxism of people's war can pose serious problems of national legitimacy for the insurgents. In the course of an insurgency, then, these asymmetries seesaw back and forth.

As for errors and reversibilities, my basic assumption is that a revolutionary insurgency is a reversible event and is not part of a predetermined dialectic of history. Building on my opening contention in this chapter that lessons come from components of events and not from their outcomes, I will note that most of these cases contained errors on one side or the other (as well as unusually shrewd moves) that were not inevitable occurrences. My first general proposition (5.2) about these contingencies is that without them, the results could have been different. This premise is what makes the issue of intervention salient. That is, from this presupposition I have posited that insurgencies can be overcome by foreign intervention (5.2a). They also can be undercut by reforms (5.2b). Further, contingencies particularly arise when one considers leadership and the competent performances it may inspire. As a concessionary third proposition (5.2c), I acknowledge that by itself such charismatic leadership might almost carry an insurgency or counterinsurgency campaign to victory and bypass the society's festering legitimacy crises. My follow-on fourth proposition (5.2d), however, is that if this leadership and performance are not rooted in the institutional structure and belief system of its society, the effects will not be lasting. I call such leadership Hannibalism, and it is how I interpret the Magsaysay phenomenon in the Philippines.

Finally, *What are the comparisons of the legitimacy struggles in each case with Vietnam?* For this question the focus will be on the various ways country-specific definitions of national legitimacy have affected both Western intervention and revolutionary strategy. Some will be quite like Vietnam in these effects, while others will be quite different. The basic proposition (6.1) about these comparisons, of course, is that, with respect to the intersection of insurgency and intervention, Vietnam is not the crucial or only case for lessons. Rather, it is only one of several similar cases of Western intervention in revolutionary insurgency.

The organization of each case follows the order of these questions. Each case is divided into three sections: Historical Setting, Framework Analysis, and Comparisons with Vietnam. The Framework Analysis section is subdivided into discussions of national legitimacy (question 2), revolutionary legitimacy (question 3), foreign intervention (question 4), and dynamics of the balances in which the issues of asymmetries, errors, and reversibilities are considered (question 5). As an exception to this pattern, Cambodia and Laos are combined into one chapter and analyzed side by side. This is partly because their histories are more intertwined than those of the other cases, but it has also been done to vary the book's methodological pattern by highlighting the contrasts between the cases through a point-by-point consideration of each.

The two chapters devoted to Vietnam (plus Appendix 2) follow this same pattern, but in an elongated manner. Chapter 4 provides the historical setting out of which Vietnam's standards of political legitimacy emerged. Chapter 6 conducts a framework analysis and concludes with an essay that discusses both the dynamics of the balances and the complications to Vietnam that yields one of my major points that, *by itself*, there are no lessons to Vietnam. The appendix on Vietnam goes back over some of this same ground from the perspective of military strategy to point out that the result of the Vietnam War represented an abandonment by both sides of the political issues that animated two generations of warfare.

In the concluding part, Chapter 11 runs through the cumulative findings of the core cases with respect to the propositions enumerated here. In addition to the central lessons—the importance of elections and land reform in service of the larger belief goal of establishing moral national communities—it also reveals some unexpected findings that will require further work. The most intriguing is the uniform urban failures of the eight insurgencies. To see what remains of the lessons of Vietnam, the conclusion maps out the terrain of a new international era in the Third World, one of people's rule. This era is analyzed for the challenges and opportunities it holds for American foreign policy. Prescriptively, as a replacement for containment, I call for a commitment to global democratization in order to redeem the unfulfilled quest of America's longest war.

Chapter 2

LEGITIMACY, INSURGENCY, AND THE INTERNATIONAL CONTEXT OF THE VIETNAM WAR

Legitimacy and Insurgency

This book pivots on two questions. What is the optimal level of intervention, if any, in a Marxist people's war of national liberation? Determining this, in turn, depends on the internal or domestic question of what makes for a successful insurgency? If an insurgent group's efforts are futile and headed toward failure, from the point of view of a contemplated intervention at least, there is no need to worry. If, however, such a group is making all the right moves and appears to be on a path to victory, there is a need to know how, when, and whether the insurgency can be blunted. Determining what makes for a successful insurgency, as I have already said, depends fundamentally on what an insurgency is. Two central presuppositions about an insurgency guide my analysis: first, an insurgency is a crisis of political legitimacy; second, in its conduct, an insurgency is a revolution "on the slow burn," as opposed to the other revolutionary variant, the volcanic insurrection.

Admittedly, these two questions somewhat beg or sidestep the larger and moral question of whether Western powers *should* intervene against these insurgencies. This moral question revolves around a consideration of what role Western powers should play in the international system and how this role and its interests can best be protected. From such a basic foreign policy stance, do communist-led insurgencies threaten the fabric of a Western-protected order and are violent political struggles within Third World countries the business of Western and other "outside" powers? Clearly one can imagine answers to these moral questions falling along as wide a continuum as I depicted for the levels of intervention in the previous chapter. Whether such a debate is worth having, or continuing, depends first, at least in practical or instrumental terms, on whether Western powers *can* intervene in such insurgencies. In this book I provide a conceptual framework for deciding this. Although this book is not an explicit treatise on the morality of the war, much of its contents has obvious moral implications.

Regarding this central concept of political legitimacy, it should come as no surprise that I am in fundamental agreement with Harry Eckstein in his simple assertion that "the issue of support and opposition, legitimacy and illegitimacy . . . stands at the crux of all political study."[1] Though I have simply defined it as the basis upon which the authority of political rule is justified, legitimacy is a complex phenomenon made up of different processes and interactions and, therefore, requiring a fuller definition. The scholar who is most responsible for the modern usage of this ancient concept is Max Weber, who understood the legitimacy of a regime to be based on a variety of motives which nevertheless clustered around the three "archetypes" he called traditional, charismatic, and legal (or rational) legitimacy. One of the many definitions reflecting this Weberian view is that of T. H. Rigby, who has observed that legitimacy brings a confidence by ruling authorities that their demands will gain the compliance of their citizens from a variety of motives, all of which are based on an acceptance of the right of the rulers to make these demands.[2] According to this formulation, legitimacy involves an exchange between the rulers and the ruled over the right of the few to govern the many.[3] With respect to this exchange, Lucian Pye presciently observed that "the great illusion of politics is that power presumably flows downward from the ruler . . . to the masses, whereas in actual fact the process is precisely the reverse." Legitimacy, he notes, is achieved only when the people bow to this presumption and that the terms for this acceptance vary "from culture to culture."[4]

Legitimacy, then, goes beyond coercion, habit, or mere self-interested calculation. It is a margin of respect that adheres to a regime that earns this respect at three levels: first, at the highest level (belief), by upholding the society's fundamental "constitutional" arrangements and historical traditions; second, by being itself duly constituted by these arrangements and performing the group functions prescribed for it (opportunity); and, finally, by being acceptably competent in the discharge of its duties and policies (interest). In a fully developed political community, there is a broad consensus about standards at each of these levels, and, as H. L. Nieburg has put it, the degree of legitimacy a regime has depends on the "vitality of this underlying consensus" that it can command.[5]

As the basis for the justification of the authority of political rule at different levels of respect and support, some features of legitimacy are worth highlighting. First, it is, as Max Weber has already told us, multifaceted and built on different motives, requiring in its elicitation, therefore, different appeals. This feature is what undergirds the division of legitimacy into three levels of appeal in my analytical framework. Second, for the legitimacy of a regime to take hold, among this concept's different facets, there must be motives above mere calculations of interest by the people. Another way of saying this is that there must be a normative or moral judgment in favor of a regime's right to rule. As Emile Durkheim simply put it, "every society is a moral society."[6] This central moral component to legitimacy, then, is something every government or regime needs to sustain its power and long-term ability to rule.[7] Finally, a state can rule without legitimacy, but not well. Without it, it is hard for a government to withstand serious challenges from its people to make needed changes for improvements, such as to promote economic growth or to ameliorate social tensions. The Batista regime in Cuba, for example, fell to Fidel Castro's puny force of two thousand men in 1960 because its lack of legitimacy left it with no margin of respect among the Cuban people for withstanding the challenge. Such brittle rule I term *nonlegitimacy*. I discuss it further in the next chapter.

An insurgency, then, is a challenge to authority. Basically, it is my argument that an insurgency is a *political* challenge to a regime's authority by an organized and violent questioning of the regime's claims to legitimacy. Thus, in Bard O'Neill's words, an insurgency is "a struggle between a nonruling group and the ruling authorities in which the former consciously employs political resources and instruments of violence to establish [its] legitimacy." In an insurgency, the intersection of legitimacy and the use of force is central and often very delicate. This makes the state or government, of course, and most particularly its military forces and police, the most conspicuous targets of the insurgents. Apropos of this link, Hedley Bull has reminded us that what distinguishes a government from other institutions is that "it possesses a near monopoly of the legitimate use of force. . . . It is just as important to a government that its use of force be legitimate as that it should be overwhelming. . . . Insurgent groups show that they understand this interconnection when they devote as much attention to undermining the government's right, in the eyes of the population, to use force, as to combating that force with force of their own."[8]

There is no getting around the fact that an insurgency is a revolution, a violent attempt to overthrow the state and the social order dependent on it. But revolutions divide into two types, the volcanic insurrection and the more slow-burning insurgency. It is the insurrection that embraces most of the spectacular qualities commonly associated with the term *revolution*, as when George Petee intoned, a revolution "begins simply with a sudden recognition by almost all the passive and active membership that the state no longer exists." Similarly, Theda Skocpol showed the influence of this anarchic eruption of an insurrection when she concurred with Wendell Phillips's epic phrase, "Revolutions are not made; they come."[9]

Herein lies the critical difference between the two types. Insurrections can just happen (and be taken advantage of by revolutionaries), but insurgencies have to be made. For a revolutionary bent on power, one road is to ride to the crest of an erupting insurrectionary volcano and seize it. If, however, the regime that is the obstacle or target cannot be so easily or instantly dislodged, then the other road is to bide one's time and start stoking the social order with the coals of an insurgency, a revolution "on the slow burn." This distinction can come out sharply when set against Lenin's classic definition of a revolutionary situation. It exists, he said, "only when the *'lower classes' do not want* the old way and when the 'upper classes' *cannot carry on in the old way.*"[10] An insurrection can be mounted if both of Lenin's conditions pertain, but an insurgency is the only path possible to the same goal if the ruling classes and their institutions are not ready to fold, that is, if only the first of Lenin's conditions holds true. Along these lines, Samuel Huntington has pointed out that it is this latter insurgent condition that has been the more typical setting of revolutions in the Third World.[11]

This insurgent condition of being blocked by an obstreperous regime places a far higher premium on strategy than does an insurrection. Because no immediate prospect for success is at hand, such as a convenient upheaval, insurgent groups must have a credible plan or strategy to get to the top. Indeed, their revolutionary strategy becomes a critical part of their own legitimacy in attracting recruits. As mentioned in Chapter 1, several different insurgent strategies appeared in the Third World after World War II. One was Leninist, which centered around a conspiratorial organization whose activities were strengthened by active support from key social groups. Another was a strict urban strategy like that attempted by the Tupamaros in Uruguay in the 1960s. Still another strategy was the "focalist" one employed by Fidel Castro and Ché Guevara in Latin America. It concentrated on striking a military fist first as a means of igniting a political rebellion afterward.[12] The most successful of all these strategies, however, has been that of the Marxist people's war of national liberation. Indeed, the very use of such a strategy can be seen as one of the first danger signs of an insurgency's threat to a regime. Revolutionary strategy, then, is a key variable or factor in my analysis because an insurgency has to have one to hold itself together. Insurrectionists, sometimes, can get away with "winging it."

Before moving on to other explanations of insurgency, one brief but critical caveat needs to be stressed: not all legitimacy crises result in insurgencies. If just particular policies, rulers, or power arrangements are in question, most societies have a range of political mechanisms to deal with them. Policies can be either amended or abandoned; rulers can be voted out or thrown out in a coup d'état; and constitutional arrangements can be amended. Because of the availability of such mechanisms, Chalmers Johnson insists that an insurgency is something that "ought never to occur." When it does, however, it is a legitimacy crisis that has turned revolutionary.[13]

Other Explanations

Despite this focus on insurgency as a crisis of political legitimacy, there are other explanations. Though I readily acknowledge that they all have a place in the broad understanding of the phenomenon, I still insist that they remain secondary to one based on the overarching struggle of political legitimation.

Perhaps the most prominent of these alternative explanations is that an insurgency is best understood as a manifestation of the East-West struggle. Indeed, D. Michael Shafer contends that it was precisely such a containment vision that led the United States into what he describes as a paradigm of "contentless universalism" in which every local conflict was analyzed for its contribution to, or impact on, the great struggle of the Cold War. Herbert Tillema, in his study of interventions, lends support to this view with his finding that the one strong predictor of a U.S. intervention was the specter of communism, which was based on "the root assumption that all new Communist governments do, in the long run, threaten the U.S." Scholars of the period seemed to echo this opinion, with James Rosenau, for example, seeing "internal wars" as a regulating mechanism for the bipolar international system: "Internal Wars are thus a testing ground in which East and West convey to each other the extent of their aspirations and the depth of their resolve. They are . . . a roundabout way of coordinating mutually exclusive objectives in order to preserve a modicum of international stability."[14]

With such attitudes, it was certainly true that from 1945 to 1975 some form of external involvement developed in nearly all "local wars." In two studies, one covering the years from 1944 to 1969 and the other from 1967 to 1976, István Kende found a growing trend of foreign intervention in civil wars, a trend that became even more pronounced in his second study. Indeed, Evan Luard, in his investigation of thirty-three civil wars, made the remarkable observation that since 1963 no rebel groups have came to power without foreign help.[15] It is also true that once beset by an insurgency, virtually no incumbent regime in the Third World has been able to suppress one without foreign help.[16] In brief, no one has been allowed to have a civil war in peace.

Nevertheless, if the Vietnam War has shown anything, it is surely that the internal political dynamics of an insurgency cannot be ignored. Indeed, for whatever purpose, for an intervention to be successful, these internal political factors must be manipulated and respected. If an intervention is done only for reasons of external or international policy and runs roughshod over these factors, at best they can be held in abeyance as long as the will of the intervenor persists—a will that never has proven to be eternal.

Another explanation is that insurgencies are basically a police or military problem, suppressible without engaging such intractable political problems as the nature of authority in a society. As Lucian Pye has pointed out, the British, for example, have long viewed counterinsurgency as police work.[17] But, in so doing, they have certainly developed a respectable record of accommodating themselves to local political factors.[18] Clearly, military and police measures are not inconsequential to the course of any insurgency. The size, composition, disposition, training, technology, and tactics of the contending military forces are critical variables. Virtually all modern students of insurgency are still in agreement with Katherine Chorley, for example, that no revolution can succeed unless the regime's army can be either defeated or corroded. Technologically, the helicopter transformed the nature of warfare in Indochina, allowing American GIs to avoid many of the tactically elegant communist stratagems that had so often ensnared the ground-bound French in the 1940s and 1950s. Tactically, the painstakingly brilliant Viet Cong sapper attacks on U.S. installations were a serious worry to the enormous and vulnerable American logistical system. Similarly, in Afghanistan, the introduction of the Stinger missile by the United States in 1986 significantly altered the battlefield situation in favor of the insurgent Mujaheddin. Nevertheless, even the U.S. military has come to appreciate the centrality of political factors to an insurgency. To quote one author in a military journal: "In an insurgency there is the overriding question of the moral right of a governing regime to exist. The root causes of insurgency are longstanding political, economic and social injustice. . . . [An insurgency is a] 'war for the right to govern.'"[19]

As a further explanation, in any revolutionary saga much is always made of leadership and organization as central causes of either success or failure.

Thus biographies of romantic guerrilla leaders quickly proliferate, though, in an asymmetry of romance, precious few are done of the generally more colorless incumbent rulers. Psychological studies seek to isolate the key factors that drive the revolutionary personality, as E. Victor Wolfenstein has done for Vladimir Lenin, Leon Trotsky, and Mahatma Gandhi. Indeed, so important do leaders loom that sometimes even in their lifetimes they can become sources of legitimacy in their own right. So pervasive is this phenomenon in societies undergoing some form of drastic change that Max Weber has identified this charismatic presence and authority as one of his three types of legitimacy. What accounts for the actual appearance of a charismatic leader, nevertheless, remains the same mystery that it was for Plato in explaining why the head-turning philosopher, in his Myth of the Cave, turned his head in the first place. For both incumbent and insurgent leaders in the modern world, Mostafa Rejai and Kay Phillips nevertheless propose an interactive theory according to which leadership personalities are those who are able to establish a visible and compelling link between themselves and the context of their social environment.[20]

Turning to organization itself, it was no less a figure than Lenin who said, "Organization. This is one of the sorest questions confronting us."[21] Subsequent communist revolutionaries have devoted almost obsessive attention to proper principles of organization and legitimate revolutionary strategies. Western scholars have also scrutinized revolutions for that master organizational touch that carried the movement over the top. For the Vietnam War, Douglas Pike's *Viet Cong* remains the classic exposition of the elaborate organizational principles, strategies, and structures developed by the Vietnamese communists.[22]

As a prior condition, however, to gain their charisma and organizational efficacy, both leaders and their organizations had to appeal to, and identify with, something that gave them an audience in the first place — something that gave them a basis upon which to mobilize and channel their followers. In my view, this prior "something" is a set of principles of political legitimacy, whether old or new.

One final explanation, however, remains as a serious rival to political legitimacy in accounting for insurgency: the economic drive for a better material life. Insurgency in this book is centrally linked to the phenomenon of development. In John Walton's words, insurgencies are "developmental revolutions" and therefore can be well understood in terms of the literature on development.[23] Development is more often than not defined in terms of material improvement — for example, in rising per capita incomes — and therefore economic variables pervade the development dynamic and are unavoidable in any aspect of the process, including insurgency.

Indeed, most of the modern strategists of counterinsurgency have remarked on this dual political and economic aspect to insurgency, though they still stress the greater importance of the political issues. Otto Heilbrun, for example, ascribed what he called "partisan warfare" to "nationalism and discontent," and considered nationalism by far the steadier and more intractable factor. This centrality of ideas over interest (to pervert Mao's "men over weapons") comes down to us from the legendary T. E. Lawrence, who stressed the drive for freedom as the core of Arab motivation in his desert campaign against the Turks in World War I: "We were an influence, an idea. . . . Our kingdom lay in each man's mind, and as we wanted nothing material . . . we offered nothing material. . . . [Despite their material superiority] the Turks would need six hundred thousand men to meet the combined ill wills of all the local Arab people."[24]

In fact, where economic factors predominate, it has proven difficult for an insurgency to develop the tenacity to go the distance. Lucian Pye found a strong emphasis on economic factors in his interviews with former guerrillas in Malaya.[25] In the Philippines, the Huk peasantry in the rural *barrios*, to the great chagrin of the fanatical urban politburo in Manila, all too often exhibited Lenin's sin of "economism" (the failure to appreciate the central political nature of one's economic grievances). In Vietnam, by contrast, strong political commitments were evident in the Rand interviews of Viet Cong ralliers (guerrillas who came over to the government side).[26] The not too subtle point here is that the more economic guerrillas of Malaya and the Philippines were not as successful as their more political cousins in Vietnam. In my analytical framework, I acknowledge the presence of both economic and political factors through the ascending calculations of interest, opportunity, and belief. The overriding importance of the political is revealed by the economic factors lying more at the lower end of the ascending continuum of legitimation (at interest and opportunity levels) and the political ones lying more at the higher end (at opportunity and belief levels).

The General Historical Trace of Legitimacy

The centrality of legitimacy to the origins of, and justification for, the state has a long history. As Dolf Sternberger has observed: "The desire for legitimacy is so deeply rooted in human communities that it is hard to discover any sort of historical government that did not either enjoy widespread authentic recognition of its existence or try to win such recognition." Traditionally, a first step in establishing legitimacy was to create (or accept) a set of myths that developed and reinforced identities and norms of conduct for the society. Hence, in classical Greece, Solon is said to have divided Athens into tribes, provided each of them with a myth of founding and distinctive attributes, and given the city-state a set of laws.[27]

From the myths, the different sections that constitute the society are provided their functions and proper way of doing things. These standards, obviously, also establish the reverse: what is not right (or just) and what violates the proper way to do things. Such violations, if uncorrected or unreformed, eventually provoke challenges to the violators. Thus, in ancient Israel, after Saul got off to a bad start by becoming king illegitimately in offering a religious sacrifice himself after promising to let Samuel the high priest perform it, he compounded this offense by ruling with a heavy-handedness that led the Israelites to embrace the challenge of David, one of history's first insurgents: "And everyone that was in distress, and everyone that was in debt, and everyone that was discontented gathered themselves unto him, and he became a captain over them" (1 Samuel 22:1).

Legitimacy, or standards of it—whether developed by some process of a contract (as is intimated above) or as the result of something more inherent to the very nature of human society, as Aristotle would have it—is what holds a state together. The history of the West has been one of a gradual progression theoretically from numinous (divine) to civil sources of legitimacy.[28] In brute fact, it has been a bloody struggle. The first dispute was between the fledgling post-Roman kings of Europe with the pope over the font of political authority. As the kings gained in their struggle with the church and consolidated their temporal power, they had to contend increasingly with the dawning and rising secularist instincts of their own people. This led to the epic moment of Western political development that Michael Walzer has called the transition from regicide to revolution, which, as explained by S. N. Eisenstadt, was that "the tendency to substitute one (good) ruler for another (bad) ruler and to condone rebellions against bad rulers gave way to the notion . . . of reconstruction . . . of the entire sociopolitical order."[29]

For most of Europe, at least symbolically, this transitional moment was met in the French Revolution (1789–94) in which the Third Estate threw out the Bourbon monarchy under the justifying (or legitimating) banner of "Liberté, Egalité, et Fraternité." In so doing, the revolutionaries grounded authority, and legitimation for it, fully in civil sources, under some notion of a social contract, and created a society, no longer between ruler and subjects, but between representative leaders and participatory citizens. The English came to similar political conclusions somewhat differently in their Glorious Revolution (1688–89), and the Americans even more differently, more temperately, as Hannah Arendt has described it.[30] In this general Western historical progression to the contemporary world, as Samuel Huntington has concluded, "Modernity is thus not all of a piece."[31]

Nevertheless, this revolutionary transformation of politics became the dynamic reality of the modern European state and, along with the economic sinews of the industrial revolution, became the source of its expansive strength. The French Revolution also brought legitimacy to the fore as a central issue in domestic European politics. Indeed, the term was first coined by Talleyrand in a directly political sense at the Congress of Vienna (1815), when he called for a return of the Bourbons after Napoleon under the slogan "Restoration, Legitimacy, and Compensation."[32] Stephen Holmes has pointed out that the persistence of this question in nineteenth-century Europe—in the case of France, whether to continue with the new politics brought in by the revolution or to return to monarchical principles—forced each country self-consciously to search for new sources of legitimation for its government. If the question, Why obey the laws? could not be answered by appeal to divine or monarchical fiat, or just because they *were* laws, then the society had a legitimacy crisis. On the Continent this was resolved either by a subservience to restored monarchies or by the development of new "constitutional" orders. Constitutional monarchies in some form emerged as the usual compromise. Whatever the form, as Melvin Richter has observed, European politics, not without spirited debate and spasms of violence, eventually settled on the distinction that what was legitimate tended toward democratic politics and what was not tended toward authoritarian and totalitarian control. Thus, in this resolution, Bonapartism became the first modern illegitimacy.[33] Despite the crudeness of such direct European analogies, it would still not be inaccurate to describe much of the politics in the Third World today as mired in Bonapartism.

As nineteenth-century politics settled down and beliefs in democratic sources of legitimacy worked their way into the political tissues of each European state, such participatory politics soon became the hallmark of the vigorous spirit of progress and modernity. Max Weber provided a scheme for such a democratic march by arguing that sources of legitimation went through a series of progressive stages, from the traditional to the charismatic to the legal (i.e., rational). The last stage Weber identified with the Western bureaucratic state, in which the ungoverned energy of charisma lifting a society away from tradition had finally been routinized by rational bureaucratic procedures. Weber's notion of progress to the self-fulfilling prophecy of the Western state found its echo in the twentieth-century growth-by-stages theories of such scholars of political development as Walt Rostow, A. F. K. Organski, and William Kornhauser.[34]

In any case, it was this system of democratic and bureaucratic states that the West writ large across the globe in the heyday of its imperial expansion, which, at least in political terms, Westerners deemed to be the very essence of their White Man's Burden, *mission civilisatrice*, or Manifest Destiny. Other parts of the world, of course, had their own institutions, historical traditions, political thought, and principles of legitimacy. African tribes legitimated rule through rituals of "enstoolment."[35] Rulers in ancient India had on their shoulders the harsh responsibility of *danda*, the upholding of a religiously sanctioned coercive order.[36] And Confucian emperors in China had the daunting obligation of embodying in their rule the Mandate of Heaven.[37] But these conceptions of politics and the institutions that grew from them were unable to stand against the politically expansionist, fully mobilized industrial states of the West. The dilemma of entering the modern world for Third World societies became how to hold their own in an international system of European creation. By holding their own, to be fully sovereign, they had to develop power that could earn European respect in ways that were still authentic, or legitimate, in their own societies.[38]

In brief, what makes insurgencies today so different from their apolitical cousins of the nineteenth century is their very essential political nature. Insurgencies in the postwar era, beyond the goal of political power or national liberation, have also, as S. Neil MacFarlane has emphasized, the added objectives of economic growth and independence, profound social change, and cultural liberation and redefinition.[39] This, of course, has been touched off, or inflicted on the Third World, by the earlier ferment and expansive redefinition of politics in Europe growing out of the French Revolution. The struggle for their own form of people's rule hangs heavily over societies in the Third World as they search, sometimes in an insurgency, for new forms and principles of legitimation as an aftershock to this earlier search in the West.

International Context

CONTAINMENT

Thus the international context for this pursuit of the lessons of Vietnam is that the Vietnam war and the other insurgencies studied here were part of a larger, international-level duel between the U.S. foreign policy of containment, and its promotion of evolutionary development, and the communist strategy of people's war, and its call for revolutionary insurgency, over which was the best way in the Third World to bring about some equivalent to this earlier political transformation in the West. In the case of the Vietnam War, what brought the United States into the struggle was the perceived imperatives of its foreign policy of containment, which was designed to halt the postwar spread of communism. For the revolutionaries in these insurgencies, what internationalized their struggles was the outside communist help they received by virtue of their use of the hallowed strategy of Marxist people's war in behalf of advancing the global revolutionary tide.

Turning first to containment, the significance of World War II cuts across most aspects of postwar life, but for the United States, clearly, the war marked the end of its isolationism. The world had become too interdependent, and through these linkages America's participation in the international system could no longer be episodic. Hitler and the Japanese had compellingly shown that this was too dangerous. A steadying, constant hand was needed, and the Yankee Atlas, with remarkable domestic consensus, took up its global burdens at the United Nations, in the North Atlantic Treaty Organization (NATO) and at Bretton Woods in the construction of a new system of international trade and development. But it took some time for the actual shape of postwar international politics to emerge. Two realities soon dominated the thinking of American foreign policy makers: the growing difficulties with the Soviet Union and the rapid decolonization that was beginning in the Third World. To integrate these two concerns into a coherent global foreign policy, the United States developed the policy of containment.

With respect to the Soviet Union, after some initial confusion, virtually all sectors of opinion (except for Walter Lippmann) found reason enough to rally around George Kennan's famous "X" article on "the sources of Soviet conduct." He argued that Soviet Russia was an expansionist power for both nationalistic and ideological reasons. Because of its ideology, Soviet expansionism was more patient and tenacious than that of Hitler. Consequently, the best policy was one of "firm and vigilant containment." He also concluded that America's surest defense rested in making its democratic dreams come true at home.[40]

Kennan and others were somewhat hazy on how to apply containment to Asia and the rest of the world. The early conceptions, such as they were, involved an extension of what Akira Iriye has called the Yalta System, which was built on plans for an independent China guaranteed by a balance of power (particularly of outside powers) in East Asia. Thus the balance between China and Japan was to be echoed by a balance between the United States and the Soviet Union in this theater. South and Southeast Asia were to be left to the responsibility of their colonial rulers: the British, French, and Dutch. Throughout this early period, Kennan worried that his fellow countrymen were oversentimentalizing their concerns about Asia. Possessed of a strong geopolitical sense of the limits to American power, he sought to confine American security interests in Asia to Japan and the Philippines.[41]

Kennan's views, however, were not the only ones circulating in Washington. By 1950, this hazy Yalta System had been washed away by a rippling tide of events. In August 1949 the Russians exploded an atomic bomb, which conveyed visions of a global reach to Soviet power. To most Americans this vision quickened in October 1949, when China fell to the communists. In this setting, South and Southeast Asia seemed to beckon to the communists as a power vacuum. The British had given independence to India, Pakistan, Ceylon, and Burma. The Dutch had withdrawn from Indonesia. The French were locked in a revolutionary war of independence with the communist Viet Minh in Indochina. Communist insurgencies also threatened the British in Malaya and the newly independent Philippine government. Paul Nitze, George Kennan's successor as head of the National Security Council, wrote in his famous memorandum, NSC-68, "The assault on free institutions is world-wide now, and in the context of the present polarization of power a defeat of free institutions anywhere is a defeat everywhere." [42] A grand geopolitical pincers move seemed manifest when, in June 1950, the North Koreans invaded the South. This invasion was almost unanimously perceived in the United States as having been launched at the instigation of the Soviet Union. This perception brought up the specter of Munich. Dominoes seemed on the verge of falling to aggression everywhere. Containment was now immodestly global.

Global containment, under the rubric of Nitze's more expansive view of American power in NSC-68, proceeded along two tracks. One was a series of direct East-West confrontations and disputes between the Soviet Union and the Western powers, and the other was a competition for the "hearts and minds" of the emerging and underdeveloped countries of the Third World. With respect to the Soviet Union, these confrontations and disputes led to an almost institutionalized Cold War in which the two blocs set up two opposing alliances — the Warsaw Treaty Organization versus the North Atlantic Treaty Organization — and drew a "line" between themselves on the European continent, the Iron Curtain. Both alliances built up their conventional forces, and the United States and the USSR transformed themselves into superpowers by acquiring massive nuclear arsenals with mutually destructive capabilities.

For the Third World, containment meant building up prosperous and democratic societies that would become impervious to communist revolutionary appeals based on poverty and class tensions. In the 1950s a foreign aid program was inaugurated and the U.S. secretary of state John Foster Dulles sought to build on NATO by stringing together a global necklace of containment treaties — CENTO and METO in the Middle East and SEATO in South and Southeast Asia. The arc was completed with the ANZUS treaty (between Australia, New Zealand, and the United States) and bilateral American treaties with Taiwan, Japan, and South Korea. The 1960s were proclaimed the Development Decade, and President John F. Kennedy called for an Alliance for Progress to stimulate democratic aspirations and economic growth in Latin America. Winning hearts and minds, then, meant development and nation-building in an evolutionary rather than a revolutionary way. On the darker side, Soviet Premier Nikita Khrushchev's "Wars of National Liberation" speech on January 6, 1961, acknowledged that general and local wars with the United States and its allies were too dangerous, but he proclaimed that wars of national liberation remained open as a promising path to a global revolutionary future.[43] Theories of counterinsurgency mushroomed to thwart what Walt Rostow called, in this process of development, "the scavengers of modernization."[44]

In the bipolar first track, containment held up because of the drastic realignment of European politics resulting from the upheavals in Soviet society that crystallized in 1989. These upheavals have led to an essential liquidating of the Cold War mostly on Western terms. Even when the American foreign policy consensus broke down during the Vietnam War, few in American domestic politics quarreled with the proposition that the Soviets remained a principal adversary and that NATO was a commitment the United States must continue to honor. Kennan had written his "X" article, after all, principally to explain Soviet behavior.

Regarding the second track, however, the United States was operating under at least four debilitating handicaps. These handicaps, furthermore, were not independent of each other but piled up on each other to produce the era's worst cumulative result: the debacle in Vietnam.

Mention has already been made of the centrality of World War II to the structure of postwar international politics. As a first handicap, historical legacies from this war created enormous difficulties for the United States in the Third World. In Asia, the poor initial military performance of the Western colonial powers against the Japanese doomed an easy postwar reimposition of their imperial rule. Despite their ultimate defeat, the Japanese had exploded the myth of Western military superiority and ended the seeming naturalness of colonial rule. In the period of rapid decolonization that followed World War II, the United States, as a Western power, was partially stuck with someone else's colonial legacy. Thus in the NATO alliance's goal to contain the Soviet Union in Europe, the United States formally aligned itself with the premier prewar imperialist powers (Britain and France). In propaganda terms, therefore, it was relatively easy to depict any American intervention in areas of the "second track" as an extension of neocolonialism rather than as a defense of containment.

American policymakers in the immediate postwar period were not unaware of this problem. Both Russell Fifield and Evelyn Colbert have pointed out that these policymakers did appreciate the importance of nationalism in the Third World and that American foreign policy had to strive to be on the right side of this force. Doing this, they also understood, meant a distancing of the United States from colonialism because anticolonialism was one of the most powerful motivators of these nationalist sentiments.[45]

There were, however, limits to this appreciation. As dangerous as it was to be tagged as an imperialist in an anticolonialist Third World, this danger was overshadowed by another historical legacy of World War II: Europe First. As in the prosecution of the campaign against the Germans in Europe and the Japanese in the Pacific, in the two tracks of containment it was also Europe first. That is, holding the line against the Soviets in Europe was always paramount over supporting Third World nationalism. A classic example was the American support of the futile French attempt from 1946 to 1954 to regain control of Indochina from the communist and nationalist Viet Minh. In the 1950s, a loss in the second track by standing in the way of a successful anticolonialist revolution in Asia was viewed as an acceptable cost to the greater global goal of preserving European unity in the first-track containment of the Soviet Union. By supporting the French in Indochina, the Americans hoped to gain vital French support for a European Defense Community. In the 1960s, however, there was a larger cost to these priorities: having stood squarely against nationalism (albeit a communist nationalism) and with the French colonialists in the 1950s, it strained the credibility of the Vietnamese for the Americans suddenly to portray themselves as champions of Vietnamese nationalism.

A second handicap was that the objectives of containment in the Third World were never clear. Containment, as John Gaddis has so brilliantly analyzed, was no monolith. Throughout the postwar period, he argues, it swung between psychological and geopolitical strategies, which in the Third World meant lurches between the defense of peripheral areas almost everywhere in the case of psychological containment and only the defense of industrially important strongpoints in the case of geopolitical containment.[46] Thus where in the Third World containment should be applied and where it should not was always subject to conflicting interpretations.

Furthermore, for much of this period the foreign policy of the Soviet Union (the intended target of containment) lacked a true global reach, and its activities in the Third World were episodic and often inconsistent. For example, though the Soviets supported Cominform forums that called for wars of national liberation, they provided no support whatever for such wars in Malaya and the Philippines and did little to help the beleaguered communist insurgents in Greece during the late 1940s. Indeed, some of the same handicaps hampering the Americans also applied to the Soviet Union. Although the Soviets were mostly successful in dodging the label of being imperialists, their objectives were not always clear either and they, too, were unsure of themselves on the ground. Despite the constancy of their commitment to the communist cause in Vietnam, in neighboring Laos they backed themselves into a corner by supporting both the neutralists and the Pathet Lao communists, who promptly turned on each other with Russian weapons. In the 1962 Geneva Conference on Laos, the Soviets, looking somewhat silly, essentially got out of Laos altogether.[47]

Also the Chinese, whom the Americans feared so much, had a mixed reputation in the Third World. Sometimes the fulminators of fiery revolutionary rhetoric, they were also viewed as a fellow backward people whose leaders, especially at the Bandung Conference in 1955, could speak movingly of Third World solidarity. Thus containment in the second track, as David Mozingo has shrewdly observed, lacked the indispensable condition that made containment so successful in Europe: an agreed-upon external threat.[48]

Even if agreement could be reached between these contending strategies of containment on where in the second track to apply it, such a happy consensus was usually debilitated by a third handicap: once on the ground with containment, nobody knew how to make it work. Frequently, then, U.S. missions in individual countries found themselves in a dilemma over whether the role of the American "containers" was to uphold the domestic political order against the threat of communism or to weaken the local appeal of communism, at the sacrifice of a little order, by promoting internal democracy and pushing for social reforms.[49] In Vietnam in 1963, for example, some American officials supported the coup against the South Vietnamese president Ngo Dinh Diem to open the social order to reforms, while others, fearful of communist exploitation of the ensuing instability, opposed it. This confusion could often lead to tragedy, as in the case of Diem, who was murdered, an outcome neither American faction wanted. As a result of this confusion and the clear dangers that accompanied it, containment, as exercised in the "field," developed a penchant for stability.[50]

In such a murky environment it was understandable, though tragic, that a fourth handicap naturally followed: the United States was not sure of the extent or limits of its power in the Third World. Early formulations were very modest. Mention has already been made of George Kennan's limited conception of confining containment to key strongpoints (Western Europe, the Middle East, Caribbean, Japan, and the Philippines). Inexorably, however, the rhetoric of containment slipped into Paul Nitze's more expansive ("free institutions anywhere") language of universal empire. The sheer size of its economy and its frightening inventory of nuclear weapons gave America, in former senator William Fulbright's memorable phrase, the "arrogance of power" to think of its reach as truly global in scope. Along with this power came a plethora of theories on how to use it diplomatically and militarily to achieve such goals as "deterrence," "compellance," "escalation dominance," and "coercive diplomacy." Yet the guiding images were conflicting. Counterbalancing the heady victory in World War II, which Americans saw themselves as leading, was the more sobering stalement in Korea. Unfortunately, in this second track, American power and its theories required an empirical test.[51]

Thus in pursuing the policy of containment in the Era of People's War, Americans sought to champion leaders or political forces that could above all guarantee order and after that hopefully be hospitable to private enterprise, reform, and democratic politics which might eventually create the preconditions for more open societies. Such men were Fulgencio Batista in Cuba, Anastasio Somoza in Nicaragua, the Shah in Iran, Syngman Rhee in Korea, Ngo Dinh Diem in Vietnam, and Ferdinand Marcos in the Philippines. In this second track, then, not only did the American knights of Camelot have a difficult time making their foreign policy work, they also compromised the very democratic ideals they were espousing against the totalitarian Soviet Union.

PEOPLE'S WAR

With such a list of champions, a significant challenge to this policy was not long in coming. It came from the Vietnamese countryside and in the form of the strategy of Marxist people's war. For a test of power in the jungles, rice paddies, and hills of Vietnam, containment was a poor match, or choice of weapons, in a duel with such a strategy. Though the precise definition, origins, and permutations of people's war have been amply treated elsewhere,[52] at this juncture it would be useful to recall the breakthrough Mao Zedong's strategy achieved in fundamentally altering the calculus of political and military power in the Third World. It was a strategy born out of the desperation of Mao's predicament in China upon barely surviving the Long March in 1935 after breaking out from his Guomindang adversary's Fifth Encirclement Campaign to "exterminate" the Chinese communist revolution. His predicament was that as the head of a dispirited remnant of ten thousand communist guerrillas facing a powerful Guomindang government war machine, and, two years later, a terrifyingly modern Japanese army as well, he needed a strategy with which he could cajole his troops into staying in the field with a credible chance of success for "men over weapons."

Essentially, Mao's formula of people's war consisted of seven components. First, it must be led by a *communist party*. Second, it must have an *armed force*, but one strictly controlled by the party. Third, it must establish a *united front* to broaden the people's war's base of support. (These first three points come straight from Lenin's strategy of a revolutionary insurrection and establish Mao's communist "orthodoxy." The remaining components are Mao's own.) Fourth, it must champion the *mass line* to gain the support of the people. Fifth, it should set up *base areas* for support, regroupment, and pilot demonstrations of the revolutionary future. Sixth, to the extent possible, it must be *self-reliant* lest it lose touch with its ultimate source of strength and support, the people. Finally, a people's war must rely on a three-staged military strategy of *protracted war*. For Mao this involved building his forces through three intensifying stages of warfare: hit-and-run guerrilla attacks, blows by larger mobile columns skillful in maneuver actions, and culminating set-piece conventional offensives.

Mao's strategy acquired its power through the political mobilization of the peasant masses in support of, and actually into, his military forces. This support was achieved by first determining what issues were salient to the peasantry and then vigorously championing them, or, in Mao's words, promoting the "mass line" of his fourth point.[53] In time, less emphasis was given to clear distinctions among the three stages, and, as a people's war reached its final stages the role of guerrillas would naturally lessen. Mao, and his later fellow strategists in Vietnam, however, insisted that active participation by these guerrillas was necessary throughout because these peasant guerrillas were the very fountain of support for the war itself. The payoff was the military key to Mao's strategy of "men over weapons": a virtual intelligence monopoly in the countryside.

In following this strategy to an ultimate seizure of power in Beijing in October 1949, Mao fundamentally altered the calculus of political and military power in Asia. Essentially, he ended the long-standing gulf between elites and masses that had so enfeebled the countries of Asia (and of the Third World) and made them such easy prey for the nineteenth-century European imperialists. It is hardly an exaggeration to say, then, that Mao's triumph was the Oriental equivalent of the French Revolution. The Vietnamese communists were quick to seize on Mao's insights and fashion their own application of people's war first against the French and then against the Americans.

Legitimacy

In such an era of decolonization and development—and of insurgency and intervention—the summoning of the image of the French Revolution should provide the international context for my central presupposition, namely, that the postwar period (1945 to 1975) witnessed a globalization of the earlier European legitimacy crisis so critical to the formation of the modern Western state and to the consolidation of its power. In the rapid transfers of political authority and in the stimulation of productive forces of economic growth, the "emerging nations" were similarly confronted by basic questions of societal definition—who should rule and on what basis of authority? what should the purpose of rule be and how should it be carried out? and what were acceptable standards of performance?—questions all of legitimacy.

Chapter 3

ANALYTICAL FRAMEWORK OF LEGITIMACY, INSURGENCY, AND INTERVENTION

Development, Insurgency, and Legitimacy

Whatever development or modernization means—to be like the United States, or like the Soviet Union, to be so prosperous as to be free of material want (to have solved the production crisis), to be democratic and industrial, or maybe to be bureaucratic in a technocratic way—above all else, for countries of the Third World (which are not like any of the above), it means to change. As these brief images suggest, it is a process of "expanding choice."[1] In societies undergoing the changes, the problem for the ruling elites is how to manage these comprehensively expanding choices and keep them under control: control in the sense of keeping the unruly waves of change moving toward the beach in a way that also keeps the regime from getting upended and overthrown by a revolutionary insurgency.

Such a process of change, or development, has received numerous portraits in the literature. First characterizations were dichotomous, that is, development involved, most simply, a transition from traditional to modern societies. For the structural functionalists of sociology, Talcott Parsons posited a set of five "pattern-variables" that constituted a social system and were described as being placed on a dichotomous continuum. Development, then, was portrayed by Parsons as moving from one set of variables to the other, from the traditional to the modern.[2]

Later theorists, heavily influenced by Walt Rostow's three stages of economic growth (from the preconditions to the takeoff to the final stage of sustained and automatic growth), saw it as progressing in stages.[3] From this perspective, theorists of political development characterized developing countries as transitional societies caught between the persistent hold of tradition and the beckoning of modernity. Fred Riggs, for example, called these transitional societies "prismatic," viewing the process of development as movement from traditional "fused" societies through an intermediate "prismatic" stage culminating in a modern, fully "diffracted" society. By a "fused" society, Riggs meant a society with essentially one undifferentiated set of values secured by one traditional authority structure. A "diffracted" society is a completely modern society with a set of differentiated and pluralistic values and with pluralistic and competitive authority structures to match. The intermediate stage, a "prismatic" society, is marked by conflicting subsystems in which some values and institutional structures are tightly fused and others are in the process of breaking up and diffracting into modernity.[4] Thus prismatic societies are ones plagued by political, social, and economic bottlenecks that can offer themselves as wonderful grist for the mill of an insurgency.

Indeed, insurgencies have often come to be a characteristic of development or modernization. Samuel Huntington has gone so far as to contend that development cannot occur without violence.[5] Somewhat more modestly, the studies of both Ivo and Rosalind Feirabend and of Douglas Hibbs have noted that transitional societies do exhibit greater internal violence than either backward or fully modern societies.[6] Orthodox economic theorists like Albert O. Hirschman have described economic growth as being, inevitably, an imbalanced process resulting in frequent bottlenecks as the pendulum of effort, striving for balance and stability, swings between forward and backward linkages (investment in infrastructure and then in services to this infrastructure).[7] In many different ways, insurgencies occur as a result of the bottlenecks to this process of development, and they impede further political progress. Either the regime will break through the political and military challenge represented by the insurgents and move on, or it will eventually be overwhelmed by the insurgents, who will have to establish their own justification for rule (legitimacy) and themselves move on to the next challenge. In any insurgency, the period in the middle when it is unclear whose claim to, and brand of, legitimacy will triumph can seem to be an endless and hopeless interregnum.

A difficult concept and goal in the best of circumstances, legitimacy is particularly elusive in an insurgency where at least two sides try to establish exclusively their own version of legitimate rule. The government has to defend both its vision and its performance of legitimacy, whereas the insurgents, at least at first, seek only to destroy the government's capability to perform. They, in turn, often have a vision that is vague, lacks authenticity in the culture, or is better hidden. Marxism-Leninism, after all, is a European import saddled with such unpalatable tenets as atheism and agricultural collectivization. Buffeted by these two forces, an insurgency grows out of a legitimacy crisis of a second degree, that is, a crisis both as to who the possessor of its mantle should be (first degree) and as to what the very terms of legitimation should be (second degree).[8]

As a second-degree legitimacy crisis, insurgencies are struggles over which side has the superior basis for the justification of political authority. Thus insurgencies are revolutions in that the insurgents seek not only to show that their claims to legitimate authority are superior to those of the incumbents but also to recast the justifications for political authority on a entirely different socio-politico-economic ordering of society. (Incidentally, in this work, the term *society* is used for this comprehensive socio-politico-economic order of a country; *state* or *government* refers to the institutional complex that provides political rule for a country; and *regime* designates a particular set of power holders in a country.) Insurgencies are distinguished from other forms of revolution by their temporal dimensions and their socioeconomic groups of origin. Unlike insurrections, which are cataclysmic, sudden, and quick, insurgencies are revolutions that move "on a slow burn." That is, in facing an initially strong and resistant government, insurgencies build their movement gradually, either from remote places or with peripheral groups, until they are strong enough to mount a frontal challenge to an incumbent regime. Thus insurgencies, unlike the Russian, French, or American revolutions, do not build their movements close to, or upon, groups central to a society's structure of power, but on outlying, peripheral, minority, or low socioeconomic groups that require a long-term political and military strategy for gaining access to this societal center so that a direct bid for power can be made.

Nonlegitimacy

As briefly mentioned in Chapter 2, it is possible to rule without legitimacy. Indeed, for a time, a ruling group, at least in personal terms, can profit immensely from its absence. Such a ruling group, however, has very thin margins when confronted with determined challenges. Politically, in fact, a central goal or even definition of development is the creation of rule and authority rooted in solid sources of legitimacy. The transition to new and modern sources of legitimacy, nevertheless, can be traumatic to any ruling group because it will undoubtedly entail some crucial accommodations with, and even sacrifices to, all the new groups clamoring for their share of these "expanding choices." Sidney Verba and Gabriel Almond have defined this new and nearly universal demand to take part in the political process as a "participation explosion" and regard it as the driving force of modernization.[9]

Even when the literature on development was most confident and the policy pronouncements the most grandiose — in the early 1960s before Vietnam — there was still a recognition that not everyone was going to make it. Joseph Strayer, for example, concluded: "Building a nation-state is a slow and complicated affair . . . [and] most of the political entities created in the past 50 years are never going to complete this process." Thus, to be very frank, there are many regimes in the Third World that persist without legitimacy, that is, they are nonlegitimate. In part, this is only to recognize Theda Skocpol's point that states or incumbent regimes can have a separate existence and set of interests apart from that of its society.[10]

Such a nonlegitimate condition can exist only where the ties between this ruling structure and its populace are such that very little is expected of the government one way or the other. That is, the state is neither expected to underwrite the welfare of its citizenry nor to be responsible for any of its problems.[11] Usually these regimes form into cliques around a central personality where "charisma . . . has been bastardized by 'personalism.'"[12] Beyond simple coercion and venality, a nonlegitimate regime lacks institutional mechanisms for dealing with problems or challenges that can survive the blows of these clumsy weapons. When the challenges persist, nonlegitimacy quickly manifests what Samuel Huntington called "praetorianism," a world in which "the wealthy bribe; students riot; workers strike; mobs demonstrate; and the military coup."[13] Lacking any reserves of political legitimacy, a nonlegitimate regime is easily crippled by praetorianism and becomes a soft target for anyone bent on a regime change.

A more persistent nonlegitimacy is a regime that has a relationship of distant nonlegitimacy with the general society but creates a network of mutually supportive ties of loyalty and "inside advantages" for a privileged favored elite. This is a legitimacy for the few at the expense of the many. Its persistence depends both on the many's continued low expectations from the regime and/or ignorance of this basic condition and on the few's ability coercively to assure the many's compliance with this arrangement. The classic example of such a persistent nonlegitimacy is the former white-run South Africa, but Saddam Hussein's Baathist regime in Iraq for minority

Sunnis at the expense of Southern Shi'ites and Northern Kurds, as well as the Philippines of Ferdinand Marcos, can also serve.[14] In this regard, it has to be observed that if there is an international influence to political developments within individual nation-states, it is surely that the persistence of such states will become increasingly difficult.

These freezes of nonlegitimacy can occur at two stages in the process of development. One is during the rot of a very traditional and backward society kept in a condition of complete stagnation by the authorities for their own venal purposes. It is a stagnation in which both GNP growth and access to the political system are at a nearly complete standstill. What circulation there is of anything—money, jobs, status, position, and influence—takes place exclusively within a ruling clique. Though true examples of such stasis in the real world are hard to find, such countries as Burma and Paraguay (until recently) come to mind.

A freeze may also take place further down the road in a case of arrested development, whether deliberate or accidental. Such a freeze is described well by David Apter. This second freeze typically takes place after a considerable amount of growth, even a boom, has occurred. Perhaps progressive land reforms or other green revolution improvements have sparked a surge in primary production. Light industries may have sprung up in the cities as well. A surge of urban squatters, however, may overburden social services and put the middle class under various forms of taxation and other social pressures. As Apter goes on "Caught between the growing power and prestige of a bureaucratic and technologically elite and downward mobility pressure, mobility displacement rather than incorporation occurs in sectors close to marginalized groups. The more a bourgeoisie is subject to such pulls, the more it will change from a class in itself to a class for itself, a circumstance favoring authoritarian political regimes."[15]

The distinguishing characteristic of this arrested nonlegitimacy is that although there may be overall economic growth and some expanding political participation in the system, it is selective (often along ethnic and religious lines). The small middle-class and monetized world of the cities may grow while the suburban shantytowns and rural backwaters continue to stagnate. Some new middle-class aspirants are welcomed into growing businesses, bloating bureaucracies, and the officer corps of an increasingly top-heavy military, but elsewhere social access is blocked.

This second condition is not dissimilar to the bottlenecks described earlier. As shall become clearer as this study progresses, insurgencies are far more likely to occur during a second "arrested" freeze than during a first "stagnant" one. A second freeze, with its all-too-frequent insurgent consequence, also underscores Huntington's warning that development, once started, cannot be assumed self-confidently to be on a linear inevitable march of progress. Instead, sadly, the process can be arrested by nonlegitimate decay or derailed by insurgent revolution.[16]

The General Transition

This general historical transition from traditional to modern society can be illustrated by the flow chart in Figure 3.1. Fundamentally, it shows the place of an insurgency in the course of this transition. Two caveats about the focus of this flow chart need to be understood. First, this general transition is not unilinear. Indeed, the specification of modern society is left outside or beyond the chart. Insurgencies, in their resolution, produce either nonrevolutionary or revolutionary rule, which may or may not complete this historical transition. Second, in this transition, there are many more possible alternative paths than depicted on the chart. The one alternative path shown is designed to be merely illustrative to preserve this focus on insurgency. In this transition, then, when a disruptive bottleneck occurs for whatever reason, one possible result is a legitimacy crisis that can provoke an insurgent challenge to the ruling regime. The outcome to this insurgency will determine whether this transition will continue under revolutionary or nonrevolutionary rule. It is this "insurgency box" that is broken down for further analysis in Figures 3.2 and 3.3.

The flow chart does depict other possibilities for the resolution of a bottleneck. As was discussed in Chapter 1, a legitimacy crisis can be resolved without a body politic erupting into an insurgency. More optimistically, a ruling regime might be able to remove a bottleneck and make rapid progress toward becoming a modern society. It also may face further bottlenecks that it will either solve or confront another legitimacy crisis and possible insurgency. Similarly, a society that has just come out of an insurgency will not necessarily be immune to more bottlenecks before it has achieved the transition to modern society. In Malaya, for example, after the defeat of the communist insurgency in 1960, the subsequent rapid progress was disrupted by the bottleneck of bloody ethnic rioting in 1969. Pessimistically, a bottleneck may produce neither insurgent conflict nor rapid progress but a stagnant quagmire presided over by a nonlegitimate regime. Alternatively, an insurgency may become so destructively prolonged that rather than any side winning, a nonlegitimate regime can develop that will carry on against the ineffectual sputtering of a group of insurgents whose original political ideals have degenerated into a causeless addiction to plunder and violence. Nonlegitimacy and stagnation, however, can also serve as way stations for a total reconceptualization of political goals—away from this seemingly in-

Figure 3.1. Transition from Traditional to Modern Society

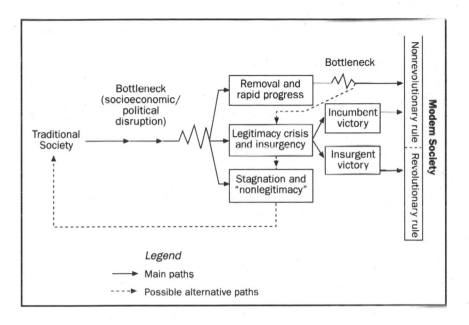

Legend

→ Main paths

----▸ Possible alternative paths

evitable march from traditional to modern society to a recapturing of some golden traditional past. Thus after their revolution against the Shah of Iran in 1979, the Muslim *ayatollahs* sought to redirect their society to the spiritually pure days of Abu Bakr of the sixth century. What they achieved was to mire their society in a decade of political terror and economic stagnation. Similarly, the Sendero Luminoso of Peru proclaims a forward-looking revolution of people's war to achieve the backward glories of the Inca Empire.

Three Levels of Legitimation—First Cut

Under the threat of insurgency, the acquisition of legitimacy—and in substantial amounts—would appear to be a clear imperative of political development. Legitimacy gives a regime authority, a resource it can call on beyond the mere numbers of its soldiers or size of its budget. Soldiers and budgets are just part of its raw power. If it has legitimacy, as challenges arise, a regime can invoke willing obedience, acts of loyalty, and deeds of self-sacrifice. That is, it can put esprit de corps in the army and a reforming zeal in the bureaucracy, and it can inspire gestures of support from broad sectors of the citizenry.

What follows is an attempt to describe, analytically, how this legitima-

Table 3.1. Domestic Legitimacy

Legitimacy Type		Legitimacy Appeal	Legitimacy Level	Legitimacy Object	Legitimacy Issues (Measures)
I. National-Traditional — Active legitimacy		Belief	National/leaders	System/traditional order	Nationalism, mandate of Heaven, "throw out foreigners," etc.
		Opportunity	Subgroups/cadres, NCOS, officers, public servants	Regime/administration/incumbents	Communalism and land reform
Passive support		Interest	Mass/individuals	Policies: popularity and effectiveness	Personal security
II. National-Modern — Active legitimacy		Belief	National/leaders	System/constitutional order	Modern nationalism, modernization; sometimes equated with democracy and industrialization
		Opportunity	Subgroups/cadres, etc.	Regime/administration/incumbents	Societal access (education, jobs, status, land reform); Political participation (elections, interest groups, parties);
Passive support		Interest	Mass/individuals	Policies: popularity and effectiveness	Physical security: obtain rewards— "Honda economy," avoiding punishments up to "Establishment" terror

Revolutionaries { *Incumbents* { }

Table 3.1. Continued

Legitimacy Type	Legitimacy Appeal	Legitimacy Level	Legitimacy Object	Legitimacy Issues (Measures)
III. Revolutionary Active legitimacy	Belief	National-international/leaders	*Organization*—Leadership strategy	High road of revolutionary strategy (People's War) and national liberation
	Opportunity	Subgroups/cadres	*Organization*—Cohesiveness, "democratic centralism," party discipline	Mobility in a new world where previously frustrated
Passive support	Interest	Mass/individuals	*Organization*—Outreach, the "mass line"	Obtaining physical rewards, life in liberated zones, avoiding punishments up to terror

Revolutionaries

tion is achieved. Essentially, it involves three interactive processes that take place together and are presented in Table 3.1. First, I will present legitimacy singly as a process of legitimation marked by three degrees of intensification: from legitimacy of interest (a merely passive support of the regime) to legitimacy of opportunity (calling for an active commitment to the regime) to legitimacy of belief (resulting in a basic belief in the regime's right to rule). Second, although legitimacy appeals move along a single upward path of intensification, along this path itself, I will describe how the basic nature and definition of legitimacy itself is shifting, dualistically, from traditional to modern sources, thereby requiring the appeals (and appeal-makers) to adapt themselves in their ascent to a simultaneous shift from the traditional to the modern. Third, if in the midst of this maelstrom, an insurgent revolution crops up, I will show how the revolutionaries, in turn, must develop a strategy that allows them both to recruit people away from the traditional and maybe partially modernizing order and to elicit from them commitments to a novel, yet not totally strange, revolutionary legitimacy. Passing an insurgent-ridden society through such a tripartite analysis permits an assessment of how the two sides, relatively, are doing—and can form the basis for a decision on the efficacy of an external intervention into such a struggle. Thus, these three processes, in their combined effects, permit analysis of a fourth process: the interjection of an intervention into an insurgency caught up in this threefold dynamic.

Adapting this general framework of legitimacy to the particular second-degree legitimacy crisis of an insurgency, in an insurgency, two sides, the incumbents and the insurgents, struggle for the prize of legitimacy as a basis of justification for political power. They struggle between themselves over who should possess this mantle, but they also struggle with the concept and goal itself, trying to frame it in such a way as to attract the populace to their side. An insurgency, then, when viewed as a legitimacy struggle, can be seen as a race up "Mount Legitimus" by the two claimants who are making appeals on three intensifying levels of calculation or commitment for the support of the people.

To begin with the first single process analytical cut, the most basic calculation or level of support is that of interest. Here the individuals and the masses move with the prevailing winds. They calculate their personal security to blend in and become inconspicuous to both sides. At this level, they take personal advantage of those programs and policies that benefit them and grumble about and evade those that do not. This "legitimacy" of interest, at best, offers passive support to the contending sides.

A second or intermediate level of support is that of opportunity. Here some individuals and groups calculate that real advantages can be had by actively joining one side or the other, whether for the opportunity of command and influence with the insurgents or for riches and prestige with the incumbent regime. Calculation at this level requires an active commitment to the side of choice and produces the tier of dedicated cadre leaders or reform-minded bureaucrats and civic-spirited citizens so vital to any side's quest for legitimation. This is basically the level at which organization, participation, and mobilization take place.

Finally, at the summit, there is the appeal to ideology or belief. This requires a transcending of calculations of individual interests and opportunity to ones that sublimate these individual and even group concerns to a largely selfless devotion to "the cause" and the good of the country as a whole. Few in a society, on either side, will rise to this level of support, but, as Andrew Molnar has pointed out, an insurgency gains staying power only insofar as it is able to transform its earlier, cadre-level commitment of opportunity to a deep conversion, for a fair percentage of these stalwarts, to its cause and ideology.[17] This requisite of a core number of "true believers" applies equally to the incumbent regime.

An insurgency and a reacting counterinsurgency, then, is a three-tiered struggle. To return back down the mountain, it is a struggle most fundamentally for a working minority, "a steel frame," of true believers who can both inspire and articulate a vision of legitimacy and a strategy for attaining it. For this effort, second, they must count on a dedicated organization that offers enough opportunities to enlist active commitments toward sustaining its activities. Finally, it entails providing for an acquiescent mass support base whose calculations of interest will respond to appropriate policy stimuli, whether ones of the carrot or the stick.

National Legitimacy: Traditional and Modern— Second Cut

Turning to my second and dualistic analytical cut, an insurgency is a national legitimacy crisis "of sorts" that arises from the challenge of a revolution "on the slow burn." As the two sides struggle for the mantle of authority at three levels of legitimation, it is important to understand that this struggle is over a concept (national legitimacy) and attendant institutional structure (amorphously speaking, the state) that are themselves undergoing a profound transition from traditional to modern political concepts and principles of societal organization. Such a quest for national legitimacy presents the challenge of steering a passage between calls for renewed loyalties to historical ideals and the beckoning of a new age model of a better life. Though this transition may be one way to define the general process of development, in each nation the degree, pace, and quality of this transition to the modern world will be shaped by its own history and traditions.

Ernest Gellner has defined nationalism as a sentiment of political belief that the political and national unit should be one. This sentiment is aroused when this principle is being violated, through foreign or illegitimate rule, and satisfied when it is being fulfilled. In Gellner's sense, nationalism has become tantamount to a standard of legitimacy.[18] As part of the process of development, however, these sentiments are in a state of transition. It is critical that the claimants to these sentiments appreciate where these sentiments lie and where they are headed so that they can devise a strategy either to shift these sentiments to, or preserve them for, their respective sides. For the Asian cases in this book, for example, taking a stand in World War II as to whether the Japanese occupations violated these nationalist sentiments or helped in their fulfillment became very important for claims of legitimacy after the war. Obviously, those individuals and groups who chose to collaborate with the Japanese made a cripplingly wrong choice.

In analytically dividing national legitimacy into traditional and modern sources, two qualifications must be kept in mind. First, no society is fully traditional or fully modern. The distinction is one of degree and nature of appeal. Second, then, traditional and modern behaviors, motives, and institutions are often hard to separate. In fact, the very notion of a transition suggests that political motives, and institutional expressions of these motives, will involve various and individual combinations of these tugging calls and beckonings. Perhaps the best example of this is Fred Riggs's "clects," which he has defined as organizations in transitional societies which combine traditional and modern values. That is, they may have modern structures but run on traditional principles. The word itself is a combination of clique and sect, and he meant the term analytically to describe bureaucracies, political parties, and labor unions as they function in the Third World.[19]

With a dualistic view of national legitimacy (traditional and modern), the components or issues that make up these legitimation appeals may be taken up with a greater range of freedom. Our climb up Mount Legitimus now can be seen more as a meandering path than a straight highway. To begin with, at the low level of "legitimacy" of interest, for both traditional and modern forms, the responses fall far short of granting legitimacy to the regime. Instead it involves a granting of mere passive support, of going along. In traditional terms, such support centers around the measures of personal security and, in modern terms, of physical and material security.

To be personally secure is to have cloaked around you the fused relationships (in that they subsume all of a person's social roles) of the patron-client ties that characterize the rural world of what anthropologists call the Little Tradition.[20] Although this village world is by no means monolithic—indeed, much of the rural prescience of communists worldwide is that they were among the first to appreciate this politically[21]—it has been generally portrayed as a universe embodying a cognitive orientation of "limited good." George Foster has explained this orientation for these villagers as "an unverbalized, implicit expression of their understanding of the 'rules of the game' of living imposed upon them by their social, natural, and supernatural universes." The limited good is that in this orientation it is held as a given that "all of the desired things of life such as land, wealth, friendship, . . . respect . . . power . . . and safety, *exist in finite quantity* and *are always in short supply* . . . [and] in addition there is no way directly within peasant power to increase *available quantities*." Further, it is a world bounded by the past and the authority of its traditions. In such a traditional world, personal security is achieved by choices and actions that are congruent with this cultural universe.[22]

The process of political development, however, has challenged this closed village cosmos and opened up a new set of calculations, modern ones of a more material security. Actually, Edward Shils has conceded that for many people of the Little Tradition, their attachments to their culture were tenuous and ripe for alienation. Further, he has acknowledged that there is a slice of rural beliefs that are free of traditionality and form a "rational zone" that is susceptible to new ideas and influences. It is precisely this rational zone that beckonings of modernization appealed to and opened up the new grounds for calculation (or orientation) which James Downton has described as "transactions." In such a rational orientation, people make straight-up cost-benefit analyses of proffered choices, whether positive ones of expected rewards or negative ones of anticipated punishments.[23] Thus, in an insurgency, positively, both sides can compete by offering various rewards: a poor but less repressive life in a liberated zone or, in government areas, the blessings of a "Honda economy."[24] Negatively, of course, both sides can punish and force submission through terror and counterterror. People responding to such measures at this level of appeal, especially to the positive ones, are doing so on the basis of a rational maximizing of their utilities based on the relative advantages of the structures presented to them. In this modern sense, they are rational actors, or as Samuel Popkin has named them, "political entrepreneurs."[25]

In larger societal terms, the rural population, in an insurgency, is being pulled into a struggle over the development and definition of a national legitimacy that is shifting from traditional to modern components. Two outside paths into this struggle open up for them, of varying degree of welcome: one to capitalist markets and, hopefully, some measure of political participation, and the other to the spartan life and opportunities for power in a revolutionary insurgency.[26] Nevertheless, the significant feature of this passive level of support is that though peasants may go along with one side or the other and take advantage of the measures of individual policies and incentives available, they have made no active commitments. They have not yet done anything to stand out or get into trouble. The grass still bends with the prevailing winds. Finally, at this level, people respond as discollected individuals; or, in a general sense, this is the mass level in Table 3.1. No groups have yet mobilized themselves for organized political or economic purpose. Politics are still passive, and crossover points lie ahead.

Active commitments are made, however, when people jump off this stony fence of passivity in response to the galvanizing appeal of opportunity. The primary goal of this level of appeal is cadre recruits for the revolutionaries and the military officers, noncommissioned officers as well as public servants for the incumbents. Though the motivations and calculations may be individual, the effect is nevertheless a group one in that such recruits are channeled into the organizations that constitute the structures of the two sides. Such recruits are now committed to one side or the other and help to provide their side with active legitimacy in that, for whatever personal reasons, they have offered general support to their chosen side. At the outset, these groups do not respond so much to appeals of ideology, nationalism, and the grand cause as they do to intermediate and group causes that are more pragmatic and relate more to the competing social and economic structures of the two sides: rank, pay, prestige, identification. Such people, nevertheless, form the hard-core activists of the two sides and play the role of intermediaries—the "Middle Tradition"—between a society's Great Tradition and Little Tradition. Issues here are of local grievance and subgroup identity.[27]

In traditional terms, the evaluative standard at this level is not high-flown appeals of an often distant nationalism or a murky Marxism but local and immediate communalism. Although there are other issues and indicators, probably the most important measure for communal legitimacy in the rural Third World is land reform. A quick glance at Figure 3.2 will confirm that land reform also appears as an opportunity measure for modern legitimacy. Again, this is owing to the dual purpose and role of land reform. Traditionally, land reform can be a way for traditional leaders to reestablish old virtues of justice and patronage. In modern terms, it can bring about a redistribution of income, and, through the granting of legal titles to these parcels of land, open up access to a dawning modern world.

In its most comprehensive sense, a land reform is the breakup of an agricultural system in which farm land is concentrated in the hands of a small landholding elite. The breakup involves an expropriation of these large estates—either without compensation or, usually with foreign assistance, some subsidized purchase arrangement—and a redistribution of these holdings to peasants with little or no land of their own. In addition to the redistribution of the land itself, successful land reforms require such further measures as legal grants of title, fair taxes, the provision of technical assistance, and the availability of affordable credit.

There is a debate in the literature over which category of peasant is most likely to be the instigator of rural revolt. Eric Wolf has argued that it is the middle peasants; Bruce Russett, that revolt comes from peasants for whom land is unfairly distributed; Jeffrey Paige, from sharecroppers working for monetary wages in the highly fluctuating export markets; and Roy Prosterman has emphasized that rural protest comes from the utterly destitute and propertyless tenant farmers.[28] A recent global study on this issue has concluded that for an insurgency "agrarian inequality is relevant only to the extent that it is associated with inequality in the nationwide distribution of income."[29] What is relevant, no matter which category of peasant is more rebellion-prone, is that land reform of some kind or other—even as an equalization or rationalization of rural with other sector incomes—is critical either to preventing an insurgency in the first place or to blunting one if it has started.

In modern terms, the key to how development, defined as "expanding choice," is managed centers on how easy and fair the access is to this opening world. In David Apter's words, "choice can be operationalized in terms of *access* [italics added] through networks of roles, classes, and institutions . . . these networks connect choice to hierarchy. . . . How to control access to choice and promote the sharing of it according to approved rules and conditions of equity has been the special political concern of development." [30] Further, because most Third World countries have been drawn up according to "divide and rule" colonial legacies, access is often unfairly divided among ethnic, religious, and regional groups.

For the purposes of analyzing insurgencies, access is best broken up into the two components or measures which I term *societal access* and *political participation*.[31] For societal access, I refer to such operational indicators as relatively open access to education, jobs at all status and income levels, organizations set up to promote these goals (labor unions; training programs and schools that are widely available, with financial aid and "reserved seats"; and professional associations), and, especially in an insurgency, land reform. Symbolically, societal access in most insurgencies focuses on land reform in the countryside and labor unions in the cities. For political participation, I refer to such operational indicators as local action groups, organized political parties, and voting, as well as rates of participation in both local and national elections. Obviously, these two sets of indicators can overlap—land reform, for example, certainly can deal out new cards of political power and participation—but clustering them around these two terms of societal access and political participation highlights an important point about insurgencies. As Samuel Huntington and Joan Nelson have pointed out, along any continuum of access there can be differences between political "commodities" and social and economic "commodities" that can form bottlenecks in themselves. In Huntington's view, it is precisely in the gap between economic growth and political languor that development decays into violence.[32]

As the central measure of political participation, elections must be fair to provide this aspect of legitimacy. In their most comprehensive sense, fair elections require a franchise open to all adult citizens from whatever subgroup in the country, a campaign process open to all parties and viewpoints without intimidation or unequal conditions of campaigning, and, at the actual balloting, competitive choices that attract at least half the registered voters to the polls. Further, the polling itself should be free from violence, intimidation, vote-buying, and fraudulent counting of ballots. In the real histories of many countries, what constitutes fair balloting can become a relative and contextual matter. Thus in Vietnam, though communists were unfairly barred from all elections, the 1967 presidential elections were far more fair than were the elections of 1971 because the former, at least, gave the voters several candidates to choose from, whereas the latter offered the voters only a one-candidate referendum.

Essentially, at the opportunity level, groups have been formed by people who have broken out of their initial passivity and made active and consequential commitments to one group or other to advance their fortunes and those of their groups. A quick look at the groups, issues, and measures at this level should make clear that with all these bubbling and often randomly coalescing participatory groups, something beyond the agenda of each group must be appealed to if some overall coherence and common societal purpose is to be developed and maintained. This is where the highest level of legitimation comes in, that of general beliefs and attendant programmatic and rationalizing ideologies. At this level, the tenets of these ideologies and the degree of their acceptance become the measures of legitimacy. Talcott Parsons, for one, has insisted that true legitimation of power occurs only when a society's institutional structure is linked to the core values of its culture. When justified in such normative terms, legitimation is of the highest order.[33]

Preeminently, in an insurgency, the leadership group of both sides responds to, and indeed shapes, this level of legitimacy appeal (as shown in column 3 of Table 3.1). In this group are both the charismatic and supremely dedicated leaders and the fanatic followers: Eric Hoffer's "true believers," South Vietnam's Buddhist martyrs, the sacrificial public servant, and the person exemplified in Mikhail Bakunin's "Catechism of a Revolutionary"— in Vietnam, the suicidal Viet Cong sapper. Obviously, not everyone who actively supports an incumbent regime or an insurgent revolution is going to rise to this level of selfless belief, but in an insurgency this is the steel to the frame upon which both sides must depend.

As at other levels, legitimacy of belief is also undergoing a transition from traditional to modern objects and issues (again, as shown in Table 3.1, columns 4 and 5). Traditional beliefs in many countries of the Third World may still be strongly held and consist, for example, of a deeply rooted anti-Western xenophobia of "throw out the foreign devils" sentiment, embody long-standing political principles such as the Confucian Mandate of Heaven, or require an upholding of the elaborate strictures of the Hindu caste system. Sadly, this traditional base often may be split among diametrically opposed subgroups (Hindus and Moslems in India or Sinhalese and Tamils in Sri Lanka, for example). At the same time, all countries of the Third World have been affected, in varying degree, by European standards and ideas of legitimation that involve some mix of nationalism, secularism, industrialism, and participatory politics. As Lucian Pye has observed about Southeast Asia, images of legitimate authority are bifurcated, "one part informed by the models of authority and power introduced by Western colonial rule, and the other rooted in the traditional cultures that have been kept alive by the vitality of religious beliefs in the region."[34]

Parenthetically, this elusive separability and shifting transition of legitimacy from traditional to modern sources, at all levels, should make clear just how tricky a foreign intervention in such a definitional contest, or insurgency, can become. In the nineteenth century, when outbursts against the colonial regimes never became full-fledged political revolutions, C. E. Callwell, for example, could propose numerous military and administrative measures free from any political considerations about beliefs in the basic right of the British imperium to rule. Thus, though Callwell recognized the importance of intelligence, he did not detain himself with any political factors in getting it.[35] Indeed, the nineteenth century's one political approach to "pacification"—the *tache d'huile* (oil slick) strategy the Frenchmen Joseph Gallieni and Herbert Lyautey developed with such success in Algeria and Indochina—essentially involved a combination of administrative reforms and punitive police actions (at no more than our interest level of calculation) that attracted the populace away from rebel areas.[36] The political mobilization accompanying a Maoist people's war, however, has long since made mere "good government" like this an insufficient remedy for an insurgency and has substantially raised the commitment, costs, and political sophistication necessary for a successful intervention.

In the transition of developing countries from traditional to modern sources of legitimacy, if tradition has been too negatively and statically portrayed, modernity, nevertheless, poses a dilemma in the Third World in that it is inherently caught up in Western ideas about, and institutions of, the state. As was noted in Chapter 2, the contemporary framework of international relations is a product of a European global expansion: the industrial revolution, political imperialism abroad and rising levels of participatory politics at home, and the European state as a mechanism, both domestically and internationally, to regulate economic progress and social order. Indeed, as Ernest Gellner has pointed out, industrial society is the "only one ever to live by sustained and perpetual growth" and, in so doing, "to invent the concept and ideal of progress, of continuous improvement." He has observed further that it also involves a high level of employment mobility (societal access) and, with it, a vast interconnecting web of professional communication (political, economic, and social). This web has been spun on a proliferation in the number of decisions necessary to keep the society functioning and in the number of people both involved in, and affected by, these decisions, in other words, political participation.[37] Essentially and symbolically, then, modern legitimacy has come to mean, at the highest level, a belief in the tenets of economic growth or modernization (industrialism, whether capitalist or collectivist as long as it grows) and in political *democracy* (as shown in the last column of Table 3.1).

Before settling on this equation for modern legitimacy, the terms must be properly understood. Whenever a country or ruler embarks on a new political order and definition of legitimacy, such rulers and societies cast about for models or standards. In the past, Confucius harkened back to the Duke of Chou and the Golden Emperor. Jews of the diaspora recalled the glories of David and Solomon. Charlemagne had himself anointed as a second Constantine. And the leaders of the French Revolution surrounded themselves in the ethos of democratic Athens and in the image of the citizen of the Roman Republic. What stands out in this historical list of "redefiners" is that their models and standards all came from backward looks. Modern legitimacy, however, interwoven as it is with industrial progress, measures all societies as moving along a backward to forward, traditional to modern, continuum. As Reinhard Bendix has observed, countries identified as backward look forward to countries that seem to represent the best approximation of all of what it means to be modern.[38]

In some cases, a single model has been adopted, as the Chinese communists first tried to do with the Russian Revolution. A more sophisticated approach was the elaborate studies of Western countries made by the Japanese of the Meiji Restoration (1868), who, in preserving a traditional Shinto frame, borrowed from the British for their parliament, the Americans for their stock market, and the Germans for their bureaucracy.[39] In any case, though Western in its ideas of progress and democracy, modern legitimacy can turn to several different models, including communist ones. Communism, after all, is a product of, or at least a reaction to, the industrial revolution of the West and offers a competitive system of modern political legitimacy to that of the liberal democracies.[40] Yet even communists hold to the two hallmarks of modern legitimacy. They, too, have a view of history rooted in a "dialectic" of material progress, and, as modern revolutionaries, the common inspiration of the French Revolution forces them to invoke for their revolutionary regimes the terminology of democracy: whether of a "people's republic," a "people's war," or a "union of socialist republics." Whatever its practicing reality, communism is an ideology of Western progress and of some notions of democracy. Thus, at all levels, national legitimacy remains at root an unbreakable bond and dilemma between the traditional and the modern.

Revolutionary Strategy and Legitimacy—Third Cut

In resolving this traditional versus modern dilemma, as T. H. Rigby has pointed out, there are two ways to recast political legitimacy: one is to re-invigorate traditional norms and another is to change the norms.[41] If the weight of effort shifts to the latter (or if one or more significant subgroup seeks this shift), this becomes a legitimacy crisis of the second degree, and, in political terms, is what a revolution is all about, to "aim at supplanting the entire structure of values and recasting the entire division of labor," as Chalmers Johnson has written.[42] The introduction of such revolutionary goals requires, therefore, a third analytical cut to my framework of legitimation, a revolutionary one (which is presented in the bottom row of Table 3.1).

In both proclaiming and creating a whole new world, however, any revolutionary confronts the enormous problem of never being able fully to separate himself from the social context of his own national society. Perhaps in an outburst of frustration over this dilemma, in 1848 Karl Marx raged: "The chief mission of all nationalities . . . and peoples is to perish in the universal revolutionary storm. They are . . . counter-revolutionary."[43] It soon became apparent (even to Marx himself) that his unbending attitude toward nationalism was futile. Lenin's genius lay in his ability to build a flexible strategy of revolution around Marx's rigid ideology. Especially in the "Colonies and Semi-Colonies," he appreciated that the dominant issue in which the class struggle had to germinate was the struggle for national self-determination. Indeed, his ability to manipulate Russia's nationalities to his own revolutionary ends was absolutely foundational to the creation and persistence of the Soviet state. Nevertheless, his successful slogan, "Nationalism in Form, Socialism in Content," revealed the embarrassment of this historically awkward alliance.[44]

Pulled in one direction by traditional resistance, communist revolutionaries also have to contend with the beckonings in another direction from a modernity to which, both intellectually and historically, they are Johnny-come-latelies. Hence they are to some degree forced to speak the diluting (if not polluting) language of democracy. As part of this language, communists have acknowledged the necessity of coming to terms with legitimacy and have recognized that even for a revolutionary state it "depends importantly on its performance conforming or not conforming to the beliefs and values of its subjects."[45]

In sum, revolutionaries are obliged to contend with their incumbent adversaries over the same puzzle of traditional versus modern legitimacy at the three levels of legitimation discussed in the two previous sections. As revolutionaries, however, they are also dedicated to attracting people and institutions to a program and a vision of a new social order. In doing so, they face at least two further problems beyond the Clausewitzian "friction" or drag of the old order. First, according to the conventions of any society, to join and perhaps then lead a revolution is a bold, if not a desperate, act. Though disinterested calculations of rational utility may not be entirely absent, it takes some passion of zealous belief, gripping fear, or wild excitement to overwhelm conventional sanctions and restraints against anyone who embarks on a path of killing. Pitirim Sorokin's early work on revolution sets forth in chilling detail the barbaric disintegration that a revolution brings to any society, a process which he contended amounted to a gross societal perversion. While admitting that revolutions are socially wasteful, Leon Trotsky perhaps spoke for all committed revolutionaries when he dismissed these costs as "one of the overhead expenses of historic progress."[46] Nevertheless, the point is that, even for lower echelons, joining a revolution is not a move one undertakes casually or for the mere sake of argument.

Second, an insurgent (as opposed to an insurrectionist) faces the added obstacle of a resistant regime, against which he is comparatively weak. As mentioned in the previous chapter, in an insurgency only half of Lenin's revolutionary situation exists: some of the lower classes may not want the old way, but the ruling class shows a very insufficient willingness to give up this same old way. Compared to that for his insurrectionist comrade, the prospective payoff is far more distant. Commitments, therefore, have to be more sustained, and the need for a credible plan (or strategy) is a sine qua non.

In the storm of a revolution, everyone is desperate not to become lost. This is especially true for a revolutionary who has offered himself and his program as means to an utopic promised land. He needs a strategy that reaches out to individuals and can reward and justify the resort to violence. The strategy then has to provide institutional mechanisms that cut channels for the flood of violence to take and, finally, must articulate an ideology for sustaining belief in this new order. In a reflection of this, Lenin is often quoted as saying: "Revolution is organization, organization, organization." His elaboration of this was equally stark: "In its struggle for power the proletariat has no other weapon but organization . . . the proletariat can become an invincible force only through its ideological unification on the principles of Marxism being reinforced by the material unity of organization." Lenin's formulary also readily corresponds to the three levels of revolutionary appeal in Table 3.1. Turning to my framework more specifically, in their quest for revolutionary legitimacy, as a measure at the level of passive support, revolutionaries, in traditional terms, must at least establish a presence with the peasantry in ways they understand. As James Downton has made clear, though the reaction of individuals to such an outside intrusion will be highly varied, revolutionaries can get nowhere if they and their organization are not available. In more modern terms, our "present" revolutionaries must do more than absorb the local culture; they must "empirically" discover the immediate issues of salience to their intended recruits as Mao did so presciently in his famous Hunan Report.[47] From this investigation, a political structure must be developed that can offer the incentives and punishments necessary to achieve the minimal goal that any insurgent group requires in getting off the ground: the silence of the villagers to the government about its presence.[48]

Though terror may be effective in procuring this silence and, thereby, the human sea in which the guerrilla fish can hide, it undermines higher stages of legitimation. Thomas Thornton has put it well: "Agitational terror is not the sort of activity that can be used effectively over a protracted period of time. It tends to lose effectiveness with familiarity . . . and it is not appropriate to the legitimacy that an insurgent group must at least claim to have."[49] The Chinese communists, for example, were relatively free of terror in their revolution and became highly critical of the Viet Cong for their far too heavy reliance on this weapon.

Making the transition to an opportunity level of appeal is of critical importance to the revolutionary strategist. At this level, he must be careful not to trample on traditional sensitivities while, in modern terms, he attempts to organize parallel hierarchies to that of the incumbent regime, ideally in secure base areas. A delicate handling of land reform is usually the measure over which this issue must be finessed. Mao Zedong had to restrain his radicals over land reform in the Jiangxi soviet in the famous Futian Incident of the late 1920s. The same issue cropped up again in Yanan a decade later. Handling traditional leaders also becomes a delicate matter. Mao, again, profitably incorporated the secret society warrior Zhu De into his command, whereas the Viet Minh in 1947 made the almost irretrievable blunder of assassinating the highly venerated leader of the Hoa Hao sect of the Mekong Delta.

In a modern sense, Alexander Groth has identified access, particularly elite access, as the measure that spells the difference between reforms and mere coups d'état on one hand and violent revolutions on the other. If access to the ruling elite is blocked, then frustrated leaders develop alternative structures of their own.[50] They carry out their own land reform, pass out titles of "land to the tillers," issue "liberation bonds," and even declare "provisional governments."

Finally, at the highest level of belief or ideology, the leadership core appreciates the importance of being able to interpret the confusing course of political events from a cohesive revolutionary worldview. Traditionally, they must portray themselves as the true upholders of national values, even though they are revolutionaries. A good way to do this, in many societies, is to entice some foreign power into an intervention so that they can reinforce their claims to being heroic patriots. Though this entails obvious risks, the hope is that these risks will be short term, and, over the long run, the intervention will rebound to their legitimating credit. Domestically, the trick is to bridge the material opportunity motives of many of their cadres with a moral philosophy imbuing the insurgency with long-term purpose. This is the critical basis for revolutionary unity, but it can be a dangerous Achilles' heel to a revolution. In the case of the Philippines, for example, the urban politburo in Manila was committed to a radical Maoist transformation. The rural rank-and-file Huk insurgents were not, and the government's land reform and elections drove a fatal wedge between the two.

Foreign Intervention—Fourth Cut

Insurgencies, in brief, are long, tumultuous affairs. They contain so many opportunities for mischief that sooner or later the question of foreign intervention looms. In the postwar era, intervention became a prominent international issue after Nikita Khrushchev's famous "Three Wars" speech on January 6, 1961. He declared that in the nuclear age "general" and "local" wars were no longer acceptable as means for advancing the cause of socialism but that "wars of national liberation" were. As Roger Hilsman recalled, the speech was widely interpreted in Washington as amounting to a declaration of war by such means. The speech was also seen as a tacit lesson by the Russians and as a message for the Chinese that even conventional, "local" wars like Korea were too dangerous, but that interventions in behalf of insurgent revolutionaries were a way to carry out their "internationalist duty" with little risk of global conflagration.[51]

Despite Washington's recognition of this "new" challenge, intervention ran counter to the dedication of all Western states to sovereignty, a principle that was institutionalized as one of the centerpieces to the U.N. Charter. Modern definitions of intervention, then, have been typically couched in negative language. William V. O'Brien, as an example, has defined it thus: "Intervention is extraordinary interference in the internal or external affairs of another state in such a manner as to affect its government's exercise of sovereignty and alter the normal relationship between the parties involved."[52]

Though a respect for sovereignty was at the heart of the nurturing of the European state, historically interventions were still justified on two grounds: interventions for justice (morality) and interventions for international stability (preservation of the balance of power). The eighteenth-century jurist Emer de Vattel offered the classic defense for a moral intervention: "If a prince, by violating the fundamental laws, gives his subjects a lawful cause for resisting him, if, by his insupportable tyranny, he brings on a national revolt against him, any foreign power may rightly give assistance to an oppressed people who ask for its aid . . . whenever such dissension reaches the state of civil war, foreign nations may assist that one of the two parties which seems to have justice on its side. But to assist a detestable tyrant, or to come out in favor of an unjust and rebellious people would certainly be a violation of duty."[53]

The classic justification for a balance of power intervention came most cogently from the Austrian Prince Metternich:

> Every state is absolutely sovereign in its internal affairs. But this implies that every state must do nothing to interfere in the internal affairs of any other. However, any false or pernicious step taken by any state in its internal affairs may disturb the repose of another state, and this consequent disturbance of another state's repose constitutes an interference in that state's internal affairs. Therefore, every state — or rather, every sovereign of a great power — has the duty, in the name of the sacred right of independence of every state, to supervise the governments of smaller states and to prevent them from taking false and pernicious steps in their internal affairs.[54]

These two "traditional" standards of intervention retain their currency today. In an especially thought-provoking article on the need for the exercise of moral considerations in decisions on interventions (and obliquely criticizing the Europeans for letting this moral standard fall into disuse), Richard Cooper and Joseph Nye argue that a statesmen owes it to his own citizens to act in accordance with his personal code while at the same time serving as a trustee of the rights of others and to intervene to protect these rights. And Prince Metternich's thesis of great power stewardship finds a clear modern echo in Eliot Cohen: "America's need to prepare for small wars flows directly from its role in the postwar world as the preeminent maritime power and the leader of the Western bloc of nations. Such a position requires a readiness and a capability to fight small wars to maintain its world position and the global balance of power outside the continent of Europe."[55]

Out of these two traditions, some fairly explicit formulas for intervention developed in the postwar interventionist era. All of these formulas sought to emphasize the exceptional character to an intervention because the principle of sovereignty was seen as a sacred cornerstone to international stability. Thus, in addition to these traditional justifications, modern theorists of intervention added the necessity of a prior intervention by an offending power.[56] These two traditions came to be boiled down to two principles for intervention in a system of otherwise sovereign nation-states: an interven-

Figure 3.2. External Legitimacy Effects

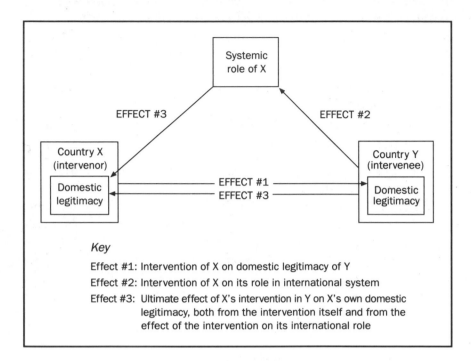

tion must be preceded by that of an adversary (if it is to maintain Metternich's balance of power), and the intervention must be in behalf of a regime or rebel group that is democratic, or at least espouses such principles, and respects human rights (if it is for Vattel's interventions on behalf of justice).

Thus, in a Western intervention in an insurgency, there is a fourth legitimacy cut, that of the external effects shown in Figure 3.2. Foreign intervention, whether on the side of the incumbent or of the insurgent, raises the stakes of the struggle and fundamentally alters it in at least three ways. First, most obviously and most crucially in the immediate arena of the struggle, there is the impact of the intervention on each of the various domestic legitimacies. To begin with, the intervenor can readily affect legitimacy in positive ways relating to legitimacy appeals of interest and opportunity. With regard to interest, through such measures as commodity import programs, massive construction projects, and foreign aid that lowers rates of rural credit, for example, the intervenor can help make it rational for the masses to stay with the government in the creation of the already mentioned Honda economy. For opportunity, the intervenor can also be of help in devising and financing land reform programs, in promoting elections, and in pushing other measures toward improving political participation and societal access for previously blocked subgroups and social strata.

It is at the level of ideology or belief, however, that an intervenor may run afoul of legitimacy and utterly negate whatever successes he may have achieved at lower levels. In contemplating an intervention, it is at the level of belief that the intervenor must assess the legitimacy of his intervention in an overall context. This assessment must come from a careful reading of the historical and emerging definition of national legitimacy within the society in question, as well as from a determination of the levels of intervention (for instance, at the level of dispatching ground combat troops) at which the legitimacy of the regime itself may be undermined by the scale of the intervention.

Similarly, it is only through such careful analysis that the intervenor can avoid the political trap of having its intervention tainted by an excessive identification with a nonlegitimate or even illegitimate regime. When an insurgency surfaces, the local regime slides into a legitimacy crisis. In confronting this crisis, if left to its own domestic devices, such a regime faces a set of choices it cannot shirk: reform, fight, or perish. It is a sad truth, however, that one way it can shirk these choices is to entice a foreign power into an intervention. By relying on an obliging foreign power, the regime can avoid being beholden to anyone locally and can count on its ally's respect for its "sovereignty" to ensure the continued enjoyment of its venal ways. This is especially true if the intervenor dispatches ground combat troops whose presence seals an identification of the intervening power with the destiny of the "hapless" regime. This trap is an illegitimacy lock. The nuances of this trap are discussed further in Chapter 5 in the analysis of the Saigon regime because it serves as an all-too-perfect example.

Second, an external intervention also affects the legitimacy of the intervenor's role in the international system. Because of the lack of uniform norms and institutional authority in the international system (that is, a world government), this effect on systemic legitimacy may be rather weak, but Hedley Bull makes it clear that great power status confers certain minimal standards of legitimacy or behavior expectations. To ignore these standards, Bull argues, will eventually entail real costs to the violator's foreign policy and basic international role.[57] Thus an intervention must be "right" internationally as well, or at least not be too blatantly "wrong." This effect is noted in Figure 3.2.

The third legitimacy effect of an external intervention might be called a sleeper, and this effect usually awakens at the cruelest of times during a long-sputtering insurgency. In the case of Vietnam, this sleeper—the reverse impact of the intervention on the domestic legitimacy of the intervening state

—awoke in the middle of the Tet offensive. At some point, then, the domestic legitimacy and politics of the intervenor and intervenee become intertwined. Thus, in relation to El Salvador, one saw Roberto d'Aubuisson, a candidate during El Salvador's 1984 presidential election campaign, picnicking with U.S. Senator Jesse Helms, and Senator Helms, in turn, being vilified for his action in his own subsequent senatorial campaign. Meanwhile, José Napoleon Duarté, the Salvadoran government's presidential standard-bearer, alternatively rallied around the highways and byways of El Salvador and then came to Washington to "meet the press" and lobby in the corridors of Congress. Through it all, Guillermo Ungo of the insurgent Farabundo Marti Liberation Front argued for a U.S. visa.

It is at this juncture, where the domestic politics of the intervenor and the intervenee become intertwined, that, from the perspective of the intervenor particularly, an intervention becomes sticky. This rebound effect from two directions is shown in Figure 3.2. Usually this point is reached when ground combat troops are dispatched. In the case of Central America, however, thanks to the persistent nightmare of Vietnam, this point was reached in the United States much earlier.

Summary: Variables, Measures, and Numbers

In summary, then, this analysis requires four analytical cuts or procedures on the intersection of insurgency and intervention. The first procedure is to analyze an insurgency as a competitive quest for legitimation, in general terms, at different levels of intensification (of interest, of opportunity, and of belief). In recognition of the dynamic character of this quest, the second procedure analytically recognizes that the fundamental nature of legitimacy itself is undergoing a definitional transition from traditional to modern sources so that one must go back over the three levels of legitimation to assess them for traditional and modern components. The third procedure is undertaken in appreciation of the fact that an insurgency throws a curve of complication into the whole process. The complication is that in this quest for legitimation, insurgents try to redirect this definitional transition to the delineation of a new social order, a revolutionary one, making an insurgency become a legitimacy crisis of the second degree. Finally, one way or another, an insurgency usually attracts or invites foreign intervention. The fourth procedure is to analyze the intervention in terms of its effects on these different levels and shifting definitions of legitimacy.

These four procedures will be what the framework analysis section of each of the cases will conduct. In each case, however, the first two cuts will be analytically combined. They can be summarized by Figure 3.3 on insur-

Figure 3.3. Insurgency: Exogenous and Independent Variables

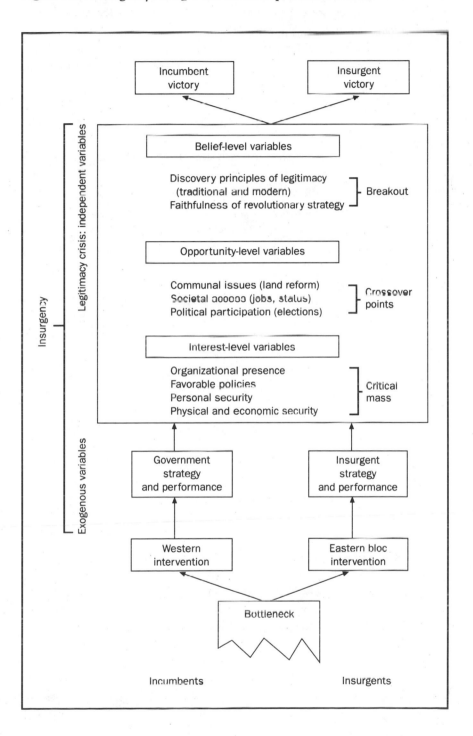

gency. Taking the same insurgency box of Figure 3.1 (which was broken out in Table 3.1), in this figure the insurgency box becomes the legitimacy crisis of three levels of independent variables which are acted on by two sets of competing exogenous or conditioning variables. The first set is the competing strategies and performance of the incumbents and insurgents in solving the legitimacy crisis that the insurgency represents. The other is the relative amounts of foreign intervention the incumbents and insurgents receive and the value of this assistance to the resolution of this legitimacy crisis in their respective favors.

For these variables there are a set of indicators by which the performance of the incumbents and insurgents can be measured. Turning to the independent variables in the legitimacy crisis box first, at the level of interest there are the measures of organizational presence, favorable or unfavorable policies, personal security, and physical and economic security. For organizational presence, the indicators are the numbers and types of government and insurgent personnel in the general and specific areas of conflict. Such personnel are local government officials, school teachers, police, soldiers, and militia for the incumbents; and, for the insurgents, their civilian supporters, political cadre, part-time fighters, and main force guerrillas. Indicators for policies are the specific measures the two sides employ to win support or force their control over the target society. On both sides, these can be both various and numerous. For incumbent regimes, a variety of measures will fall under a rubric of rural development: rural credit, cooperatives, schools, and the like. Beyond these political incentives, police activities and military campaigns will define more coercive indicators. Police will issue identity cards and set up other population control practices. Soldiers will set up patterns of patrol and basing that will have either a positive or negative impact. Personal security, as discussed earlier in Table 3.1, refers to the strength and comfort enjoyed by villagers in their traditional patron/client ties. And physical and economic security, also discussed earlier, measures more modern attributes of basic well-being.

Insurgents, of course, will be measured competitively against the incumbents for their ability to deliver on the same indicators above, or on some equivalents. For example, if insurgents are not able to offer villagers the blessings of a Honda economy, they must offer something else competitive with this, such as the status of serving as a functionary in a liberated revolutionary base area.

The opportunity-level variables revolve around such measures as communal issues, societal access, and political participation. Though these, too, have been discussed in connection with Table 3.1, they divide into the traditional and modern issues that together become the basis for the institutional competition between the two sides as both individuals and groups make active commitments to the two sides. Communal issues refer to the traditional group-level goals people are likely to pursue collectively. Most often this is land reform. Societal access, obviously, is a measure of the openness of the modern sector to those seeking a part in it, whether for employment or social status. This can also mean land reform, but more often it refers to labor unions, higher education, government quotas and/or discrimination, and other institutions that either promote or block this access. Political participation is the political side of economic and social access. Most directly, it means free, fair, and competitive elections and with them the development of political parties, robust legislators who perform a variety of policy and constituent services, and citizens who involve themselves in this process at various levels.

Insurgents, again, will have to offer attractive equivalents of their own. Communal issues mark the point at which they will have to show their political perspicacity. In revolutionary parlance, it is here where they will have to make a correct choice for a mass line. If the government has no land reform program, they have a clean shot on this issue. If there is a government land reform program, however, the insurgents will either have to ruin it or offer a better alternative. For societal access and participation, insurgents will either have to redirect the populace toward their own set of institutions or work within the government's system and hope to win anyway. Most adamantly try the former alternative.

The belief level has two grand variables: discovery principles of legitimacy and faithfulness of revolutionary strategy. As for legitimacy, when specified by country-specific definitions, the principles become measures of whether the two sides deserve to claim the mantle of legitimacy for which the insurgency has been fought. At this level, the principles of legitimacy emerge, and continue to emerge, from an inductive pursuit of historical discovery, which are provided in the "Historical Settings" sections of each chapter. Both sides try to shape and claim these principles for their own. The challenge for both sides is that part of what ignites the very insurgency they are fighting is that the definitional principles of this legitimacy are in a state of flux from traditional to modern sources. Hence, in Vietnam, both sides sought to legitimate their claims to rule on their fulfillment of the Confucian Mandate of Heaven while at the same time creating the foundation of modern rule in a constitutional republic. Along with this struggle, the insurgents, as revolutionaries, are trying to recast their society on a new sociopolitical foundation. In so doing, then, the revolutionaries have the added obligation, while fighting the incumbents, of being true to their revolutionary vision. For the cases of this study, this means being faithful to Mao's seven principles or measures of a Marxist strategy of people's war.

What affects or conditions this legitimacy crisis are the efforts of the two sides to manipulate in their favor the independent variables that constitute this crisis. Each one of these variables or issues, then, constitutes a contest or obstacle that the two sides need to overcome or solve in their race up Mount Legitimus I described earlier. Regarding government strategy and performance, the markers for this are the components and effects of its strategy at all three levels, as well as its leadership and military efficacy. For its strategy at the interest level, one needs to ascertain the nature of its presence, the purposes of its policies, and the effectiveness of both. At the opportunity level, the institutional design and group effects of government programs need to be specified—whether of land reform, elections, or labor unions. Finally, at the belief level, each case will delineate the grand cause for which all these efforts serve.

Whatever the strategy, leadership is what directs it. One indicator for leadership, beyond the articulation of a strategy, is the organization a leader can both design and establish to carry out the strategy. Critical to the functioning of this organization are the inspirational qualities (another indicator) a leader can bring to bear to elicit motivated and competent performances from his followers. Since an insurgency is a struggle of organized violence, the acid test of leadership will be on its prosecution of the armed struggle against its adversary. As discussed in Chapter 2, military efficacy results from an aggregation of such indicators as the size of its armed forces and police, its composition and equipment, how it is disposed throughout the country, its technology, and its training, motivation, and tactics. These same indicators pertain to the insurgents. They as well will need to follow a strategy under good leadership that can create a superb fighting machine. For this study, what stands as further indicators are whether the strategy the insurgents follow is a Marxist people's war and how single-mindedly they pursue it.

A second exogenous or conditioning variable to a legitimacy crisis erupting into an insurgency is foreign intervention. The measures for a foreign intervention are its level, constancy, and legitimacy impact. The level refers to the continuum of intervention laid out in Figures 1.2 through 1.8. The constancy of an intervention is also important. Does an intervention continue at a sustained level throughout the life of an insurgency, or is it irregular or withdrawn completely somewhere before the end? It is only fair to observe that despite the massive level of American assistance to the governments of Vietnam, Laos, and Cambodia, the lack of constancy of this assistance negated the value of this general amount of support. Finally, of course, there is the impact of this intervention on the claim of its clients to legitimacy. The centrality of this has already been underscored and will receive special attention in all the cases.

These struggles do involve numbers. Setting forth some numbers as markers for achievements at the three levels of struggle can certainly aid in diagnosing the progress and prospects of an insurgency or its opposing counterinsurgency. At the right of the legitimacy crisis box in Figure 3 3 are the three benchmarks for insurgent success of critical mass, crossover points, and strategic breakout. Though these are quantitative indicators, they roughly correspond to the three levels of legitimacy to their left. A critical mass is a microcosm of what the insurgents hope they can generalize across their society. It will consist of a leadership core of true believers, an organized cadre and armed force, and a mass of sympathizers. Thus all calculations of legitimacy are present in a critical mass, making it a nut that cannot be cracked by coercive measures alone. A critical mass, however, has not yet found a broad-based program around which it can mount a momentum of societal expansion. When it makes such a discovery, the yeast of a critical mass rises along a trajectory of crossover points. In so doing, the insurgency will have garnered opportunity-level commitments from numerous individuals and groups to the legitimacy of its claim to rule. To reach a strategic breakout an insurgency must successfully address itself to the national belief-level issues animating the entire society. With all their strategic nuances, this is what the numbers of a breakout reflect.

In determining these numbers, two concepts I have relied on are Thomas Greene's "critical mass" and Jeffrey Race's "crossover point." Though Greene acknowledges that precise numbers, particularly as rules for comparison across cases involving different cultures and histories, are too dangerous to mention, his basic observation is that the business of both mounting and suppressing insurgencies involves only a minority of a society's population. Further, every insurgent group is divided into a hard core of a leadership organization and its combatants and a larger network of "soft-core" civilian supporters. Thus a critical mass for an insurgency's sustenance is relatively low compared, say, to the percentage of the vote necessary for a political party to win a mandate in a democratic election. Along these lines, Jeffrey Race has argued that after the early stages of an insurgency, there comes a point, the "crossover point," when the insurgency has achieved enough staying power so that a purely coercive solution is no longer possible for the authorities. In other words, at this point, defeating an insurgency is no longer a matter of brilliant police work and deft military ambushes. Instead or in addition, further political solutions and reforms must come forth to undercut the grounds of the insurgent movement.[58]

From these concepts of critical mass, crossover point, as well as T. Robert Gurr's "strategic crisis," I have developed three quantitative benchmarks for charting the course of an insurgency.[59] These roughly correspond to the three levels of legitimation of my analytical framework (interest, opportunity, and belief). The danger in setting out such numbers is that they can be taken too literally and seized on too quickly. It must be emphasized, then, that their purpose is to reveal trends of underlying political forces rather than to establish mathematical formulas for calibrated military responses. With this warning in mind, a critical mass exists when an insurgent group has recruited a hard core of five to ten thousand armed fighters supported by a network of civilian sympathizers ten times the size of this force. These numbers pertain for countries with populations of ten to twenty million. In larger countries, a critical mass would have to be scaled up, but even in a larger country, these original numbers would have at least a regional significance. The political point about a critical mass is that breaking up such a guerrilla movement will require more than military and police work; it will need a package of policies and programs that separate the guerrillas from this civilian (and, therefore, political) base of support.

The next benchmark of crossover points is based on a ratio rather than a fixed number. It is an upward sliding ratio (or a downward one) in pursuit of the next fixed number and benchmark: the strategic breakout, if upward; the critical mass, if downward. For insurgents, crossover points refer to a condition in which the size of their military forces and civilian support base is expanding at a greater rate than the incumbent government can contract it. For incumbents, of course, crossover points chart a reverse trend. As a benchmark, crossover points signify momentum. It is the fluid interregnum in an insurgency that corresponds to Mao Zedong's second stage of people's war, that of strategic maneuver. It is a period when the trend of this point can advance, get stuck, retreat, and advance again. Crossover points can be advanced or arrested by military campaigns that have had their way paved by major political and economic reforms.

Insurgents reach the final benchmark of the strategic break-out when they have put themselves in a position to launch a frontal bid for power. Such a point has been reached when the insurgency attracts a following exceeding 10 percent and moving up to 20 percent of the adult population, provided that this 10 to 20 percent is widely distributed—both geographically and ethnically (if this is important to a society's social mosaic)—and penetrates key political and economic groups. Among our cases, breakouts were achieved by the Chinese communists and Greek communists immediately after World War II. Vietnamese communists similarly reached a breakout in 1968 and again in 1972 and 1975. In Laos and Cambodia breakouts came only at the very end, and in Malaya and the Philippines the insurgents never got beyond short-lived cross-over points in their favor.

On the down side, for an incumbent regime to have less than 50 percent—certainly no less than 30 percent—of the adult population willing to commit themselves to at least some active gestures in its support will require either or both major political measures and massive foreign intervention to avoid a serious danger of overthrow. Empirically, once insurgents have reached a breakout, usually only a foreign military intervention can throw the scales back for the incumbents. British troops had to rescue the Greeks in 1945, and in Vietnam foreign interventions repeatedly staved off the final day of reckoning. One of the very few mostly political defeats of a breakout came in 1986 with Corazon Aguino's "People's Power" dislodging of President Ferdinand Marcos in the Philippines, which had the side effect of freezing the near breakout of the New People's Army against the Marcos regime. The discrepancies in these numbers between insurgents and incumbents are due to the differences in the tasks facing the two sides. The insurgents, at least at the level of law and order, have merely to tear down and disrupt. The incumbents, however, have the duty both to continue normal governance and to root out the insurgent threat to this order.

It must be stressed that in every case these numbers have to be nuanced for critical sub-issues and measures. For example, within an overall 10 percent support base, locally wherever guerrilla forces operate they have to count on a near monopoly of intelligence support. Minimally, this translates into a guarantee of popular silence to the government as to their whereabouts, and, maximally, it means the provision of hard information as to the whereabouts and plans of the government's army. It is a little difficult to put firm numbers on achieving this. Also, whatever the problems in morale, training, and equipment an incumbent regime may have with its army, it has to at least maintain its force levels. For all its problems, the South Vietnamese army did maintain its force levels up to the final battle, for example, but these levels for the Afghan army dropped precipitously after the Soviet occupation, suggesting a significant difference in the relative legitimacy of the two "puppet" regimes in Saigon and Kabul. But armies also have to fight well, which, at the end, the South Vietnamese army did not. The numbers, again, become tricky. Further, in the support base of both sides, some groups are more important than others. For an incumbent regime in the Third World, William Wriggins has listed the following groups as key: the bureaucracy, military, landowners, business leaders, unemployed intellectuals, union leaders, and press and radio organizations.[60] For the insurgents, the sine qua non is a discontented peasantry and a leadership organization (probably drawn from the unemployed intellectuals) capable of mobilizing it. The basic point about these numbers and benchmarks is that they are symptoms, not causes. That is, these numbers are merely signs of the underlying political struggle between incumbents and insurgents for the mantle of properly legitimated rule.

In all these numbers, there is an important limitation, even danger, to interventions in these insurgencies. Interventions, in Figure 3.3, are portrayed as feeding into their clients' strategy and performance. It is from this second tier of boxes (of strategy and performance) that the line enters the big legitimacy crisis box. The point of these lines is that an intervention should be supportive of a local client's main effort and not go into this main box directly and become a substitute for this effort. Historically, however, the scale of foreign intervention has almost had this effect. This was particularly true in Vietnam. The problem is that no amount of interest and opportunity-level intervention can procure a belief-level legitimacy for a client. Whether incumbent or insurgent, this legitimacy they have to get for themselves in the context of their own society. Former secretary of state Dean Acheson recognized this a long time ago. During a press conference in January 1950, called to rebut criticism that the Truman administration had "lost China," he issued his "missing component" warning: "American assistance can be effective when it is the missing component in a situation which might otherwise be solved. The United States cannot furnish all these components to solve the question. It cannot furnish the determination, it cannot furnish the will, and it cannot furnish the loyalty of a people to its government. But if the will and if the determination exists and if the people are behind their government . . . American help can be effective and it can lead to an accomplishment which could not otherwise be achieved." [61]

Sorting out "all these components," missing or otherwise, is precisely what this chapter's analytical framework is designed to do. Eight cases await its scrutiny, first, Vietnam, the deviant one.

PART II
Vietnam,
the
Deviant
Case

HISTORICAL SETTING: THE EARTHLY STRUGGLE FOR HEAVEN'S MANDATE

Legitimacy in Vietnam

For the Vietnamese the idea of legitimacy is most clearly subsumed under the Chinese concept of the Mandate of Heaven, which embodies several time-honored duties. The principal task of any holder of this mandate has been the preservation of Vietnamese identity. The Vietnamese have always been borrowers from other cultures, but the borrowing has had to be Vietnamized by the ruling establishment so that the people would not lose their identity as Vietnamese. More tangibly, it has always been the sacred charge of Vietnam's rulers to rid the country of foreign invaders and meddlers. The longest tradition in this respect was the struggle against the one thousand years of Chinese domination (ca. 100 B.C. through A.D. 900). After the Vietnamese finally secured their independence from the Chinese, this imperative continued against the Portuguese, Dutch, French, and, finally, the Americans. Part of this striving drove the Vietnamese south for space in a long march to the Camau Peninsula (at Vietnam's southern tip) that began in the fifteenth century. The march added regional variants to their identity and gave them a well-deserved reputation in Southeast Asia as both a giant slayer and a military bully.

Although protecting the Vietnamese culture and fatherland from external adversaries was one of their charges, Vietnamese rulers further gained legitimacy by dispensing justice internally. In a predominantly agrarian society this meant ensuring an equitable distribution of land so that the peasants on whom the social order was based not only had enough to provide for their families but also had a place to cultivate the memory of their ancestors and a communal site (*dinh*) to keep alive the traditions of their villages.

This, then, was traditional Vietnam; however, as Vietnam moved into the modern world, the nature of this legitimacy changed. The French came, and the dual economy and dual political system they imposed shook the Confucian order to its foundations. As Vietnamese nationalists struggled with Western ideas, values, economics, and institutions, they were handicapped by the lack of anything in their own history potent enough to counter this Western challenge. The last Vietnamese dynasty, the Nguyens, had permanently sullied their mandate by their disastrous cooperation with the French. But the French found it increasingly difficult to stay on, and if World War II meant just one thing in Asia, it was that the mandate of the white man was fast ending. In this uncertainty the communists stepped in to offer an entirely different political order with which to recreate Vietnamese society.

Still, until the revolution was complete, the communists had to justify their claims for an active legitimacy in the Vietnamese context, that is, in terms that squared with rightful rule as it was traditionally understood and as it was evolving under the shocks of the twentieth century. Herein lay (and still lies) the struggle in Vietnam for legitimacy.

Traditional Vietnam

Early Vietnamese history is dotted with legends of genies, dragons, and fairies. The founding myth of the Vietnamese people is that they are the offspring of the mating, four thousand years ago, of a male dragon from the sea and a female fairy from the land. After a period of independence, they fell under the yoke of the early Han dynasty of China in 111 B.C. The thousand years of Chinese domination which followed left a profound impression on Vietnamese culture. Nevertheless, the period was punctuated by revolts whose leaders are remembered today as Vietnam's first heroes and heroines. In A.D. 939 Ngo Quyen finally achieved Vietnamese independence by trapping and burning a Chinese fleet in the shallow waters of Haiphong harbor.[1]

A capital city was established in Thang Long (Hanoi) and a strong dynasty, the Tran, secured the Vietnamese Mandate of Heaven until 1400. Its great hero was Tran Hung Dao, who, from 1282 to 1289, defeated three attempts at Chinese reconquest by the Mongol general Kublai Khan. With the collapse of the Tran dynasty, the ever-present threat of Chinese intervention returned in the reoccupation by the Ming dynasty from 1407 to 1427. Once again a hero, Le Loi, rose up to drive the Chinese out after a ten-year guerrilla campaign. He founded the Le dynasty and crowned himself the "Prince of Pacification." The domestic side to his claim to rule was assured by his prompt redistribution of land to the peasants. The Le dynasty lasted until 1788 and reached its apogee under Le Thanh Tong (1461–1497), whose reign is remembered as the golden age of Vietnam. His conquest of the Indic kingdom of Champa along the central Vietnamese coast paved the way for Vietnam's famous Nam Tien (march to the south), a slow-motion version of America's westward movement, when villagers sent their surplus population to start pioneer settlements in the south. These settlements produced a chain that finally reached the Camau peninsula in 1757.[2]

The classical political order of the Les was undergirded by a Confucian ideology that bestowed legitimacy on an emperor by Thien Minh (the Mandate of Heaven). To the Vietnamese there were two components of this concept that were embodied in the two Vietnamese words for ruler. One was *hoang de* (emperor), which reflected the Confucian and Chinese emphasis on hierarchy and correct social relations. The other was *vua* (king), which was more of a Buddhist term used by the peasants for a patriotic protector who was sentimentally close to them. On a political and cultural level, this meant that the emperor's mandate was to introduce Chinese institutions and ideas but to Vietnamize them at the same time. The emperor ruled the villages through his mandarins, whose power he always tried to curtail so as to prevent warlordism and insurrection. The villages were relatively self-sufficient communities that carefully safeguarded their autonomy, as pointedly expressed in one of Vietnam's oldest political proverbs: "The laws of the emperor yield to the customs of the village."[3]

By the early sixteenth century, the Les could no longer hold the centripetal forces of their expanded kingdom in check. Baronial families from the north and south fought for real control under nominal Le rule. By the seventeenth century these feuding families had called in foreign advisers and support, the northerners from the Dutch and the southerners from the Portuguese. After a century of relative quiet, a nativist revolt against all this meddling, led by the Tay Son brothers of central Vietnam, sought to overthrow the Le dynasty. After driving out the southern ruling family, the eldest, Nguyen Hue, proclaimed himself emperor and marched on Hanoi.

Undaunted by a Chinese force sent to rescue the Le emperor, Nguyen Hue crushed the invaders in a surprise offensive during the Tet celebrations of 1788.[4]

The triumph of the Tay Sons was cut short by Nguyen Hue's untimely death in 1792. Waiting for such an opportunity, Nguyen Anh, the defeated southern ruler, returned from Thailand with a unit of French artillery and a complement of French military advisers. By 1802 he had defeated the Tay Sons and established Vietnam's last royal dynasty, the Nguyen, at a new imperial capital along the central coast at Hue. Though the Nguyens were the first rulers to achieve central control over all of Vietnam, their rigid Confucian orthodoxy and reliance on foreigners ran into a current of opposition still flowing from the nativist ferment of the Tay Sons. Consequently, the Nguyen court never gained the fundamental legitimacy accorded the Les. Problems came to a head during the reign of Tu Duc (1847–83). Peasant uprisings in the 1840s and 1850s drove the dynasty to the safety—and isolation—of urban fortresses. Behind these walls, Tu Duc was plagued by court intrigues and plots from his own family. From 1854 to 1866 the vacillating poet-king ended up killing his elder brother and the brother's entire family. His throne "secure," Tu Duc, racked by guilt and ill health, was a broken man. At just this inopportune time, the struggling Nguyens were forced to confront another challenge—the French.[5]

The French

The nineteenth century, of course, marked the heyday of European colonial expansion. Though the Annamese coast had been sized up by numerous colonial prowlers since 1540, it was the French who proved to be the most determined. Attempts by a French admiral to safeguard the rights of a persecuted Christian minority led to a cession of Vietnam's six southern provinces by Tu Duc to France in 1867. In the north, initially looking for an inland route via the Red River to the rich interior of China, the French developed an interest in Vietnam itself. With a total force of three thousand men, the French bombed Hue into submission in 1883 and imposed on Tu Duc's hapless successor the Patenotre–Nguyen Van Tuong Treaty of June 6, 1884, in which the French established a protectorate over Annam (central Vietnam) and Tonkin (northern Vietnam) and the Nguyen court publicly disavowed the camel's seal that had symbolized China's tributary delegation of Heaven's Mandate in Vietnam to the court.[6]

French rule lasted until March 9, 1945. Its effect was to create half a revolution. That is, it destroyed the traditional order but ultimately failed in the crucial task of replacing it with a legitimate new one. The Vietnamese, as a society, were pushed into the twentieth century stumbling and off balance. Through an unusually large colonial bureaucracy, the French had fashioned a society of "structural dualism." Economically, they pulled from the traditional agricultural countryside a modern trading sector tied to metropolitan France. Politically, they ruled the colony through two administrative structures. Cochinchina they ruled directly, but in the protectorates of Annam and Tonkin the Vietnamese court was allowed to keep its mandarin bureaucracy, while the French resident superior watched over this structure with his own system of residents and province officials.

Though this system of Vietnamese impotence further discredited the imperial court and its mandarin bureaucracy, French rule had its limits. At the village level, attempts in the 1920s to "reform" rural administration with democratic councils and progressive taxation led to so much resistance that the reforms were repealed in 1941. Thus the French also discovered that their rule could not penetrate the customs of the village. Unlike the British in India, the French tried to suppress all nationalist political activity. In this, too, they were unsuccessful.[7]

Modern Vietnamese nationalism grew out of a three-waved resistance to French rule. The first wave of resistance was by traditionalists who supported the Can Vuong (aid the king) scholar-patriots in the late nineteenth century. In the second wave were those who in the early twentieth century could be called transitionalists and split into those who merely wanted to overturn the feudal Nguyen regime in Hue and those who yearned to restore the independence of the court by throwing out the French. Succeeding the transitionalists were the moderns, both communist and noncommunist, who sought to establish a modern equivalent or substitute for the Confucian Nguyen court.[8]

The only point to note about the traditionalists is that they sparked several revolts against French rule which, despite their ineffectiveness, continued the time-honored legacy of struggle against foreign rule. The most notable of these revolts was the eight-year rebellion of the scholar Phan Dinh Phung, who was hunted down and executed by the French in 1896. The first two decades of the twentieth century belonged to transitionalists, centered around the figures of Phan Chu Trinh (1872–1926) and Phan Boi Chau (1867–1940). Phan Chu Trinh was an intellectual who tried to rid Vietnam of Confucianism and the trappings of the imperial court. He opened a school in 1908 to expose the Vietnamese to Western ideas. Though he was exiled by the French, his ideas survived in the Constitutionalist party. It was the only party officially tolerated by the French, and in the 1920s and 1930s it lost to the communists and Trotskyites in the Saigon municipal elections.[9]

Phan Boi Chau is still regarded by many communists and noncommunists as the father of modern Vietnamese nationalism. His one passion was to rid the country of the French, but as a transitional figure his ideas for realizing his passion were contradictory. Though he wanted the French out, he also sought to restore the imperial court. In addition to people within the royal family, he looked for support in Can Vuong remnants and guerrilla bands. He also vigorously pursued foreign assistance in restoring Vietnamese independence, first from the Japanese and later from the Chinese. Neither country was particularly responsive. Phan Boi Chau, nevertheless, was a man of action. Though bitterly disappointed by the failure to transform a tax revolt in 1908 into a general uprising (or *khoi nghia* to the Vietnamese), he went on to launch an assassination campaign against French officials in 1912 and 1913. In his last effort, he turned to mobilizing Vietnamese colonial militiamen in two unsuccessful uprisings in 1916 and 1917. The French were able to thwart all these efforts with a force of only two thousand men of their own.[10]

The modern wave of nationalism flowed out of the intellectual and spiritual ferment that gripped Vietnam in the mid-1920s much as it had seized China during the May Fourth movement from 1914 to 1920. Buddhism and Confucianism underwent revivals and two new politico-religious sects, the Cao Dai and the Hoa Hao, grew up in Cochinchina that have large mass followings to this day. Explicitly political groups had to go underground. The largest and best organized was the Nationalist party, or VNQDD as it was known by its Vietnamese initials. It was similar to China's Guomindang party and followed a strategy of military takeover followed by a period of political tutelage leading eventually to constitutional government. It focused on organizing the noncommissioned officers of the colonial militia and prepared an elaborate uprising against the French. The plan erupted, prematurely, into the famous Yen Bay mutiny of February 9, 1930. Genuinely alarmed, the French were ruthless in their reprisals after it was put down. Many of the party leaders were executed and most of the rest fled to China.[11]

The baton then passed to the communists and Ho Chi Minh (1890–1969), or Nguyen Ai Quoc (Nguyen the patriot), as he was known at the time. Ho had become a communist in France in 1920 and returned to Asia under the sponsorship of the Comintern. A year after the Yen Bay mutiny, he brokered an agreement by which Vietnam's quarreling Marxist groups united under the banner of the Indochinese Communist party (ICP). Just as the ICP was getting under way, peasant uprisings that produced the Nghe-Tin soviets erupted in June 1930. Although communist organizers were everywhere, the party could take only partial credit for them. Nor could it keep a focus or direction to the uprising's violence. The French suppressed it bloodily.[12]

In the 1930s Ho was out of the country and the ICP swung to an urban strategy under the direction of a more internationalist set of leaders. Under Léon Blum's "democratic front" government in France, more open political activities were permitted in the colonies which obviously facilitated this approach. In the south, however, the ICP found itself in a vicious struggle with a vigorous and intellectually sophisticated Trotskyite party to which it was losing ground. It was, therefore, a thinly disguised blessing when, in 1939, the French thought better of this liberalization and ordered a halt to these urban political movements. Both groups went underground, but only the communists resurfaced.[13] Indeed, there is considerable evidence that the communists collaborated with the French to undermine their rivals.[14]

The resurfacing of the communists was symbolically achieved by Ho in a meeting of the ICP Central Committee which he convened in May 1941. In it, he signaled some key shifts in strategy. He announced a shift to a rural strategy of mobilization, a switch from a revolution of class struggle to a nationalist and internationalist fight against imperialism, and the formation of a broad-based political front, the Viet Minh, to orchestrate it all. The communists were certainly fortunate to have had Ho Chi Minh as their leader. He was tactically flexible, an astute organizer, a unifying conciliator, and always sure of his ultimate goal. In resurfacing at this juncture, as nearly all their rivals had not, the communists had much for which they could be thankful: their tactical adroitness in making this shift to the countryside, the mistakes of the other nationalists, and the repression of the French, which polarized Vietnamese politics to the extremes of collaboration or revolution. In 1941, as William Duiker has said, "The movement, the man, and the moment converged."[15]

In 1941 World War II began in Asia. The war imposed a crucial choosing of sides for all the competing nationalist groups of the continent. The clear consequence was that those who sided with the Japanese generally wound up as losers in the postwar grants of independence. The situation in Indochina was complicated because, unique to their Greater East Asia Co-Prosperity Sphere, the Japanese tolerated the continuation of the French colonial administration in exchange for the use of the colony's resources and facilities for their war effort. The various rivals of the Viet Minh decided on either collaborating with the Japanese, continuing to work with the French, or going into exile in China under the sponsorship of the Guomindang government (while the fatherland was under occupation by two foreign powers). Though seemingly foolhardy at the time, in traditional national terms, the Viet Minh made the correct choice of opposing both the French and the Japanese from within Vietnam. In view of the choices made by their rivals, the fact that they actually did very little to fight either the French or the Japanese did not matter very much.

They were, however, organizing, and by war's end the communist military leader Vo Nguyen Giap had trained and equipped a force of five thousand men. A true interregnum came to Vietnam in 1945. Realizing that the war for them was over, the Japanese on March 9 staged a lightning coup de force against the French colonial regime by disarming its troops, interning its officials, and, perhaps cynically, granting the Vietnamese independence under a puppet Manchukuo-like regime.[16] With the French rendered impotent, the Japanese defeated, and everyone else quite literally out of the country, the communists decided that this was a moment to be seized. They called it the August Revolution, and it stands out as a high-water mark in the lexicon of Vietnamese revolutionary struggle. With the official Japanese surrender on August 15, victory rallies scheduled in Vietnam's major cities were taken over by Viet Minh agitators. Heeding the calls of the ralliers for a new government, the emperor Bao Dai abdicated and handed over the official camel seal of tribute to Viet Minh representatives. On September 1 Ho Chi Minh entered Hanoi to accept Heaven's Mandate from a cheering throng of half a million. It was a genuine *khoi nghia* (the general uprising that Vietnamese call a "righteous revolt").[17]

It was also illusory. With the war over, the French were determined to return. First, however, the Japanese needed to be disarmed and sent home. Pursuant to the plans laid out at the Postdam conference in July 1945, British and Chinese troops began to arrive to reoccupy Vietnam: the British south of the sixteenth parallel and the Chinese north. Negotiations between the French and Viet Minh on the future of Vietnam began in the fall of 1945 and continued until September 1946. Though they were able to work out logistical arrangements for the departure of the Chinese and British, they were at loggerheads over the future political direction of Vietnam. While they talked, the two sides feverishly built up their forces so that by December 1946 each side had one hundred thousand men. At root, the communists were sure they could hurl the French into the sea, and the French were bent on annihilating the Viet Minh.[18]

The War with France

The French returned first in the south, taking over from the departing British. Hostilities broke out when they tried to reassert control in the north. Exasperated by the harassments that attended these efforts, on November 23, 1946, the French gave the Viet Minh two hours to clear out of Haiphong. When the deadline passed, general fighting erupted. In its course six thousand fleeing civilians were killed by barrages from a French cruiser that had mistaken their flight for an assault on an airfield. In December the fighting spread to Hanoi, and the war began. The first phase was a fierce contest in the north for the cities. Between December 19 and February 7, at a cost of nearly two thousand killed, the French pushed the Viet Minh back into the hills. In the fall of 1947, the French launched a major offensive of sixty thousand men against the Viet Minh, which included the paratroop drop Operation Leah to capture the Viet Minh leadership. The Viet Minh eluded both the offensive and the raid. By year's end, the French were certainly not in the sea, but the Viet Minh were by no means annihilated. The nature of both politics and warfare had changed in Asia.[19]

Defeated in the cities, the Viet Minh retreated to their strongholds in central Annam, the southern Mekong Delta, and the six northern provinces of the Viet Bac. The Viet Bac (northwest of Hanoi) was the heart of the Viet Minh resistance, and the provisional government installed all its government departments in the limestone caves surrounding the town of Thai Nguyen. By the end of the war, nearly ten million of Indochina's twenty million people lived in Viet Minh zones. In their Resistance War against the French, the communists sought to wage a three-phased protracted war of guerrilla attacks, battles of maneuver, and final conventional assaults with the whole enterprise fueled by the political mobilization of the peasantry.[20]

Under pressure from the right for a military solution and from the left for a negotiated settlement, French authorities tried both. Politically, the formula they hit upon was to grant Indochina "independence within the French Union" and to deny a role for the Viet Minh through the "Bao Dai solution." In the case of independence, the French moved far too slowly, which only exacerbated the unreality of any settlement without the Viet Minh, the one nationalist group actually fighting for independence. In the Elysée Agreement of March 8, 1949, between Emperor Bao Dai and the French president, the French formally conferred "independence" to Vietnam as an Associated State of France. The "details" of independence were left till later. These "details" were not perfected until full independence was granted on April 28, 1954. By then, it was too late.[21]

Militarily, in addition to bringing in their own regular forces and foreign legionnaires from Europe, the French recruited Vietnamese into the Expeditionary Corps and militia to defend static positions and free French forces for offensive actions. As a result of communist excesses and poor handling of the Cao Dai and Hoa Hoa sects in the Mekong Delta, the French enjoyed some success in recruiting the sect armies to their side. Indeed, despite intensive efforts, the communists were never able to control more than one-third of the delta's population. Nevertheless, the need for the French to expand their conventional forces grew rapidly. In the Elysée Agreement the French agreed to create a separate Vietnamese army both to slake this requirement and to make a show of independence. Progress, however, was slow. The Bao Dai regime's lack of genuine independence made recruitment difficult. The French, furthermore, did not have any enthusiasm for an independent Vietnamese army. Despite ambitious plans, by 1952 only one division had been organized.[22]

While the French built up their forces, tried their political manipulations, and dithered on "Vietnamization," the Viet Minh were busy organizing and mobilizing. According to official party sources, the Viet Minh embarked on the second phase of maneuver right after the failure of the French campaign in the Viet Bac in late 1947. The culmination of this phase came in a series of lightning attacks from May to October 1949 against a string of French border posts along the Chinese frontier which were preventing a linkup with the friendly forces of the victorious Chinese communist army. In abandoning these forts, the French ran into bloody ambushes as attempts to reinforce these garrisons marched into disaster. Seven thousand French troops were lost. General Vo Nguyen Giap announced in February 1950 that these triumphs meant that the time was ripe to launch Mao's third stage in the fall.[23]

The French, clearly alarmed, summoned the colorful General Jean de Lattre de Tassigny, the commander of French forces in Europe, to take charge of their war effort. Giap was delighted by the challenge and responded: "The French are sending against the People's Army an adversary worthy of its steel. We will defeat him on his own ground." In December Giap led his men out of the Viet Bac, and in January 1951, he threw a total of thirty battalions at Vinh Yen, on the fringes of the Red River Delta. He was repulsed with six thousand casualties. Two other major assaults were beaten back with equally heavy losses. Giap withdrew to the Viet Bac and warned the French to expect a protracted guerrilla war. In being set back to phase two, the communists had lost one-third of their regular army. General Tassigny, however, was not able to savor his victories. He died within a year of cancer.[24]

Both sides, perceiving that they were in a stalemate, sought a breakthrough by elevating the struggle to an international one, thereby gaining foreign support. Their efforts were successful, and for both the Viet Minh and the French the extent and nature of this support was considerable and critical.

Chinese aid began as early as the linkup between the two communist armies along their common border. Indeed, some accounts insist that the border fort attacks succeeded because of Chinese training of the Viet Minh attackers.[25] In any case, the Military Trade Agreement of January 18, 1950, provided the Viet Minh with a steady stream of military supplies and a large training mission in southern China that served to both put forty thousand highly trained Viet Minh regulars into the major battles of 1952 and 1953 and to provide an essential rear base and safe haven for communist troops.[26] Chinese help at the war's epic final battle of Dienbienphu was especially critical. The minimalist position of George McT. Kahin and John Lewis concedes that "only" the heavy artillery used in the siege came from China. A maximalist, Hoang Van Chi, asserts that a Chinese general took actual command of the battle. Other accounts say that Chinese advisers and artillery units were involved in the battle.[27] To this day, the Chinese insist that the Viet Minh could never have carried that day without their help.[28] At various points, the Vietnamese have acknowledged this. In 1960 Le Duan, the Lao Dong (Labor) party secretary said, "The inestimable help of the Chinese people to our people's resistance war made an extremely important contribution to the success of the resistance war."[29]

The French, realizing after Giap's offensives that a greater effort was required than they themselves were capable of, sent General Tassigny to Washington in September 1951. He secured substantial American aid by portraying the Indochina War as an anticommunist crusade. In the early postwar years United States policy toward the French was ambivalent. Washington, in fact, displayed very little interest in Indochina until late 1949, when the communist triumph in China radically altered the picture. To Americans, Bao Dai suddenly was seen as a staunch Vietnamese patriot, and a massive military and foreign aid program was set up. From 1950 to 1954, the United States sent $2.6 billion in aid. By 1954 this money was underwriting 78 percent of the French war effort. American military equipment was critical in the French successes in holding off the Viet Minh attacks of 1952 and 1953. At Dienbienphu, however, the United States demurred when the French pleaded for direct military intervention.[30]

All this outside help caused the war on the ground to heat up considerably. In 1952 and 1953 the Viet Minh mounted ever larger assaults. The French were able to hold off the attacks, but were also obliged to withdraw gradually and consolidate their positions against these onslaughts. When Henri Navarre became the French commander in chief in the spring of 1953, both sides were feverishly building up their forces. In May the balance of forces stood at 463,800 men on the French side to 350,000 Viet Minh fighters. Nevertheless, Navarre was appalled at the extent to which French forces had become tied down in static defense. He embarked on his eighteen-month Navarre Plan to augment his forces with a buildup of Vietnamese soldiers to take over these defensive roles, freeing French units to form maneuver striking groups. This process was called Vietnamization, but it overlooked the termitelike way the structure of French power was being eaten away in the villages. Donald Lancaster has asserted that in north Vietnam the Viet Minh controlled five thousand of the seven thousand hamlets and villages. In the south, Kahin and Lewis reported that, outside of sect areas, 60 percent of the countryside was under communist sway.[31]

Something more dramatic was required to convince the French that they were finished. Part of the Navarre Plan was to lure the Viet Minh into a major set-piece battle wherein French air and artillery power could be used to best advantage. Remote Dienbienphu on the northeastern Laotian border appeared to be the perfect place to block Viet Minh columns moving into Laos and to trap them into a fight. In November 1953 French paratroops landed and set up camp. Mountains three miles distant were deemed too far away for Viet Minh artillery. Meanwhile, according to a communist party history, the Central Committee decided at a December 1953 meeting to move over to the final phase of their war and seize the bait at Dienbienphu. Giap took direct command of the battle. By March 1954 the Viet Minh had surrounded the camp and placed it under a methodical, unrelenting fifty-five-day siege lasting until May 7, when the white flag of French surrender fluttered over the command bunker. The French had committed sixteen thousand crack troops, which were overwhelmed by forty thousand Viet Minh regulars. At Dienbienphu, Giap at last defeated the French on a ground of their choosing.[32]

Although fighting continued elsewhere until July, Dienbienphu had convinced the French to divest themselves of their Indochina albatross. The war had cost the French forces 92,707 killed, 76,369 wounded, and 30,861 missing. The Viet Minh did not publish their casualties, but Bernard Fall estimated them to be in excess of half a million killed. Total civilian casualties were approximately a quarter million.[33]

Even before Dienbienphu, the war had reached such intensity that both sides had begun to explore the possibility of a negotiated settlement. On November 29, 1953, a Swedish newspaper leaked a statement by Ho Chi Minh that expressed his willingness to study cease-fire proposals. Realizing that after a year the Navarre Plan was going nowhere, on March 9, 1954, the French Assembly voted to negotiate. Negotiators for a Big Four Conference on Germany in Geneva agreed to accommodate these talks starting on May 8 (as it happened, the day after Dienbienphu fell).[34]

The talks lasted until July 21, and to describe them as complicated hardly does them justice. Throughout the talks the Western allies were disunited, and the American delegation was at cross-purposes. The French government of Joseph Laniel fell in the middle of the conference because the French Assembly was impatient with the lack of progress. Pierre Mendès-France immediately formed a government and announced that he would resign if there were no cease-fire by July 20. His shock tactics injected some unity into the Western side, and the Viet Minh suddenly became more forthcoming. Although the communist side was at least outwardly harmonious, the Vietnamese were discomfited by Soviet machinations with the French over a trade-off on European issues that produced the startling Soviet endorsement of a two-year delay to nationwide elections, one of the key sticking points in the talks.[35]

When the conference closed on July 21, 1954, the "accords" consisted of six unilateral declarations, three cease-fire agreements, and an unsigned final declaration. The elections were provided for only in the final declaration, and the fledgling government of South Vietnam specifically repudiated them. The Americans refused to sign any of the agreements, but promised not to disturb them. In addition to an end to the fighting, the basic achievement of the accords was to end French rule and leave Vietnam as a divided state at the seventeenth parallel.[36]

Considering their situation, the French did well at Geneva, having secured an honorable exit with only the loss of north Vietnam to the communists. Geneva marked only a partial completion of Ho Chi Minh's revolution. Inexorably, it would continue, but the communists carried with them the memory that at Geneva they had been outmaneuvered, and they vowed never again. Ho was criticized for accepting the accords. He derided his critics as leftist deviationists who saw only the trees, not the forest, and warned: "They see only the French, not the Americans."[37] It would not be too long before all Vietnamese would see more than their fill of Americans.

The War against the Americans until Tet 1968

Some important conclusions about Vietnamese national legitimacy emerge from this evolution (and discovery) of Vietnamese history on the eve of the American involvement. The most fundamental point is that all of Vietnam's history continued to be important to the Vietnamese as they tried to establish a "right" modern society. Although, in a land racked by war, physical security increasingly became their immediate concern, traditional features of their sense of well-being remained. Ultimate security to the Vietnamese still depended on the Mandate of Heaven. Despite the emerging of a modern society with modern standards of legitimacy, it was still incumbent on the power holders to preserve Vietnamese identity, maintain correct social relations, protect the fatherland from foreign intervention, and dispense justice through equitable redistributions of land.

In the development of more modern forms of legitimacy, the importance of the French colonial period and the nationalistic reactions to it cannot be overemphasized. The very success of the French intervention did much to discredit the old order represented by the Nguyen dynasty. It made the Vietnamese susceptible to the precepts of a new mandate. The values, ideas, economics, and institutions of the West flooded Vietnam, touching off a ferment from which the Vietnamese have still not recovered. In the attempted fusion of the principles and values of the new Western order with their own traditional verities — a process that can serve as a definition of modern nationalism—the Vietnamese experience, along with that of the Chinese, was unique in Asia in that it was the communists who eventually secured the role of champions and framers of this new mandate.

Yet I, for one, do not subscribe to the view that the Americans had lost the struggle even before they arrived. The history of the communists' rise to power had created a riptide against them. Even though they were the national salvation heroes, they had nevertheless alienated large numbers of their countrymen. The allegations about the communist treatment of Phan Boi Chau and the Trotskyites raised questions, their deception of Catholics and other nationalist groups in the Viet Minh Front caused defections, and their brutal treatment of the sects and other leaders in the Mekong Delta created enemies. In brief, especially in the south there was a real, if inchoate, base of anticommunism.

One person who strove to fashion this base into a coherent political spear was the fledgling Republic of Vietnam's first president, Ngo Dinh Diem. After Geneva, no one held high hopes for the longevity of this infant republic. An overconfidence in the certainty of the collapse of the Saigon regime no doubt explains both the communist passivity in the late 1950s and, for all their loud protests, their complaisance over the failure to hold nationwide reunification elections in 1956.[38] Thus the successful consolidation of control by Diem from 1954 to 1956 came as a surprise to virtually everyone. The communists, who recognized him as a nationalist and had sought to lure him to their side, were perplexed by his stubbornness. The French were piqued by his hostility. South Vietnamese rivals were blindsided by his organizational skills and ability to manipulate American support. Americans, who had all but written off South Vietnam after Geneva, were supremely grateful. A group of American admirers, which included Senators Lyndon Johnson, John Kennedy, and Mike Mansfield and Justice William O. Douglas, formed a society called the Friends of Vietnam.[39]

By 1960 the miracle was wearing thin. The communists had decided that the revolution could be completed in the south only by armed struggle. Southern cadres who had been regrouped to the north after Geneva began to reinfiltrate back. Incidents began to pick up, and a new war dribbled in. Not all of Diem's growing problems could be blamed on the communists. An enigmatic man in the best of circumstances, this Catholic mandarin did not handle opposition well. In April 1960, eighteen old-time politicians called on the president in a manifesto to guarantee democratic liberties to ensure public support for his government. Diem jailed them. More serious threats came from the military. In November 1960, he managed to turn back an elaborate coup mounted by several military units. Despite his subsequent efforts to forestall further cabals by close attention to key assignments and frequent rotations of commanders, his palace was bombed in February 1962 in another abortive rebellion. Increasingly, his regime became a family affair, and his brother Ngo Dinh Nhu acquired more and more power through his control of the National Police and semisecret Can Lao party. At the regional level, his brothers Ngo Dinh Can and Bishop Ngo Dinh Thuc had carved out a fief for themselves in the central provinces of old Annam.[40]

Diem found himself in an isolated position, especially from the population's Buddhist majority. This isolation was most exposed at the village level in the shambles of the Saigon regime's Strategic Hamlet Program begun in February 1962. The idea was to deny the Viet Cong "fish" its "human sea" of support by regrouping the rural population into protected and fortified villages linked by strategic highways that would give the villagers a "new life" through the infusion of modern social services. The scale of the program was vastly overambitious, and because many peasants were torn from their ancestral burial grounds and traditional communities, the program was bitterly resented.[41] Underwriting all this activity was a massive American aid program, which necessarily involved the United States in the fate of the Diem regime. Wanting to contain the communists but also to promote "nation-building," President Kennedy sent out repeated study and fact-finding missions to make recommendations on how to manage this delicate balance of tasks. The advice was contradictory, and as the situation deteriorated, the U.S. military presence grew. Year-end totals for the number of military advisers mark this escalation well: 1960 — 875; 1961 — 3,164; 1962 — 11,326; 1963 — 16,263, and 1964 — 23,210.[42]

Despite American efforts, Diem's isolation increased. The beginning of his end came on May 8, 1963, the anniversary of Buddha's birthday. Government troops fired on a procession of celebrants in Hue waving Buddhist flags in defiance of a ban on the display of religious flags. Nine people were killed. The killings sparked nationwide protests that included dramatic self-immolations by Buddhists monks which Madame Nhu tactlessly derided in public as "Buddhist barbecues." Spurred by the scent of Diem's vulnerability to these emotional public outbursts, a cabal of generals began to plot again. The third leg to the awkward triangle that toppled Diem, the Americans, began tentatively to weigh in as well. Though the U.S. administration in Washington and its mission in Saigon were deeply divided over Diem, the Buddhists, and the generals, the Central Intelligence Agency (CIA) kept in contact with the plotters. Over the summer President Kennedy cut off agricultural aid after Diem refused to take measures to ameliorate the crisis. Undaunted, Diem's brother Nhu launched brutal raids against Buddhist pagodas in August.[43]

That did it for just about everyone. On August 24, a vaguely worded and controversial cable from middle-level officials in Washington authorizing official U.S. links to the conspirators was interpreted by the U.S. Embassy in Saigon to the plotters as a green light for the coup. On November 1 the conspirators struck and, whether intentionally or not, both Diem and Nhu were murdered. Though no one on the American side intended these tragic deaths, it is clear that the U.S. administration had become convinced that the Diem regime had to go.[44] The affair, nevertheless, was sordid. Then Vice-President Lyndon Johnson later lamented: "The worst mistake we ever made was getting rid of Diem."[45] In any case, the removal of the Diem regime did not produce the desired stable, legitimate political order committed to American-sponsored reforms. Instead, to the near despair of the American mission, it ushered in a two-year interregnum of political chaos in which the war in the countryside was all but forgotten. Before the flashy Air Vice-Marshal Nguyen Cao Ky stepped in on February 10, 1965, and finally stabilized the situation, there had been nine changes of government.[46]

Both sides now made a series of decisions that brought on a major war. It was the North Vietnamese who made the first important move in the spiral of escalations that led to direct combat between their soldiers and American troops. In December 1963, after the fall of Diem and the assassination of President Kennedy, the Lao Dong party made a decision to capitalize on the chaos in the south and escalate the war in the coming year by going over to Mao's second-stage war of maneuver. The communists effected this process in three ways. First, by the end of the next year, Hanoi had sent down three regiments of a regular North Vietnamese army division. Second, on July 20, 1964, the communists in the south—the Viet Cong, as they were called—announced a nationwide mobilization to build up main force units. Finally, they put in place a civil structure of eight to ten thousand cadres that was nearly nationwide in scope.[47]

The Americans, meanwhile, were drawing up to a Rubicon River of their own. As the number of their advisers grew, in early 1962 the proscription against field advisers taking part in combat was withdrawn. President Kennedy also authorized harassing covert activities against North Vietnam. These activities led to the famous 1964 Gulf of Tonkin incident in which, under confusing circumstances, one and possibly two attacks on August 2 and 4 were launched against American destroyers by North Vietnamese torpedo boats. From this incident President Johnson secured the Gulf of Tonkin resolution from both houses of Congress (in the Senate by a vote of 88 to 2 and in the House by 416 to 0) authorizing him to take military action.[48] Though the river had been crossed, how to implement this authorization at first was not clear. Politically, the announced goal was to protect the independence of South Vietnam by convincing the North it could not achieve its goals by force and to encourage the establishment of constitutional government in Saigon. The decision to commit ground combat troops in large numbers (175,000 initially and 100,000 more later) did not come until July 1965 after the presentation of General William C. Westmoreland's three-phased plan to defeat the communists on the ground through a war of attrition.[49]

From July until the spasm of the Tet offensive in 1968, the war went through its period of fiercest struggle, with both sides hotly contesting at all levels. This was in large part because, until the massive American intervention, the communists were close to a takeover. The forces of the Army of the Republic of Vietnam (ARVN) were being chewed up at a rate of a battalion a month and national politics were paralyzed. Communist forces were able to procure 80 to 90 percent of their supplies locally and to recruit most of their manpower in the south. This was difficult to sustain against the American buildup, however, and the escalation created a growing political crisis for the communists in which the National Liberation Front (NLF) had to demand even more of peasants, who were already driven beyond the limits of their support. The NLF was soon forced to phase out its 1964 mobilization and reduce its "taxes." Nevertheless, the Viet Cong continued to make a game effort at southern recruitment. From early 1965 to August 1966, total VC/NVA forces rose from 116,000 to 282,000. This put an army of 177 main force battalions in the field, 96 of them southern. Half of this stupendous increase came from southern recruitment, the rest from northern infiltration. But increasingly the burden shifted to the north, as reflected in year-end infiltration figures: 1964 — 12,400, 1965 — 36,300; 1966 — 92,287; and 1967 — 101,263.[50]

By the end of 1966, allied forces had risen to a total of 1,018,000 (including 375,000 Americans), giving them a better than three-to-one numerical edge in troops, and the lavish American resources in firepower made the overall combat edge far greater. The United States also had amassed the largest aerial armada in Asia. At its peak it consisted of more than six thousand aircraft, which dropped more ordnance over Indochina than in all of World War II and the Korean War combined. To secure an attrition rate greater than the replacement ability of the communists, General Westmoreland used his forces to launch search-and-destroy sweeps in an effort to trap VC/NVA main force soldiers into big-unit battles to effect maximum casualties and to push these forces back away from populated areas to permit "nation-building" in pacified areas. This priority given to big-unit war produced an obsession with the body count of communist dead.[51]

More than anything else, this obsession turned Vietnam into a numbers war. Three sets of numbers formed the charts by which progress in the struggle soon came to be gauged: reports of the Hamlet Evaluation System (HES), the body count of communist dead, and the numerical strength of VC/NVA forces. Though the latter two are self-explanatory, HES surveys grouped the country's twelve thousand villages and hamlets into five categories along a secure, insecure, contested, enemy-infested, and enemy-held continuum. Progress here was measured by shifts toward the government side of the spectrum. All three sets of numbers had enormous problems in the way they were collected and interpreted. The recent *Westmoreland v. CBS* trial over the huge disparity in the reported size of Viet Cong forces between his command's figure of three hundred thousand versus a CIA analyst's number of six hundred thousand is merely one illustration.[52] If taken with a large grain of salt and viewed comparatively over time, however, the numbers did show that communist casualties were indeed heavy. They also showed that the communists had a potent political structure and presence that could not be wished away by HES figures measuring government "control" that largely missed the political issues fueling the insurgency.[53] This is not to say that these massive operations and bombings had no effect on these issues. As David Hunt observed, the insecurity brought on by these campaigns raised questions about the legitimacy of a Viet Cong mandate by disproving their ability to protect populations under their control. This rural insecurity started a pronounced trend of urbanization as peasants fled to safer government areas. On the eve of Tet, the communists' human sea was rapidly evaporating.[54]

As the fighting raged, Premier Nguyen Cao Ky attempted to impose political stability and to attain legitimacy for his regime. He was unable, however, to contain the rivalries among his generals, particularly those between Nguyen Van Thieu and Nguyen Chanh Thi. Thi was the commander of I Corps (in the north), and he soon made the quarrel public by openly siding with the militant Buddhists of the Struggle Force in Hue and Danang from 1965 to 1966. This brought the new nation to the brink of civil war. By June 1966 the Buddhists were brought under control and Thi forced out. But to secure this peace, Thieu and Ky, as new co-leaders, had to agree to elections for a Constituent Assembly.[55]

From September 11, 1966 to October 27, 1967, six sets of nationwide elections were held in South Vietnam. The ones for a Constituent Assembly were the first and held out great promise. The delegates drafted a constitution for a Second Republic (after Diem's first) that provided for a president, Supreme Court, and bicameral National Assembly. However American in structural appearance, the flow of power was more in the image of a Charles De Gaulle with a president who could dissolve the Assembly and rule by emergency decree. The cresting election of this tide was the presidential election held on September 3, 1967, which somewhat tarnished the promise of the Constituent Assembly elections. The Buddhist slate was disqualified, communists were not allowed to participate, and what opposition remained was splintered among nine tickets. The military, after a tearful and tense meeting that revealed some deep splits, agreed to a single slate with the more senior Thieu as president and Ky as vice-president. Thieu and Ky won over their fractured opposition with 35 percent of the vote and, despite these problems, won a measure of legitimacy to their government, both in the South and in the United States.[56]

The combination of these political developments with the relative communist quiescence by late 1967 before an American military machine in Vietnam that had grown to over half a million men gave rise to some optimism. General Westmoreland's intelligence staff had concluded that the "crossover point" over communist forces had been achieved in June 1967, and, at a National Press Club audience in November, the American commander offered the opinion that "we have reached an important point when the end begins to come into view." He followed this remark with even more bravado by telling an interviewer: "I hope they try something . . . because we are looking for a fight."[57] He certainly got one.

Much like the siege of Dienbienphu at the end of the war with France, the communist Tet offensive, which lasted from January 31 until mid-June, 1968 was the landmark event of the American war. Unlike Dienbienphu, which produced a clear winner and loser, everyone—Americans, South Vietnamese, Viet Cong, and North Vietnamese—could point to the other side as the loser at Tet. It changed the nature of the war fundamentally. Although still fiercely contested, the struggle was no longer so well-rounded or strategically straightforward. Mao's classic stages and Westmoreland's neat phases had to be abandoned, and the politics that was fueling the insurgency and counterinsurgent nation-building came to be increasingly suspended.

The main political achievement of the government and forces of South Vietnam was that they survived. Despite an uneven performance, ARVN units did not disintegrate or defect (as government forces did in China in the 1940s and in Afghanistan in the 1980s), nor did the people rise up against the government in any sort of khoi nghia. Instead, when it was all over, the communist forces had been badly beaten, and President Thieu, who initially thought the offensive was a coup being launched against him by Ky, was able to exploit the attacks in the consolidation of his own power. He was able to rouse the shaken urban populace somewhat and announced a mobilization that eventually doubled the size of ARVN from 670,000 to 1,100,000.[58]

As Robert Sansom has argued, from the perspective of the southern communists, or Viet Cong, Tet was designed to demonstrate forcefully that they could not be shut out of the political process, that they retained the popular support they had earned against the French, and that the villagers should return from the cities by convincing them that no place was safe under the Thieu government.[59] To the contrary, the political result of Tet in South Vietnam was to cast the government in the image of a winner, and the trend of urbanization increased.

Nevertheless, at the international level, the Tet offensive was a profound political shock to the United States, and the orientation of the American leadership, nervous about the rising polarization of its own domestic politics over the war, shifted away from further escalation. Hanoi, its forces momentarily shattered and its revolutionary strategy in shambles, agreed to President Johnson's offer to hold talks and adopted a policy of "fighting while negotiating."

The War against the Americans from Tet to Liberation

The period just after the Tet offensive was a low point for the communists. Their soldiers, at least, had expected a quick victory, and it was difficult to convince them to resume the drudgery of protracted guerrilla war. As part of their negotiating strategy, the communists proclaimed the Provisional Revolutionary Government on June 6, 1969, as a rival government to Thieu's. But neither the negotiating nor the fighting went well. An offensive launched in the fall of 1969 to lift the spirits of the aged Ho Chi Minh was a complete failure, and Ho died in September, right in the middle of it.[60]

Meanwhile, Richard M. Nixon came to the White House in January 1969 with a "secret plan" to end the war. Actually, his plan consisted of twin measures that had been visible parts of the Vietnam debate for years, but he gave them new twists. The first measure was to continue the public negotiations started by Johnson, but Nixon also made it a first priority to open parallel secret talks. The other was to continue the program of Vietnamization, but more rapidly and with greater fanfare than it had received under Johnson. Coupled with this, he began a phased withdrawal of American troops (which had reached a peak of 543,000 in April 1969) that deescalated the war for the United States. By the end of his first term in November 1972, Nixon had pulled out all but 25,000 of the American GIs, thereby reducing the number of casualties and winning for the White House a degree of domestic support for its handling of the war.[61]

On all fronts, 1969 and 1970 were probably Thieu's best years. American support, despite the troop withdrawals, was solid. Communist activity was low. Regional forces were built up, and at this level the government improved its position in the Central Highlands and Mekong Delta. In the Mekong Delta this was largely because of the psychological impact of the March 1970 land-to-the-tiller land reform legislation, long a priority item of the U.S. Agency for International Development. Financially underwritten by the United States at a cost of $725 million, in its essential features the program provided for a free grant of land to the tiller with full legal title and a cessation of rent payments for all of the country's rice land (which was 80 percent of the land under cultivation). Basically, tenant farming was ended and no one was allowed to till tracts of more than fifteen hectares.[62] With due allowance for the mushiness of HES statistics, these measures certainly played a role in the improved proportion of people living in secure hamlets from 47 percent in 1968 to 71 percent in 1969 to 75 percent in 1970 to 84 percent in 1971.[63]

But failures in war and politics by late 1970 and 1971 made Thieu's best years brief. In the war, a long-standing irritant to the American command was the communist use of border areas across the Cambodian frontier for its elusive Central Office of South Vietnam (COSVN) headquarters (which directed the southern war effort) and for bases for the resupply and recuperation of its soldiers. To ensure that these areas would not be used to stage attacks against the withdrawing American troops, on April 30, 1970, Nixon announced that U.S. and ARVN forces had launched an incursion into Cambodia to destroy the communist headquarters and destroy the communist buildup in supplies for another offensive. Though COSVN headquarters was not captured, thousands of tons of communist supplies and equipment were destroyed by the June 30 withdrawal of American troops. The ARVN troops, however, remained in Cambodia, and the war now became an Indochina War.[64] Whatever boost ARVN morale received from the Cambodian adventure was largely nullified by a disastrous thrust across the Ho Chi Minh Trail in Laos in 1971 by two of ARVN's best divisions.[65]

But the most serious repercussions were felt in the United States. Student demonstrations and protests erupted all over the country, most dramatically at Kent State University, where four students were killed. Thus, though the incursion into Cambodia may have brought time on the ground in Vietnam for an orderly withdrawal of American troops, at home it fanned the old flames of opposition and burned away whatever margins of time Nixon's twin policies had bought for him earlier. Thieu's American support was no longer solid.

The failures in politics had been building for some time. In upper house elections held in August 1970, a militant Buddhist slate of candidates beat one favored by Thieu by 1,148,000 votes to 1,107,000. Two other slates received nearly one million votes apiece as well. Despite these impressive vote totals, there remained the damning fact that only 1 percent of the adult population belonged to any noncommunist political group. Thus, despite the numerous nationwide elections since 1966, the failure of these elections to produce organized political parties that could meaningfully share and compete for power resulted instead in a large but utterly fragmented opposition to Thieu.[66]

By the time of the October 1971 presidential election (or, more correctly, referendum), it was no wonder that Thieu was able to outmaneuver his opponents and achieve a one-man race. Donald Kirk has argued that the withdrawal of his two principal opponents from the campaign was a clear demonstration of the political power Thieu had amassed in a Charles De Gaulle style. However it was interpreted in South Vietnam, the one-man race seriously tarnished Thieu's legitimacy in the United States. If, in South Vietnam, Thieu could have counted on active support beyond the circles of his own partisan supporters, perhaps he could have shrugged his shoulders, but as one factional leader observed after the election: "All the system is based on American aid." [67]

Inspired by these mounting difficulties in Saigon, the Hanoi politburo decided that it would be advantageous to launch another offensive in 1972. Accordingly, Le Duan, the party general secretary, made an extended trip to Moscow in the fall of 1971 and secured the necessary assistance in heavy weaponry. Despite plans for Nixon's historic trip to Beijing, the Chinese also agreed to help.[68]

On Easter Sunday, March 20, three North Vietnamese divisions struck across the demilitarized zone mounting a conventional Korean-style invasion supported by two hundred Soviet T-54 tanks and scores of 130-millimeter long-range artillery pieces. In an offensive that lasted until the middle of September, the North Vietnamese eventually threw fourteen divisions and twenty-six independent regiments into the onslaught (virtually the entire armed force of North Vietnam). This time, except for the area around Saigon, virtually no local Viet Cong units participated. If this was still a people's war, hardly any of them were southerners. Also, this time on the government's side the responsibility for the ground fighting rested exclusively on the shoulders of ARVN and the small network of American field advisers. In most instances, the South Vietnamese held their ground, but it was difficult to call this conclusive proof of Vietnamization. American airpower was massively employed and accounted for half of all communist casualties and tank losses. Moreover, in the north, the combination of the aerial bombing campaign Linebacker I (which was much more effective than previous campaigns because of the lifting of numerous targeting restrictions and the use of new "smart" bombs) and the mining and blockading of North Vietnamese ports reduced the flow of supplies from the north to a trickle. In addition to a small district town north of Saigon and unpopulated border regions, the only accomplishment of the offensive was the seizure of Quang Tri, the capital of South Vietnam's northernmost province. When ARVN paratroopers and marines retook it on September 15, the invasion was over. Communist casualties were reported to be one hundred thousand killed.[69]

There is very little doubt that the failure of the Easter invasion made the Paris Peace Agreement possible. Stymied in the guerrilla war earlier, Hanoi was convinced by the huge costs of this conventional invasion that it could not militarily defeat the combination of Nguyen Van Thieu and a Vietnamese military machine backed by American firepower. At least one term of the equation had to be taken out, perhaps now by negotiation.

Though the secret talks had been going on since August 4, 1969, it was not until after the recapture of Quang Tri that the talks held out the possibility of an end to the war. In these talks, the longtime objectives of Nixon and his national security adviser Henry Kissinger (who conducted the talks for the American side) were to bring about a cease-fire to extricate the United States from Vietnam and to secure the release of American prisoners of war as well as to guarantee the political independence of South Vietnam. Kissinger's opposite, Hanoi's politburo member Le Duc Tho, chiseled away the firmness of this latter guarantee. Up until Quang Tri, the sticking point was Hanoi's insistence on the resignation of Thieu. The big break in the talks came on September 26, 1972, eleven days after the recapture of the city, when Le Duc Tho dropped the demand for Thieu's departure. Letting himself get too far in front of events, no doubt because of the pressures of the U.S. presidential election, Kissinger went on television to announce on October 26 that "peace is at hand."[70]

It was not. What was not in hand was the concurrence of the South Vietnamese government. Hanoi, having been assured that this support would be automatic, was angered by Thieu's public posturing and even more by the $2 billion in military equipment that poured into Saigon in November and December. Though Kissinger finally brought Thieu into line, Hanoi balked and began to withdraw some of its earlier concessions. Now Nixon was angry, and on December 15 he threatened to bomb North Vietnam within three days if the deadlock were not broken.[71]

It was not, and Nixon was true to his word. From December 18 to 30, he unleashed the "Christmas bombing" on Hanoi and Haiphong. Known also as Linebacker II, it was designed to paralyze the North Vietnamese economy and bring the agreement to a conclusion. In twelve days of bombing, 2,000 sorties were flown (including 720 by strategic B-52 bombers) hitting targets in the heart of both cities. Though the damage was unprecedented, civilian casualties were relatively low. Estimates ranged from 1,300 to 4,000 killed.[72] Since the bombing, a bitter controversy has swirled around its efficacy in securing the Paris Peace Agreement. In his analysis of the negotiations, Gareth Porter viewed Linebacker II as a great failure that revealed Nixon's weakness and forced him to return to Hanoi's draft proposals of October. This conclusion has been hotly disputed by Sir Robert Thompson, who asserted that Hanoi was brought to its knees by the bombing. More soberly, Allan Goodman simply concluded that the bombing was instrumental in achieving the final agreement.[73]

On January 8 Hanoi agreed to return to the bargaining table. In effect, both sides returned to where they were in October, and on January 28, 1973, the agreement was signed in Paris. Its essential provisions were for an immediate cease-fire, the release of all prisoners as well as a complete withdrawal of the remaining American soldiers within sixty days, the establishment of a National Council of Reconciliation and Concord to set up elections for a new government in the south, a commitment to peaceful reunification, the establishment of an International Commission of Control and Supervision, one-for-one replacement of military equipment and supplies, and a promise from the United States to assist in the reconstruction of North Vietnam.[74] In a significant omission, the 145,000 North Vietnamese troops in the south were allowed to remain. Yet the communists were not much of a threat by the time of the agreement. Even *Nhan Dan*, the official Hanoi newspaper, conceded that the Saigon government was "comparatively more stable and better organized from the central to the village and hamlet levels than the army and government which existed at the beginning of the Diem period."[75]

On the verge of collapse in 1965, when the United States intervened with its own combat troops, South Vietnam found the tide in 1973 decidedly in its favor for what, according to the Paris Peace Agreement, should have been the next stage: the struggle for the political loyalty of the South Vietnamese people. A question, however, hung heavily in the air: Was Thieu ready for a straight political struggle with his communist adversaries?

Because his government descended from a position of considerable strength to total defeat in slightly more than two years, the obvious answer is no. But the story of Saigon's fall—or liberation—is a saga interwoven with several strands.

To begin, the Paris Peace Agreement had been concluded with a great deal of hypocrisy and forced marriages of convenience. The Americans, though concerned that Saigon be given a "decent interval," basically wanted out. The South Vietnamese had been unwillingly forced into the agreement and Thieu had no intention of carrying out its political provisions. The communists, who needed a respite, wanted to grant the Americans their wish so that the struggle could be resumed without their interference. From the beginning, the pact was violated, and the fighting never stopped. The only peace achieved in Paris was peace for the communists from the Americans.

This peace came soon. Nixon had secured Thieu's acquiescence by promising to unleash further bombings on Hanoi if its violations of the agreement were massive. They were, and in March the president twice warned Hanoi to stop its huge build-up in the south.[76] Plans were laid for bombings in April. Just then John Dean began talking to Watergate prosecutors, and the project was canceled.[77] The congressional cutoff of all funds for U.S. military action in Indochina effective August 15, 1973, and the War Powers

Act of November 7, 1973, requiring the approval of the Congress for the deployment of troops overseas after thirty days sealed Thieu's isolation. Nixon could no longer deliver.

More than Watergate, however, was involved in this rancor on Capitol Hill. Despite Hanoi's obvious violations, many in the Congress were displeased with Thieu's failure to cooperate in carrying out the political provisions of the agreement. Furthermore, though he made some phlegmatic efforts to expand his New Democracy party to the "rice-roots" level, Thieu reserved his greatest efforts for a vigorous military land-grabbing campaign against the communists which brought an additional one thousand hamlets under government control.[78] The effect, nevertheless, was a cut in American aid to South Vietnam. In 1973 Congress approved $2.2 billion in aid, but in 1974 this was cut to $900 million and in 1975 to $700 million. Meanwhile, communist aid to Hanoi, according to Richard Falk, held constant at $300 million in 1973 and $400 million in 1974, although China's claim in 1979 (which went unrefuted by Hanoi) to have provided $10 billion in aid to North Vietnam suggests that these figures may be understated. More recently, reports in the press have stated that Soviet advisers participated in combat operations against American air attacks and that China's aid actually totaled more than $20 billion, including combat troops fighting in both north and south at a loss of four thousand killed. George McT. Kahin, with a little more restraint, has cited U.S. intelligence reports of fifty thousand Chinese soldiers in North Vietnam itself and the construction of a major Chinese military complex just over the North Vietnamese border.[79] If nothing else, these figures should illustrate how much of an international undertaking the continued prosecution of the Vietnam War had become.

Meanwhile, in South Vietnam, the entire American-devised system of firepower superiority and maneuverability had broken down under the aid cutbacks, supply bottlenecks, and Vietnamese inability to keep sophisticated equipment functioning. The cutbacks most critically resulted in drawing down ARVN ammunition stocks. The quadrupling of oil prices worldwide in October 1973 made tactical field operations inordinately expensive. On top of this, at any one time more than half the helicopters and planes were grounded with maintenance problems. These were not auspicious conditions for an aggressive military approach of land-grabbing, and Thieu would have been better served if he had husbanded his military resources by expending greater energies in the political sphere.[80]

But Thieu cannot be judged in a vacuum. He was not alone in spurning the politics that had once fueled this struggle in Vietnamese society. Hanoi, too, after the agreement, embarked on a decidedly military course. Van Tien Dung, a senior communist commander, has admitted that a huge military buildup was begun in 1973 in preparation for another offensive. After some probes in late 1974 that produced no American reaction, it seemed that the coast was clear. President Gerald Ford, sensing the imminence of another communist move, submitted to Congress on January 7, 1975, an emergency request for $300 million in military aid to Saigon. Before Congress acted, the communists struck on March 10, in the Central Highlands, opening their final Ho Chi Minh campaign.[81]

Three highland provincial capitals were captured, and ARVN forces were put into a rout that proved irreversible. What was missing this time was the crucial component of American firepower. On April 10, ARVN forces made a determined stand at Xuan Loc just sixty miles northeast of Saigon. On April 21 the town fell, and Thieu fled the country the same day. North Vietnamese soldiers marched into Saigon on April 30 and renamed the tired capital Ho Chi Minh City. The war was over, at a staggering cost to everyone. Guenter Lewy's careful analysis of war casualties has put total war dead at 1.3 million, including 282,000 allied soldiers. He estimated that communist military deaths ranged from 444,000 to 666,000, and civilian deaths, both in the north and south, from 365,000 to 587,000. For the Americans, 55,000 troops were killed in a war effort that cost $150 billion.[82]

After a thirty-five-year struggle for power, the communists, in a modern version of *Nam tien*, had finally taken full possession of their country after fighting the French, the Americans, and their fellow countrymen. Yet this was not the triumph of a balanced political and military revolution like the August Revolution or the subsequent Resistance War against the French. Such an attempt had perished in the rubble of the Tet offensive. By 1971 the politics of this struggle had become suspended as the revolution degenerated into a military slugfest propped up by international benefactors. Saigon fell, not to the popular uprising of a revolution but to the conquering invasion of a conventional army.

Chapter 5

FRAMEWORK ANALYSIS: THE WAR WITHOUT A LESSON?

The Legitimacy Crisis

At the heart of the war in Vietnam lay the quest for legitimacy between two social orders (and supporting international movements). On both sides, communist and nationalist, the combatants had no doubt of their national identity as Vietnamese. What was disputed was the very nature of authority for the nation, a classic crisis of legitimacy. The origins of this dispute date back at least to the French defeat but can be traced earlier to the rise of the communist party, or even to the impact of the French and the waves of resistance to them. At the time of the French defeat, however, a tension existed between two points of view within the Vietnamese elite. Traditionalists viewed the Viet Minh victory as a signal to return to traditional values and structures, but the modernists saw it as an opportunity for Vietnam to embark on a program of rapid development and modernization.[1] The dilemma confronting the traditionalists was that the traditional hierarchical relationship of patron and client, all the way down to the landholder and his landless laborers, had been too badly shattered to be revived.

The patron at all levels was simply not strong enough to do what he was supposed to do—provide personal security. For the modernists, with the French gone, the problem was how to use Western ideas without compromising Vietnamese nationalism.

Subsequent governments of South Vietnam could not decide on which of these two approaches to follow. The result was a sense of drift similar to that besetting Tu Duc's court in the face of the first threat from the French. There was no such drift in the new communist government lodged in Hanoi. It turned its back on the traditional order in recruiting its leaders (though the men themselves were mostly from the former mandarin class), knowing full well that the path to modernity involved "critical changes in legitimacy from transcendental to immanent sources."[2] Thus the communists unveiled Marxism as a new secular and ideological culture to replace the traditional Confucian virtues and social order. Yet the prime constituency of the revolution remained the peasantry, which for all the blows rained on the authority of the royal court still adhered to traditional concepts. Therefore, the communist revolution had to be translated into Vietnamese by the age-old formula of the Mandate of Heaven.

As we have already seen, the communists took pains to portray their actions as a heroic exemplification of this formulary. As the new emperor (*hoang de*), care was taken in 1945, for example, to have Bao Dai publicly abdicate to the communists in the August Revolution to ensure orderly succession and correct hierarchical political relationships. But there was more to a mandate than maintaining a structure; the responsibility of rule was to further a righteous cause, or *chinh nghia*. For the Vietnamese the most righteous of all causes was for their king (or *vua*) to advance the *phuc duc* of Vietnam, which Stephen Young has described as the superego of the Vietnamese ethnic experience.[3] What better way to pursue this then to secure "national salvation" for the people from the French barbarians by means of a righteous revolt (*khoi nghia*) and redeem this pledge by pressing on against the American "imperialists." Yet the king as protector still had to guarantee the protection of the people. In this, at least during the American war, the communists were less successful. The creation of an elaborate organizational network of political links and associations was only partially successful as a substitute.

In this struggle for legitimacy, the communists were not invulnerable. Although they were careful to follow traditional formulas in their path to power, the order they sought to establish was a modern, socialist one inimical to traditional leadership groups. This obviously guaranteed some opposition. Paradoxically, as avowed modernists, the communists were not as successful in winning over other modernists, who also wanted to modernize Vietnam, but along more democratic lines. It is noteworthy that urban intellectuals, for all their cynicism toward the Saigon regime, never flocked en masse to the banner of the National Liberation Front.[4]

Saigon, for its part, did take some steps to establish a writ of legitimacy, at least in modern terms. The Constituent Assembly elections of 1966 and the presidential elections of 1967 appealed to modernists by going much further than Hanoi in establishing legitimate constitutional government. Many legislators in the National Assembly honestly saw themselves as modern ombudsmen and developed links with constituents. The crux of the South Vietnamese government's difficulty in establishing its legitimacy, however, was the common dilemma facing the fledgling governments of all developing states—its very weakness. It was caught in a vicious circle in which the regime lacked the political support and participation of the citizenry in its system—the very support necessary to encourage bureaucratic and political services dynamic enough, in turn, to stimulate this participation. The clearest reflection of this dilemma is that in 1970, according to Allan Goodman, only 1 percent of the South Vietnamese populace belonged to a noncommunist political group while the membership in the then decimated southern communist party, as Douglas Pike has conceded, was much higher.[5]

What is perhaps most striking about this war that was a struggle for national legitimacy in Vietnam was how much of its burden was carried by the United States. The creation of a noncommunist portion of Vietnam at the 1954 Geneva accords was a tribute to French diplomacy. Its preservation for nearly twenty-one years was the gradually shouldered burden of the United States. Ngo Dinh Diem's rise to power would not have been possible without the Americans, nor would the maintenance of all the subsequent Saigon regimes. That Nguyen Van Thieu could not survive without the Americans was made starkly clear in the two painful years after the 1973 Paris Peace Agreement. In playing Atlas, the United States was struggling to stand with its burden against the flow of a communist historical tide. Yet during this period of artificial propping, some strides were made to reverse this tide. A measure of political stability was achieved, a major land reform program was enacted, fair elections were held, and Hanoi's military wolf was kept at bay.

In fact, those efforts made such an impact that, even as the American Atlas grew tired and finally shrugged off the burden, the communists, in achieving their victory in 1975, were forced to abandon the high road of their lofty revolutionary ideals and strategy of people's war (if not of their *chinh nghia*, at least their *khoi nghia*) and settle for the far less ideologically salutary victory of a simple military seizure of power. Any victory is savory at first, but that of the communists has left the bitter aftertaste of unresolved questions of national and revolutionary legitimacy. Since 1975, they—and their revolutionary comrades elsewhere—have discovered that power and legitimacy may indeed overlap, even for a long time, but they are not, ultimately, the same thing.

Framework Analysis

NATIONAL AND REVOLUTIONARY LEGITIMACY

Breaking the Vietnam War into the three levels of legitimation portrayed in my Domestic Legitimacy Chart (Table 3.1) at the level of interest, and its passive support, the Viet Cong were very careful to create the "sympathetic environment" described by Jeffrey Race and missed by the "security" measures of the HES statistics.[6] The representatives who established the communist presence in the villages were invariably local people who knew the villagers and were sympathetic with their "communal" concerns. In the new system of traditional patron-client ties that they established both in the cells of the communist party and in their various liberation associations, the NLF took pains to preserve a sense of belonging among the peoples brought into this order. This effort was reinforced by scaring away or, if necessary, killing those who attempted to maintain a GVN presence that would compete with this community.

In such traditional terms, the approaches of the GVN were generally terrible. The presence it established was distinctly alien. That is, the officials who were appointed, even at the village level, were from urban backgrounds and all too often corrupt and conspicuously lacking in *uy tin* (traditional Vietnamese "virtue," the hallmarks of which are ability, concern for others, and personal austerity).[7] Further, some of the large-scale activities of the government were disruptive to village life. Sweeps by ARVN soldiers in the countryside were often accompanied by destruction and larceny of property, disrespect to women, and harassing interrogations of men. The two Hamlet resettlement programs of 1959 and 1962–64 wrenched villagers from their ancestral homes and largely failed to follow through with any of the promised compensatory social services. Earlier, villagers in the Mekong Delta in particular were alienated by President Diem's partial land reform program of 1956 that obliged peasants to take out loans to pay for land that had already been "given" to them by the Viet Minh during the Resistance War.

Despite this interest level of legitimacy, in traditional terms, falling to the communists, it was not completely one way. The communists had made mistakes in the sect areas. The strong local organizations of Catholic villages made them hard areas for the communists to penetrate. Further, the government tended to improve as time went on. After Tet, the GVN provided M-16 rifles to the Regional Forces/Popular Forces (who were local soldiers) and who, despite some unevenness in performance, were the most cost-effective military force in the country, accounting for 30 percent of communist casualties at only 4 percent of the total allied war costs.[8] From 1967 to 1972 the pacification program, particularly in its elected village officials and delegated budgetary authority, did provide villagers with some popular policies and leaders.[9] In 1974, however, President Thieu decided to supplant these officials with a special corps of junior army officers loyal to him.

Though the communists, for the most part, could boast of a sympathetic environment achieved through the passive support of the villagers' silence, they found it difficult to intensify this support to higher levels because the modern aspects of this interest-level support, physical and material security, were hard for them to accomplish. The increasing ubiquity of ARVN and American troops made it difficult for the Viet Cong to offer much physical protection. Indeed, harm did come to many contested villages from bombing and shelling, activities controlled by the government. If the villagers wanted to avoid this capricious damage, the pragmatic solution was to move to the cities and other government-controlled areas. The sporadic mortaring of government areas was a communist attempt to prevent this.[10] On a larger scale the Tet offensive can be seen as a desperate attempt to halt this migration.

As for material security, against the Americans, the communists were never able to set up liberated zones to show the people a better way of life.[11] In contrast, the massive U.S. aid programs, especially the provision of readily available rural credit, did bring substantial material improvements to the peasantry. Further, the creation of a Honda economy in the cities brought in transfer payments to the countryside from urban relatives. At the level of interest, the Viet Cong's attempts to disrupt these new patterns were largely futile. As long as this aid continued, the Vietnamese were willing to go along with, and individually take advantage of, this government world of American creation. In a passive sense, the HES statistics measure this. It was in this sense that in 1973 the communists conceded that the GVN had regained the position enjoyed by the Diem regime.

Nevertheless, despite these modern drawbacks, the revolutionary strategy of the communists was more than successful at this level. Thanks largely to the freshness of the war against the French, the Viet Cong were able to achieve a "takeoff" from a critical mass in this second round very quickly. Significantly, the world of the villager remained largely traditional, and in attracting support the Viet Cong could bank on the national legitimacy they had earned against the French as well as on their ability to champion a "mass line" because of their closeness to the concerns of the peasantry. They were able to establish a widespread presence. In coercive terms, hundreds of local officials were assassinated at the beginning, and by 1965 the Viet Cong were collecting "taxes" from nearly all of South Vietnam's forty-four provinces.[12] Almost from the start, then, a purely suppressive solution against the communists was not possible.

This was particularly true because at the group level of opportunity the communists had long-standing advantages left over from the Resistance War against the French. Again, communist strengths were more in the traditional area than in the modern. The structures and associations the Viet Minh left behind offered real opportunities for advancement among the peasantry. Communist reports that 85 percent of their middle-level cadre leadership came from the local peasantry have not been disputed by anyone.[13]

The traditional components of this level of appeal proved to be an enduring problem for the GVN. Diem at least understood the importance of establishing organizational links to the countryside, and the National Revolutionary Movement, Madame Nhu's Women's Solidarity Movement, and Ngo Dinh Nhu's Can Lao party did offer conduits for participation in the Diem order. But these organizations were only halfway measures that embodied Fred Riggs's concept of the "clect": modern in outward form but traditional sectlike in actual functioning. The organizations themselves were turned into warlord preserves of Diem's closely knit family entourage. Diem himself never understood the communal issues that animated the peasantry to whom his links tried to lead. He lived in a very Catholic world of elite French ideas. The talk was always of nationalism, but in a very Western sense of the word. The more indigenous patriotism, what the Vietnamese called *mat nuoc* (save the country), he subtly betrayed by his isolation and his alien ideas.[14] Two conspicuous examples of his lack of sensitivity were his Land Reform Act of 1956 in which he provided loans for farmers to buy land from absent landlords that the Viet Minh had already redistributed to peasants as outright grants in exchange for their loyalty,[15] and his breaking with tradition by making direct appointments of all rural officials. In stark contrast to communist cadremen, they were virtually all urban dwellers and culturally from a different world.

Though he never set up the organizational links that Diem did, Nguyen Van Thieu, during his presidency (1967–75), was one southerner who appreciated the importance of the countryside. In the 1967 presidential race, for example, he gained more of his support from the countryside than the cities.[16] Land reform was a project he embraced, and the March 1970 Land Reform Act made critical encroachments on the communists' traditional superiority. As has been mentioned, however, these advantages came late, when the political issues were being superseded by the larger, conventional military struggle.

In modern terms, the GVN made much more headway, but it was not enough. The progress in elections illustrates this best. In holding local, legislative, and presidential elections that permitted competitive candidacies, important steps were taken. But from electoral blocs of candidates, modern political parties, with their critical acceptance of a sharing of power and thereby allowing for the creation of a national political community, never developed. At the local level, the various organizations of the Revolutionary Development Program that were part of the Accelerated Pacification Program from 1968 to 1970 almost screamed for the formation of broad-based political parties as the national capstone to these efforts. Indeed, when one of the political parties, the Tan Dai Viets, tried to build a national following, Thieu blocked it.[17] Despite all this effort, then, the net result was a non-communist "society" in which only 1 percent of the adult population had any active or organizational national allegiance.

The importance of a middle tier group of leaders with at least opportunity-level commitments to the regime had a special significance in the military. This point was stressed by General Matthew B. Ridgway in his own successful buildup of a strong South Korean army: "What I want to stress above everything else is the foundation of an Army—its officer corps. With one, any problem can be overcome; without one, all other efforts are in vain. . . . No amount of equipment or numbers of personnel can be substituted for the basic ingredient of leadership."[18]

The truth of this, both positively and negatively, was visited on the Vietnamese army many times during the war, but the negative instances outweighed the positive. Unlike the Korean case, commanders were not relieved as often as they should have been. As Thayer has pointedly observed, this was owing both to a lack of will and outright political fear by President Thieu and to American failure to push this issue vigorously enough. Very simply, the South Vietnamese government's power rested in the army, and, in this power center, every national leader saw nightmares of his own image and fate—a bubbling caldron of coup-prone leaders, each with no more basis for legitimate authority than his own initial claims. In brief, there was no real evidence of strong opportunity-level commitments to the GVN. By 1975, with most of the ARVN leadership either cowed or off balance by Thieu's final blundering, it was "every man for himself." Tentative calculations of opportunity quickly reverted to those of mere interest.

By contrast, the communists had a huge organization in place that offered opportunities for advancement for those willing to make a commitment. In fact, they were better organized and had a wider following than any political movement on the government side. Were it not for the massive U.S. presence and the pervasiveness of the South Vietnamese army, the government could not have competed at this level. The elections and steps toward legislative politics were just beginnings rather than a clear alternative to a communist society. The size of both the military forces of the communists and of the some three hundred thousand members of the NLF made it clear that they had the active support of at least the 10 to 20 percent of the population I said was necessary for the building blocks of the critical threat to the regime of a strategic break-out.

But the communists were not without their own problems at this level. For one thing, they never successfully penetrated the cities, and, as the population became increasingly urban as the war progressed, this weakness became more serious. Their most conspicuous failure lay in labor organization. Thanks to both American and West German trade union assistance, the four major government labor organizations were successful in preventing the communists from capturing the loyalties of the urban work force.[19]

Beyond their failure with the proletariat, the embarrassing urban silence in the Tet offensive laid bare a deeper communist weakness. As Gerald Hickey has pointed out, an insurgency that had such a strong component of terrorism was effective in keeping the government off balance, but it also produced among the citizenry a survivalist ethic whose self-interested defensiveness militated against any active or voluntary commitments of opportunity to the revolution.[20] On the communist side, this survivalist "sitting on one's hands" posture was exacerbated after Tet when the dominance of the communist structure by northerners became more pronounced.[21]

Thus, at this level, the success of the GVN land reform program in the countryside and even the failed strides in electoral politics were significant in that some societal access and political participation were achieved. Though they may not have been enough, at least in the modern sector, it is by no means clear that the communists could have done better. This, of course, is the great advantage of being the challengers: they didn't have to prove this until after they had won.

At the highest level of belief, the legitimation of the GVN never took hold against the prior claims of the communists. Especially in traditional terms, there is the stark fact that all of Saigon's military rulers had served under the French. Even in Confucian parlance, a society dominated by soldiers was evidence of a polity from which the Mandate of Heaven had been withdrawn. Only Diem started with nationalist credentials. In contrast, at the start of the American war, the communists were fresh from their triumph against the French. The *phuc duc* of the country had been heroically advanced by the successful pursuit of their *chinh nghia* by means of a genuine people's war and *khoi nghia* (righteous revolt). Furthermore, their leaders exhibited *uy tin*.

As I have pointed out earlier, however, even in traditional terms, the communist claims for legitimation had their vulnerabilities. Ngo Dinh Diem held out some possibilities for a challenge. He came from a prominent Confucian family of the mandarinate class, which was also deeply Catholic. Diem was caught in the French intellectual ferment of the 1930s that included Manet's personalism, reform Catholicism that reached out to the laboring classes, and Vietnamese nationalism, all of which were easily reconcilable with the ethic of the Confucian gentleman-scholar. Indeed, Diem himself projected some of the same *uy tin* as his communist adversaries. But Diem's entourage was deeply offensive in both traditional and modern terms. His brother Nhu acted like a fascist, brother Can like a Nguyen warlord, and Nhu's outspoken wife, Madame Nhu, and her grasping family were an acute embarrassment. Diem refused either to distance or to separate himself from his family. Though something of a transitional figure, in the end he refused all compromise and made it utterly impossible for either the Americans or the South Vietnamese to continue with him.

Nguyen Van Thieu, in my opinion, was an improvement over Diem, and his administration held out the possibility that some legitimation of belief might develop around the Saigon regime. Like all his peers, Thieu served under the French. Though he was politically cagey in the coup against Diem, artillery units under his personal command overcame Diem's Presidential Guards. For this, Thieu always retained the respect of the line (as opposed to staff) officers of the ARVN military. Once in power, he reached out in many ways and places that Diem had not. Though a convert to Catholicism, he preserved ties to the Buddhists through such gestures as permitting a Buddhist chaplaincy in the military and ending all government harassment of religious activities. He assiduously courted the Cao Dai and Hoa Hao sects in the delta. He came from a poor part of central Vietnam, and rural issues and the countryside were important to him. The 1970 land reform has to be granted to him as a significant accomplishment. He certainly was a better alternative to Diem than the flashy Air Vice-Marshal Nguyen Cao Ky, who could not suppress public statements of admiration for Hitler, and his stewardess wife, who offended traditional sensitivities with her retrofitted American body. Thieu's wife was more circumspect, though her extensive business activities were never above suspicion. Nevertheless, in the end, Thieu, as well, failed to measure up. Though he submitted to democratic politics, he was as unwilling as Diem to share the meager political power he held. When the time came in 1973 to take up the political struggle in earnest, he could not break out of either his military mold or his deep dependence on the Americans.

It is hardly surprising, then, that at this belief level, there were very few die-hard commitments to the GVN. Perhaps one very clear indicator of this lack is a response to a Vietnamese survey conducted on the eve of the Paris Peace Agreement in which only 1 percent of the respondents said they would refuse to live in a communist-controlled area after the war.[22] Nguyen Cao Ky has often asserted that social relations turned upside down in the Vietnam War.[23] There were as many prostitutes as bureaucrats in Saigon, and the former generally made better money.[24] Thus it could hardly be said that correct social relations were being maintained. Nor, as was obvious to all Vietnamese, was the country free from foreign meddling. Conspicuously, Vietnamese identity was not being safeguarded. Land reform, however, was finally redressing rural grievances, but it came very late in the war.

In modern terms, real efforts had been made to create a modern political community, but they fell short of the final achievement of a democratic political community and were hardly sufficient to inspire commitments of belief in the fledgling system. In this arena, the communists hardly tried at all, and where they did (such as in labor organizing) they were even less successful than the GVN. Actually, as modernizers both sides were failures. During the war, however, the GVN, with the responsibility of rule, was the side forced into global and national scrutiny. The similar communist incompetence was the great blind spot of the Vietnamese revolution.

Regarding revolutionary strategy, two points are salient about communist beliefs. First, in their overall commitment and fundamental belief in the *chinh nghia* of seizing power over the entire country, as leaders, and as an organization, they never wavered.[25] A basic unity of will and purpose was never broken. People's war, as a coordinating and coherent strategy, proved to be a highly useful a vehicle to achieve their goal from 1946 to 1968. This raises the second point, however. The strategy was defeated in 1968 and their victory in 1975, as single-minded as it was, was achieved by a dramatic switch away from revolutionary politics to nearly outright military conquest. This is what is explained in detail in Appendix 2.

This qualification of the communist victory has provoked various reactions. One is dismissive. The communists won anyway, and, as William Duiker has acidly observed, this qualification has given the new communist rulers "few sleepless nights."[26] Nevertheless, another reaction that bears repeating is that, for purposes of drawing lessons, such strategic abandonment disqualifies Vietnam as a confirming case for the efficacy of people's war as a revolutionary strategy. Finally, it left the fundamental political issue undergirding the insurgency—that of legitimacy—unresolved. This latter point has been highlighted by the wretched record of governance the new communist rulers have unwaveringly maintained since their seizure of power.[27]

THE SCALE OF INTERVENTION

Turning to external legitimacy effects, the scale of the interventions on both sides was massive and had an enormous impact on the domestic struggle. At all levels of legitimation, foreign intervention was present, and it became an important and complicating ingredient in everyone's calculations. In fact, it is the very scale of these interventions that puts the Vietnam

War into a nearly singular category. Much of the problem in analyzing the war was its antinomous character, that is, it was simultaneously a conventional war and a guerrilla insurgency. It was also both a national war and an international war. Such a dual antinomy is what makes lesson-drawing so difficult. No other twentieth-century insurgency had developed so much revolutionary activity only to have it thwarted by such a massive Western intervention.

In addition to its own direct involvement of half a million men and $150 billion spent in support of them, the United States kept the South Vietnamese economy afloat through a commodity exchange program that dampened inflation, a foreign aid program that built up an imposing infrastructure of roads, airfields, and harbors, made rural credit cheap, and directly underwrote 80 percent of the costs of South Vietnam's war effort.[28] On the other side, while not quite on the same scale, support to the Vietnamese communists was at unprecedented levels. Soviet and Chinese aid came to billions of dollars.[29] The aid Hanoi received more than covered the costs of both replacing its equipment losses suffered in the war and maintaining its large force structure in the south.[30] More critically, none of the major offensives of the war (Tet 1968, Easter 1972, and Ho Chi Minh 1975) would have been possible without outside help.[31] Though getting this help was not free of problems and Hanoi often found itself caught in the rival communist jockeying between Moscow and Beijing, Douglas Pike is certainly correct in observing that Hanoi basically got what it wanted.[32]

For the United States, a critical problem for the international legitimacy of its intervention was that it was justified mainly by Vattelian moral rhetoric, namely, to protect freedom and democracy in South Vietnam, whereas in actual intention it was more of a Metternichian balance-of-power enterprise. The most often-cited evidence of this is the famous John McNaughton percentages in the *Pentagon Papers* of U.S. war aims:

70% — to avoid a humiliating U.S. defeat (to our reputation as a guarantor).
20% — to keep SVN (and the adjacent) territory from Chinese hands.
10% — to permit the people of SVN to enjoy a better, freer way of life.[33]

Whenever geopolitical justifications were used, they centered on the image and thesis of falling dominoes, a line of reasoning that was accepted only by right-wing circles in the United States.

This gap created enormous problems in external legitimacy effects two and three of my chart: for the legitimacy of the systemic role of the United States in international relations and for the legitimacy of the intervention itself in domestic American politics. For the world community, the moral basis for an intervention in behalf of an obviously corrupt client state and the use of unprecedented levels of naked military force, most dramatically in the bombing campaigns, was not persuasive. Perhaps the clearest measure of the cost to the United States of the bankruptcy of such a rationale, and of the Vietnam War, to its international position was its deteriorating position in the United Nations compared to the Soviet Union. Through the Cuban Missile Crisis of October 1962 it is fair to say that the General Assembly and Security Council were "bully pulpits" to stage global embarrassments of the Soviet Union. After this Soviet debacle in Cuba and with the gradual rise of Vietnam as a major international issue, however, the tables began to turn. In 1967 the U.N. Secretary-General U Thant (a Burmese) condemned the United States for its bombing campaigns. Similar condemnations soon rained in from all quarters, and the United States, in effect, retreated to the citadel of the Security Council and protected itself with its veto. More Metternichian arguments, furthermore, were not persuasive to European allies, though they made some sense and provided reassurance to friends of the United States in Asia.

Partly as a result of these reverberations in international politics, but equally on their own intrinsic defects, both Vattelian and Metternichian arguments held less and less legitimacy back in the United States. Even in the best of times (from the perspective of the Johnson and Nixon presidencies), the moral case for the war was too often refuted by political realities in South Vietnam and occasionally by instances of American misconduct in the war. Hence, although the Tet offensive was a major military, strategic, and political victory for the South Vietnamese and Americans, right there on television before the American public it was a little too bloody to be believed. It was difficult to see how the proclaimed "light at the end of the tunnel" came in the juxtaposed images of such destruction.

This fundamental shift in domestic sentiment against the war in 1968 came far more from these ambiguities than from the antiwar movement, despite the professed gratitude of communist leaders to it. In 1968, for example, a majority of Eugene McCarthy's supporters who were so critical in forcing Johnson from the presidency carried their protest votes into a balloting for the super hawk George C. Wallace in the November elections.[34] Furthermore, Michael Mandelbaum found that during the Nixon years disgust for war protesters seemed to outweigh the public disgust for the war itself. Every time there was a major demonstration against the war by bearded hippies, support for the war experienced a momentary rise in the polls.[35] Yet the overall slope of public support for the war was ever downward, and by 1972 congressional pressure on the White House began seriously to constrain American options. As was mentioned in Chapter 4, the Cooper-Church Amendment to an appropriations bill cut off funds for U.S. military activity in Indochina by August 15, 1973, ending the president's unilateral power for war making. These restrictions were further codified by the War Powers Act of November 1973, passed into law over Nixon's veto. It will never be clear whether this path to such executive branch impotence would have occurred without the events of Watergate.

Parenthetically, the Vattelian legitimacy of the Chinese and Soviet interventions in the Indochina War never ran into any of the difficulties that plagued the United States. The extent of the American involvement almost guaranteed a constancy and even competition among the two powers as to who was the more steadfast in taking up their "internationalist duties." In both cases, however, problems developed in the fulfillment of these revolutionary duties in the face of growing and larger Metternichian interests in detente and some basic accommodations with the Western world. Clearly, despite their continued military support by both the Chinese and Russians, the lack of continued enthusiasm for the war played an important role in Hanoi's acceptance of the Paris Peace Agreement. As Douglas Pike has speculated, the Chinese really wanted a stalemate all along, and the Soviets became impatient with the war's global costs to themselves and with Hanoi's failure in the Easter invasion.[36]

To the American public, the intervention in Vietnam was murky. It was on the first external legitimacy effect, however—the effect of the intervention on the legitimacy crisis within Vietnam—that the intervention ran into the most trouble. At the level of interest, the American intervention was very important to the struggle, particularly in modern terms. The United States established the framework for the Honda economy that brought the Vietnamese countryside a considerable measure of prosperity, even in wartime. Rural credit was made easy, and new "appropriate technology"—particularly the profusion of water pumps in the Mekong Delta—set up a strong institutional network and array of incentives for developing interests in the South Vietnamese government.[37] In traditional terms, however, the United States was stuck with the miserable performance of the GVN, functions that had to be done by the Vietnamese in any case.

It was at the level of opportunity that the U.S. intervention had its greatest impact and nearest success. In traditional terms, the United States was not a colonial power and was careful to respect Vietnamese sovereignty. The Vietnamese armed forces were separate and under their own independent command. Americans who worked with Vietnamese were advisers, not resident superiors. Nevertheless, their presence in such large numbers made the traditional legitimacy of the Vietnamese government difficult to uphold, however necessary these numbers may have been to the survival of the government. In brief, appearances simply overwhelmed the attempted circumspection. The near success rather lay in the development of modern legitimacy. Certainly the Americans went much farther in this regard than the French. They helped establish a single national government that for the first time reached all strata of society. An attempt was made, with some success, to train and equip a national army. Its repulse of the Easter invasion of 1972 did show the promise of an effective armed force. But there were chinks in this armor, which were fully exploited by the communists in their final 1975 offensive. Also, important strides were made in expanding societal access and political participation in the land reform financed by the United States and in the several sets of national elections that were held under the American-backed (and even inspired) Second Republic. But the land reform came too late; the elections failed to produce a true political community in which power could be shared among mass-based political parties; and the struggle shifted in the end to a lesson-frustrating military solution.

The near success was turned into ultimate failure by the inability of the Saigon government to develop this opportunity level of legitimation into a fundamental belief in its right to rule. No South Vietnamese government ever presented to the Vietnamese a *chinh nghia* equal to that of the "national salvation hero" communists. In part, this difference lay in something fundamental to these governments. They were all products of the French rule, were mostly urban in their social orientations, and were out of touch with the rural society's traditional roots. A tragic illustration lay in the leaders' publicly cited models. Nguyen Cao Ky professed his admiration for Hitler and Mussolini, Nguyen Van Thieu for Charles De Gaulle, and General Vo Nguyen Giap, significantly, for Nguyen Hue (though other communist leaders talked extensively of Marx and Lenin).

In larger part, this lack of legitimacy was owing to the trap the scale of the U.S. intervention created, the embrace of an illegitimacy lock. Recall that at the outset of the Tet offensive, Thieu's initial fear was that Ky was pulling off a coup, and he was relieved that it was *only* the communists launching an offensive. His fear is illustrative of this dangerous political embrace awaiting an intervenor. Though a regime's long-range solution to an insurgency lies in legitimate rule, immediate threats to its rule come from its own military. That is, the ruler's power can be seriously threatened only by one of his generals. Thus he was preoccupied with keeping these generals happy or at least under control. Although undercutting the grounds of the insurgency may depend on addressing the popular issues fueling it, the people per se rarely posed an immediate threat. Nor did the insurgents offer an immediate threat until they were powerful enough to storm the national power centers. Ensuring that this point was not reached was delegated to the obliging foreigners. This created the lock, though. As long as the foreigner was willing to provide this margin, the politics in the capital city could go on as usual in, from the regime's point of view, a happy stalemate.

Put from the perspective of the ruling clique: to win an insurgency is to lose because it will result in a call for broad-based civilian rule. More pragmatic victory lies in losing imperceptibly and staving off the ultimate reckoning with a circumspect, respectful intervention. Obviously, it is a program for survival built on a fraud because when the foreign help is withdrawn, the deck of cards collapses. Although this may be overstating the cynicism of the South Vietnamese government, it is not far off the mark. If people's war is the Oriental equivalent to the French Revolution, the illegitimacy lock is the Oriental equivalent to *après mois, la deluge*.

THE LESSONS OF INTERVENTION

The level of intervention in the Vietnam War, with its large numbers of American ground combat troops, will always be a subject of controversy. More than anything else, it was the commitment of these troops that trapped the United States in the embrace of the illegitimacy lock. Certainly, the scale of this intervention grew to be far out of proportion to larger American interests as a global power. At the height of the war, the United States had committed to Vietnam 40 percent of its combat-ready divisions, 50 percent of its tactical airpower, and 33 percent of its naval forces.[38] This was an overwhelming presence in South Vietnam that smothered any regime's claims to independent national legitimacy. Sad as it is to say to Americans, even according to their own polling services, the "Yankees" (civilian and military) were uniformly disliked by the Vietnamese.[39] Before being tempted to declare a proscription against interventions with ground combat troops as a lesson, it is worth recalling that without them Saigon would have fallen in 1965, could not have survived the Tet offensive in 1968, and, without them, did fall in 1975.

Beyond the issue of the level of the intervention, at least in retrospect, the United States, both in military and political terms, was overly cautious. Two events after World War II played a powerful role in inducing this timidity: the Korean War and the ease of the communist takeovers in Eastern Europe through initial coalition governments. Though it may be the "forgotten war" today, at the time of the American intervention in Vietnam, still powerful nightmares of Korea were instrumental in stamping the U.S. Military Assistance Command in Vietnam (MACV) with a tactical conservatism. In the Korean War (1950–53), it is important to remember, the American command suffered two serious, large-unit defeats, first by the North Koreans and then by the Chinese, which almost resulted in "the big bug out."[40] Twice the capital city of Seoul had been lost. Important lessons were learned from Korea, particularly at the small-unit level, that permitted, for example, a vast improvement in nighttime fighting in Vietnam, but the one that was most important to MACV —and to General Westmoreland (a Korean War veteran) — was, at all costs, not to permit any large-unit defeats. Though MACV was

successful in this objective, this preoccupation helped to put a more domi-
nantly military emphasis to the limited war in Vietnam that was at least at
the beginning much more of a revolutionary insurgency.[41]

The United States was also politically timid in Vietnam. Bad experiences with postwar coalition governments in Eastern Europe (particularly
the communist coup in Czechoslovakia in 1948) made Washington overly
gun-shy about admitting communists into the political process. In Vietnam, however, when the United States intervened in force in 1965, the time
had passed for completely precluding the communists from the political
process in the south. In a major study for the State Department, Samuel
Huntington analyzed the sociopolitical mosaic of South Vietnamese society
and concluded that in a political competition with the communists, there
were constituencies upon which a "hollow majority" for the GVN could be
built. Huntington recommended that such a majority be vigorously pursued
politically.[42] The study was too frightening for policymakers and was quietly
shelved. Nevertheless, this was also the conclusion of Allan Goodman in his
book *Politics in War*, in which he also cited the pressing need for the establishment of mass-based, competitive parties to create a political community
that could fully compete with the politically well-entrenched communists.[43]
William Colby, a CIA station chief in Vietnam, openly called for a coalition
government in Saigon and argued that this would not automatically result
in a communist takeover.[44]

In my opinion, bringing the Viet Cong into the political process would
have been the only way to get political parties going in the south. A thoroughly fragmented opposition to President Thieu in the National Assembly
could oppose the president only as elite blocs of legislators. Under a communist participatory threat, with its large mass membership, the opposition's survival would have depended on the formation of competitive political parties. This, though, is another easy lesson from hindsight. In Vietnam,
from 1967 to 1972, the chaos of 1964–66 was too immediate a nightmare,
and, intrinsically, for the Americans the rubric of containment still saw
coalition governments with the communists as tantamount to defeat.

DYNAMICS OF THE BALANCES

Students of revolution and of intervention always debate about volun-
taristic reversibility versus revolutionary determinism. In the Vietnam War
there were several dramatic moments of reversal, even though it was nevertheless true that deterministic legacies weighed heavily in bringing about the
war's final result. First, the success of Ngo Dinh Diem in 1956 in consolidating his control over the south reversed an almost universal expectation at the
Geneva Accords that the south would soon be absorbed by the north. Again,
in 1964 and 1965, it appeared that the anarchy in Saigon and the disintegra-

tion of the army in the countryside would precipitate a communist takeover. The American intervention with ground combat troops at least held this day off. The double defeat of the Tet offensive, whatever else it did, took the war down such a jarringly different path that any lessons from the war may have been permanently shattered. Finally, the stunning collapse of the Thieu regime from 1973 to 1975 exceeded the fondest hopes of Hanoi's leaders.

Yet historical forces and events constraining the independent freedom of this war were considerable. The handicaps of containment at the international level have already been discussed. Within Vietnamese society, when the insurgency resumed against the Americans in the 1960s, the Viet Cong did not have to contend with the usual and many asymmetrical difficulties in getting an insurgency started because they had a deeply rooted organization left in place from the war against the French. Indeed, Thomas Thayer has shown that the Viet Cong's greatest areas of strength, even at the end of the war, were precisely in the same areas where the Viet Minh had made their greatest inroads against the French.[45] Further, the polarization of Vietnamese politics fostered by the French between themselves and the communists — because it was just the confrontation the French thought they could win — left South Vietnam without viable alternative parties and leaders when the French lost. The Viet Minh went one step further in ensuring this by assassinating scores of southern nationalist leaders in 1946–47. Thus it was not surprising that the subsequent leaders of South Vietnam (except for Diem) had all been collaborators with the French.[46] In this second race up Mount Legitimus in Vietnam, the communists started with a significant lead: they had a critical mass from the beginning.

Still, even in Vietnam, there were some historical openings for catch-ups. In their drive for national independence from the French, the communists enjoyed the least success in the south. An ill-advised uprising against the French in the Mekong Delta in 1940 left the southern communist leadership decimated, which is why, in the subsequent postwar struggle against the French, the bulk of the leadership and communist effort shifted to the north.[47] In the Mekong Delta after the war, the communists were never able to make up for their egregious blunderings against the powerful Hoa Hao and Cao Dai sects, which eventually gave their loyalties to Nguyen Van Thieu. The Roman Catholic community (15 percent of the population) became an almost natural enemy of the communists, an enmity reinforced by the communist practice of singling out Catholic villages for terrorist attacks. Noteworthy as well is that, though the Saigon government has been often criticized for failing to reach out to Vietnam's amorphous Buddhist majority,[48] the communists similarly failed to take much advantage of Buddhist dissent.[49] Nevertheless, it is fair to say that these historical openings were not fully exploited by the United States or its Vietnamese ally. It is also fair to say that in comparison with other cases, these openings for reversibility were never so slender as in Vietnam.

Related to the issues of reversibility and asymmetries is the balance of errors between the two sides, which I mentioned in Chapter 3. For all the shrewd moves and massive efforts in the Vietnam War, mistakes and failures were important to the outcome as well. Though both sides made their share of mistakes, at the end, the momentum was shifted decisively by a series of blunders by President Thieu just as the communists made some important rectifications in their strategy. To recapitulate the odyssey of crossover points, as I have mentioned, in the course of their revolution against the French, the Viet Minh made some mistakes in the south that opened up the possibility of an alternative society. These mistakes were compounded by a communist overconfidence immediately after the Geneva Accords. The failure to launch armed struggle against the vulnerable Ngo Dinh Diem was an invaluable gift to him in his struggle to consolidate his position against other sources of opposition. Diem's advantage in this consolidation were frittered away, however, by his increasingly heavy-handed rule and final stubbornness that led to his downfall. Diem's demise only made matters worse, as the anarchy in the capital from 1964 to 1965 led to a serious neglect of the war and opened up the countryside to a growing revolution. The complete collapse of South Vietnam was avoided by the curious failure of the communists at the national level to exploit either the post-Diem urban anarchy or the Struggle Force of the Buddhists and, internationally, by the American commitment of ground combat troops.

The Tet offensive was an epic error all around. For the communists, it was the failure of a revolution. For the United States, it was the failure to see this. Ultimately, the American error was more serious. It meant that any hope of immediate victory was over and that security for South Vietnam could come about only through long-term political and economic development that would have to be guaranteed by a prolonged American military commitment. The only such commitment the United States has ever made has been to NATO, and Vietnam was no NATO. Of all the generous American resources committed to the war, the one that proved to be in shortest supply was time. For the communists, though the southern revolution had been crushed, this defeat did not rule out a seizure of power by the north through other means.

As the communists searched for these other means, ARVN's bungled incursion into Laos in 1971 could not have been more inopportune. It gave Hanoi too many ideas. Militarily, a raid in force is exceeded in difficulty only by the orderly withdrawal of large units under determined enemy attack. The two-divisional thrust mounted by ARVN was too small a force to hold its positions athwart the Ho Chi Minh Trail for long, and too large a force to make its hasty withdrawal look like anything but a rout. The vulnerabilities of Vietnamization, in brief, stood revealed. Though these vulnerabilities were certainly not absent in the Easter invasion of 1972, Hanoi's offensive dissipated under its own strategic and tactical misjudgments and from the power of American bombing.

After this, though, the crossover points rose to a strategic breakout under a rush of American and South Vietnamese mistakes. First, Thieu failed to press the political struggle for which the Paris Peace Agreement of 1973 had set him up. Instead he embarked on a course of political repression reminiscent of the last days of the Diem regime and on a military land-grabbing campaign that seriously overextended his forces. Such an overextension was particularly ill-advised because Thieu's ultimate source of support, President Richard Nixon, became politically crippled by the self-inflicted wound of Watergate. Then, when the strategic breakout came in the Ho Chi Minh campaign of 1975, a spiteful U.S. Congress sat on its hands and went on an Easter recess rather than respond to President Ford's desperate entreaties for supplemental military assistance. Finally, Thieu panicked and, in desperately trying to save his own political position, committed irretrievable military blunders for the defense of the country as a whole. In military terms, I can only offer the Armed Forces High Command in Hanoi the compliment that in 1975 it made no mistakes.

Conclusion

Whether one can prune from such a balance of errors any clear historical lesson is problematic because a mistake is by definition something not to be repeated. Mistakes, as axiomatic negatives, however, do not necessarily have automatic opposite positives. To find lessons in mistakes, there needs to be a common thread. In the case of Vietnam, for all their mistakes at interest and opportunity levels, the communists never lost sight of their ultimate goal. They always retained a belief in the revolutionary and national legitimacy of their *chinh nghia*. The "nationalists," however, for all their gradual improvements at interest and opportunity levels, never really developed this ultimate belief in their cause. In the end, it was every man for himself as the deluge descended. The problem with this neat dichotomy, however, is that in Vietnam, the nature of the conventional communist victory — essentially one of revolutionary abandonment — was a victory that could have been readily prevented.

Nevertheless, the breakthrough that the South Vietnamese failed to achieve was the creation of a legitimate political community. Strides were made through a process of democratic elections that involved large numbers of people, momentarily, in the process of government. Institutions were built up of a military, economic, and political nature that did link people to the regime. Land reform was finally carried out. But the final step of organized competitive, mass political parties that might have created a society legitimate in both opportunity and belief was not completed. In time, it might have happened, but everyone's patience ran out, and the matter was settled by the sword. The only ones to have outlasted everyone else, and who had not been brought to a downward momentum of crossover points, were the North Vietnamese.

Finally, there is the curious irony that in all the debates over American options in the Vietnam War, the more fruitful ones may have been those which, at the time, seemed to have been the more fainthearted. In the debate over the McNamara Line across the Ho Chi Minh Trail, the more modest idea of a blocking force favored by McNamara himself was spoiled by the more vigorous supplement of following on with thrusts across the North Vietnamese panhandle that was favored by General Westmoreland and more recently by Colonel Harry Summers.[50] The suggestions by Samuel Huntington, Allan Goodman, and William Colby that a political community would have to come through some coalition process was overwhelmed by the conviction that a Vietnamese nationalist society could be built around a vigorous right-wing, pro-American containment alliance. And the reliance on a more long-term commitment of vulnerable U.S. field advisers was squashed by secret pledges of "safer" massive bombing. All these more "wimpy" alternatives would have required a reliance on a sophisticated political wisdom of American limits rather than on military force to provide the margins for these choices. In this sense, then, the U.S. intervention in Vietnam *was* a true "arrogance of power." This was especially embarrassing at the end, when, through national self-emasculation, the United States had no power left to bear on Indochina.

If confusion continues to surround the quest for lessons, it is understandable. Despite the anchor of legitimacy to an understanding of the Vietnam War, the lack of fruit to the electoral process, the seeming lesson of no combat troops, and the various balances of error and crossover points, by itself, there are no lessons to the Vietnam War. Passing the deviant case of Vietnam through a comparative prism of cases from elsewhere, however, contains possibilities.

PART III
The
Comparative
Prism

Chapter 6

CHINA, 1920–1949: THE LONG MARCH TO LIBERATION

Historical Setting

Though never a formal colony like Indochina, China in the second half of the nineteenth century became an arena of imperial competition for spheres of commercial and political influence. Such unwelcome foreign pressures posed an increasingly serious threat to the legitimacy of the Qing (Manchu) Dynasty (1644–1911). The traditional requirements of the Mandate of Heaven, spelled out for Vietnam earlier, came from China, after all, and were wrapped in the rhythm of the dynastic cycle from the Han, to the Sung, to the Tang, to the Ming, and, finally, the Qing. They were for the Son of Heaven to preserve social and political harmony by upholding proper hierarchical relationships epitomized by the virtue of filial piety at home and the exacting of suitable tribute from peoples abroad. The emperor was also to dispense rural justice through periodic land redistribution and provide virtuous administration through a mandarinate recruited among scholars examined in the ancient Confucian classics. Above all, the heavenly mandate demanded keeping unwanted foreign influence and power out of the Middle Kingdom.

The Manchus were foreigners themselves (that is, from beyond the Great Wall of the Han Chinese), the mantle of rule never settled securely on their shoulders, and the repeated penetrations of the foreigners were doubly discomfiting. Indeed, the demonstrated superiority of European arms and manufactures in the nineteenth century touched off a ferment of irresolution in the court. Outside the court, it provoked protest. Four major rebellions scarred this unhappy century. The addition of natural disasters and military defeats at the hands of the British and the Japanese turned the court grimly to reform and to the incorporation of Western ideas. The last decade of Manchu rule ushered in a frenzy of reform as the dynasty sought to stave off collapse. They included the abolition of the Confucian examination system, a commitment to Western education and the building of a nationwide network of such "new schools," and a promise of democratic government under their monarchy. They even held provincial elections as they planned for an elected national assembly to establish a parliament.[1] But other modernizers had more republican ideas, and the Qing Dynasty finally lost the Mandate of Heaven on October 10, 1911, to the machinations of the Revolutionary Alliance (the precursor to the Guomindang [Nationalist party]) under Dr. Sun Yat-sen. As Mary Wright observed, "Reform destroyed the reforming government; it could not control the forces to whose acceleration its own policies had contributed."[2]

The path from a traditional to a modern China, which ultimately led to the triumph of the Chinese Communist party (CCP) in 1949, was not without wrenching twists and sharp turns. The turbulence arose from a welter of warlord irredentism, modern nationalism, industrial expansion in the face of a calamity-stricken countryside,[3] the depredations of foreigners (especially the Japanese in their 1937–45 invasion), and, through it all, the competing visions for a modern China of the Communist and Guomindang (GMD) parties in their long struggle for the mantle of rule.

The spark that ignited and inspired these visions was the May Fourth Movement. The specific incident inciting the movement was the demonstrations on May 4, 1919, protesting the decision taken by the European powers at Versailles to transfer German rights in Shandong province to Japan. More than just an outburst against the Japanese, the movement was a cultural ferment of national self-examination extending roughly from 1914 to 1921, whose call was "down with the old, up with the new."[4] The three groups caught up by the movement — Westernized intellectuals, businessmen, and industrial workers[5] — went through a gamut of slavish praise of Western ideas and democratic ideals to virulent anti-Western nationalism, settling finally on the distaff line of the Western tradition, Marxism and even fascism.[6]

In this process, the Guomindang and the Communist party emerged as the dominant political forces in China. The Guomindang was founded by Sun Yat-sen in 1912 and was dedicated to his Three People's Principles of Chinese nationalism, constitutional democracy (to be realized after a period of tutelage), and "people's livelihood" (an ill-defined form of socialism in the cities and "land to the tiller" in the countryside). It got caught up in the fervor of the movement from the beginning and became a mass party in 1919, reaching a peak membership of 442,000 in 1929.[7]

The communists came in on the tail end of the movement. An organized study of Marxism did not begin until the spring of 1920. But the forces unleashed by the May Fourth Movement led to their rapid expansion in the 1920s, reaching sixty thousand by 1927. The point to note here is that both sides drew members disproportionately from the politicized intellectuals of the May Fourth Movement.[8]

From their start as a study group in 1920, the communists met in Shanghai in July 1921 under the direction of the Comintern agent Gregory Voitinsky and formed a party with an initial membership of fifty. The fledgling party faced two disadvantages: the small proletarian base in Chinese society and its own small numbers.[9] It embarked on two efforts to remedy deficiency: a program of labor organization, and from 1922 to 1924 it sought an alliance with the Guomindang to share in the benefits of the latter's "bourgeois democratic revolution." Party members joined the Guomindang first as individuals, hoping eventually to take over the organization by "boring from within." Both tasks were pursued energetically. Through its National General Labor Union, the communists led 150,000 workers in more than one hundred strikes in 1922. Although set back in the bloody suppression of the Hankow railway workers strike in 1923, they still succeeded in wresting control of radical workers away from anarchists by 1925.[10]

They were even more successful in their "bore from within" strategy in the Chinese Communist party–Guomindang Alliance. By 1922 the momentum of the Guomindang had stalled and Sun Yat-sen sought Russian help. The Russians were only too willing to oblige, and the result was the Sun-Joffe Agreement of 1923 in which the Russians provided financial support, training missions, and assistance in the reorganization of the Guomindang along Soviet lines.[11] As part of this effort, Sun had to let communists join the Guomindang as individual members while still being allowed to retain their membership in the Communist party. They joined in large numbers. At the Second Guomindang Congress held in 1926, 100 of the 256 delegates were communists as were 7 of the 35 Central Executive Committee members.

In addition, the communists dominated the mass activities of the Guomindang, controlled the propaganda and peasant bureaus, and were well-placed in the training centers. Mao Zedong, for example, was the deputy director of the GMD propaganda bureau.[12] From 1925 to 1927, the communists increased their own party's membership from one thousand to sixty thousand.[13]

During this time, the control of the Nationalist government was confined to the area in southern China centered around the city of Canton. Large warlord territories and armies, which in total numbered over one million men, posed a significant threat from the north. Determined to meet this threat head-on and well aware of the factional strife within the warlord cliques, the new Guomindang leader General Chiang Kai-shek launched the Northern Expedition in 1926 against the warlords with the one-hundred-thousand-man National Army, which had been trained and equipped along European lines. Upon embarking on the campaign, he said, "I expect to win the war thirty per cent by fighting and seventy per cent by propaganda."[14] He might also have given some recognition to communist support. The communists were enthusiastic participants in the Northern Expedition. According to Lucien Bianco, they organized 1.2 million workers and eight hundred thousand peasants along the route of march. A working-class uprising in Shanghai, orchestrated by the skillful communist organizer Zhou Enlai, allowed Chiang Kai-shek to enter the city without firing a shot.[15]

The successes of the communists proved to be their undoing. Unlike his predecessor Sun Yat-sen, Chiang had become increasingly suspicious of the ultimate intentions of the communists. In 1926 he expelled a large number of Soviet advisers and demanded a list of Communist party members in the Guomindang. In the midst of the Northern Expedition, the Guomindang split into a right and a left wing, and the left wing established a rival government in Wuhan. The left wing, under the mercurial Wang Jing-wei, focused on the Guomindang party as the arena of central effort rather than Chiang Kai-shek's National Army and Government. In this split, the communists elected to join the Wuhan government.

Then, in rapid succession, two blows fell on the CCP which destroyed the "bore from within" strategy. First, upon entering Shanghai, Chiang Kai-shek launched a surprise "White Terror" against communist workers which quickly grew into a nationwide pogrom. Mao Zedong later acknowledged to Edgar Snow that forty thousand party members were killed.[16] By the end of the year party membership was down to ten thousand.[17] Second, despite the disaster, Stalin urged the CCP to stay with the left-wing Guomindang and try to take it over.[18] A copy of Stalin's instructions came into the possession of Chiang Kai-shek, and their publication thoroughly discredited the left wing of the Guomindang. Shortly thereafter, both the left wing and the communists were expelled from the Guomindang, the latter permanently.

With the communists in full retreat and Chiang now in complete control of the Guomindang, he turned his attention to consolidating the nationalist government's hold over the northern warlords. In a two-year effort labeled the Reorganization War (1928–30), Chiang managed to persuade most of the warlords to let their remaining 700,000 soldiers become part of a 900,000 man "reorganized" nationalist army. The campaign, however, was not entirely bloodless. Thirty thousand Guomindang soldiers were killed and the warlords lost 150,000 in killed and wounded.[19]

Meanwhile, the communists, their urban strategy in ruins, gradually and reluctantly embraced the unorthodox peasant strategy of Mao Zedong, termed a "marginal exotic trend" by Benjamin Schwartz.[20] They installed themselves in rural base areas, which they called "soviets," and set about rebuilding the party on the basis of various land reform measures designed to win peasant support. Mao established himself as chairman of the Jiangxi soviet, which became the largest. He had to contend with opposition from more radical Marxists and even had to suppress a revolt, called the Futian Incident, which he did with a bloody vengeance.[21] Nevertheless, by 1932 the Jiangxi soviet contained 2.5 million people, and, nationwide in 1930, CCP membership stood at 122,000 and its new Chinese Workers and Peasants Red Army numbered 65,000.[22]

Once again, the success of the communists attracted Chiang Kai-shek's unwelcome attention. With the Reorganization War behind him, the Guomindang generalissimo determined to eliminate them. Over the next four years, the rural soviets endured five nationalist "extermination campaigns." The first four failed, the third because of the distraction of the Japanese invasion of Manchuria in December 1931. For the last campaign, Chiang marshaled a force of 900,000 (400,000 targeted against Jiangxi) under his personal command supplemented by German military advice and planning. With an initial total of 180,000 men, 120,000 communists managed to break out of the Guomindang encirclements in October 1934 and set out on the famous, year-long six-thousand-mile Long March to Yanan in Northwest China.[23]

Harassed all the way by pursuing nationalist troops, faced with formidable physical barriers, and beset by grave internal problems, the Long March became the legendary epic of the Chinese Revolution, and participation in it became a must for political leadership even a generation after the communist seizure of power in 1949.[24] Amid all the adventures were two important meetings: one at Zunyi in January 1935 south of the Yangtze River and the other a split meeting at Lianghoku and Maoerhkai in July 1935 southwest of Yanan toward the end of the march. The Zunyi meeting, thanks to a crucial switch in position by Zhou Enlai, established Mao as the undisputed leader of the First Front Army's Long March. The second meetings took place in conjunction with the rendezvous of Mao's and Zhang Guotao's forces. The meetings centered on a struggle for leadership between Mao and Zhang (who was the leader of another rural soviet) over the destination of the Long March as well as the future direction of the party. Mao favored a closer northwest base from which a guerrilla war could be launched against the Japanese in central China whereas Zhang urged a western course to re-build under Russian assistance and tutelage. Although Zhang struck out on his own, he ran into Guomindang ambushes and was obliged to rejoin Mao in his journey to Yanan.[25]

The communists arrived in Yanan a pitiable remnant of their former selves. Of the approximately 120,000 who started on the Long March with Mao, a mere 7,000 to 8,000 made it.[26] Total communist forces numbered only 30,000, and party membership had plummeted to 40,000.[27] Bound and determined to prevent any further dramatic resurrections of the CCP, Chiang Kai-shek laid plans for a final extermination campaign in 1936–37. But General Zhang Xueliang, the former warlord of Manchuria commis-sioned to lead it, balked at the order because he favored a united front with the communists to oppose Japan, and instead he kidnapped the generalis-simo when he came to make plans at Xian in December 1936. The country was stunned, but sufficient pressure was soon exerted on the kidnapper to secure Chiang's release.[28] Chiang Kai-shek, however, was forced to agree to an earlier call by the communists for a united front against the Japanese and to stop his campaign against the CCP base areas.

Freed from Guomindang harassment, the CCP, in the eight years (1937–45) of the war against the Japanese, got a third lease on life and transformed itself once again into a formidable political organization. In 1937 the party had only 40,000 members, an army of 92,000, and held sway over 1.5 mil-lion people in Yanan. The Guomindang, by contrast, had 500,000 soldiers under its central command as well as the nominal control of most of the country. By the time of the Japanese defeat in August 1945, the commu-nists had grown into a political colossus of 1.2 million party members (with another 5 million in peasant associations), an 860,000-man army, and the control of base areas containing 100 million people (one-fifth of China's total). By this time the armed forces of the Guomindang had grown to 3.7 million.[29] The communists accomplished this huge growth by appealing to nationalistic sentiments in fighting against the Japanese and by providing an effective, reform-minded government in the countryside, thereby breaching an age-old gap between all previous Chinese governments and the villages. That the latter was true became clear as the Guomindang was driven from its urban base by the Japanese and proved unable to develop an alternative administration in the countryside. In the struggle against the Japanese, even though the Guomindang put up occasionally stiff resistance, particularly at

Shanghai,[30] and refused to negotiate with them, its continued hostility to the communists in face of a national anti-Japanese struggle, especially its clash with the communist New Fourth Army in 1941, only rebounded to the nationalistic credit of the CCP.[31]

With the defeat of the Japanese in August 1945 — outside China — and the withdrawal of their 1.9 million troops inside, the stage was set for a show-down between the Guomindang and the CCP. Both sides scrambled to fill the vacuum left by the Japanese: the communists, thanks to the Russians, getting most of the Japanese military equipment in Manchuria, and the Guomindang, thanks to American air transport, taking most of the cities. A year long mission by the American general George C. Marshall to mediate the dispute ended in failure in June 1946, essentially because neither side really wanted to compromise. Hostilities resumed in the summer of 1946. The Guomindang retained the initiative until the spring of 1947, posting gains throughout Manchuria and northern China, even seizing Yanan in March 1947. By mid-1947, however, the communists went over to the offensive in Manchuria and by the end of the year controlled much of that region. In 1948 the massive communist guerrilla infiltration of the countryside began paying the dividend of confining Guomindang troops to their urban garrisons. In the summer the first cities fell to the communists — Loyang and Kaifeng. At the end of the year, the eventual coup de grace was delivered to Chiang Kai-shek in two stunning blows. First, in a two-month campaign launched in September, the communist general Lin Biao took all of Manchuria and inflicted four hundred thousand casualties on the Guomindang. Even more devastating was the Huai-hai River campaign of November 1948–January 1949 in which, after sixty-five days of fighting, fifty-one Guomindang divisions were defeated, suffering losses of nearly six hundred thousand men.[32] Parenthetically, it should be noted that, despite the conventional character of the fighting, communist guerrilla forces continued to play a key role in these final campaigns by disrupting supplies and blocking Guomindang re-inforcements.[33]

These two blows turned the balance of forces decisively in favor of the communists. The Guomindang was unable to replace either its human or material losses and could muster only 1 million men against the 1.5 million People's Liberation Army (PLA). In 1949 the Guomindang lost the stomach to resist because American aid was sharply reduced, inflation ran out of control in the cities, and general after general made his accommodation, most notably Fu Zo-yi in Beijing, who allowed the imperial capital to fall on January 23.[34] The collapse of the Guomindang then proceeded at a brisk pace, and on October 1, 1949, the People's Republic was proclaimed in Beijing over all of China. It was the world's first triumph of a Marxist people's war. The epitaph by Major General David G. Barr, the senior U.S. military adviser to Chiang Kai-shek, however, dwelt more on the shortcomings of the Guomindang: "Their military debacle, in my opinion, can all be attributed to the world's worst leadership and many other morale-destroying factors that led to a complete loss of the will to fight."[35] As just one point of evidence, of the total five million Guomindang casualties claimed by the communists, 75 percent of them were prisoners.[36]

Framework Analysis

NATIONAL LEGITIMACY

As a brief introduction and review for this analysis, after the fall of the Manchus (the Qing Dynasty), the mantle of legitimacy was assumed by the Guomindang of Dr. Sun Yat-sen. His antiforeignism and somewhat hazy vision of a modernized China helped the Guomindang retain the loyalty of most Chinese with an active interest in national politics, at least through the Xian Incident of 1936. The United Front proclaimed after this incident gave the communists an equal opportunity in proving their patriotism and public service to the people—an opportunity they pursued with vigor and to great profit. They emerged from World War II as a truly significant national power. In the civil war that followed, the relentless communist momentum proved too much for the weary and ever more dispirited Guomindang, and the Mandate of Heaven settled easily and almost naturally on communist shoulders in October 1949.

At the level of interest, the split between the GMD and the CCP turned into a struggle between the cities and countryside. A modern world was opening up in the 5 to 10 percent of the population who lived in the cities, and the two parties fought hard for primacy in this arena. Here the Guomindang won. It allied itself with the business interests already in place and, ironically, even co-opted the labor movement away from the communists. For the city dweller it paid to go along passively with the Guomindang. Nevertheless, the communists made a fight of it. Their ideology, certainly, compelled them to struggle for the proletariat. But their efforts at labor organizing, at coordinating nationwide strikes, and even at setting up Paris-style communes all failed to provide enough personal or physical security to win them support. In the Shanghai massacres of 1927, the communists were essentially forced out of the cities and, seemingly, were blocked from any access to the modern world.[37]

It was in the countryside that the CCP finally planted its seeds of power successfully. But it was a garden whose cultivation had a rocky history. For one thing, like the communists in the cities, the Guomindang did not automatically surrender in the countryside. The rule of Chiang Kai-shek reached to the rural counties. For his presence, however, he relied on the traditional rural elites: the magistrates, landlords, and gentry—the very class of people most responsible for the well-documented pressures that cramped peasant life in the late nineteenth century. In the post-Manchu period, these included the arbitrary actions of local magistrates, price-fixing of agricultural produce by "gentry capitalists," the double taxation by provincial officials to finance their separate activities from the national government, and the sharply increased land rents and curtailed services of the landlords.[38] Thus, although working through the established elites succeeded in the cities for the Guomindang; in the countryside, it did not.

Nevertheless, it took the communists a while to exploit this nationalist weakness. In his Hunan Report of 1927, Mao realized, as Chiang Kai-shek did not, that a modern world in the countryside could open up only if the local elites were displaced.[39] Mao further appreciated, as his more radical comrades did not, that broad support from most classes of the peasantry was necessary to build a revolution strong enough to seize national power. It was such tensions over rural policies in the Jiangxi soviet that exploded in the Futian Incident. At Yanan Mao had his way and base areas were set up that grew under favorable policies such as rent reductions rather than land expropriations that specifically reached out to the middle peasantry.[40]

Both sides continued their struggle for group commitments at the opportunity level. The Guomindang was a truly national organization in scope or presence. It was well financed by a relatively prosperous national business community, particularly from Shanghai.[41] The party, military, and government bureaucracy, as well as an emerging industrial economy, provided both societal access and some political participation. In 1934 Chiang Kai-shek sought to expand this opportunity structure to the countryside through the New Life Movement. In theory, it was an adroit blend of traditional and modern appeals. Traditionally, the generalissimo called for a renewed dedication to the four cardinal Confucian virtues. A cadre of "Blue Shirts" fanned out to the countryside establishing Sun Yat-sen schools whose curricula propounded nationalist ideology, the three R's, cooperative farming, and scientific agriculture. The New Life Movement also promoted land reform by returning property to original owners while providing usage rights for peasants already on the land. In practice, the movement was manipulated by local elites for their own purposes, and it foundered.[42]

In contrast to the rural fumbling of the Guomindang, the communists came into their own at the opportunity level. The vast spaces left by the patchwork coverage of Guomindang rule left large areas for communist penetration and experimentation. Forced into the countryside as they were, the communists came to share with the peasants the bond of grain as the staff of life. The communists exchanged surplus grain for their lifeblood of supplies, light industries, and munitions plants.[43] To promote a productive peasantry, the communists ended the Guomindang double tax, guaranteed subsistence agricultural prices in market towns, reduced rent or developed share-rent arrangements for the land, and recruited landless peasants into Red Army agricultural production units. Furthermore, in the Yanan period, while displacing local elites, the CCP established a "three-thirds system" of local government in their base areas. This was a sharing of power among the communists, Guomindang (party, not local gentry), and nonparty elements.[44] To the peasants, any reestablishment of the nationalist government in the countryside essentially meant a return of the landlords and other sociopolitical obstacles that the communists had removed.

Despite this communist victory at opportunity levels in the countryside, the struggle in the arena of national beliefs went on for a long time. And for a long time, the advantage was held by the Guomindang. The first nation-wide hero of nationalism and modernization was Dr. Sun Yat-sen. On top of his Three People's Principles, in 1924 he established a political organization, the reorganized Guomindang under Russian sponsorship, and articulated an ideological program to fulfill his vision of a democratic, independent, and modern China.[45] This gave legitimacy to the Guomindang party as the vehicle to this destiny and bestowed on Chiang Kai-shek the mantle of the party's helmsman. At this level, the communists could only be swept along as part of this journey.

The flip side of this advantage was that Sun's ideology provided some basic criteria for judging subsequent Guomindang performance, and to its own self, the Guomindang was increasingly less true. First, the inability of the nationalists to provide "equal livelihood" has already been discussed in the failure of the New Life Movement. Second, and equally serious, Chiang Kai-shek gradually lost grip on the one issue that originally had been his greatest strength: nationalism. Nationalism had come to have a variety of meanings, but the irreducible minimum was an antiforeign "China for the Chinese." [46] Simply put, Chiang Kai-shek's constant turning on the communists became the source of his eventual downfall on this vital issue. The Xian Incident of 1936 reaffirmed the preeminent position of Chiang Kai-shek as national leader but also warned him to retain proper nationalist priorities, namely, to put the common national enemy, the Japanese, above his partisan differences with the communists.

In this regard, Chalmers Johnson was right: the communists used the Japanese intervention to excellent nationalist effect. In championing a strong anti-Japanese rhetoric and at least some violent resistance to match, the communists built a viable nationalist place for themselves during World War II even beyond their growing interest and opportunity-motivated base areas. By the end of the war, intellectuals and the various national institutions they controlled, accepted the communists as a legitimate nationalist force, even if they did not fully support Marxist ideology. In addition to their record of resistance, a key document in gaining this acceptance was Mao's pamphlet *On New Democracy*, first published in 1940 but reemphasized by the party in 1945. In it, Mao declared a communist willingness to participate in a postwar coalition government and promised to treat all social classes evenhandedly.[47] Chiang Kai-shek, however, was not willing to enter into such a coalition government, and his stubborn refusal to cooperate with the plans of the Marshall Mission, in the face of a professed desire by all other strata in China for some form of "union government"—from communist to liberal to the "party" section of the Guomindang—alienated Chiang from this widening circle beyond the narrowing clique of his loyal followers.[48]

Third, Sun called for a democratic China built through a step-by-step process both from the local to the national levels and from phases of military consolidation to political tutelage under a national administration culminating in the formal establishment of constitutional government. In cataloging Chiang Kai-shek's record of failure, it must be said, in fairness, that the communists had not developed much political democracy either. Other than an expressed willingness to enter into coalition rule at both local and national levels and a vague support of Sun's ideology, the communists had never made explicit commitments to constitutional democracy as had the Guomindang.

For a time, the Guomindang did make some democratic efforts. Following the Northern Expedition, in 1928 the nationalists ended military rule and established the Guomindang dictatorship of political tutelage. At its party meeting the next year, the nationalists declared that tutelage would end in 1935. In furtherance of this objective, local elections were held, provincial assemblies were installed, an increasing share of Guomindang party delegates were elected, and constituent assemblies were convened for national elections. The culminating elections themselves, though, never seemed to take place. Insufficient political tutelage as a rationale for a dodge was clever at first, but it grew thin. At its fifth party congress in 1935, the Guomindang claimed the Japanese intervention of 1931 had slowed the process of tutelage and required postponement. In 1945, as the war drew to an end, the nationalists renewed their pledge for a democratic China. Despite the failure of the Marshall Mission in 1946, in November 1947 the Guomindang at last declared political tutelage to be over. In April 1948 nationwide elections established a National Assembly, which elected the generalissimo president. This certainly came as no surprise because the communists were excluded from the balloting and the Democratic League was outlawed. What made this "final" election doubly meaningless was Chiang Kai-shek's sidestepping of the whole process through rule by emergency decree, which especially angered urban intellectuals.[49]

Thus, on all three counts, by 1948 Chiang Kai-shek had sundered himself from Sun's legacy. Chiang was a man, like much of China itself, caught between two worlds. Like the elect of Fred Riggs's "imprismned society," Chiang had had a modern education and the rudiments of a modern vision, but his skills and support all lay in the manipulation of traditional factions for the commanding heights of elite entrenchment. Even within his own organization, Chiang drew his support from the military and administrative elites and kept his distance from the Guomindang party and its more participatory cadres. After World War II, just when he most needed to reach out to reformist pressures, Chiang became "a holder with no goal but to hold."[50]

REVOLUTIONARY LEGITIMACY

In revolutionary legitimacy, the strategy of Marxist people's war originated with Mao Zedong as a long-term plan that offered his comrades hope of eventually overcoming both the Japanese and the Guomindang in the face of their near helplessness in Yanan. The Long March to Yanan, however, had been a journey forced on the party by error. An urban strategy failed in 1927. A doctrinaire approach to the countryside rendered the Jiangxi and other rural soviets vulnerable in the 1930s. But in Yanan, Mao was able to demonstrate and articulate, at both opportunity and ideological levels, a viable alternative path to the future, both from his internal opponents and from the Guomindang.

What is impressive is that, leaving aside the question of foreign support, in essential details the Chinese communists followed Mao's script. Three aspects of the Chinese revolution are particularly noteworthy. First, the Chinese under Mao's leadership mapped out and followed, in people's war, a revolutionary path independent from Moscow, foreshadowing the unlikelihood of any lengthy subordination to the Russians after liberation. Second, fueled by the political support of people's war, unlike the Vietnamese, the Chinese made critical use of guerrilla forces and tactics right up to the moment of liberation. Finally, Mao's long march to power vindicated his fundamental premise of people's war, the primacy of men over weapons, a point seconded by General Barr in his bleak assessment of Guomindang leadership.[51]

As a fellow modernizer, Mao saw, as Chiang did not, that securing the "people's livelihood" would require displacing local elites. The hallowed cry of the May Fourth Movement — "Down with the old, up with the new" — meant, simply, a revolution. Mao also saw, as his radical comrades did not, that any tearing down of the old still required maintaining the position and livelihood of the middle peasant. Ironically, Chiang was able to rule the modern cities with the traditional politics of elite manipulation, but the "traditional" countryside could no longer be ruled by traditional methods. A dramatic shift in this equation came after the war, when, upon returning to the cities, the Guomindang found that the rampant wartime inflation made it impossible to resurrect the traditional props to its rule.[52] Further, Mao had "Sinified" Marxism to the point that both its record and its ideology were no less nationalistic than those of the nationalist Guomindang. On the count of democracy, the communists were more vulnerable to the Guomindang, but on this potential strength, the nationalists ultimately failed to deliver. In the end, Mao's communism was truer to Sun Yat-sen's modern democratic vision than was Chiang's fascism.

INTERVENTION

Illustrative of another chink in the armor of the Guomindang's legitimacy was a couplet that circulated in Chinese teahouses during the civil war:

> Chiang Kai-shek has a stubborn heart,
> America is his father and mother.[53]

Even though antiforeignism was a central part of the Guomindang platform, it always relied on some form of foreign support. First, there were the Russians. As a result of the Sun-Joffe Agreement of 1923, a host of Russian advisers descended on the Guomindang. They founded the Whampoa Military Academy, provided financial assistance, and tried to mold the Guomindang in their own image. Russian assistance ceased with the collapse of the CCP-GMD Alliance in 1927 but resumed in 1937 with the establishment of the United Front. From 1937 to 1940 the Russians provided the Chinese with their only source of foreign aid, and until 1941 the Soviets remained the Guomindang's principal provider of foreign assistance. It included half of the planes of Chiang Kai-shek's air force, a $250 million loan in 1938, and another $250 million loan in 1940, which the generalissimo used to outfit six divisions. The aid was cut off again with the collapse of the United Front in 1941.[54] Then there were the Germans. In 1928 the Weimar Republic agreed to provide Chiang Kai-shek with a staff of military advisers, especially for the Whampoa Military Academy. German advice and equipment were helpful in the extermination campaigns, but the assistance was halted in 1937 when the Germans began to forge links with the Japanese.[55]

Dwarfing all this assistance was the aid of the United States. Starting from flood and famine relief loans in the 1930s, in 1940 a $75 million loan was extended to the nationalist government, which was followed by a $500 million loan in 1942. After the Cairo Conference in 1943, U.S. aid was dispatched to China at a rate of $25 million a month. In the first year after the war, $600 million in lend-lease aid was given Chiang Kai-shek. This was supplemented by another $400 million in the China Aid Act of 1948.[56] Over and above this, after the war Chiang Kai-shek was allowed to purchase $900 million worth of surplus military equipment for $175 million.[57]

More than just the money and equipment, American personnel, both civilian and military, provided a variety of services that helped to prop up the regime. A team of American financial advisers helped Guomindang officials double their customs tax collections in the 1920s and 1930s.[58] The colorful Claire Chennault built up the Chinese air force to a force of five hundred planes and trained Chinese pilots from a nucleus of 150 American pilots. In the war his "tigers" shot down six hundred Japanese fighters and destroyed seven thousand ships along the Chinese coast. But it was the military mission of General Joseph Stilwell and the 95,500 men of the China-Burma-India theater (CBI) that kept Chinese nationalist resistance alive in World War II. They kept the supply lines to China open and equipped and trained thirty-nine Chinese divisions. Stilwell himself briefly served as chief of staff for the Chinese army. In late 1943, given personal command of three GMD divisions, he annihilated one Japanese division and chewed up another.[59] Finally, immediately after World War II, half a million nationalist troops were ferried by American planes to Shanghai, Nanking, and key cities in Manchuria to preempt a communist bid for control of those areas.

But it was not enough, or else it was to much. When Madame Chiang Kai-shek flew to Washington and requested supplemental assistance of $3 billion in December 1948, she was turned down and all further aid was suspended.[60] By this time, 75 percent of the American equipment furnished the nationalists had fallen into the hands of the communists.[61] As in the subsequent case of Vietnam, America decided to cut its losses. If Chiang Kai-shek was perceived in the teahouse couplet to be the child of the Americans, the Americans lamented their lack of any leverage over this basically antiforeign Chinaman.[62] Yet the very amount of the American assistance, in the eyes of the Chinese, made his Chinese patrimony and his legitimacy suspect.

In contrast to the Guomindang, the Communist party made a virtue of its self-reliance. There is reason to believe that it made this a virtue more out of necessity than of choice. The success of Mao's third stage of people's war depended on foreign support, and in 1935 he thought he could count on Soviet assistance because "we are bound together in a common cause."[63] It was not forthcoming. Repeatedly in crises, the communists had to rely on their own devices.

Direct material aid to the CCP was indeed meager. Initially until 1927 most of the aid it received was channeled through Comintern agents affiliated with the CCP-GMD Alliance. After 1927 the monthly Comintern stipend of $15,000 was insufficient to maintain an urban apparatus and was part of the reason for moving the Communist Party Central to the Jiangxi soviet in 1931.[64] The United Front period (1937–41) brought much needed assistance to the CCP, but, ironically, most of it came from the Central Government of the Guomindang. Government subsidies were crucial to the early building period of the communists in Yanan. In 1940 they reached a high of $10.4 million. By keeping administrative costs low, the communists were able to use this money both to build up the Eighth Route Army and to keep taxes light.[65] After the New Fourth Army Incident of 1941, the subsidies were cut off and the CCP was on its own again.

Despite the lack of material aid, the CCP never lacked for Russian advice. Indeed, the party itself was founded at the urging of Comintern agents. It both joined and persisted in the alliance with the Guomindang at Stalin's behest. Comintern representatives journeyed on the Long March and stayed on in Yanan as advisers until 1943.[66] And it was Stalin who pressured the communists into working toward the release of Chiang Kai-shek at Xian.[67] The last piece of Soviet advice was to suggest in 1949 that the PLA halt its advance at the Changjiang (Yangtze) River and leave southern China for the Guomindang.[68]

Beyond the direct aid to both sides, which by itself cannot be said to have been determinative of the outcome, there were other forms of intervention which were critical to the struggle and certainly do complicate any analysis based on domestic legitimacy alone. First, the Japanese intervention in Manchuria from 1931 to 1937 and their subsequent invasion of China proper from 1937 to 1945 critically compromised one of the Guomindang's three planks of legitimacy, nationalism. In deciding that his most vital foe was the communists rather than the Japanese, Chiang Kai-shek's numerous attempts to crack down on the communists, who had cloaked themselves in a mantle of anti-Japanese nationalism, and his own frequent evasion of the Japanese, gave the communists the opportunity to "Sinify their Marxism" at Guomindang expense. With respect to the postwar question of a democratic "third force" alternative, it is worth noting that the left-wing Guomindang under Wang Jingwei and other liberals committed an even more serious nationalistic error than Chiang Kai-shek by actually going over to the Japanese or collaborating with them, leaving their legitimacy irreparably suspect.

Second, it was not the Chinese, communist or nationalist, who defeated the Japanese, but the Americans—and, in Manchuria at least, the Russians. In China, by 1942 the Kwangtung army's "Three Alls" strategy of counter-insurgency had sharply reduced the size of communist forces and the base areas under their control.[69] Though the Japanese became too extended to keep up this pressure, as late as their Ichigo offensive along the Chinese coast at the end of 1944, they were able to sweep everything before them. Even by the precepts of people's war, it was something of an embarrassment to have the third stage victory over the Japanese commandeered by foreigners.

Third, both the United States and the Russians helped their respective clients in the critical jockeying for position immediately after the war. The United States flew nationalist troops to the cities of north China. The Russians allowed the PLA to seize the arms of the Japanese soldiers who had surrendered to them in Manchuria and facilitated the consolidation of a communist position there. This gave the communists both their initial conventional military capability and first industrial base, which enabled them to challenge the Guomindang in open warfare.[70]

Finally, the United States dispatched the Marshall Mission to China, where, for a year, it endeavored to provide the nationalists and communists with an eleventh-hour opportunity for a coalition government. The failure of Marshall's endeavor put China's future on a fated course, whose result touched off a subsequent political whirlwind in domestic American politics, the anticommunist wave of McCarthyism. The long march of the communists to power, then, was an inseparable drama of national and international politics, of insurgency and intervention.

DYNAMICS OF THE BALANCES

As in all insurgencies, there were asymmetries in China. The communists deftly overcame the critical mass problem of getting their revolution started by riding piggyback on the Guomindang's own period of organization in the Comintern-directed bore-from-within strategy. Chiang, of course, turned on them, over and over, but then the Japanese turned on both of them. The Japanese intervention and invasion fell heavier on the Guomindang, as the incumbents, than on the communists. This asymmetry was a particularly heavy blow in the invasion of China proper because the nationalists were rooted out of the very citadel of their strength: the cities, and especially Shanghai. Unable to make much of Sun Yat-sen's principle of "people's livelihood" for China, Chiang Kai-shek was more particularly unable to carve out much political livelihood for his regime in the rural hinterlands outside of Nanjing and Chongqing. In any case, the burden of incumbency to provide rule over all China was too heavy for the Guomindang under such stress.[71] In the interstices of this wartime emergency, the thin and interrupted spread of nationalist rule, even taking into account the Japanese presence, left plenty of cracks for the nurturing of revolution.

Nevertheless, despite the "unfair" yoke of incumbency, the Guomindang contributed to their own undoing by an unfavorable balance of error. Committing themselves to a path leading toward democracy, the nationalists never went the distance. Part of the reason for this failure was a misplacement of the groups within the nationalist camp. The ascendant cliques around Chiang Kai-shek at the national level kept the left-wing Guomindang and other liberals, who did advocate democracy and a more inclusive political community, out of the tent. At the local level, the New Life Movement failed to provide a rural base of support as at least a reserve for the Guomindang to fall back on during World War II. In general, as Lloyd Eastman observed, Chiang Kai-shek "never transcended elitist politics and trapped himself in the practice of ruling through the balance of weakness."[72]

In the war, the generalissimo devoted most of his time to international diplomacy, in stark contrast to the feverish party-building of the communists, and did little to strengthen his domestic position. Immediately after the defeat of the Japanese, the Guomindang threw away a chance to broaden its support by removing the large cadres of Japanese collaborators in the wartime municipal bureaucracies. Willfully, the party also failed to adjust politically to the strengthened position of the communists.[73] It followed that the nationalists would squander the opportunity in 1946 for a coalition government with the communists. The subsequent military disasters seemed to tear out readily along the same unraveling political seam.

The communists certainly made mistakes of their own, but they learned from them. The doctrinaire errors of a Comintern-directed urban strategy and then the rigid approach to land reform in the Jiangxi soviet cleared the way for Mao's more pragmatic and nationalist strategy in Yanan.[74] As I have argued about revolutions generally, as a process they can be reversed. Certainly in the case of China, there were alternative, reversible directions. Most of the changes in direction, however, were done by the communists, who switched in time to survive for another day: in 1924 by joining the GMD, in 1927 by fleeing to the countryside, and then marching even further in 1934 to Yanan, where they took up the beat of the flexible strategy of people's war.

In all the oscillations of these shifting crossover points, two points stand firm. First, regarding the question "Who Lost China?," apart from wondering if it is fair to say that anyone ever had it, the "stubborn heart" of Chiang Kai-shek must stand at the center of an answer. Poignantly, though he spread the responsibility around some, concurrence came from Chiang himself in a speech in January 1948: "To tell the truth, never, in China or abroad, has there been a revolutionary party as decrepit . . . and degenerate . . . as we are today; nor one as lacking spirit, lacking discipline, and even more, lacking standards of right and wrong as we are today. This kind of party should long ago have been destroyed and swept away!"[75]

Second, though, it is not fair just to say that the Guomindang lost. Whatever the vicissitudes and fortuitous circumstances of international politics, the communists persevered, adapted, and exploited opportunities to earn their breakout. As Suzanne Pepper concluded: "Politically, therefore, the

CCP's victory was as genuine as the GMD's defeat. . . . The Communists did not just happen to be in the right place at the right time to benefit from the GMD's debacle. They did not win an unqualified mandate in 1949 to establish one-party Communist rule in Mainland China. But their achievements had been substantial enough to provide the basis for a transfer of popular allegiance to the new Communist-led government."[76]

Comparisons with Vietnam

Of all the cases to be discussed in this comparative prism, the Chinese revolution is the most similar to the Vietnamese. With the notable exception of self-reliance, the Vietnamese followed the Chinese people's war script quite faithfully against the French as well as against the Americans until the Tet offensive in 1968. They both had to contend with the conventionally superior armies of industrial states. The endings of the two struggles in 1949 and 1975 make Nguyen Van Thieu appear to be a living reincarnation of Chiang Kai-shek. Yet there were differences. Mao was not opposed by any Western troops as was General Giap. Also, Mao had the vastness of China's geography and population from which to set up his base areas for a people's war, advantages not enjoyed by the Vietnamese, who had to face their enemy "cheek to jowl," which made the establishment of secure base areas almost impossible. In fact, only the Greek communists were able to duplicate this Chinese advantage. More imponderably, the Chinese did not have to contend with the technological revolution in American firepower and what it portended for a basic premise of people's war, the superiority of men over weapons (most notably, the instant response capability of armored helicopters and gunships and the effect of long-range bombings on attempts to create base areas).

For comparisons with Vietnam, three main issues emerge. First, the saga of elections and democratization seems to come to the same dismal fate in Vietnam and China, in Vietnam whether it was against the Viet Minh or the Viet Cong. All the attempts of the French to confer meaningful independence and democracy on Indochina were like the phlegmatic efforts of the Guomindang, too little and too late. Against the Viet Cong, elections that excluded the National Liberation Front in the face of such a hopelessly fragmented and politically disorganized opposition to the Thieu government meant that any national political community was impossible, as it was without a coalition government in China. Despite bugaboos of fear drawn from European experience, it is by no means clear that coalitions with the communists in China in 1946 or in Vietnam in 1973 would have automatically produced communist takeovers. In any case, communist participation in coalition regimes might have blunted the revolutionary momentum by tarnishing the communists as well with the yoke of incumbency.

Second, one cannot help but be struck by the centrality of legitimacy to the struggle in China. Part of the reason it lasted so long was that, at least until 1937, the Guomindang had a genuine purchase on national legitimacy, traditional and modern. Chiang Kai-shek symbolized this by the solidifying role he was forced to play in the Xian Incident. From then on, however, the legitimacy of the nationalists waned while that of the communists waxed at all levels. After World War II, Mao had such a lock on legitimacy and Chiang Kai-shek was stumbling so badly that no amount of foreign intervention would have made any difference. It was the prescience of General Marshall, at the end of his mission, to see this. The United States, therefore, in ending its aid in 1948 was wise enough to escape the embrace of Chiang's illegitimacy lock.

Finally, what is most striking about China as a different ending (despite common communist victories) was that the communist victory was a political one all the way through to the military end. When the Marshall Mission failed, Chiang Kai-shek abandoned all pretense of politics and opted for his favorite weapon, the sword. But, like Henri Navarre shortly after him, Chiang set himself up for his own Dienbienphu.

Chapter 7

GREECE, 1941–1949: THREE ROUNDS TO ALBANIA

Historical Setting

While Guomindang troops were fleeing head over heels to Taiwan and the opium fields of Southeast Asia's "Golden Triangle" (Thailand, Burma, and Laos), the shoe was on the other foot in Greece, where ragged bands of communist forces were struggling over stark mountain trails into Yugoslavia and Albania to internment at the hands of no longer sympathetic communist authorities. American advisers could take some credit for this defeat, and their experience in Greece shaped the doctrine for future U.S. counterinsurgency operations.[1]

If any country meets Karl von Clausewitz's requirement for people's war of "difficult and remote terrain," it is Greece. Sixty percent of mainland Greece is mountainous. The terrain along the six hundred miles of its northern border is especially arduous, and, like the borders of South Vietnam's Central Highlands, is "unguarded and unguardable."[2] From these remote mountain redoubts, Greek brigands, known as Klefths, repeatedly raided and plundered their hated Ottoman Turk overlords and kept alive the

"Great Idea" (Megali Idea) of the panhellenic Byzantine Imperium. During the nineteenth century, the dream of Greek independence also captured the imagination of the Great Powers: Britain, France, and Russia. Their naval actions against the Turks were critical in helping the Greek uprisings realize national independence in 1832. In gratitude and in emulation of the form of government in vogue in Europe, the Greeks proclaimed a king, Otto of Bavaria, as their head of state.[3]

As a state born of external intervention, little stigma was attached to it, and Greek politics soon reflected the rivalries of the Great Powers. The monarchy, however, ran into problems rooting itself in Greek society, particularly among the interior population (including the Klefths), where loyalties were local and ties to a national society, let alone a foreign king, proved difficult to foster. Revolts occurred in 1843 and again in 1863. In 1913 the king, George I, was assassinated.[4] Despite these upheavals, the chief task of all Greeks was the pursuit of the Megali Idea. At the time of independence, only seven hundred thousand of the three million Greeks lived in the new state.[5] Their cause's big advance came in the Balkan Wars of 1912–13 with the defeat of the Turks at the hands of the Greeks, Serbians, Montenegrins, and Bulgarians. The Greek spoils of Macedonia, Crete, and part of Thrace increased their territory and population by two-thirds. But the continued pursuit of this quest by King Constantine in an expedition into Asia Minor from 1920 to 1922 ended in disaster. The 1923 Treaty of Lausanne finally stabilized the territory and population of Greece. The treaty called for an exchange of population in which some 380,000 non-Greeks (mainly Turks) departed and 1.3 million ethnic Greeks arrived to add to the existing population of 4.5 million Greeks.[6]

This population exchange only exacerbated the central issue of division in Greek politics: the monarchy. Political lines had polarized during World War I, when Prime Minister Eleutherios Venizelos favored the Entente, and King Constantine I, married to the kaiser's sister, supported the Central Powers. Greece finally sided with the Entente and entered the war in 1917. The king was driven into exile but was recalled by a plebiscite in 1920. His disastrous campaign in Asia Minor, however, obliged him to abdicate in 1922. With the king discredited and the influx of 1.3 million refugees in 1923 with no ties to the monarchy, Venizelos was able to establish a republic in 1925.

The rest of the 1920s and early 1930s were a period of instability punctuated by military coups intermingled with elections split between the Populists (or royalists), who favored the monarchy, and the Republicans (or liberals), who opposed it. In 1935, however, another plebiscite brought back Constantine's son, George II, to Greece. A national crisis followed from the 1936 National Assembly elections, which deadlocked the two major parties at 143 seats to 141 with the Communist party holding the balance with its fifteen seats. Fearing another military coup — the General Staff clearly signaled that it would not tolerate communists in the government — the king turned the government over to the royalist general John Metaxas, who suspended the constitution and ruled as a dictator until his death on January 29, 1941.[7]

As a small part of this larger picture, communists made their first appearance in Greek politics in 1918 as the Socialist Labor party. Started by a clique of Greek intellectuals and students, the organization sought followers among tobacco, railway, and industrial workers. It received its biggest boost from the uprooted, new arrivals from Asia Minor, who had no attachments to the existing political system. In 1924 the organization openly took the title of the Communist Party of Greece (KKE). Nationally, however, the KKE remained a small, unpopular party, never achieving even 10 percent of the popular vote in the elections of 1926, 1932, 1933, and 1936. It had made virtually no inroads in the countryside and labored under the nationalist disadvantage of its expressed ideological support for the Balkan Communist Federation, which advocated autonomy for Macedonia and Thrace. In the Metaxas era, KKE membership remained at a mere five thousand.[8]

On the eve of the three rounds of civil war, Greece faced the explosive bottleneck of an interwar economic boom even as national politics had stalemated into a full-blown crisis of legitimacy.[9] While an economic boom of small-scale industries created both an expanding middle class (even into the countryside) and a set of tensions between an industrial work force and a class of capitalists, questions of political legitimacy swirled around the traditional Megali Idea, the modern drive for a truly democratic government, and the desire, in all these struggles, for stability. These three themes came to pivot on the monarchy.

In traditional terms, Greece received a German king as part of its "guarantee" of independence. The basic schism in Greek politics was over the acceptance of this alien monarchy. To some Greeks, the royalists, accepting a foreign king was an attractive symbol of their participation in the larger European order. But to the republicans, the monarchs were not only foreign but also unrepentant in their Protestantism and, therefore, unsuitable as rulers over a devoutly Greek Orthodox society. On a secular level, however, these alien monarchs did have a consistent record as champions of the Megali Idea: the belief that Greece was more than the territory of a single kingdom but existed wherever there were Greeks and places touched by Greek culture.[10]

If, with respect to the Megali Idea, the sentiments of the monarchy were at least in the right place, on the modern desire for democracy, its record was poor. Though Greece's foreign kings accepted democratic institutions and political parties, in World War I Constantine aroused suspicion by siding with the undemocratic German kaiser. These suspicions were heightened by the numerous military coups in the interwar years that always bore the stamp of royal complicity. On top of this, as new territories came into the Greek kingdom from the 1870s on, the king administered them directly through royal governor-generals. These governors were autocratic, corrupt, and unpopular.[11] In brief, the king had far greater support in areas where he was a symbol (in the Peloponnese and central Athenian plain) than where he was a ruler (in northern and eastern Greece).

By the 1930s, the repeated crises precipitated by this schism produced a growing concern for, and insistence on, political stability. It was on the back of this "third force," interestingly, that the monarchy was able to appropriate for itself the role of a stabilizing institution. In the 1935–36 parliamentary paralysis, King George played a central part in mediating between the political parties and the military. Indeed, the parties themselves finally endorsed the end of parliamentary rule in favor of the Metaxas dictatorship.[12] As Greece plunged into three successive rounds of civil war in 1941, the three legitimating planks (or measures) of the Megali Idea, modern democracy, and political stability held the key to their resolution, even though, during these rounds, their definitions changed profoundly.

For all the countries in this study, the "external" phenomenon of World War II became an internal crucible of vital domestic struggle for claims to the mantle of postwar political authority. During the war, Greece, in addition to the Italian invasion attempts and the depredations of the German occupation, endured two rounds of bloody civil war between the communists and those opposed to them.

First Italian and then German invasions brought the war to Greece quickly and forcefully. Attempting to steal a march on the blitzkriegs of Hitler in the north, Mussolini struck the Greek army from Albania in October 1940 with a force of 120,000 men. But the action quickly departed from the script of his German colleague. By December, Mussolini experienced the humiliation of being driven back thirty miles into Albania. Metaxas and the Greek National Army deserved the domestic credit they received for upholding the national honor. In March 1941, the Italians launched a second invasion only to be repulsed again, this time with the help of 74,000 British troops sent to aid the Greeks. Realizing that the disgrace of the Axis had gone far enough, Hitler sent his armies south. The unexpected surrender of Yugoslavia on April 17 caught the Greeks by surprise, and on April 22, 300,000 Greek soldiers (half of their mobilized strength) were captured and disarmed by the Germans. The day before, 50,000 British troops had been evacuated hastily from the fighting, and on April 27 the Germans entered Athens. The British forces and Greek government withdrew to Egypt where a government in exile was established. The Germans, with the help of the

Bulgarians, Italians, and a Greek puppet government, settled in Greece for a three-and-a-half-year occupation.[13]

Organized resistance sprang up quickly on the Greek mainland. In September 1941, the KKE banded with other groups to form the National Liberation Front (EAM). It in turn formed a National Liberation Army (ELAS), whose initials, patriotically, rhymed with Hellas. The National Liberation Army soon grew to be the largest resistance organization. From their inception, EAM and ELAS were controlled by the KKE. Nevertheless, the communists did not enjoy a monopoly in resistance movements. Also in late 1941, liberals with republican sympathies formed a resistance movement under Colonel Napoleon Zervas. It was called the National Republican Greek League (EDES). In time the antimonarchical passions of EDES abated, though those of the communists remained steadfast. Other noncommunist resistance groups were the Liberation Struggle Command (AAA), under the political direction of George Papandreou, who became prime minister in the last stages of war, and the Front of National and Social Liberation (EKKA).[14] The most significant action of the resistance was the sabotage of the Gorgopotamos Bridge in November 1942 by elements of both ELAS and EDES under the leadership of British demolition experts. In the course of this operation, the British decided to favor EDES over ELAS. This discrimination did little to stop the growth of ELAS. By October 1943 it numbered fifteen thousand regulars and ten thousand reserves, while EDES stood at five thousand men and EKKA at only one thousand.[15]

Despite the presence of a common enemy, tensions grew between the communists and noncommunists, especially in the Peloponnese Peninsula, where German reprisals were blamed on the KKE and Greek peasants began to join the Security Battalions of the puppet regime in Athens to retaliate against the communists. The first round of fighting between the two sides broke out in October 1943, when ELAS and EDES clashed all over Greece. Initially, ELAS punished EDES forces severely, but EDES eventually beat back the communist attacks and by January 1944 the fighting reached a stalemate. Round 1 was finally ended by the Plaka Bridge Armistice of February 28, 1944.[16]

Far from ending the civil strife, the cease-fire merely transferred the struggle to the political arena. British plans for a landing in Greece (Operation Noah's Ark) precipitated an intense jockeying for position in a postwar order. The KKE established its own provisional government on March 14, 1944, the Political Committee for National Liberation (PEEA), as a rival to the official government in exile. To underscore the Cairo regime's lack of an electoral mandate, PEEA held a nationwide "one-party" election for a National Council in May.[17] On the ground, the communists entered this struggle in a strong position: the national army had been defeated and was mostly with British forces in Egypt, and ELAS now numbered some fifty thousand fighters to EDES's roughly ten thousand.[18]

The first attempt at a political agreement was the Lebanon Charter signed on May 20, 1944. It called for a reorganization of the military both inside and outside Greece, a punishment of collaborators, an understanding that King George II would not return until a plebiscite was held, a coalition government, and an end to the communist "reign of terror."[19] The EAM organization, however, denounced the charter and the actions of its own representatives and countered with further demands. A second political arrangement, the Caserta Agreement, was concluded on September 26, 1944. Its essential accomplishments were two. First, agreement was reached to set up a Greek Government of National Unity with full participation by EAM. Second, all parties (the government in exile, EAM, and EDES) recognized the military authority of the British to exercise command in Greece. This authority was recognized in the international realm by Joseph Stalin's famous concurrence, in conversations with Winston Churchill on October 9, 1944, with the latter's formula for dividing interests between the British and Russians in the Balkans. The formula for Greece was ninety to ten in favor of Britain in exchange for better Soviet proportions elsewhere.[20]

Meanwhile, for Greece, the war was coming to an abrupt conclusion. Prompted by Soviet intrigues, a coup in Bulgaria brought in a pro-Russian government on September 9, 1944, which caused the Germans quickly to evacuate Greece. Prudently waiting for the departure of the last German units, British paratroopers landed in Athens in October, bringing with them the government in exile of George Papandreou. It was sworn in on October 21, 1944, with twenty-three cabinet portfolios: fourteen of the new prime minister's choosing, six from EAM (later seven), two Liberals, and one Independent.[21] Thus the wartime resistance ended. At its peak, forty thousand Bulgarians and three hundred thousand German soldiers (who suffered between five thousand and fifteen thousand deaths) had been tied down at a cost of five thousand to twenty thousand lives for ELAS alone. In addition, some seventy thousand civilians were executed.[22]

The end of World War II in Greece did not end its civil war. When the Papandreou government arrived in Greece, the political situation had been all but taken over by the communists. From their commanding position in March, they were now dominant. With a force of 80,000 men, ELAS controlled three-fourths of the territory and one-half of the population of Greece. EAM claimed over one million members, 450,000 of whom were communists. In opposition were the 30,000 men in EDES and 8,500 men in various military units available to Papandreou. In October 1944, the British had a mere 4,000 men in Greece. By the end of November, this force had increased only to 23,000. With this precarious base, the writ of the Papandreou government was confined to the cities of Athens, Petras, and Salonika.[23]

Hence, despite the common acknowledgment of British authority, the British and the Greek government lacked the means to enforce their orders. The determination of the British to assert this authority and of Papandreou to lead a government of all Greece in fact as well as in name led to a second round of fighting, mostly in Athens, from early December 1944 to January 15, 1945. The catalyst was the ELAS commander's blunt refusal on November 29 to disarm his men. This defiance was seconded by its Civil Guard (EP), which rejected an order by Papandreou on December 1 to hand over its police duties to the new National Guard. The next day KKE-organized riots erupted. The police fired on the crowds, killing seven and wounding at least one hundred people.[24]

Fighting then broke out between the British and ELAS units that had been infiltrated into the city. The ferocious communist resistance was a surprise to the British, who were obliged to muster a force of seventy-five thousand and to conduct a month-long house-to-house campaign before dislodging the insurgents from the city. In their withdrawal, they abducted an estimated thirty thousand civilian hostages, four thousand of whom were killed. Furthermore, perhaps to compensate for their loss in Athens, ELAS turned on EDES in the countryside and destroyed it.[25]

Nevertheless, in addition to their military victory in Athens, several political developments strengthened the negotiating hand of the British and of the Greek government in the discussions following the cease-fire on January 15, 1945. First, the atrocities of the KKE's Units for the Protection of the People's Struggle (OPLA) and the mass killings of the four thousand Athenian hostages not only added to the growing revulsion of the Greek populace toward the communists but also horrified a visiting delegation of the British Trade Union Congress, which effectively dried up British leftist support for the KKE. Second, Churchill's trip to Athens in late December led him to drop his long-standing (and politically damaging) insistence that the monarchy be restored immediately.[26] Finally, at the Yalta Conference in February, Stalin reaffirmed his continued acceptance of the course of events in Greece, thereby dooming any KKE avenue of international appeal.[27]

Accordingly, the Varkiza Agreement of February 12, 1945, which ended the second round, secured not only the withdrawal of ELAS troops from all urban centers and the Peloponnese Peninsula but also its general demobilization. The agreement further called for a plebiscite on the return of the monarchy, national elections for a new parliament, and the punishment of collaborators. Some forty-three thousand firearms were turned in by ELAS (more than had been called for), but, ominously, 4,000 guerrillas slipped into Albania and Yugoslavia and cached some forty thousand additional weapons. Casualties in the second round were relatively light (the only precise casualties were 237 British troops killed; less specific were the 680 casualties and 6,000 "disappearances," presumably from desertions, suffered by EDES, as well as the hundreds of unrecorded ELAS casualties). Overall in World War II, however, some half million Greeks perished (two-thirds from starvation). The International Labor Office assessed the physical destruction at $8 billion, which, at $1,000 per capita, was second only to the losses suffered by the Soviet Union.[28]

Yet the end was not in sight. As one communist leader put it, "the KKE had decisively lost the battle of Athens, but the national government . . . had not won the battle of Greece."[29] Instead, a third round of fighting began in early 1946 after a year of rising tension over unsettled questions about the role of the monarchy and of the communists in the postwar political order. During this time, a wave of anticommunism swept the country and the royalist "X" organization bloated to a membership of two hundred thousand.[30] Significantly, former collaborators in the civil administration were mostly left undisturbed. Furthermore, the Greek government permitted royalists to gain control of both the new Greek army and the government bureaucracy. Alarmed at this casual government attitude toward the Varkiza Agreement, the KKE decided in February 1946 to organize for a new armed struggle, this time with the support of Marshal Tito of Yugoslavia. Nevertheless, the March 31, 1946, parliamentary elections, boycotted by the communists, gave the royalist Populist party 251 of the 354 seats. These royalist sentiments were reemphasized in the September 1, 1946, plebiscite in which King George II, over communist and liberal opposition, received 68 percent of the eligible vote.[31]

Rebuffed politically, the communists took to the hills. By the fall of 1946, their hit-and-run attacks forced the government to put northern Greece under martial law. At year's end, it was clear that external assistance was playing a significant role in sustaining the communist war effort, and in response to charges to this effect by the Greek government, a U.N. Commission of Investigation agreed.[32] Behind a campaign of calculated terror in the countryside, conducted from mobile base areas within Greece and from secure bases in Yugoslavia and Albania, the communists were aiming to build an army of 50,000 men from the 50,000 members in the Yiafaka (communist cells) and its 250,000 sympathizers. The commander Markos Vafiades figured that with such a force he could fight the dispirited Greek army to a standstill. By the end of 1946, however, the Democratic Army (DA) stood at a mere 8,000.[33]

Although the Greek army totaled 120,000 men, both the military and the civil government were riven and demoralized by dissension. In the summer of 1947, the government grew desperate and made 10,000 wide-scale arrests and conducted 462 summary executions. Under international protest and American pressure, the executions were halted, the "X" organization was disbanded, and, most significantly, a more moderate Liberal-Populist coalition government assumed power and lasted through the end of the civil war.[34] Meanwhile, to attract greater international support, the DA, in the same summer of 1947, attempted to seize six different towns as the seat for a rival government. All the attacks failed.[35]

Edgar O'Ballance characterized the next year, 1948, as a stalemate. The fighting was heavy, and the Greek army's casualties in killed and wounded totaled twenty thousand. Even though the DA lost thirty-two thousand men in killed, wounded, and prisoners, its strength remained stable at twenty-three thousand by the end of the year. Most of these casualties occurred in Operation Summit, an only partially successful government drive to clear the DA out of its northern mountain redoubts of Vitsi and Grammos.[36]

In 1949, however, the struggle took a decisive turn in favor of the government. This shift resulted both from communist errors and a new government strategy. In June 1948, Yugoslavia was expelled from the Cominform by the Soviets and the KKE dutifully, if reluctantly, endorsed the action. In retaliation, the Yugoslavs shut off supply lines and closed their border to the DA on July 10, 1949, a move seconded by anti-Soviet Albania in August. On top of this political blunder, the DA decided to switch strategies and make a conventional stand at Vitsi and Grammos. Coupled with these communist moves, the Greek National Army underwent a change of command that revitalized the military under a British-American strategy of conducting a south-to-north sweep of the country.[37]

The combination of this strategy and the communist errors produced dramatic results. By the end of January, the Peloponnese Peninsula was cleared. In a final campaign to drive the communists from their Grammos and Vitsi strongholds, called Operation Torch, the Greek army and its American advisers totally defeated the Democratic Army. At the start of the battle in the summer, the Greek army was able to concentrate six of its eight field divisions against 12,000 desperate defenders. By August their mountain citadels had been smashed and their numbers reduced to 3,710. All resistance ceased by the end of the year.[38]

Thus, similar to the Chinese, the Greeks finally were liberated, but it was a liberation from communism, not under it. In this last round, the cost in battle deaths alone was 38,000 communists and 15,000 government soldiers. In all three rounds of civil war, 158,000 Greeks lost their lives.[39]

Framework Analysis

Contrary to the other cases of this study, the Greek civil war was one of three rounds, and the framework balances among them are so different that each round can almost be considered a separate case. Yet they tied together in the end to produce the decisive communist defeat in 1949.

At the level of interest, the wartime years of Axis occupation imposed upon the Greeks a period of misery. A growing interwar economy plunged downward in the chaos, and at least three hundred thousand Greeks died of starvation. To put the civil war and resistance in some perspective, then, this political contest was not the first priority of citizens' lives. For all Greeks—rural and urban—keeping the wolf of starvation at bay and surviving in the midst of three occupying armies was their central preoccupation.[40] In truth, except in disparate localities, none of the resistance organizations did much. This was in sharp contrast to Yugoslavia, for example, where partisan warfare raged across the country and posed a serious threat to the German occupation. Nevertheless, the wake of terror that followed the German withdrawal in 1944 did wreak havoc in peoples' lives. In the Peloponnese in particular, the population was cowed as it was whipsawed between communist executions of collaborators and personnel in the security battalions and the counterterror of hastily organized right-wing retaliatory groups. Security, both personal and physical, held sway over any political commitment.[41]

Still, in the last two rounds of the civil war, the communists started with the stronger hand. In the vacuum left by the departing Axis armies, EAM was on the ground and better positioned than the long-absent government. Indeed, as late as mid-1948, U.S. Army maps showed the government in control of only half the countryside.[42] Gradually, however, calculations of personal interest shifted to the government as it rebuilt its political administration and massive foreign aid revived the war-shattered economy. This shift began in the cities and slowly spread to the countryside, leaving a communist presence, finally, only in marginal areas of ethnic minorities.

At the level of opportunity, the story is similarly varied in the three rounds. By 1940 the Metaxis government had nearly shattered the KKE. It had splintered into three bickering groups, and most of its leaders were jailed.[43] But the dictatorship and the onslaught of the war had leveled the playing field of Greek politics. The major political parties, "suspended" by the dictatorship, were not structured or equipped to serve as military resistance organizations and virtually ceased to exist during the war.[44] As a result, the government in exile had few active links with political groups in Greece.

With the shearing off of the national government and the defeat and withdrawal of the Greek National Army, World War II provided a golden opportunity for the previously all-but-irrelevant Communist party. The KKE cannot be accused of failing to seize its chance. It built ELAS around a cadre of competent former army officers. To attract a mass following, it set up the National Liberation Front (EAM) that, though controlled by the KKE, included other political groups such as the Socialist party. More than this, it set up a complex of institutions that allowed widespread societal access to their order: a trade union that carried the initials EEAM, a youth organization (EPON), and the popular EAM red cross (EA) for women. All told, some two million people joined these organizations as the KKE's own membership swelled to 450,000.[45] With the pronouncement of its own government PEEA, the KKE had set up a regime for political participation as well. Though the KKE did not have a political or military monopoly in Greece, by late 1944 it had built a momentum of crossover points that brought the communists to the brink of a strategic break-out.

The thirty-three-day military offensive of the second round in Athens, however, spelled political disaster for the entire institutional structure of EAM. As a result of both the offensive itself and the civilian executions conducted by ELAS, the socialists dropped out of the front, leaving it exposed as an unambiguous communist organization. The agreements of 1945 forced ELAS to demobilize, militarily defanging the communists. Their decision not to participate in the elections of 1946, furthermore, left them out of the political re-institutionalization of Greek society. Noncommunist labor unions were formed, the political parties rebuilt, and a bloated bureaucracy, a "parastate," ensconced itself in Athens and all the towns — all to the opportunity-level exclusion of the KKE.[46]

The new government of Greece was not without its problems. The Greek National Army was hardly a source of national inspiration, and the political parties, though rebuilding, lacked strong leadership. Through 1948, changes in government were frequent.[47] Indeed, for all the blows rained on the KKE since Athens, in almost a classic restatement of my three levels of legitimation, a report of the Greek military in February 1948 found that the rural people were passive, "they would not fight for the guerrillas nor would they provide the army with information." A large number of people, though not communists, were "so confused in their ideological thinking" that they were sympathizers. Finally, about 150,000 people followed the "KKE line consciously and actively" and constituted a "potential army" for the DA.[48]

But by late 1948, the national government had developed a stable coalition, and the military was being rejuvenated by General Alexander Papagos. The DA, meanwhile, failed to build up to its desired strength of fifty thousand and increasingly relied on forced conscription and large numbers of women. In the end, only in Macedonia (and among the 1 percent of the Greek population that was ethnically Macedonian) could the communists elicit voluntary commitments. Overall, their opportunity structure had crumbled.[49]

Behind this crumbling lay a communist failure, in their quest for legitimation, to throw any grappling hooks over the summit level of belief. Before World War II, the KKE was irrelevant to Greek politics because of its twin assaults on the traditional dream of the Megali Idea and its modern repudiation of Greece as a democratic state. In its 1931 Central Committee Plenum, for example, the KKE declared: "Greece is an imperialist country which has conquered by force whole regions populated by other nationalities."[50] That the KKE was firmly antimonarchical, in light of these assaults, helped only a little.

On October 30, 1940, Nikos Zakhariadis, the jailed KKE secretary-general, wrote a widely published appeal to the government for a united resistance: "Everyone in the fight, each to his post, victory belongs to Greece and its people."[51] The party had finally identified itself with nationalism, and it was on the back of this appeal that it built up to the high levels it attained in 1944. But the party also began to do things that raised questions about its newfound nationalist credentials. Every time it struck against fellow Greeks—when it mounted a mutiny within the Greek army in Egypt, when it proclaimed a rival government, when it wiped out EKKA in the middle of the Lebanon talks, and, indeed, when it launched Round 2 against the British and its own national government—the party tarnished these claims. By the time of the March 1946 elections, the communists had depleted their stock of nationalist credits and their momentum of crossover points had sharply reversed.[52]

Three issues of belief were pivotal to the changing definition of national legitimacy occasioned by the civil war. The most important was the fashioning of a compromise on the monarchy so as to remove it as a divisive issue in Greek politics. The checkered history of the monarchy had become less checkered. In World War II, the king remained closely allied with the British. Indeed, no major party or leading political figure collaborated with the Germans. Also, the new King Paul I and his beautiful Queen Frederika became enormously popular, and the king played a key role in fashioning the coalition governments of 1947 and 1948.[53] In the midst of war, the king had become a symbol of stability. The Republicans accepted the monarchy and the king accepted the supremacy of parliamentary politics. This compromise gave birth to a solid middle ground for the establishment of a stable political community built upon the monarchy and modern democracy. It also deprived the communists of their one entrée issue into this community.

Second, the ending of the Great Schism (at least until the late 1960s) led to a transformation of the Megali Idea, particularly on the part of intellectuals, to an identification of the plight of Greece in civil war with the global struggle for democracy between East and West.[54] Interestingly enough, this modernization of an irredentist theme of Greater Greece was dramatized most powerfully by the American commitment to the Greek government. The maiden voyage of the Truman Doctrine's global policy of containment set sail for Greece, and it was a flattering tribute to the Megali Idea.

Against these two ideological achievements, finally, the communists dug their own graves during the third round in what amounted to a deal with the devil. Desperate for Soviet military aid, during talks between Yugoslavia and Bulgaria in August 1942, the KKE endorsed the Soviet-sponsored call for a Balkan Federation that would carve out an independent Macedonia from Greece, Bulgaria, and Yugoslavia. This, of course, was nationalist heresy in Greece. It also angered Yugoslavia. In the final break between Moscow and Belgrade in 1948, the KKE again sided with Moscow. But Moscow offered no rewards for this support, and the Yugoslavs, predictably, severed all ties with the KKE. In February 1949, the DA made a desperate appeal for Macedonian recruits. Fourteen thousand signed up, making the communist forces two-thirds Macedonian. With such a success, Greek communists left the KKE in droves.[55] There can be no mystery as to why the communists failed to reach their minimal goal of an army of fifty thousand.

REVOLUTIONARY LEGITIMACY

The quest of the Greek communists for revolutionary legitimacy, then, is a tale of unraveling. What started out as a clear strategy with organizational cohesiveness and a large mass following degenerated into strategic blundering, organizational disintegration, and political isolation.

The communists, first of all, orchestrated a tremendous political performance in World War II. Keeping their options open as to whether ultimately to pursue power through confrontation, infiltration, or parliamentary politics, during the war itself they wrapped themselves tightly in nationalism. Accordingly, they set up a national front to broaden their appeal. In this front, the intent of the KKE was one of concealment, to be "always faceless" (as the People's Revolutionary Party was in the National Liberation Front of Vietnam). Thus as John Loulis has concluded, "the nature of EAM eluded thousands of Greeks." Finally, they used national liberation slogans rather than class grievances in their mobilization campaigns. In the grudging concession of Evangelos Averoff-Tossizza, the party "achieved prestige."[56]

Both in the offensive of Round 2 and in its aftermath, however, the communists showed a crippling hesitation over their three options. In launching the December attacks, did they want to seize full power through climactic confrontation or just secure a prominent role in national politics through infiltration—that is, to follow the Varkiza Agreement and press for the "basic ministries" (interior, justice, and defense)—for gaining power by parliamentary processes?[57] In its confusion, the KKE quickly ruined its chances for the latter two. By destroying EKKA during the Lebanon talks, it put any peaceful hope of gaining the "basic ministries" beyond its reach. By turning on EDES in the middle of the offensive, it ripped open the concealment of its intentions. It also made no attempt to justify its executions while withdrawing from Athens.[58] Finally, by boycotting the elections of 1946, far from discrediting the government, the KKE sealed itself off from the democratic political process. It was a swift fall from nationalist grace.

Thus, for the third round, the only choice remaining to the communists was armed confrontation. In this choice, the question has arisen as to whether the communists followed a Maoist strategy of people's war. Mao's writings were familiar to Greek communists, and Markos Vafiades certainly followed a guerrilla strategy by developing his partisan bands into larger units in the countryside.[59] Whether explicitly Maoist or not, the communists did a poor job of implementing their strategy. Actually, through 1948, the Democratic Army can be credited with holding the government to a stalemate, despite the huge size of the national army and civilian bureaucracy. Indeed, the leadership of General Vafiades earned the grudging admiration of even Averoff-Tossizza, who served in the government during the civil war. He described Vafiades's defense of Vitsi and Grammos in 1948 as brilliant.[60] But Zakhariadis became impatient with Vafiades's guerrilla tactics, and, in January 1949, he was fired. In opting for a conventional stand that would place an even higher premium on outside support, the KKE then doomed this strategy by embracing a Soviet-line position on Macedonia that cut the DA off from Yugoslav and Albanian support as well as from its own people.[61]

Equally important was that Greece lacked a popular base for a people's war strategy. People's war, practically or organizationally speaking, is built on the grievance of land reform. That issue had been stripped from Greece by the Venezelan land reforms of 1917 and 1923. Thus, by the end of the civil war, some 92 percent of Greek farmers were small landholders.[62] Essentially, there was no rural lumpenproletariat in Greece. To be sure, peasant indebtedness and taxes were high, and these burdens did motivate enlistments in the DA.[63] But they joined as individuals, not groups. Greece lacked a grand rural issue for the opportunity-level organization of groups. It was the only Balkan state, for example, without a peasant party.[64] Instead, a process of petite-bourgeoisification had spread from the cities and towns to bind all of Greece into a babble of small tradesmen.[65]

INTERVENTION

The case of Greece illustrates both how determinative a foreign intervention can be in the resolution of an insurgency and how important a country-specific definition of legitimacy can be in analyzing an intervention's impact.

For the Greek communists, Russian assistance and patronage were deemed essential, and proved to be continuously frustrating until, finally, the party was put in an untenable position. As Peter Stavrakis has observed, "the divergence between Soviet and Greek communist interests devastated the KKE."[66] Two factors dominated Russia's unhappy revolutionary performance in Greece. First, regarding Eastern Europe as a whole, there was the famous percentages agreement between Churchill and Stalin in which Stalin conceded a ninety-to-ten role for Britain in Greece in exchange for greater relative Soviet interests elsewhere. Thus, despite an immediate postwar split in the politburo between Andrei Zhdanov and Georgi Malenkov over how vigorously to confront the West, Stalin left this concession on Greece undisturbed in the final round.[67]

Second, this regionally generated restraint was reinforced by the low regard the Soviets held for the Greek communist guerrillas during World War II. Especially in contrast to Tito's audacious 180,000 partisans, the 25,000 men of ELAS were "tactically conservative." Indeed, a Soviet military mission concluded that ELAS was "just a rabble of armed men, not worth supporting."[68] For both reasons, then, Stalin often counseled the KKE to go along with the Greek government. In fact, much of the blame for PEEA's excessive concessions to Papandreou during the Lebanon talks (in the view of the KKE politburo back in Greece) must rest with Stalin's irritated communication to the delegation to cooperate with the government.[69] Then, in dismissing any suggestion of Soviet intervention in Round 2 in Athens, Stalin dismissed the ELAS fighters as "Trotskyites."[70]

Nevertheless, in the final round, Moscow relented a bit and even provided some direct assistance. The Greek communists simultaneously acknowledged this aid and complained of its parsimony.[71] Indirectly, however, the Russians supported the initial deal the KKE made with Yugoslavia, Albania, and Bulgaria to establish a secure supply network in these countries for its campaign in the third round. But the flow of this critical system was broken up by the split between Yugoslavia and Russia and by the final act of Yugoslavia and Albania sealing their borders to the Democratic Army of Greece. Siding with Moscow was a double blunder for the KKE because Moscow had already decided, at the time of the split, to write off the Greek civil war.[72]

Just as the communists foundered on their foreign support, the Greek government would not have survived without first British and then American help. The British, in the first round, favored EDES over ELAS and, in so doing, ensured that the wartime resistance was not totally communist dominated. This allowed the emergence of a postwar noncommunist leadership with valid nationalist credentials. Such a stand was important because in other ways the performance of the British was spotty. The government in exile, for example, lacked any electoral mandate and was unduly beholden to the British. This was embarrassingly underscored by the British suppression of mutinies in the Greek armed forces in Egypt.[73] Nevertheless, on the ground in Greece, the English were popular. When their troops arrived in Athens in October 1944, they were met with the greeting, "[Lord] Byron has come again."[74]

In the second round, the vigorous British military intervention in the thirty-three-day battle prevented a certain communist takeover in a Tet-like offensive. Like Tet, this military victory for the British was not free from political problems. Until the extent of communist atrocities became clear, Churchill had to undergo considerable criticism from the British left. Further, the British leader had more liberal critics to mollify, which he did by retreating from his support of the monarchy and agreeing to let the Greek people decide the king's return in a plebiscite.

In the third round, Western military and economic assistance was pivotal at both interest and opportunity levels. The financial costs of this assistance were staggering. From liberation in 1944 to the end of the civil war, Greece received $2 billion.[75] At the beginning, the responsibility was largely British, and their military assistance from 1944 to 1947 totaled $152 million.[76] The last two years of the war turned into an American undertaking, and U.S. military assistance alone was some $480 million. All told, American aid in those two years amounted to 50 percent of the entire gross national product of Greece.[77]

The institutional programs that followed in this financial tide set in motion three processes — political, socioeconomic, and military — that denied the communists a postwar breakout from their World War II momentum of crossover points. First, politically, this assistance provided Athens the wherewithal to set up its parastate, the bloated civil bureaucracy that presided over reconstruction. From a "normal" civil service of 55,000 in 1940, government administration boasted 144,000 public employees in 1949. When various other forms of quasi-public employment are taken into account, one-third of the nonagricultural labor force was dependent on the state.[78] Simple calculations of individual interest, then, accompanied the expanded state.

This interest was reinforced by the general economic recovery spurred by the financial assistance. During the third round of the civil war, nearly ten thousand new enterprises were formed that doubled industrial production from 1946 to 1950. Though real wages declined some and urban unemployment remained high, inflation was kept in check by the American aid.[79] Thus the stage was set for an important institutional, or opportunity-level, effort of the United States to drive the communists out of organized labor in Greece. Through financial incentives and manipulative efforts by American trade union officials, noncommunists gradually took over the General

Confederation of Labor.[80] In modern terms, thanks to this assistance, the government was thus able to provide societal access and political participation while the communists could not. Essentially, in the last round, the communists were forced out of the cities.

Finally, militarily, in the countryside, the lack of an effective communist rural strategy coupled with an infusion of U.S. aid and a reinvigorated leadership in the Greek army drove the DA and KKE into further isolation. The huge American aid that began to arrive in 1948 made a difference both in equipment and strategy. Rather than send in increments of American troops, the Americans flooded the Greek army with equipment that vastly improved its firepower in the field and built up the size of the Greek armed forces. An important component of this firepower was the provision of Hell diver fighter-bombers that helped to dislodge die-hard communist defenders from Vitsi and Grammos.[81] Also, the government gave its military commander Alexander Papagos a free hand in revamping the army leadership and vigorously prosecuting an American strategy of driving the DA into the Vitsi and Grammos "corrals."[82]

What is also noteworthy about Greece, as opposed to Vietnam, is that this huge flood of American aid did not drown the belief legitimacy of the Greek government. Though the British stumbled over the issue of the monarchy, the United States, with its distinctly republican form of government, was accepted in Greece as more neutral on this issue. Thus the passing of the baton from Britain to America assisted the domestic healing of the Great Schism that was already under way. Indeed, this direct American commitment transformed the Greek civil war into a central act of the West's global struggle with communism, making this assistance a flattering homage to the Megali Idea.

On the international level, while the Soviets engaged in internal discussions over how vigorously to contend with a postwar expansive capitalism, the decisive American intervention under the rubric of the Truman Doctrine precluded Greece from entering into these discussions. At the same time, however, the refusal of the United States to succumb to Greek pleas for direct commitments of American troops deprived the Soviets of an excuse, in their discussions, for similar interventions elsewhere in Europe.[83] Thanks to the strong consensus supporting the Truman Doctrine, U.S. intervention in Greece was blessed domestically on both moral (Vattelian) and balance-of-power (Metternichian) grounds.[84]

DYNAMICS OF THE BALANCES

With respect to the inevitable asymmetries of insurgent warfare, again, in Greece, World War II provided the boost to the communists in achieving a critical mass to get their revolution off the ground. The German victory and occupation removed the Greek government from the field, offering the remaining communists a political opportunity for a positioning for power that had always seemed far beyond their reach, especially under the vigorous repression of Metaxis. They wisely chose to use this opportunity to champion a struggle against the Germans in the name of nationalism. The huge numbers that flocked to the EAM banner and the commanding position achieved by ELAS by 1944 testified to the success of the insurgency in building a momentum of crossover points and to the clear emergence of communism as a major political force in the national life of Greece.

With this wartime accomplishment, the weight of asymmetry at the opportunity level shifted to the returning national government. The government in Athens overcame this enormous disadvantage of the postwar position of a near communist breakout through a process of political and social reinstitutionalization as well as economic growth that was immensely facilitated by Western aid. The various aspects of this process have been touched on, but politically, thanks to the fortuitous communist boycott of national elections in 1946, Republicans and Populists eventually were able to form a government of national union in 1948. The return of the monarchy following the plebiscite in 1946, whose solidifying position was boosted by the accession in 1947 of Paul and Frederika, essentially ended the issue's divisiveness in Greek politics and permitted a revalidating of political authority around the legitimating themes of nationalism and democracy. In this "resynchronization" of legitimacy, the communists gradually were pushed off the stage on which they at one point commanded the spotlight. The falling numbers of communist forces and followers dramatized this shift. From their dominating position in 1944, they were reduced by 1949 to forced recruits and Macedonians in fielding a pitiable force of nineteen thousand for their final stand. In the final round, the crossover points and finally the critical mass built up by the communists crumbled.

The story behind these falling numbers can be illustrated by a balance of errors that tipped heavily at the end against the communists. The government, however, made enough mistakes at the beginning to make it a contest. After a heroic stand against the Italian invasion, the Greek army, against the Germans, failed to coordinate its defense plans with the British, and the two partners were defeated. Nevertheless, in the vacillation of Greek politics between the civil war's first and second rounds, the hollowness of the government in exile had at least one steel thread in men like Papandreou who retained links to the resistance. Then, during the tense period of the Lebanon negotiations, the communists made the mistake of exposing their bad nationalist manners by turning on EKKA in a bloody military attack. The communists stumbled further under Russian pressure to go along with the government in exile.

Despite these communist missteps, the new government that came to Athens in October 1944 was not strong enough to stand on its own. For all their blunderings on the ground in their Round 2 offensive, the only real mistake the communists made was to count on the British not to interfere. Had the British been more cooperative, the Athens offensive would have been a crowning communist victory. The basic achievement of the British in their thwarting action was to create a level playing field for postwar Greek politics. In this setting, the fundamental communist mistake was to boycott the pair of elections in 1946. In so doing, the communists hoped both to discredit the electoral process and to avoid public exposure of the political damage they suffered in the Second Round. The elections, however, held.

Taking up armed struggle in a third round, through early 1949 the Democratic Army made a determined business of fighting, against overwhelming odds, an indecisive government and an ill-prepared army. If not explicitly, an implicit rural-based people's war strategy helped. In 1949, however, the communists delivered to themselves two fatal blows. In the face of the vigorous turnaround of the Greek army, the Democratic Army, first, obligingly abandoned its wily guerrilla formations and tactics in favor of large units concentrated for a conventional stand. For this stand, the KKE then took the suicidal second step of siding with Russia (and its largely rhetorical support) against its matériel supplying Yugoslav and Albanian allies, thereby depriving the DA of the very lifeline it needed for this conventional stand. Because both mistakes were fatal, it is difficult to apportion blame for the communist defeat in Greece between domestic factors of insurgency and foreign factors of intervention. The communists buried themselves in a self-inflicted over-kill of error.

There were, nevertheless, reversibilities in the Greek civil war. By 1940 the Metaxis dictatorship had all but destroyed Greek communism. The intervention of the Germans in World War II, however, drove the government into exile and the army out of the country. The German occupation provided the KKE with a cause around which it could reincarnate its organization and recast its mission. And in the first stunning reversal, on the eve of the war's end, the communists commanded the heights of Greek politics. But the intervention of the British in Athens reversed the communist reversal. The papering over of the great national schism of Greek politics, through both national elections and coalition government, turned the communists back almost to their prewar position. The subsequent and final communist attempt to reverse their fortunes ultimately foundered on their insufficient and not always useful foreign support and advice, the strong foreign assistance received by the government, and their own political and strategic blundering.

From the communist side, the story of the Greek civil war was that of a determined mountain climber scaling a cliff. At one point, he seized a solid purchase on national legitimacy, and then his grip slipped.

Comparisons with Vietnam

China is the case most like Vietnam and Greece is the one least like it. The Megali Idea and the Mandate of Heaven (Thien Minh), as sources of legitimacy, carried dramatically opposite political electrical charges on their respective foreign interventions. Greece, under the buffeting storms of insurgency and intervention, retained a solid middle ground of national politics which commanded the loyalties of established (if not too well-entrenched) political parties. In Vietnam, nothing similar had ever been established. But Vietnam did have land reform as an issue and an aggrieved peasantry around which a people's war strategy could be fashioned. For the purpose of lessons, the case of Greece highlights three issues: legitimacy and intervention, elections and political community, and revolutionary strategy.

Chapter 2 discussed legitimacy as a general concept particularly defined in each society. The traditional concept of the Megali Idea coupled with the modern beckoning of a fuller democracy accommodated an enormous Western intervention, bolstering opportunity-level commitments to the government without endangering the legitimacy of belief in the government. The American assistance, in particular, justified as a common Western crusade by the Truman Doctrine, played up to a Greek sense of pride in being on a global stage that provided modern justification to the Megali Idea.[85] In Vietnam, on the contrary, a similar scale of American assistance undermined belief in the Saigon regime's right to rule despite the improvements at the opportunity level. Unlike the Megali Idea, Thien Minh was not flattered by this dependence and attention; it was ashamed.

A second critical issue is that in stark contrast to both Vietnam and China, Greece had a solid political and economic middle ground regarding both opportunity and belief, upon which a national community could be built in the final third round. During World War II, there were at least some elements of established political groups in the resistance, and, unlike China and Vietnam, none of them collaborated. In particular, the monarchy avoided any embarrassing repeat of World War I and kept its hands clean for a brighter future after this war. The two elections of 1946 essentially confirmed this community, and the subsequent coalition government of national union sealed the communists from any entrance to it. It must be admitted that both this coalition and this community were often very tenuous. The communists may well have broken this seal with more successes on the battlefield.

Thus the communist failure in military strategy dealt the deathblow to the KKE not only militarily but politically as well. Though some have argued that the DA was following the rough outlines of a Maoist people's war strategy, it was, in any case, poorly done overall and definitively abandoned with the firing of Markos Vafiades. In the third round, the lack of a clear overarching strategy caught the communists without effective counters to the opportunity-level government organization-building in the cities and towns. They held aloof from the electoral forms of political participation and lacked the resources, strategy, and appeal to provide a societal access of their own. In the countryside, normally a more fertile field for insurgency except for some unique political conditions in Greece, the communists gradually isolated themselves from the Greek national peasantry in favor of a strategy designed to win foreign support for a conventional strategy that forced them to champion the cause of ethnic Macedonians.

During the "bloody December" of 1944 in Athens, there was a true Tet in Greece. But in 1949, when a Dienbienphu came to Vitsi and Grammos, it was the communists who were inside the beleaguered barricades. Put another way, when the guerrillas were defeated in Greece, as they were also defeated in Vietnam, there was, in Greece, no regular North Vietnamese army to slam across the demilitarized zone to the rescue. There were only donkey trails to Albania.

Chapter 8

THE PHILIPPINES, 1946–1956: LIBERATION DEFLECTED

Historical Setting

Shortly after the Greek communists faded away into Albania and Yugoslavia, an uprising of the communist Huks (actually Hukbong Mapagpalaya ng Bayan—People's Liberation Army) reached its peak in the Philippines. On March 20, 1950, the politburo in Manila declared that a "revolutionary situation" existed thanks both to the "illegitimacy" of the presidential election of 1949 and to the size of the party's political and military organization. Fifteen thousand Huk fighters were in the field supported by a network of one hundred thousand communist party activists and perhaps another half million sympathizers.[1] One wave of an offensive in March overran two towns and eighteen villages in Central Luzon, and, in a second wave in August, Huk forces swept into two provincial capitals and held a police base long enough to conduct a massacre at the camp hospital.[2]

Although it lacks a mainland, the Philippine Islands possess the same rugged and difficult terrain for people's war as does Greece. Two-thirds of it is either hilly, covered with jungles, or both. Its seven thousand islands, however, have made it difficult to hold in one political piece. Though 94 percent of the people live on just eleven of these islands and some 85 percent of the population are ethnically Malay and Indonesian (what the Spanish called Indios) and three-fourths were rural in 1948, several differences undermine such homogeneous statistics.[3] The eleven populated islands divide into three distinct regions: the big island of Luzon (42,000 square miles out of 116,000 for the whole country) in the north, a belt of middling sized islands across the center collectively known as the Visayas, and the second big island of Mindanao (38,000 square miles) in the south.[4] Further, these ethnically homogeneous Malays and Indonesians came in scattered tribal migrations over the centuries. Eventually, eight major languages developed around these tribal groups. In 1960, Tagalog, the largest as the mother tongue of 20 percent of the population (though some 37 percent could speak it), had to share honors on Luzon with Iloko (14 percent), Bikol (18 percent), and Pampanga (3.7 percent), as well as with the three Bisayan languages of the Visayas (counting for 44 percent of the population).[5] Finally, at the time of the insurgency, Filipinos were unequally divided economically and geographically. The rich made up 5 percent of the population, the poor, in both city and countryside, 70 percent, and those in between 25 percent.[6] Onto Luzon crowded nearly half the population (47.3 percent), while the Visayas held 34 percent and Mindanao only 12 percent.[7]

Beyond these divisive statistics, Philippine history has provided for no common Filipino identity. The Spanish conquest began in 1565, aborting a process of political centralization that was just beginning under the Muslim sultans of Sulu and Borneo. Manila, their largest outpost, had just two thousand people.[8] For purposes of traditional legitimacy, then, the Filipinos had no glorious precolonial past to summon up for nationalist consecration.

What the Spanish found was a quasi-feudal system of hierarchical relations among the *datus* (political chiefs and landowners), *maharlikas* (independent warriors who served their *datus* and held land), and two gradations of economic dependents. These communities, or *barangays*, were held together by the moral debt of *utang na loob*, which constituted the vast network of gratitude community members owed for services mutually rendered but personalized by allegiance to the *datu*. To be insufficiently grateful at key moments when loyalty was required was to risk the dread accusation of *walang hiya* (shamelessness).[9] The Spanish did little to disturb this system. They stopped the incessant warring among the *datus*, incorporating them as their governors and tax collectors. Along with the Spanish priests who fanned out from Manila on God's evangelical business, the *datus* and *maharlikas* became the *principales* of the colony, its ruling local elite. Through this network, the Spanish converted 80 percent of the population to Roman Catholicism, binding the people in settlement, soul, and taxation to a

nationwide network of churches and haciendas. Yet they divided the islanders in speech. The government taught Spanish only to its officials, and, in
prohibiting the Indios from leaving their *barangays* (now called *poblacións*),
separated their languages from a common communicable base.[10]

The nineteenth century reverberated with shocks that brought fundamental changes to Spain's Philippines. Stripped of its New World colonies
in the 1820s, Madrid suddenly found the Philippines important as more
than a spiritual outpost. The islands were opened up to world trade as lands
were cleared for a host of commercial and agricultural enterprises. Exports
jumped from 4 million pesos in 1841 to 33 million in 1894, and Manila grew
to a metropolis of 220,000 by century's end.[11] Politically, the Spaniards gin-
gerly experimented with the liberalism of Europe by beginning public education in the islands and discussing some form of Filipino representation in
the Spanish Cortes in Madrid.

As a modern society began to emerge, the definition and direction of
Filipino consciousness became a central question. The first expressions were
narrow: a Filipino was a European Spaniard born in the Philippines.[12] Brief
military revolts erupted in 1821 and 1872 over keeping the officer corps
Spanish. When the Jesuits returned in 1859 (after being forced out earlier by
Charles III), it was in part to restore positions in the church to Europeans.
Three resisting local priests became the first martyrs as "Filipinos" in 1872.
But the economic growth in the nineteenth century brought a more expansive view of the term from two overlapping quarters. First, the commercial-
ization of the economy created a new social and economic intermediary between the Indios and these business haciendas, the Inquilinos, who were the
beginnings of a middle class and who, politically, gradually became a part
of the *principales* previously dominated by the *datus*. Second, socially these
vigorous newcomers were mainly Chinese mestizos who by 1900 numbered
5 percent of the population.[13] Thus the local *principales* began to develop a
national view, and, influenced by the Propaganda Movement in Spain, those
who saw themselves as Filipinos, in wanting full rights as Spaniards in the
Cortes, called themselves *ilustrados*.

Their chief spokesman was José Rizal, but other islanders, such as Andrès
Bonifacio and Emilio Aguinaldo, parted with the *ilustrados* and saw the Philippines as an independent nation. As David Sturtevant has observed, had
the Spaniards accommodated themselves to the *ilustrados*, they might have
held on to the islands.[14] The Spanish, however, executed Rizal for his imper-
tinent definition, and Bonifacio and Aguinaldo revolted for their even more
insolent one in 1896. By 1898, when the American admiral George Dewey
sailed into Manila Bay to take the Philippines as a prize in the Spanish-
American War, the Spanish were about to be overthrown on the ground by
Filipinos.

The Americans inserted their rule into this confusion and definitional wedge but only after suppressing a tenacious insurrection led by Aguinaldo from 1899 to 1902. The Americans won through the combination of General Arthur MacArthur's mailed fist and William Howard Taft's deft political glove. MacArthur attacked Aguinaldo from two sides in Central Luzon and then hit him in the rear with an amphibious landing of marines at Lingayen Gulf.[15] Aguinaldo broke up his forces and fled deep into the mountains, only to be caught in a daring raid by Colonel Frederick Funston as a result of an intelligence windfall.[16] Officially, four thousand American soldiers and twenty thousand *insurrectos* were killed, as were at least two hundred thousand civilians.[17]

Politically, Taft realized, as the Spaniards had not, that American rule would have to be based on an "attraction" of "the Philippines for the Filipinos." By Filipinos Taft meant the *ilustrado* elite that was giving Aguinaldo's insurrection some nationalist luster but who were rapidly becoming disenchanted with the movement's militarist cast. Taft deliberately recalled the reformist dreams of José Rizal and promised that they could be realized under American rule. In exchange, the "attracted" *ilustrados* "demanded from the alien rulers good government for the Philippines."[18]

In attempting to fashion a political community "in our image," the American raj was dedicated to democratic principles of constitutional rule that had five foundations. First, the Americans implemented their principle of the separation of church and state that allowed them deftly to strip the Catholic church of its political functions and even confiscate some of its large landholdings while preserving for the church its role as a source of unifying spiritual values. Second, the centerpiece of the American imperium was its expansion of public education in English. Half the colonial budget went into this system. As early as 1910 more Filipinos knew English than any other language compared with the less than 2 percent who had been privileged to know Spanish. By the 1930s more than half the population was literate. The Filipinos had a common language once again, which was a vehicle for a widespread exposure to democratic political values.[19] Third, the Filipinos were allowed to practice these values through the establishment of political parties and nationwide elections. The Federalist party was founded in 1900 by *ilustrados* with a platform indistinguishable from the Propaganda Movement, and the Nationalist party was started in 1907 with a platform calling for eventual independence.[20] The first national elections were held in 1907, and their regularity made political campaigning the fiestas of American rule. In 1946, the franchise (based on literacy) had expanded to nearly half the adult population.[21] Fourth, the Americans were quicker than any other colonial power to make good on the promise of a "Philippines for the Filipinos." By 1912 and 1913, over 90 percent of the municipal and provincial offices were filled by Filipinos as were over half of the insular-wide positions. Both houses of the colonial legislature and even the ruling Philippines Commission had Filipino majorities. Under a Commonwealth Constitution of 1935, the Filipinos elected their own president and were promised independence in ten years.[22]

These ruling Filipinos were almost exclusively drawn from the *principales* of the Spanish era. This, of course, was the fifth principle, or fundamental deal, of American rule: that Americans would continue the Spanish practice of ruling through the Filipino elite. The Americans were fully aware of its negative features and even had a bad word for it, *caciquism* ("bossism"). Indirectly, they sought to undermine this stranglehold of the elite through education and expansion of the franchise. This created a social, political, and economic leakiness to Philippine society that was more democratic than the elite wanted. David Sturtevant has estimated that some 20 percent of the population directly benefited from American rule (way up from the 2 to 3 percent under the Spanish), but for the rest of the population in the countryside these visible benefits only made their stagnation seem worse.[23] This faltering fifth foundation, then, opened up a wedge for agrarian protest and a further expansion of Filipino identity.

The landed elites were attracted to the modern sectors politically and economically developed by the Americans, but the tenant farmers were excluded. Many landowners moved to the towns and cities, abandoning their traditional *utang na loob* responsibilities to the rising middle-class intermediaries of the late nineteenth century, the Inquilinos, and their modern financial institutions. Under the old order, tenants enjoyed the security of easy access to credit in exchange for personal services to the landowner. In traditional terms, the peasants were left stranded as they faced a new order of cash loans from Inquilinos at cruel interest rates.[24]

As a result of this breakdown of rural society, the barrios of Central Luzon roiled in armed protest and political agitation. In the 1920s a series of rural revolts erupted under cultic leaders that were all vigorously suppressed by the Philippine constabulary. The most spectacular of these armed uprisings was the May 2–3, 1935, insurrection of the Sakdalists. They were organized as a pro-Japanese political party in 1933 and claimed a membership of three hundred thousand. In the 1934 elections they won some local offices in Luzon as well as three congressional seats. They boycotted the vote on the constitution. Instead, sixty-five thousand mostly unarmed men seized several towns in Central Luzon, but they were suppressed by the constabulary in a little more than a day.[25]

Politically, the peasants vented their grievances in the 1930s through strikes organized by their unions to protest against the unilateral changes in tenancy relationships imposed by the landowners. The largest of these was the National Society of Peasants in the Philippines (KPMP), which, by the late 1930s, had the support of perhaps half the peasantry in Central Luzon. The 1940 elections in particular demonstrated the growing political strength of the peasantry. The Popular Front ticket consisting of these rural labor unions, socialists, and communists won nine mayoralty races and majorities on eight municipal councils.[26]

In this growing politicization of the countryside, the communists came to play an increasingly prominent role. The Communist Party of the Philippines, or Partido Komunista ng Pilipinas (PKP) was founded on August 26, 1930, under the direction of the Comintern. The party, however, was beset with difficulties from the beginning. The secretary-general, Crisanto Evangelista, was arrested in 1931. The next year the party was outlawed by the Philippine Supreme Court and survived only under the cover of various front organizations. The Socialist party was formed in 1933 and had strong communist leanings. Its constitution accepted the principles of scientific socialism as enunciated by Marx, Engels, Lenin, and Stalin. The leader, though, was the quixotic Pedro Abad Santos, who admired Gandhi, Leon Blum, and Norman Thomas as much as Marx, and whose main objective was land reform. Nevertheless, the outlawed communists and two affiliated peasant unions, the KPMP and AMT, joined the Socialist party. These mergers essentially permitted a communist takeover of the party, yet noncommunists did retain powerful positions. Santos, for example, became vice-chairman. Although this consolidation strengthened the hand of the PKP in rural politics, the diluting presence of noncommunist leaders and organizations also set the stage for a history of party disunity.[27]

The bombing of Pearl Harbor on December 7, 1941, brought World War II to the Pacific, and the rapid collapse of the American defense of the Philippines, despite a brave stand at Corregidor, left the islands under the yoke of Japanese occupation. As in other countries, the communists rose to the occasion. In February 1942 the PKP organized a United Front among peasant and urban groups under the leadership of Dr. Vicente Lava, the new PKP secretary-general. On March 19, 1942, the Front established a military arm, known as the Huk, with Luis Taruc as commander. Taruc was a peasant leader from Pampanga and a protégé of his fellow Pampangan Pedro Santos.[28]

The Huks, however, were only one of several guerrilla commands. In Luzon alone there were a dozen separate guerrilla organizations. By the end of 1944, 180,000 Filipinos were serving in the resistance, and the loyalty of all of these fighters, except the Huks, was to General Douglas MacArthur and the late Philippine president Manuel Quezon. Only one-sixth, or 30,000, were Huks. Nevertheless, primarily because of an order from MacArthur to avoid combat, the Huks, who ignored the order, were the most active.

Japanese reprisals were quick and brutal, and their 400,000-man occupying force (ten times their force in Indochina) persuaded even the Huks to lie low by the end of 1943.[29]

The only hope left to the Filipinos was MacArthur's promise: "I shall return." He did. Commanding an invasion force of 280,000, he captured Manila in March 1945 after a month's heavy fighting, which, excluding D-Day, was the largest American land campaign of the war. One hundred thousand Filipino civilians were killed by the Japanese in their Manila defeat.[30] All told, perhaps as many as 1.1 million Filipinos lost their lives in World War II.[31] More than just the numbers in the nine-month campaign — 200,000 Japanese were killed at a cost of only 8,000 American lives — Mac-Arthur's redeemed pledge became the heroic epic of the Philippines, and those who fought for him in the resistance "shed the psychology of being colonial subjects."[32]

The euphoria of liberation, however, quickly wore off as the political atmosphere in the Philippines turned poisonous over three issues that finally goaded the Huks into armed revolt against the independent government. The first was the failure of American authorities to recognize Huk units. Though Huk units helped prepare the way for the returning GIs, after liberation, the Americans turned on them, arresting their leaders and disarming the men. In one extreme instance, the Malolos massacre, American officers looked the other way while Philippine soldiers gunned down 105 disarmed Huks.[33] Despite the creditable record of the Huks during the war, other resistance units disliked them both for their political organizations and for their refusal to come under MacArthur's command. The Filipino elite was implacably opposed to the Huks. Nevertheless, four Huk units were eventually extended recognition for veterans benefits, and, despite pleas by the elite for their suppression, MacArthur refused: "I haven't the heart to go after them. If I worked in those sugar fields, I'd probably be a Huk myself."[34]

The second issue was the very sensitive question of collaboration. It was sensitive because of the harshness of the Japanese rule and because "the list of collaborationists in Manila read like an honor roll of prewar Filipino leaders."[35] MacArthur had vowed to punish all collaborators, but once in Manila he lost heart a second time. Among the five thousand interned collaborators was Manuel Roxas, his close personal friend. Fervently insisting that Roxas had performed heroic services as a double agent for the resistance, MacArthur rehabilitated his comrade.[36] Roxas went on to win the 1946 presidential election and promptly pardoned all collaborators. Quite naturally, this act stirred up a cloud of resentment among all who had resisted the Japanese.

The smoldering third issue was the growing rural unrest caused by a rise in tenancy and a continued dispute over its terms. From 1903 to 1939 the population of the Philippines grew from 7 to 16 million, and by 1948 it had reached 19.2 million.[37] Nowhere was this pressure felt more strongly than in the four provinces of Central Luzon. Thus, though nationally the tenancy rate grew from 20 to 37 percent from 1918 to 1948, in Central Luzon the corresponding figures were 29 to 75 percent.[38] When landowners returned to their properties after the war, they immediately became involved in disputes with their tenants over the still unsettled issues of crop shares, interest rates, and evictions.

Such a tempest is the perfect breeding ground for a critical mass for revolution, and the communists were quick to take up the Leninist call to organization. While the fighting was still raging in Manila during March 1945, they put together the Committee of Labor Organizations (CLO), which served as the nucleus for a series of trade unions eventually representing one hundred thousand members, one-fifth of the urban labor force.[39] On the rural front, they combined two unions into the National Peasants Union (PKM). Its membership grew to five hundred thousand, making it by far the country's largest peasant organization.[40]

These resentments also made excellent political fodder for the Democratic Alliance, which was formed in July 1945 as a liberal political movement devoted to agrarian reform and bringing collaborators to book. Though communists joined the alliance as part of their united front strategy, it was not a communist-controlled organization. The alliance did very well in the April 1946 elections, winning six congressional races. One of the victors was Luis Taruc, the former Huk commander. The triumph, however, turned bittersweet when the six were unseated by the full Congress, and, despite the outrage over this act, the alliance fell apart by the November 1947 elections.[41]

Nevertheless, the alliance's brief existence marked a successful effort in bringing the peasantry into the national political process, and the unseating of its congressmen was the first of two acts in 1946 that triggered the second rising of the Huks. The other, the immediate causus belli, was the slaying of Juan Feleo, a communist and the leader of the PKM, on August 24 by military police. Luis Taruc returned to the barrios and called the Huk guerrillas to reactivate their two-hundred-man squadrons. Until the end of 1949 the PKP was of two minds on how to proceed politically. One faction wanted to continue a legal struggle as well while the other argued that the armed struggle of the Huks was the only course left.[42] They did both. To manage these two struggles, until 1950 the communists had two parallel politburos, one in Manila and one in Central Luzon.[43]

President Roxas (elected in April 1946) responded to the insurgency in the fall both with an iron fist, vowing to crush it in sixty days, and with a velvet glove, promising to enact a "70:30" law for the tenant farmers. But the insurgency continued inconclusively for two years. In March 1948 Roxas outlawed the National Peasants Union and the Huks, but he died the next month. The new president, former vice-president Elpidio Quirino, sought to end the insurgency politically by granting a general amnesty over the summer and negotiating a settlement with Luis Taruc. The talks got nowhere, and the insurgency continued along its irresolute course.[44]

When Quirino was elected president in the November 1949 elections, however, the fraud and brutality that accompanied this polling galvanized the Huks into stronger action. By 1948, the three Lava brothers had taken firm control of the Communist party organizations and Huk commands and in 1950 (over some dissent from Luis Taruc) declared that a "revolutionary situation" existed. Their plans were ambitious. They hoped by the end of 1951 to expand the Huk forces to 172,000 supported by a mass base of 2.5 million sympathizers and to wage mobile war against the Manila regime. After this, they planned to establish provisional revolutionary governments in liberated areas, redistribute land, and build the Huks into a conventional military force for a final attack on the government. It was to have been a textbook people's war.[45] But despite their two waves of attacks in 1950, the Huks could not sustain the pace or build any momentum of crossover points.

Much of the credit for breaking their stride belongs to the reinvigorated Philippine Defense Department under its new secretary, Ramon Magsaysay, a congressman and former guerrilla leader, who took office in September 1950. Before his accession, the brunt of the fighting had been borne by the Philippine constabulary and military police units. The Armed Forces of the Philippines (AFP) had deployed only two infantry battalions against the Huks. Magsaysay got the defense budget tripled and immediately reorganized the department and its war strategy. The Philippine constabulary was both reduced in strength (to 7,600) and put under AFP control. The released men were absorbed into the AFP, which by 1951 had expanded to 53,700 men. These men, in turn, were reorganized into twenty-six mobile Basic Combat Teams (BCT) battalions of 1,000 fighting men each. Civil Guards remained in the *barrios* for static defense, and, adding to the speed and small unit maneuverability of the BCTs, 7,700 men were organized into Scout Ranger Teams (of five to ten men each) and special intelligence units.[46]

Magsaysay did not waste time in pursuing his adversaries. His first blow was an intelligence raid in Manila on October 18, 1950, that netted 105 communist leaders, including the entire Manila branch of the politburo. This effectively ended the urban struggle, leaving the Huks in Central Luzon to carry on alone.[47] In the field that year, BCT units crisscrossed "Huklandia" (the four rice-growing provinces of Central Luzon) in repeated battalion- and company-sized sweeps, killing Huks at the rate of 50 a week for a year-end total of 2,500.[48] By 1953 the back of the resistance was broken. In the spring of 1954, during a sweep through the field headquarters of the Huks, the "supremo" himself, Luis Taruc, surrendered. Three years later, with most of their leaders captured, Huk forces numbered only 600 men in scattered and isolated bands, and in 1958, their continued pursuit was turned over to the municipal police. Official casualties in the Huk uprising stood at 31,465 for the Huks (9,695 killed, 1,635 wounded, 4,269 prisoners, and, significantly, 15,866 who defected) and 2,994 for the government (1,578 killed and 1,416 wounded).[49]

The Huks were not suppressed by military measures alone. A series of agrarian reform measures and a relegitimation of national elections in 1951 and 1953 further deflected and finally sealed the doom of the Huk uprising. The reform that drew the most attention was Magsaysay's Economic Development Corps (EDCOR), a program that offered amnestied Huks twenty-five acres and a house on Mindanao. Though the operation was on a small scale — only 250 Huk families were actually given land — symbolically it deprived the Huks of a monopoly on their slogan "land for the landless."[50] More widespread programs followed. Some reforms came as a result of U.S. pressure in the Quirino-Foster Agreement of 1950, and others grew out of the Agricultural Tenancy Act of 1954 and the Land Tenure Act of 1955. David Wurfel has estimated that seven hundred thousand tenants benefited from these measures.[51]

In addition, when the congressional elections of 1951 came, the army surprised everyone with its evenhanded supervision of them. Earning credit for this, Magsaysay bolted from the Liberal party in 1952 and ran for president in 1953 under the Nacionalista banner. In an inspired campaign, he swept everything, including the boycotting Huks, by carrying forty-eight of fifty-two provinces. Magsaysay's landslide was significant because it rested not so much on a switch in voter sentiment as on the massive numbers of peasants newly brought into the political process by his barrio campaign.[52]

Militarily and politically, then, as a PKP spokesman acknowledged, "Between 1950 and 1956, under the impact of the imperialist counter-offensive, the Huk armed struggle was defeated."[53]

Framework Analysis

NATIONAL LEGITIMACY

At the level of interest, what was at stake, particularly for the peasantry of Central Luzon, was the viability of the traditional patron-client relationship of *utang na loob* and *compadrazgo*. (The latter is a Catholic custom built on blood compacts whereby a family finds godparents for its children. It acts as a booster to *utang na loob* in that clients seek powerful patrons as godparents and patrons accept, reciprocally, to expand their influence. Such fictive-kinship ties crisscross the islands).[54] Before World War II, population pressures, the rapid urbanization around Manila and other cities, and the growth of a modern, capitalist intermediate economic sector created a crisis in the traditional terms of personal peasant security. During the war, both the Huks and noncommunist resistance groups had built up followings in the countryside. The Huks had promised "land to the landless" after the war and the American-led resistance had been issued IOUs and assurances of titles to their land. Upon MacArthur's heroic return, the prosaic questions animating the peasantry were whether they would get compensation for their sufferings and commitments during World War II and what kind of relationship with landlords they could count on when they went back to working the land.

Though the Americans did pay out some $400 million in compensation for IOU and other claims, the easy counterfeiting of these IOUs led to inflated claims, mistaken awards, and tragic denials.[55] Further, the independent government did a poor job of processing land title applications. The Huks, by contrast, could not give out any land until they had taken it in the first place.

In more modern material terms, the devastation and loss of life in the Philippines during the war were enormous. The only Allied city whose level of destruction equaled that of Manila (80 percent of the buildings leveled) was Warsaw.[56] The years from 1946 to 1950, then, were dominated by rebuilding the cities, reviving the economy, and establishing the new government. The communists, in turn, sought to reach people through their mass actions, as they had been doing in the 1930s, in both the countryside and the huge urban area of Metro Manila with its one million inhabitants.[57] By 1950 most of the economy had recovered, and the period from 1951 to 1956 was one of great growth in which the boats of all groups—urban and rural— rose. Agricultural production grew at a rate of 7.2 percent a year and urban manufacturing by 12.1 percent.[58] During this period, average agricultural wages increased a total of 25 percent. Though urban wages declined some, a minimum wage law passed in 1951 was vigorously enforced bringing some 1.6 million workers under its protection.[59] By the 1950s, then, the advantages of this modern material security had shifted to the government.

As the Huks took up arms again, both sides, at the opportunity level, energetically sought committed followers. Their organizations and institutions were like competitive magnets trying to draw the people to their side of the struggle. The Huks had ambitious plans of creating loyalties through two parallel structures: one, in the countryside, of peasant unions and rural support groups for the Huk squadrons; and the other, in the cities, of labor unions that would provide the Communist party a following that would struggle politically against the two major parties. At the height of the rebellion, the Huks collected taxes, set up schools, and fielded highly mobile guerrilla squadrons that in 1950 were overrunning provincial towns. Concentrated in the Pampagueno- and Tagalog-speaking areas of Central Luzon, they had, nevertheless, made efforts to expand into Mindanao and the Visayan islands of Panay and Negros, though the government was quickly able to break up these moves.[60]

But it was at this level of opportunity that the government made its most concerted efforts both in traditional and modern terms. In a modern sense, the government approach was one of nation-building: of setting up institutions infused with funds for economic growth that would create the strong middle class that citizens as long ago as Aristotle had said would be the bulwark against revolution. As Robert Stephens pointed out, however, the peasants wanted social justice even more than general economic growth.[61] Sometimes directly, and often by osmosis, nevertheless, the nation-building efforts that expanded both societal access and political participation did alleviate the rural injustices felt by the peasantry. Government efforts across three broad fronts deflected the Huks from realizing their ambitious plans: a vastly improved military performance, a panoply of programs improving societal access in both rural and urban areas, and the elections of 1951 and 1953 that brought political participation to the barrios.

First, Magsaysay's reorganization of the AFP that specifically brought the Philippine constabulary under army control and curtailed the harassment of the peasantry reduced the immediate source of local alienation from the government. Further, the BCT organization gave the AFP the mobility to attack Huk units at both large and small unit levels, leaving static duties to the constabulary and civil guards. As defense minister, Magsaysay, like Papagos in Greece, effected major changes in leadership, giving the BCTs aggressive commanders such as Napoleon Valeriano.[62] Quirino, Magsaysay's thoroughly jealous president, meant to disparage his defense minister with the epithet, "He is only good for killing Huks."[63] It wasn't just the killing; Magsaysay's continual sweeps kept the Huks off balance and prevented them from establishing the intelligence monopoly so critical for an insurgent force in building self-sustaining crossover points. At such a delicate transitional phase, ambivalent peasant sentiments like the following were fatal: "I sympathized with the Huks, but the police were always passing through. I couldn't afford to take risks. I gave rice to the guerrillas and answered the cops truthfully."[64]

Second, of all the programs designed to undercut the Huks, the most symbolic was EDCOR. Despite its meager results, it represented a government commitment to the peasantry. By itself it might have been a hollow shell, but the government made good on its commitment in other ways. Laws establishing a basic crop split and land tenancy rights not only were passed but were then enforced by rural judges. Though the government was slow to establish peasant organizations to replace the outlawed communist PKM, 225,000 peasants did join cooperatives for 8 percent loans and guaranteed prices.[65] In a sense, a new *utang na loob* was set up by the government.

Again, as in Greece, the communists were shut out of the cities. In Manila, the communists attached great importance to promoting the CLO among workers and to working out "united front" electoral alliances. But the government outlawed the CLO in 1951 and, in the Industrial Peace Act of 1953, provided for independent labor unions with democratic rules of governance and strengthened the bargaining position of unions against management. In three years the number of unions jumped from 838 to 2,000. With a minimum wage law and better bargaining terms, the number of strikes rose as workers showed their commitments to, and preference for, this form of opportunity-level struggle.[66]

Finally, the national elections of 1951 and 1953 have been given the most credit for turning aside the Huk rebellion. What is curious, however, is that even these fair elections, at the opportunity level, worked mainly in a traditional way. Parties and electioneering were orchestrated through the traditional mechanisms of *utang na loob* and *compadrazgo*. For example, in Magsaysay's first congressional campaign in 1945 under the Liberal party banner, his victory was built on a nucleus of former resistance fighters for whom, as their *datu*, he promised to get veterans benefits. The vote was the grateful moral payment of his constituents.[67] In his 1953 presidential race, Magsaysay spread a web of *utang na loob* so vast that patron-client ties were replaced by a state-client tie.[68] Though, in Stanley Karnow's words, "his restless energy, uncommon honesty and personal charisma restored the faith of the population in government," [69] such a traditional system is vulnerable because too much depended on the quality of the man at the apex of the network. In more modern terms, Filipino political parties as institutions amounted to little more than expanding and contracting patronage networks that "lacked both the ideological and organizational basis to survive." [70]

Thus the belief level was problematic for both sides. Especially in traditional terms, Filipinos lack a clear formulary of national legitimacy. In modern terms, the 1935 constitution gave the Philippines a liberal democratic regime based on American political values disseminated by the system of public education. But these principles had not been effectively translated into social and economic reforms for the peasantry. Nor had the American period of rule provided a definitional answer to the nationalist question of who was a Filipino and of what Filipino nationalism consisted. In the Philippines, there were groups; there were values; there were heroes; but, as Lee Young Leng has observed, there was no binding "state idea." [71] At this level, *utang na loob* and *compadrazgo*, which put a personalized stamp to politics, were more of a hindrance than a help.

Important traditions and political associations have clustered around tribal and linguistic loyalties. Tagalogs, who live in and around Manila, have become dominant because of their role in fighting the Spaniards and then in ruling through the Americans. The Pampaguenos of Central Luzon have had a tense relationship with Tagalogs and have been resented by all Filipinos for their close collaboration with the Spaniards. The Visayans of the middle islands have always held aloof from the rivalries of Luzon. The Muslim tribes of Mindanao and the southern islands were never fully incorporated into Spanish, American, or even subsequent Philippine rule. Also, the Pampangan/Tagalog composition of the Huks created some awkwardness both internally and externally.[72]

Yet mitigating these group cleavages has been the essential leakiness of Philippine society. Despite the clannishness of most groups, Tagalogs and Ilocanos (from Northern Luzon) have a counter pattern of settling all over the islands. In addition, *utang na loob* and *compadrazgo* have created loyalties cutting across all groups. Finally, the lingua franca of English forms the silk to these "leaking" webs.[73] Thus, even though there have been no clear lines of ethnic and social conflict, such a social mosaic has made the organization of a common purpose or the definition of a single national identity a difficult task indeed. It facilitated Spanish rule and American rule on the one hand, just as it allowed frequent rebellion on the other. But it could not create anything larger. In his failure to organize a resistance to the Spaniards, the Sultan Suleiman's lament in 1565 remains the plague of Filipino politics: "You must understand that there is no sole authority in this land. Everyone has his own opinions and does what he likes."[74]

During the Huk rebellion, the values of Filipinos clustered around the unlikely trinity of, first, Roman Catholicism from Spain, second, democratic constitutional politics from the United States, which were, third, socially managed by the traditional Philippine pyramid of *utang na loob*. Thus legitimacy in the Philippines was grounded not in the necessity or virtue of a traditional authority system of patron and client, but of national politics running according to American constitutional rules in which competing patron-client networks masked as modern political parties conducted periodic electoral rituals as if they were secular fiestas.

Defining and defending both the historical and ideological sources for this trinity, however, has been a big problem. For the government, did it hearken back to José Rizal and the benefits of American rule? Perhaps. But where was there anything Filipino in this? José Rizal wrote a book called *Noli Me Tangere* (the motto of Boston's Sons of Liberty), had an English wife, and led a movement, the Propagandists, which wanted Filipinos to be accepted as Spaniards.[75] For the Huks, where were the heroes or the indigenous civilization untainted by contact with Western colonialism? Having led the fight against both the Spaniards and the Americans, Emilio Aguinaldo deserves to be treated as a genuine national hero. Indeed, one Filipino historian has proclaimed him the Philippine Napoleon.[76] But his behavior was erratic, and his reputation remains controversial among Filipinos.[77] In the Philippine insurrection, after being hunted down and captured by the dashing Colonel Frederick Funston, he praised his captors with the damning words: "Is there no limit to what you Americans can do!"[78]

Not liking the idea of an elite anyway, an alternative route to nationalism for radical historians has been to glorify the patriotic fervor of the Philippine masses resisting colonialist oppression against the repeated treachery of their own elite.[79] Glenn May has noted that at least in the Philippine-American War, the masses stayed a full step behind the elite leaders of the insurrection. When the leaders gave up, so did the masses.[80]

More generally, taking a stand on the legacy of American rule was not easy. Certainly there were negative features, most notably the failure to redress the economic cleavages in the countryside, but, compared with other colonial regimes, the Yankee imperium lacked obvious targets. It had no odious plantation labor recruiters as the French did in Indochina; there was no equivalent to the cynical British opium trade; and, more to the point, there were no exploitative friar estates as there were in Central Luzon during Spanish rule. Indeed, four of its five foundations (separation of church and state, public education, parties and elections, and "good" administrative government) stood as positive legacies by any reckoning. Also, at the international level, it was readily apparent that there were predatory wolves lurking in the shadows of the American campfire. For such interwar leaders as Sergio Osmena and Manuel Quezon, this comparative preference for Washington over such alternatives as the Germans, British, Dutch, Chinese, or Japanese became an *ultima ratio* for American rule.[81] This preference was all too graphically confirmed by the brutal Japanese occupation.

Because of this, the one sensitive belief-level issue the Huks seized on immediately after the war was the collaboration of the elite. Indeed, the length of the list of prewar leaders who served the Japanese was a plain embarrassment: seven of the eleven-member Commonwealth Cabinet, ten of twenty-four senators, one-third of the representatives, virtually the entire judiciary, and 80 percent of the Philippine army's officers.[82] Three complicating factors, however, prevented the communists from getting a firm grip on this issue. First, the list of those in the resistance, including the elite, was also large, and the wartime Huks accounted for only one-sixth of the total. Second, the very existence of the resistance depended on a pervasive net of collaborators serving as double agents. Indeed, militarily, General Donald Blackburn's account of his command's activities in the resistance makes clear that his successes would not have been possible without well-placed double agents in the Japanese Bureau of Constabulary.[83] Thus in the publicized case of Manuel Roxas, his assertion that his visible collaboration concealed patriotic services to the resistance was not dismissed out of hand by his fellow countrymen. Finally, and more profoundly, collaboration was what the Filipino elite had made their profession for four hundred years. Thus to have been too hard on collaborators would have indicted the entire authority structure of Filipino society. With the significant exception of the Huks, Filipinos were not ready to be without an elite. It is David Steinberg's contention, however, that the collaboration of the elite left a legacy of cynicism and ready moral accommodation to corruption.[84] Whatever the dark clouds, more directly, to MacArthur and his promise, Filipinos felt a debt of *utang na loob*. Collaboration, then, was an exhibition of *walang hiya* (shamelessness). But the sin was washed away in the "American Caesar's" heroic and forgiving return.

Thus, despite an impressive list of immediate grievances with which to launch their armed struggle, the Huks lacked a sustaining grand cause. Rather than matching competing heroes, myths, and ideologies, theirs was a war of program-for-program, ambush-for-ambush in a struggle at the opportunity level for organizational dominance. At the level of belief, the Huks foundered. Magsaysay, in taking out the opportunity-level sting of the insurgency, also, at least in modern terms, restored the belief-level legitimacy of the faltering Philippine political system. He explicitly upheld the foundations of American rule, and, by bringing his programs of reform to the barrios and winning the peasantry to his side in the elections, he even shored up the one weakness of the American legacy.

REVOLUTIONARY LEGITIMACY

In broad outline, the Huks did follow a Maoist people's war strategy. It was certainly a movement based on the mass line. In his interviews, Benedict Kerkvliet found that Huk origins were at the "grass roots," in Central Luzon barrios, before building up into larger organizations. Initially, this larger organization was the KPMP, which was taken over by the PKP in 1938. Kerkvliet has estimated that 30 percent of the peasantry in Central Luzon joined the KPMP and that during the war support for the Huks was widespread.[85] The legacy of this popular backing sustained the Huks in the first few years of their uprising. As Frances Starner concluded, "There can be little doubt that the Huk rebellion was popularly based as far as the peasantry of Central Luzon was concerned."[86]

The Huk movement was part of a larger rural ferment for agrarian reform whose organizations eventually came under communist control. Despite this control, many of the peasant leaders had a melange of views that, at critical moments, fissured this organizational control. Santos and the socialists revered Gandhi as much as Lenin. Luis Taruc was devoted to communism, Catholicism, his guerrillas, and his press conferences.[87] The Lava brothers in Manila were dedicated to their ideological brilliance and their backstage political maneuvering.[88] What was missing in the Philippines was the old-fashioned communist discipline that Stalin, Mao, and Ho successfully imposed on their revolutions.

Though the three mass bases (the KPMP in the countryside, the CLO in the cities, and the PKP for United Front politics) were supposed to feed into one revolutionary fount, the essential dualism to the PKP in its organization proved crippling. To begin with, none of these mass bases developed the group monopolies they needed for their organization-building. In the field, the Huks were kept off balance by Magsaysay's sweeps. In the cities, the CLO faced too much competition from noncommunist labor unions. Further, the successful raid against the politburo in Manila was a product of the urban Communist party's lack of social distance from the ruling elite.[89] Despite this crippling of the urban struggle, the urban Lava brothers still took command of the reconstituted party in Huklandia and stripped Taruc of his command.

Yet the division persisted, which was only too fully illustrated in the confusion that gripped the party over the 1953 elections. Elections had been one of their strongest issues. By being unseated in 1946, the members of the Democratic Alliance became martyrs. Given the fraudulent character of the elections, the communists only added luster to their cause by boycotting the elections of 1947 and 1949. But in the 1951 elections, the government redeemed itself, and the communists were taken off balance. The 1953 elections, with Magsaysay's candidacy, opened all the divisive sores of a historically and fundamentally riven organization. The Lava brothers rigidly stuck to a boycott line. The purged but still active Taruc campaigned for Quirino to thwart the too dangerous Magsaysay. The only effect was to leave the communists isolated; the people voted for Magsaysay in droves.[90]

In the countryside, though William Pomeroy (an American communist who fought with the Huks) has insisted that the agrarian issue was a national rather than a local or sectoral issue,[91] when the government's opportunity-level programs effectively overwhelmed the Huks on this front, the communists had no further claims of belief to justify a call to arms. Thus, after the government revalidated its electoral system after the collaborationist issue disappeared, the communists turned to spiteful internal bickering.

Interestingly, the PKP made no direct attacks on the disjunctive trinity of Philippine society but only on its imperfect social manifestations. No doubt not wanting to draw attention to its atheism, the party was silent on Catholicism. Instead, it attacked the Spanish legacy of rural inequality. Nor did it touch democracy, just the unfair elections. On the traditional pyramid of *utang na loob*, it made no comment but railed against its corruption.

When these corroding manifestations were programmatically corrected, the societal trinity was left in place. This left the Huks naked at the belief level. Mao had warned: "Marxism must take on a national form before it can be applied. There is no such thing as abstract Marxism, but only concrete Marxism. What we call concrete Marxism is Marxism that has taken on a national form."[92] In the Philippines, the Huks could not find one.

INTERVENTION

In a profound sense, Philippine society is the product of 350 years of Spanish intervention and 50 years of American. The Spanish kept the traditional elite-mass/patron-client authority system in place even while they laid the foundation for a national society around a common Catholic religion. The Americans provided the institutional structure for such a society and encouraged democratic values and practices through public education and a secular "church" of political parties and electioneering fiestas. In their rule, the Americans also expanded the access of their imperium to a growing middle class, economically and politically adding to the social leakiness of Philippine society. Though this diluted the authority of the elite, the expansion opened up the eyes of the still neglected masses to how much they had been missing. Into this wedge of near-term grievances and long-term injustices over foreign intervention, the Huks made a bid for power.

The U.S. intervention (or reintervention) in support of its foundling former colony was massive but, in important respects, modest. From the very beginning, Roxas's iron fist policy was based on a reliance on American military aid. Until mid-1948 this assistance came to $73 million. In addition, from 1946 to 1950, the United States provided $700 million in reconstruction aid. The United States was also financed much of Magsaysay's military expansion and agrarian reform measures. From 1951 to 1956, U.S. assistance totaled another $500 million ($383 million in economic aid and $117 million in military help).[93]

At the interest level, all this assistance provided the wherewithal for putting the Philippine economy on the road to recovery from 1946 to 1950 and for the record economic growth in the early 1950s. Beyond the money, at the opportunity level, the United States played an important role in shaping the institutions that deflected the insurgency with conduits for commitments to the government. All of the agrarian reform measures and labor legislation were American-designed. Indeed, American pressure was often instrumental in their implementation. The BCT concept, as well as military strategy and equipment that came with it, all came from the Joint U.S. Military Advisory Group (JUSMAG). American involvement in the Filipino election campaigns of 1949 and 1951 was massive, both in the CIA's establishment of an organization to monitor the freedom of the elections (NAMFREL) and in Colonel Edward Lansdale's strenuous efforts in behalf of Magsaysay's 1953 campaign that earned him the nickname of "Colonel Landslide."[94] In so doing, the United States helped redeem the belief-level legitimacy of a political system of its own creation.

Despite Quirino's complaint that the Americans had interfered too much in Filipino politics, there was one thing the United States did not do in its intervention that made it modest. As in Greece, it sent no troops and thereby deprived the Huks of an issue for nationalist exploitation. The JUSMAG never amounted to more than an El Salvador–sized advisory effort of fifty-eight officers and men.[95] The twenty-five thousand sailors and airmen on station at Clark Air Base and Subic Bay were on duty for America's global mission. Even the Huks acknowledged that they played no role in the insurgency.[96]

Overall, perhaps the best assessment of the American contribution came from a Philippine army officer who said that "30 percent of the credit for stopping the Huks goes to the U.S."[97]

In Vattelian and Metternichian terms, the U.S. assistance to the Philippines certainly had no negative impact in the United States or on its role in the international system. During the Huk rebellion, the United States was locked in combat with communism in the Korean War and making a large financial commitment to the French in their war in Indochina while the British were chasing communist guerrillas in the jungles of Malaya. It was a time of crusading—and of Metternichian alliance-building. The Manila Pact, establishing SEATO, was signed in September 1954. The Philippines, then, was another stop after Greece in the global voyage of the Truman Doctrine.

In contrast, the conspicuous point about external assistance to the Huks is that they got almost nothing. The Russians praised them for their role in the "global struggle against the U.S." but did not back up these kind words with any material support.[98] What assistance they received came mainly from the Chinese, though, interestingly, the American Communist party sent a small subsidy.[99] Some Chinese communist members helped in organizing the Huks, and Luis Taruc reportedly was trained by Chinese communists.[100] But despite their use of Mao's people's war strategy, the postwar Huks were on their own. Far from welcoming this self-reliance, the lack of assistance became one of the chief explanations in Huk postmortems of their defeat.[101]

DYNAMICS OF THE BALANCES

Asymmetries, again, play an important part in understanding the dynamic balance of forces between the Huks and the government. As in all postwar insurgencies, the Huks had the benefit of World War II in overcoming the asymmetric difficulties in getting an insurgency off the ground.

The advantages gained by the communists in their mobilization activities in the Philippines, however, were far slenderer than elsewhere. Domestically, there were many other resistance groups operating in the islands, and, from overseas, the American return was overwhelming both in its numbers and in its heroic reclamation of the legitimacy of American rule—and of the elite who served it.

From 1945 to 1949, the Huks, nevertheless, had a full list of grievances for stoking the coals of their insurgency. By 1950 they had in place an impressive revolutionary structure and strategy. From this point on, at the opportunity level, the Huks were overwhelmed. Not only were they overwhelmed institutionally, but, in the face of such a deluge, they were unable to proclaim a higher belief-level appeal for an even greater commitment for their stalwarts to stand fast in the storm.

Also, in the Philippines, balances of error, or striking successes, illustrate the seesaw drama of insurgency and counterinsurgency. The Huks got off the ground with a critical mass because of a series of errors by the government from 1945 to 1949: the unseating of the Democratic Alliance congressmen, the hasty pardoning of collaborators, the unequal trade provisions between the United States and the Philippines in the Bell Act of 1946, and the fraudulent elections of 1947 and 1949. But just as this momentum picked up steam, the teeter tottered the other way. Indeed, in 1949, just when the government, and its electoral system in particular, was exposing a venal and fraudulent soul, the Huks revealed a ruthlessness in their ambush and slaying of Aurora Quezon, the widow of the Commonwealth's first president.[102] This act gave pause to those Filipinos who were beginning to give thought to an alternative revolutionary system.

After this pause, the Huk side crashed to the ground in a cascade of error (or government success). The Manila politburo raid caught nearly the entire urban leadership of the communists and essentially finished their urban struggle. Left with only the option of rural struggle, similar to Greece, the remaining politburo stripped the Huk fighters of their ablest commander, thereby confirming a breach in the long-simmering dispute between the ideologies of the party organization and the agrarian reformers of the rank and file.

This led to the two final errors of the Huks that confined and then thoroughly confused them. First, though ethnic cleavages in the Philippines are porous, the Pampagueno-Tagalog focus of the Huks was both an internal communist problem and an outreach mistake in that it made it difficult for the Huks to spread their revolution beyond Central Luzon. Such confinement gave the army the advantage of being able to use 90 percent of its BCTs to chase and corral the Huks in one small piece of terrain. Second, faced with fair elections in 1951 and 1953 and the massive electoral mobilization in the countryside of Magsaysay's barrio campaign, the communist boycotts of the 1947 and 1949 elections turned into confusion. In this paralysis of leadership, the Tagalog Huks essentially bailed out of the insurgency and voted for Magsaysay, leaving the Pampagueno Huks ethnically and electorally isolated.[103]

In an insurgency, however, nothing is inevitable, and, to a point, there are opportunities for reversibilities. In the Philippines, from the government's point of view, the most fundamental reversal was the traumatic shock of the Japanese occupation and the triumphant American return that deflected the growing social tensions of the 1930s and even smothered the sensitive issue of the wartime collaboration of the Filipino elite. But the path of corruption and fraudulent elections on top of more long-term abuses just as certainly set the stage by 1950 for a possible reversal to a revolutionary transformation. Then the blazing comet of Magsaysay, supported by a massive but somewhat in-the-background American intervention, deflected the course of events from such a reversal.

Comparisons with Vietnam

For the purposes of filtering lessons of Vietnam through comparative cases, six messages from the Philippines are of special salience: again, the overarching importance of legitimacy, for the communists the twin needs of a socially monopolistic environment for the early nurturing of an insurgency and the subsequent requirement of maintaining organizational unity and discipline, the idiosyncratic role of Magsaysay's leadership, the Achilles' heel of elections, and the revolutionarily frustrating leaky and cross-wired nature of Philippine society.

First, regarding this central but culturally different impact of legitimacy, the massive American intervention in Vietnam undermined the Mandate of Heaven (Thien Minh) of the Saigon regime, even though this intervention was vital to its survival. Such a dilemma did not exist in the Philippines because there was no nationalist principle or traditional formulary that the American intervention violated. Had the United States intervened with ground combat troops, the communists might have articulated some beliefs that the presence of these troops might have violated and been used as an inspiration for enraged redress by the masses. The United States, however, judiciously declined to offer such a temptation. More like Greece, then, the large U.S. intervention at the interest and opportunity levels did not offend any indigenous beliefs of legitimation at the ideological level.

Second, in reviewing the cases of Vietnam, China, and Greece, what comes out with sharp clarity in the Philippines is the requirement for an intelligence monopoly, that is, a place to nurture an insurgency through the awkward stage of building it to an opportunity level in a social and physical place free from competition. For all these cases, the occupations by Axis powers created such a space. In the Philippines, the space for the Huks was too small. Following on this, third, at the opportunity or organizational level, revolutionaries must maintain unity and discipline as an illegal movement against an incumbent government. The diluting institutional mergers of the 1930s that created a leadership of varied inclinations made it impossible for the Huks in their uprising to meet the challenges they faced with a unity of voice, purpose, or strategy. A similar failure dogged the communists in Greece and in China until Mao's leadership was established in Yanan. In Vietnam, the unity and discipline under Ho and his revolutionary comrades were never in question.

Fourth, for the purpose of lessons, there remains the problem of assessing how much of the government's success can be attributed to Magsaysay's leadership alone. Though the question of leadership cannot be focused on Magsaysay exclusively because, like Papagos in Greece, he effected comprehensive changes in both military and civilian leadership, he nevertheless did so much that it could almost be argued that he defeated the Huks by himself. Indeed, his career illustrates the problem of Hannibalism. A single leader can go a long way with his charisma, and, never minding his society's meager political institutions and systems, gain his symbolic Cannae (216 B.C.) against the disoriented but more solid Roman Republic. If, however, this charisma is not routinized in the society's system of institutions and beliefs in a Weberian sense, this problem or factor is a mercurial will-of-the-wisp. When the Roman Republic finally produced a Scipio Africanus, even Hannibal was driven from the field at Zama (202 B.C.). In the Philippines, Magsaysay may have been enough to deal with the faction-riven Huks, but if the institutional mechanisms he set up and the beliefs he stood for were not incorporated and to a considerable extent realized in more routine ways in Philippine society, then the same factors that fueled the first uprising were likely to ignite another. Indeed, the corrupt course in Philippine politics after Magsaysay's untimely death in 1957 has sadly confirmed this.

Fifth, the Philippines, more clearly than any other case, reveals the Achilles' heel of bona fide elections to a communist insurgency. For reasons already discussed, this vulnerability was not fully exploited in Vietnam or China. But it was in Greece. In the Philippines as well, the communists were utterly outmaneuvered by the elections of 1951 and 1953. At root, people's war, as a strategy of political mobilization, has no agreed-upon answer for national elections that competitively serve the same strategic goal.

Finally, elections, more fundamentally, are a manifestation of a political community. Following Alexander Groth's contention discussed in Chapter 3 that revolutions come from blocked societal and economic access, what is noteworthy about Filipino society is its leaky and cross-wired social structure, with elites and masses on both sides of the revolutionary or dialectical fence. This continual possibility of treachery, or co-optation, has always made revolution difficult in the Philippines: from Funston's hunting down Aguinaldo to Magsaysay's dashing politburo raid. In the future, this very leakiness and socially cross-wired split may form the basis for the pluralist politics of a single national community. In Vietnam, by contrast, the cleavages had become too wide, and the possibility of a middle-ground political community between communist and nationalist had disappeared after the Tet offensive.

In the Philippines, rather than a military Dienbienphu, Magsaysay made himself into a political Dienbienphu and challenged the communists to a duel at the polls. Confused and divided, they dithered and faded away into the oblivion of banditry.

Epilogue: The Insurgency of the New People's Army

The struggle of the New People's Army (NPA) against the Philippine government has marched along a road of incredible déjà vu to that of the earlier Huk uprising. Though there have been some important and different new twists, they ultimately did not cause a break from this path of yesterday.

Following Magsaysay's tragic death in 1957, the Philippines returned to the corruption, economic stagnation, and lawlessness that characterized the islands before his meteoric appearance. By the mid-1960s the rising extent of this lawlessness brought Ferdinand Marcos to the presidency on a platform of law and order. The reactivation of insurgency in the formation of the New People's Army in 1969 and the spectacular Plaza Mirando bombing during an election rally in downtown Manila in 1971 triggered a declaration of martial law and a suspension of the constitution. Firmly established in his rule by this fear of anarchy, Marcos, nevertheless, saw his grip on power gradually slip as the economy and society stagnated and his own ruling circle became enmeshed in networks of corruption, aptly called "crony capitalism."

In many ways, the NPA began much better than the Huks did. There was no split politburo between Manila and the countryside this time. José María Sison was kicked out of the Philippine Communist party. He linked up with a similarly discredited former Huk military commander, Bernabe Biscayno. Together, they made a new and unified revolution in the NPA. This time they fanned out to nearly all of the provinces and islands of the Philippines. Finally, they integrated their revolution around the belief-level appeals of an explicit Marxist people's war strategy in the noble tradition of the Chinese and Vietnamese global anti-imperialist struggle against the United States.

In this cause, Sison called for an international Ho Chi Minh Trail to the Philippines. Though this appeal fell on geopolitically deafened Chinese and Soviet ears, this new revolution had developed a critical mass on a much broader base and by the early 1980s was building a momentum of crossover points in its favor.[104]

Perhaps nothing better illustrates how a strategic breakout occurs than the trajectory of Philippine politics from the assassination of Benigno Aquino on the tarmac of Manila airport in August 1983 to Marcos's call for presidential elections in October 1985. This outrageous murder and the blatantly fraudulent behavior of a commission of judicial inquiry brought about, in the parlance of Chalmers Johnson, a dramatic "power deflation" to the authority and legitimacy of the Marcos regime. As the economy, in tandem, plummeted, by the fall of 1985 the NPA had twenty thousand fighters in the field, a support base of one million sympathizers, and control of 20 percent of the villages.[105] Still lacking was a strong presence in the cities for a strategic breakout.

Like the Huks, here is where the NPA made its big mistake. When Marcos made his snap call for elections, Corazon Aquino, Benigno's widow, mounted a vigorous campaign against the president. The large leftist front orchestrated by the communists, Bayan (New Nationalist alliance), decided to sit the campaign out. This freed leftist labor union members and inspired Catholic youth (urged on by Vatican II–generation priests) to work for what turned out to be Mrs. Aquino's almost divinely inspired "People's Power" seizure of power. Again, the communists were left out in the cold, as they were after the elections of 1955. Cory's last-minute "intervention" against a likely communist breakout had an effect similar to the British intervention in Athens in the second round of the Greek civil war. This time, though, it was reversal by reform abetted by a colossal communist error caused by a congenital Marxist Achilles' heel — elections.

During this power deflation in the Philippines, it was my assessment that the country was at least headed toward some form of anti-Western socialism. With the internationalist flavor to Sison's ideology, it was my further fear that any direct American intervention would have triggered a full-scale revolution. In the event, American diplomatic maneuvering was deft and critical to both Mrs. Aquino's accession to power and her weathering of some dozen coup attempts afterward. The recent declaration by the NPA of standing down its insurgency because of the U.S. withdrawal from Clark Air Base in December 1992 has to be seen as an excuse rather than a reason. After Mrs. Aquino's accession to power and the utter disintegration of any global socialist community to be moved to calls of international duty, the NPA, like the Huks, found itself without any rallying set of beliefs. By 1988, its base of sympathizers had sunk to less than half of what it was in the last days of Marcos.[106]

In the early days of Mrs. Aquino's rule, I also argued that she would never stabilize her hold on power until she had instituted comprehensive land reforms, well beyond the symbolic measures and rhetorical promises of Magsaysay. Elections have clearly carried heavier weight than land reform; nevertheless, as the two aspects of opportunity-level legitimation of rule, they must, by some point, go hand in hand. Until then, the breeding ground for insurgency remains fertile. The land reform law of 1988 has all the right legal provisions and safeguards, but there are still some miles to go before these promises are kept.

Chapter 9

MALAYA, 1948-1960: THE UNMAKING OF AN INSURGENCY

Historical Setting

While population pressures built up in Central Luzon and accompanying rural grievances made the appeals of the Huk rebels attractive, communists in the more sparsely populated country of Malaya launched their own bid for power. As in the case of the Philippines, the Malay Peninsula, except for a 275-mile northern border with Thailand, is isolated from external sources of supply. Inside the 50,700-square-mile country (equal in size to England or New York State), 75 percent of the land is given over to dense and mountainous jungles inhabited only by some forty thousand aborigines.[1] Despite all this jungle, Malaya is the most prosperous country of Southeast Asia. At the time of the Emergency (1948–60), it was meeting 40 percent of the world's rubber requirements and was the world's largest producer of tin.[2] Though Malaya imported two-thirds of its rice, the cost was easily borne by these export earnings.[3]

This is hardly a fertile environment for insurgency. But Malaya is divided into three communities: ethnic Malays, who are the peninsula's native residents, and, as such, recipients of political privileges; Indians, largely Tamilians, who were brought in by the British at the turn of the century to work in the rubber plantations; and Chinese, who migrated on their own and had come to dominate Malaya's economy. In 1951, of a population of 5,337,000, 2.6 million (49 percent) were Malays, 2 million (38 percent) Chinese, and 600,000 (12 percent) Indian.[4] If the economic health of the country as a whole did not encourage an insurgency, the interrelationships among these communities did. Though two-thirds of the population derived its income from agriculture,[5] the urban/rural and occupational groupings revealed three communities that earned separate fortunes and lived insulated lives. Geographically, the Malays predominated in the more backward East and North and shared space with the concentrations of Chinese and Indians along the economically developed West Coast.[6]

Even where space was shared, they kept apart. In general terms, 79 percent of the Malay population was agricultural, whereas only 50 percent of the Indians and 47 percent of the Chinese were similarly engaged.[7] Their rural pursuits, though, were different. Most Malays grew rice on lands reserved for them, while Chinese worked the tin mines and Chinese and Indians together toiled on the rubber plantations.[8] Majorities of the Chinese and Indians lived in the cities during the Emergency while only 11 percent of the Malays were urban dwellers. In the aggregate this made the cities 64 percent Chinese, 21 percent Malay, and 14 percent Indian.[9] Here as well, they kept apart. The Chinese and Indians worked in the commercial sector both as owners and workers, and the Malays were employed by the government. The simple effect of these complicated splits was enormous economic and political disparities. Economically, per capita annual income in 1947 was $219 for Chinese, $187 for Indians, and only $86 for Malays.[10] Politically, however, the Malays were compensated with safeguards that discriminated against the "foreign" communities. These disparities, in brief, fueled opportunity-level resentments that fanned the coals of insurgency.

Until the fall of Singapore in 1942, however, the Pax Britannica, which had created these disparities, had also managed to stitch these three communities into a socially stable and economically dynamic colony. The first principle of British rule was a recognition of the special social and political position of the Malays. Quite unlike the Malays of the Philippines when the Spanish arrived, when the British first probed the settlements along the Straits of Malacca, they found a well-established, though crumbling, political order. Peninsular Malaya had been part of the Indic and Hindu kingdoms of Sri Vijaya centered in across-the-straits Sumatra in the seventh century and of Java's Majapahit Dynasty in the fourteenth century. By the thirteenth century, Islam had become a major political force in the peninsula. The Malays of Malaya and Indonesia soon became as Muslim as their

Philippine cousins became Christian. Independent Muslim sultanates rose up in the fifteenth century. The most prominent were Malacca and Johore. In this historical trinity of Islamic rule, under Hindu principles of kingship, which conformed to traditional Malay *adat* (customs), the Malays claimed the peninsula to be preeminently theirs as *bumiputras*, "sons of the soil."[11]

But no Southeast Asian country can claim its history as fully its own. Indians came with their principles of kingship and illustrious kingdoms. The Chinese, in the sixteenth century, saw in Malaya an El Dorado of gold, or at least of tin. In the next two centuries the Europeans came — Spanish, Portuguese, French, and Dutch. For them, a piece of the "Spice Islands" was prize enough. English interests were more strategic. The narrow Straits of Malacca sheathed the carotid artery of the exchange of Indian opium for Chinese tea. From their cockpit in Singapore, which Sir Stamford Raffles seized in 1819, the English sought to broker this commerce. They also set up an entrepôt trade between English business concerns that broke down bulks of European manufactured goods for distribution into the interior and Chinese business *kongsis* that packaged Asian commodities for export to Europe.[12] This economic symbiosis with the Chinese was the second principle of the Pax Britannica in Malaya. As in the Philippines, the value of this trade soared. By 1864 it was five times what it was in 1825. In 1869 total trade to and from Malaya amounted to $28 million, and by 1920 it had risen to $156 million.[13] Thus Malaya became the "dollar arsenal of the empire."[14]

As nineteenth-century Malaya was marked by this economic growth in Singapore, it was also pockmarked by political disintegration in the interior. Attracted by this commercial expansion and the opening of new tin mines, waves of Chinese lapped into Singapore and streamed on into the peninsula. In the intensely mined sultanate of Perak, the nucleus of nine thousand Chinese tin miners in 1877 grew to ninety thousand residents by 1897.[15] The Malay sultans tried to keep control of Chinese miners and their secret societies, but the fighting among these groups soon exceeded their capabilities.[16]

From 1874 to 1914, the English gradually stepped in to impose the stability of the Pax Britannica over the entire peninsula. In seeking both to promote the economic expansion from Singapore to the interior and to safeguard the social stability of the rural Malays, the British extended their third principle of political rule through their tried formulary of "divide and rule" by "direct and indirect" government. The Straits Settlements of Penang, Malacca, and Singapore, which were centers of the entrepôt trade and had non-Malay majorities, were ruled directly as crown colonies. The western Malay sultanates, with significant commercial activities (tin mines and rubber plantations), were set up as Federated Malay States: Perak, Selangor, Negri Sembilan, and Pahang. Those sultanates lacking in such activities and with large Malay majorities were protected as Unfederated Malay States: Perlis, Kedah, Kelantan, Trengganu, and Johore.[17]

By 1921, the population mix of the Malay Peninsula had stabilized at 49 percent Malay, 35 percent Chinese, and 14 percent Indian, proportions that held to the Emergency.[18] The turnover among both the Chinese and Indians, however, was high. In 1921, only 21 percent of the Chinese and 12 percent of the Indian populations were Malay-born.[19] In the 1920s and 1930s, then, most Chinese and Indians were more politically wedded to events in their homelands than in the peninsula. For the Chinese, these apolitical proclivities were fortunate because the British were quick to suppress political activity by them. In the late nineteenth century the British had broken the conspiratorial hold of the Chinese secret societies — the *imperium in imperio* — and replaced them with looser kinship associations.[20]

Indians were brought over by the British to work in the rubber plantations and to serve as functionaries for the apparatus of British rule, but more particularly in the early twentieth century they were intended as a counterweight to the Chinese. Those Indians who broke into the middle class and developed political sympathies for independence took their cues from the Congress party in India and were content to pursue their interests legally.[21]

In allowing in the Chinese and bringing in the Indians to help build their "dollar arsenal," the British developed a symbiotic political relationship with the Malay ruling class to shield the peasant society of the Malays from the socially disruptive effects of this economic growth. The abundance of unoccupied land afforded the raj the luxury of clearing jungle for European and Chinese mining and plantation enterprises while also setting aside large tracts of rice land as exclusive Malay reservations.[22] The capstone of this special relationship was the elite Malayan Civil Service (MCS) of the British, which recruited native subordinates from among the younger generation of Malay aristocrats who had received suitable Western educations. These aristocrats invariably retained their ties to their sultanate and village *kompongs* and, as administrators, were still able to perpetuate their traditional prince-peasant links through the structure of British rule.[23]

Largely because of this privileged position with the British, the Malays in Malaya did not support the independence struggles of the Malays of Indonesia. In particular, the classless egalitarianism of their nationalistic cousins across the straits was not something the Malay elites were eager to import. Similarly, the Muslim reform movement that grew out of the Islamic renaissance in Egypt and Turkey was ultimately rejected because it was non-Malay. More than being non-Malay, such a renaissance would have brought under uncomfortable scrutiny the non-Muslim nature of many Malay customs, especially the distinctly Hindu principles of kingship that still underlay the "Muslim" sultanates.[24] Instead, in the 1930s Malay associations were formed. These organizations were ethnically chauvinistic at root. They were almost as staunch in their support for British rule, viewing it as a bulwark against the demands of the Chinese and Indians. Nevertheless, they foresaw a time when Malaya could become independent.[25]

In this environment, the communists were a small, struggling conspiracy groping for an issue with which to gain a political foothold. Their attempts to reach the Malays and Indians were not successful. Comintern agents from China were then dispatched to Singapore to organize a general strike among the Chinese proletariat. The success of such an effort in 1930 provided the impetus for the founding of a Malayan Communist party (MCP) in the same year. In proud attendance was the Comintern's ambassador-at-large, Ho Chi Minh.[26]

From the beginning, the party was outlawed and its members hunted down by police. Nevertheless, under the organizational skills of Lai Tek, an ethnic Chinese from Vietnam, the party built a following by casting itself as a traditional and outlawed secret society. It enjoyed particular success among the Hailams from Hainan Island.[27] When the Japanese invaded the Chinese mainland in 1937, the party found its issue. A host of party-inspired associations attracted young Chinese from Malaya to support China's United Front. By 1940, thirty thousand Chinese had joined these groups, and the number of party followers swelled to forty thousand, though only seventeen hundred were full members.[28]

It was not these communist machinations that upset British rule. Rather, it was the Japanese invasion of the Malay Peninsula and subsequent conquest of Singapore on February 15, 1942, that inflicted upon the British, in Prime Minister Winston Churchill's words, "the worst disaster and largest capitulation of British history."[29] The effect of this event and the three-and-a-half-year Japanese occupation that followed was to unhinge the fundamental social, political, and economic balancing act of British rule. For surrendering over one hundred thousand men in a supposedly impregnable fortress to a Japanese campaign of just two months, the British suffered a tremendous loss of face. The myth of British protection was cruelly deflated. Though militarily the British redeemed themselves in neighboring Burma in 1944, this occurred "offstage," from a Malayan perspective. Operation Zipper, a campaign for an English return planned for September 1945, was scrubbed by the Japanese surrender in August, and the British were deprived of their heroic return.[30]

Despite the general harshness of the Japanese occupation, the Malays, again, were particularly favored. In a show of independence, the sultans and many Malay civil servants refused to leave with the British.[31] The Japanese retained the sultans and these civil servants and also set up numerous support organizations among the Malays.[32] The occupation, nevertheless, was unsettling to the Malays. After initially lumping Malaya and Sumatra into a single administration, the Japanese abandoned this but then sheared off the four northern sultanates and gave them back to Thailand.[33] The remaining Malays were left with their ultimate demographic horror: becoming a minority in their own land. In this Malaya made-in-Japan, the Chinese were 48 percent of the population and the Malays only 34 percent—an almost exact reversal of their positions in 1940.[34]

The Chinese and Indians, however, came to know the meaning of a truly harsh alien rule. For the Indians, the occupation was an unmitigated disaster. Inspired by the Quit India campaign of the Congress party in India and locally angered by the brutal British suppression of rubber plantation strikes in 1941, many Indians welcomed Japanese rule. Some 80,000 joined the Indian National Army (INA) set up under the aegis of the Indian Independence League (IIL) (which drew another 350,000 followers), cynically sponsored by the Japanese and led by the fiery Indian nationalist exile Subhas Chandra Bose. Politically, the IIL took the Indians nowhere, in India or Malaya, and, militarily, the INA dissolved in desertions to the British when it was sent off to Burma. Those who declined to join these organizations were treated brutally. Some 150,000 Indians were conscripted as laborers to build such projects of no return as the Burma railroad. From its wartime experience, the Indian community lost all taste for confrontational political adventure.[35]

In sharp contrast, the Chinese were inspired by their wartime experience into further confrontational politics. In 1939 President Chiang Kai-shek called on the Chinese of Malaya to unite with the British in resisting the Japanese. One thousand men volunteered and fought well in the futile defense of Singapore. In prompt retaliation, more than forty thousand Chinese were killed by the Japanese. The British, nevertheless, appreciated this loyalty. In fact, just before the fall of Singapore, the British made a secret agreement with Lai Tek to train and equip a "stay-behind" guerrilla force recruited by the MCP. From the initial training group of two hundred, the Malayan People's Anti-Japanese Army (MPAJA) grew to a force of ten thousand by the war's end. It was exclusively Chinese. For this defiance, the Japanese singled out the urban Chinese for harsh treatment. As many as one million fled the cities and took up subsistence agriculture along the jungle peripheries. These squatters provided the support base for MPAJA guerrillas.[36] Though perhaps an overstatement, MPAJA claimed that it fought 340 engagements against the Japanese and inflicted twenty-three hundred casualties.[37]

The destabilizing impact of the Japanese occupation on the social peace of Malaya cannot be overstated. The occupation itself brought an end to the out-migration of Chinese and Indians, and both communities came to link their postwar destinies to politics in Malaya.[38] Even though the three communities contemplated a permanent association, the war had stung their visions with the smoke of smoldering communal animosities.

As in the other cases, the war greatly strengthened the position of the communists. The MPAJA emerged from the jungles feeling triumphant and, therefore, petulant about the firm British insistence that it disband. Nevertheless, 6,800 stood down, although more than 3,000 went underground and dispersed into a Chinese community that gave them warm support for their wartime resistance.[39] In the country at large, however, MPAJA overplayed its hand. During the interregnum before the reestablishment of British authority, guerrilla bands took over towns, proclaiming the abolition of the sultanates and vowing to make Malaya part of China.[40] From March to August 1945, MPAJA guerrillas killed 2,542 "collaborators," mostly Malay. In defense, the Malays formed the Red Bands of the Sabillah (Holy War) and outpaced MPAJA in a brief orgy of communal killing. Indeed, the intensity of this communal violence sealed in the minds of Malays an identity of communism with the Chinese, and, therefore, as a threat to both Islam and the Malay community.[41]

The British did not ease their return by creating the Malayan Union in April 1946. Designed to put Malaya on a path to independence and a national community among the three communities, it gave full citizenship rights to Chinese and Indians born in Malaya and dissolved all the sultanates into one secular union. Though the Indians and Chinese were amenable, the Malays were apoplectic. They saw the union as a disintegration of all their safeguards as *bumiputras*. Not one Malay ruler attended the inaugural ceremonies. Instead, the Malays were roused, in their dissent, to form in 1946 the United Malay National Organization (UMNO). The Chinese, by contrast, held to the union as a rightful reward for their wartime resistance. These tensions contributed to a two-year deterioration of law and order and provided the then legalized MCP with the opportunity to organize in hope of seizing political power.[42]

With the ubiquitous Lai Tek still at the helm, the MCP launched a preparatory legal phase. Its first objective was to build a national base for the revolution by establishing the Pan-Malayan Federation of Trade Unions (PMFTU). By April 1947, it claimed 264,000 members. This was half the urban work force and included Chinese as well as Indians—but few Malays.[43] A debate over whether to seize on this success and launch an armed struggle was interrupted by Lai Tek's dramatic disappearance with party funds in the midst of contradictory accusations of his being a Japanese collaborator and a British double agent during the war.[44] A twenty-six-year-old militant named Chin Peng seized the secretary-generalship and dedicated himself to inciting an insurrection through a campaign of general strikes. More than three hundred strikes ripped into the civil peace that year.[45]

To defuse the unrest, the British reversed themselves on the Malayan Union and on February 1, 1948, announced the creation of the Federation of Malaya. The traditional prerogatives of the sultans were reinstated and the previous safeguards enjoyed by Malays as *bumiputras* were restored. Though this act rekindled the resentments of Chinese and Indians, the Malays were pacified. Politically the Federation plan undercut the attempts by the MCP to win over the Malay community.[46] The British responded to the challenge from labor by suppressing the strikes, requiring government registration of all existing unions, and organizing additional unions of their own. The PMFTU, furthermore, was outlawed in June 1948. The immediate response of the MCP to the banning of the PMFTU was to raise a call to armed struggle. After an immediate campaign of terror directed against the mines and plantations in which three European planters were killed, the British declared an Emergency on June 18, 1948. Under its powers, they promptly jailed thirty thousand activists and deported another fifteen thousand to the inhospitable arms of Guomindang authorities in China.[47]

When the Emergency was declared, the MCP had its organization in place. Its 3,250 combatants were dubbed the Malayan Races Liberation Army (MRLA). Aiding the MRLA were the approximately 10,000 members of the Minh Yuen (People's Organization), half of whom were armed. It conducted sabotage and terrorist attacks and furnished intelligence and logistical support to MRLA units. Supervising these activities at all levels were cadres drawn from the 3,000 full-fledged members of the MCP. Supporting this tight organization were some 60,000 active party followers who were able to enlist the willing and unwilling cooperation of about half the one million rural Chinese. In short, the MCP launched its armed struggle with a critical mass already achieved, but although well-organized, the *armed* insurgent forces never grew to large numbers. At its peak in 1951, the MRLA numbered just 5,500.[48]

This situation was fortunate for the British because at the outset of the Emergency they did not command a very large force either. It consisted of a 10,233-man police force (mostly Malay) and a regular military force of thirteen battalions (of roughly 700 men in each) of British, Gurkha, and Malayan troops. In the first few months, the British recruited 24,000 Malays into a Special Constabulary for static defense that freed the soldiers for offensive operations. Later a part-time Home Guard of 50,000 was recruited to support the constabulary.[49]

The first task of the authorities was to protect the plantations and mines so that production would not be disrupted. For two years it was tough going. The grim situation was exacerbated by differences among the top

British leadership. In fact, the high commissioner, Sir Edward Gent, had to be brought home because of his inability to control this bureaucratic infighting. These feuds continued under his successor, Sir Henry Gurney, because the commissioner of police, Colonel W. N. Gray, and the military director of operations, Lieutenant General Sir Harold Briggs, were unable to agree on basic strategy.[50]

For the communists as well, things were not going according to plan. They had hoped that their declaration of armed struggle would have touched off an insurrection enabling them to carve out a "People's Republic" by August 1948.[51] By December, it was clearly evident that there would be no popular uprising in Malaya. In early 1949, the party shifted to a people's war strategy and withdrew to the jungles to carve out Yanan-like base areas. By the end of the year, even this was not going well and the MRLA resumed offensive operations, leaving the setting up of base camps to the Minh Yuen.[52] But in these operations the MRLA still massed in formations sometimes as large as four hundred men and got chewed up, most notably in the ill-starred assault on the railroad town of Kuala Krau in March 1950.[53]

In the fall of 1951, Chin Peng ordered the MRLA to break down into platoon-sized units and launch more scattered attacks. This made the guerrillas both more difficult to find and more disruptive in their activities. Although roads were not cut as in Vietnam, heavily armed convoys were necessary. Train service became unreliable and production in the rubber plantations finally began to suffer. The prize of this new strategy was the assassination of Gurney on October 6, 1951, in a well-planned ambush.[54]

In spite of this blow, the British were soon able to organize their war effort effectively. Both Gray and Briggs had departed by the end of 1951. Before he left, Briggs had devised a plan for his successor to carry out. The plan was literally the blueprint of the British military success. A strong reason for this success was that the successor, General Sir Gerald Templer, was given the full authority needed to enact the plan. Upon his arrival in February 1952, he was named both high commissioner and the military director of operations.

The plan's purpose was to neutralize the support the MRLA was receiving from the five hundred thousand Chinese squatters left over from World War II. Its heart was the resettlement of the squatters in "New Life Villages" in which social amenities were provided, organizations with ties to the government established, and full titles to the land passed out for the squatters who resettled. The military point of these villages was to separate the guerrillas from their source of food. Unlike Vietnam, the communists could not support themselves in the jungles, and the necessity of having to come out to these open villages made them vulnerable to ambush. In all, about five hundred thousand squatters were resettled in some five hundred villages.[55]

Establishment of the villages was only the first level of the plan. Briggs also called for the coordination of civil, police, and military activities at all echelons. Accordingly, district, state, and national war executive committees were established. Representatives of each of these activities served on these committees as did invited Malay, Indian, and Chinese community leaders.[56] Supporting this coordinated war effort was a military force that by 1953 numbered 40,000 British, Malay, and Commonwealth troops (25,000 British), 45,000 regular and special police, and Home Guards that had swollen to 350,000.[57]

Militarily, the back of the insurgency was broken from 1952 to 1954 in what Templer called "a struggle for the hearts and minds of men."[58] Police squads went deep into the jungles to flush out communist fighters still trying to establish base camps. Army units as well broke down into smaller formations and stayed out on longer patrols hunting down guerrilla bands. The communists were never strong on seasoned military leaders, and in 1952 four of their top commanders were killed, as were fifteen hundred guerrillas. British troops dealt a serious blow to the morale of the MRLA when, in the spring of 1953, Chin Peng was forced to evacuate his headquarters to north of the Thai border.[59] From 1952 to 1954, two-thirds of the guerrilla forces were eliminated. Overall, from 1951 to 1957 total MRLA casualties outpaced new recruits at a rate of three to one (nine thousand to three thousand) so that its net strength fell from eight thousand to two thousand.[60] The flow of crossover points had reversed.

Despite the importance of the Briggs plan and its attendant military campaign, the British owed their success to political initiatives as well. The culminating gesture, of course, was the grant of full independence on August 31, 1957. This was the capstone to a process of party organizing and electioneering that was creating something of a national political community in Malaya. Following the creation of the UMNO in 1946 for Malays, Indians banded together in the same year to found the Malayan Indian Congress (MIC). At Gurney's suggestion in 1949, Chinese businessmen started the Malaya Chinese Association (MCA) to draw poor Chinese away from the MCP. In 1951 the colorful Tunku Abdul Rahman took over the UMNO and was bent on creating a national coalition. In the next year he effected an alliance with the MCA and MIC and established the Malayan Alliance party (MAP), which was called the Triple Alliance. Also that year, the British granted citizenship to all aliens born in Malaya. This immediately affected 1.2 million Chinese and 180,000 Indians.[61]

With all these parties, the only thing left to do was hold elections. Indeed, as a precondition for granting independence, the British insisted that elections be held for a Malayan government. Though the ethnic communities had quarreled over the form of the state, whether it should be a union or a federation, they were united on the goal of *merdeka*, or independence.

Hence, when the British granted citizenship to so many Chinese, the Malays were forced to take account of Chinese interests. When the British decided to begin with local, city elections in 1952 before national ones in 1955, this necessity became urgent. Because the Chinese formed majorities in most cities, the UMNO faced defeat if it did not work with the MCA. It did, and the Triple Alliance swept to victory against the Independence of Malaya party (IMP), a more exclusive ethnic Malay party. Despite some intense intercommunal jockeying, the alliance held together to win a victory in the national elections of 1955 and again in the 1957 and 1959 elections.[62]

The MCP viewed this electoral process from the outside. Realizing that these elections were leading to genuine independence, Chin Peng wanted the party to regain its legal status so that it could compete in them. He agreed to talks with the *tunku*, which were held at Bailing in December 1955. The Malayan leader offered a general amnesty to the MRLA but made the legalization of the MCP conditional on the disarming of the MRLA. Chin Peng refused, and the talks were broken off. In April 1956 he offered to negotiate again, but the *tunku* refused this time, saying any further talks had to be contingent on the MRLA disbanding.[63]

The communists were facing serious difficulties, and the negotiations were their last grasp at survival. In a combined civil, military, and police campaign, the British were focusing on eliminating the MRLA region by region (as the Americans had done in Greece). Templer declared Malacca to be the first "white" area in September 1953. By the end of 1954, a "white belt" girdled the peninsula. The British were grinding down the insurgency through three programs. One was a campaign of food denial operations through defoliation and ambushes at supply points. Not only did these operations induce widespread guerrilla surrenders, they also produced the windfall of forcing Minh Yuen cadres to expose themselves, and, in this sunlight, remaining guerrillas were cut off from their support.[64] Another program was the vigorous efforts of the police, the Special Branch in particular, to disrupt and even halt the MRLA's communications. The most spectacular of these was the capture of the entire courier network of Chin Peng.[65]

Results from these two programs brought the MRLA to the brink of ruin. At the end of 1956, half the population lived in white areas, and by August of the next year, only a strip along the northern border and the southern state of Johore remained "unwhite." The third program delivered the coup de grace. Through vigorous personal "recruitment" by generous cash and other inducements by Special Branch officers, the guerrillas were being lured out of the jungles. In May 1958, Hor Lung, the MRLA commander in Jahore, surrendered and brought out 160 ranking colleagues with him. Mass surrenders followed everywhere, and by year's end all the MRLA had left was 250 ragged stragglers along the Thai border.[66]

On July 31, 1960, the Emergency was declared to be over. It had cost the Anglo-Malay side $850 million. A total of 11,048 people had been killed: 6,710 guerrillas, 1,865 security forces, and 2,473 civilians.[67]

Framework Analysis

NATIONAL LEGITIMACY

On the brink of the Emergency, the traditional political order was crumbling for everyone. That a more modern world would have to be fashioned was clear to all, but what shape this world should take was the question that framed the politics of the Emergency. That independence, or *merdeka*, would be the centerpiece of this new order was one answer all agreed on. For the British, after their disastrous defeat in Singapore, it was a reluctant and inevitable concession. Though the Malays had thought about independence, the protection of the British raj had given them comfortable advantages. But the British inability to stand against Japan and the treachery of the Union plan had made this protection both uncertain and unreliable. Independence would certainly give the Malays rule, but with it would come the responsibility of keeping the Indians and Chinese at bay.

This was a troubling prospect because the war brought permanent changes to these communities. Chinese and Indians no longer saw themselves as economic interlopers. They wanted a full political role in Malaya. But both communities were divided. The Indians still had their traditional leaders — chamber of commerce presidents in the cities and labor supervisors on the estates — who related to the British in the style of the Congress party, that is, legally. More modern activist leaders had emerged after the war, however, who spoke the language of labor organizing, job actions, and strikes. The larger Chinese community contained a similar but more ominous split. All Chinese sought political participation: some, through traditional organizations, followed leaders like Tan Cheng Lock for democratic rights; others, through their experience with the resistance and exposure to communism, clamored for revolution.

In this dangerous disagreement over whither modern Malaya, at least for noncommunists it was fortunate that the British not only presided over the resolution to this question but also committed themselves to obliging all three communities in their common goal of *merdeka*.

At the level of interest, devastation from the war had been minimal. Though the economy had suffered under Japanese occupation, the British were quickly able to reestablish Malaya's position as the dollar arsenal of their now waning empire. Indeed, the Emergency fortuitously coincided with an economic boom stimulated by an American stockpiling of tin and rubber for the Korean War. From 1948 to 1960, per capita income rose 160 percent. Rural employment expanded and wage increases were steady. The availability of well-paying jobs certainly helped the government's efforts to build alternative lives for squatters against the outreach activities of the communists.[68] The highlight of these favorable winds of material interest for the government side is that the MRLA drew 70 percent of its recruits from these same squatters.[69]

The boom also brought modest urbanization to Malaya. The 19 percent of the population that were city dwellers in 1947 rose to 26 percent by 1957.[70] The communists naturally sought to create their revolutionary situation first in the cities by organizing workers into unions for strikes and insurrection. But winning workers over to the dislocations of strikes in an environment of rising wages was difficult.[71] To ensure that these unfavorable winds of modern interest did not change, the government either arrested or deported most labor activists and replaced them with Indians. In more traditional terms, the bulwark against communist urban inroads into the Chinese community was formed by the personal security of the continued patron-client ties of the dialect/regional associations, the leaders and service activities of the *kongsis*, and the Guomindang party.

Mostly outmaneuvered in the cities, the communists turned to the countryside, and particularly to the squatter settlements from which MPAJA had drawn its wartime support. A new ingredient to the MRLA's outreach was terror. If not a reservoir of sympathy, the communists were at least determined to achieve a monopoly of silence against the government. It is significant, then, that of the 1,942 civilians killed by the MRLA as of April 1952, 1,250 were Chinese.[72] Thus, despite the small number of armed insurgents, if not a sympathetic environment (in Jeffrey Race's terms), the MRLA certainly had created an intimidated population.

Clearly, the Achilles' heel for the British was the Chinese community in the countryside. Despite all the efforts made to co-opt Chinese, their essential passivity remained striking. Few worked for the government, and their response to recruitment in the police and armed forces was abysmal. When Sir Henry Gurney announced a conscription of 290,000 into the Security Forces, only 1,800 who entered service were Chinese.[73] Also, despite the importance of political participation to their leaders, the Chinese masses were slow to take advantage of their political rights. In the 1955 federal elections, of the 600,000 Chinese declared eligible to vote (half their adult population), a mere 143,000 (less than a quarter) registered.[74] Perhaps this was because of communist intimidation, but it was more likely owing to a persistent economic raison d'être to the Chinese community.

Attempts by both sides to inspire greater Chinese commitments were certainly not lacking at the opportunity or organizational level of legitimation.

After their legalization in 1945, the communists were quick to embark on their classic path to power of labor organization, strikes, and revolutionary insurrection. With a large urban work force of Chinese and Indians (Malays made up just 17 percent of industrial workers), the MCP did extremely well. At one point, the PMFTU claimed to control or influence between 80 and 90 percent of all unionized workers.[75] This, of course, permitted the successful and immobilizing strikes of 1947 and 1948. In this year of decision, however, the British countered with some organizing of their own that ultimately crushed the communist labor movement. Aided by experts from the British Trade Union Council, the colonial government put in place an alternative set of unions more to its liking. By the end of 1948, as a result of the government banning of the PMFTU, most industrial workers had "deunionized." The British then set up unions of their own: in 1950 the Malayan Trade Union Council for industrial workers, in 1954 the National Union of Plantation Workers (soon to become the largest union in Southeast Asia), and in 1957 a union for government employees with 232,000 members. Essentially, over the urban proletariat, the British recreated their formula of divide and rule. The public union was a Malay preserve and the private sector unions replaced Chinese members with Indians. By 1961 Indians made up 65 percent of all unionists.[76]

At this institutional or group level, the struggle revolved around efforts to provide and maintain societal access and political participation for all. Regarding the former, access to modern jobs for all groups was guaranteed by an educational system in the native tongues (Malay, Chinese, and Tamil) as well as in English that preserved ethnic identity in these "native" tongue schools and provided access to professional positions in the English schools for those, like the Chinese, who sought them. A related factor, not lost on the Chinese of Malaya, was that nothing was done by the authorities to deprive the Chinese of their economic position in an emerging, modern Malaya. Such security, notably, was not enjoyed by their comrades in Indonesia, Thailand, or Indochina. Also, in 1952 the colonial government opened up the prestigious Malayan Civil Service to non-Malays.[77] Finally, as the struggle moved increasingly to the countryside, the institutional complex of the Briggs plan sought to provide social and economic access for the squatters to this emerging Malaya and enlist commitments from them to the campaign against the MRLA.

For the Malays, the Federation of 1948 and the constitution of 1957 recommitted a modern Malaya to the traditional safeguards enjoyed by the Malays as *bumiputras*. Ten states were retained, each under the continued rule of a Malay sultan. In tandem, the British turned over control of the elite Malayan Civil Service to Malays by making it three-fourths Malay. Economic security and ethnic identity were further preserved in the countryside by retaining the Malay reservations of choice rice-growing lands for Malays. Since the squatter settlements and New Life villages had encroached on some of this land, the government set up a low-interest loan program for rice farmers. Thus whatever the larger national system of citizens and elections that the constitution established, modern Malaya also enshrined the traditional prince-peasant tie that bound the Malay aristocracy to its rural *kompongs*.[78]

Nevertheless, it was the building of institutions and rituals of political participation that began to develop in the three groups a single political community, at least at the elite level. The Malayan Indian Congress, under John Thivy's leadership, became very conservative and Gandhian during the Emergency. It was distinctly antiunion, and Indian union leaders and members tended to join the intercommunal Labor party.[79] The UMNO was similarly socially conservative. It was primarily a rural organization and was built on traditional lord-peasant bonds. The MCA was a combination of three groups: Westernized professional and business leaders (the "Baba Chinese"), various wings of the anticommunist Guomindang, and the traditional voluntary associations that preserved a separate Chinese identity. After initial difficulties with membership, by 1953 its rolls had reached 250,000.[80]

The precursor to the formation of the Alliance (MAP), however, was the Communities Liaison Committees set up by the British in June 1949 to help coordinate the civilian side of the war effort. They got the leaders of the three communities into the habit of working together to solve political problems. The national symbol of this newfound political cooperation was the amicable relationship between Tunku Abdul Rahman, the leader of the UMNO, who was a British-trained lawyer and the son of a sultan, and Tan Cheng Lock, the head of the MCA, who was a "Baba Chinese" rubber baron.[81]

With such institutions, habits, and relationships as precursors, the prospect of local elections in 1952 led the *tunku* to form the alliance with the MIC and MCA. Bluntly, though his dream was to form a truly national party, the start of the electoral process in the cities prevented him from getting his plans off the ground without Chinese help. The triumph that these elections brought turned this marriage of convenience into a more enduring alliance lasting through their winning electoral campaigns of 1955, 1957, and 1959. It was a symbiosis of the *tunku's* charismatic hold over Malay votes with the MCA's financial support, administrative services, and delivery of the Chinese vote, eventually even in the squatter settlements.[82]

In the opportunity-level competition with the communists over societal access and political participation, the British countered the challenge of the Emergency by creating a political middle across communal lines as a bulwark against a radical political and ethnic fringe. Specifically, this middle was a political community of moderate Malays and conservative non-Malay business and traditional interests against radical Chinese who could not break out of the peripheral Chinese squatter settlements. With their political flanks secured, the British and the Malayan government were able to treat the MRLA as a police and military matter.

These political flanks that were secured at the group level for the subsequent military scattering of the insurgency flowed from a national deal, or constitutional contract, struck at the belief level. This contract emanated from a British commitment to *merdeka*, which came to fruition in the adoption of the Federal Constitution in 1957. After the debacle of the Union plan, the British came to realize that moderate Malays would stay on their side only by a commitment to independence.[83] The importance of this commitment to British military success is highlighted by the *tunku's* assertion that this success was enabled by the full cooperation of the public, which was not forthcoming until this political promise.[84]

Independence, however, could not be just for Malays. Half the population, after all, was Chinese and Indian. Indeed, in the 1930s a Chinese member of the Legislative Council had already asked the dreaded question: "Who said this is a Malay country?"[85] A more plural answer was embodied in the constitutional contract culminating in the Federal Constitution. In exchange for a grant of citizenship to the Chinese and Indians, the Malays were still entitled, additionally, to their special position of *bumiputras*, defined, in the traditional way, as those who habitually spoke Malay, professed Islam, and conformed to traditional Malay customs (*adat*). The Chinese and Indians were also permitted language rights in return for an eventual acceptance of Malay as the national language. Thus full political participation was guaranteed for all and was sealed by the elections of the 1950s. For the economic and social side, societal access was assured by committing the new government to providing Malays access to the modern economy and, eventually, to a proportionate share of its wealth, without depriving the Chinese and Indians of the gains they had already achieved.[86] Thus, as K. J. Ratnam has observed, the constitution "appears to have done justice . . . [by] giving the Malays and non-Malays an approximation of what they expected."[87]

At the belief level, the communists were blocked from a grand appeal for their revolution by a government-designed trinity encompassing both traditional and modern legitimacy. For the Malays, there was *merdeka*: *merdeka* for all certainly, but for the Malays especially, because their privileges as *bumiputras* were continued. In addition to their relative economic wealth, for the Chinese and Indians there was participation in a modern democracy that came with citizenship and elections. Finally, to mold a plural community among these groups, there was a constitutional contract that justified equitable opportunity-level arrangements of political participation and societal access.

There is no question that Chin Peng and the MCP were pursuing a Maoist, people's war strategy after the failure of the urban, insurrectionist strategy in the strikes of 1947–48. In following the mass line of a united front policy, the MCP established the Minh Yuen. It was recruited from among Chinese sympathetic to the wartime MPAJA and served as a source of intelligence and logistical support for the MRLA. It was tightly organized into a hierarchy of committees responsible to the MCP. As an added measure of party control of the "gun," one thousand MCP members fought in the MRLA.[88]

Chin Peng's plan for liberation also followed the Maoist progression of protracted war. Starting from jungle bases, he intended to liberate the rubber estates along the jungle fringes and then extend his control over neighboring villages to establish a network of "people's republics" (or soviets). From this second stage, he planned to build up the revolution's political and military strength for a final confrontation with the British in open, conventional warfare.[89] In the event, despite a critical mass organizational base and reservoir of support left over from World War II, a campaign of terror lasting until 1952 failed to provide the MRLA with the conspiracy of silence it required as a minimum, at the interest level, for its revolutionary strategy. In this regard, a comparison of the first three years of the Emergency with the first three years of the armed struggle of the Viet Cong is instructive. In Malaya, those killed by MRLA terror went from five hundred in 1948, to seven hundred in 1949, and to twelve hundred in 1950, but then the annual toll went into a sharp and uninterrupted decline. In Vietnam, by contrast, the Viet Cong killed seven hundred civilians in 1957, twelve hundred in 1958, and twenty-five hundred in 1959. In 1960, instead of falling off, the death chart jumped to four thousand and kept climbing.[90]

More seriously, the MCP, despite its formidable organization, could not inspire sufficient opportunity-level commitments to this organization for a momentum of crossover points into a second phase of people's war. The British had rendered the Malays impervious to communist appeals, which was confirmed by the communal violence immediately after the war. Some Indians were willing to go along with strikes and job actions, but when the call came for armed struggle, they dropped out. Such a "shut out" made a people's war difficult because the rural population, except for the squatters, was overwhelmingly Malay. The essential problem of the communists was that their natural base of support lay in the towns and cities, where their fortunes were ruined. Like the Guomindang, when it was driven out of the coastal cities by the Japanese in China, the MCP could not develop a rural base. Even among the squatters, the government was able to squeeze the MRLA away from the Minh Yuen and destroy it in detail.

At the belief level, despite a clear strategy and a unity of leadership under Chin Peng, the very Maoist ideology of the MCP only confirmed its un-Malay ambitions. Besides communism, the only other appeal the MCP could lay claim to was *merdeka*, and that had already been guaranteed by the British to the moderate and electoral politics of the Alliance. This paucity of a larger message came out in the Bailing talks when Chin Peng endorsed the *tunku*'s achievement of independence and wanted to participate in electoral politics but still refused to disarm.

With independence, the MCP became an ethnic embarrassment to those Chinese who had joined the MCA and the Triple Alliance to learn how to be good "Malays."[91] In the traditional prince-peasant society of peninsular Malaya, one thing that was not being a good "Malay" was to embrace a call for a classless, Godless society.

INTERVENTION

Though Mao's strategy of people's war stresses the virtue of self-reliance, it is equivocal as to whether, in the last stage, it can succeed without outside help. Indeed, no people's war has, not even Mao's own. For the communists in Malaya, none was forthcoming. What foreign assistance they received, ironically, came from the British. It was the British who raised and equipped the MPAJA and trained the leadership that became the nucleus of command for the MRLA. During the Emergency itself, over 70 percent of the MRLA weapons were British.[92]

As for their fraternal socialist allies, though the Russians encouraged the MCP to launch a violent struggle against British colonialism, their support was purely verbal. Nearby China was not much better. During the war, there was some indirect Chinese communist assistance in that some of the MPAJA guerrillas had fought with Mao's armies in the 1930s. After the communist seizure of power in China, rhetorical support for a people's war in Malaya was warm, but the rare attempts to smuggle in weapons by sea were easily blocked by Royal Navy patrols.[93]

It is hard to imagine how the communists, hemmed in by their ethnic isolation and political misplacement in the countryside, could have won with any amount of help, but the scope and significance of British assistance to the new nation of Malaya is beyond dispute. More than material support, British programs and political direction unmade the Malayan insurgency. Sir Gerald Templer had an explicit understanding that his task as high commissioner was to put Malaya on a crash program in nation-building that would bring it independence in five years.[94] From New Life villages at the rice-roots level to local coordinating committees among the three communities, and, finally, to national political parties and elections, the British nudged the peoples of Malaya into a reluctant, plural nation. At first blush, in the face of such massive assistance, including the use of British combat troops, it seems amazing that the English did not compromise the legitimacy of the fledgling state of Malaya. Yet political legitimacy in Malaya at the belief level was of British design, namely, that of a constitutional contract which provided the abstract gifts of *merdeka* and democracy in concretely equitable portions.

When the British first came to Malaya, they established a colony of separate development that provided a social peace as the guarantor of the peninsula's economic prosperity. They left trying to fashion a single political community for all Malayans under their own leaders. In having the wisdom to step aside midcourse in the Emergency, the British stepped out of the long shadow of Dienbienphu.[95]

DYNAMICS OF THE BALANCES

Asymmetries, again, in the balances between the insurgents and incumbents played their role both in getting the insurgency off the ground and then in thwarting it. The harsh treatment meted out to the Chinese by the Japanese in the war and the collapse of economic life in the cities created a rural flotsam of Chinese squatters that became the breeding ground of the MRLA. Because of wartime sympathies, a critical mass (of, say five thousand armed guerrillas and a support base ten times the number of fighters) was easily achieved for beginning the insurgency. The promise of a strategic breakout (a broad-based threat to the regime itself) was encouraged by the confidence-shattering debacle of the fall of Singapore. Deprived of a re-solidifying reconquest, the British return to Malaya was tenuous.

Though the insurgency thus profited at the start, its fuel lines quickly became clogged because it got off the ground only in one community. This inability to break out of one ethnic preserve produced the fundamental asymmetry of the Emergency. As universal as its language tried to be, people's war was still seen in Malaya as a Chinese strategy with dubious objectives and no message for traditional Malay nationalism. The MRLA was never able to free its lines of this ethnic obstacle, and its flight crashed in a downward spiral of crossover points.

Though regarded as a textbook counterinsurgency campaign, the story of the Malayan Emergency is as much one of a balance of errors as it is of dashing triumphs. The most fundamental error made by either side, of course, was the failure of the communists to break out of the Chinese community. Communism itself was a more primary mistake because as a belief system it was a poor choice for establishing links to the dominant Malay community. Communist ideology, bluntly, scared traditional Malays, who took comfort in their aristocratic and religious social structures. The general mistake of this poor political choice by some Chinese was compounded by the specific offense of the MPAJA pogrom against rural Malays immediately after the war. Among Malays, communism ever afterward was held in deep suspicion.

As the Indians emerged from World War II as a more permanent presence, their credentials as Malayans were sullied by their wartime activities. The large numbers that joined Japan's Indian National Army and supported the Indian Independence League revealed to Malays some rather un-Malay political aspirations. After the war, when Indians joined in Chinese-sponsored labor union organizing, they aroused further Malay suspicions that Indians were becoming tools of the Chinese. The more conservative Indian leaders who founded MIC did so to make common cause with the Malays and to distance their community from the armed struggle launched by the Chinese. Atoning for their mistakes in this manner, the Indians remained relatively impervious to communist appeals throughout the Emergency.

The story of British error is one of initial mistakes followed by a learning process that produced timely rectifications. The fall of Singapore, of course, was an epic military and political disaster that shook the foundations of the empire. Militarily, despite the lack of a glorious return, in the intense jungle warfare against the Japanese in neighboring Burma, the British learned some invaluable lessons for their subsequent campaign in Malaya. Over half the English officers who served in Malaya had fought in Burma, as had six of the nine British and Gurkha battalions that were first deployed to Malaya.[96]

Politically, in this shock, the British came to see the inevitability of *merdeka*. Their first plan for independence, the Malayan Union, however, nearly paralyzed the British return. It was hatched in India during the war by a colonial office that had come to the conclusion that postwar colonial states would have to abandon imperial principles of divide and rule and embrace features of the egalitarian modern state.[97] Whatever the enlightenment of such thinking, it was a political vision that ethnic Malays in particular were not ready to accept. Awaking to local realities on their return, the British came to their senses in the Federation. Nevertheless, they became distracted in internecine bureaucratic warfare from 1948 to 1950 that gave the communists space to get their insurgency started. The rectification provided by the Briggs plan and its united implementation under Templer, though, allowed the British to break the back of the insurgency in the next two years.

Faced with oblivion, Chin Peng made the final mistake of spurning the *tunku*'s hand at the Bailing talks. People's war as a revolutionary strategy is a rural one, and, with the MRLA's failure to reach the rural Malay *kompongs*, its sole constituency became the Chinese squatters. Separated from this constituency by the Briggs plan, the communists could survive only by returning to the cities—and to the politics of competitive elections. In spurning this path by refusing to disarm, Chin Peng disemboweled his insurgency and again revealed the Achilles' heel of people's war: elections.

Without any outside help, it is hard to imagine a communist takeover in Malaya, but some shifts in direction, or plausible reversibilities, could have seriously complicated the government's position. Indeed, shifts in direction by the British were vital to the continued failure of the communists. Ethnically isolated by their own mistakes, the communists, nevertheless, might have made inroads into the Malay community had not the British quickly abandoned the Union. Also, despite the successes of the British, it remained true that large numbers of Chinese were disaffected by the political process and stood aloof from the Triple Alliance. Had Chin Peng seized the opportunity to switch from fighting to balloting, he way well have laid claim to fair proportions of the Chinese and Indian electorates.

Finally, however solid the British achievements were in corralling the Malay community and co-opting enough Chinese and Indians to fashion their solid political middle ground, these achievements partly rested on a delicacy of timing and sequence. At the beginning, the alliance between the UMNO and the MCA was tentative. In the local elections of 1952, the UMNO faced a serious rival in the IMP. Membership in the IMP was at first open to all communities (as the UMNO and MCA were not), and many Chinese were favorably disposed to the IMP. But in Kuala Lumpur, where the local elections began, the Chinese leader was not, and he embraced the Triple Alliance instead. The alliance swept the elections, and the coalition of expedience solidified into the "community" that swept to power in 1955. To survive, the IMP spurned further overtures to the Chinese and became more ethnically chauvinistic than the UMNO. As Donald Horowitz has presciently observed, had the order of elections been reversed, the course of Malayan politics in the Emergency would have been much more unpredictable.[98]

Comparisons with Vietnam

The case most often thrown up as a counter to the American debacle in Vietnam is the British suppression of the communists in Malaya. Indeed, the parallels for lessons are compelling. Both incumbent regimes faced bands of guerrillas espousing Mao's strategy of people's war. Both governments were assisted by Western powers countering their insurgencies through programs of nation-building. In both cases, Western combat troops were dispatched to fight the insurgents. As a visible symbol of this link, Sir Robert Thompson, a young aide to Templer, became one of President Nixon's official advisers on the Vietnam War.

Another surprising similarity between Malaya and Vietnam (and true also of the rest of the cases) is that the people's wars that the two Western powers faced were preceded by communist failures to mount successful proletarian insurrections in the cities. The differences lay in the fact that in Vietnam and China the communists found a favorable rural environment for switching to a people's war strategy but did not in Greece and did in only one community in Malaya and in only one region in the Philippines.

There are other differences in comparing Malaya to Vietnam. Fundamentally, the nature of opportunity and belief legitimacy was different in the two countries, producing different political effects on the presence of Western combat troops. In Malaya the ethnic split among the three communities created a divided group basis for the legitimation of rule. These divisions were first mediated by British rule and then transferred to an independent intercommunal alliance. The Chinese and Indians, in traditional terms, accepted British "protection" even as the Malays depended on the British to safeguard their special position as *bumiputras*. In this sense, the armed struggle of the MCP was seen as a unilateral bid to upset this system and, within the Chinese community, as an attempt to overthrow its own leadership. The British "intervention," then, even with ground combat troops, was seen as a legitimate effort to resynchronize these traditional arrangements. In Vietnam, the American intervention in behalf of the Saigon regime was a slap in the face of the traditional Mandate of Heaven, particularly because the claim of the regime to this mandate was slender.

In modern terms, the age of the white man was fast receding, and the British, prompted by Singapore and reminded by Dienbienphu, agreed in the middle of their intervention to let go of their rule. The Triple Alliance was thus able to seize *merdeka* as its own, and the MCP, by spurning the offer extended at the Bailing talks, lost a chance to claim a part of it as well. By this grant, the British staved off whatever remained of the issue of British troops undermining the legitimacy of the new Malayan government.

The French, in refusing to make a similar grant, destroyed any chance of legitimacy for the hapless Emperor Bao Dai. The situation facing the French, however, was different. Any grant of genuine independence in Indochina would have meant turning the colony over to the communists. Either way, they lost. The Americans inherited from the French something of this same dilemma. The harder they fought with their combat troops to stave off an immediate South Vietnamese military defeat, the more this very effort undermined the political legitimacy of the Saigon regime — trapping the United States in the clutches of an ever more desperate illegitimacy lock by the regime's ruling circle.

Nation-building for new avenues of societal access and political participation was the key task that both the British and the Americans set for themselves, but there were differences in scale and quality. The program most admired in Malaya was the Briggs resettlement plan. Similar schemes in Vietnam were disasters. The Briggs plan was a modest one for a half million Chinese squatters who had no titles to their lands and had been uprooted from their previous occupations, conditions totally dissimilar from the long-entrenched peasants of the Mekong Delta. In Vietnam, President Diem intended to resettle seven million peasants into 5,753 hamlets within a year, a task utterly beyond the bureaucratic capacity of any developing country.[99]

The Briggs plan also laid the foundation for the military success of the British, primarily through breakthroughs in intelligence. Again, however, negative military comparisons between the performance of the Americans and British are unfair without reference to their respective adversaries. As in the U.S. vice-presidential debate of 1988, when Lloyd Bentsen acidly observed that Dan Quayle was no John Kennedy, so also was the MRLA no Viet Cong. After the death of its chief military leader one month after the start of the Emergency, the MRLA had few remaining competent commanders and, in the field, had no weapons larger than machine guns. The Viet Cong, by contrast, were well led and equipped with rockets, mortars, and even heavy artillery.[100] Also, if the adage is correct that armies always fight their last wars, then Burma was a better last war for the British in Malaya than Korea was for the Americans in Vietnam.

The success of the British, however, does raise the question of leadership. Richard Clutterbuck, for example, has pointed with pride to the "three-staged leadership rocket" of Briggs, Templer, and the *tunku*.[101] On the government side, one is hard-pressed to think of similar figures in Vietnam. Some names at the intermediate level come to mind—Nguyen Be, who ran the Revolutionary Development Cadres; Ngo Quang Truong, who commanded I Corps; and the colorful American adviser John Paul Vann—but these men were not in a position to determine the basic course of the war. Although the precise role of leadership is difficult to assess, in Malaya this "rocket" acted as the steward of an institutionalizing process set in motion by the British government.

The capstone of nation-building in both countries was the birth of a democratic society through competitive elections. But in these countries the scale of the communist threat to these elections was dramatically different. The Viet Cong already had the largest political organization in the country when the Vietnamese constitution was adopted in 1966. Rather than face up to this challenge, Nguyen Van Thieu balked and disqualified the communists from the 1967 elections. In Vietnam, however, the communist strength was so large that no political community could be achieved without them. In

Malaya, though, at the Bailing talks the MCP was still in the fledgling position of a political beggar. Rather than take up the challenge of participating in the Constitutional Contract and its path to people's rule, Chin Peng drew back and retreated to the isolation of his people's war—dooming his vision of a Malayan Dienbienphu to a will-of-the-wisp. The British stepped out of the shadow of Dienbienphu and unmade an insurgency by making a democracy.

Chapter 10

CAMBODIA'S "AUTOGENOCIDE" AND THE DISAPPEARANCE OF LAOS, 1949–1975

Cambodia and Laos are treated together in this chapter because they shared a common colonial heritage as contiguous backwaters to the French Empire. Before the colonial era, they also partook of a common Theravada Buddhist political culture, which Stanley Tambiah has called a "galactic polity."[1] Thus their traditional standards of legitimacy came from common sources and their exposure to modern political values followed similar paths. Moreover, barring exceptional periods of historical glory, both have been small powers in which foreign intervention, however resented, has been an intrinsic part of their destinies. This vulnerability has been reinforced by their status as the most backward and poor countries of this study. Per capita income in Laos during its insurgency was less than $100 per year, and it was only slightly more in Cambodia. The figure for South Vietnam was at least three times that of Laos, and Vietnam had undergone greater institutional development. Like Malaya, both Cambodia and Laos were underpopulated. With 89,000 square miles, Laos was the largest of the Indochinese states, followed by Cambodia with 71,000, and South Vietnam with 66,000; yet, in the 1960s, Laos had only 3 million people and Cambodia 6 million compared to South Vietnam's 15 million and North Vietnam's 17 million. Over 80 percent of the Cambodian and Lao populations were engaged in some form of agriculture, but less than half the land was under cultivation. Though there were rural grievances aplenty, land reform was not one of them.[2]

For all these commonalities, their struggles for national liberation were strikingly different. Both these struggles, nevertheless, became enmeshed in the far larger and overshadowing war in Vietnam. From the American point of view, this confusion only magnified the tragedy of the three results. For the communists, in this revolutionary backwash, the Cambodians committed a bloody and senseless suicide while the Laotians quietly disappeared. In addition to the thematic questions driving this study as a whole, this chapter, in a brief epilogue, will address a more case-specific question as to why, relatively speaking, the Cambodian revolution was so bloody, the Laotian so gentle, and the Vietnamese so orderly.

Historical Setting

Cambodia and Laos are the proud possessors of moments of precolonial glory. In A.D. 802 Jayavarman II broke his feudal ties to the Majapahit kingdom of Java and established an independent Khmer dynasty in Cambodia. By the thirteenth century, its majestic capital of Angkor Wat contained the largest religious building that has ever been built. In the fourteenth century, Fa Ngoum founded the first Lao kingdom, Lan Xang (Land of a Million Elephants). The glories of both Angkor and Lan Xang, however, were fading by the seventeenth century. Indeed, Laos had split up into three principalities, and in 1827 the king of Thailand sacked the city of Vien Chang, destroyed its royal line, and seized Lao territory up to the Mekong River. This seizure permanently upset the demographic balance between the Lao and the mountain tribespeople they were conquering. Most Lao lived west of the Mekong, and those east of the Mekong faced a fifty-fifty split with the tribals. As late as 1957, five million ethnic Lao lived across the river in Northeast Thailand and only a million and a half resided in Laos proper.[3]

Nevertheless, both societies had several centuries of independent rule. Both also had their founding myths. For Cambodia, a Brahmin prince from India married a local princess, drained the swamps with his magic sword, and formed the kingdom of Kambuja around the big lake Tonle Sap. For Laos, it all began at Dienbienphu, where a gourd from a vine revealed to the first ruler the hierarchical ordering of heaven, nature, and human society. Indian principles of governance, first Brahmanic and then Theravada Buddhist, came to legitimate the rule of the two kingdoms. Sacred objects were brought to each capital to undergird the king's authority as a *devaraja*, a god-king. For Cambodia, it was the scale and munificence of Angkor Wat itself. The Laotians took a statue of Buddha from Angkor Wat and placed it in a temple they triumphantly built over the previous spiritual center in Luang Prabang of a local animist religion. This temple of the Phra Bang Buddha is the cultic symbol of the Lao nation.

Thus there developed a trinity of national identity for Laotians and Cambodians centered in king, Buddha, and country. The king was to protect and support the *sangha*, or Buddhist clergy and temples. In return, the clergy aided in the selection of the king and reinforced his claim to a divine mission in upholding the axis between the heavenly and earthly cosmos. The king automatically held this role both by the Hindu laws of *karma* and the Buddhist notion of merit. According to the former, the king merited his position by his obviously worthy behavior in previous lives. To his countrymen, then, his authority was automatic. Beyond this automatic authority, according to the latter, the king earned the merit of his people's favor by further acts of virtue, both religious and political. Traditional legitimacy, in brief, provided a bonus for performance such as in the building of temples, roads, and canals; ensuring bountiful harvests; adding to the realm through military conquests; and promoting the spread of Buddhism. If he did all this, he could call himself a *chakravartin*, a universal emperor.[4]

From the Thais, both monarchies incorporated the practice of dual lines of rule. For the Laotians the second king was institutionalized as a viceroy (*maha oupahat*). In Cambodia the practice was more one of alternating rule between two closely tied families.[5] Nevertheless, both societies were organized hierarchically in descending tiers of royalty, nobility and Buddhist clergy, commoners, and various categories of slaves. In Laos, there was the added distinction of the ethnic lowland Lao (Lao Loum) from the original *Lao Theung* (called *kha*, or slaves) and the more recent eighteenth-century migrations of Hmong and Yao peoples from South China called Lao Seung. Also, though Luang Prabang was the symbolic capital of Laos, the monarch had to contend with the independent proclivities of his principalities.[6] In Cambodia, the monarchy was more centralized and its subjects far more ethnically homogeneous, but it was constrained by several checks. Because of the system of two royal lines, the king directly ruled only forty-one of Cambodia's fifty-six traditional provinces. The former king, the designated heir, and the queen mother were entrusted with the rest. Provincial officials themselves, the *okya*, had a long tradition of independence, and, back in court, the king had to contend with the "advice" of a powerful Council of Five Ministers.[7]

Despite these structural and demographic differences, by the nineteenth century both of these once proud kingdoms were being battered at will by the Vietnamese and the Thais. Whole provinces were being ingested at both ends of Cambodia, and in Laos the ruling family disappeared in the sacking of the principality of Vien Chang. Then the French appeared. In their search for a flanking river into the Chinese interior around the British ports on the Chinese coast, the French, though they never made it to China, established protectorates over Cambodia and Laos (in 1863 and 1893 respectively). In so doing, they saved both countries from extinction.

In good Khmer tradition, the French built a magnificent palace complex at Phnom Penh, centrally situated at the confluence of the country's great rivers. The dynasty obligingly moved in from its previous capital. The royal Cambodians were mostly grateful to the French, but out-group lines frequently intrigued with the Thai. Popular revolts fanned by culturally outraged Buddhist monks were more serious. The Buddhist *sangha* was less closely tied to the monarchy than in Thailand or Laos and, as in Vietnam, represented a focal point of traditionalist protest.[8] In Laos, the French imperium was extremely light. The colonial government had only one hundred positions compared to the forty thousand in Cochinchina alone. When the French established their residency in Vien Chang (renamed Vientiane), a political vacancy obligingly created by the depredations of the Thais, there was no protest from either the king or his *sangha*. But the tribal minorities were another matter. Both the Kha and the Hmong broke out into revolts, and the French were both hard-pressed and brutal in suppressing them.[9]

Even in these backwaters, the French introduced some trappings of modernity. In Cambodia they used French education for the elite to create a "responsive" colonial administration. To these urban centers of France's *mission civilisatrice* (mainly Phnom Penh and Vientiane), they also brought in a cadre of Vietnamese clerks and bureaucrats. A vigorous trade developed by Chinese merchants along the Mekong River that the two countries shared bound them to the world economy.[10] In eastern Cambodia, the French extended the network of rubber plantations they had started in Cochinchina to compete with the British in Malaya. Similarly, they opened up tin mines in Tonkin and even one in Laos. Politically, aside from the vast tribal areas in the mountains, the French found extending the sway of their rule in Laos easy. The power of the king, they discovered, was more ritual than real. Cambodia was more complicated, and the French sought to stay on top of the endemic aristocratic intrigue by alternating rule between the Sisowath and Norodom royal lines. Prince Norodom Sihanouk has always been proud of his family's French reputation of having been the more difficult of the two.[11]

As in all our cases, this mixing of the traditional and modern socioeconomic orders touched off the political ferment that gave birth to modern nationalist movements, including communist ones. The trigger events of the modern political struggles of both Cambodia and Laos came during World War II.

One early nationalist impulse came from the bizarre and syncretistic Cao Dai sect that began in 1925 in Tay Ninh, a Cochinchinese town close to the Cambodian border. The sect was immensely popular among Khmer Krom (ethnic Cambodians living in Vietnam) and quickly spread into Cambodia. The Buddhist *sangha* felt deeply threatened by this new faith, and the French, who had had more than their fill of Buddhist revolts, became eager to promote Buddhism. They built and repaired pagodas and established in Phnom Penh a national Institute for the Study of Buddhism. This institute attracted both Buddhist theologians and political nationalists. The fiery editor of its journal, Son Ngoc Thanh, was distinctly in the latter category and, despite his subsequent association with the CIA, was one of the first modern Cambodian nationalists.[12]

The sudden collapse of France in World War II and the installation of a pro-Nazi Vichy regime in Paris produced a near fatal crack in the foundations of French rule in all of Indochina. In the Greater East Asia Co-Prosperity Sphere that was established by the Japanese, Vichy French rule in Indochina was allowed to continue, as long as it did not disturb this new Japanese order. In managing this delicate mission, the Vichy high commissioner for Indochina, Admiral Jean Decoux, faced a succession crisis in Cambodia with the death of King Sisowath Monireth in 1941. Hoping to have someone on the throne malleable to French interests, Decoux picked an eighteen-year-old playboy prince who was of the Norodom line but had a Sisowath mother.[13] Norodom Sihanouk was certainly flexible, but he was not malleable. If malleable means bending to the will of others and flexible means bending to get one's will, Sihanouk's career over the next fifty years became a vivid demonstration of this definitional difference. Coronated by the French, Sihanouk was loyal to them during the war. For this he earned the lifelong hatred of Son Ngoc Thanh. Thanh led anti-French demonstrations in 1942 and then fled to Japan. When the Japanese struck the French with their March 9, 1945, coup de force, Sihanouk declared Cambodia's freedom from the French. But he thought better of it when the Japanese installed Son Ngoc Thanh as prime minister.[14]

With the start of the Resistance War in 1946 against the reimposition of French rule in Vietnam, Cambodians found themselves caught up in it as well. Son Ngoc Thanh founded his own guerrilla force, the Khmer Isarrak (Free Khmer), and fought against both the king and the French in the south and west with Thai help. Some of these guerrillas went over to the Viet Minh, who set up a resistance against the French in the northeast. In the cities, the passed-over Sisowath line founded the Democratic party and fought Sihanouk politically. Meanwhile, Sihanouk gambled on being able to achieve independence diplomatically. In a series of moves from January to October of 1953, he persuaded the French to give Cambodia independence while their attention focused on their deteriorating position in Vietnam. Thus Sihanouk succeeded where all his opponents had failed.[15] As one communist source lamented, Sihanouk had stolen their revolution from them.[16]

In Indochina, Laos was the most vulnerable to the delicate arrangements between Vichy France and Japan. Neighboring Thailand became Japan's wartime ally. From this alliance, Japan used Thailand as a springboard for its further conquests. Thailand, in turn, saw this alliance as a means to regain territories it had lost to earlier colonial encroachments, particularly in Laos. In short order, it launched an offensive that regained the two Laotian provinces west of the Mekong. Indeed, the Japanese were willing to let all of Laos become a Thai "protectorate." To prevent this, the French launched a crash "Lao awakening" program to steer the Lao elite away from the lure of the pan-Thai movement in vogue in Thailand. Seven thousand schools were built to develop a Lao consciousness, and the French, for the first time, acknowledged that the king of Luang Prabang was the ruling dynasty of all Laos.[17]

The war, nevertheless, produced a split in the Lao elite. Most, of course, went along with the Vichy French and, by extension, the Japanese. But others sided with the Free French. This split produced a confusion over the Japanese coup de force on March 9, 1945. The king of Luang Prabang was ordered by the Japanese to declare independence. Instead he proclaimed an uprising against the Japanese, who immediately suppressed it. Nevertheless, the viceroy, Prince Phetsareth, and his two younger brothers, Souvanna Phouma and Souphanouvong, organized the Lao Isarra (Free Laos) and eventually persuaded the king to declare independence from both the French and Japanese.[18]

By the end of 1945, however, the French announced their intention to reestablish French protection over Laos. Prince Souphanouvong was made commander in chief of the Lao Isarra. In March 1946, the Laotians made a stand against the French at the town of Thakek and were decisively defeated. Three thousand were killed and the prince was wounded.[19] The king and viceroy entered into negotiations with the French and agreed in August of 1947 to a unified kingdom of Laos under French protection. With this agreement, the Lao Isarra dissolved. Souphanouvong, in protest, founded a Neo Lao Isarra in 1949 under the sponsorship of the Viet Minh. The French were still able to raise a substantial army among the Lao, and a Lao-French force beat back two Viet Minh drives on Luang Prabang in 1953. At the Geneva Accords of 1954, both Laos and Cambodia participated as independent states.[20]

In the middle of this ferment, communism in Cambodia and Laos had modest beginnings. As mentioned in Chapter 4, the Indochinese Communist party (ICP) was founded in 1930 in Shanghai by Ho Chi Minh at the behest of the Comintern. Despite its regional rubric, for all practical purposes, it was a Vietnamese party. Indeed, until the late 1940s, Cambodians and Laotians were mere tokens in the history of the ICP. The Viet Minh began its own military activity in Laos October 1945. Prince Souphanouvong did receive support from the Viet Minh in the stand of the Lao lsarra at Thakek. Souphanouvong was not satisfied with the May 1947 constitution with the French and continued in the resistance with the Viet Minh. In February 1949, however, Souphanouvong started his own resistance, the Neo Lao Isarra. For this he was promptly expelled from the Lao Isarra, which then disbanded.[21]

Committing his organization to a firm path of revolution, on August 15, 1950, Souphanouvong convened the First Lao Resistance Conference in which he structured his Neo Lao Isarra into a front similar to the Viet Minh. The front took the name Neo Lao Hak Sat (National Liberation Front). It, and its military arm, became more widely known as the Pathet Lao (Land of the Lao). The front was supposed to be guided by the communist People's party of Laos, but how firmly this nucleus organization was established has never been clear. With the Viet Minh in a dominant political and military position, the need for such a party was hardly pressing. Indeed, the Viet Minh took over two northern Laotian provinces, Sam Neua and Phong Saly, and set up their own political administration with Pathet Lao as training apprentices. Similarly, they helped recruit and train a Pathet Lao military force that grew to fifteen hundred by the end of the Resistance War.[22]

The origins of communism in Cambodia followed the same confusing path as in Laos. On April 17, 1950, two hundred delegates (half of them monks) met in Southwest Cambodia for the First National Congress of Khmer Resistance organized by Achr Mean, a former monk who was a member of the ICP. What was confusing was that the organization this congress founded was called the United Issarak Front (UIF), which sounded like Son Ngoc Thanh's Khmer Issarak. Indeed, at this congress Achr Mean adopted the nomme de guerre Son Ngoc Minh, a not too subtle but ideologically perplexing combination of Son Ngoc Thanh and Ho Chi Minh. The next year, Cambodian communists established the Khmer People's Revolutionary party (KPRP) as the vanguard to their front. The structure of this party followed guidelines established by the Viet Minh, and it was submitted to them for their approval.

Some fifty-seven hundred Cambodians fought with the UIF against the French. The Viet Minh stationed three thousand of their own guerrillas in Cambodia to run the headquarters for their operations in Cochinchina. After the French gave independence to Cambodia in November 1953, a combined Viet Minh–UIF force attacked Northeast Cambodia in March 1954 (during the height of the siege at Dienbienphu). An outraged King Sihanouk personally commanded the counterattack that scattered the guerrillas. At Geneva, the communists in Cambodia got nothing. In fact, as a result of the Geneva Accords, along with the twelve thousand Viet Minh regroupees, Son Ngoc Minh and one thousand UIF guerrillas accompanied these regroupees back to North Vietnam.[23]

The history of Cambodian communism, however, had another strand. From 1949 to 1953 a wave of students from the Cambodian elite were sent to Paris. A group of these students were drawn into the Marxist-Leninist circle of a young Cambodian aristocrat.[24] Ten of them became the Paris group that would eventually and vengefully gain control of the party. The group included Hu Nim, Hu Yuon, and Khieu Samphan all of whom earned Ph.D. degrees. Two others, Ieng Sary and Saloth Sar, were not so successful. Indeed, Saloth Sar (later Pol Pot) flunked an electrician certificate program twice at a technical college. The latter two became close friends when they married two sisters in their group. At a Berlin Youth Festival in 1951, some of them met communists from the UIF who led them to the necessity of armed struggle at home.[25]

Back in Paris, they excitedly plotted their return. In 1952 they circulated a letter critical of King Sihanouk and promptly had their scholarships pulled.[26] Before they returned home in 1953, Saloth Sar brought his more intellectual friends down to earth with the declaration: "It is I who will direct the revolutionary organization! I will become Secretary General, I will hold the dossiers, I will control the ministries, and I will see to it that there is no deviation from the line fixed by the central committee in the interests of the people."[27]

When Cambodia and Laos emerged as independent kingdoms after the Geneva Conference, they sought to establish themselves as modern constitutional monarchies. Actually, this modern polity was something of a hybrid in that the traditional monarchical lines continued in a new context of democratic national assemblies patterned after the French republic. Indeed, the kings were to maintain a regal aloofness on a Thai model as the details of governance were left to others.

The Laotians followed this model for twenty years until 1975. In Cambodia, Sihanouk was too restless for such detachment. He abdicated in 1955 and turned the throne over to his father so that he could rule directly. As Prince Sihanouk, he became the head of state. The first thing he did was to found his own political party, the People's Socialist Community (Sangkum Reastr Niyum). Though as king he had spurned electoral politics, in the 1955 National Assembly elections his Sangkum won every seat, taking 80 percent of the vote to the Democrats' 12 percent (a right-wing party allied with the Sisowath line) and the communist-front Pracheachon's 4 percent.[28]

Sihanouk's best years as head of state were from 1955 to 1963. He owed his success to his remarkable political agility in managing the three simultaneous games of Cambodian politics. Because 85 percent of the population was rural, the foundational sine qua non of Cambodia, or its first game, was the passive support of the peasantry for the national leader. In sharp contrast to President Diem, whose rare and awkward rural forays only emphasized a rural-urban alienation, Sihanouk's frequent rural travels, with his rambling expositions on "Buddhist socialism," constantly recemented the passive, but vital, traditional king and country bond.[29]

The second game was staying on top of the politics among the urban elites. Here active group commitments were necessary because in this arena governments could be overthrown. Therefore, the line between this and the third game — that of using various foreign interventions — often became blurred. The more players there were in the cities, the better Sihanouk did. With everyone in town, Sihanouk's Sangkum allowed him to preside over a nearly one-party state. Business interests, however, were allied with the Democratic party, the Sisowaths, and, somewhat loosely, with the Thais. Sihanouk kept the military close to him, but the officer corps also felt a loyalty to the United States. Leftists were split between supporting the Pracheachon or working directly for the outlets of the KPRP. In the National Assembly elections of 1958, the Sangkum gained 99 percent of the vote, a feat Sihanouk repeated in a referendum on his policies the next year.[30]

But votes were not everything. One person who did not return to the cities after independence was Son Ngoc Thanh. Instead, he opposed the prince with a guerrilla force, the Khmer Serei (Free Khmer), that was backed by Thai interests and to some extent funded by the CIA. When Thanh staged a brief rebellion in 1959, Sihanouk embarked on what he called his "long war with the CIA."[31] With the far right beaten down, Sihanouk turned on the far left, suppressing communists in both the country and the cities in 1959 to 1960. He split their forces by co-opting some of the open leftists into his government. Thus Hu Nim, Hu Yuon, and Khieu Samphan remained as public figures, which had the effect of neutralizing the Pracheachon.[32]

From 1963 to 1967, however, Prince Sihanouk began to cut his maneuvering room from under his feet. The Pracheachon was neutralized by Sihanouk's nationalizing in 1963 of both the domestic banking industry and the foreign trading concerns. These were measures that all three communist cabinet ministers had called for in their writings. This, of course, deeply alienated the modern business sector, what Sihanouk called the Khmer Bleues. In the international game, the prince was determined to keep Cambodia out of the Vietnam War. It was his judgment that the way to do that was to fix his star to China both to outlast the ephemeral American presence and to keep the more permanent Vietnamese at bay.[33] In 1963, he suspended all American aid, and in 1965 he broke diplomatic relations with Washington. The same year he sponsored an Indochinese People's Conference, with Beijing's blessings, to denounce American imperialism.[34]

But Beijing's blessings did not translate into enough material assistance to offset the loss in American hardware. The royal army, in particular, was badly hurt by these cuts. In 1967 its weakness compelled it to look the other way when Sihanouk agreed to let the North Vietnamese extend the Ho Chi Minh Trail throughout eastern Cambodia and use the port of Sihanoukville to provision the Tet offensive. As the economy deteriorated, Sihanouk lost control of the slate of candidates for his Sangkum party. Thus the right-wing slate of the Sangkum party that swept the elections of 1966 forced on Sihanouk a hostile National Assembly. The prince confessed to being depressed about Cambodia's political system.[35] His problems went beyond a political headache when, in April 1967, peasants erupted into open revolt in Sumlaut, Battambang province. With the boards of Cambodia's three political games breaking under his feet, Sihanouk faced both revolt and revolution even as Cambodia was swept into the tide of a wider war.

In the several party histories laying out the Maoist stages to the communist revolution, the years from 1950 to Sumlaut were the "era of political struggle."[36] The struggles were numerous, and the disappointments were many. During this period, the Cambodian communists struggled in four groups. The main organization that had founded the party under Viet Minh tutelage continued to build a base in the countryside. Some returned to the cities, where they divided into two groups. Hu Nim, Hou Yuon, Khieu Samphan, and others joined the Pracheachon party, where they took part in the open politics of the government. More directly, Saloth Sar and Ieng Sary took up the revolutionary struggle, organizing party cells among students and workers and publishing revolutionary tracts. In 1959, the movement suffered a devastating blow when Sieu Heng, the leader of the rural-based communists, defected to Sihanouk. Over the next year, 90 percent of the party cadre was lost.[37] The South Vietnamese communists had suffered a similar devastation in the late 1950s under President Diem, but the Geneva Conference regroupees reinfiltrated back to South Vietnam to keep the revolution alive. Despite the crisis back home, the Cambodian regroupees in North Vietnam with Tran Ngoc Minh (the fourth group) waited another ten years before they returned.

What was left of the party, mainly those in Phnom Penh, reconstituted themselves in September 1960 as the Workers party of Kampuchea. Though the absent Tran Ngoc Minh was the titular head, Touch Samouth, who was sympathetic to the Vietnamese, became secretary-general. Saloth Sar and Ieng Sary (the direct party workers) became third- and fifth-ranking members of the politburo.[38] In 1963 Touch Samouth disappeared, and, at a party conclave in February, Saloth Sar became secretary-general (as he predicted) and Ieng Sary number three in the politburo. Five of twelve politburo members were from the Paris group. Most of this direct revolutionary group went underground in 1963 during Sihanouk's crackdown on leftists. With the election of the right-wing National Assembly in 1966, the open election competing group did as well.[39]

Though party histories insist that the Sumlaut uprising was the product of careful party preparations,[40] the event bore the mark of a spontaneous rural revolt that the communists were quick to take advantage of, just as the fledgling ICP did with the Nghe Tin soviets of 1930–31. At Sumlaut, peasants from the Southeast were promised newly irrigated land in Battambang province, where, unfortunately, peasants were already settled. The peasants on this land were growing rice under contract with the Vietnamese but were abruptly ordered to sell their rice to the Cambodian army at half the contract price. When the army and the two groups of peasants met, there was a clash. However it came about, for the communists, the long period of preparation was over. The armed struggle had begun.[41]

As a fully independent country after the Geneva Accords, Laos held its first elections for the National Assembly in 1955. Despite a boycott by the Pathet Lao, Katay Sasorith became prime minister and his Progressive party won twenty-one of thirty-nine seats. Prince Souvanna Phouma, however, emerged as the dominant figure in Lao politics in the succeeding years, and he was determined to bring the Pathet Lao into a coalition government.[42] As part of his efforts, on January 18, 1958, fifteen hundred Pathet Lao troops (out of some three thousand) were integrated into the twenty-five thousand-man Royal Laotian Army (RLA). Then supplementary National Assembly elections were held in May. The Pathet Lao's political organization, the Neo Lao Hak Sat, won nine of the twenty-one seats and an allied party won four. The most popular candidate in the election was Prince Souphanouvong, who was declared president of the National Assembly. Pro-government candidates won in only eight races. In part, this was because the pro-government vote was split among four or five parties. Overall, the government won 549,000 votes to 450,000 for the Pathet Lao, and another 278,000 votes went to independents. Thoroughly alarmed at this leftward turn of events, two government parties merged to create the Rally of the Lao people and formed a government with twenty-nine seats under a rightist prime minister, Phoui Sananikone. Spearheading this rightward reaction was an extragovernment organization called the Committee for the Defense of National Interests (CDNI).[43]

Angered at this turn to the right in spite of its electoral victory, one of the two Pathet Lao battalions in the Royal Laotian Army slipped into the hills in the spring of 1959, and in July Pathet Lao units began a military campaign against the RLA. More determined than ever to remove all vestiges of the Pathet Lao from the government, the anticommunists set up elections for April 1960. The CDNI formed itself into the Paxa Sangkhom (PS — Social Democrats) and won thirty-five seats in an election that Martin Goldstein labeled a "model of fraud and dishonesty." Souvanna Phouma called them a sham. The communists did not win a seat.[44]

Souvanna Phouma's outrage was shared by Captain Kong Le, a paratroop battalion commander, who staged a lightning coup in August and seized Vientiane. Kong Le's blow was struck for more than sympathy for the Pathet Lao; it was also a moral outburst against the official corruption that accompanied the high volume of American aid ($417 million from 1954 to 1962).[45] Having made his point, he lacked a political direction. Soon, however, he came under the tutelage of Quinim Pholsena, a neutralist with Pathet Lao leanings.[46] Sensing a revolutionary opportunity in the resulting confusion, the Russians began sending aid to both the Pathet Lao and the Neutralists. By the spring of 1961, the Neutralists and Pathet Lao, under the titular leadership of Souvanna Phouma, controlled half the people and could call on a force of twenty thousand to the government's thirty-five thousand. After much infighting, three princes (Boun Oum for the rightists, Souvanna Phouma, and Souphanouvong) agreed in October to establish a coalition government.[47]

No sooner was the agreement concluded than it was upset by renewed fighting in northern Laos around the garrison at Nam Tha. Against American advice, the Lao defense minister reinforced it with five thousand of his best troops. After a two-day assault spearheaded by North Vietnamese troops, the post fell. The military balance was destroyed, and, with the specter of the Pathet Lao being able "to sweep across Laos as unopposed as a bolt of lightning slashing across the sky,"[48] President Kennedy dispatched five thousand U.S. troops to Thailand and warned the Pathet Lao to stop fighting. The fighting soon did subside as all parties, both international and national, returned to the bargaining table. On July 16, 1962, the Plain of Jars Agreement was concluded in which a coalition government was set up with Souvanna Phouma as premier and Souphanouvong and Phoumi Nosavan as vice-premiers. Under this arrangement the Pathet Lao was given four cabinet ministries.[49] A few days later (July 23) in Geneva, the Russians, Chinese, British, French, Americans, North and South Vietnamese, Laos, and others announced the Declaration and Protocol on the Neutrality of Laos. It prohibited the introduction of foreign troops and called for the withdrawal of all such forces in seventy-five days.[50]

Despite all the international attention, this set of agreements did not stick. Although the United States withdrew 666 of its military personnel within the stipulated time, Hanoi withdrew only 40 of its estimated 10,000 troops in Laos.[51] On the political front, the Pathet Lao withdrew from the coalition government in April 1963, when Quinim Pholsena was assassinated. The Pathet Lao turned on the Neutralists and by the spring of 1964 had dislodged them from the Plain of Jars. The chief contestants in the now full-fledged civil war once again were the communists and anticommunists, with Souvanna Phouma at the head of the government.[52]

Despite the retrospective declaration by communists in Cambodia that Sumlaut launched their armed struggle, for three years this armed struggle did not go well. During the Tet offensive in Vietnam, Sihanouk ordered an all-out attack on communists in which Saloth Sar was nearly captured. Like Giap before him, he fled to the hills and began to recruit an army among the tribal population in the Northeast. By the end of 1969, all he had to show for it was a force of five thousand—enough for a critical mass, perhaps, but not much more.[53]

It was enough, however, to alarm Sihanouk because from 1967 to 1970 his hold on power was weakening. Like Marie Antoinette's scandalous diamond necklace in the French Revolution, accusations surfaced in 1968 that Princess Monique was corruptly enriching herself and that the queen mother was running a brothel. The prince did not help matters by opening a gaudy casino in Phnom Penh to raise government revenue in early 1969. By the end of the year, Sihanouk started to backpedal. He acquiesced to a rightist denationalization program. He reestablished ties with the United States and agreed to accept American aid. He even "acquiesced" to the secret fourteen-month U.S. bombing campaign Operation Menu (begun in March 1969) to drive Vietnamese communists out of their border sanctuaries in Cambodia. But it was too late.[54]

True to ancient Cambodian auguries of drastic cosmic transformations, stories of white crocodiles swimming in the Mekong wafted into Phnom Penh in March 1970. When an anxious Queen Mother Kossamak drew a sacred sword of Angkor to divine these portents for her Riviera-vacationing son, the blade emerged blackened from its scabbard.[55] Indeed, on March 18, 1970, Sihanouk was "legally deposed" by a variety of factions led by Sisowath Sirik Matak, Tran Ngoc Thanh, and General Lon Nol. To some extent, the CIA lent its hand to support this intrigue.[56] With General, soon to be Marshal, Lon Nol as its eventual head, the new regime proclaimed Cambodia a republic, the monarchy dead, and "staked its legitimacy on a vow to rid the country of the threat from the Vietnamese Communists."[57] On a wave of anti-Vietnamese enthusiasm, Cambodia's army swelled from 35,000 to 110,000 in two months. The Marshal then launched two epic campaigns, Chenla I and II (named after Cambodia's first independent kingdom), against the traditional enemy. After the end of first campaign, he had given up half the country to the North Vietnamese army. By the time the second campaign ended in December 1972, his army was shattered. Except defensively behind barricades, it would fight no more.[58]

For the communists, 1970 to 1973 were every bit the transitional years of multiple crossover points that 1967 to 1970 were not. Three dynamics propelled this growth. First, with no place else to go, Sihanouk joined forces with the communists. On March 23, he announced the formation of the Khmer National United Front (FUNK), and in May he proclaimed a joint government with the communists. Peasants joined the Front in droves and government soldiers deserted, including the entire garrison in Kratie. In the same period that the government's army tripled, the Khmer People's National Liberation Armed Forces (PFLANK) also grew threefold to a force of fifteen thousand supported by fifty thousand irregulars.[59] During the Chenla offensives, perhaps as many as a million peasants came under their control.

Second, during this period the communists actively courted the peasantry. Collectives were established and extensive land reform was carried out in the Southeast. Agricultural productivity doubled in revolutionary areas.[60] Among a list of "precepts" distributed to party cadres for handling peasants, the third one admonished: "If one wrongs the people, he must beg their pardon."[61] Through Sihanouk's defection and these policies, the communists built the political base for their people's war.

Finally, militarily, the communists benefited mightily from the enlargement of the war. Lon Nol's directly confrontational stance toward Hanoi marked a sharp break with Sihanouk's desperate efforts to keep Cambodia out of the war. When the Americans launched their sixty-day "incursion" into Cambodia in April 1970, it stirred up a hornet's nest of North Vietnamese troops. Within months, they had sheared off the northern half of the country. Behind this shield, the Cambodian communists built up their forces. After the defeat of Chenla II in December 1972, the North Vietnamese turned the fighting over to a PFLANK force that had grown to fifty thousand.[62]

Behind this growth, however, was a riptide of factional strife that eventually exploded into paranoid frenzy. At the outset, one particularly unwelcome development, at least to the controlling Paris group, was the return of Tran Ngoc Minh and his regroupees. Though they provided essential military training, Pol Pot and his entourage regarded them as proxies for Vietnamese influence. They were gradually eliminated, many of them as cannon fodder for the American bombing blitz of 1973.[63] Another source of discomfort to this group was its heavy dependence on Sihanouk for rural mobilization. Indeed, in this growth, the party lacked the cadres to supervise it.[64] The problem was that the Sihanoukists were not sufficiently hostile to the Vietnamese and their Cambodian regroupees. All this inhibited the ability of the ruling group to assume control of their own revolution. Another problem was that the rapid military growth brought with it a decentralization of the PFLANK command into seven military regions each with its own autonomous commanders. The Paris group was sure of its control over the Northeast, East, and Southwest regions, but not the others.[65] The root of this problem of control lay in an imbalance of numbers. By liberation in 1975, PFLANK had seventy thousand fighters for a communist party of only fourteen thousand members. Controlling this revolution was a party cadre of merely one thousand.[66] Though very few, they were very dedicated.

Whatever the problem the communists were having, the Phnom Penh that Sihanouk had left behind continued to rot. After the failure of the Chenla offensives, Lon Nol ordered elections in late 1972 to relegitimate his rule. A respectable liberal politician won in Phnom Penh, but the overall result went to the marshal in a charade of ballot corralling in the countryside.[67] But in the interests of the larger war, the Americans held the Lon Nol government afloat. From 1970 to 1975, U.S. aid totaled $2.3 billion. With it, President Richard Nixon pledged his "all-out support" for the Khmer Republic.[68]

From 1973 to 1975, everything turned nasty in Cambodia. After faltering in January, the communists opened up a coordinated attack on Phnom Penh in February 1973 that ran into a firestorm of American bombing. From February to August 15, when the U.S. Congress cut off funding for all U.S. military action in Indochina, 253,000 tons of bombs fell over Cambodia. When it was over, the offensive was beaten back with perhaps half the besieging force of twenty-five thousand killed.[69] As the communist forces returned to the countryside to lick their wounds, they were determined not to lose control of the peasants under their control. They stopped begging their pardons and, instead, eliminated those who sided with Sihanouk or the Vietnamese. The "killing fields" began early in the countryside.[70]

In January 1975, the communists launched their final offensive, which was relentless thanks both to Vietnamese artillery and a sky completely empty of American bombers. It was full of symbols, though. In February, President Ford ordered a massive airlift reminiscent of the famous one to Berlin in 1948. But Phnom Penh, to the U.S. Congress, was no Berlin, and, under congressional pressure, Ford ordered a halt on April 14th.[71] Three days later, under a final artillery assault on the airport, Khmer Rouge soldiers broke through the last government barricades, and Phnom Penh was theirs. Over this revolutionary road from 1970 to 1975, six hundred thousand Cambodians lost their lives.[72] Rather than being a liberation for Cambodians, this nasty two-year revolutionary path broadened into an avenue of horror. For the ruling communist group, seizing Phnom Penh was just an incidental part to a final campaign of purification. In this three and a half years of subsequent purification, the white crocodiles of the Mekong turned blood red.

The path to the liberation of Laos was more placid. It also followed a predictable pattern that was, until 1973, bound by some tacit parameters. Politically, this translated into a balance between the two sides. Souvanna Phouma was left in full charge of the government with the solid backing of the Americans, which included a critical American role in turning aside two rightist coups in 1964 and 1965.[73] On the other side, though the Soviets did abandon a direct role in Laos after Geneva, the slack in supporting the Pathet Lao was more than picked up by the North Vietnamese and the Chinese.

Militarily, the northwest-southeast diagonal axis of Laos split into two separate wars. The war in the south was a clear extension of the Vietnam War. Forty thousand North Vietnamese troops, increased to sixty thousand by 1973, protected and maintained the intricate Ho Chi Minh Trail that traversed the Annamite mountains of southern Laos into South Vietnam.[74] Systematic U.S. bombing began in January 1965, and over the next four years 455,000 tons of ordnance fell on this trail (a figure almost equal to the total tonnage that fell on Cambodia). Despite this campaign, by 1970 half a million North Vietnamese troops had traversed the trail. At most, the bombing only stopped 20 percent of the supplies shipped down the trail. When the bombing finally ended in February 1973, two million tons had fallen on Laos. This figure exceeded the total U.S. aerial ordnance dropped in all theaters of World War II. On a per capita basis, Laos thereby earned the distinction of being the most heavily bombed country in human history.[75]

The war in the Northwest was a seesaw battle for control of the strategic Plain of Jars plateau. The royal capital of Luang Prabang immediately to the northwest on the Mekong was vulnerable to being cut off from Vientiane were the plain to fall. In this contest, there were many military fingers in the pie. Depending on the season, the North Vietnamese sent ten thousand to seventeen thousand troops into northern Laos to bolster a Pathet Lao force that had grown from fifteen thousand at the time of the Geneva conference to thirty-five thousand in the early 1970s. Opposing the communists were a Royal Laotian Army of fifty-six thousand, a Meo irregular army that fluctuated between twenty-five and forty-thousand, and Thai mercenaries that varied from seven to twenty-one thousand, depending on the size of the Meo force.[76] The pattern was for the communists to take the offensive during the dry season at the start of the year and for the government, backed by U.S. airpower, to recover the communist gains during the rainy season. In the mid-1960s, when this began, the government held nearly half the territory and two-thirds of the population, which is roughly what it held in 1970. In both areas, the fighting was in the mountains, leaving the ethnic Lao of the Mekong River virtually unscathed.[77]

Indeed, Norman Hannah, an American State Department official, has contended that the key to America's failure in all of Indochina lay in a "tacit understanding" worked out by Averell Harriman at the Geneva Accords on Laos that held the country's two wars in balance. In exchange for the United States not cutting off the Ho Chi Minh Trail in the south with ground forces of its own (thereby ultimately letting the personnel and supplies slip through), the North Vietnamese would not overrun the country in the north (and repeat the horror of Nam Tha).[78] Thus the United States never extended the McNamara Line into Laos, and the Pathet Lao, though they encircled Luang Prabang from three sides in 1969, declined to take the defenseless capital.[79]

Whatever agreement there was broke down in 1970. The fighting intensified as the North Vietnamese army (NVA) introduced two full combat divisions in the north and in the south mounted attacks far west of the Ho Chi Minh Trail.[80] From then until the February 1973 peace agreement, the government gradually lost ground. The communists seized Attopeu in southern Laos, their first province capital. Shortly thereafter, neighboring Saravane fell. In the Plain of Jars, the NVA almost drove Meo irregulars off the strategic plain. The next year, in a tremendous effort backed up by massive American air support, the Meos took most of the plain back. Despite all this and the infusion of Thai mercenaries, however, in 1972 the NVA posted gains all over the country, nearly taking the Meo headquarters of Long Tieng. By October 1972, the Pathet Lao controlled two-thirds of the territory and held a fifty-fifty split with the government on population.[81]

From this position of strength, the Pathet Lao were ready to hold peace talks. The talks concluded with the signing of the Vientiane Peace Agreement on February 21, 1973. The terms reflected this improved communist position. More than this, with the withdrawal of further U.S. support, it represented an upending of the basic balance in Laos. On February 9, Souvanna Phouma told Secretary of State Henry Kissinger that Hanoi would respect a peace agreement in Laos only if the United States would continue its military pressure against the communists. The purpose of the meeting, however, was for Kissinger to inform the prince that U.S. military assistance was ending and that Souvanna Phouma should conclude whatever agreement he could.[82]

It wasn't much of an agreement. All foreign troops were to be withdrawn in sixty days. The United States and its Thai mercenaries complied. As had been true of the Geneva Agreement of 1962, the North Vietnamese did not. Souvanna Phouma had to agree that in the formation of a Provisional Government of National Union (PGNU) there would only be two sides, the "Vientiane administration" and the Pathet Lao, because the Neutralists had been absorbed into the government side. Ministerial posts were to be equally divided, with Souvanna Phouma to continue as prime minister assisted by a vice-premier from each side. Finally, the Pathet Lao was permitted to administer its "zone of control" from Sam Neua, while in the Vientiane zone the Pathet Lao participated in the governing and policing of Vientiane and Luang Prabang. This prompted the saying, "What is ours is ours, and what is yours is half ours."[83]

In any case, the downward slide of the Royal Lao government became dramatic after the agreement. The Provisional Government of National Union was formally established on April 5, 1974. With Prince Souphanouvong as the chairman of a National Political Consultative Council, a set of eighteen principles of national unity, drafted by the Pathet Lao, was accepted as the basis for a new constitution. Despite this fleetingly hopeful start, by year's end rightist troops mutinied and the prime minister had to call on the Pathet Lao to suppress them. Fighting then broke out between the Pathet Lao and Meos in March 1975, which left the irregulars isolated in Long Tieng. Souvanna Phouma refused to let the air force help the Meos for fear of causing Pathet Lao casualties. The struggle shifted to Vientiane, where demonstrations were held in April and May against the United States. The rightists left the government in protest, and U.S. aid was terminated on June 30, 1975. Although Souvanna Phouma stayed on as prime minister, the Pathet Lao convened a National Political Consultative Conference on November 26 in which top-level bureaucrats were told that the government had been taken over. Souvanna Phouma announced his intention to step down. On December 4, the Lao people were told of the abdication of King Savang Vatthana, though the two traditional leaders were retained as an "adviser" and "guide" to the new regime of commissars.[84] Nineteen years earlier, at his father's funeral, the king had remarked to Prince Sihanouk, "Alas, I am doomed to be the last King of Laos."[85]

In this more or less quiet disappearance of the Kingdom of Laos, more than 20,000 Meo irregulars lost their lives, as did another 15,000 soldiers of the Royal Lao Army. Some 750,000 civilians, mostly in tribal areas, became refugees. Civilian casualties in Laos, despite the heavy bombing, were relatively light because most of it took place along the remote Ho Chi Minh Trail or in the Plain of Jars, whose population had been "relocated." In 1960, 150,000 people lived in this plain, but only 9,000 were left in 1970. On the other side, "many thousands" of North Vietnamese and Pathet Lao soldiers were killed.[86]

Framework Analysis

When the French abandoned their attempt to reimpose their "protection" over Indochina at the Geneva Accords of 1954, the former colonies sought to reclaim their precolonial political traditions even as they tried to build modern nation-states. Cambodia and Laos, in particular, endeavored to fashion a bond between traditional Buddhist principles of kingship as symbols of national identity and the modern republicanism of a Charles De Gaulle and the professionalism of the Ecole Polytechnic as foundations for functioning modern states. Both embarked on a creditable path of national and local elections to build the ties and sentiments of a middle-ground-based polity. But the fractures engendered by this transition were too great for these bridges, and, by the mid-1960s, in both Cambodia and Laos, this process of nation-building had frozen up. Instead, they were swept over first by a wave of revolution coursing over peninsular Southeast Asia and then by a second wave of foreign interventions as the two global power blocs struggled to turn this first wave to their own geopolitical channels. The drowning effect of these waves can be seen most clearly in the analysis of the asymmetries, errors, and reversibilities to the Cambodian and Laotian revolutions. They were so bound up in the larger war in Vietnam that none of the changes discussed really could have been possible unless they were tied to changes originating in the Vietnam War itself. As terrible as they were to their own people, the revolutions in Cambodia and Laos truly were "sideshows."

As for national legitimacy in Cambodia, at the interest level, the government was able to provide material incentives, both positive and negative, that were sufficient until 1963 to keep the lid on revolutionary activity. This was reflected by Prince Sihanouk's ability to smash the rural network of cadres in 1959 and either repress or co-opt the communists in the cities. According to the communist theoreticians Hu Nim, Hou Yuon, and Khieu Samphan, the years 1963 to 1967 brought increasing misery to the peasantry. Landholding became more concentrated, and poorer peasants were forced by their indebtedness to become sharecroppers, perhaps as many as 25 percent. Other studies cast some doubt on this thesis of rural misery. Jean Delvert found rural indebtedness a greater problem than land, and a cooperative movement did mitigate this somewhat. This fragmentation of landholding may also be explained by a marked shift from 1963 to 1968 away from rice paddy to the farming of cash crops. These were all cultivated on smaller plots but yielded double to quadruple the returns of paddy. There was, however, a discrepancy in rural and urban incomes, which caused tensions.[87]

Whatever the rising or falling of peasant misery, the communists showed no capabilities of exploiting it. Even the tinderbox at Sumlaut merely served to rouse the communists momentarily. For the next three years, except in tribal areas in the Northeast, they floundered. The 1970 coup and the five-year war that followed brought two changes to the sociopolitical landscape, besides the Sihanouk crossover. First, people flocked to the cities. In 1970, Phnom Penh was a picturesque "French provincial town" of six hundred thousand. At war's end, it had bloated to over 3 million. Despite the tightening communist noose around the cities, in April 1975, four and a half million Cambodians lived in them.[88] Second, the bombing and ground fighting concentrated the rural population that was left, leaving broad swaths of land abandoned. This made mobilization and "land reform" easier for the communists.[89]

The basic deal of Sihanouk's rule was that in exchange for ensuring the traditional but passive support of the peasantry, he felt free to pursue a more activist set of nation-building policies in the cities.[90] At the opportunity level, he cultivated the Buddhist *sangha*. As long as the prince kept this link tight, the communists found rural mobilization almost impossible. Until 1970, they had to content themselves with building support in tribal areas and in regions in the Northeast under Vietnamese communist control. In the cities, Sihanouk concentrated his efforts on controlling the National Assembly through his Sangkum party. For a while, he was absolutely dominant. The Sangkum's winning ways were a reflection of his coalition of military officers, high-ranking bureaucrats, Buddhist monks, some business interests, and even urban intellectuals. In addition to all this political participation, his expansion of the educational system and the economic growth of the early 1960s opened up societal access as well. The communists tried to compensate for the dismal electoral performance of their front party, the Pracheachon, by mobilizing workers and winning over students to revolutionary activity.

Shanouk's dominance slipped as soon as the political participation and societal access he had helped to expand choked under his own policies. In placating and co-opting leftists, he deeply alienated the right wing and business interests by his pro-Chinese foreign policy and his nationalizations. When he lost control of his own party in 1966, the prince and the National Assembly were at loggerheads. Indeed, the 1970 coup that ousted Sihanouk was mounted by figures within the National Assembly and the military, the very institutions, in modern terms, he had depended on most heavily. His switch after the coup to the communist side, however, created a powerful revolutionary *troika* of Sihanouk royalists, Cambodian communists, and Vietnamese communists. It was a combination strong enough to overwhelm the foundationless Lon Nol regime but not sufficiently cohesive to assuage its own internal differences in the mere accomplishment of victory.

At the belief level, all of the political players tapped into parts of the ethos of Cambodian political legitimacy, but only Sihanouk, for a while, managed to embody all of it. As king, of course, he started out with much built-in legitimacy. He added to this by having the best of both worlds in stepping down as king and becoming chief of state. The monarchy, as an institution, could remain aloof in the person of his father, while he either earned more "performance" legitimacy through his policies or buffered the monarchy from any taint of his errors. He lost this cushion with his father's death in 1963.

Through his party, Sihanouk preached a "Buddhist socialism." Indeed, the Sangkum's full name was People's Socialist Community.[91] With these views, he modernized Buddhism, justified his nationalizations, and, perhaps unwittingly, socialized Cambodians to Marxist rhetoric. Though as king Sihanouk suspended the National Assembly from 1949 to 1953, when he saw the regal ways in which Charles De Gaulle manipulated republicanism in France, as a prince he embraced this legislative arena almost as fervently as Buddhism. By 1966, however, he had grown tired of modern parliamentary politics. The 1970 conspirators, nevertheless, legitimated their overthrow of the prince in the name of republicanism. For a few months, in fact, the cities were enthusiastic about Lon Nol—as they were, for a few hours in 1975, about Pol Pot.[92]

For all his flexibility, there is one principle of Cambodian political legitimacy to which Sihanouk was constantly dedicated: the independence of Cambodia. He played his cards right against the French, and, if he did not play them well in the Second Indochina War, he nevertheless played them true. Lon Nol came to power because he felt the game should be played harder against the Vietnamese. He succeeded only in making things worse and found himself totally dependent on the United States. The corruption that came with this dependence speeded his departure.

Regarding national legitimacy, the communists, too, made much of reviving the ancient Khmer identity. They talked of Angkor, of the Sangha, and of the degeneration of urban life. They were particularly effective in highlighting the corruption of Sihanouk's last years in Phnom Penh. Indeed, they talked about everything but communism. Ironically, the branch of the party dependent on the Vietnamese was quite effective in winning over Buddhist monks.[93] Pol Pot's most favored revolutionary nomme de guerre was one that meant "original Khmer."[94]

In Laos, the light hand of French rule and the fragmented, buffeted state of the political situation before that made for a very late blooming of nationalism. In fact, it was not until World War II that some form of Lao consciousness developed in Charles Rochet's "Lao awakening." Unlike Cambodia, in this growing consciousness there was a keen recognition that the continued need for protection would always place limits on this growth. As Prince Phetsareth observed in 1945, "We still have a need to lean on a strong power in order to protect ourselves against the designs of our neighbors."[95]

This feeling of modern Lao consciousness branched off in two directions. They are best symbolized by the careers of the two half-brothers Souvanna Phouma and Souphanouvong. Although both received excellent French educations and were motivated by a desire to modernize Laos, their visions were different. The prime minister essentially had Western tastes while his younger brother was always the rebel. Nevertheless, both brothers served in the Lao Isarra, Souphanouvong was the military commander, and it was Souvanna Phouma's repeated demands that finally persuaded the French to grant Laos full independence on October 15, 1953.[96] Thus both brothers and parties, communist and anticommunist, had valid roots to their claims of national legitimacy.

At the interest level, in Laos the gap between the elites and the mass of peasantry living in the country's ten thousand villages was vast. Indeed, 95 percent of the population was engaged in agriculture, the illiteracy rate was 85 percent, and only 10 percent earned and spent money.[97] Thus the ties between the villagers and the cities were meager. Except for Luang Prabang, the towns and cities were over half Vietnamese and Chinese. Though all Laotians knew and took pride in the traditions of Lan Xang, perhaps no more than half realized they were living in a modern state called Laos. Surveys showed that 94 percent of the villagers could not name their national leaders and 81 percent could not identify the king, who, in 1959, had reigned for fifty years. But they all knew their canton chief, village headman, and local military commanders.[98] For personal security in Laos, then, villagers continued to rely on their traditional patron-client ties. For modern material security, interestingly, they were actually supported by either the Americans or the North Vietnamese, who kept afloat the administrative shells of the Royal Lao Government or the Pathet Lao zones.

What made security easier in Laos was that, except along the Ho Chi Minh Trail, the war was not a guerrilla one. The Pathet Lao confined their military activities to expanding their zones of control in tribal areas. In the lowlands, they attempted political organization but did not conduct terrorism or guerrilla campaigns. In this gentler revolution, officials of the government often doubled as Pathet Lao cadres.[99] The many layers of people's war in Laos did not scratch deeply at the rice roots.

It was much more of a contest at the opportunity level. Here there was a two-way split to Laotian politics. First, among the ethnic Lao, there were splits between the cosmopolitan French-educated elite of the cities and the Buddhist *wat*-educated leaders of the villages. What was frustrating for the much larger latter group was that all the best jobs in the civil service and military went to the former group. In addition, the modern economy was dominated by Chinese and Vietnamese. Obviously, there was an opportunity here for the Pathet Lao. They also found it in a fracture that had developed in the *sangha* in the 1940s and intensified in the 1960s. In the 1940s a reform Buddhism, known as Thammayut, swept into Laos from Thailand to challenge the dominant national Mahanikai sect. Though it eventually took root only in the south, it touched off a storm of debate, in part because of Thammayut's support from right-wing interests in Bangkok. On nationalist grounds, the Pathet Lao championed the national sect.[100]

The other major split was the gulf between the ethnic Lao and the mountain tribal groups. Though these tribals make up their own mosaic, politically and culturally they divide into two main groups: the Lao Theung (or Kha) and the Lao Seung (the Hmong and the Yao). The Lao Theung are a Mon-Khmer people akin to both Cambodians and the South Vietnamese montagnards. They make up 25 percent of the population and live in the southeast, near Luang Prabang in the northwest, around the Plain of Jars, and along the Vietnamese border in the northeast. The focus of settlement for the 10 percent of the population that is Hmong (or Meo) is the Plain of Jars.[101]

In this tribal mosaic, the Royal Lao Government and the Pathet Lao struggled to extend their writ. In truth, the Americans were responsible for most of the effort on the government side. Loyalties among the Hmong were by clans, and the Americans won over Vang Pao and his cousin Touby Lyfang. Because of clan rivalries, this alignment permitted the Pathet Lao to attract the third major clan chieftain, Fay Dang. This success among the Hmong was a boon to the government but was a tragedy to the tribals themselves. They bore the brunt of the fighting.[102] Outmaneuvered among the Hmong, the Pathet Lao succeeded in winning over large numbers of Kha. Their big coup was recruiting Sithone Komadam, son of the great Kha chief who led the highland revolt of 1901–7.[103] This very success, however, was also the source of a political weakness of the Pathet Lao: its ethnic imbalance. Though its political leadership and officer corps was overwhelmingly ethnic Lao, 70 percent of the population in their zones was highland minorities as were, by some reports, 60 percent of their soldiers.[104]

On the government side, genuine attempts were made to build a modern state through the political participation that elections provide. Following the constitutions of 1949 and 1957, municipal councils, provincial councils, and a National Assembly were created that did conduct periodic elections.[105] Specifically, National Assembly elections were held in 1955, 1958, 1960, 1965, and 1967. Among these, the 1958 elections were a fair reflection of the political balance in the country. The Pathet Lao received 35 percent of the vote, though as late as 1968 the Communist party itself had only fourteen thousand members.[106] Souvanna Phouma's Neutralist party had a membership of thirty-three thousand, and, in the 1967 elections, candidates allied to him won a majority of the National Assembly.[107] Still, Martin Stuart-Fox and Rod Bucknell are surely correct that at this institutional level, the government had failed to effect an integration of the country's institutional complex (the monarchy, military, *sangha*, civil service, and political regime).[108]

At the belief level, if both sides could stake a valid claim to national legitimacy, they both also had problems. In the modern world of the cities, the absolute dependence of the Royal Lao Government on the Americans was glaringly obvious. Indeed, the Kong Le coup of 1960 and the subsequent rise of neutralism were sparked by a popular, traditional revulsion to the corruption that came with this dependence.[109] The government only compounded its problems by then pressuring the *sangha* to serve as a mouthpiece for its political propaganda. The unintended effect was to open a wedge for the Pathet Lao to do the same by exploiting the sectarian split within the *sangha*. This politicization of Buddhism was self-destructive to everyone. Forced into the partisan debates of earthly politics, the standing of the *sangha*, in providing the far more important cosmic legitimacy to the government's writ, was diminished. The spiritual authority of the monks in the village *wats* was also eroded.[110]

The unusual vitality of neutralism in Laos was inspired by the equal dependence of the Pathet Lao on foreign benefactors. With the government and Pathet Lao equally compromised, on the issue of independence, the Pathet Lao, initially, handled their claims to national legitimacy with some skill. With the establishment of the Provisional Government of National Union in April 1973, the Pathet Lao won widespread modern and traditional support for their eighteen-point program of national unification. It called for a liberal democratic state, a constitutional monarchy, and a Buddhist *sangha* protected by the state. Indeed, the popularity of this facade became an acute embarrassment after the takeover in 1975.[111]

In traditional terms, the communists in Laos, at first, were as careful and circumspect as their Cambodian comrades were rude and bloody. The break with the monarchy was softened by the "red prince" Souphanouvong serving as president of the new regime as well as by Prince Souvanna Phouma serving honorifically as a "national guide" until his death in 1984. The king, in fact, was kept on as an "adviser" until 1977, when both he and his son were deposed and arrested after being implicated in a coup attempt.[112] In these first few years, the Pathet Lao used the *sangha* as a vehicle both for grass-roots communication and for a national literacy campaign. But with the overthrow of the king, relations with the *sangha* turned sour. The sacred ivory fans of monastic abbots were smashed, and in 1978 the *Dhammaraja* of the *sangha* (like Tibet's Dalai Lama) fled across the Mekong into Thailand.[113] C. J. Christie wrote about a Laos caught between three nationalisms — rightist, neutralist, and communist — with the revolution destroying the first two.[114] Surely the aftermath has destroyed the third as well.

What is particularly noteworthy about Laos, nevertheless, is the genuine vitality of a "third force," neutralism. In all the other cases, such a middle ground was stretched apart to polarized opposite sides. Kong Le galvanized a strong Buddhist and traditional outburst even as Souvanna Phouma lent it a modern dignity. The United States did well in 1964 to break with the rightists, whose ties with Thailand were too much like those of the Pathet Lao with the Vietnamese. In Laos, there *were* grounds for a locally legitimate intervention.

REVOLUTIONARY LEGITIMACY

Both the Cambodian and Laotian communists framed their revolutions in the explicit terms of a Marxist people's war, in what Don Fletcher and Geoff Gunn have called its "fourth generation."[115] Both these "fourth-generation" renderings, however, compromised the principles of this strategy. Put simply, the people's war in Laos was not much of a revolution, and the one in Cambodia was far too much of one.

In their two contradictory official histories, the Cambodians relied on Mao's three stages of protracted war to chart their path to liberation. Indeed, the Paris group that sought to dominate the revolution was thoroughly steeped in the writings of Stalin, Mao, Lin Biao, Giap, and Robespierre. They were inspired by Stalin's "Socialism in One Country" (because of its autarky), the various formulations of people's war by Mao, Lin Biao, and Vo Nguyen Giap, and the radical Jacobism of Robespierre that sought to create social equality through terror.[116] There was no lack of beliefs among these revolutionaries. The problems lay in the execution. For one thing, at the mass level of interest, there was no "mass line" to exploit. Land reform and rural misery were not strong enough issues to turn the revolutionary key. At the organizational level, they were unable to compete on their own with the government. Their electoral fortunes in the National Assembly earned them a marginal role similar to that of the Greek communists.

What got the Cambodian revolution off the starting blocks into a momentum of crossover points, of course, was the traditional belief level of appeals that came to the communist side with the defection of Prince Sihanouk and the opportunity groups that came with him. To the fanatical and unified Paris Group at the top, this dependence struck at the heart of their burgeoning paranoia: their inability to control their own revolution. Militarily, it was the rival Cambodian communist returnees who recruited and trained the guerrillas in base areas protected by the North Vietnamese. In further defeating Lon Nol's Chenla offensives, the North Vietnamese took care of the first two phases of the protracted war for the Cambodians. Having decisively defeated the government forces, Hanoi turned the third phase over to the Cambodians, who carried the battle to strategic breakout and victory (with the continued assistance of Vietnamese artillery).[117]

Like the Russian Revolution, the Cambodian revolution was a product of several genuine and conflicting political forces that required a settling of accounts after victory. In Phnom Penh, victory brought no peace to the victors or to the Cambodian people. Instead, it was merely the opening round in an ever more bloody spiral to gain the absolute control that the revolution itself did not bring. The party's "mass line" by which the Paris group mobilized the peasantry was not their own. The urban world they conquered in 1975 was almost a Martian environment to them.[118] Indeed, their control over their own party and military was incomplete, and the degree of Cambodian dependence on the Vietnamese for the success of their revolution was an embarrassment.[119] By all definitional criteria, the purity of their people's war victory was tarnished.

To gain mastery over their revolutionary victory, there were circles of enemies that would have to be eliminated, one by one. First, they emptied out the cities to eliminate "class enemies." Phnom Penh was evacuated in six days, Battambang in fifteen hours. In all, half the population (3.5 million people) was scattered. This served two purposes: it disorganized and essentially eliminated any remnant "capitalist" sources of opposition.[120] More important, it broke the decentralized administrative capacities of the military regions and forced the commanders to go to the party central committee for a nationwide solution. In July, Pol Pot announced the achievement of a central military command, which cleared the path for consolidation. As such, certain nationalist encumbrances were no longer needed. Sihanouk was forced to abdicate and, in his own words, "spit out like a cherry pit."[121] In revealing its Marxism for the first time in 1977, the party tried to eliminate Buddhism. During the party's three-and-a-half-year reign of terror, only a thousand monks survived from the prewar total of forty thousand. They also turned on the ethnic Chinese and Vietnamese in the cities and on the Muslim Cham minority that had given Pol Pot much of his earliest support. Half of all three groups were killed.[122] So much for "class enemies."

Second, despite the military consolidation and the elimination of noncommunist opposition, the party itself was in a state of factional confusion and in sore need of purification. In this purge, Pol Pot's modus operandi was to use the forces of one region against another. The Northern Zone had shown weaknesses during the revolution, and forces from the Eastern Zone, with their distinctive gray uniforms, were called in to purge this zone. Another weak link was the perennially capitalist Battambang of the Northwest Region; so the Southwest Zone forces, the largest, marched to purge the weaklings of Battambang. These intraparty purges did not take place without considerable resistance. Ieng Sary later claimed that four "illegitimate" coups struck at Pol Pot in 1976 and 1977.[123] His major smoke screen was to provoke the Vietnamese so as to rally the party and people around this ancient and overriding paranoia.[124] For allegedly failing to block Vietnamese border provocations in the second half of 1977, Eastern Zone forces were ordered to attack Vietnam to redeem themselves. They failed utterly. When they returned, Pol Pot unleashed Ta Mok's Southwestern forces on the routed guerrillas in gray. By July 1978, more than one hundred thousand had been killed. Though the zone commander was killed, some of his lieutenants escaped to Vietnam. When the smoke screen returned as a real Vietnamese military fire in January 1979, these Eastern Zone escapees were installed in Phnom Penh.[125] With Pol Pot and his regime of butchery dispatched into the jungles, the "killing fields" ended, but not before as many as two million Cambodians had been killed in a harvest of 30 percent of the population.[126]

Beyond this organizational insecurity, these killings were also driven by a set of fanatical beliefs. Other Asian revolutions had to contend with groups of zealous European-trained intellectuals whose devotion to their ideals outran the traditional constraints of their homelands. The difference was that in these other revolutions the foreign-trained radicals ran aground with their foreign fanaticism once they returned home. In China, Wang Ming and his "28 Bolsheviks" pushed a pure urban strategy and rigidly ideological program of land reform that the more pragmatic Mao Zedong was easily able to outmaneuver and suppress. In Vietnam, Tran Van Giau, fresh from the "Toilers of the East University" in Moscow, promptly launched a suicidal uprising against the French in the 1930s that decimated the party in Cochinchina.[127] Though similarly suicidal, Cambodia's "Bolsheviks" got much farther. As a point of revolutionary legitimacy, these fanatics shared a failure to appreciate the need to ground this legitimacy societally in General Giap's precept: "Marxism-Leninism never disowns the history and great constituent virtues of a nation . . . it raises them to new heights."[128]

The first point of departure of the Cambodian fanatics started out being harmless enough. From the doctoral dissertations of Khieu Samphan and Hu Nim came the observation that Cambodia owed its backwardness to its inextricable linkage to, and dependence on, a capitalist and neoimperialist world system. To their less intellectual comrades Pol Pot and Ieng Sary, this meant the Cambodian revolution should cut itself off from this link and be self-sufficient. As Catherine Becker has commented, "Being pure became Pol Pot's chief idea."[129] The second turn to their boundless fanaticism started with their initially innocuous admiration of Chinese revisionism. They admired the attempts of the Chinese ideologically to leap ahead of their Soviet revolutionary progenitors in the Great Leap Forward (1958–62) and Cultural Revolution (1966–69). This admiration was made less innocuous by their desire to go on leaping. On a visit to Peking in 1975, Khieu Samphan and Ieng Sary's wife reportedly told a dying Zhou Enlai that they would take their revolution even further than the Chinese and bring pure communism to Kampuchea in "one fell swoop."[130] To this end, Pol Pot had gathered around himself a core of dedicated cadre that he planted like cancerous seeds throughout the seven military regions.

The effect of these two twisted points was a realization of Friedrich Nietzsche's worst nightmare of modernity: men of no traditional values or restraints playing with their own divinity. Indeed, Pol Pot averred that their revolution was "the work of God, for it is too imposing for mere humans."[131] Mere humans, then, were clearly expendable. Having used the social values of these humans to gain control over them—namely, their monarchy and their religion—they then tried to bury these traditions in the killing fields as well. This insanity ultimately brought on a sacrifice of the one tradition they, and what remained of their people, still believed in: national independence from the Vietnamese. By seizing Phnom Penh, the Vietnamese saved the Cambodians from themselves. In this fateful mix of ideological fanaticism with organizational insecurity, Cambodia gave birth to a new word in the lexicon of political horror: autogenocide.

From a revolutionary point of view, Laos is a very difficult setting in which to create revolutionary consciousness. It is a country of sparse population and little exploitable wealth. Hence there are no groups consigned to lives of conspicuous relative misery, no tradition of agrarian revolt, and no industrial proletariat.[132] In brief, the ingredients of the class struggle are not developed. Nevertheless, following the advice of their North Vietnamese mentors, the Pathet Lao did embark on a strategy of Marxist people's war. Tapping the mass line was attempted in the united front organization of the Neo Lao Hak Sat. In the election that it contested in 1958, it did very well. The front was duly controlled by the People's party of Laos, but the party was more shadowy than other communist parties. It was reported to have been founded in 1954. Interestingly, with the North Vietnamese already providing ample political direction, its founding took place in the midst of a debate as to whether it was even necessary.[133]

Nevertheless, in broad outline, the Pathet Lao did follow Mao's three stages of a protracted war. Following a long period of preparation of a critical mass from 1946 to the 1958 elections, armed struggle broke out in 1959 when two Pathet Lao battalions fled into the hills to begin a first phase of defensive guerrilla warfare. This stage of crossover points had no sooner begun when it was interrupted or reversed by the Kong Le coup of 1960 that ushered in conventional battles among rival military groups. With the collapse of the 1962 Geneva Agreement, the fighting moved to Mao's second stage of mobile or equilibrium warfare in 1964 and lasted until the end of 1972. The Vientiane Peace Agreement of 1973 offered some respite, but with the fall of Phnom Penh and Saigon in April 1975, the Pathet Lao opened Mao's third stage of the general counteroffensive with the call in May for a breakout political uprising that toppled the Vientiane administration.[134]

The actual pattern to the fighting in Laos did not develop in the way Mao envisioned. The guerrilla phase was never fully inaugurated. The central feature of the subsequent war in the Plain of Jars was that of road-bound columns of North Vietnamese and Pathet Lao light infantry pushing back the retreating guerrilla bands of Vang Pao, who were protected by American air strikes. At the zenith of these advances, Vang Pao's guerrillas would hit communist supply lines with rear ambushes to force these columns to withdraw. In the south, CIA-recruited guerrillas from among Kha tribal groups harassed the southward infiltration of conventional North Vietnamese military units.[135] In Laos, it was not the communists who were fighting a guerrilla war. Indeed, their final political uprising was not that of Mao's positional warfare, but that of a much more successful replay of the 1945 August Revolution of the Vietnamese.

Despite this unorthodox pattern, in most respects the Pathet Lao were faithful to a people's war strategy: the party did keep control of the gun, the revolution was conducted by a Marxist-Leninist party which established a United Front to champion the mass line, and base areas were established to build the three levels of armed forces for a protracted war. But self-reliant they were not. All the essentials of revolution-making—organization, leadership, strategy, money, weapons, and most of the fighting—were provided by the North Vietnamese. Further, in a "people's war" where 70 percent of the population under its control were tribal highlanders, the Pathet Lao remained a displaced ethnic Lao movement.[136] In fact, on both sides, almost everybody except the ethnic Lao were fighting the war in Laos. It was a strange revolution.

Strange or not, some of the benign effects of this dependence are worth noting. Though perhaps making a virtue out of necessity, the Pathet Lao did try to create the consciousness of a common Laotian nation among the hitherto unintegrated mountain tribals. Also, whatever their dependence, the leadership of the Lao People's party has had a remarkable history of unity. In 1990, its politburo was dominated by the same seven members who began the Neo Lao Isarra in the 1940s. Much of this unity stemmed from their willingness to serve "in an apprentice relationship to Vietnamese mentors" and to recognize that "they may not distinguish a Lao national interest as distinct from a Vietnamese one."[137] Despite this dependence, the writ of revolution never cut too deeply into Laotian society. If Laotian revolutionaries suffered from a modesty of ambition, it was a modesty that spared the Laotian people from the carnage of revolutionary purity in Cambodia.

Living in the shadow of Vietnam, the revolutions in Cambodia and Laos became bonded to this larger war. The very weakness of these two states made foreign interventions decisive to the outcomes. Put very simply, the continuity of North Vietnamese assistance to the revolutionaries was as determinative of their "national liberations" as were the breaks and disjunctures of American aid to the downfalls of the incumbent regimes.

In developing a modern independent state, Cambodia received assistance from the United States that helped string together a web of individual interests and group opportunities for access to, and participation in, the government. But in preserving Cambodia's independence against Vietnam, Prince Sihanouk felt China was a better patron than the United States, and he suspended American aid in 1963. Chinese aid, however, was never sufficient to compensate for this American loss, and, too late for his own immediate political career, the prince relented in 1969. The republican coup that ousted Sihanouk in March 1970 was very pro-American in its sympathies. The United States was quick to pledge its undying support. For a while, so did a lot of other groups within Cambodian society. But these enthusiasms soon waned as defeats mounted in the field, and a pall of corruption rose up over Phnom Penh. Political groups of all stripes became alienated from the regime.

This left the United States in the grip of a vicious illegitimacy lock by Lon Nol. American military aid was the lifeblood of the army, which became Lon Nol's sole base of support. Massive U.S. bombing staved off a defeat in 1973, even as two other U.S. interventions only hastened the regime's downfall. The Cambodian incursion of 1970 to capture COSVN headquarters and buy time for the Vietnamization program unleashed a hornet's nest of maddened North Vietnamese soldiers on an ill-prepared Cambodian army. The secret B-52 bombing campaign just inside the Cambodian border to cut off communist infiltration into South Vietnam only inspired an outraged U.S. Congress, when news of it became public, to cut off all American military activity in Indochina on August 15, 1973. This did not stop Washington from continuing to furnish weapons and provisions to the besieged regime. But, in an urban replay of the American refusal to bail the French out of Dienbienphu, the now thoroughly righteous U.S. Congress would entertain no thoughts of renewed U.S. bombing to silence the Vietnamese artillery closing in on Phnom Penh. One cannot help but observe that this is not the preferred way of breaking an illegitimacy lock.

On the communist side, Pol Pot attributed his victory to

1. "The efficient and correct leadership" of the KCP.
2. "Our people are very courageous. . . ."
3. "Of secondary significance [was] increased production and supply of food to the rear areas."
4. "Not to be forgotten though it is only of secondary significance [is] the support we received from the world."[138]

Leaving aside his failure to mention Prince Sihanouk, the ordering of Pol Pot's list does not seem right. To begin with, the Communist party in Cambodia was established under the direction of the Vietnamese ICP. Militarily, the Khmer Rouge achieved a critical mass in base areas behind a shield of elements of five NVA divisions.[139] These same divisions then took care of the second maneuver phase of people's war by breaking the back of Lon Nol's army in its disastrous Chenla I and II campaigns. Even when the Khmer Rouge took over the fighting for the last breakout phase, it was still North Vietnamese artillery that battered down the final defense perimeter of Phnom Penh.

Laos was America's "secret war." It was a secret because after the 1962 Geneva Agreement, foreign forces were supposed to leave Laos. The North Vietnamese never left but said they weren't there, just as they never admitted to being in South Vietnam. It was a point of honor for the Americans not to be in Laos with ground forces because Geneva told them not to, even if they were there in every other way. In 1971, official U.S. assistance to Laos was $284 million, and $162 million of it paid for the entire Laotian defense budget. (This does not include the expenditures of the CIA or of the bombing campaigns.) Even so, this assistance came to $141 per person in Laos, double the country's per capita GNP. Official U.S. aid peaked at $374 million in 1972.[140] With this aid package, the United States underwrote the functioning of the Laotian economy as well as the entire institutional complex of the Royal Lao Government.

Militarily, short of ground combat troops, American involvement in Laos ran the gamut of everything else. The number of U.S. military personnel in Laos after 1962 hovered at six hundred. The military assistance program to Laos was funneled through the Military Advisory Group in Thailand, which outfitted and trained Laotian, Meo, and Thai mercenary units operating in Laos. Hence the numbers of U.S. forces involved with the war in Laos was much higher than the six hundred "in-country" personnel. Operating under an Agency for International Development cover, the Central Intelligence Agency ran one of its largest "special operations." Three hundred CIA operatives coordinated the activities of both General Vang Pao's Meo irregulars and the ten thousand Thai mercenaries. This latter program alone cost the CIA $100 million a year. For logistical support, the agency relied heavily on Air America, a CIA "company" with several hundred planes, twenty thousand employees, and two hundred American pilots.[141]

The wide scope of these activities translated into a very powerful American political influence. The United States was able to shore up the right wing and to bring it to heel on several occasions, to wit, in gaining support for the 1962 Geneva Conference, quelling the coups in 1964 and 1965, and stopping talk about a coup in 1973. After making up its mind about Souvanna Phouma, the United States was able to provide him with steadying support. Despite all this assistance, Souvanna Phouma did not have his nationalist credentials tainted by the American embrace.

But this happy state of affairs in Laos was upended by a tidal wave that crashed in from the larger war in Vietnam. The signing of the Paris Peace Agreement on January 27, 1973, provided that all U.S. military personnel were to be withdrawn from Vietnam in sixty days. Decent interval or not, Washington wanted out of Southeast Asia. As the Laotians negotiated their own agreement during this withdrawal period, Kissinger paid his fateful visit to tell Souvanna Phouma that American military assistance was ending and that the prince would have to take whatever agreement he could get out of Hanoi. With this message, the long-nurtured chance for a noncommunist Laos disappeared.[142]

If the Laotian government's dependence on the United States was overwhelming, the Pathet Lao were equally beholden to their foreign patrons. Some of the assistance came from the Soviet Union, at least in the early stages. After Kong Le's coup in August 1960 provided them with an opportunity, Kennedy charged that the Russians flew one thousand planeloads of supplies and equipment to the Pathet Lao between December 1960 and March 1961. After the 1962 Geneva Conference, however, Soviet aid was halted.[143] The Chinese also dispatched military provisions to both the Pathet Lao and the North Vietnamese in Laos. Ironically, in response to an initial request from Souvanna Phouma in 1962, the Chinese launched a road-building program in the northern province of Phong Saly, where the prime minister sought to strengthen his own neutralist influence against a strong Pathet Lao presence. This program developed a mysterious life of its own, however, with thirty thousand Chinese engineer soldiers building roads that never seemed to get finished, lead to any destination, or serve any purpose. Though they made everyone nervous, the roads never had a direct impact on the war. In 1978, the Chinese said their task was done and left.[144]

These distractions aside, the bulk of the assistance the Pathet Lao received came from the North Vietnamese. From the very beginning, when separate parties were created for each Indochinese state in 1951, the Lao Dong party of North Vietnam maintained supervisory rights over its junior fraternal parties. The Cambodians, obviously, fought this, but the Laotians did not. Indeed, a State Department White Paper on Laos in 1959 reported that the North Vietnamese controlled the administration of the Pathet Lao provinces of Phong Saly and Sam Neua and also provided political guidance to the Pathet Lao.[145] From their headquarters in Sam Neua, North Vietnamese military and political "advisers" planned military strategy for the Pathet Lao and directed the policy of the People's party of Laos.[146]

Militarily, in addition to running the vital Ho Chi Minh Trail, the North Vietnamese sought to stiffen the military performance of the Pathet Lao in the Plain of Jars. To do this, they used their own regulars as a shock force in initial assaults, leaving the mopping up for the Pathet Lao. This was the case in Nam Tha in 1962. Marek Thee confirms this pattern by listing other battles fought in this manner.[147] From a force of a few thousand in the early 1960s, the size of the NVA contingent in Laos grew to forty thousand in 1968 and reached a high of seventy thousand from 1970 to 1972 before tapering off to forty thousand again in 1974.[148]

Clearly, the Laotian communists could never have come to political power without the North Vietnamese. As one Pathet Lao leader quickly admitted, "Vietnamese aid was essential" to the revolution.[149] Although this dependence posed no general belief-level problems for the Pathet Lao because they accepted the practical reality of foreign dependence as readily as did the government side, for ardent Laotians, both sides had demonstrated a lack of national legitimacy. Indeed, this is what gave real vitality to neutralism in Laos. This lack of legitimacy, in this dependence, was compounded by the postrevolutionary behavior of the Pathet Lao. The eighteen-point program of the Third Coalition was one of widely popular national union and independence. Despite this rhetoric, after liberation the Pathet Lao abolished the monarchy and by 1978 became confrontational toward Buddhism. Laos, in short order, became a country without national institutions: "a country without a parliament and without a constitution, a country where the only law . . . would be that of the party."[150] Furthermore, this was a party whose only ideological blueprint was that of the Vietnamese theoretician Le Duan's "three revolutions."[151] In winning, the Pathet Lao became too Vietnamese to be Laotian anymore. Thus, somewhere in all this excessive intervention in Laos, Laos itself disappeared.

DYNAMICS OF THE BALANCES

The fundamental asymmetry for both Cambodia and Laos is that their revolutions were bound up in the larger revolution in Vietnam. Thus they both were not masters of their own revolutionary destinies. The difference was that the Laotians accepted this gracefully; the Cambodians did not. In this asymmetry there was a further imbalance to the two sides. To the Americans, Cambodia and Laos were "sideshows" to their basic commitment to South Vietnam. To the North Vietnamese, Cambodia and Laos were basic to their revolution in the South. Laos provided the territory for their vital logistical supply line. Until 1970, the Cambodian port of Sihanoukville also played a crucial role in provisioning communist forces in the Mekong Delta. On an ideological plane, the North Vietnamese always sought to embrace these two countries in their common Indochinese revolution. At this belief level, the Americans were ambivalent. The resultant difference was a constancy to North Vietnamese support of their revolutionary comrades that was distinctly lacking in the assistance of the United States.

This inconsistency became apparent in Cambodia when the U.S. Congress cut off the bombing in August 1973 even though the North Vietnamese continued their assistance all the way to liberation, despite the tensions with the Cambodian communists over their elimination of the Cambodian Hanoi returnees. It was magnified by the fact that Hanoi's contributions in Cambodia were on the ground, while those of the Americans were in the skies. After the cutoff, only two hundred American military and civilian officials were permitted in the U.S. Embassy in Phnom Penh.[152]

In Laos, this U.S. ambivalence resulted in acquiescence to the large North Vietnamese troop presence in Laos that defied the Geneva Agreement of 1962. A further asymmetry in Laos was the imbalance of the war's ethnic burdens. For all but the last seven months of the war, the Laotian communists fought their revolution in the territory of tribal minorities using them as the foot soldiers in their "Lao" people's war. The Americans responded with a campaign in the Plain of Jars on the backs of the hardy Meos. Indeed, speaking of the Meos, one American official admitted, "in Laos we were pushing people beyond their limits."[153]

The overpowering presence of the Vietnam War does not mean that errors of real consequence were not committed in Cambodia and Laos. In Phnom Penh, Prince Sihanouk played a pivotal political role, and he drew errors to himself like nails to a magnet. Three he committed himself, two simultaneously. By both nationalizing the banks and siding with Peking, he set himself up for a coup d'état. Then, third, when the coup happened in 1970, he mistakenly thought he could regain control of his country by siding with the communists. In the latter event, the coup plotters would have done better to have forced the prince to change policies rather than to have forced him from office, as Lon Nol originally wanted.[154] In any case, Prince Sihanouk had developed so much hostility toward the CIA, because of its complicity in this and a previous rebellion, that political moderation was a difficult course for him to consider at the time of the coup. These errors of politics were compounded by the military blunder (for Cambodia) of Nixon's 1970 Cambodian incursion, which transformed the sleepy North Vietnamese logistical base areas into launchpads of conquest for angered NVA troops.[155]

Perhaps the most poignant error was the failure of either Washington or Cambodian republicans to heed Ith Sarin, the Cassandra of Phnom Penh. Ith Sarin was a government civil servant who defected to Pol Pot. In studying to be a cadre, he saw the true horror of this revolution and returned to Phnom Penh to write a book of warning, *Regrets for the Khmer Soul*. The book was suppressed and he was jailed.[156] What made this revolution the horror that Ith Sarin foresaw was the failure of the two wings of the party, the "Cambodian" and the "Vietnamese," to reach a comradely accommodation.

In Laos, there were also American errors of politics. Because the rightists didn't win, the United States did not support the results of the 1958 National Assembly elections or Souvanna Phouma's attempts to create a national community with the Pathet Lao. Instead the United States undermined his position by buying the elections of 1960.[157] Though on this score the United States did see the error of its ways, it, in effect, recommitted the same error in 1973, when it refused to continue its critical military support for the Vientiane government.

On the other side, the Soviet Union had the decency to quit Laos after making a fool of itself on the Plain of Jars. Initially, the Soviets had airlifted conventional military equipment to the Pathet Lao to ensure their survival against government forces and then similarly equipped Neutralist forces for their survival. But the Pathet Lao got jealous and turned their Russian weapons on the Neutralists, who wanted more Russian weapons to save themselves from the communists. Though the Russians quit, the Chinese kept on building their roads. Whether the Middle Kingdom was making a big mistake with these roads will have to await a future revelation of China's still very opaque intentions. One thing is not opaque: the North Vietnamese made few mistakes in transforming the Pathet Lao into their good puppets. The Pathet Lao ensured this outcome by stripping themselves of what remained of their Lao identity: the monarchy and the *sangha*.

The question of reversibilities in Cambodia and Laos is problematic because, with the Vietnamese revolution so powerfully present, it is not clear there were any. Two remain as possibilities. First, with all the domestic and international forces dissecting Cambodia, Prince Sihanouk played a pivotal role as a source of unification. Thus, which way this mercurial but legitimate leader jumped was critical. Had the United States recognized this political quality that attached to him, he might have been treated more sensitively, and, perhaps, stayed with the government in 1970. Second, in Laos the United States belatedly recognized the error of its ways and saw in Souvanna Phouma what it had failed to see in Sihanouk. The problem was that, once seeing this, in its indecent haste to exit from Vietnam, the United States failed to see its newfound prescience through, and abandoned Laos in 1973.[158]

Comparisons with Vietnam

In any comparison of Cambodia and Laos with Vietnam, problems arise whether they are treated separately or together. Separately, neither revolution had sufficient strength by itself to develop an independent history from the overshadowing revolution in Vietnam. The Cambodians could not have started without the Vietnamese nor could the Pathet Lao ever have completed their revolution without Hanoi's sustenance. On the other side, America's vital assistance to the Phnom Penh and Vientiane regimes was only an extension of its primary commitment to Saigon. But trying to fold these two revolutions into the Vietnamese revolution has created other problems. The North Vietnamese saw these revolutions as part of their larger Indochinese revolution. The consequence was the complete disappearance of an independent Laos and a nearly complete hostility between Vietnam and Cambodia. Washington, too, saw these wars as one, resulting in at least one unfortunate consequence. Though Nguyen Van Thieu probably deserved his fate in Saigon as did Marshal Lon Nol in Phnom Penh, Souvanna Phouma in Vientiane did not. In brief, greater American sensitivity to the differences in these struggles might have at least salvaged something in Laos.

From this book's central perspective of legitimacy, it is my tenet that none of the communist victories in Indochina gained the victors the prize of either national or revolutionary legitimacy. The Vietnamese communists went the farthest. They mounted a successful people's war and nationalist campaign for independence against the French and carried their revolution on as far as the ashes of the Tet offensive in 1968. Against this revolutionary tide, the nationalists were not able to develop an alternative that was competitive on its own against the communists. But the political dispute between them was still settled by blows, leaving the issue of legitimacy unresolved in 1975 — as it remains unresolved today. In Cambodia, Prince Sihanouk handled the transition to modernity badly, but he was badly handled in return — first by the Americans, then by the communists. All along, in the mindless, postliberation destruction of tradition and subsequent abandonment of modernization to chaos, he held the key to national reconciliation and to any possible redefinition of legitimacy. When the tide of revolution swept over Laos, it was more of a feudal entity in the midst of differences within its ruling elites and two royal lines than a modern state ripe for revolution. This family feud was rendered irreconcilable by the interference of this larger struggle. In this larger struggle, any distinctive Laotian definition of legitimacy disappeared.

The revolutions in Indochina were won at the organizational or opportunity level, backed by steadier foreign intervention. This did not mean that the communists provided full answers to communal land reform, societal access, and political participation. It did mean that when these political struggles froze up and became suspended until the military battles were resolved, the superiority of the insurgents in their strategy and performance was able to carry the day. This said, in Cambodia and Laos, there were real defects to the communist accomplishments. Land reform never became an issue in either Cambodia or Laos, although the Cambodian communists did redistribute land in areas they held. Societal access in both these societies was guaranteed by foreign patrons, though new opportunities were created by the communists for tribals in Laos and for peasants and students in Cambodia. In Laos, the Pathet Lao was able to lay claim to about a third of the Laotian electorate, but what was noteworthy was the far larger share earned by the Neutralists. In Cambodia, the electoral fortunes of the communist-front Pracheachon were disastrous. Such politics were not the forte of the Pol Pot group either. As Ith Sarin observed, "As for general elections, they have no ideas."[159] Finally, like all the other revolutions treated in this book, the rural people's war strategies in Cambodia and Laos were born out of the fruitlessness of revolution in the cities.

If these were defective victories at the opportunity level, there was virtually no belief-level legitimacy to either of these revolutions. In the penultimate paragraph to *The Communist Manifesto*, Karl Marx intoned: "The Communists disdain to conceal their views and aims."[160] But in Laos and Cambodia they won by stealth and deceit. The Pathet Lao shared power in 1973 through popular promises to safeguard national institutions. When they seized power in 1975, however, they abolished the monarchy and turned on the Buddhist *sangha*. The Cambodian communists trumpeted the glories of Angkor Wat in their struggle for national liberation even though afterward the party attacked Cambodia's long line of kings as "corrupt anachronisms who had always sucked the blood of the people."[161] As vampires, the Cambodian communists did not reveal themselves as communists until they were two years into their bloodletting.[162] Though the communists in Vietnam did not win by stealth and deceit, they had similar problems of opportunity and belief-level legitimacy, particularly in its modern aspects.

Having joined in the revolutionary struggle in Indochina, the United States withdrew prematurely before strong enough foundations for modern nation-states had been built. If Vietnam is not illustrative of imperial overstretch, Cambodia and Laos certainly are. In a larger global scheme of things, they were pawns readily sacrificed in a bigger game. But American responsibility for the fate of Cambodia and Laos is nevertheless heavy. Even on the larger stage, Washington's behavior in the Mekong River interior raises questions about its ability to undertake long-term commitments away from areas of strategic interest. America's intervention in Indochina began under the immodest Nitzean assumption that "an attack on free institutions anywhere was an attack on free institutions everywhere" and ended in a return to the "vital strong points" becoming to a Kennanesque modesty, which left Cambodia and Laos abandoned by a pious U.S. Congress in a fit of abstemious noninterventionism.

From a Western perspective, until the Vientiane Peace Agreement of 1973, the war in Laos represented a fairly successful, low-cost intervention. As Chalmers Johnson put it, "The Laotian approach did not actually make the situation worse, which was an achievement of sorts."[163] For a change, after some faltering, the United States had backed a leader with legitimate national appeal. The struggle within Laos might well have led to some accommodation if the Laotians had been left to themselves. Real independence, of course, was practically impossible in a country like Laos, but if outside forces could have been kept evenly balanced, a great deal of internal latitude might have emerged.

The tragedy of Laos is that it might have been avoided had not the United States been so overpowered by the analogy of its own contemporary experience in Vietnam. When the North Vietnamese failed to withdraw their troops in 1973, there was no reason for the United States to withdraw its weight from the balance. The United States may well have been standing on the winning side in Laos even as it stood on the losing side in Vietnam and Cambodia. Souvanna Phouma was a widely respected figure as Nguyen Van Thieu and Lon Nol were not, and, ultimately, to recall Phetsareth's verity for a moment, the Laotians probably preferred a distant protector to a near one. In short, Laos represented the first misreading of the lessons of Vietnam and induced the Americans to snatch defeat from the jaws of a workable stalemate.

Although Laos has disappeared under Vietnamese hegemony, there is at least a chance to redeem Cambodia in the U.N. Peace Agreement signed in Paris on October 23, 1991. Even at sixty-nine, Prince Norodom Sihanouk remains pivotal to national unity. Just as having the Khmer Rouge communists inside this new national tent is critical to giving the prince the room for maneuver he needs to counterbalance Cambodia's four internal political groups, it is just as important for all the foreign patrons to hold fast their ropes to the tent poles lest the tent collapse once more on the dancing prince. Hence, as the Vietnamese support the Heng Samrin regime (of the old Eastern Zone) and the Chinese the Khmer Rouge, the United States must stay with the returned prince and the noncommunists to ensure that the mistake of Souvanna Phouma is not repeated.

As a modern Rip Van Winkle, Prince Sihanouk returned to Phnom Penh on November 14, 1991, aboard a coughing 1963 Chevrolet Impala, a car dating from the year official American aid to the prince's regime was cut off.[164] In Buddhist-Hindu mythology, the splendor of a god, or a god-king, came as much from his festooned vehicle as it did from his regally dressed personage. Thus Vishnu flew on Garuda the Eagle; Lord Shiva rode astride Nandi the Bull; and the fair Saraswati glided on a graceful Swan. Surely our prince in Phnom Penh deserves a more "legitimate" vehicle than a twenty-three-year-old Chevrolet. The fact that his son was the chief vote-getter in the U.N.-supervised elections of May 1993 seals the proof to his claims.

Epilogue

This chapter began with the question, Why was the Cambodian revolution so bloody, the Laotian so gentle, and the Vietnamese so orderly?

One of the most fatuous theses that has been proposed is that the bloody tragedy in Cambodia, according to Gareth Porter and George Hildebrand, "should mainly be attributed to the American bombing."[165] Ben Kiernan has amplified this conclusion by contending that the level of bombing—twice that sustained by Japan in World War II, as he has fondly pointed out—aroused intense peasant hatred toward the Americans and this rage helped Pol Pot consolidate his control over both the peasantry and the disparate groups of his revolution.[166] The official explanation given by Ieng Sary for the evacuation of Phnom Penh and the other cities was that the Khmer Rouge found the cities on the brink of starvation and they could not provision them because the transportation network had been destroyed by the bombing. Further, he has alleged that the CIA was planning to use the urban chaos to stir up rebellion and bomb the cities in support of a Lon Nol counterattack.[167]

This entire thesis simply cannot stand up under scrutiny. Laos takes top honors for being the most heavily bombed country in the war. The two million tons of bombs that it received was equal to the total U.S. bombing in all theaters during World War II.[168] Not to be outdone, North Vietnamese politburo member Le Duc Tho has insisted that "the amount of U.S. bombs dropped in Laos and North Vietnam was much more than that dropped in [Cambodia]."[169] In fact, despite the bombing for two hundred days and nights that Cambodia suffered in 1973, the most sustained bombing campaign of the war was the 1.2 million bombs that fell mostly in South Vietnam to help roll back the Tet offensive of 1968.[170] Further, though civilians were certainly killed by the bombing and artillery-rocket cross fire, most of the U.S. bombing in Cambodia was directed at North Vietnamese forces and installations employed in the war in Vietnam.[171] Ironically, the bombing itself did not prove its worth in producing the results attributed to it. After touring the countryside in April 1973, during the most intense period of bombardment, Sihanouk observed that the "intensive bombing . . . was manifestly ineffectual."[172] The supposedly outraged peasants told Francois Ponchaud that "most of the time they were bombing the forests, where there was nobody."[173] Finally, neither starvation, nor bombing, nor stay-behind agents, nor wild fears of American reintervention can justify the evacuations and killings that followed Phnom Penh's liberation. None of the major cities liberated in World War II were evacuated. Moscow and Leningrad were on the brink of starvation when their sieges were lifted and their transportation network was similarly destroyed, but, unlike the Cambodians, the Russians were willing to accept international help. And stay-behind agents by themselves did not warrant fears of a new war from U.S. bombers grounded by congressional fiat. Bombing was something all Indochinese countries had in common and cannot account for the different courses their revolutions took.

Rather, as this chapter has demonstrated, the evacuations and killings in Cambodia's bloody revolution were done for internal control by a cadre too small to be sure of its strength but still too strong, in its victims' divided fears and suspicions, to be stopped. Pol Pot and his entourage masked their organizational weakness by ideological ambitions stoked by the purifying fires of Cambodian corpses. As Martin Diamond has written: "The political pursuit of impossible dreams leads to terror and tyranny in the vain effort to actualize what cannot be."[174] The Laotian revolution was comparatively gentle because, despite the Pathet Lao's similar organizational weakness, its ambitions were modest and its dependence on outsiders was readily accepted. Finally, the Vietnamese revolution was more orderly because, once the Americans were gone, the Vietnamese communists had enough military and organizational depth to carry out their plans, rather than dreams.

PART IV
Lessons

Chapter 11

FINDINGS FROM THE PRISM AND AN APPLICATION: SENDERO LUMINOSO OF PERU

The Findings

Insurgencies are revolutions "on the slow burn"—they are protracted. As such, they must appeal to a mixture of motives to sustain them: to intensifying individual interests, group opportunities, and societal beliefs. Because insurgencies erupt as bottlenecks to the overall transition in the Third World from traditional to modern society, the fundamental nature of such disputes is over the basis upon which political authority should be justified. In other words, insurgencies are crises of political legitimacy. This, at least, is the paradigmatic presupposition of this study.

In the last analysis, beliefs about political legitimacy are more determinative and sustaining to the enduring outcome of an insurgency, for both incumbents and insurgents, than are calculations of interest or opportunity. In building an insurgency, calculations of interest attract tentative followers. Commitments of opportunity mobilize groups as active participants even as such motivations create the organizational leaders or cadres of both sides. Professions of belief about "the cause," however, sustain both leaders and mobilized followers down the long road of sacrifice an insurgency entails. Thus, without these beliefs, an insurgency lacks the elasticity to protract. Also, beliefs about political legitimacy, rather than being generally determined, are the idiosyncratic products of each society's history and political culture. These, anyway, are the undergirding findings that have emerged from the cases of this book.

DIAGNOSIS OF THE BENCHMARKS OF INSURGENT SUCCESS

To gauge which side is on a more likely trajectory to success (in response to the basic question of what makes for a successful insurgency), I have developed the diagnostic tools of the three rising benchmarks of insurgent or counterinsurgent success which roughly compare to the three levels of motives: critical mass to interest motives, crossover points (the establishment of momentum) to opportunity motives, and strategic breakout to belief motives. They also compare with Mao's three stages of people's war. These comparisons are certainly not exact. In real life, insurgencies are dynamic and comprehensive struggles in which the most appropriate place to portray these motives, benchmarks, and stages is on a pinwheel in a hurricane. For example, for a critical mass to exist among a collection of followers, there will have to be an organization of opportunity-level cadres to employ these followers and fanatical leaders of belief to inspire the organization itself. Though opportunity-level analysis focuses on groups and organizations, individuals make the commitments that coalesce into these groups. Finally, fanatical leaders of elevated beliefs are certainly not above self-interested calculations of interest nor are they immune to the opportunity manipulations of the groups and organizations within and outside their movements. Insurgencies, nevertheless, are built (as well as defeated) by an intensifying process of rising motivation, organization, and scale that can be usefully separated analytically into the stages and levels presented in this work.

Figures 11.1 through 11.8 illustrate the paths followed in our cases from critical mass through unpredictable gyrations of crossover points to either strategic breakout and victory or to a downward loss of this momentum and defeat. Certainly no mathematical precision is intended for these curves, but for heuristic purposes they do provide a rough map of each case's history. They also offer some generalizations from this typology for possible application elsewhere. Before turning to the individual cases, it is worth recalling the numbers suggested as measures for the benchmarks of insurgent success at the end of Chapter 3. In countries of ten to twenty million, a critical mass exists when an insurgent group commands a hard core of five to ten thousand fighters and a network of sympathizers ten times as large. Crossover points, a range marked by brackets to the left of each of the figures, refer to momentum, either upward toward a breakout or downward to a smashing

Figure 11.1. Benchmarks of Insurgent Success: Vietnam I

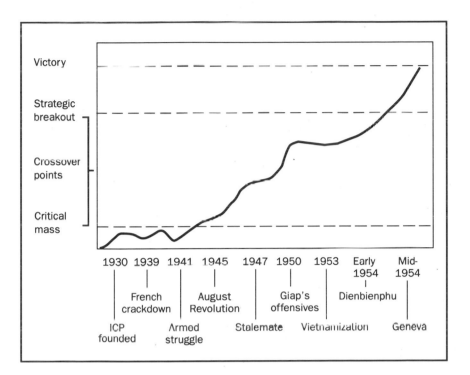

of the initial critical mass. A strategic breakout occurs when an insurgency has attracted enough support to pose a genuine crisis of rule and has jockeyed into a position to launch a frontal bid for power. Roughly speaking, such a point has been reached when 10 to 20 percent of the adult population join the insurgent cause (provided this number is widely distributed and includes key political groups) and active support for the incumbent government dips below 50 percent.

Turning to the cases themselves, in all of them (except for Vietnam II), the struggle both to achieve and to lift off from a critical mass was prolonged. In no case was it less than ten years, and in Cambodia and Laos a secure liftoff took nearly thirty years. Vietnam II started from above a critical mass because of the legacy of the earlier Resistance War against the French. For most of the cases, this liftoff occurred only with the fortuitous external intervention of World War II and the defeat and removal of incumbent regimes that came with this war. Mao's revolution in China did manage to rise above a critical mass on its own internally; however, it was beaten back down by Chiang Kai-shek in the mid-1930s. It was the Sino-Japanese War (which merged into World War II) that provided the lasting impetus to Mao's rising momentum of crossover points. The very length of the struggle

Figure 11.2. Benchmarks of Insurgent Success: Vietnam II

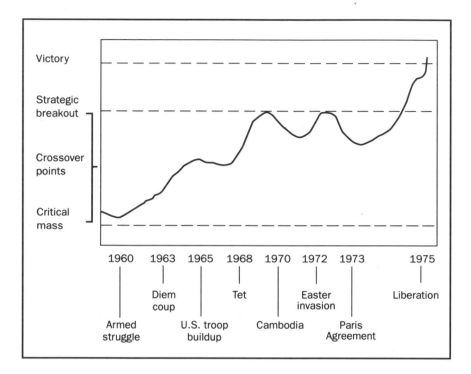

out of critical masses for Cambodia and Laos reflected the weaker boosting effect of World War II there. An extremely important point of contrast with these experiences today is the absence of such a ubiquitous booster (or its equivalent) in the emerging post–Cold War order.

The main point about the momentum of crossover points, in the vast middle of these figures, is their volatility. There is nothing preordained about any of these revolutions. The momentum can go up, it can go down, or it can stall as it did in Laos from 1961 to 1971. As in Mao's second phase of protracted war, crossover points are as fluid as his campaigns of maneuver. But these figures do show two different patterns to these fluidities. Momentums of crossover points that flow from conventional military offensives, whether purely domestic or as a result of foreign interventions, follow sharper, steeper curves. The most dramatic case is Greece, but the Tet offensive and Easter invasion of Vietnam are also good illustrations. Lower-level guerrilla activity and incumbent programs of reform follow a more gradual pattern of rising and falling. The best examples are the Philippines and Malaya. Occasionally, a dramatic political event, whether internal or external, can also provoke sharp curves. The Sihanouk defection in Cambodia

Figure 11.3. Benchmarks of Insurgent Success: China

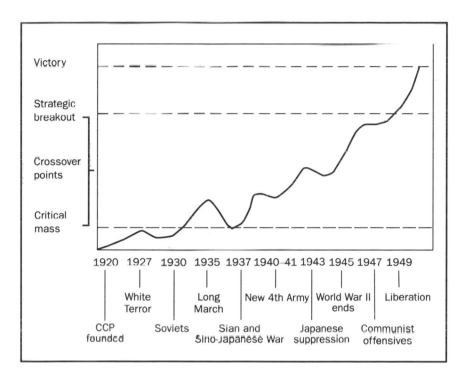

(1970) and the American sellout of Laos in the Vientiane Peace Agreement (1973) are perhaps the most noteworthy of these exceptions.

One clear commonality from these cases does emerge about strategic breakouts. Despite the focus on the politics of insurgencies in this book, the only thing that throws back an insurgency that has reached a breakout is a sharp military action. Political reforms work only at lower benchmark levels. In these cases, the only breakouts that were turned back were in Greece and in Vietnam at the Tet offensive and Easter invasion. Absent these interventions, insurgents are likely to win at this stage, as they did in Vietnam in 1975 with no American reintervention. But the differences between the Greek and Vietnamese cases are also instructive—particularly to those contemplating interventions, such as in Bosnia. The political receptivity to the British intervention in Greece was far more favorable than it was to the American in Vietnam, creating far shallower reversals for the Viet Cong in Vietnam than the plunge taken by the guerrillas in Greece.

THEMATIC QUESTIONS: THE RESULTS

Chapter 1 presented a set of six thematic questions and attendant propositions to guide the analysis of the cases. The first question was a contextual

Figure 11.4. Benchmarks of Insurgent Success: Greece

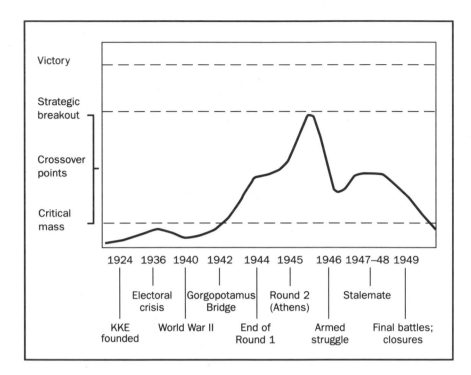

one: *What was the historical setting out of which each insurgency developed and from which the country's specific definition of political legitimacy arose?* The point here was to underscore the essential or historical nature of such definitions. This was demonstrated descriptively in the historical settings of each case. Each case highlighted the centrality of World War II to these definitions and to the initiation of each insurgency (proposition 1.1). The fact that the international context for insurgencies is now quite different is taken up in the conclusion (proposition 1.2).

The second question asked, *How did the incumbents and insurgents fare competitively according to the terms of our analytical framework of legitimacy?* As for achieving a critical mass at the interest level, it is always difficult for an insurgency to get going because it is illegal and thereby entails high risks and costs. In all of our primary cases, this asymmetry was not overcome until the fortuitous advent of World War II, which destroyed the suppressive capabilities of the governments and compromised their belief-level legitimacy. In China, Chiang Kai-shek was chased by the Japanese from his power base in the cities. In Greece the government was driven into exile. And colonial rule was either eliminated or seriously compromised in the Philippines, Malaya, Vietnam, Laos, and Cambodia. Except for Cambodia and Laos, the

Figure 11.5. Benchmarks of Insurgent Success: Philippines

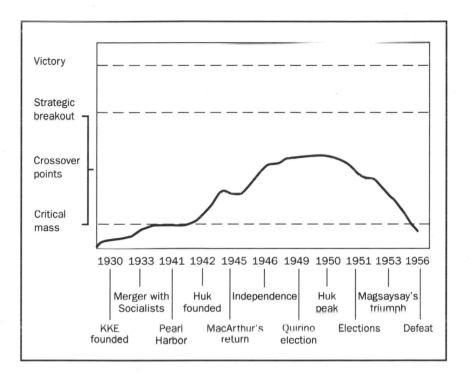

insurgents took full advantage of this wartime interregnum and by war's end had built a strong momentum of crossover points in their favor.

At this opportunity level of struggle between and within subgroups for maintaining or reversing the direction of this momentum, domestically the key was to undercut the other side with reforms that opened up opportunities at the same time as these measures helped certify a belief-level legitimacy for the reformers. In these cases, two reforms that proved critical were land reform and elections: land reform because it opened up societal access both traditional and modern in the countryside and elections because they provided avenues of expanding political participation nationwide. In China, both sides seized on land reform as an issue, but Mao did it better. Though the communists did not engage in much electioneering, they did work at coalition-building among groups. Chiang Kai-shek did stage elections, but his manipulations of them made them of dubious value. In Greece, land reform had been disposed of as an issue before the insurgency, but the elections of 1946 were important in confining the guerrillas to the countryside where, essentially, they lacked a motivating issue. In the Philippines, the land reform issue worked in favor of the Huks in the single region of Central Luzon even as elections worked to the nationwide advantage of the govern-

Figure 11.6. Benchmarks of Insurgent Success: Malaya

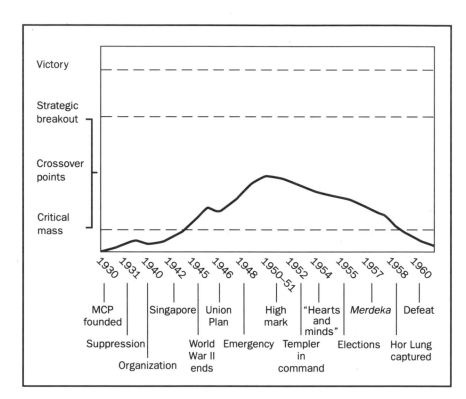

ment. In Malaya, both land reform and elections were appropriated by the government. The MRLA never developed a political response. In Vietnam, both land reform and elections were pursued by the government, but for the former, it was too late, and for the latter, they were unconvincing. Members of the National Liberation Front, for example, were barred from voting. In Cambodia and Laos, neither land reform nor elections played a determinative role in the outcomes of these insurgencies. Here an exogenous variable to a legitimacy crisis—namely, intervention—carried the day.

Another key variable of societal access is, simply, jobs. What is remarkable in all our cases is the success of the incumbents in unionizing the urban workers away from the communists and thereby driving them from the cities, their ideologically preferred revolutionary seedbed. In every case, this success was achieved by Western home-country labor organizations rather than government agencies. For the promotion of elections, this would suggest that relying on the State Department and CIA may not have been the best instrument.

At the belief level, insurgencies are fought between two groups trying

Figure 11.7. Benchmarks of Insurgent Success: Cambodia

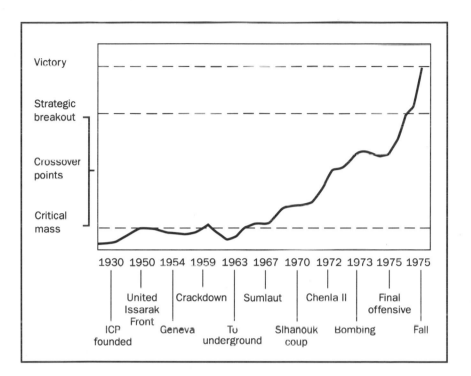

to create a middle ground for a political community based on common national or newly agreed-upon principles of political legitimacy. Among our cases, as depicted in Table 11.1, the results at this belief level were mixed. Mao's long march to power demonstrated his own premise that revolutions are "actualized by nationalism." In his case, he married the interest- and opportunity-level commitments of the peasantry to the belief-level quest in China for freedom from all forms of foreign intervention. In Vietnam, the Viet Minh replicated Mao's accomplishment in their triumph over the French and continued in this path to the disaster of the Tet offensive against the Americans. After Tet, however, the communists abandoned their people's war strategy and neglected the political appeals upon which such a strategy is built, thereby settling for a politically compromising victory based on military means alone. The liberation of Saigon, then, as a stellar exhibit of both revolutionary and national legitimacy, was, at best, controversial.

In Greece the balance of national legitimacy switched between the two sides. During the war, the insurgents cashed in on the discredited government's defeat and retreat into exile. Given a second chance by the British intervention, the government reclaimed its legitimacy through two elections

Figure 11.8. Benchmarks of Insurgent Success: Laos

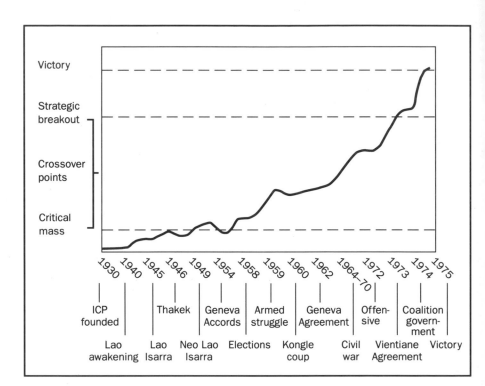

and a coalition government among the noncommunist parties. The attempt of the communists to regroup politically around appeals of Macedonian irredentism only hastened their final military debacle at Vitsi and Grammos. In this regard, the momentums in the Philippines and Malaya were roughly similar in that the communists never rose above opportunity-level appeals (regional ones of land reform for the Huks and ethnic ones for the Chinese peasant squatters of Malaya) while the governments swamped the insurgents with elections in the Philippines and with a constitutional contract and *merdeka* in Malaya. In the Philippines, however, the government's accomplishment at the belief level lacked a solid grounding, but the challenge of the Huks was not serious enough to reveal this weakness. Though belief-level appeals did play a role in attempting to legitimate political rule in Cambodia and Laos, various forms of foreign intervention threw these two struggles completely off balance. The fates of these two insurgencies, then, were ultimately decided beyond their borders.

Thus, apart from Cambodia, Laos, and the controversy over Vietnam, wherever the insurgents were able to make successful belief-level appeals to national legitimacy, they won, as in at least one Vietnam case and China;

Table 11.1. Comparative Legitimacy

Cases	Incumbents				Insurgents			
	Interest	Oppor-tunity	Belief	Vic-tory	Interest	Oppor-tunity	Belief	Vic-tory
Vietnam I	+	+	o	o	+	+	+	+
Vietnam II				o				+
To Tet	+	+	?		+	+	+	
After Tet	+	+	?		+	+	?	
China				o				+
Up to WWII	+	+	+		+	+	+	
After WWII	+	?	o		+	+	+	
Greece				+				o
Round 1 and 2	+	+	?		+	+	+	
Round 3	+	+	+		+	?	o	
Philippines	+	+	?	+	+	?	o	o
Malaya	+	+	+	+	+	?	o	o
Cambodia				o				+
Pre-1970	+	+	+		+	?	o	
Post-1970	+	+	o		+	+	?	
Laos	+	?	?	o	+	?	?	+

Key
+ = Present
o = Absent
? = Partial or controversial

and wherever such appeals eluded them, as in Greece, the Philippines, and Malaya, they lost. Thus, it is my proposition (2.1) that though most activity in an insurgency takes place at the opportunity level and its institutional and group contest for societal access (land reform) and political participation (elections), the outcome to an insurgency depends more critically on the belief level.

To these legitimacy crises, of which these insurgencies were manifestations, there were the exogenous or conditioning variables of the strategy and performance of the two sides and the amount of foreign intervention in their behalf (as depicted in Figure 3.3). Accordingly, the third question asked, *How closely did the insurgents follow a Marxist people's war strategy and what was its impact on the claims of the insurgents to both national and revolutionary legitimacy?* The fourth was, *What was the impact of Western intervention on the legitimacy crisis animating each insurgency?* I turn to the exogenous variable of intervention first because, as much as legitimacy, this

Table 11.2. Comparative Intervention

| | On Behalf of Incumbents | | | | |
	Amount	Level	Constancy	Legitimacy Effect	Outcome
Vietnam I	+++	+++	+	−	Loss
Vietnam II					Loss
To Tet	+++	+++	+	−	
After Tet	+++	+++	−	−	
China					Loss
Up to WWII	++	++	+	o	
After WWII	+++	++	−	−	
Greece					Win
Rounds 1 and 2	+	+++	+	+	
Round 3	+++	++	+	+	
Philippines	+++	++	+	o	Win
Malaya	+++	+++	+	+	Win
Cambodia					Loss
Pre-1970	+++	+	+	o	
Post-1970	+++	++	−	−	
Laos	+++	++(+?)	−	o	Loss

Key

Amounts:	Level:
+++ = Massive ($1 billion +)	+++ = Ground combat
++ = Moderate ($ millions)	++ = Direct support short of combat
+ = Low	+ = Material support

is a study of the intersection of insurgency and intervention. In this regard, intervention has been analyzed along four axes (and is presented in Table 11.2): first, the sheer material amount of the foreign assistance; second, the level of intervention, as depicted along the vertical continua of Figures 1.1 through 1.8 (the balance of intervention charts); third, the constancy of the intervention; and, finally, the effects of the intervention on legitimacy in three areas—on the legitimacy of the government challenged by the insurgents, on the intervening state's international position, and on the domestic legitimacy of the intervening state's intervention.

Overarching all these axes is the commonality that in none of these insurgencies were any of the participants, whether incumbents or insurgents, successful without some intervention in their behalf. At least in these cases, insurgencies do intersect with intervention. The successful insurgencies in China, Vietnam, Cambodia, and Laos all received critical outside help.

	Amount	Level	Constancy	Legitimacy Effect	Outcome
+++	++	+	+	Win
					Win
+++	++(+?)	+	+	
+++	++(+?)	+	?	
					Win
+	I	−	o	
++	+	−	o	
					Loss
+	++	+	+	
++	+	−	−	
o	o	o	o	Loss
o	o	o	o	Loss
					Win
+	+	+	?	
++	+++	I	?	
+++	+++	+	o	Win

Constancy:
  + = Present throughout
  − = Episodic or withheld at
      key moments
  o = No aid

Legitimacy effect:
  + = Positive
  o = No effect
  − = Negative
  ? = Controversial

Though the Chinese came the closest to the autarkic people's war ideal, at critical points, particularly during and after World War II, intervention in support of the revolution was invaluable. Similarly, the successful counter-insurgencies in Greece, Malaya, and the Philippines received important help from Britain and the United States. Also, in the two cases in which one side in the struggle received no help at all, as was true for the communist sides in the Philippines and Malaya, the nonrecipient sides were easily defeated.

Nevertheless, the effects of these interventions were not simply those of free-floating mathematical balances. Though interventions certainly weighed in at interest- and opportunity-level calculations of legitimacy, the table shows that the strongest effect of an intervention was felt at the belief level (which is proposition 4.1 to the fourth question). Further, at this highest level, this effect on a client's quest for legitimacy could be positive (and enhancing) or negative (and debilitating), depending on the specific definition of belief-level legitimacy in the society in question. The analysis of each case paid considerable attention to making this assessment. This finding comes out the strongest in Vietnam and China. In both of the Vietnamese insurgencies and in China, the incumbents received far more assistance than did the insurgents, yet the insurgents won. In large part this was because this support hurt the belief level legitimacy of the incumbent regimes. The Mandate of Heaven in both China and Vietnam was sullied by the incumbent regime's excessive dependence on foreigners. Interestingly enough, the cases of Cambodia and Laos produced a stand-off on this question. In Laos, both sides were so heavily compromised by their degree of foreign dependence that the political neutralists held the balance. In Cambodia, the communists fraudulently proclaimed their loyalty to national beliefs and hid their overweening degree of dependence on the Vietnamese until after "liberation" while the Americans found themselves caught in Lon Nol's illegitimacy lock because Prince Sihanouk and the belief-level legitimacy he offered had danced away from them into even more treacherous communist arms. Finally, in Greece, Malaya, and the Philippines, Western interventions, even with ground combat troops in the cases of Greece and Malaya, did not affect the claims of the incumbent regimes to legitimacy.

Along these axes of intervention, there are some further findings. Regarding the levels of intervention from rhetorical support to formal control (as depicted in the balance of intervention charts in Chapter 1), the introduction of ground combat troops proved to be a flashpoint (proposition 4.2). For one thing, nothing more symbolizes the identification of an intervening state with its client state than the presence of these forces. The global military prestige of the intervenor is now on the line in the client state. Within it, nothing is more revealing of either side's external dependence than the obvious presence of foreign troops. However efficacious this intervening force, two internal traps await the unwary. One is a specific illegitimacy lock of sycophant leadership, and the other is a general and variable belief-level legitimacy effect. The United States avoided an illegitimacy lock in China by backing away from Chiang Kai-shek in his last crisis but then fell into the embrace of Nguyen Van Thieu in South Vietnam. With so many troops and its prestige on the line, Washington felt it could not afford the risks of pushing for the reforms that would have created political alternatives. Similarly, in Cambodia, Washington's "all-out commitment" to Lon Nol put it in an isolated position when Prince Sihanouk took his constituency over to the communist side. More fortunately, in Laos, when the United States finally recognized the bankruptcy of the rightists, a solid middle ground was waiting in Souvanna Phouma and the Neutralists.

The general effects of these interventions on local legitimacy varied according to the country's specific definition of this legitimacy. In China and

Vietnam, the provision of safeguarding the fatherland against the depredations of foreign powers ensured that any regime heavily dependent on "foreign devils" would have its right to rule seriously questioned, although in Vietnam, after the Tet offensive, the political credentials of the communists lost their luster. In the Philippines, had the United States sent ground combat troops to aid President Magsaysay, the Huks might have been given a national issue to seize on similar to the Japanese invasion of China that Mao used so well. As it was, they could not break out of the purely regional and opportunity-level claim of land reform, and the massive but subcombat troop level assistance of the United States did not have an appreciable negative effect on the legitimacy of Magsaysay. Cambodia and Laos are the two cases in which the insurgents received levels of intervention on their behalf that discredited them just as much as Western assistance discredited the incumbent regimes. In Greece and Malaya, however, Western combat troops by the thousands enhanced the belief-level legitimacy of the incumbent regimes. Obviously, there were different beliefs at play. In Greece, British troops flattered the Greek sense of their global importance embodied in their Megali Idea. In Malaya, ethnic Malays were grateful to the British forces for keeping in place the upstart Chinese community, and the grant of *merdeka* won the support of all.

Where interventions can make a positive effect on the legitimacy crisis (or perhaps overwhelm the negative effects), they have to be constant because insurgencies are, by definition, protracted. Vietnam is a classic of ambiguity on this question. Though American aid undermined the legitimacy of the Saigon regime, it was also massive enough to keep it propped up. But in 1973 Washington faltered, and in 1975 it dropped the baton. Left to his own devices, Thieu by 1975 was so lacking in legitimacy that he didn't stand a chance without American reintervention. Also, when Congress cut off the bombing in Cambodia in 1973, the more constant communist pressure and Vietnamese communist support gave the "victory" to the side with the steadier outside hand. Because of the lack of legitimacy to these two client regimes, the U.S. withdrawals from Saigon and Phnom Penh may have been cases of prudently cutting off an endless tap of pouring good money onto bad. But the withdrawal from Laos was different, and less excusable, because there were solid grounds for a legitimate noncommunist regime in Vientiane.

On this matter of constancy, ground combat troops (and aerial bombing) were a flashpoint to the legitimacy of the intervention within the intervening state as well. In the United States, on the matter of containing communists, whether on tanks in Europe or on Land Rovers in Southeast Asia, there was a basic agreement on the legitimacy of this enterprise. When the latter case went beyond foreign aid and nation-building to the dispatching of troops, however, the agreement fell apart. Under the banner of containment, the previously isolationist conservatives became knee-jerk interventionists. Liberals were far more wary, wanting to commit only to reform-minded governments. Conservatives, already committed, were eager to finish off the insurgents and were irritated by the restraints imposed by liberals, who, in turn, became increasingly outraged by the moral stigma attached to the use of Western force championed by conservatives. In spite of their feelings of liberal betrayal, conservatives, by this point, became willing to call the whole thing quits on the grounds of pragmatic resignation. The flashpoint to this domestic paralysis over the legitimacy of an intervention was the commitment of treasure, prestige, and blood involved in the dispatching of combat forces. Indeed, it was just such a paralysis in the United States, brought on by the Cambodian Incursion of 1970, that unraveled the entire American commitment to Indochina.

This flashpoint of combat troops, however, was avoided by the United States in both Greece and the Philippines (and in Cambodia and Laos as well) and, more recently, in Central America. This had a few useful effects. Since such subcombat troop level interventions were less costly and controversial, they gave Washington the steadiness it needed to see these commitments through. Because its prestige was less on the line, the United States also retained more leverage over the besieged regimes in the Philippines, Greece, and Laos.

As for interventions in support of the communists, people's war as a revolutionary strategy was an elaborate belief system stressing the self-reliance of the insurgents. What help they received was always painted as supportive of their own forces who were in the vanguard roles and still able, therefore, to appeal to a sense of traditional nationalist honor. With Western help usually so massive and obvious, the revolutionaries were successful in both excusing and hiding their own foreign dependence, despite the high levels of this assistance in Cambodia, Laos, and even Vietnam.

The second exogenous set of variables to the outcomes of an insurgency, as depicted in Figure 3.3, is the strategy and sheer quality of the performance of the two sides, or leadership. Leadership (seen as a combination of strategy, organization, and inspirational command) can make an enormous difference, both positively and negatively, in the outcome of any political event, including an insurgency. As such, it is the rogue elephant of the social sciences because its origins and inspiration remain as mysterious as it was for Plato in his Myth of the Cave. In this study, it almost serves as an alternative explanation to legitimacy. Marxists, nevertheless, have sought to dismiss leadership as accidental, and therefore incidental, to the inevitable fulfillment of dialectical materialism.[1] For the insurgent side, the third thematic question was, *How closely did the revolutionaries follow a Marxist people's war strategy and what was the effect of this strategy on their claims to legitimacy?* With respect to this strategy, I advanced three propositions in the first chapter. The first two are interrelated. The first (3.1) was that a Marxist people's war strategy is the most potent insurgent strategy because it is rooted in popular mobilization as the fount of its power. This, of course, poses a direct challenge to any incumbent program of nation-building because it is built on a similar effect of mobilization under the rubric of expanding political participation and societal access. The second and related proposition (3.2) is that a successful people's war will have to be couched in appeals resonant with the society's particular precepts of national legitimacy, which Mao called discovering the "mass line."

In the cases of this study, both Chinese and Vietnamese revolutionaries showed the power of this leadership strategy, though the Vietnamese abandoned it after the Tet offensive. After being routed from the cities, the communists in Greece were never able to rally around a unifying strategy. The Greek counterexample underscores the value of people's war and also illustrates the importance to any revolutionary strategy of rooting its appeals in national ideals of political legitimacy, not, in the case of Greece, in appeals for Macedonian autonomy to win Soviet support. In the Philippines, beyond appeals of opportunity embodied in land reform, the Huks were never able to develop a set of country-wide beliefs, leaving them vulnerable to Magsaysay's country-wide elections. Similarly, in Malaya, the MRLA became trapped in an ethnic Chinese box, while the government was able to create a constitutional contract fostered by elections that built some national bridges across the three communities. Finally, the promise of a people's war strategy was perverted in Cambodia and never fully developed in Laos.

The third proposition (3.3), or requirement, for insurgent success is the need for revolutionary unity, a unity that may be forged or frayed by opportunity-level groups but cemented only by belief-level principles. The importance of this requirement is demonstrated most clearly by the three cases in which this unity was most conspicuously lacking: Greece, the Philippines, and Cambodia. The communists in Greece were split into three points of view that were never resolved: whether to advance their cause by armed struggle, or infiltration and sabotage, or open competition in the government system. This lack of a unified strategic vision led to both military and political catastrophe. The mass mobilization of the Philippine countryside in the 1930s included groups whose beliefs were so irreconcilable that the Huk insurgency which followed was led by a split politburo that could not contend with a unified Philippine government under Magsaysay. Briefly, though the insurgents in Cambodia "won," their fundamental lack of unity produced a paranoid reaction in victory that engulfed them in a flood of blood.

In contrast, the Vietnamese and Chinese revolutions illustrate the power of insurgencies dedicated to, and united under, a common set of beliefs. Indeed, Mao fashioned his strategy of people's war to provide a set of instrumental principles of strategy and fundamental beliefs about revolution in Asia to unify and inspire his dispirited and faction-riven comrades in Yanan. The Vietnamese communists adopted and modified this strategy for the same purpose. Even though they abandoned the strategy after Tet, they retained sufficient common faith in the revolution itself to win against an adversary whose political beliefs had yet to take root in Vietnamese society. Nevertheless, that revolutionary unity is a necessary but not sufficient condition for insurgent success is shown by the cases of Laos and Malaya whereby the Laotians maintained unity by a common acceptance of an almost complete (and delegitimating) dependence on the North Vietnamese and the Malayans commonly agreed on a suicidal ethnic strategy.

The issue of strategy and leadership provides a good background for the fifth thematic question: *What are the contingencies to these cases regarding their asymmetries, errors, and reversibilities?* The asymmetries to an insurgency recognize that the rhythms of the music for the two sides are different and disjunctive. At the beginning, it is difficult for an insurgency to achieve a critical mass (proposition 5.1a). This achievement came only after a prolonged period in all the cases. But once an insurgency lifts off from a critical mass, it is hard to stop (proposition 5.1b). With momentum achieved, an incumbent regime is obliged to take drastic measures to blunt and reverse this momentum, whether through a major military effort or through reforms that may well endanger the regime's own mainstays of political support. Finally, once an insurgency reaches a strategic breakout where belief-level appeals become more prominent, the Marxism of people's war can pose serious problems of national legitimacy for the insurgents (proposition 5.1c). This is especially true of insurgencies that hide these beliefs, like that of the Khmer Rouge.

Nevertheless, far from being deterministically inevitable, insurgencies can be reversed (proposition 5.2). They can be reversed by interventions (proposition 5.2a), as they were in Greece and Malaya. Alternatively, insurgencies can be won by interventions, as they were by communists in Cambodia and Laos, and in Vietnam, if we regard the North Vietnamese army as an intervening force. In addition, insurgencies can be undercut by reforms (proposition 5.2b), as they were in Greece, Malaya, and the Philippines. On the other side, it was communist reforms in China that built Mao's revolution up to a strategic breakout just as similar reforms did in Vietnam against the French and against the Americans up to the Tet offensive.

Further, what makes any insurgency ultimately unpredictable is that either side can make mistakes that can be fatal, even at the last minute of a strategic breakout. Indeed, in every case, neither side was error-free. If there was anything analytically useful to these discussions of error, it was that one side was usually more prone to making errors than the other. Mistakes flowed more freely from the side whose struggle was less surely grounded in the principles of legitimacy to its society. The most prominent example is the hapless communists of Greece who neither fully accepted guerrilla strategy nor understood that the Megali Idea would not be honored by the Machiavellian embracing of Macedonian separatism. Further, though all sides made mistakes, one side proved more adaptable in learning from its mistakes rather than compounding them. The communists in China made one mistake after the other until they finally adopted Mao's strategy of people's war, even as Chiang Kai-shek seemed congenitally incapable of breaking out of the elitist politics of China's vulnerable urban centers. In Malaya, the British were able to recoup militarily from their disastrous defense of Singapore and quickly rebound from the political error of the union plan while the communists, all the while, remained frozen in the mistake of their single ethnic preserve.

Finally, in all of our cases, leadership has been important, for both incumbents and insurgents, and in some of them it has been almost singly decisive. Indeed, charismatic leadership might almost carry an insurgency or counterinsurgency campaign to victory and bypass the society's festering legitimacy crisis (proposition 5.2c). The most obvious such example is Ramon Magsaysay of the Philippines, who almost single-handedly turned around a corrupt political system through military reorganizations, political reforms, and national elections to undercut the Huk insurgency that was regionally near a strategic breakout in Central Luzon. In Malaya, the government had its "leadership rocket" of the *tunku*, Briggs, and Templer. Laos had its solid but tragically handled Prince Souvanna Phouma and Cambodia its mercurial Prince Sihanouk, whose political gyrations kept everyone off balance. In short, leadership is a difficult factor to bring under analytical control whether one is trying to account for its origins, the direction of its effects, or its intensity.

At least for this study, there is some hope that this rogue elephant of leadership can be made analytically useful in that the type of leadership that has the most lasting effect is that which is rooted in belief sources of national legitimacy and has an institutional grounding. Otherwise it becomes the chimera of what I have called Hannibalism (proposition 5.2d). Magsaysay gathered around himself a trove of inspirational beliefs, but left no political organization as a legacy when he died in 1957. Thus the Philippines were exposed to the possibility of a new insurgency, a possibility that was realized with the start of the New People's Army in 1969. Malaya's military "rocket" could never have achieved what it did without the political arrangements of the constitutional contract that kept the MRLA politically isolated and thus militarily vulnerable. In Greece, the energetic General Papagos could not have cornered the communists at Vitsi and Grammos without the elections and coalition agreement that sent the insurgents packing into the hills in the first place.

Indeed, in Table 11.3, quite naturally whichever side had the clearly superior strategy and leadership won, although this is not clear in the cases of Vietnam II and Laos. What makes Vietnam controversial is that, although the communist leadership was definitely superior, the communists abandoned their own strategy in favor of an American one. Similarly, in Laos it is not clear that the victorious Pathet Lao really had any strategy of their own. Their revolution was won for them by the North Vietnamese. What keeps leadership from being an independent explanation is that for all of the cases, except for Cambodia and the continually idiosyncratic Vietnam II, the successful leadership strategies were inextricably tied to the principles of legitimacy within their societies. Whatever the dedicated leadership that gave the communists their "victory" in Cambodia, it was not a leadership tied to Cambodian national legitimacy, except for the presence on their side of the hapless Prince Sihanouk. In Vietnam, both sides abandoned politics after Tet in favor of a contest decided by force of arms. Power can come this way, but legitimacy is not an automatic bride to such a suitor.

For those interested in lessons for interventions in insurgencies, the best kind of leadership can be termed bridge leadership. Because insurgencies, as revolutions "on the slow burn," pose the problem for activist groups competitively to outmobilize an apathetic middle, the leadership each side needs is one that can build bridges of activism to this middle mass and its constituent groups. This, of course, is done by appealing to societal standards of political legitimacy. What the prospective intervenor is looking for are the leaders, organizations, and strategies that can be these bridges. Almost by himself, Magsaysay was such a bridge in the Philippines. Though there was no such flamboyant political personality in the third round in Greece, a bridge to the middle was built around elections and a coalition government that cut the communists off from this middle and confined them to minority appeals. What the *tunku* did in Malaya with his Alliance party was to build bridges among the three ethnic communities that left the Malayan Communist party outside of the tent and blocked from entrance. In Laos, Souvanna Phouma was a bridge leader who commanded a strong middle and might have stayed in control of that middle with a steadier helping hand from the outside. But in Cambodia probably no amount of outside help

Table 11.3. Alternative Explanation: Leadership/Strategy (L/S)

Cases	Incumbents L/S Superior	L/S Tied to Political Legitimacy	Victory	Insurgents L/S Superior	L/S Tied to Political Legitimacy	Victory
Vietnam I	o	o	o	+	+	+
Vietnam II			o			+
To Tet	o	o		+	+	
After Tet	o	o		?	o	
China			o			+
Up to WWII	?	+		?	+	
After WWII	o	o		+	+	
Greece			+			o
Round 1	o	+		+	+	
Round 2	+	+		o	o	
Round 3	+	+		o	o	
Philippines	+	+	+	o	?	o
Malaya	+	+	+	o	?	o
Cambodia			o			+
Pre-1970	+	+		o	+	
Post-1970	o	o		+	?	
Laos	?	?	o	?	?	+

Key

+ = Present

o = Absent

? = Partial or controversial

could have helped Marshal Lon Nol. Artificially propped up by American aid, with most of the political middle wrapped up in the prince he deposed, he spent most of his five years in power burning bridges to what was left of this middle rather than building them.

In the middle of insurgencies, it is sometimes difficult to decide who and which side has the better claim to this leadership. At the Sian incident in China in 1936, it was still not easy to decide between Mao Zedong's communists and Chiang Kai-shek's nationalists. Mao was building a movement based on rural mobilization but remained on the fringes in Yanan and had virtually no presence in the cities. Chiang, on the other hand, was a national figure in command of the cities and was at least attempting an outreach in the countryside. After the war, however, the relative claims were clear: Mao's rural mobilization had built bridges to a solid command of the countryside while Chiang had retreated to his urban strongholds and an ever-narrowing circle of elitist cronies.

Whether to "sink or swim with Ngo Dinh Diem" at the start of the Vietnam War in 1963 posed a terrible dilemma for American policymakers. A man who began his career with real bridge-making possibilities and was even heralded as "the George Washington of Asia" had, by that year, cut himself off from the Buddhist majority and refused to break away from his elitist family ruling circle. As I argued in Chapter 5, for all his faults, Nguyen Van Thieu went much farther as a bridge leader. Two factors, however, make rendering a verdict problematic: first, the Viet Cong had already seized much of this middle ground by virtue of their previous performance in the Resistance War against the French, and, second, this political contest was thrust aside in favor of a purely military "solution." In any case, the lesson for a would-be intervenor is this: if you don't see any bridge leadership material in the country, don't go in; but, if, for whatever reason of high national purpose, you insist on going in anyway, avoid those flatterers who would trap you in an illegitimacy lock, and make it a central goal of your intervention to encourage such bridge leadership.

The sixth thematic question asked, *What are the comparisons of each case with Vietnam?* The premise undergirding this question was that lessons from Vietnam could emerge only from placing this insurgency in a clearly defined comparative context. Thus a typology of eight cases was created on the basis of a similar set of two conditioning factors or variables: first, insurgencies following an explicit Marxist people's war strategy and, second, incumbent regimes, beset by such insurgencies, receiving the support of substantial Western intervention. The eight cases meeting these criteria produced different outcomes. That is, in five cases the insurgents won (China, Vietnam I, Vietnam II, Cambodia, and Laos), and in three the incumbents won (Greece, the Philippines, and Malaya).

The central theoretical proposition driving this investigation is that insurgencies are one manifestation of a crisis in political legitimacy. From this, I have advanced the hypothesis that what accounts for the differences in the outcomes within this set of cases is the relative success enjoyed by the winning side in resolving this crisis. I do acknowledge other factors (or exogenous variables) beyond legitimacy as playing a role, namely, intervention as well as strategy and performance (or leadership) as depicted in Figure 3.3. This has not followed the more orthodox pattern of a test between two theories, however, because both these exogenous factors are depicted as conditioning variables having impact on the three sets of variables that make up a legitimacy crisis. In this book, then, they have not been given the analytical independence necessary for competitive theory testing. Rather, this book has been a probe of the explanatory power of this one theoretical proposition across eight cases.

In these eight cases, the different results of five and a half of them can be explained by the hypothesis of legitimacy as the central explanatory variable to the outcome of an insurgency. First, in China, Mao grounded his successful people's war on a superior claim to the Mandate of Heaven as did the Viet Minh, second, against the French in Indochina. As a half, the Viet Cong followed a similar path of legitimacy against the Americans until the loss of legitimacy was buried in the debacle of the Tet offensive. Third, on the other side, the postwar government of Greece reclaimed the legitimacy of the Megali Idea in defeating the blundering Greek communists as did Magsaysay in the Philippines, fourth, against the regionally isolated Huks and the British in Malaya, fifth, over the ethnically stranded MRLA.

Two and a half cases, however, do not fully support this hypothesis. In Vietnam, as has been argued at some length, after Tet the political issues fueling the insurgency were abandoned in favor of a purely military solution. Hence legitimacy as an explanatory variable works only until Tet, making it only half a case. This half-cased quality to Vietnam is what has made it such a difficult war for lessons and is why, in the intersection of insurgency and intervention, Vietnam should be treated as only one case among others for comparative analysis (proposition 6.1).

Though appeals to national legitimacy were an important part of the debate in Cambodia, the outcome was more centrally determined by Vietnamese communist support of the Khmer Rouge and by the ultimate withdrawal of American support from the Lon Nol regime. Similarly, in Laos, both sides were held up, even run, by foreign support, and, when the Americans stopped watering its side of the garden in 1973, it quickly withered and died. Laos and Cambodia, further, are not well explained by my analytical framework because their very weakness as societies made them vulnerable and too dependent on the events and actors in the overshadowing war in Vietnam. Legitimacy in these countries was too fragile to withstand these outside shocks. Thus insurgencies fought and won in societies without firm definitional groundings to legitimacy are as likely to destroy legitimacy as to capture and redefine it.

An Application: Sendero Luminoso of Peru

DECAPITATION

On September 12, 1992, Peruvian police, tipped off by a captured guerrilla and alerted by the unusual character of the garbage at 459 First Street in Lima, swooped into the house and found Abimael Guzman, the leader of the Sendero Luminoso (Shining Path) insurgent revolutionary movement, quietly reading a book.[2] A short time later, authorities rounded up ten other members of the movement's Central Committee and scores of other cadres. Following these arrests, a police official warned: "It is like a wounded animal. We cannot say that the Shining Path has been finished. The head has been hurt. But the arms continue to be active and they can do a lot of harm."[3] More simply, Guzman later said, "It was my turn to lose."[4]

Such an act of decapitation had both killed Ché Guevara in Bolivia in 1967 and ruined his insurgency. Guevara, however, was using a different strategy, a focalist one, which emphasized leadership and the primacy of military blows to political barriers.[5] Similar blows against Marxist people's wars have been less successful. The French failed to end the Viet Minh insurgency in early 1947 when Ho Chi Minh eluded the airborne raid of Operation Leah. Through five encirclement campaigns, the Goumindang never caught Mao Zedong in China. The Americans, also, bungled their attempt to capture COSVN headquarters in the incursion into Cambodia in 1970. Even where such decapitation blows *were* successful, they did not spell the immediate end to the insurgencies. In Malaya, the top military commanders of the MRLA were killed in 1952, but the insurgency sputtered on for another eight years. In the Philippines, though nearly the entire politburo was captured in Manila, the Huks continued on in the countryside for six more years. For the fourteen-year-old insurgency in Peru, the question, then, is, How fatal a blow is the capture of the movement's charismatic leader?

Historical Setting

With over 22 million people living in 496,000 square miles (equal to Alaska), Peru is one of the largest and most populous countries in Latin America. It is also one of the richest in resources, although, like Malaya, it is not self-sufficient in food production because only 15 percent of its rugged territory is suitable for agriculture. Peru is a leading producer of copper, lead, silver, and zinc and has significant deposits of gold, iron ore, and petroleum.[6] For the Spanish conquistadors, Peru was a true El Dorado.

Today it still has more Indians than any other country in South America, most of them descendants of the proud Incas. Current estimates are that 45 percent of the population is Indian, 37 percent mestizo, 15 percent white, and 3 percent African, Chinese, and Japanese.[7] Indeed, many Peruvians, not just Indians, harken back to the Inca Empire as a golden past of urban and architectural splendor and of rural prosperity and communitarian harmony. The largest political party, Popular Revolutionary Alliance of America (APRA), still manipulates Inca symbols for sloganeering consumption. And the founding father of Peruvian Marxism, José Carlos Mariategui, grounded his dialectical analysis of "Peruvian Reality" in the "true myth" of a rapacious Spanish urban coast whose feudatories exploited an inland Indian socialist Sierra.[8]

Whatever the nostalgia for Peru's pre-Columbian past, the reality of modern Peru under siege by Sendero Luminoso is grim. Despite its generous endowment in resources, at the start of the insurgency in 1980, per capita GNP was $1,070 out of a GNP of $20 billion, and, in the southern highlands, a per capita GNP of $200 put the region on a par with Bolivia and Haiti, the poorest countries of the hemisphere.[9] After some healthy growth in the early 1970s, the economy began to sputter, and from 1977 to 1980 it experienced a 1.5 percent average annual decline.[10] In the 1980s, again after some initial growth, the economy went into a tailspin. From 1985 to 1990 average annual "growth" was a negative 9 percent. In 1990, it was negative 4.6 percent. Under newly elected Alberto Fujimori, the economy grew again by 2.4 percent in 1991.[11] A more serious blow was the rate of inflation. At the start of the insurgency, it was a modest 73 percent. By the end of the decade, the rate had rocketed to 4,600 percent, although Fujimori brought it back down to a respectable 67 percent by the end of 1991.[12] The cruelest impact of inflation is on real wages, and in urban areas they had fallen by 57 percent in 1988.[13] Such inflation gave rise to an "informal" sector of the economy that by 1990 was estimated to have equaled 40 percent of the official GDP. Adding to national instability, it was a sector dominated by criminal activity and violence.[14]

This misery, of course, has not been evenly shared. The southern Sierras around Ayacucho, which was the initial focus to the insurgency, had a per capita income of only $200 a year. The area was also neglected by government services. It received only one-third of its proportional entitlement. Worse yet for the peasantry, a much heralded land reform program from 1968 to 1980 did not distribute much tangible benefits to the southern Sierras. Although the huge coastal plantations were broken up and haciendas in the northern Sierras redistributed, estates eligible for such redistribution in the south were few, and promised accompanying social reforms never made it to Ayacucho.[15] The improvements in the countryside elsewhere only made the largely Indian peasants of the south more frustrated and prone to insurgency.

This Peru of poverty-stricken frustration that ignited the Sendero Luminoso insurgency was a far cry from the mighty Inca Empire of the sixteenth century. To Francisco Pizarro and his 180 conquistadors in 1532, the wealth of this powerful but plague-ridden and strife-torn empire beckoned as El Dorado. It was. After overcoming an Inca army of thirty thousand the Spanish plundered this wealth in earnest. Until 1800, the estimated value of this booty to Spain, in 1900 dollars, approached $6 billion.[16] The burden of this exploitation crushed the Indian population. By 1600, the toll of disease and forced labor in the mines reduced the 12 to 32 million inhabitants of the former Inca Empire to 2 million.[17] As in the Philippines, the Spanish ruled through what was left of the Inca aristocracy, the *kurakas* (governors). The *kurakas* were able to act as a buffer between the Indians and the worst features of Spanish rule. Agricultural production was restored under the Inca system of communal plots called *ayllus*. Gradually, the Indian population was restored to 60 percent of the total of Peru by the late nineteenth century.[18] But the Catholic church employed the Inquisition to destroy the Inca religion.

In 1780 the Indians mounted one last, convulsive revolt. They killed whatever Spaniards they could, indeed, anyone who was white, and even extended their butchery to white-colored chickens and dogs.[19] But the Spaniards responded with equal frenzy. The *kuraka* class, and, with it, any chance of Spanish-Inca reconciliation, was destroyed. In the war for hemispheric independence against Spain in the 1820s, both of the leading revolutionists, José de San Martin and Simon Bolivar, fought important battles in Peru against the viceroyalty in Lima. But the white domination of the Inca was undisturbed by independence in 1824.[20]

Under independent Peru, a Spanish *criollo* elite controlled a trading economy of cash crop plantations on the coast (some owned by foreign enterprises) and haciendas in the Sierras owned by *criollos*, managed by mestizos, and tilled by Indians. The chief economic effect of the end of Spanish rule was to open up Peru to British and French investors and, with the construction of the Panama Canal, to American as well. From 1890 to 1920, Peru experienced an export boom that established a "traditional" order of a coastal oligarchy that allied itself with the landowners of the Sierra haciendas and with increasingly American foreign business interests.[21]

In the 1920s a reaction to this oligarchic order sprung up in two powerful political movements. The larger one was Raul Haya de la Torre's APRA. Founded in 1928, it was the first mass-based political party in Peru and drew its support from the lower middle class, students, and urban and rural workers—basically, from those affected by this capitalist boom and who resented its unequal distributive effects. Interestingly, with respect to Chinese analogies in Peru, de la Torre took inspiration from the Three People's Principles of Sun Yat-sen and admired the Soviet organization of the Guomindang party.[22] Also, in 1928, José Carlos Mariategui established the Peruvian Socialist party based on a Marxist examination of Peruvian society. In this examination, he concluded that the Indian campesinos were the best vehicles for socialist liberation in Peru and prophesied: "The Indian proletariat awaits its Lenin." [23] Mariategui, however, died that year, and the Comintern turned his party into the Peruvian Communist party in 1930 and organized it on a more conventional urban proletariat basis. Both parties staged violent protests against this oligarchic order, and in 1930 and 1931 both were suppressed and banned from electoral politics, which were developing under a very restricted franchise.

From then until the 1960s, the military became the mainstay of support for the oligarchy. This "traditional" system did bring about general economic growth, but it was a growth that also gave Peru the most unequal landholding structure on the continent.[24] These economic inequities gradually produced fractures in the political system. Three centrist parties developed in the 1950s and 1960s that generally supported these military-backed regimes: Popular Action, the largest, the Popular Christian party, and the Christian Democrat party. The communists split into several groups, but the divide finally came between a legal left and a violent left. The legal left consisted of at least eight parties that eventually coalesced into an electoral alliance in 1980 called the United Left (IU, Izquierda Unida). The violent left had at least five armed groups, the most potent being the Sendero Luminoso. Long shut out from the political process, APRA split into a right wing with close ties to Washington and the Lima oligarchy and a left wing that was deeply impressed with Castro's Cuba abroad and pushed a populist reform program at home. In response to this ferment, the Peruvian military divided as well, among left-wing reformers, right-wing defenders of the oligarchy, and "technical" officers in the middle.[25]

This system received a jolt in the mid-1960s when middle-class students and professionals from Lima (many from the left wing of APRA) took to the Sierras as the Movement of Leftist Revolutionaries (MIR) and mounted an insurgency following Ché Guevara's focalist strategy. None of them spoke Quechua (the Incan language), and the military, using American-trained counterinsurgency units, put the movement down in two years. But by the mid-1960s, the composition of the officer corps had switched more to lower-class mestizos from the provinces, many of whom were reform-minded and antioligarchic. Riding on this sentiment, in 1968 General Juan Velasco Alvarado, a mestizo proud of his Indian heritage, seized power with a pronounced reformist agenda.[26]

Under Velasco (1968–75), the principles of a modern Peru debated in the 1920s became something of a reality. The real changes that independence did not bring began to come now. In 1968, three-fourths of the mining and two-thirds of the banking industries were in foreign hands. By 1975, half of the mining enterprises and two-thirds of the banks had been taken over by state-owned concerns, although most manufacturing companies still remained in foreign hands. With a host of new state-run activities, corporatism became fully established in Peru, and a solid middle class began to grow around this interlocking of business interests and the state bureaucracy.[27] It was in land reform, however, where the changes were the most sweeping. From 1968 to 1980, Peru underwent a more wide-ranging land reform than anywhere else in Latin American, except for Cuba. Nine million hectares of land were expropriated, which completely eliminated the plantations of the coast and broke up most of the haciendas of the northern and central Sierras. These redistributions affected 35 percent of the farm land. Twenty-seven percent of rural families were direct beneficiaries.[28]

Two drawbacks, however, prevented these reforms from creating a harmonious modern Peru. First, economically, neither the land reform nor the corporate nationalizations were managed well. Follow-up technical assistance and economic services for redistributed land did fan out into the coastal regions but were never established in the southern Sierras.[29] In 1975, another military coup brought in a regime of the "technician" faction under Francisco Morales Bermuda. But this regime could not halt the slide either. Through the Constituent Assembly elections of 1978 and the national elections of 1980, the military seemed relieved to return the country to civilian rule. Second, because much of the Indian land of the southern Sierras was communally held to begin with, the benefits of the land reform for the country's Indians were minimal. Hence, by 1980, for the country as a whole, half of the peasants who needed redistributed land had received it, but in the southern Sierras this figure stood at a mere 15 percent.[30]

Revolutionaries as far back as Lenin have insisted that in such regional and ethnic disharmony, every revolution needs an igniting spark. In the misery of Ayacucho, this spark was provided by the University San Cristóbal de Huamanga, which was reestablished in 1959 by the government to bring education and social reform to the Andes. With a Marxist rector, it soon became a school of revolution attracting Marxist academics from all over the country.[31] One of them was Abimael Guzman (1934–), who cofounded Sendero Luminoso at the university in 1970. Guzman and his confederates mounted cabals to dominate university politics, but they also built revolutionary cells in the countryside by learning the Quechua language and establishing *compadrazgo* ties (as in the Philippines) with the campesinos.[32] Drawn to the revolutionary strategy of Mao Zedong and the mystic Andean vision of Mariategui, for Guzman, Huamanga University served as a commodious version of Mao's Yanan "base area" of the 1930s.[33] Although he was rebuffed in university politics, Guzman's revolution-building went much better. While the rest of the country was distracted by the 1980 national elections, Sendero Luminoso launched its armed struggle on May 17 by attacking three polling stations in Ayacucho.[34]

From these initial strikes, Guzman's people's war quickly spread to three provinces in Ayacucho Department. Following a dramatic guerrilla attack on the Ayacucho city jail, President Fernando Belaunde Terry, in late 1982, declared a Military Emergency Zone in these three provinces. But the military's strategy amounted to nothing more than repression. In justifying instances of indiscriminate slaying of peasants in this zone, one commander replied: "If the army kills 60, at least six can be expected to be Senderistas." [35]

Though forced out of Ayacucho, by 1983 the insurgency had spread to several other regions in the country. It did so under a three-staged strategy, reminiscent of Mao's protracted war: a first stage of armed propaganda that would conduct sabotage and consolidate areas of influence in the countryside, a second stage in which liberated zones would be established, and a third stage of a conventional war from the countryside surrounding and attacking the cities.[36] Under the rubric of these stages, the Senderista insurgency actually waged four separate campaigns: one in the Military Emergency Zones against the army, a second outside these zones against the police, a special third campaign in the coca-growing Upper Huallaga Valley, and a fourth campaign to build a network for urban struggle.[37]

In 1985, Alan Garcia united both wings of APRA and won the presidential elections, giving Peru's largest party its first mandate of rule. During Garcia's administration (1985–90), the insurgency escalated. Pragmatically, the Senderistas discovered another fertile rural base in the El Salvador-sized Upper Huallaga Valley in central Peru. There it championed the cause of peasants growing coca against Columbian drug lords, government police, and American antidrug efforts. By 1987, Sendero Luminoso had forced all other outside groups from the valley. The government's response was to form a second Military Emergency Zone. By the late 1980s, 50 percent of Peruvian territory and 64 percent of the population lived under some form of martial law.[38]

As a result of the fighting in the countryside, the people flocked to the cities. Two-thirds of the population became urban, leaving only 15 percent in the southern Sierras. In response, in 1985 the Senderistas declared a new strategy which emphasized the cities as a new field for people's war. The countryside was by no means abandoned, but the war was now to be waged as a synergistic whole, rather than as a rural-to-urban progression.[39] In 1989, following this shift to the cities, Guzman declared that the stage of consolidated base areas had been reached, and in 1991, he boasted that Peru's people's war had reached Mao's second stage of strategic equilibrium.[40]

Though Guzman was overconfident in these proclamations, President Garcia had not been performing well, either as president or in fighting the insurgency. He began his administration with a massacre of Senderista prisoners during a prison riot that earned him wide condemnation. Though he was energetic in cracking down on the drug lords, he did so in ways that only helped the insurgents. His direct response to them was one of repression. He turned to Argentine and Israeli secret service operatives for advice.

Their principal effect was to add a new column of "disappearances" to the casualty figures that had grown fearfully high, twenty-two thousand killed by 1990.[41] Garcia, meanwhile, had lost control of the economy as well. Inflation had soared to 4,600 percent by 1990. At the end of his regime, Garcia was rocked by scandals and plagued by an insurgency that had grown to a core of ten thousand armed fighters and a base of active sympathizers in the hundreds of thousands.[42]

Alberto Fujimori, the son of Japanese immigrants, swept into power in 1990 with a self-declared mandate to heal Peru's ethnic strife and defeat the insurgency. Despite his lack of a political organization, Fujimori's election, as an obviously successful candidate of color, was a setback to Sendero Luminoso. Furthermore, the Senderistas were running into problems in the cities. Unlike Ayacucho, the cities contained competition, and the government had a more potent network of agents for rooting out "subversives." Also, the Senderistas were not proving flexible enough to move toward the political middle to secure a vantage point for an urban appeal.[43]

Initially, Fujimori had trouble securing support from the political parties for his counterinsurgency program, and in early 1992 some elements of the military staged a partial coup.[44] The new president, however, staged a dramatic comeback. He dissolved Parliament in February 1992, which restored his support in the military, and his forces captured Guzman and many of the key leaders of the insurgency in September and October. He then reestablished democracy with national elections in November 1992 and local elections in May 1993. In this comeback, Fujimori, who vowed to defeat the Senderistas by the end of his term in 1995, has become the most popular national leader in the Western Hemisphere.[45]

In a war that has cost twenty-five thousand lives, and, by some estimates, inflicted $20 billion worth of damage to the Peruvian economy,[46] the question is, Has the back of the insurgency of Sendero Luminoso been broken, or, like Mao Zedong himself, can the Senderistas, through their strategy of people's war, reverse this downward momentum of crossover points and rise to a strategic breakout?

Framework Analysis

NATIONAL LEGITIMACY

Observers of modern Peru have often remarked on the dual character of Peruvian national identity. The need to discover a basis for a merger of these two Perus stems from, among other things, a white and mestizo guilt over the violence done to the pre-Columbian order and its inheritors, the indigenous survivors of the Inca Empire. Modern national legitimacy, then, has become a quest for creating an absolving blend of these two worlds. Its requirements include a more equitable distribution of social and economic resources between the indigenous interior and the cosmopolitan coast, a fairer apportioning of the socioeconomic pie between Indians and the whites and mestizos, and more national control over the mining, manufacturing, and financial sectors of the economy. Corporatism over the economy, land reform across the country, and a democratic political system for everyone have become the central principles for harmonizing the two faces of Peru.

At the interest level of favorable policies and performances, along with accompanying incentives of rewards and punishments, the deterioration of economic conditions and the resultant withdrawal of government social services in many areas provided a general and even country-wide attraction for the insurgency. This general appeal was exacerbated by the particularly harsh impact of these conditions on the campesinos of the Sierras and the poor of the cities. In addition, the dizzying financial growth of the illegal cocaine market in the United States provided too strong a temptation for coca leaf farmers of the Upper Huallaga Valley, and the Sendero Luminoso profitably exploited the issue.

At the opportunity level of active commitments coalescing into group action, the results achieved by the Senderistas have been mixed. Clearly, active commitments to the insurgency have been made by enough groups to have created a real problem for the government. This is a problem, however, that still lacks the ingredients of a strategic threat. One careful study of Senderista activists found that what propelled them into these commitments were an ideological alienation by students in the cities and the disparities of income among different groups by campesinos in the country, a mix of belief and opportunity motives.[47] The measure of land reform is both important and difficult to judge in Peru. Its successful redistributive effects in breaking up plantations on the coast and haciendas in the northern Sierras have made these areas relatively impervious to Sendero Luminoso.[48] Since well over half the population lives in these regions, this has given the government significant insurance.[49] It basically puts a strategic breakout out of reach for the insurgents. The relative failure of land reform, however, in the southern Sierras, because there were so few haciendas to break up, is what gave Sendero Luminoso its opening for achieving an initial critical mass.

With respect to the key measure of modern societal access, employment, the record of Peru during the insurgency has been terrible. At the end of 1989, official unemployment stood at 8 percent, and underemployment was as high as 74 percent of the work force.[50] Under the impact of murderous inflation, the real wage-earning power of urban workers has plummeted. Nevertheless, Sendero Luminoso has made very little headway in the labor movement, an area in which both the legal left parties and APRA are still the main competitors.[51] Indeed, the success of the Senderistas, except for their triumph in the Upper Huallaga Valley, has been confined to areas where they had no competition.[52] They have been thwarted in the northern Sierras by Campesino Rondo (peasant self-defense groups) and in the cities by a welter of "new social movements," including lay Catholic organizations.[53]

Regarding the measure of political participation, the Senderistas used the distraction of the 1980 national elections to launch their insurgency. It is ironic that these were the elections that opened up the Peruvian electorate to a mass base for the first time in that the Spanish-language franchise requirement was eliminated. While APRA boycotted these elections, the legal left joined both the 1978 and 1980 elections and gained 19 percent of the vote in 1980.[54] The Senderistas have been implacably hostile to elections. In fact, one of their central goals has been to disrupt and destroy electoral politics so as to create a so-called "New Democracy."[55] In meeting this goal, they enjoyed some early success. The intimidating effects of the Senderistas were felt most strongly in the municipal elections of 1978, 1980, and 1983, when large numbers of voters either stayed away or cast defective ballots.[56] But their attempts to disrupt the national elections of 1990 and congressional and municipal elections of 1992 and 1993 were largely ignored by the electorate.[57] As is the case for many other insurgencies, this isolation from the electoral process remains a key barrier to further progress for Sendero Luminoso.

At the belief level, Sendero Luminoso struck national legitimacy in Peru in its most vulnerable feature: the continually elusive goal of creating a common community between the coast and the highland interior and the antagonistic populations of the white and mestizo world brought in by the Spanish against the remnant world of Inca culture. The land reform that ran from 1968 to 1980, which was an opportunity-level program designed to produce a belief-level reconciliation, failed in the southern Sierras, even though it enjoyed general success in the rest of the country.

Despite the insurgents' successful exploitation of this regional and ethnic failure, in other areas the Vargas land reform and industrial nationalizations did provide a significant purchase of two of the principles of belief-level legitimacy for the government. Reform-minded sections of the military and APRA, in fact, had been longtime champions of this oligarchic breakup. In addition, a more democratic basis to Peruvian politics was developing throughout the years of the insurgency. In this expansion of the political system, the legal left, in contrast to the Senderistas, carved out for itself a viable place within the national process of furthering the principles of corporatism, land reform, and democracy. The violent left — and there were other groups besides Sendero Luminoso[58] — sought to exploit the embarrassing anomaly of this success. Although this charge of failing to incorporate the Indians of the Sierras into these three principles is serious, by itself it is an appeal with definite limits and certainly not sufficient to carry the Senderistas to a strategic breakout.

REVOLUTIONARY LEGITIMACY

Abimael Guzman founded the "Peruvian Communist Party—for the Shining Path of José Carlos Mariategui" under an explicit Marxist people's war ideology. Guzman's Senderistas declare him to be "the Fourth Sword of World Revolution," following Marx, Lenin, and Mao.[59] At the interest level, Sendero Luminoso has established its presence throughout most of the country. Especially where the presence of the government was weak to begin with, the Senderistas have been successful in recruiting a base of sympathizers. These bases are fed by the obvious failure of the economy to reach its poorer strata. Some 80 percent of Peru's population is identified as lower class, and over half the population has slipped below the national poverty line so this is a large reservoir to draw on.[60] Also, in the Upper Huallaga Valley, the Senderistas have earned at least interest-level support from coca-growing peasants for their policy of helping the peasants get higher prices for their produce from Columbian drug lords. Sadly for the peasants, the violence from both sides has been excessive. This punishment has intimidated the peasantry into a stalemated silence. As a Bolivian journalist put it: "To be a Senderista suspect is dangerous. To be on the side of the government is also dangerous. Not to be either can be mortal."[61] Such violence cuts both ways in an insurgency, that is, even though it can be instrumental in achieving an initial critical mass, its continued use can frustrate further progress. There were, nevertheless, ample issues available for promoting a mass line in Peru.

At the opportunity level, the revolutionary record of Sendero Luminoso has been uneven. On the plus side, the failure of land reform in the southern Sierras has given the movement a solid foothold among Indians. As the Indians have migrated to the slums of Lima and other cities, they found that government services in these peripheral areas had broken down. The Senderistas, naturally, have brought their organization into the cities to fill the void. Although the insurgents have faced a more competitive environment, this mobility has gained them a core of activists. In the Upper Huallaga Valley, it is still difficult to tell how much of a following of activists Sendero Luminoso has recruited from among its interest-level supporters of cash-hungry coca farmers.[62]

Elsewhere in Peru, the movement has been markedly less successful precisely because it has been more like Mao the postrevolutionary radical of the Cultural Revolution (1966–69) than Mao the more pragmatic leader of a United Front in his long march to power from 1920 to 1949. Before 1949, Mao was careful, in his people's war, to discriminate among the peasantry in its several subclasses, most of whom he sought to make eligible for revolutionary recruitment. Except in the Upper Huallaga Valley, Sendero Luminoso has not shown such sophistication and has tended to treat the peasantry as a single class.[63] Although such bluntness has been successful in the abject misery of Ayacucho, elsewhere in the country, where the rural social mosaic is more diverse, the Senderistas have been unsure of themselves. They have been blocked from the small landholders of the northern Sierras and from the broken-up plantations of the coast. Thus, even in the countryside, their movement lacks a national base.

During his revolution, 85 percent of China's population was rural, and Mao's strategy was rural. Even though over half of Peru's population lived in all the Sierras as late as the 1960s, by the mid-1980s this figure dipped below 40 percent and the southern Sierras were home to only 15 percent of the population. Pragmatically, Sendero Luminoso shifted its strategy to include the cities as well.[64] In waging a national strategy of revolution, Mao followed Lenin's policy of a broad-based united front. Also, when the Viet Cong made a strong appeal for urban participation before and during the Tet offensive, it unveiled a welter of front organizations designed to incorporate bourgeois and proletariat city dwellers. Although Sendero Luminoso has shown some signs of prudential shifts to such a policy, it has not been a full-hearted effort.[65] The Senderistas remain hostile to, and estranged from, the legal left. Even more serious, they have yet to make any headway in the labor movement of Peru, either in the cities or the countryside. Their attitude towards the bourgeois remains murderous. As late as 1988, one mid-level cadre warned, "The genocide which we have accepted, they will have to accept."[66] Thus, at the opportunity level, their success in societal access has been confined to specific areas in regard to land reform and has not been at all successful in the modern measure of employment. Finally, they have been hostile to Peru's expanding process of political participation under the legal political parties.

At the belief level, Sendero Luminoso has been trying to follow the orthodox precepts of Marxist people's war. Guzman and his confederates *had* traveled to China, and Mao would have readily recognized the stages articulated by the Senderistas in their strategy.[67] Because of the demographic shift to the cities and also because they were forced out of their Ayacucho base, they revised their strategy to include the cities in their activities. Certainly Mao would not have faulted his pupils for this mutation. But in other key respects Mao's pupils have failed to measure up to his ideological standards. The use of Inca symbols and a national nostalgia for these symbols as a central basis for recruitment appeals is hardly the foundation for Mao's future construction of "socialist man." Though the contention of some Peruvian scholars that such an irredentist Andean mysticism is not the object of the

Senderista insurgency may well be true,[68] the movement's reticence in publicly acknowledging its Maoism is reminiscent of the similar secrecy of the Khmer Rouge before its triumph, when it manipulated traditional royalist symbols around the supportive, but coerced, figure of Prince Sihanouk. What was missing for Sendero Luminoso, as it was missing for the communists of Greece, was a national cause around which to rally followers from all over Peru, as Mao did so well in China and Ho Chi Minh did in Vietnam. Even the necessary factor of revolutionary unity, as the communists in Malaya discovered and the Senderistas are discovering, is not sufficient without it.

FOREIGN INTERVENTION

The exogenous variable of Western intervention in support of the government is more muted in Peru than in the other cases, and Eastern bloc support of Sendero Luminoso is conspicuously absent. Moving from a background to foreground continuum, the United States supported Peru, to a limited extent, in four ways. First, American investments in Peru are considerable. One-third of Peruvian trade is with the United States and half the foreign investment in Peru is American. It was mainly American companies that built a modern Peruvian economy from 1890 to 1920, and today, despite the wave of nationalizations under Vargas in the late 1960s, American concerns, particularly in manufacturing, remain an important prop to the Peruvian economy.[69] International Monetary Fund loans, heavily influenced by Washington, also play a critical role in the economy. Second, this private sector involvement is reinforced by official United States government assistance to Peru. Though modest, it has given the United States some stake in the country: from 1970 to 1989, American assistance amounted to $1.7 billion while other Western assistance for the same period was $4.3 billion.[70] The effect of this economic role, of course, is that Washington serves as an interest- and opportunity-level guarantor of the Peruvian elite.

More in the foreground, third, as in other Latin American countries, the United States has helped Peru's security services. The Agency for International Development has trained police officers, and hundreds of military officers have received training in the United States. Throughout the postwar period, a modest flow of military assistance has supported the 120,000 personnel of the Peruvian military. In the 1960s a military aid team of sixty-six helped in its delivery and training.[71] Though the United States has not been involved in the government's general campaign against Sendero Luminoso, it has, fourth, directly involved itself in the antidrug program in the Upper Huallaga Valley. This involvement, bluntly, has been an unmitigated disaster. The American program to induce the farmers to convert their coca acreage to other cash crops was a pronounced failure. Land conversion plummeted from 4,830 hectares in 1985 to 355 in 1987, after which the program was discontinued.[72] Further, the obvious American presence of Drug Enforcement Agency agents and army Special Forces troops in Blackhawk helicopters only contributed to the Senderista success in the valley.[73]

In pristine Maoist fashion, Sendero Luminoso has not received help from anyone. The people's war of the Senderistas has been pure in its self-reliance. The record of people's war, however, in all the cases of this book, has shown that pure self-reliance and insurgent success have *not* gone hand in hand. Even Mao himself was equivocal on this point in that he was prepared to accept help in the third stage of protracted war. In fact, in the Chinese revolution, Mao's forces did profit from foreign intervention in the chaos of the immediate aftermath to World War II.

Actually, the Senderistas have shown some pragmatism on this matter. They moved into the cities partly to be on hand to exploit the possibilities of coups mounted by others.[74] In the coup-strewn wreckage of Latin American politics, this is certainly not a fond hope. In another respect, their pragmatic venture in the Upper Huallaga Valley, where they play the role of middlemen agents between Columbian drug lords and the coca farmers, has earned them some $30 million a year, which might be considered a fair proxy for foreign support.[75] However pragmatic in the short term, this windfall undermines the purity of their revolutionary credentials both elsewhere in the country and in their claims to a belief level of legitimacy.

CONTINGENCIES: DYNAMICS OF THE BALANCES

As has been stressed throughout this work, insurgents face the opening asymmetric disadvantage of getting an insurgency going until it reaches a self-sustaining critical mass. For the other cases, this barrier was overcome by the incumbent regime-shattering Axis occupations of World War II. No such advantage was available to Sendero Luminoso. Instead, the near equivalent of such an advantage was afforded by the government's founding of a reform-minded university in the high Sierras. More than reform, many of the eager young professors and students came to transform Huamanga University into a government-sponsored Yanan base area for the cradling of revolution. In any case, it was a perfect environment for cultivating the yeast of revolutionary cells in that the government presence in the southern Sierras was always meager and easily dislodged. In ten years, the cells multiplied to the point that an armed struggle could be launched.

From its Ayacucho base, Sendero Luminoso spread throughout the country in a rising momentum of crossover points so that by 1991 Abimael Guzman could declare that his insurgency had reached a strategic equilibrium, Mao's second stage of people's war. As has been noted elsewhere, however, moving to a strategic breakout shifts the asymmetries back in favor of the incumbent side. This is because maneuvering for a final bid for power requires a shift in strategy to accommodate and incorporate larger numbers of people and groups into the revolutionary organization, including groups that might have been targets in the earlier stages of the insurgency. In its continued ideological purity, except in the Upper Huallaga Valley, the Senderistas have not shown enough of this necessary flexibility.

Regarding the balance of error, with the capture of Guzman and much of his leadership group, the weight of error sits heavily with the insurgents. The essential error of Sendero Luminoso is that it picked the wrong Mao Zedong for its ideological beacon. Rather than the pragmatic young Mao bent on power from the Yanan caves, Guzman fixed on the radical old Mao bent by his fanaticism into the self-destructive purge of the Cultural Revolution in the hands of his overzealous confederates, his wife and the Gang of Four radicals. Mao, the pragmatist, had insisted on a drive to power under the banner of a united front strategy that deemed 90 percent of the rural population as acceptable for revolutionary recruitment.[76] Guzman's error has been to eschew a united front approach and confine his movement to the radicals of his carefully nurtured cells. This has made it difficult for him to broaden the base of his insurgency, and it has left him without allies in the far more competitive political terrain of the cities. In fact, this urban myopia led to his capture. Interestingly, this same secretiveness and insistence on exclusive control over his cell organization brought about Guzman's earlier expulsion from the Red Flags in 1970 for "occultism."[77]

At the belief level, the appeal to Inca imagery has its limits, particularly in populous urban areas, as to the number of opportunity-level groups that will respond to such a message. At the interest level, the reliance by Sendero Luminoso on both indiscriminate and discriminate terror has been excessive. Its discriminate killing of elected officials often has gone beyond terror to popular revulsion, as in February 1992, when Maria Moyano, the deputy mayor of Villa El Salvador, was wounded while leaving a party and then dragged to a public square where she was blown up with five sticks of dynamite.[78] In the countryside, the use of violence against a peasantry defined too broadly without subclass distinctions would not have won approval from Mao, who was critical of any reliance on terror.[79] But the government has been equally bloody. One particularly unwelcome recent development has been the rise in "disappearances" as the result of advice received from Argentine advisers who "perfected" such methods in their "dirty war" against dissidents in the 1970s. More than any of our other cases, this terroristic violence by both sides has made the civilian populace the principal victim of Peru's insurgency.

Regarding the variable of strategy and performance, beyond simple repression, the government has had no strategy. Indeed, a former commander of the first Military Emergency Zone warned that the guerrillas could not be defeated unless the government coupled its military efforts with political reforms. With respect to the insurgency of Sendero Luminoso, the essential error of the government has been its failure vigorously to extend the benefits of its otherwise impressive land reform to the Indian peasants of the southern Sierras. It is these two essential and continuing errors (following the wrong Mao for the insurgents and a still unequal land reform for the government) that have produced the stalemate between the two sides.

The reversibilities will be taken up in more detail in the next section because they constitute the grounds for qualified predictions, but for both sides these factors are volatile and offer real opportunities as well as dangers. For the government, the opportunities come from the possibilities of improved performance through increased American aid and the rewards awaiting the extension of land reform to the southern Sierras, while danger lurks in the ever-present specter of a coup d'état in Lima. For the Senderistas, a distinctly improved position awaits their seizing the possibility of a modus vivendi or even alliance with the legal left. If the seizure of such an Aristotelian middle is accompanied by a nervous military coup in reaction, there is a clear opportunity for a strategic breakout. The danger for the guerrillas lies in their failing to see this possibility and succumbing to causeless banditry if their political grievances are moderated by further government reforms, which could also threaten to break up their critical mass.

COMPARISONS AND PROGNOSIS

Earlier Robert Jervis was cited as insisting that lessons in foreign policy can come only from passing candidate lessons through an array (or prism) of competing analogies. Following his advice, a prognosis for the insurgency of Sendero Luminoso in Peru can best be developed by first weighing it against the eight cases of this book.

The Senderistas have been almost devotional in comparing their insurgency to Mao Zedong's successful revolution in China. Abimael Guzman explicitly sought to inherit Mao's mantle of revolutionary legitimacy by being declared the Fourth Sword of Marxism. If Guzman's sword had been true to Mao's steel, the regime of Alberto Fujimori would be in trouble. The steel of Guzman's sword, however, is flawed. First, Sendero Luminoso has never proclaimed a nationwide cause to which all Peruvians can rally, as Mao did in his anti-Japanese, peasant nationalism. Guzman's appeal to Andean indigenism has created an ethnic basis for his revolution, but it is an appeal with limits. Second, the Senderistas have yet to embrace the United Front strategy of the pragmatic revolutionary Mao. Thus they have failed to move to an Aristotelian middle ground through offering the necessary bridge leadership for a strategic breakout. Third, the use of excessive violence has produced a stalemate that is self-defeating to the legitimacy of both sides.

Despite their failure to measure up to Mao's standards, the Senderistas are still not as bad as the hapless communists of Greece. Though, like the Greeks, the Senderistas lack a national cause, they have not committed any error equivalent to the embrace of Macedonian separatism. Indians, at least, make up half of Peru's population, whereas Macedonians in Greece amounted to a mere 1 percent of the total. Also, an earlier land reform program in Greece in the 1920s was successful in precluding land reform as an opportunity-level issue for the communists. In Peru, an earlier land reform was uneven enough in its effects to open up the southern Sierras for opportunity-level commitments to insurgency. Finally, for all their fanaticism, the Senderistas have yet to be plagued by the fatal disunity that eventuated in the implosion of the insurgency in Greece.

Indeed, a quick comparison with Malaya offers encouragement to Sendero Luminoso. In Malaya, the MRLA was stymied because it could not break out if its ethnic Chinese preserve, which constituted only one-third of the population. Though largely white and mestizo-led, the Senderistas have drawn most of their rank-and-file recruits from the Indian campesinos of the Sierras. Indians, all told, make up nearly half the population of Peru, similar to the dominant position of the ethnic Malays of Malaya. In this ethnic reversal in Peru, then, the Senderistas should be poised for a strategic breakout. The ethnic divisions in Peru, however, are not nearly as airtight and compartmentalized as those in Malaya. In fact, Peru's ethnic groups are more analogous to the socially "leaky" mosaic of the Philippines. As in the Philippines, *campadrazgo* networks link mestizos and Indians in fictive kinship relationships. Indeed, it was precisely through establishing social *compadrazgo* ties with Sierra Indians that mestizo Senderista activists cultivated their political revolutionary cells. As Mao discovered about the peasantry of China, the peasantry of Peru has its own distinctions and stratifications. A fair number of Indians, for example, who are called *chollos*, have identified themselves with mestizos by adopting Spanish occupations, language, and dress.[80] These differences, of course, have created divided loyalties and aspirations among the Indians and seriously complicated Senderista attempts at building an ethnic monopoly among the Indians.

Thus, on closer examination, the insurgency that is probably closest to that of Sendero Luminoso is the New People's Army (NPA) in the Philippines. Like the NPA, the Senderistas have broken out of the single regional enclave that hobbled the earlier Huk insurgency in the Philippines and freed themselves from the single ethnic preserve that doomed the MRLA in Malaya. Both the NPA and the Senderistas, then, have built a broader base than that of these preceding insurgencies. In addition, with the exception of China just after World War II, the only other insurgency accompanied by a sharp economic downturn was that of the NPA. All the others had economies that were rising or at least stagnant (as in Cambodia and Laos). Quite generally, this is something Western assistance was able to accomplish. More negatively, the Senderistas share with the NPA the same fatal blind spot to elections. Finally, both these insurgencies lacked an open, belief-level grand cause for rallying their respective countrymen. With the collapse of the NPA insurgency in 1992, such a close comparison is not auspicious for Sendero Luminoso.

To be fair, on this issue of a grand cause, it is not, of course, that the NPA and Senderistas lacked a grand cause but that both groups have been compared—and aptly so—to the Khmer Rouge of Cambodia. That is, just as the Khmer Rouge kept their true grand cause carefully hidden during their revolution, the Senderistas have been content, until recently, to remain opaque as to their postrevolutionary plans. Instead, they have preferred to attract recruits through appeals to Andean indigenism.[81] With the Khmer Rouge having shown the world the horror of its postrevolutionary intentions in 1975, however, such a Cambodian comparison has not helped Sendero Luminoso preserve the secrecy of its own unpleasant postrevolutionary plans. Also, although Sendero Luminoso has not shown any of the paranoid disunity of the Khmer Rouge, the Senderistas have received no foreign help whereas the Khmer Rouge was the beneficiary of vitally important foreign support from the Vietnamese communists. With this support, despite its disunity, the Khmer Rouge won. Without any support, despite its unity, Sendero Luminoso is too weak to make a frontal challenge against the government in Lima.

One insurgency to which Sendero Luminoso rarely has been compared is Vietnam. In fact, the Senderistas have been openly disdainful of the conduct of the communists in Vietnam. One *El Diario* article ran the headline, "There will not be another Vietnam in Peru." This headline was provoked by the Senderista author's insistence that there could be no compromise with capitalism such as has been made in Vietnam in the Paris Peace Agreement of 1973. The sin of Hanoi was that it had consented to the division of Vietnam, giving the Americans a partial victory.[82] Ironically, "another Vietnam in Peru" may work better in Peru than it did in Vietnam. The Tet strategy, after all, was one of dramatic transformation to an urban offensive built on a preparatory network of urban front organizations. In Peru, Lima is a far more pivotal center of national power than Saigon was, and, with the absence of a large garrison of American troops and the ever-present possibility of the engineered chaos of a coup, such a culminating urban assault would have a far better chance of success.

With these comparisons as a guide, my prognosis is depicted in Figure

Figure 11.9. Benchmarks of Insurgent Success: Prognosis on Peru

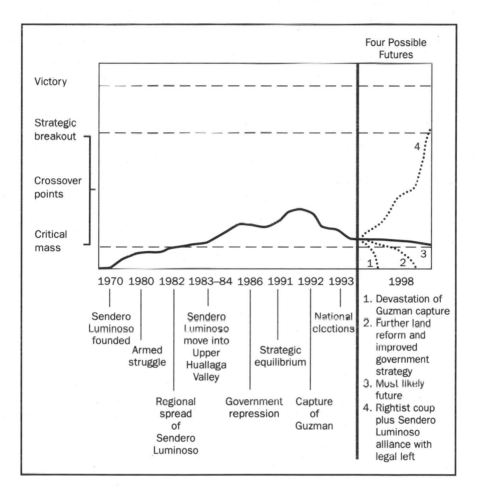

11.9. Following the rough indicators of my benchmarks of insurgent success, Sendero Luminoso, by any reckoning, remains far short of achieving a strategic breakout. At best, when Abimael Guzman proclaimed the attainment of Mao's "strategic equilibrium" (the second stage of protracted war) in 1991, the Peruvian insurgency had done no better then rival the zeniths of the Huks in the Philippines and the MRLA in Malaya or equal the stalemate in Laos from 1961 to 1971. Briefly, to review its historical record, when Sendero Luminoso launched its armed struggle in 1980, it is doubtful that the insurgents had achieved a critical mass. Such a point, however, clearly had been crossed when the Senderistas broke out of their Ayacucho base in 1982 and spread to other parts of the country. An upward surge of crossover points occurred when they moved into the Upper Huallaga Valley. After a setback following the bloody suppression of Senderista prison riots in 1986, another upward momentum of crossover points grew out of a monopoly in the Upper Huallaga Valley by Sendero Luminoso in 1987. By expanding its activities to urban areas, the insurgency capitalized on the graphic deterioration of the urban economy and the failure of government services to meet the needs of the growing impoverished class. This expansion sustained the insurgency's momentum until the slow economic turnaround and antiguerrilla program of President Fujimori arrested this growth. The subsequent capture of Guzman and sets of national elections have decidedly reversed the direction of this momentum.

Four possible futures await the insurgency of Sendero Luminoso. Relying on the proposition derived from the analytical framework of this book and the comparisons just made, in my view, the third is the most likely.

The first possibility is the rapid breakup of the insurgency because of the catastrophic blow of the loss of Sendero Luminoso's leader. This will occur if I have underestimated the role of leadership. In effect, this future would make Peru a case of Hannibalism in reverse. That is, Guzman would be the equivalent of Magsaysay in the Philippines, and the staying power of the insurgency would collapse without his spellbinding leadership. Although leadership as a factor is a rogue elephant and cannot ever be confidently dismissed in politics, the very employment of a Marxist people's war strategy by the Senderistas makes such an overpowering effect of leadership unlikely. Though a focalist strategy has proven to be vulnerable to decapitation (witness the case of Ché Guevara in Bolivia), as all the cases of this book have shown, Marxist people's wars have proven their resiliency in times of devastating loss. In Peru, the Senderistas are dispersed and entrenched broadly and deeply enough in their society so that the capture of Guzman and many of his confederates alone will not be enough to destroy the insurgency. Moreover, the political issues providing the basic fuel for the insurgency remain unresolved.

The second possibility, pertaining to the two exogenous variables of this study, is that the extension of meaningful land reform to the southern Sierras accompanied by improved economic performances in the cities and a more effective military strategy in the countryside will gradually defeat Sendero Luminoso. A key ingredient to this improved government performance, practically speaking, could be American assistance. Such intervention would have to avoid the flashpoint of ground combat troops. The intensely negative popular reaction to American helicopter crews in the government's antidrug efforts in the Upper Huallaga Valley should serve as sufficient warning on this score.[83] In other ways, however, American assistance could make tangible contributions. Gordon McCormick has observed that Peru has a limited road network that creates vulnerabilities similar to those the Soviets encountered in Afghanistan. Washington could help expand and diversify this transportation network so that Lima, for example, would not be so vulnerable to guerrilla strangulation. McCormick has also observed that the Peruvian military has generally not broken its field soldiers into small, mobile units capable of extended patrolling in the countryside. American training, similar to that undertaken in the Philippines, could certainly remedy this problem.[84]

As attractive as this future is, at least to the government, it is still not likely. First, the Fujimori regime has shown no interest in furthering land reform, in large part because the regime's urban power base is centered in right-wing business interests and sectors within the military more focused on repression then reform. Second, the insurgency does not yet pose a serious threat to the government, and, absent a coherent U.S. foreign policy on Third World intervention in the post–Cold War order, Washington is not likely preemptively to extend itself with such a program of assistance.

The most likely future is the third possibility, one of a very gradual decline (almost a stalemate) in the fortunes of the insurgency. Failure to undertake a final land reform in the Andes means that the Senderistas cannot be destroyed, despite the loss of their swordsman. They have purchased too strong a base within Peru's impoverished Indian community for any breakup of its critical mass. Yet the fortunes of the Senderistas are not likely to improve. At the interest level, the economy is slowly turning around. Inflation is again under control and the GDP actually rose by 2.4 percent in 1991.[85] This economic improvement accounts for the slight downward slope of the line in Figure 11.9. At the opportunity level, the government system retains the support of the solid middle of Peruvian society: business interests committed to national control of capital, labor unions and leftist political parties committed to participatory politics and modern societal access, a military behind Fujimori's counterinsurgency emphasis, and even highland Indians outside of the southern Sierras. Sendero Luminoso has thus far disdained to compete for this middle ground. As for beliefs, a democratic system of competitive elections seems to have finally won broad support in Peru. The expansion of the electoral rolls in 1979 to include all Indians has given them a political stake in the system, a stake confirmed by the participatory power they demonstrated in electing Fujimori, a man of color, against a white candidate in 1990.[86] For all Peruvians, Sendero Luminoso has offered no belief-level appeal that can break it free from the stalemated corner it has painted itself into. Nevertheless, the April 1995 presidential elections resulting in another landslide victory for Fujimori confirmed the continuation of the economic recovery without reform and the persistence of the insurgency even without its "decapitated" leader.[87]

The fourth possibility is the least likely, at least in the short term, but it cannot be completely ruled out. It represents a lethal combination that could catapult Sendero Luminoso to a strategic breakout. The combination consists of a right-wing military coup provoked by an ineffective government response to a declining economy and seriously disruptive urban terror. If this coup bungles into further repression of the political system, it might provoke an alienated legal left (with its 20 percent plus of the national vote) to join with the Senderistas and reformist elements within the military to produce a fundamental crisis of rule in Peru. Though the current system appears to have enough safeguards to keep such a combination from occurring, worse things have happened in Latin America.

The Lessons

From all these cases it should be clear that insurgencies are dynamic phenomena. They are not subject to deterministic laws. Even at the eleventh-hour moment of a strategic breakout, they can be reversed by intervention, by reform, by leadership — whether that of strategic brilliance or of colossal blunder — or they can just stall. I have advanced an analytical and diagnostic framework that captures this process. It is a framework built on the paradigmatic presupposition that insurgencies are manifestations of crises in political legitimacy.

My presupposition about legitimacy is that societies in the Third World, in one way or another, are attempting to move from a traditional to a modern order. The latter order, whatever institutional or constitutional form it takes, does presuppose a belief system about politics that is reflected in broadened patterns of societal access and expanded opportunities for political participation. Such an undergirding assumption does not suggest that every country will achieve this condition or that what will evolve in these societies will always be equivalent to a liberal Western democracy. Thus, even successful insurgencies or counterinsurgencies do not mean these results will equate with modernization. Further achievements and perhaps more bottlenecks lie ahead. Similarly, the outcomes may sidetrack into a trap of prolonged stagnation, or even "regression" toward a traditional, anti-modern purity (as in the cases of Cambodia, Afghanistan, and Iran).

As for this study's cases, Mao's long march to power did fashion a revolutionary variant of modern legitimacy. Lying ahead, however, were the further bottlenecks of the Great Leap Forward, the Cultural Revolution, and the grand achievements of the 1980s marred by the butchery in Tien An Minh square. As frequently noted, the Vietnamese seconded these revolutionary achievements against the French and then against the Americans until the Tet offensive. Their triumph in 1975 ushered in a long period of managerial incompetence and economic stagnation that is finally beginning to show signs of easing. In Greece, the government neutralized the issue of legitimacy by means of elections and a parliamentary coalition, thereby depriving the communists of any hope of a competing national issue. The end of the civil war, however, traced a path of growing military political influence, the overthrow of the monarchy, and a very gradual return to democratic politics. The Philippines was a triumph of democratic politics over revolutionary politics, but it was so much the work of one charismatic figure that the islands had to face another insurgency after his death. In Malaya, *merdeka* and a constitutional contract embracing the country's three communities succeeded in isolating an insurgency that was unable to free itself from its single ethnic group moorings. Subsequent Malay politics, however, were marred by ethnic rioting and tense renegotiations of the constitutional contract. The revolutionary legitimacy of the Cambodian communists was a fraud and perversion whose triumph visited untold horrors upon their people. Finally, the victory of the Pathet Lao in Vientiane was so heavily guaranteed by the North Vietnamese that after the revolution the state of Laos all but disappeared. Thus the traditional to modern transitions in these societies, of which these insurgencies were episodes, did not follow along similar linear paths.

A basic lesson of this book is that the essence of all these struggles was the quest for an Aristotelian middle for the grounding of the politics of these "new" societies. The three rising benchmarks surfaced in this study to chart these struggles form an arch to this middle keystone. This keystone is a set of common beliefs that create a community of groups and individuals who cooperate on the basis of them rather than contend and fight with each other over either different beliefs (with revolutionaries) or the complete absence of common beliefs and interests (with separatist groups).[88]

This key to finding and defining such a middle ground is one lesson that holds for most of the cases of this study. In China, Mao gradually took this ground away from Chiang Kai-shek, who retreated into an elitist lair of Guomindang party cronies and foreign patrons. The effect of the Resistance War against the French in Vietnam was to earn the middle ground for the communists, a ground to which the various "nationalist" regimes in Saigon were never able to develop a full access. After World War II in Greece, the government reclaimed this ground from the nearly successful communist seizure of it during the war. This middle ground is precisely what was secured against the ethnic Chinese in Malaya and the regional Huks in the Philippines. In Cambodia, however, the middle ground represented by Prince Sihanouk was rendered impotent by its initial manipulation and subsequent cavalier rejection by the communists. Similarly, in the hinterland kingdom of Laos, the middle ground personified by Prince Souvanna Phouma was betrayed by an imbalance of intervention.

Table 11.4. Candidate Lessons

	Factors Important to Victories					
	Belief Legiti- macy	Inter- vention	Elec- tions	Land Reform	Revolutionary Strategy (Faithful People's War)	Bridge Leader- ship
Incumbent Victories						
Greece	+	+	+	o	o	+
Philippines	?	+	+	+	o	+
Malaya	+	+	+	+	o	+
Insurgent Victories						
Vietnam I	+	+	o	+	+	+
Vietnam II	?	+	o	o	o	?
China	+	?	o	+	+	+
Cambodia	?	+	o	?	+	+
Laos	?	+	o	o	o	?

Key
+ = Yes
o = No
? = Controversial

This centrality of the struggle for the middle ground is illustrated by Table 11.4. Bridge leadership and belief legitimacy emerge as important factors in all but a handful of the victories. An even stronger lesson is that intervention is an important factor in all of the victories but one. Indeed, it is so important that it is responsible for undermining somewhat the importance to communists of belief legitimacy, land reform, and faithfulness to revolutionary strategy. The most dramatic lesson of this table, however, is that elections were important to all of the incumbent victories just as for the insurgents it was the one factor that played no role in any of their victories. All of the incumbents who lost were unable to carry off legitimate elections to validate their rule.

For lessons on the intersection of insurgency and intervention that emerge from our cases, two points are striking. First, though all the factors discussed in this chapter are important in at least sustaining an insurgency or counterinsurgency campaign, for victories, a few stand out as almost sufficient in themselves. Second, these "stand-out factors" are not always the same for incumbents and insurgents. Again, this highlights the fundamental asymmetries between the two sides to these "internal wars." The factor of elections just mentioned is the most obvious illustration. Incumbents need to justify their rule to the Aristotelian middle, and, playing by the rules of modernizing, would-be constitutional states, elections are the best way of corralling pledges to the system. Insurgents, on the other hand, are bent on winning the struggle by redefining legitimacy. For them, there are other ways to do this than elections. The fact that in Table 11.4 none of these other ways have the same exclusive claim over insurgents that they do over incumbents suggests that insurgents are freer to select a mix of these factors. Apart from a perfect zero on elections, none of the other factors required complete performances by all the cases for victory. Nevertheless, as a pointed lesson for the Senderistas in Peru, insurgents have to do something to legitimate their insurgency with the Aristotelian middle of their societies, whether by appeals to belief legitimacy, demonstrations of land reform, or exhibitions of bridge leadership.

Victorious incumbents, however, with the exception of revolutionary strategy, appear to have to do it all. The task of incumbents is to uphold the rules, and they have to live by them as well. It is worth briefly noting in Table 11.4 that the zero for land reform in Greece is only because there was a successful one before the insurgency, and the question mark for belief legitimacy in the Philippines is what rendered Magsaysay's victory over the Huks unstable and led to further trouble down the road. Despite the importance of "everything" for incumbents, what stands out as primary is belief-level legitimacy. Given the absolute necessity for incumbents to hang on to the Aristotelian middle to defeat an insurgency, elections, land reform, and bridge leadership are functional avenues to this middle, whose possession is certified by the conformance of a regime's rule with its society's particular principles of legitimacy. Because insurgencies are won or lost by relative performance on this question, if an insurgency does not mount too serious a challenge, as the Huks failed to do in the Philippines, this keystone of belief legitimacy, for the moment, may not be necessary, as long as some of the other functional factors have been secured. Such victories, however, tend to be tenuous.

For both sides, then, insurgencies are difficult challenges. In fact, in the economically poor and politically weak societies of the Third World, it is too much of a task to manage alone. Thus none of the victors in any of our cases was able to win without outside help. A closer examination of the question able case of China shows that a considerable amount of foreign assistance was provided to Mao. In a sense, this makes nonintervention as determinative of outcomes as actual interventions. Our cases, however, reveal a different effect of intervention on the two sides. For insurgents, interventions do not seem to have as sensitive an impact on their legitimacy as they do for incumbents. Thus, despite the controversy surrounding the legitimacy claims of insurgents in Laos, Cambodia, and Vietnam II, the strong amounts of foreign intervention they received did not further undermine their claims to legitimacy. They merely guaranteed their victories. Though, as discussed in some detail, these "purchased" victories created their own problems, these two and a half victories by intervention have upset the unanimity of this book's presupposition that insurgencies are crises of political legitimacy and are won or lost by those who solve the crisis better.

The presupposition, however, has worked unanimously for incumbents. This means, of course, that interventions in behalf of incumbents do have to be sensitive to the effects of the intervention on the domestic legitimacy of the client regime. Although in all eight of our cases the incumbent regimes received massive amounts of foreign assistance—in every case, considerably greater than, or at least equal to, the amounts received by the insurgents—the incumbents won in only three of the insurgencies and lost in five. In the three that they won, the interventions buttressed the belief-level legitimacy of the client regimes, and, except Laos as a stand-off, for the other four cases, this assistance crippled the legitimacy of the client regimes, and they lost. Given the importance of the question of intervention for great powers like the United States, the discussion earlier in this chapter paid considerable attention to laying out the various components to an intervention so that such decisions can be sensitive to their effects: the scale, the amount, the constancy, and, most important, its impact on the domestic legitimacy of the client regime.

Even here, however, I cannot offer general-law predictions. Rather, I have developed a set of diagnostic tools for assessing the intersection of insurgency and intervention as a crisis of political legitimacy in the specific historical context in which these intersections occur. I have done this by developing a three-tiered framework of legitimacy itself that also shows the traditional to modern transition of this concept as well as the impact of both competing strategies and interventions on this country-specific transition. To measure these dynamic effects, I have offered two sets of gauges. One separates political legitimacy into passive and active intensities of support and commitment based on demonstrable calculations of interests, opportunities, and beliefs along a continuum of rising or falling benchmarks of insurgent success. I have stressed land reform and elections (with an emphasis on the latter) as key marks of these legitimacy claims. The other, for interventions, identifies the clues or markers of the illegitimacy lock (as something to avoid), Hannibalism (as something to ground institutionally), bridge leadership (as something to promote), and the flashpoint of combat troops (as a measure to consider very carefully).

This book has analyzed a tightly defined set of typological cases: cases of Western interventions in Marxist people's war during the Cold War, or, in the Third World, the Era of People's War. Of the several forms of insurgency,

Marxist people's wars became a criterion for selecting cases because the mobilization emphasized by this strategy brings legitimacy to the center as the target for revolutionary appeals as well as for democratic reforms. Also, during this period, the very invocation of a communist ideology served as an incendiary trigger to Western intervention.

This analytical framework, nevertheless, can certainly be useful for insurgency more generally and for other types of intervention. In such broader cases, naturally, there will be more intervening variables and contexts with different definitional parameters. For example, in Table 1.1, the separatist insurgencies in Ethiopia, Morocco, Sri Lanka, Burma, and Timor are certainly a different breed from the cases analyzed here. As separatists, they are not interested in claiming any middle ground to a society from which they wish to withdraw. But among their own chosen people, they will still have to make their appeals based on accepted ideas of legitimacy. And interventions can similarly be charted for the effects and markers noted in this analysis.

Through the prism of these comparative cases, this book provides one overriding caution for foreign policy. On the question of foreign interventions in domestic insurgencies, the Vietnam War is only one of many relevant cases. In fact, in many ways, it is the most deviant and least relevant analogy to the very phenomenon that it is most often invoked as a lesson.

Conclusion

THE NEW ERA:
WILSON'S TRIUMPH
OVER LENIN

The New Era

"The old order changeth, yielding place to new," wrote Alfred, Lord Tennyson in his *Morte d'Arthur*, lamenting the death of King Arthur and the passing of his kingdom at Camelot. So also might such departed revolutionary elders as Mao Zedong and Ho Chi Minh lament the passing of the old order of people's war and its yielding to a new one of people's rule. Both with regard to U.S. relations with the Third World and to domestic political struggles within these countries, a major theme of this book is that the era when the triumphs of communist insurgencies in China and Indochina raised the specter of their continued and inevitable success is being replaced by a renewed global struggle for democratic participation, in what Samuel Huntington has called the "third wave" of democracy.[1]

To fix meaning to the times they live in, people and societies resort to periodization. Such labels as the Era of Good Feelings, the Great Depression, the Cold War, and the Spirit of Camp David declare the *weltanschauung* of a particular period or event by distinguishing it from other periods when conditions and trends were demonstrably different. In international relations, such *weltanschauungs* provide the set of perceptions about the environment upon which foreign policies are based. During the Cold War, foreign policies worldwide became oriented around the struggle for domination between two power centers and belief systems: the United States and its principles of liberal democracy and the Soviet Union and its communist ideology. In this struggle Washington developed a foreign policy of containment against what it perceived to be a globally expansionist Soviet power bloc. Following the dictates of this policy, any insurgency that declared a Marxist people's war strategy was bound to provoke at least some level of American intervention against it.

In the 1960s and 1970s there was a trend or burden of proof in favor of the triumph of wars of national liberation. As William Overholt has observed: "In countries as disparate as Indonesia and South Korea, it was widely assumed by leftists, neutralists, and pro-Western analysts alike that the communist forces possessed a kind of natural and inexorable superiority that could be overcome only by overwhelming external pressure from the U.S. The degree to which this perception predominated was so great that it is difficult to communicate to a generation that never experienced it." [2]

Thus at the outset of the Vietnam conflict no one questioned General Vo Nguyen Giap when he advanced the proposition: "If it proves possible to defeat the 'special war' tested in South Vietnam by the American imperialists, this will mean that it can be defeated everywhere else as well." [3] After the result in 1975, there seemed to be no answer to Ho Chi Minh's prophetic utterance six years before Saigon's surrender: "Imperialist aggressive wars are bound to be defeated, national-liberation revolutions are bound to be successful." [4] Americans and communists alike in this era, then, shared a common belief in dominoes. The struggle was to make them lean the other way. With the communist triumph, Vietnam, to a traumatized American polity, quickly became a Clorox that bleached out discrepant cases (such as, in the 1950s, the British defeat of the Malayan communist insurgents and the U.S.-assisted suppression of the Huks in the Philippines) to create a trend of people's war in the Third World during the 1970s.

Most fundamentally, my point in asserting that the victorious Era of People's War has yielded to one of people's rule is that we live in a more sober period in which historical forces in the Third World between incumbents and insurgents (or reformists and revolutionaries) has become more evenly matched. Indeed, at least momentarily, it has shifted heavily in favor of this new wave of democratization. Several factors account for the favorable conditions of this new era.

First, Marxist-Leninist revolutionaries no longer have the advantage of asymmetrical comparisons between the promises of revolutionary utopias versus the obviously lacking performances of struggling incumbent regimes. Revolutionaries have seized power in enough places now (Vietnam, Laos, Cambodia, Ethiopia, Mozambique, Angola, Zimbabwe, Southern Yemen, Iran, Cuba, and, for a while, Nicaragua) to be held accountable for their own miserable performances as well. In other words, instead of measuring promise against performance in an unequal contest of vision versus reality, performance can squarely confront performance. Simply, what this means today is that revolutionary demagogues no longer have the soft target of a sleazy Saigon versus the promise of the comradely utopia of "socialist man." Now the sleazy Saigon of the past can be compared with the ghoulish Ho Chi Minh City of the present. Such a murky contrast deflates the rhetoric a bit. Indeed, enlarging on this point in 1989, the Armed Forces of the Philippines, in a media campaign against the NPA, showed the film *The Killing Fields* about Cambodia with telling effect to horrified rural audiences.[5]

Second, accompanying this parity of comparisons has been a redressing of the imbalance between incumbents and insurgents over the traditional to modern transition. Ironically, since revolutionaries seek to overthrow traditional orders, communist insurgents, in some of our cases, were more successful in their appeals to traditional legitimacy than their incumbent adversaries. This was certainly true for both the Vietnam cases and China, though less true for Cambodia and Laos, and not at all true for Greece, the Philippines, and Malaya. The global reason for this relative success was that a hallmark of the Era of People's War was the tidal wave of decolonization that accompanied it and, with it, a repudiation of Western culture and political institutions. In some quarters, this repudiation even extended to the very goal of modernization itself. In global terms, this created a cross-current to containment as a legitimating ground for Western intervention. Thus, even as containment provided a justification, to domestic American politics and to the foreign policies of its allies, for interventions against systemically hostile communist insurgencies, the tide of decolonization cheered on elsewhere made such Western interventions appear to be reincarnations of this bankrupt imperialism. This cross-current put noncommunist nationalists on the defensive, especially if they had to accept dramatically obvious Western help (like combat troops) against their insurgent challengers.

Thus the insurgents were able to take advantage of this tide by dressing up communism as a non-Western alternative to modernization via liberation struggles against colonialism that also promised vague restorations of precolonial glories. Pol Pot conjured up images of Angkor; Mao took advantage of the Japanese invasion to call for a national salvation struggle; and Ho called for a classic *khoi nghia* against the French and the Americans. This, of course, was part of Lenin's two-staged revolutionary strategy whereby communists reveal themselves and their distinctly nontraditional intentions only after they have seized power. Though admittedly the communism of the Chinese and Vietnamese revolutionaries was clear enough (both, however, did hide behind united fronts for extended periods), in Cambodia Prince Sihanouk's traditional presence was discarded like "a cherry pit" after the revolution and the Laotian character to the Pathet Lao disappeared into the Three Revolutions of the Vietnamese theoretician Le Duan. From the high traditional ground as the chief upholder of the honor of Hellas against the Axis occupiers, ELAS in Greece plunged from this summit after World War II to the treacherous championing of Macedonian separatism to curry Soviet favor in a doomed bid for survival. Communist revolutionaries in the Philippines and Malaya were unable to build any momentum in large part because such galvanizing traditional appeals eluded them.

With respect to this balance, what has also become clear is that for all their clamorous championing of lost traditional ideals, revolutionaries were largely silent about the modern legitimacy to which all Third World societies were aspiring to transit. As Ith Sarin observed about the Khmer Rouge, "As for general elections, they have no ideas."[6] Instead of proposing any specific program for achieving this transition, apart from their general ideological appeals and their admittedly specific calls for land reform, they mostly chose to attack the soft target of the numerous vulnerabilities of the incumbent regimes. Such deceits could be continued during the revolutions, when the governing performances of the incumbents were under attack, but not afterward.

Given this imbalance, the Western interventions of this period posted a creditable record of three wins (Greece, Malaya, and the Philippines) and five losses (China, Vietnam I, Vietnam II, Cambodia, and Laos), with the latter three losses occurring under controversial circumstances. What stood out as a mitigating factor during this bleak period was the beacon of the ballot box. As a beacon, it at least laid bare and sometimes actually solved the sociopolitical crises that sparked and fueled the insurgencies of the era. Thus even fraudulent or restricted elections often provided an important service by highlighting the thinness of a regime's writ of legitimacy and revealing the constellations of groupings either behind or outside of a ruling regime. As usual in this study, Vietnam stands out as the ambiguous case. Honest and open elections for a constitutional convention in 1966 were followed by a 1967 presidential election in which communists were barred. The next presidential election in 1971 presented the spectacle of Nguyen Van Thieu running against himself after his two main rivals withdrew, revealing both his political strength in ruling circles and his regime's isolation from the large civilian population that remained either disdainfully aloof or retained a reservoir of sympathy for the communists. In the Philippines, the fraudulent elections of 1946 and 1949 only made the insurgency stronger.

In Laos, the chicanery marring the 1960 elections, after such honest ones in 1958, revealed both the narrowness of the support base of the rightists and the continued strength of the Neutralists and Souvanna Phouma. Similarly in Cambodia, Marshal Lon Nol's attempt in 1972 to legitimate his seizure of power with an electoral mandate only exposed his lack of it by his defeat in Phnom Penh City having to be reversed by stuffed ballot boxes in the countryside.

More honest ones posed serious dilemmas for insurgents and often forced them into serious division and major error. Instances abounded of increasingly honest elections deflecting the quest of insurgents for power. The twin elections of 1946 in Greece created a national consensus around the monarchy and recertified the parliamentary system of government. This forced the once-powerful communists into the countryside, where they searched in vain for a new rallying issue and unifying strategy. Following the corrupt elections of 1946 and 1949 in the Philippines, Magsaysay brought millions of new rural voters into the electoral process in the 1951 and 1953 elections and drowned the insurgency of the Huks in Central Luzon. José Maria Sison found his NPA insurgency similarly swamped by Corazon Aquino's presidential campaign in 1986. The electoral path in Malaya was trickier, in that much of the Alliance's success rested on the local to general sequence of Malayan elections, but the ultimate communist refusal to participate in them sealed their political isolation. Because the MRLA's initial support base was confined to peripheral Chinese squatter settlements, this refusal denied them a critical avenue of access to a larger constituency. Finally, despite President Fujimora's temporary assumption of dictatorial powers in Peru, the persistence of electoral politics, in the face of vicious terroristic campaigns of disruption, is a source of enraging frustration to Sendero Luminoso guerrillas, as most recently reflected in the successful elections of 1995.

This shift in the balance between incumbents and insurgents over promises versus performances in the traditional to modern transition has set up the third factor marking out this new era, namely, a shift in the political agenda of the Third World. The question at the top of the list is no longer how to acquire political power but how to manage it. For the United States, in particular, this historical shift from appeals of revolution to principles of governance represents an opportunity to shift its own image from that of a master to a model. During the Era of People's War, revolutionaries sought to sweep the United States and its clients from the scene in a tide of such epithets as "neocolonialist masters," "running dogs of imperialism," and "puppet lackeys." With the ebbing of this tide, what remains is what always has been: a United States that is a model for certain clear principles of democratic rule.

To George Kennan, it was these democratic principles that would be the final line of defense in the containment of the Soviet Union and communism. Indeed, it was to these very principles that Mikhail Gorbachev desperately turned in a futile attempt from 1985 to 1991 to save the Soviet Union. The implosion of this empire has done far more than redraw the boundaries of Europe; it has caused, in Reinhold Bendix's terms, the disappearance of the socialist image of the future for nation-building and modern legitimacy.[7] On how to seize power from alien, colonial rulers, communism had much to offer, but on how to rule once power had been seized, its long record of rule turned up no answers. In truth, the light of this "brave, new world" has gone out.

The fourth factor that has ushered in the era of people's rule is that with this new emphasis on rule over revolution has come a fading of one of the two romances of World War II—the romance of the guerrilla. The heroic resistance fighters of World War II turned into the independence fighters of the postwar period struggling against the continued tyranny of alien rule, whether directly colonial or indirectly neocolonial. This romance guaranteed at least a critical mass and often the boost of a momentum of crossover points to postwar insurgent movements. Indeed, such a romantic boost clearly accrued to the insurgencies in China, Vietnam, Greece, the Philippines, and Malaya.

The other romance, that of democracy, has worked a little slower. It was, after all, the democracies of the United States and Great Britain (leaving aside the Soviet Union) that triumphed over the global menace of Nazi and fascist tyranny. Both powers held aloft their political principles as the motivational inspiration to their triumph. After the war, of course, both powers sought to commend these principles as the basis for the building of new nations in the Third World. The ballot box served as a beacon of this democratic romance during the storm of the guerrilla's dominance.

These two romances, moreover, have now interacted in such a way as to create their own new conditions for international relations. The fading of the romance of the guerrilla from World War II has reestablished the earlier difficulty of any insurgency: the asymmetrical disadvantage of getting one going. The gift of World War II, then, is over. Also, these two romances were never completely separate. That is, it is becoming clear, to stand Marx on his head, that the triumph of people's war contained the seeds of its own destruction: democracy. In the mobilization of the peasantry and of their concerns into the cause of communist revolution, the peasantry has not wished to be demobilized in the postrevolutionary era from its acquired participatory habits. Finally, with democracy at the fore, the blinders of containment have come off and outside patrons can search more analytically for the bridge leadership that emerges from honest elections and avoid the trap of illegitimacy locks from Bonapartist sycophants.

The Promise and the Danger

For the people of the Third World, the twentieth century opened to the struggle between Vladimir Lenin and Woodrow Wilson for their hearts and minds. In addressing the breakup of the empires of Europe at the end of World War I, Wilson touched the hearts of more than just Europeans when he declared in his "Peace without Victory" speech on January 22, 1917: "No peace can last, or ought to last, which does not recognize and accept the principle that governments derive all their just powers from the consent of the governed. . . . Any peace which does not recognize and accept this principle will inevitably be upset. . . . The world can [not] be at peace . . . where there is not tranquility of spirit and a sense of justice, of freedom, and of right."[8] Indeed, he reiterated his commitment to this principle in the fifth of the famous Fourteen Points he took with him to the peace treaty conference at Versailles (1919).[9] But at Versailles, under the pressure of international diplomacy, Wilson was forced to turn his back on his own declarations in the awarding of the Shandong Peninsula of China to the Japanese.

As discussed in Chapter 6, the disillusionment over Wilson's treachery did much to touch off the May Fourth Movement. This movement opened the way in China to modern revolution and put the spotlight on Vladimir Lenin and his revolutionary strategy, ironically, as a better means of realizing Wilson's ideals. Lenin argued that countries in the backward colonies and semicolonies had become the new exploited proletariat of Western capitalism and that, in throwing off their chains to this system, they could bring about the destruction of capitalism itself. In these global backwaters, modernizers, now turned revolutionaries, were less interested in this, but they were interested in their own independence and in doing in their foreign overlords.

It has taken the better part of a half-century for people in the Third World to see through Lenin's siren calls. With the disintegration of the Soviet Union and the bankruptcy of Lenin's promises, the way is once again clear for a redemption of Wilson's legacy. Democracies, however, are not immune to failure, particularly to failures of imagination and perception. The United States, for example, could once again snatch defeat from the jaws of victory, as it did in Laos from a workable stalemate. By falling victim to a Patrick Buchanan's political call for "America First" or the more academic "Europe First and Only" dissertations of "hyperrealists," Americans can fail to see what they have done.[10]

The often-remarked-upon American quality of separating the military from the political and of not seeing how the two interact has led the United States to grief more than once. General Dwight D. Eisenhower's refusal to march on the political objectives of Berlin, Vienna, and Prague at the end of

World War II is just one example. Similarly, this book has highlighted the American failure to see what it accomplished in the Tet offensive. More than just dealing a sharp military defeat to communist forces, MACV destroyed an entire political-military strategy, a revolution of Marxist people's war. In its Cold War triumph in the 1990s, the United States stands on the brink of another Tet, as a blundering Cyclops failing to see what has fully been opened up to it: in the vanished future of communism, a concrete opportunity for the globalization of democracy.

If, in this study of insurgency, political beliefs about legitimacy have proven to be primary and economic principles of performance secondary, it is nevertheless true that the secondary can grind down the primary and eventually overturn it.[11] Thus, though elections have proven marginally more important than land reform in these studies, no regime is beyond insurgent challenge until political legitimacy is supported by solid policy and economic performance. In the Philippines, for example, a third round of insurgency cannot be precluded until a thorough land reform is equitably dispensed.

If democracies fail in the Third World and elsewhere, rather than the close of the twentieth century marking the "end of history" in the triumph of the liberal democratic state, as Francis Fukuyama has contended,[12] a new round of fascism might take hold in the Third World. The weakness of the Weimar Republic in Germany after World War I was swept aside by a powerful Nazi performer that forestalled the triumph of democracy in a horrible cycle of domestic violence and world war. If there is a peace dividend to the United States that settles down to a reduced defense burden of 3 percent from the Cold War's 6 percent of Gross National Product, it does not seen immodest to propose that 1 percent of this savings be dedicated to this global project, especially when one recalls that the Marshall Plan after World War II claimed 2 percent of GNP.

This may lead the United States to further interventions. Preferably such occasions could come under the rubric of a collective action such as Wilson first envisioned for his League of Nations. Whatever the global rubric, this book's basic warning still stands: in large measure, the efficacy of an intervention will succeed or fail on the basis of its effect on the definitional grounds of political legitimacy in the affected society. The difference between a Viking's raid for plunder and a posse's ride for justice lies in the legitimacy with which the venture is viewed in the receiving demographic terrain.

The basic lesson of Vietnam and its companion prismatic cases remains the beacon of democracy, and of a vigorous promotion of it by the United States. The surest way to recapture a positive legacy from Vietnam is to make a reality of General Norman Schwartzkopf's declaration of the *best* of our intentions in that war: "I think we went to Vietnam . . . for the principle of democracy . . . I'm not saying that's what turned out . . . I'm only saying that this is the principle we went to Vietnam for."[13]

As the global agenda has shifted from people's war to people's rule, even in Vietnam this intention can yet triumph. When it does—when voters cast their ballots in Saigon in free, fair, and competitive elections—something of this pledge of my fifty-seven thousand fallen comrades can be redeemed and the lesson of this agonizing war be fulfilled.

Appendix 1

THE LITERATURES
OF THE FRAMEWORK

Rational Choice and Revolution

The three-tiered analytical framework of legitimacy, insurgency, and intervention presented in Chapter 3 cuts a swath through several bodies of literature, including that on legitimacy, development, revolution, and intervention. Two of them merit separate discussion here so that the academic perspective of this book can be properly understood as well as its implications for foreign policy: first, rational choice and revolution, and second, intervention.

In the second analytical cut in Chapter 3, I proclaimed opportunity-level calculations or commitments as the repository for rational actions and the area where rational actor theories had their greatest "utility." Throwing a revolutionary situation into this chart, however, greatly upsets a rational actor theoretical apple cart. At least in political science, perhaps the basic standard of rational behavior is provided by John Rawls's conception of it as action in conformance with, or in furtherance of, one's life plans.[1] When, in a revolutionary situation, it is difficult to carry out any life plan at all, including basic survival, the very development of a life plan becomes a fundamental crisis. To commit to one side or the other, then, involves a leap of faith to a life plan whose sense, or rationality, depends on being in harmony with the historical direction of the society at large, an assurance that can be only very tenuous. Thus what is rational behavior in a revolution is bounded by the course of the revolution itself. The hope is that one's little pocket of rationality grows with the course of events.

Saigon on April 29, 1975, for example, had turned into a society of irrational, panic-stricken rats. What was rational was growing behind the advancing columns of the North Vietnamese army just as it was rapidly disintegrating in the capital city's frenzied chaos. The next day, when North Vietnamese tanks slammed through the gates of the Presidential Palace, the tanks brought with them their own rationality and, to the Saigonese, a restoration of at least one kind of humanity. Rationality in any society, then, depends on a mutual agreement as to what it is. In a revolution of any kind, this is one of the many subjects under violent dispute.

Regarding this growing pocket of rationality, James De Nardo has presciently observed that in such disruptive situations people search for safety in numbers. With power quite literally lying in these numbers, for leaders its key turns on designing strategies that corral them for their side.[2] From my perspective, his discussion of these strategies is similar to building the momentum of crossover points. Earlier, I noted that Margaret Levi deliberately steered clear of chaotic situations in which basic societal rules and the numbers supporting them remained in contention. What she really wanted to avoid was a direct analysis of periods when the terms of political legitimacy were in question. Though she has acknowledged the importance of legitimacy for the support of political rule, the concept for her was too methodologically troublesome.[3]

De Nardo and Levi, nevertheless, are reflective of a fifth wave of modernization theory. In this literature, I first mentioned a shift from an approach of a dichotomous transition to a view of development as progressing through stages. Both approaches still had in common the tradition to modernity transition presented in Chapter 3. This "classic" modernization literature (of two "waves") came under attack from two directions. One source (a third wave) questioned either the whole value of modernization itself or at least whether Western models of development were appropriate.[4] A larger source (the fourth wave), creating a corpus of literature known as the dependency school, raised the argument that what was holding back Third World countries was not their lack of internal development but the exploitative structure of the international system. In Migdal's parlance, what was needed was not a change of rules within these societies but a change in the terms of economic exchange and political power between the developed and lesser developed countries.[5]

Despite vast ideological and methodological differences among these four waves, they held in common a macro-theoretical perspective on the problem of development. From several directions, this fifth wave has sought to recast this problem in micro-theoretic terms. Essentially, it has centered on an explanation of human behavior, including political actions, in terms of maximizing one's utilities along the indifference curves of microeconomic theory.[6] These several sources collected themselves under the rubric of international political economy and advanced a new theory of development based on assumptions of rational choice.[7] The major focus of this theory has been on the leadership elite within a state and its manipulation of subgroups for its own independent political purposes. International political economy has offered invaluable insights into these political purposes to economic policies.[8]

It has been slower to take up the question of collective violence and revolution. Margaret Levi has offered the most honest expression of this reluctance. To explain rulers as rational predators, she has preferred to put beyond her analysis nonmaterial sources of coercion (such as ideology and legitimacy) and irrational sources of compliance (such as patriotic fervor). She nevertheless has admitted that all these sources of coercion and compliance (material and nonmaterial, rational and irrational) are interwoven and even that irrational "moments of madness" are important historically. The problem is that such combinations are hard to explain by rational choice theory so it is better to separate them.[9] James De Nardo brings into his analysis much that Margaret Levi leaves out. His analysis is dynamic in that strategy is the key determinant of outcomes: whether protest can be sedated by reforms or stimulated to revolution by mobilization. He gives play to different intensities of calculations and different values for behavior (greed or fear, for example), but his explanations remain grounded in a cost-benefit analysis of behavior.[10] Because joining a revolutionary movement is both an individual and a collective act, however, and, therefore, comes from a combination of rational appeals and moral sanctions, De Nardo's fellow traveler Michael Taylor has conceded that assumptions of rational behavior in revolutions can be expressed only as a "thin theory" of individual rather than collective behavior.[11]

The chief limitation of rational choice theory lies not in its failure to account for rational behavior but in its petulant unwillingness to incorporate nonrational behavior into its overall theory of individual and collective action. One of the fathers of modern social science, Max Weber, acknowledged the multiplicity of motives for human behavior and started with this premise as the foundation for his archetypical theorizing about social reality. Much earlier than Weber, this multiplicity of motives can be traced to Plato's intellectual struggles with the elements of the soul. Despite his strong preference for reason-guided behavior, Plato was forced to concede a place to both appetite and will in his integrative soul of wisdom.[12]

Despite its macro crudeness and its Eurocentric bias, I have built my analytical framework primarily on the "classic" modernization theory of the 1960s and 1970s because it acknowledged the centrality of nonmaterial resources (such as legitimacy) to nation-building and to the issues surrounding insurgency and counterinsurgency. Also, the basic traditional to modern transition described by this theory, with all its faults, remains the central dynamic to the history of our age (both for people's war and a post–Cold War global democratization). With David Apter, I recognize that it is much more of a curvilinear than a linear path.[13] That is, it proceeds by fits and starts. Indeed, in these fits and starts lie the origins of most insurgencies. What my work offers is an analytical framework that integrates both material and nonmaterial as well as individual and collective sources of action into an explanation of the intersection of insurgency and intervention.[14]

Intervention

The intersection of insurgency and intervention has produced two approaches or levels of analysis for examining this "academic" phenomenon and foreign policy problem. They are best represented by the titles of two books on the subject, James Rosenau's *International Aspects of Civil Strife* and Harry Eckstein's *Internal War*. Rosenau's work concentrated on insurgency as it spilled over to the level of the international balance of power while Eckstein and his associates tried to confine their analysis to the impact of insurgency internally on the level of the politics of the nation-states affected.[15]

At this international level, James Rosenau, Thomas Schelling, Alexander George, and Andrew Mack all wrote compelling works relevant to the question of intervention. James Rosenau saw the postwar world as playing host to a vast proliferation of "linkages" making it both a more interdependent and at the same time a more interfering system. Thomas Schelling pointed out that, unfortunately, much of this interfering involved either outright violence or posturings about violence, which led him to characterize these patterns as amounting to a "diplomacy of violence" in which states pursued goals vis à vis their adversaries of either deterrence or compellance, that is, to prevent them from doing something or to force them to do something. Alexander George called this "coercive diplomacy" and divided it into Types

A and B. Though they were similar to Schelling's deterrence and compellance, there were subtle differences. For George, Type A merely involved stopping an adversary from doing something he hadn't done yet, whereas Type B required a state to stop an adversary from doing something he was already doing. Type B, George pointed out, was enormously more difficult and would require the marshaling of a considerable and steady resolve. The Type B variant of coercive diplomacy was clearly what was necessary for an intervention in an insurgency, and Andrew Mack made the prescient observation that "big nations lose small wars" because, as global powers with competing interests, they cannot match the total mobilization of will that small nations can summon in focusing on a single "national salvation" objective.[16]

Andrew Scott has drawn up the most specific set of principles for intervention. He started from the premise that nonintervention was impossible in an interdependent world and that intervention, in fact, was often desirable for both Vattelian and Metternichian reasons. He called, therefore, for an international regime of conditional intervention and for drawing up both military and economic codes for these conditions. He further spelled out three types of interventions: intrabloc (within a sphere of influence), interbloc (which carry too high a risk of war), and extrabloc (outside of any bloc and where there was the greatest need for such principles).[17] Insurgencies, it hardly needs to be pointed out, fell most often in zones of extrabloc ambiguity.

As perceptive as this international level of analysis was on the phenomenon of intervention, interventions ran into trouble if they were unaware of the "local" conditions in the countries that were the arenas for them. Obviously, my point is that at such an elevated level the centrality of the legitimacy crisis to the political dynamic was missed. The "internal war" literature of counterinsurgency, however, did provide an appropriate level for this political analysis. Almost all of it viewed insurgency from a Maoist framework and tried to develop countermeasures appropriate to each of Mao's stages of protracted war. Though there was a tendency to overgeneralize in much of this literature and to concentrate too much on the purely suppressive features of counterinsurgency, the very use of a Maoist framework required an appreciation of political factors. It also provided a ready-made scheme for classifying one's progress.

The best of this literature did bring political factors under close scrutiny. David Galula, for example, proposed a combined political-military strategy of scattering main force insurgent forces, establishing both a political and a military presence in affected areas both to expose and to root out the insurgent political structures, the immediate championing of local elections, ultimately organizing these leaders into political parties tied to national organizations, and, finally, contending with the last guerrillas by political co-optation or arrest.[18] By looking at insurgency from a framework of Maoist stages, counterinsurgency specialists were able to do two things. First, they had a rational scheme for calibrating the level of their interventions. Second, it made them appreciate the importance of timing, both in the development of an insurgency and in an intervention against (or for) it.

This, of course, did not prevent the United States from making a mess of its intervention in Vietnam. In fact, it destroyed the bipartisan consensus that had undergirded the foreign policy of containment. One principal effect was to sow confusion over the issue of intervention in the Third World. In 1969, before the war was even over, President Richard Nixon declared in his Guam Doctrine that the United States would not intervene again with ground combat troops in support of beleaguered friendly governments. Jimmy Carter, on the other hand, decided that in the "arc of crisis" (the Middle East), the stakes were high enough to justify direct American combat capability formed into a Rapid Deployment Force. Ronald Reagan more than embraced this capability in his doctrine of rolling back communism, and he wanted to rebuild the foreign policy consensus shattered by Vietnam. Instead, his entire presidency was plagued by congressional debates over intervention in Central America and division within his administration over the very basis for intervention. Defense Secretary Caspar Weinberger outlined six criteria for intervention grounded in public support, but Secretary of State George Shultz countered that such grants of support were impossible in the ambiguous warfare of insurgency.[19] In a valedictory address as president to West Point cadets in January 1993, George Bush sought to resolve this debate by calling for the "selective use of force for selective purposes." Although he conceded that there was no "easy formula," four conditions were critical: sufficiently high stakes with the strong possibility of success, circumstances that precluded other policies, action that could be limited in scope and time, and benefits that would outweigh the costs.[20] The lessons that Vietnam can still hold for this debate is the main topic of the conclusion to this book.

Appendix 2

A TALE OF TWO STRATEGIES: AN ALTERNATIVE EXPLANATION

Dienbienphu, madame . . .
Dienbienphu . . . history doesn't always
repeat itself. But this time it will. We
won a military victory over the French,
and we'll win it over the Americans,
too. Yes, madame, their Dienbienphu is
still to come. And it will come. The
Americans will lose the war on the day
when their military might is at its
maximum. . . . We'll beat them at the
moment when they have the most men,
the most arms, and the greatest hope of
winning.
　　　—Gen. Vo Nguyen Giap

The eventual goal throughout was
Saigon, but from the first the primary
emphasis of the North Vietnamese
focused on the Central Highlands and
the central coastal provinces. . . . [Also,
the] most logical course for the enemy,
it seemed to me, was to make another
and stronger effort to overrun the two
northern provinces, . . . the most
vulnerable part of the country.
　　　—Gen. William C. Westmoreland

Introduction: Of Dreams and Nightmares

　　Lewis Carroll had his character Alice awaken from her bizarre and somewhat frightening Wonderland with the reassuring exclamation, "Things are not as they seem in dreams." So, too, it appears, with the Vietnam War: things were not as they seemed. This tale of two strategies probes the ironic twists of fate meted out to Giap's dream of another triumphant Dienbienphu against the Americans and Westmoreland's nightmare of ignominious defeat before two simultaneous conventional thrusts by the North Vietnamese across the demilitarized zone in the north and through the Central Highlands at South Vietnam's midriff that would link up on coastal Highway 1 for a steamroller advance on Saigon.[1] In the world of events, Giap's dream of a Dienbienphu against the Americans, even in the triumph of his forces in 1975, was dashed, but Westmoreland's nightmare, after the departure of the last American GIs from Vietnam in 1973, was fully visited on the hapless remaining South Vietnamese defenders two years later.

Put simply, then, as a demonstration of a successful people's war strategy (of which a "Dienbienphu" was to be the culmination), the triumphant Ho Chi Minh campaign of the North Vietnamese in 1975 was a fraud, whereas, ironically, the fears of the American command of a South Vietnam succumbing to a conventional invasion proved, prophetically, to be well-founded.

To make such claims obviously risks confusing the already difficult task of drawing lessons from Vietnam because they dispel what has come to emerge as two of the war's fundamental "truths" for lesson-making. The first of these "truths" is that the North Vietnamese victory was a virtuoso exhibition of the strategy of people's war. The lesson is that such a strategy can serve as a model for profitable emulation by beleaguered insurgents in El Salvador, the Philippines, Peru, and elsewhere. The second "truth" is that the United States was so blinded to the guerrilla nature and underlying political issues of the conflict that it erringly chose to focus on the conventional threat of the North Vietnamese army. The lesson emerging therefrom is that the United States cannot be counted on ever to develop a foreign policy capable of dealing with insurgencies and the grievances that undergird them. Whether these emergent lessons prove right or wrong, the point of this appendix is that in order to establish themselves, they will have to look elsewhere for their foundational truths (such as to the comparative prism of this book). There is no simple Munich, then, in the Vietnam War.

Few wars can compare with Vietnam as an example of a Clausewitzian fog that has become even soupier after the war's conclusion than when it was actually being fought. The North Vietnamese claim they won by a strategy they actually abandoned after the 1968 Tet offensive. Most Americans have come to believe they lost to an insurgency that they in fact crushed. Ironically, the winning strategy was an American one used by the North Vietnamese in the name of Marxist people's war. It is not a story from which lessons readily emerge.

Building an "Atom Bomb" of People's War

At the outset, it must be acknowledged that the Ho Chi Minh campaign of the North Vietnamese army that achieved the conquest (or liberation) of Saigon on April 30, 1975, was indeed a triumph, for both the Lao Dong (communist) party of Hanoi and the more general cause of world socialism. It is hard not to admire Ho Chi Minh for his determination and faith in prophesying ultimate victory shortly before his death in 1969: "We, a small nation will have earned the signal honor of defeating, through heroic struggle, two big imperialisms—the French and the American—and of making a worthy contribution to the world liberation movement."[2] Despite the departure of American forces two years before this triumphant moment, a global significance to this communist victory cannot be denied. Giving due allowance for its hyperbole and propagandistic tone, a statement from the General Resolution of the Fourth National Congress of the Lao Dong party held in Hanoi in December 1976 is, nevertheless, on the mark: "This victory defeated the biggest and longest neocolonialist war of aggression since the end of the Second World War, upset the global strategy of the imperialist chieftain, drove US imperialism into an unprecedented predicament, further eroded and enfeebled the imperialist system, consolidated the outpost of socialism in South-East Asia, expanded and strengthened the socialist system, and further increased the strength and enhanced the offensive posture of the world revolutionary forces."[3]

From this acknowledgment of victory, however, it is quite another matter to accept the pronouncements of lessons flowing from this victory. Despite his prophetic insight, Ho's own lesson about a communist victory was somewhat grandiose. It will demonstrate, he said, "that imperialist aggressive wars are bound to be defeated, and national liberation revolutions are bound to be successful."[4] Ho, however, neglected to enlighten his readers as to what the basis was for expecting such universal success to national liberation revolutions. The inherent justice of a liberation struggle, a heroic history of resistance, and fine martial traditions all tend to depend on individual national circumstances. Presumably, strategy might provide the links for Ho's chain of universality. Indeed, General Giap and Party Secretary Le Duan have not been bashful about making such claims of strategic brilliance in behalf, of course, of their party: "Another outstanding success of our party consisted in creating and developing to a very high level the combined strength of people's war, of revolutionary war, using military attacks by mobile strategic army columns as main striking forces, combining military attacks with popular uprising, combining military struggle with political struggle and agitation among enemy troops . . . and winning total victory by means of a general offensive and uprising right in the 'capital city.'"[5] The strategy Giap and Le Duan described is one of people's war, a strategy to which they both professed their deep loyalties throughout their careers. It is not, however, the strategy that they used to gain their victory.

People's war, before its abandonment by the Vietnamese, was beginning to develop a venerable history. As has already been discussed, it was born out of the desperation of Mao Zedong's predicament in China upon barely surviving the Long March in 1935 in which he needed a strategy to cajole his troops into staying in the field with a credible chance of success of "men over weapons." Again, as has been mentioned, what gave Mao's strategy its power or force was that the strength to wage it came from a political mobilization of the peasant masses in support of, and actually into, his military forces.

The Vietnamese communists were quick to seize on Mao's insights and fashion their own application of people's war against the French. Indeed, though he is seldom given credit for being much of a strategist, some of Ho Chi Minh's writings on elements of a people's war strategy even precede those of Mao.[6] Ho's colleagues Truong Chinh and Vo Nguyen Giap, like Mao, discovered the political power of the peasantry early and remarked that "whenever they become conscious, are organized and have leadership, *they are an invincible force.*"[7] Armed with this peasant-based strategy, the communists alone faced World War II by deciding to oppose both the French colonial administration and the occupying Japanese army. With the defeat of the Japanese, the communist Viet Minh adopted a straight people's war strategy in what the communists call the Great Resistance War (1946–54) against the French. Both Giap and Truong Chinh, in their accounts of the war, went out of their way to demonstrate how their success was the result of a faithful adherence to Mao's formulary. Giap, in fact, went so far as to recount his triumphant siege against the isolated French bastion at Dienbienphu in terms of Mao's three phases of protracted war.[8]

Despite their "orthodox" adherence to Mao's formula, the Vietnamese did add some of their own touches that Vietnamized the nature of people's war. The principal ones came at the beginning and at the end of the war: the August Revolution in 1945 and the siege of Dienbienphu in 1954. The August Revolution was masterminded by Truong Chinh. It amounted to an overthrow of the fledgling national government of Vietnam under Emperor Bao Dai by a nationwide series of well-organized popular demonstrations or "uprisings." Notwithstanding the temporary power vacuum that permitted this (the French were not able to return to Vietnam in force until December), these uprisings struck a popular chord among the Vietnamese, who saw them as a resumption of the revered tradition of public protest, or *khoi nghia* (righteous revolt). At the end of the war, Giap rose to the French commander General Henri Navarre's bait of an isolated French garrison at Dienbienphu for a conventional set-piece battle and gambled on a go-for-broke confrontation. Fighting finally on Navarre's terms, Giap won. Putting these two touches together, the Vietnamese redefined the culminating stage of people's war as a general offensive (Dienbienphu)–general uprising (August Revolution). Mao would hardly have approved—it was "adventurism" pure and simple—but it worked in Vietnam.[9]

Despite the fall of Dienbienphu to Giap's protracted siege, the communists did not get what they considered to be the proper fruits of their victory in the Geneva Accords of July 1954. When it became clear that the southern regime of Ngo Dinh Diem was not going to collapse of its own weight, the Lao Dong party began to prepare for a renewal of armed struggle. In January 1959 the party's Central Committee made a secret decision to begin the southern revolution.[10] In March the Ho Chi Minh Trail was set up for the reinfiltration of southern Viet Minh cadres back to the south.[11] With great fanfare, the National Liberation Front was proclaimed on December 20, 1960. Somewhat more quietly, the Central Office of South Vietnam (COSVN), a command structure used by the Viet Minh, was reactivated by Hanoi in early 1961.[12] The publication of Giap's *People's War, People's Army* in 1961 made the intended strategy for this second round seem clear enough. He wrote: "The situation has now changed and the revolution has shifted to a new stage, and our People's Army is becoming a regular and modern army. If a new war breaks out, it will be a modern one. But on our side, this war always be, in nature, a people's war."[13]

A well-orchestrated campaign of terror and hit-and-run attacks in the early 1960s left the Saigon regime's Strategic Hamlet Program in shambles. The United States dispatched more and more military advisers, flooded the Army of the Republic of Vietnam (ARVN) with equipment, and stepped up its training activities. But to all these measures, the communist momentum seemed impervious. In January 1963, at the battle of Ap Bac (in the Mekong Delta), a Viet Cong battalion stood its ground against a far superior ARVN force, exposing, according the communists, the bankruptcy of the American "special war" strategy.[14] In any case, the Viet Cong had clearly demonstrated a capacity to move into Mao's second stage. Along with this mounting military pressure, political conditions for the Saigon regime began to deteriorate and, from this deterioration, nearly to disintegrate. South Vietnam's first president, Ngo Dinh Diem, was killed in a bloody coup in November 1963. Rather than breathing new life into the young republic, the coup ushered in a two-year interregnum of chaos.

Such conditions offer a veritable "land of milk and honey" for revolutionaries, and, in December 1963, the Lao Dong party's Central Committee, in effect, declared that the time was ripe to launch Mao's second stage: "Our main force should launch more mobile attacks in strategic areas of operation."[15] In 1964 the first regular contingents of the North Vietnamese army prepared to move as units to the south. They arrived in September, October, and December.[16] At the battle of Binh Gia (just southeast of Saigon) from December 27, 1964, to January 1, 1965, Viet Cong forces launched stage 2 with a vengeance by overrunning a hamlet and decimating two ARVN battalions. Throughout the spring, ARVN battalions were being chewed up with regularity and seemed incapable of offering effective resistance. In short, the country was on the verge of collapse.

Then the Americans came. If, upon arrival with ground combat troops in March 1965, the Americans seemed not to know what to do with their "timely" intervention; the complications posed by this radical change in the nature of the war gave the communists little time to gloat over American strategic dithering. The years 1965 to 1967 were hard ones. From a position from which victory seemed just around the corner of the next coup, communist forces now found themselves up against a modern conventional military machine. The burden of matching this force fell more and more directly on Hanoi, and whether Hanoi's own military machine was equal to this task came increasingly into question. Within the various ruling circles of Hanoi's military command, a debate over how to cope with the American intervention became a paramount concern.

Although it is not yet clear who precisely was associated with what position, three views were in contention. One sought to bow to the inevitable by reverting to guerrilla war and wait until the American storm had passed (a position probably held by southern guerrilla commanders). Another insisted on maintaining the pressure on the Americans through unrelenting large-scale engagements that would keep them bloodied and off balance (this is thought to have been the position of the COSVN commander Nguyen Chi Thanh). Finally, others (presumably Giap and the high command in Hanoi) bided patience while the ground was laid for a large and sudden offensive.[17] In any case, by mid- to late 1967, the time for debate was over, and a consensus built up around doing something dramatic to recapture the initiative from the Americans and get the revolution back on track. Perhaps by fusing Dienbienphu with the August Revolution (a general offensive–general uprising), the communists could unleash against the technologically sophisticated Americans an "atom bomb" of people's war.

Tet 1968: The Fraud of People's War

Few students of the Vietnam War quarrel with the notion that the Tet offensive was a major—if not the central—turning point of the war, but many still debate its significance, the intentions behind it, and its outcome. Militarily, it was a series of coordinated shock assaults on a national scale. Starting with their preliminary siege of the Khe Sanh combat Base (near the demilitarized zone) on January 21, the communists launched their country-wide attacks on the nights of January 30 and 31, which, in the first week, enveloped thirty-four province capitals, all seven autonomous cities, and sixty-four district towns. For this first wave the communists had amassed a force of some eighty-four thousand men.[18] Though by March 31 the offensive had been beaten back, the defenses of many of these towns and cities had been breached. Parts of Saigon were held by Viet Cong shock units for two weeks, and the citadel of Hue was occupied for three weeks. Even the grounds of the U.S. Embassy in Saigon had been briefly penetrated. The physical destruction was enormous; the fighting was fierce; and the casualties were heavy. The communists lost nearly sixty thousand killed and wounded, the Americans and South Vietnamese about ten thousand.[19] Fifteen Americans won the Congressional Medal of Honor.[20] A second wave called "Mini-Tet" was launched in May, but, despite another break into Saigon, it quickly fizzled. A final wave in August hardly attracted attention, and the communists themselves readily acknowledged that this last round was a failure. When it was over, official American figures showed that the communists had suffered ninety-two thousand deaths.[21]

Despite these heavy communist losses, the most obvious effect of the Tet offensive was that it marked the end of the escalation ladder for the Americans. In brief, a war effort designed to induce Hanoi to come to the conference table and desist from a forcible takeover of the south was instead blown apart by these shocking attacks ordered by Hanoi. The Pentagon, to say nothing of the American public, was obviously shaken by the offensive. An afteraction assessment by General Earle G. Wheeler, chairman of the Joint Chiefs of Staff, concluded that "it was a very near thing."[22]

In the very same report, Wheeler endorsed what he said was an add-on request by the U.S. military command in Saigon (MACV) for 206,756 men to turn the war around and exploit the military advantages the defeat of the offensive afforded.[23] Such a request clearly amounted to a proposal for a major change in strategy as well. An analysis of this request in the *Pentagon Papers* reveals a full understanding of this strategic Rubicon that would be faced in responding to it favorably: "A fork in the road had been reached. Now the alternatives stood out in stark reality. To accept General Wheeler's request for troops would mean a total U.S. military commitment to SVN [South Vietnam] — an Americanization of the war, a callup of reserve forces, vastly increased expenditures. To deny the request for troops, or to attempt to again cut it to a size which could be sustained by the thinly stretched active forces, would just as surely signify that an upper limit to the U.S. military commitment in SVN had been reached."[24]

To help him think through his response, President Lyndon Johnson called together a group of his most trusted advisers, inside and outside of the government — dubbed the Wise Men — who agonized over this request in February and March. In the meantime, the domestic American reaction to the offensive was not promising for any contemplated expansion of the war. On March 12, Senator Eugene McCarthy, the most visible critic of the war, garnered 42 percent of the vote in the New Hampshire presidential primary. Just four days later, a dithering Senator Robert Kennedy announced his candidacy for the presidency on a antiwar platform, giving the antiwar movement a luster it had previously lacked. The polls also began to show signs of a demonstrable shift away from support for the war. Although 40 percent of the respondents of a 1967 Harris Poll supported Johnson's conduct of the war, that support had plummeted to 26 percent in March 1968.[25] Surveying the military options and this domestic carnage to his presidency, the Wise Men advised Johnson to deescalate and seek a negotiated settlement. Reluctantly concurring, Johnson, in a televised address on March 31, explained to the American public his decision essentially to freeze the war by keeping the American troop commitment at largely existing levels and to order a partial bombing halt of North Vietnam as a step toward negotiation. Further, he dramatically announced that he was dropping out of the presidential campaign. In America's military victory, politically, Lyndon Johnson had had enough.

Had Johnson and his Wise Men's survey encompassed the perspective of the communists, their assessments might not have been so gloomy. Whatever the intentions of the communist leaders, the Tet offensive certainly did not go according to the plans they had given to their cadres and military commanders. Directives went out to all commands to instill in their troops a sense of ultimate sacrifice for this "decisive hour." All the long years of revolutionary activity had led up to this moment: "We only need to make a swift assault to secure the target and gain total victory."[26] Victory was to be achieved in three stages: first, a shock assault would be carried into the cities by largely local (i.e., southern) forces; second, a tide of both popular uprisings by the people and massive defections by ARVN units triggered by those assaults would bring about the collapse of the South Vietnamese government;[27] and finally, regular units of the North Vietnamese army would then enter the cities as a triumphant mopping-up force, obliging the outflanked Americans to negotiate their own withdrawal.[28]

In the event, of course, the offensive never got beyond stage 1. The responsibility for this stage, one recalls, fell heavily on locally recruited southerners. Pentagon sources estimated that in the first wave of Tet (January to March) only 20 to 25 percent of the North Vietnamese forces in the south were committed, whereas virtually all Viet Cong combatants were engaged.[29] With the failure of any popular uprisings and mass ARVN defections to develop in accordance with stage 2 plans, Hanoi decided to husband its resources. Though it used many of its own troops in the Mini-Tet launched in May, this second wave was much smaller than the first. The third wave in August reverted back to a reliance on local forces. As a standard of comparison, there were twenty-nine battalion-sized attacks in the first wave, six in the second, and only two in the third.[30] This is not to say that northerners went completely unscathed—they bore the brunt of the fighting at Khe Sanh and in Hue, for example—but it was the southern insurgent ranks that were decimated. The ultimate military result of Tet, therefore, was that responsibility for the continued prosecution of the war shifted to northerners. Before the offensive, 55 percent of the main force communist ranks were filled by northern regulars, but in April 1968 over 70 percent of these positions had to be provided by northerners.[31] Even Frances FitzGerald, a believer in the revolutionary unity of the communist side, admitted that after Tet the "southern movement was driven to become almost totally dependent on the North."[32]

If southern communists might be forgiven for wondering aloud about the asymmetry of regional sacrifice during Tet, northerners felt they had reason to fear for the fatherland itself and were therefore justified in conserving their troops for this challenge.[33] Indeed, after the siege of Khe Sanh was lifted by American troops in Operation Pegasus in April, two North Vietnamese divisions withdrew from the south altogether.[34] They feared a repeat of the Inchon landings.[35] Despite aspersions from southerners about the northern preoccupation with safeguarding "the great socialist rear," Hanoi's fears were not unfounded. American military planning (and desires) for cross-border operations into Laos and Cambodia to cut the Ho Chi Minh Trail and even to disrupt the north by amphibious landings that would slice across North Vietnam's slender southern panhandle was long-standing. In his memoir Westmoreland relates that he first proposed such cross-border operations in 1964. His staffers continued to draw contingency plans for these operations in 1966 and 1967. Throughout his account he expresses frustration over his failure to get clearance for these attacks, which he saw as a natural extension of his strategy.[36] It is clear from the *Pentagon Papers* that embedded in the request for 206,000 troops was a petition for a green light for moves into Laos, Cambodia, and North Vietnam.[37]

That a strategy to expand the war was behind the troop request was no mystery to Vietnamese communists. Indeed, a lead article in the March 10, 1968, issue of the *New York Times* outlined the essential features of the debate over the request. Though the tenor of the article was that the request was unrealistic, the article admitted that if it were granted, Vietnam could "no longer be called 'a limited war.' "[38] The communists, in fact, had been worried about such an expansion for at least as long as Westmoreland had been planning it. The key December 1963 resolution of the Lao Dong party to intervene directly in the war in the south contained the warning: "At the same time, we should be prepared to cope with the eventuality of the expansion of the war into North Viet Nam."[39] An intriguing 1984 interview with the deputy editor of the North Vietnamese journal *People's Army* in 1984 corroborates this preoccupation. The editor said that the siege of Khe Sanh was actually intended as a probe to see if the Americans would send troops north in response to attacks across the demilitarized zone. When no such attacks came, Hanoi went ahead with Tet.[40] It can also be inferred that with the huge losses, the failure to incite any response from the South Vietnamese populace, and the rumblings of a request for 206,000 troops (even when it was turned down), Hanoi got nervous and decided not to send "good money after bad" — even if it meant splitting the revolution and abandoning a strategy.

The meaning of Tet 1968 turns, then, essentially on the intentions of the communists. If their intentions were not to win on the battlefield but rather to launch a dramatic and devastating assault (sacrificing, incidentally, a fair proportion of their southern comrades) that would rekindle the antiwar movement to the point that the American will could no longer be mobilized for a response — and thereby induce American policymakers to deescalate the war — then the communists clearly could have called Tet a victory and even hailed it as another Dienbienphu. Indeed, it is in precisely these terms that an official account of the war portrays the offensive as a victory: Tet "bankrupted the aggressive will of the U.S. imperialists, and forced them to deescalate the war and negotiate with us at the Paris Conference."[41]

Though such intentions square well with subsequent events, it can be readily inferred from other communist writings and statements that, with such enormous sacrifices, they intended to achieve much more than a gradual American deescalation. If Tet were considered to have been such a victory, it is strange that as early as 1969 and 1970 there were thinly disguised public recriminations over the offensive at even the politburo level among such venerables as Truong Chinh, Le Duan, and Vo Nguyen Giap. In the middle of a eulogy to Karl Marx, for example, Truong Chinh pointedly reminded his colleagues that "our strategy is to protract the war; therefore, in tactics we should avoid unfavorable fights to the death."[42]

Since the war, some leading communist figures have become even more candid about Tet. That the war could have been won by pulling on the fickle heartstrings of American domestic moral sentiment and opinion is not something too many communists are eager to claim. Such a claim would almost vitiate all the sacrifices made on the battlefield, where, according to the strategy of people's war, the final test must come. Despite his praise for the U.S. antiwar movement, General Giap emphasized to Stanley Karnow "that the 'decisive' arena was Vietnam itself, where Communist success hinged on 'changing the balance of power in our favor.'"[43] Indeed, communist general Tran Do told Karnow, "In all honesty, we didn't achieve our objective, which was to spur uprisings throughout the south. . . . As for making an impact in the U.S., it had not been our intention — but it turned out to be a fortunate result."[44] Truong Nhu Tang, a southerner who was a founding member of the NLF and the justice minister of the NLF's Provisional Revolutionary Government, does not even concede the "fortunate result." What

Tet succeeded in doing, he points out, was to bring Richard Nixon, a far more formidable adversary than Lyndon Johnson, into the White House.[45]

For purposes of settling the question of intentions, the postmortem of Tet by Tran Van Tra, the leading southern general among the communist forces, is poignantly revealing:

> However, during Tet of 1968 we did not correctly evaluate the specific balance of forces between ourselves and the enemy. . . . In other words, we did not base ourselves on scientific calculation or a careful weighing of all factors, but in part on an illusion based on our subjective desires. For that reason, although that decision was wise, ingenious, and timely . . . , we suffered large sacrifices and losses . . . which clearly weakened us. Afterwards, we were not only unable to retain the gains we had made, but had to overcome a myriad of difficulties in 1969 and 1970 so that the revolution could stand firm in the storm. . . . If we had weighted and considered things meticulously, taken into consideration the balance of forces of the two sides . . . less blood would have been spilled . . . and the future development of the revolution would certainly have been far different.[46]

This failure to "correctly evaluate the specific balance of forces between ourselves and the enemy" because of subjective illusions of popular support produced profound mistakes in the deployment of communist forces during the offensive. The best example is Hue, but the pattern was true for Saigon as well. Ultimately, the communists sent some thirteen thousand troops into Hue, a force roughly equal to the number of defending Americans and South Vietnamese.[47] In purely military terms, of course, this was an insufficient ratio for a conventional assault. But this was a people's war, and the assault was supposed to have been sufficient to touch off a paralyzing popular revolt. As was the case everywhere in South Vietnam, nothing happened. With no political factors weighing into the balance, the city battle followed the dictates of the purely military balance-of-forces logic to communist defeat. Meanwhile, in a more straightforward military operation, the North Vietnamese threw two of their four divisions in I Corps into the siege of remote Khe Sanh.[48] Recently, they have admitted to tying down three of their divisions in this futile assault.[49] Had they hurled in just one of these divisions of ten thousand men into Hue instead, as General Creighton Abrams acknowledged one year later, "We'd still be fighting there."[50]

More than a battlefield loss, then, the Tet offensive was a failure of strategy and politics as well. Even the official account of the war drops its overweening tone of euphoria in its narration of Tet and does not resume its pro forma optimism until the Easter invasion of 1972.[51] Truong Nhu Tang, more forthrightly, describes the period from the Tet offensive to the Laotian cross-border operation of 1971 as one of hardship and of serious tension between southern and northern communists. This tension, he insists, could have been profitably exploited by Henry Kissinger had he had the local political vision to have seen it.[52]

Thus the Tet offensive was no Dienbienphu. Even Gabriel Kolko has conceded, "Never again was the Tet 1968 strategy repeated."[53] People's war, as a banner that had led the party through a generation of trials, was finished. Without it, the communists thrashed about in their jungles for two years without a strategy to guide them. Then hope trickled back as the glimmerings of another strategy began to emerge, an American one.

Success in Failure: Hanoi's American Strategy

Though it may have been terra incognita to the American public, Vietnam was no stranger to contingency planners in the Pentagon. As early as 1952 the Joint Chiefs of Staff mulled over the possibility of sending eight American combat divisions to Indochina's Red River Delta to free French forces for offensive actions against the Viet Minh. With the withdrawal of the French and the partitioning of Vietnam at the seventeenth parallel as a result of the Geneva Accords of 1954, a Korean War mind-set settled in on the military planners of the 1950s. Assuming the North Vietnamese were bent on reunifying the country, the planners identified three invasion routes that could link up for a culminating assault on the capital city of Saigon: the first, and most direct, was a drive across the demilitarized zone and down Highway 1 along the coast; the second passed through the Laotian panhandle and cut across the Central Highlands; and the third was a grand flanking movement originating in the northern Laotian mountains that would sweep down the Mekong River and follow it to Saigon. To counter such a presumed strategy, they envisioned a three-staged operation of their own. The first involved securing coastal and inland bases to establish enclaves of logistical support. The second called for U.S. forces to push inland and set up blocking positions astride these three invasion routes: the demilitarized zone, the Central Highlands, and an arc around Saigon's northern and westerly approaches. The final stage was a counteroffensive of combined airborne, amphibious, and ground attacks into North Vietnam.[54]

With the advent of the Kennedy administration in 1961, a concern for counterinsurgency began to play a role in military planning. Indeed, the Joint Chiefs of Staff had recognized the need to incorporate counterinsurgency capabilities into the South Vietnamese armed forces in March, 1960.[55] The Kennedy era ushered in a crew of enthusiasts for counterinsurgency strategy. Such men as General Maxwell Taylor, Walt Rostow, and Roger

Hilsman guaranteed that there would indeed be a debate with the more conventional planning of the military establishment. Michael Brown categorized the debate as being between two schools who conceptually viewed the nature of the war in diametrically opposite terms: the war school and the insurgency school.[56]

It was this tug-of-war that caused the initial indecision in 1965 over how to deploy forces in the impending troop buildup. Nominally, the debate was between a cautious pacification/enclave strategy versus a big-unit/aggressive strategy.[57] In fact, however, the military debate was overlaid by a welter of political concerns that were also argued out in this period.[58] By July 1965 a compromise strategy emerged, described by Westmoreland in his memoir:

Phase One: Commit those American and Allied forces necessary to "halt the losing trend" by the end of 1965.

Phase Two: "During the first half of 1966," take the offensive with American and Allied forces in "high priority areas" to destroy enemy forces and reinstitute pacification programs.

Phase Three: If the enemy persisted, he might be defeated and his forces and base areas destroyed during a period of a year to a year and a half following Phase II.[59]

This seemingly innocuous strategy contained important ramifications. In this strategy of attrition, provision was made for the incorporation of "pacification programs." Indeed, the PROVN study of the Army Staff, completed in March 1966, insisted that pacification be given top priority in the war. Although a variety of programs and missions were undertaken under the rubric of pacification, when all was said and done Westmoreland's strategy reflected the conventional-war emphasis that Andrew Krepinevich convincingly argues is at the core of the U.S. Army's ethos.[60] His strategy, furthermore, was little more than a reiteration of the first two stages of the three-staged operation envisioned by the Joint Chiefs planners in the 1950s to throw back a North Vietnamese invasion. It is obvious, at least from a military point of view, that the success of Westmoreland's strategy ultimately depended on the implementation of an unstated fourth phase, the third stage of the Joint Chiefs' contingency plan calling for airborne, amphibious, and ground attacks into North Vietnam.

Putting this tale of two strategies together (Washington's and Hanoi's), the Tet offensive meant two things. For the communists it was the end of people's war and, essentially, of any strategy built on guerrilla warfare and a politically inspired insurgency. For the American command, with the refusal of the request for 206,000 troops, it was the end of any possibility of a conventional military victory. A strategy of attrition alone, though it had just worked against the Viet Cong, had no possibility of succeeding against North Vietnam.[61] Both sides, then, saw their strategies turn to ashes. For the Americans there was little else to do but to deescalate the war, turn it over to the Vietnamese, and find some palliative way to negotiate themselves home. For the communists, however, there remained, lying around still unused as a strategy, an acting out of the very conventional invasion that had animated the fears of the Joint Chiefs planners of the 1950s.

Interestingly, Truong Nhu Tang cites the "incursion" into Cambodia by American forces in 1970 as the turning point of the war, rather than Tet. Although he concedes that the operation nearly succeeded in capturing COSVN headquarters intact and seriously disrupted operations in the south, because it decisively separated the American leadership from its own domestic support, it was "an enduring gift."[62] The domestic American uproar over Cambodia also ensured that there would be no unstated Phase 4 to worry about from MACV. With a conventional victory for the Americans impossible, ARVN's debacle in its cross-border operation into Laos in February 1971 (Lam Son 719) proved to the communists that a conventional war strategy was possible. Two of ARVN's best divisions, the First Division and the Airborne Division, were routed in their assault across the Ho Chi Minh Trail on Tchepone, Laos. Though no American ground troops were involved, there was generous American air support for the ARVN forces, but the communists were successful in spite of it.

In the Easter invasion launched on March 30, 1972, the communists tried out their new strategy. They dubbed it the Nguyen Hue campaign, not even bothering to call it a popular uprising. This time the North Vietnamese unleashed practically everything they had: fourteen divisions and twenty-six independent regiments (only a training division in Hanoi and two in Laos were held back). They also concentrated their forces for four major attacks: one across the demilitarized zone, one on Hue, another across the Central Highlands, and a final one on Saigon. An attempt to bring the invasion to the Mekong Delta ended in failure.[63] After seizing all of Quang Tri province just south of the demilitarized zone and overrunning Loc Ninh north of Saigon, the invasion everywhere else stalled. Though U.S. ground troops played little role in the Easter invasion, American air support was massive and often decisive. On September 15, South Vietnamese marines recaptured Quang Tri. With this, the invasion was over, at a reported loss of one hundred thousand North Vietnamese killed.[64]

Plainly, the communists had not got their new strategy down right. General Giap and his staff made two strategic mistakes that were magnified by the tactical errors of their field commanders. Although this time Giap did nothing like Tet and scatter his forces to the four winds, he nevertheless failed to concentrate them in a single blow. Instead, he attacked on four fronts at staggered time intervals. Further, after overrunning Quang Tri he ordered a three week pause. The effect of both these mistakes was to allow ARVN time to regroup and consolidate its positions. Tactically, the North Vietnamese committed a variety of conventional blunders showing an inability to conduct combined-arms warfare. That is, they were unable to get armored, artillery, and infantry units to work together. On the ground, particularly in the Central Highlands, they often threw away an initial superiority by mounting desperate human-wave assaults that left their ranks depleted and forced them to retire from the field.[65]

In 1975, in their lightning fifty-five-day Ho Chi Minh campaign, they got their strategy right. Though the communists were aided by disastrous mistakes of both strategy and tactics by the South Vietnamese and by the complete lack of U.S. air support that had always provided hefty margins of error in the past for both Americans and South Vietnamese, it was an epic military campaign culminating in the triumphant seizure of Saigon on April 30, 1975.[66] This time the communists concentrated their forces for one overwhelming thrust across the Central Highlands choosing, shrewdly, to aim at the lightly defended provincial capital Ban Me Thuot. The town fell on March 11, the day after it was attacked. On March 13, South Vietnamese president Nguyen Van Thieu convened a fateful meeting in which he contradictorily ordered the simultaneous withdrawal from Pleiku and Kontum and the recapture of Ban Me Thuot. Ban Me Thuot was not recaptured and the withdrawals turned into a general rout.

Determined not to give ARVN forces any chance to recover and regroup, North Vietnamese forces now struck across the demilitarized zone to link up with their comrades cutting across the Central Highlands. In a panic, Thieu ordered the Airborne Division south to Saigon just as the I Corps commander was setting it up to anchor his defense of Hue. Shorn of this division and with the commander further confused by Thieu and on whether to try to hold Hue and Danang, the north collapsed in chaos and panic. Hue fell on March 28 and Danang two days later. The linkup was now complete and the North Vietnamese steamroller inexorably advanced on Saigon, its tanks smashing through the gates of the Presidential Palace in Saigon on April 30, 1975.[67]

Thus, in losing a people's war, the communists went on to win the war itself. But in adopting a conventional war strategy, they won by a means that should have brought defeat. The United States, by contrast, won a war it thought it lost and lost by default what it could have prevented.

Conclusion: The Stolen Strategy

For the sake of lessons, three points from this tale of two strategies emerge. First, it was not at the hands of a guerrilla strategy or people's war by which the United States and South Vietnamese were beaten. Against the Americans, General Giap never got his Dienbienphu. He said that the American defeat would come when the Americans were at their strongest. The equivalent of Dienbienphu in the American war was Tet, not the final campaign in 1975. Although it was Giap who went down to defeat at Tet, the Americans mistakenly transformed for themselves the failed offensive into something of a political Dienbienphu. Nevertheless, despite this perception, Tet destroyed the whole crown of people's war. However spectacular the final 1975 campaign was, it was not a people's war.

What was missing from this last campaign was balance—both balance within the military components of the strategy and balance between the political struggle and the military forces that were supposed to be supported by it. Everywhere in Vietnamese communist writings on revolutionary people's war, a world of symmetry and balance was depicted. According to them, the three stages of the protracted war were flowing into and renewing each other. The war was being waged with equal vigor in the hills, forests, and plains. Efforts in the city and countryside were proceeding in tandem. The method of fighting by three prongs (armed struggle, civilian struggle, and proselytizing of ARVN troops) was well integrated. The three levels of forces (guerrilla support forces, guerrillas, and main force units) played mutually reinforcing rolls—all in a grand, beautifully orchestrated strategy of people's war. After Tet, this was a world of dreams.

Part of this discussion on people's war also hinges on what is meant by the term *people*. My definition of *people* has been confined to the people within the country of South Vietnam because that was the territory being fought over. Nevertheless, I recognize that there is an ambiguity here in that the North Vietnamese are, as they frequently said, "kith and kin brothers" to their South Vietnamese compatriots. Perhaps a resolution to this definitional puzzle can best come from the North Vietnamese themselves. Even though the war was orchestrated and controlled by Hanoi from the very outset of the armed struggle, maintaining the fiction that Hanoi was scrupulously adhering to the Geneva Accords while the Americans were shamefully violating them was an important plank in Hanoi's appeal to the larger, international audience. The line went thus: the state of North Viet Nam was being violated by American air attacks while its southern compatriots were waging a legitimate people's war of liberation against the puppets of American neocolonialism.

Throughout the war Hanoi depicted the southern communists as being in the vanguard of the fighting front, with the Democratic Republic of [North] Viet Nam serving as the "great socialist rear." Clearly, then, in all Hanoi's official pronouncements, local forces meant southern forces. After the Tet offensive, when the local people were plainly sitting on their hands, Hanoi insisted it had no forces in the south. Thus when its forces struck virtually alone in 1972 and triumphed alone in 1975, according to Hanoi's own definition of the term *people*, the victory—if it was a revolution at all—came by a revolution from without.

This is not to say the Americans are to be commended for being intelligent and wise. Despite their abandonment of people's war in the Tet offensive, the communists did enjoy for the duration of the war one of the key benefits of this strategy, an intelligence superiority in the field. Truong Nhu Tang has insisted that communist units always had advance warning of major allied operations.[68] Throughout the war, then, some of the fruits of a deeply rooted political structure continued. Consequently, U.S. forces in the field were unable, most of the time, to fulfill the basic mission of the infantry, "to close with and destroy the enemy." Also, even had the United States intervened successfully in 1975, there is no assurance that Hanoi would not have kept trying. Indeed, Hanoi's ability to fight the Cambodians in 1977 and 1978, take on the Chinese in sharp border battles in 1979, and continue to occupy Cambodia in the 1980s should refute any latent hopes that Hanoi would have fallen immediately to a Phase 4 attack. What this does say, however, is that switching to a conventional war strategy left the internal political issues that fueled the defeated people's war unresolved by both sides, not just by the Americans and South Vietnamese.

Second, the Vietnam War was a frustrating antinomy in that it was simultaneously a conventional war and a guerrilla insurgency. Compared to other insurgencies of the postwar era, then, it is more unique than it is general in its application.[69] As such, it was not wrong for American military planners or for General Westmoreland to concentrate on the conventional challenge first. Larry Cable has pointed out that in Korea the United States faced both a conventional war and a guerrilla war and when it concentrated on the conventional war the guerrilla war evaporated with the expulsion of the conventional North Korean army.[70] In Vietnam, the guerrillas largely disappeared after they rose to mount a conventional attack, and the war had then to be won by the communists in conventional, almost American, terms.

In fine, what is clear about Tet is that it was the end of a revolution. Afterward, the Vietnam War became analogous to the conventional Korean War that earlier served so inappropriately as a guide to fighting what until Tet was a genuine revolution. The irony of the Vietnam War is that for the Americans, in going into the war, the dominant Korean War analogy was mostly wrong. After Tet, it was mostly right. The U.S. judgment, however, became so "terrorized" by Tet's revolutionary fury that it failed to see how decisively this revolution had just been crushed. Instead, the Americans became so preoccupied by their own inadequacies in dealing with this revolution (which, except at very low levels, had ceased to exist) that the North Vietnamese were able to pick up virtually unnoticed the strategy of a purely North Korean–style military offensive. The fallout of this misperception, or myopic inward-looking agonizing, by the American leadership was that just as Hanoi picked up this conventional weapon in 1972 and again in 1975, the superior American military sword was mostly withdrawn in 1972 and completely gone in 1975.

This is emphatically not to say we could have won the war or solved Vietnam's legitimacy crisis by staying on, but it is hard, at least on the pivotal question of Tet and of military strategy, to avoid expressing a kindred nostalgic sentiment over this American misprision with the lamentations of the famous T. E. Lawrence over his English generals: "The men were often gallant fighters, but their generals as often gave away in stupidity what they had gained in ignorance."[71]

As for the communists, this discussion on strategy can conclude on a classical note by agreeing with the venerable Chinese strategist Sun Tzu's dictum: "What is of supreme importance in war is to attack the enemy's strategy."[72] To this eternal verity General Giap can legitimately add the postscript that it is doubly clever to steal it.

The implicit argument in this appendix is that the Vietnam War can be better explained by strategy because the struggle for political legitimacy, all around, was suspended by the failure of revolution in the Tet offensive. But this explanation on the basis of strategy has also run into an ambush. However much this skillful theft may account for the communist victory in the particular instance of Vietnam, a stolen strategy does not an alternative explanation make. Hence, finally, in this confusion of strategy and suspension of the political struggle for legitimacy, Vietnam is too different and difficult a case for generalizable lessons by itself under any explanation — except one that puts it in a set of analytical, comparative cases.

Appendix 3

ASSUMPTIONS, THEMATIC QUESTIONS, AND PROPOSITIONS

The lessons presented in Chapter 11 and the Conclusion are derived from the following assumptions, thematic questions, and propositions.

Assumptions

- Vietnam was wrapped up in a historical process of societies inflicted with insurgencies as they struggled to modernize.
- Such a definitional struggle represented a general crisis of individual national political legitimacy.
- Western powers were more likely to intervene in Marxist people's war insurgencies because their universalist claims threatened the global balance of power between the Eastern and Western blocs.
- The outcome of these insurgencies, despite all this intervention, still turned on the relative success earned by the two sides in this legitimacy crisis.
- The outcomes to these insurgencies were neither inevitable nor predetermined.
- The true basis for comparison of the Vietnam War with its companion cases is the resolution of their legitimacy crises rather than the outcome of the insurgencies themselves.

Thematic Questions and Propositions

1. What is the historical setting out of which the insurgency developed and from which the country's specific definition of political legitimacy arose?
Propositions:
1.1: I assert a historical flow wherein all core cases experienced a definitional challenge of legitimacy in the interwar years. This definitional crisis suffered a further shock in World War II that touched off insurgencies both during and after the war.
1.2: Because such a "beneficial" future shock is unlikely on a global scale, the chances for a new outbreak of insurgencies such as occurred after World War II are dim.

2. Within my analytical framework of legitimacy, how did the incumbents and insurgents fare competitively?
The summary in Chapter 3 provides indicators of legitimacy at three levels of support (interest, opportunity, and belief) as well as benchmarks of insurgent success (critical mass, crossover point, and breakout).
Proposition:
2.1: Though most activity in an insurgency takes place at the opportunity level and its institutional contest for reforms of societal access (land reform) and political participation (elections), the resolution of an insurgency lies more critically at the level of belief.

3. How closely did the revolutionary insurgents follow a Marxist people's war strategy and what was the effect of this strategy on their claims to both revolutionary and national legitimacy?
Propositions:
3.1: The Marxist people's war is the most promising strategy in response to an insurgent condition because popular mobilization is central to this strategy.
3.2: For such a strategy of mobilization to be successful, it must be couched in terms of the host society's particular precepts of national legitimacy.
3.3: Revolutionary unity is vital to the success of an insurgency, and though this will be forged or frayed at the opportunity level of cadre organization, it can be fully achieved only at the belief level of revolutionary legitimacy.

4. What was the impact of the Western intervention on this legitimacy crisis in terms of its enhancement or debilitation of its client's claim to legitimacy?
This is the key effect, but there are also the "offstage" effects of the inter-

vention's impact both on the intervenor's international position and on its own domestic legitimacy.

Propositions:

4.1: Though the visible efforts of an intervention will be at the interest and opportunity levels, the primary effect will be at the belief level.

4.2: The critical level of intervention is the dispatching of ground combat troops.

5. *What are the contingencies to these cases regarding their asymmetries, errors, and reversibilities?*

Propositions:

5.1: Asymmetries between incumbents and insurgents tend to seesaw back and forth.

5.1a: First, because it is illegal and because it requires killing, it is difficult to get an insurgency off the ground (achieve a critical mass).

5.1b: Second, once an insurgency becomes a going concern, most of the advantages switch to the insurgents (crossover points).

5.1c: Third, once an insurgency reaches the point at which belief-level appeals are important to its final success, the Marxist connections of a people's war can pose problems of national legitimacy for the insurgents (breakout).

5.2: Without errors and reversibilities, results could have been different. Most cases contained errors on one side or the other (as well as unusually shrewd moves) that were not inevitable occurrences.

5.2a: Insurgencies can be reversed by a foreign intervention.

5.2b: Insurgencies can be undercut by reforms.

5.2c: Charismatic leadership and organizational performance alone might carry an insurgency or counterinsurgency campaign to victory and bypass the society's festering legitimacy crisis.

5.2d: If this leadership and performance are not rooted in the institutional structure and belief system of their society, however, they will exhibit Hannibalism. That is, the effects will not be long-lasting.

6. *What are the comparisons of each case with Vietnam?*

The focus of comparisons is on the ways country-specific definitions of legitimacy have affected the impact of both Western intervention and revolutionary strategy. The point is that some will be like Vietnam in these effects and others will be different.

Proposition:

6.1: With respect to the intersection of insurgency and intervention, Vietnam is not the only or even the crucial case from which lessons can be derived.

NOTES

Introduction

1. Hugh Sidey, "The Presidency: Ending a Personal War," *Time*, May 12, 1975, p. 28.

2. "Weinberger Outlines Tests for Using Troops," *Raleigh* (N.C.) *News and Observer*, November 29, 1984, p. 6A.

3. Maureen Dowd, "A Renewed Bush Confronts Old Problems," *Raleigh* (N.C.) *News and Observer*, March 2, 1991, p. 1A.

4. "Retreating Iraqi Tanks Destroyed," *Raleigh* (N.C.) *News and Observer*, March 3, 1991, p. 10A.

5. Daniel Ellsberg, *Papers on the War* (New York: Simon and Schuster, 1972), p. 9.

6. William E. Connolly, *The Terms of Political Discourse*, 2d ed. (Princeton, N.J.: Princeton University Press, 1983), pp. 14–17, 97, 107–16.

7. Eqbal Ahmad, "Revolutionary War and Counter-Insurgency," *Journal of International Affairs* 25 (1970): 5.

8. Edward H. Carr, *What Is History?* (New York: Knopf, 1962), p. 80.

9. Theda Skocpol, *States and Social Revolutions* (Cambridge, U.K.: Cambridge University Press, 1979), pp. 19–24.

Chapter One

1. Ernest R. May, *"Lessons" of the Past: The Use and Misuse of History in American Foreign Policy* (New York: Oxford University Press, 1973), pp. 127–41.

2. Robert Jervis, *Perception and Misperception in International Politics* (Princeton, N.J.: Princeton University Press, 1976), pp. 281–82.

3. To support this contention of "universal particularism" for legitimacy, Reinhard Bendix has made the same point for the companion concept of nationalism: "England, France, Germany, Japan, Russia, and China have participated in a worldwide movement of nationalism and of government by popular mandate, though each country has done so in its own way. My account attempts to show that nationalism has become a universal condition . . . [but] that the problems faced by each modernizing country were largely unique." See his *Kings or People: Power and the Mandate to Rule* (Berkeley: University of California Press, 1978), p. 5. As for nationalism, so also for legitimacy.

4. Alan C. Isaak, *Scope and Methods of Political Science: An Introduction to the Methodology of Political Inquiry* (Homewood, Ill.: Dorsey Press, 1969), pp. 62–64.

5. Although Portugal, as a NATO ally, did receive American military assistance, this was in fulfillment of NATO treaty arrangements officially unrelated to the prosecution of the wars in Africa. The Portuguese, however, did employ this aid in behalf of their efforts in the three colonies.

6. Harry Eckstein, "Case Study and Theory in Political Science," in *Handbook of Political Science*, ed. Fred I. Greenstein and Nelson W. Polsby (Reading, Mass.: Addison-Wesley, 1975), 7:133.

7. The theoretical construction of this book's edifice for drawing lessons by selecting cases, choosing questions, and erecting frameworks owes a deep debt to two key works by Alexander George and Harry Eckstein. Specifically, for settling on common questions, see Alexander L. George, "Case Studies and Theory Development: The Method of Structured, Focused Comparison," in *Diplomacy: New Approaches in History, Theory, and Policy*, ed. Paul Gordon Lauren (New York: Free Press, 1979), pp. 54–57; and Eckstein, "Case Study and Theory," pp. 90–92.

8. More specifically, by *Verstehen* Weber meant "understanding the meaning of actions and interactions from the members' own point of view." To Harry Eckstein, this is the chief contribution of the case study method ("Case Study and theory," p. 81).

9. With the presupposition that an insurgency is a function of a legitimacy crisis embedded in the political norms and institutional arrangements of a society, this book certainly falls within the structuralist approach set forth by Theda Skocpol. This book, however, views this structure, in the grip of an insurgency, to be in a fluid condition. As a central challenge to power and rule, the very definition of legitimacy is undergoing either vital change or vehement revalidation. Hence this study supports the point of Chalmers Johnson that revolutions and insurgencies offer real opportunities for reversal, whether domestically or from foreign intervention. Thus the structure of legitimacy depicted in this book case by case imposes no deterministic outcomes to the course of events. This work, therefore, concurs with the rational choice theorist James De Nardo's emphasis on strategy as a key determinant of a revolutionary or repressive outcome to protest. My major contention on strategy, both revolutionary and counterinsurgent, is that its most important effect for success or failure is on the basic political legitimacy crisis that the insurgency represents. See Theda Skocpol, *States and Social Revolutions* (Cambridge, U.K.: Cambridge University Press, 1979), pp. 3–43; Chalmers A. Johnson, *Revolutionary Change*, 2d ed. (Berkeley: University of California Press, 1982), pp. 185–94; and James De Nardo, *Power in Numbers: The Political Strategy of Protest and Rebellion* (Princeton, N.J.: Princeton University Press, 1985), p. 12.

Chapter Two

1. Harry Eckstein, *Support for Regimes: Theories and Tests*, Research Monograph 44 (Princeton, N.J.: Center for International Studies, Princeton University, 1979), p. 3.

2. Max Weber, *Basic Concepts in Sociology*, trans. and intro. by H. P. Secher (Secaucus, N.J.: Citadel Press, 1962), pp. 75–83; and T. H. Rigby and Ferenc Fehér, eds., *Political Legitimation in Communist States* (New York: St. Martin's Press, 1982), p. 1.

3. For a further explanation of such an "exchange" view of legitimacy, see Reinhard Bendix, *Kings or People: Power and the Mandate to Rule* (Berkeley: University of California Press, 1978), p. 60.

4. Lucian W. Pye, *Asian Power and Politics: The Cultural Dimensions of Authority* (Cambridge, Mass.: Harvard University Press, 1985), pp. 283–84.

5. H. L. Nieburg, "Violence, Law, and the Social Process," *American Behavioral Scientist* 11 (March–April, 1968): 19. Although I have defined them differently, I am indebted to David Easton for the differentiation of legitimacy into separate levels of support. See his *A Systems Analysis of Political Life* (New York: Wiley, 1965), pp. 278–89; and his later "A Re-Assessment of the concept of Political Support," *British Journal of Political Science* 5 (October 1975): 435–58.

6. Emile Durkheim, *The Division of Labor in Society*, trans. George Simpson (New York: Free Press, 1933), p. 228.

7. This role of legitimacy as a moral factor in the power of rule is cogently expressed by Reinhard Bendix: "Power needs ideas and legitimation the way a conventional bank needs investment policies and the confidence of its depositors." See his *Kings or People*, p. 16.

8. Bard E. O'Neill et al., eds., *Insurgency in the Modern World* (Boulder, Colo.: Westview Press, 1980), p. 1; and Hedley Bull, *The Anarchical Society: A Study of Order in World Politics* (New York: Columbia University Press, 1977), p. 57.

9. George Sawyer Petee, *The Process of Revolution* (New York: Harper and Brothers, 1938), p. 100. Phillips quoted by Theda Skocpol, *States and Social Revolutions* (Cambridge, U.K.: Cambridge University Press, 1979), p. 17.

10. "'Left Wing' Communism: An Infantile Disorder" (1920), in *Lenin Reader*, ed. and comp. Stefan T. Possony (Chicago: Henry Regenery, 1966), p. 436.

11. Samuel P. Huntington, *Political Order in Changing Societies* (New Haven, Conn.: Yale University Press, 1968), pp. 144–45.

12. O'Neill et al., eds., *Insurgency in the Modern World*, pp. 26–34.

13. Chalmers A. Johnson, *Revolutionary Change*, 2d ed. (Stanford: Stanford University Press, 1982), p. 150. That a legitimacy crisis can develop into a revolution is precisely what revolutionaries attempt to engineer through various strategies, according to James De Nardo. Thus the unresponsiveness of a regime is critical for crossing over a revolutionary threshold, just as its responsiveness is crucial to the attempts of reformers to thwart this threshold. As De Nardo has observed: "According to Marx, then, the ruination of the proletariat is the pathway to its salvation." See his *Power in Numbers: The Political Strategy of Protest and Rebellion* (Princeton, N.J.: Princeton University Press, 1985), pp. 106–23, quote on p. 113.

14. D. Michael Shafer, *Deadly Paradigms: The Failure of U.S. Counterinsurgency Policy* (Princeton, N.J.: Princeton University Press, 1988), pp. 280–81; Herbert K. Tillema, *Appeal to Force: American Military Intervention in the Era of Containment* (New York: Thomas Y. Crowell, 1973), p. 196; James N. Rosenau, ed., *International Aspects of Civil Strife* (Princeton, N.J.: Princeton University Press, 1964), p. 91.

15. See István Kende, "Twenty-five Years of Local Wars," *Journal of Peace Research* 8 (March 1971): 12, 22; also Kende, "Wars of Ten Years (1967–1976)," *Journal of Peace Research* 15 (September 1978): 227; and Evan Luard, *Conflict and Peace in the International System* (Boston: Little, Brown, 1968), pp. 142–43.

16. Lucian Pye has cogently mapped out the overwhelming and asymmetric difficulties for fledgling Third World regimes in maintaining their usual governmental functions while at the same time developing the unusual measures necessary to cope with an insurgency. See his "The Roots of Insurgency and the Commencement of

Rebellions," in *Internal War*, ed. Harry Eckstein (New York: Free Press, 1964), pp. 157–79.

17. Ibid., p. 160.

18. Two good recent works on this generally good British performance are Ian F. W. Beckett and John Pimlott, eds., *Armed Forces and Modern Counterinsurgency* (London: Croom Helm, 1985); and Lawrence James, *Imperial Rearguard: Wars of Empire, 1919–1985* (London: Brassey's Defense Publishers, 1988).

19. Katherine C. Chorley, *Armies and the Art of Revolution* (London: Faber and Faber, 1943), p. 23; Max G. Manwarning, "Toward an Understanding of Insurgent Warfare," *Military Review* 68 (January 1988): 33–34.

20. E. Victor Wolfenstein, *The Revolutionary Personality: Lenin, Trotsky, Gandhi* (Princeton, N.J.: Princeton University Press, 1971). For a cogent discussion of Max Weber's types of legitimacy, especially of charismatic authority, see Reinhard Bendix, ed., *State and Society: A Reader in Comparative Political Sociology* (Berkeley: University of California Press, 1968), pp. 616–20. Mostafa Rejai with Kay Phillips, *Leaders of Revolution* (Beverly Hills: Sage, 1979), pp. 59–60. The personality structure components of leadership and the social and political organizations such leaders create first to attract and then to channel followers into their orbit is perhaps best laid out by James Downton in his *Rebel Leadership: Commitment and Charisma in the Revolutionary Process* (New York: Free Press, 1973), pp. 22–80. Andrew Molnar also has provided a clear exposition of this subject. See Andrew R. Molnar, ed., *Human Factors: Considerations of Undergrounds in Insurgencies* (Washington, D.C.: American University Special Operations Research Office, 1965), pp. 71–87.

21. Taken from his "Urgent Tasks of Our Movement" (1900) and cited by Possony, *Lenin Reader*, p. 313.

22. Douglas Pike, *Viet Cong: The Organization and Techniques of the National Liberation Front of South Vietnam* (Cambridge, Mass.: Massachusetts Institute of Technology Press, 1966). The work of William R. Andrews, however, is equally good. See his *The Village War: Vietnamese Communist Revolutionary Activities in Dinh Tuong Province, 1960–1964* (Columbia: University of Missouri Press, 1973).

23. John Walton, *Reluctant Rebels: Comparative Studies of Revolution and Underdevelopment* (New York: Columbia University Press, 1984), p. 5.

24. Otto Heilbrun, *Partisan Warfare* (London: George Allen & Unwin, 1962), pp. 9, 22, 186; Lawrence quoted by Stanley Weintraub and Rodelle Weintraub, eds., *Evolution of a Revolt: Early Postwar Writings of T. E. Lawrence* (University Park: Pennsylvania State University Press, 1968), p. 106. For an excellent, concise portrayal of Lawrence's accomplishments, see Major Oliver B. Patton, "Colonel T. E. Lawrence of Arabia," *Military Review* 34 (October 1954): 18–30.

25. Lucian W. Pye, *Guerrilla Communism in Malaya* (Princeton, N.J.: Princeton University Press, 1956), pp. 128–39.

26. John Donnell, "Viet Cong Motivation and Morale in 1964: A Preliminary Report" (Santa Monica, Calif.: Rand Corp., RM-4507/3-ISA, March 1965).

27. Dolf Sternberger, "Legitimacy," in *International Encyclopedia of the Social Sciences*, gen. ed. David L. Sills, Vol. 9 (New York: Crowell Collier and Macmillan, 1968), p. 244; Plutarch, *The Lives of the Noble Grecians and Romans*, trans. John Dryden and rev. Arthur Hugh Clough (New York: Modern Library, n.d. [ca. 1940s]), pp. 97–116.

28. Sternberger, "Legitimacy," pp. 244–45.

29. See Michael Walzer, *Regicide and Revolution* (Cambridge, U.K.: Cambridge University Press, 1974), cited by Shmuel Noah Eisenstadt, *Revolution and the Transformation of Societies: A Comparative Study of Civilizations* (New York: Free Press, 1978), p. 174.

30. Hans Kohn identified these British principles as the supremacy of the law over the king, the preponderance of parliament in lawmaking, the impartiality of justice, the security of individual rights, the freedom of expression and a free press, and religious tolerance. See his *Nationalism: Its Meaning and History* (Princeton, N.J.: D. Van Nostrand, 1955), p. 17. Hannah Arendt distinguished between the French Revolution's absolutist goal of freedom and the American Revolution's more moderate aim of liberation, with the latter producing a more enduring set of democratic political institutions. See her *On Revolution* (New York: Viking Press, 1963), pp. 22–26, 49–52, 120, 142–44, 153.

31. In Bendix, *State and Society*, p. 194.

32. Arthur J. Vidich and Ronald M. Glassman, eds., *Conflict and Control: Challenge to Legitimacy of Modern Governments* (Berkeley: Sage, 1979), p. 18. The concept itself, of course, long predates Talleyrand. It had received very sophisticated discussion by both the Greeks and Romans. The latter divided it into *legitimum imperium* (international) and *legitima potesta* (domestic). See Rigby and Fehér, eds., *Political Legitimation in Communist States*, p. 19.

33. Stephen Holmes, "Two Concepts of Legitimacy: France after the Revolution," *Political Theory* 10 (May 1982): 165, 181–82; and Melvin Richter, "Toward a Concept of Political Illegitimacy: Bonapartist Dictatorship and Democratic Legitimacy," *Political Theory* 10 (May 1982): 187–88, 210.

34. H. H. Gerth and C. Wright Mills, trans. and eds., *From Max Weber: Essays in Sociology* (New York: Oxford University Press, 1958), pp. 295–301; Walt W. Rostow, *The Stages of Economic Growth: A Non-Communist Manifesto* (Cambridge, U.K.: Cambridge University Press, 1960); A. F. K. Organski, *The Strategies of Political Development* (New York: Knopf, 1965); and William Kornhauser, "Rebellion and Political Development," in *Internal War*, ed. Eckstein, pp. 142–56.

35. Basil Davidson, *Which Way Africa? The Search for a New Society* (Baltimore: Penguin Books, 1964) pp. 22–23.

36. A. L. Basham, *The Wonder That Was India*, 3d ed. (London: Sidgwick and Jackson, 1967), pp. 113–15.

37. By far the most comprehensive discussion of the political concepts of Confucianism is that of Joseph Levenson, *Confucian China and Its Modern Fate*, vols. 1–3 (Berkeley: University of California Press, 1958–65).

38. Lucian Pye presents these dilemmas well in his *Asian Power and Politics*, pp. 320–46.

39. S. Neil MacFarlane, *Superpower Rivalry and Third World Radicalism: The Idea of National Liberation* (Baltimore: Johns Hopkins University Press, 1985), pp. 44–61.

40. [George F. Kennan], "X" "The Sources of Soviet Conduct," *Foreign Affairs* 25 (July 1947): 566–82. The sharpest criticism of Kennan came from Walter Lippmann, who wrote a series of *New York Herald Tribune* articles in 1947. He observed: "Yet the genius of American military power does not lie in holding positions indefinitely. That requires a massive patience by great hordes of docile people. American military

power is distinguished by its mobility, its speed, its range and its offensive striking force. It is, therefore, not an efficient instrument for a diplomatic policy of containment. . . . The Americans would themselves probably by frustrated by Mr. X's policy long before the Russians were." See his "The Cold War," *Foreign Affairs* 65 (Spring 1987): 875. Ironically, Lippmann has been proven to be wrong in Europe but perhaps on the mark in the Third World.

41. Akira Iriye, *The Cold War in Asia: A Historical Introduction* (Englewood Cliffs, N.J.: Prentice-Hall, 1974), pp. 119–30; George F. Kennan, *American Diplomacy*, expanded ed. (Chicago: University of Chicago Press, 1984), p. 53; and John Lewis Gaddis, *Strategies of Containment: A Critical Appraisal of Postwar American National Security Policy* (Oxford, U.K.: Oxford University Press, 1982), p. 41.

42. U.S., Department of State, "National Security Affairs; Foreign Economic Policy," in *Foreign Relations of the U.S., 1950* (Washington, D.C.: U.S. Government Printing Office, 1977), 1:240.

43. Roger Hilsman, "Two American Counter-strategies to Guerrilla Warfare: The Case of Vietnam," in *Crisis in China*, ed. Tang Tsou, vol. 2, *China's Policies in Asia and America's Alternatives* (Chicago: University of Chicago Press, 1968), pp. 269–70.

44. U.S. Army, Chief Office of Information, *Special Warfare, U.S. Army* (Washington, D.C.: U.S. Government Printing Office, 1962), p. 22.

45. Russell H. Fifield, *Southeast Asia in United States Policy* (New York: Frederick A. Praeger, 1963), pp. 10, 17–18; and Evelyn Colbert, *Southeast Asia in International Politics, 1941–1956* (Ithaca, N.Y.: Cornell University Press, 1977), p. 19.

46. Gaddis, *Strategies of Containment*, pp. ix, 28–30, 41, 91. In place of Gaddis's confusing terms *symmetrical* and *asymmetrical* containment, I have substituted *psychological* for the former and *geopolitical* for the latter.

47. For a good overview of the strengths and weaknesses of the relations of the Soviet Union with the Third World, see Roger Kanet, *The Soviet Union and the Developing Nations* (Baltimore: Johns Hopkins University Press, 1974). More recent accounts of Soviet dilemmas in the Third World are those of Jerry F. Hough, *The Struggle for the Third World: Soviet Debates and American Options* (Washington, D.C.: Brookings Institution, 1986); and Carol R. Saivetz and Sylvia Woodly, *Soviet-Third World Relations* (Boulder, Colo.: Westview Press, 1985).

48. David P. Mozingo, "Containment in Asia Reconsidered," *World Politics* 19 (April 1967): 365.

49. A very thorough analysis of this split, which he terms as one between "bolsterers" and "reformers," can be found in Douglas J. Macdonald, *Adventures in Chaos: American Intervention for Reform in the Third World* (Cambridge, Mass.: Harvard University Press, 1992). In Vietnam, Patrick Hatcher has described this split as one between Whigs and Tories. See his *The Suicide of an Elite: American Internationalists and Vietnam* (Stanford: Stanford University Press, 1990), pp. 3–31.

50. A larger treatise of this basic American preference for "safe" order over potentially destabilizing reform is Robert Packenham's *Liberal America and the Third World* (Princeton, N.J.: Princeton University Press, 1973).

51. Three useful works that both describe and point out the failure of these theories in Vietnam are Paul Kattenburg, *The Vietnam Trauma in American Foreign Policy, 1945–1975* (New Brunswick, N.J.: Transaction Books, 1976), pp. 69–106; Michael Nacht, "The War in Vietnam: The Influence of Concepts on Policy," Arms

Control and International Security Working Paper 26 (Los Angeles: Center for International and Strategic Affairs, University of California, 1980); and Wallace J. Thies, *When Governments Collide: Coercion and Diplomacy in the Vietnam Conflict, 1964–1968* (Berkeley: University of California Press, 1980), pp. 1–15, 375–420.

52. In addition to the writings of such noteworthy practitioners as Mao Zedong, Lin Biao, Ho Chi Minh, Vo Nguyen Giap, and Truong Chinh, three works by Chalmers Johnson give a good overview of the subject. His *Peasant Nationalism and Communist Power* (Stanford: Stanford University Press, 1962) provides an insightful account of the historical origins of Mao's strategy of people's war; "The Third Generation of Guerrilla Warfare," *Asian Survey* 8 (June 1969): 435–37, describes the adaptation of Mao's theory to the situation the Vietnamese communists confronted against the Americans; and, in a foreshadowing of one of this book's basic themes, his *Autopsy on People's War* (Berkeley: University of California Press, 1973) argues that, to the Chinese anyway, the utility of this strategy has ended. A more sympathetic analysis of people's war is that J. L. S. Girling, *People's War: Conditions and Consequences in China and Southeast Asia* (New York: Praeger, 1969). I have also traced the odyssey of people's war from China to Vietnam and discussed the adaptations and eventual mutations the Vietnamese subjected this strategy to in fighting the Americans. See *The War Everyone Lost—and Won: America's Intervention in Viet Nam's Twin Struggles*, rev. ed. (Washington, D.C.: Congressional Quarterly Press, 1993), pp. 138–58.

53. Mao's political discovery of the revolutionary potential of the peasantry is eloquently expressed in his famous pamphlet *Report on an Investigation of the Peasant Movement in Hunan* (1927; rprt. Peking: Foreign Languages Press, 1967). A similar discovery for the Vietnamese communists was made by Truong Chinh and Vo Nguyen Giap in their "The Peasant Question (1937–1938)," trans. and intro. Christine Pelzer White, Southeast Asia Program, Data Paper 94 (Ithaca, N.Y.: Cornell University, 1974).

Chapter Three

1. David E. Apter, *Rethinking Development: Modernization, Dependency, and Post Modern Politics* (Newbury Park, Calif.: Sage, 1987), p. 6.

2. As just two examples, regarding the variable of authority, he saw development as moving from universal (for the traditional) to specific sources (for the modern). For the variable of institutional structures or patterns, Parsons described a movement from diffuse (traditional) to specific arrangements (modern), the latter as an inevitable by-product of the industrial revolution's division of labor. An early presentation of his pattern-variable scheme can be found in Talcott Parsons, *The Social System* (Glencoe, Ill.: Free Press, 1951), pp. 58–67. He later refined this with a full description of his five dilemmas of a social system and their attendant sets of dichotomous pattern variables. See Talcott Parsons and Edward A. Shils, eds., *Toward a General Theory of Action* (Cambridge, Mass.: Harvard University Press, 1959), pp. 77–90.

3. Though Rostow actually set forth five stages of economic development (traditional, preconditional, the takeoff, the drive to maturity, and the age of high mass consumption), for the lesser developed world, only three of these were impor-

tant: the preconditions for takeoff, the takeoff itself, and a general state in which growth was sustained. See Walt W. Rostow, *The Strategies of Economic Growth: A Non-Communist Manifesto*, 2d ed. (Cambridge, U.K.: Cambridge University Press, 1960), pp. 4–11. For a description of this theoretic shift through the early 1970s, see Samuel P. Huntington, "The Change to Change: Modernization, Development, and Politics," *Comparative Politics* 3 (April 1971): 283–322.

4. Fred Warren Riggs, *Administration in Developing Countries: The Theory of Prismatic Society* (Boston: Houghton Mifflin, 1964), pp. 27–31.

5. In Huntington's words: "There may well be violence without development; but there is virtually no development without violence." See his "Civil Violence and the Process of Development," *Adelphi Papers* 83 (1971): 3.

6. Ivo K. Feirabend, Rosalind L. Feirabend, and Betty A. Nesvold, "Social Change and Political Violence: Cross-National Patterns," in *Violence in America: Historical and Comparative Perspectives, a Report Submitted to the National Commission on the Causes and Prevention of Violence*, ed. Hugh Davis Graham and Ted Robert Gurr (New York: Frederick A. Praeger, 1969), pp. 684–85; and Douglas A. Hibbs, Jr., *Mass Political Violence: A Cross-National Causal Analysis* (New York: Wiley, 1973), pp. 28, 31.

7. Albert O. Hirschman, *The Strategy of Economic Development* (New Haven, Conn.: Yale University Press, 1958), pp. 62–75, 98–103.

8. Indeed, it is Joel Migdal's observation that the key feature of politics in weak states of the Third World is "struggles over who has the right and ability to make the countless rules that guide people's social behavior." See Joel S. Migdal, "Strong States, Weak States," in *Understanding Political Development*, ed. Myron Weiner and Samuel P. Huntington (Boston: Little, Brown, 1987), p. 397. Margaret Levi's ambitious work in explaining political rule in terms of rational choice theory deliberately steers clear of situations in which these rules are unclear, which, if Migdal is correct, would include most of the politics of the Third World. In discussing compliance, for example, she admits that her analysis pertains only to normal "in period" times, rather than moments of transition when a society faces constitutional choices and confrontations over these rules. See Levi, *Of Rule and Revenue* (Berkeley: University of California Press, 1988), p. 48. Hence rational choice theory appears to work only when everyone in a society agrees on what the rules are, the very opposite condition of an insurgency. Rational choice theory is discussed further in Appendix 1.

9. Sidney Verba and Gabriel Almond, "National Revolutions and Political Commitment," in *Internal War: Problems and Approaches*, ed. Harry Eckstein (New York: Free Press, 1964), pp. 206–7. Robert H. Bates, a rational choice critic of development theory, prefers a more fine-grained explanation of development and its increasing participation. He commends a "collective choice" approach that would combine micro and macro theory into an explanation that would focus on the behavior of key groups within institutions, parties, unions, and sectors of society. See Bates, "Agrarian Politics," in *Understanding Political Development*, ed. Weiner and Huntington, pp. 181–85. Indeed, the framework of this chapter seeks to outline the behavioral effects of both individual and group actions.

10. Joseph Strayer, "The Historical Experience of Nation-Building in Europe," in *Nation-Building*, ed. Karl Deutsch and W. J. Foltz (New York: Atherton Press, 1963), p. 25; Theda Skocpol, *States and Social Revolutions* (Cambridge, U.K.: Cambridge

University Press, 1979), pp. 27–32. This point, of course, has received fuller amplification in the writings of Robert Bates and Margaret Levi. See Bates, *Markets and States in Tropical Africa: The Political Basis of Agricultural Policies* (Berkeley: University of California Press, 1981), pp. 119–32; and Levi, *Of Rule and Revenue*, pp. 2–3.

11. This is merely a restatement, from the flip side, of Gunnar Myrdal's dilemma of the "soft state," which tries to promote growth but expects nothing from its citizenry by way of discipline and sacrifice. See Myrdal, *Asian Drama: An Inquiry into the Poverty of Nations* (New York: Pantheon Books, 1968), 2:895–900.

12. Arthur J. Vidich and Ronald M. Glassman, eds., *Conflict and Control: Challenge to Legitimacy of Modern Governments* (Berkeley: Sage, 1979), p. 12.

13. Samuel P. Huntington, *Political Order in Changing Societies* (New Haven, Conn.: Yale University Press, 1968), p. 196.

14. Margaret Levi's reference to the state as a predatory organization is particularly apt here. See Levi, *Of Rule and Revenue*, p. 3. Indeed, Robert Bates, in his survey of the state manipulation of agricultural markets in Africa, has made the remarkable and counterintuitive discovery (in terms of development theory) that such manipulation has had the deliberate effect of demobilizing the African peasantry. See Bates, *Markets and States in Tropical Africa*, pp. 108–13.

15. Apter, *Rethinking Development*, pp. 32–33.

16. Huntington, *Political Order in Changing Societies*, pp. 6, 86.

17. Andrew R. Molnar, ed., *Human Factors: Considerations of Undergrounds in Insurgencies* (Washington, D.C.: American University Special Operations Research Office, 1965), pp. 71–89.

18. Ernest Gellner, *Nations and Nationalism* (Ithaca, N.Y.: Cornell University Press, 1983), p. 1.

19. Riggs, *Prismatic Society*, pp. 164–73.

20. This world is described well both by George Foster and Robert Redfield in *Peasant Society: A Reader*, ed. Jack W. Potter, Mary N. Diaz, and George M. Foster (Boston: Little, Brown, 1967), pp. 2–15, 25–35, 300–323.

21. Henry A. Landsberger, ed., *Rural Protest: Peasant Movements and Social Change* (London: Macmillan, 1973), p. 16.

22. George M. Foster, "Peasant Society and the Image of Limited Good," in *Peasant Society*, ed. Potter, Diaz, and Foster, pp. 300, 304. This is the essence of Harry Eckstein's "congruence theory" of legitimacy, which he has explained more fully in *Support for Regimes: Theories and Tests*, Research Monograph 44 (Princeton, N.J.: Center for International Studies, Princeton University, 1979), pp. 16–25.

23. Edward Shils, "Tradition," *Comparative Studies in Society and History* 13 (April 1971): 128; and James Downton, *Rebel Leadership: Commitment and Charisma in the Revolutionary Process* (New York: Free Press, 1973), pp. 75–79.

24. Such an image, in effect, is what Frances FitzGerald conveyed in *Fire in the Lake: The Vietnamese and the Americans in Vietnam* (New York: Random House, 1972), p. 466.

25. Samuel Popkin, *The Rational Peasant: The Political Economy of Rural Society in Vietnam* (Berkeley: University of California Press, 1979), pp. 259–66.

26. Jack M. Potter, "Introduction: Peasants in the Modern World," in *Peasant Society*, ed. Potter, Diaz, and Foster, p. 381.

27. The salience of this Middle Tradition as a lubricating carrier between the

"high and mighty" and the "meek and lowly" is concisely laid out by Jeffrey Race, *War Comes to Long An: Revolutionary Conflict in a Vietnamese Province* (Berkeley: University of California Press, 1972), pp. 179–80.

28. See, in order of mention, Eric R. Wolf, *Peasant Wars of the Twentieth Century* (New York: Harper & Row, 1969), pp. 268–69; Bruce Russett, "Inequality and Instability: The Relation of Land Tenure to Politics," in *Anger, Violence, and Politics: Theories and Research*, ed. Ivo K. Feirabend, Rosalind L. Feirabend, and Ted Robert Gurr (Englewood Cliffs, N.J.: Prentice-Hall, 1972), pp. 125–35; Jeffery M. Paige, *Agrarian Revolution: Social Movements and Export Agriculture in the Underdeveloped World* (New York: Free Press, 1975), pp. 58–71; and Roy L. Prosterman and Jeffrey M. Riedinger, *Land Reform and Democratic Development* (Baltimore: Johns Hopkins University Press, 1987), pp. 7–35.

29. Edward N. Muller and Mitchell A. Seligson, "Inequality and Insurgency," *American Political Science Review* 81 (June 1987): 443.

30. Apter, *Rethinking Development*, p. 16. Indeed, Seymour Martin Lipset has identified the management of this problem of access through the accommodation of Almond and Verba's "participation explosion" as the key test of the legitimacy of an incumbent regime. See his *Political Man: The Social Bases of Politics* (Garden City, N.Y.: Doubleday, 1960), p. 67.

31. Such a split is fully supported in the literature. The venerable sociologist S. N. Eisenstadt has divided up the "crucial intervening variables" of modernization into access, by which he meant economic resources, and participation, by which he meant political positions. See his *Revolution and the Transformation of Societies: A Comparative Study of Civilizations* (New York: Free Press, 1978), pp. 32–34, 240. Also, Gabriel Almond, surely one of the deans of comparative politics, has called two capacities critical to the evolution of the modern state, distribution and participation, which he has defined synonymously with my societal access and political participation. See his "Political Systems and Political Change," in *State and Society: A Reader in Political Sociology*, Reinhard Bendix et al. (Berkeley: University of California Press, 1968), p. 34.

32. Samuel P. Huntington and Joan M. Nelson, *No Easy Choice: Political Participation in Developing Countries* (Cambridge, Mass.: Harvard University Press, 1976), p. 53; Huntington, *Political Order in Changing Societies*, p. 4.

33. Talcott Parsons, "Some Reflections on the Place of Force in Social Process," in *Internal War*, ed. Eckstein, p. 57. Beyond "exercising" and "distributing" power, this is what Harold Lasswell has referred to as "shaping" it. See Harold Lasswell and Abraham Kaplan, *Power and Society* (New Haven, Conn.: Yale University Press, 1955), p. 75.

34. Lucian W. Pye, *Asian Power and Politics: The Cultural Dimensions of Authority* (Cambridge, Mass.: Harvard University Press, 1985), pp. 91–92.

35. Colonel C. E. Callwell, *Small Wars: Their Principles and Practice*, 3d ed. (London: Wyman and Sons, 1906), pp. 43–56.

36. Ian F. W. Beckett and John Pimlott, eds., *Armed Forces and Modern Counterinsurgency* (London: Croom Helm, 1985), p. 4.

37. Gellner, *Nations and Nationalism*, pp. 22, 35.

38. Reinhard Bendix, *Kings or People: Power and the Mandate to Rule* (Berkeley: University of California Press, 1978), p. 5. The Iranian Revolution of 1979, harken-

ing back to the days of Abu Bakr in the sixth century, represents a stark exception to this pattern.

39. A fascinating account of this intense Japanese scrutiny is that of Marius B. Jansen, *Japan and Its World: Two Centuries of Change* (Princeton, N.J.: Princeton University Press, 1980).

40. An excellent portrayal of modern legitimation in communist states can be found in an edited volume by T. H. Rigby and Ferenc Fehér. The essential difference they point to is that legitimacy in liberal democracies derives from adherence to a duly prescribed constitutional process of politics whereas modern communist states hold aloft a set of performance goals for legitimacy and measure their systems less by their political processes than by their abilities to move toward these goals. See their *Political Legitimation in Communist States* (New York: St. Martin's Press, 1982), pp. 10–13.

41. Ibid., p. 18.

42. Chalmers A. Johnson, *Revolutionary Change*, 2d ed. (Stanford: Stanford University Press, 1982), p. 126.

43. Karl Marx and Friedrich Engels, *Collected Works*, vol. 8 (London: Lawrence and Wishart, 1976), p. 230.

44. Walker Connor, *The National Question in Marxist-Leninist Theory and Strategy* (Princeton, N.J.: Princeton University Press, 1984), p. 37. In addition to Connor's long treatise on this incompatibility, the uneasy coexistence of these two forces is discussed by Ronaldo Munck, *The Difficult Dialogue: Marxism and Nationalism* (London: Zed Books, 1986); J. L. Talmon, *The Myth of the Nation and the Vision of Revolution: The Origins of Ideological Polarisation in the Twentieth Century* (Berkeley: University of California Press, 1980); and Peter Zwick, *National Communism* (Boulder, Colo.: Westview Press, 1983).

45. Rigby and Fehér, *Political Legitimation in Communist States*, p. 17. Will H. Moore has noted that at the village level, outside agents of mobilization can succeed only when they gain legitimacy through the support of local authority figures. See his "Rational Rebels: Overcoming the Free-Rider Problem," paper presented at the American Political Science Association convention, Atlanta, Ga., August 31, 1989, p. 16.

46. Sorokin's study is of the Russian Revolution, and he presents table upon table of statistics showing the huge increases in murder, rape, thievery, suicide, divorce, illegitimate births, divorce, and hunger that accompanied the revolution. See his *The Sociology of Revolution* (Philadelphia: J. B. Lippincott, 1925), pp. 58–170. Trotsky quoted by George Sawyer Pettee, *The Process of Revolution* (New York: Harper and Brothers, 1938), p. 4.

47. Vladimir Ilyich Lenin, "One Step Forward, Two Steps Backward" (1904), in *Collected Works*, vol. 7 (Moscow: Foreign Languages Publishing House, 1961), p. 451; Downton, *Rebel Leadership*, pp. 104–5; Mao Tse-tung, *Report on an Investigation of the Peasant Movement in Hunan* (1927; rpr. Peking: Foreign Language Press, 1967).

48. For the impressive record of the Viet Cong in achieving this supportive silence in South Vietnam's Mekong Delta, see Stuart Herrington, *Silence Was a Weapon* (Novato, Calif.: Presidio Press, 1982).

49. Thomas Perry Thornton, "Terror as a Weapon of Political Agitation," in *Internal War*, ed. Eckstein, p. 89.

50. Alexander Groth, "A Typology of Revolution," in *Revolution and Political Change*, ed. Claude E. Welch, Jr., and Mavis Bunker Taintor (North Scituate, Mass.: Duxbury Press, 1972), pp. 30, 36–37.

51. Roger Hilsman, "Two American Counterstrategies to Guerrilla Warfare: The Case of Vietnam," in *China in Crisis*, vol. 2: *China's Policies in Asia and America's Alternatives*, ed. Tang Tsou (Chicago: University of Chicago Press, 1968), pp. 269–70.

52. William V. O'Brien, "Special Operations in the 1980s: American Moral, Legal, Political, and Cultural Constraints," in *Special Operations in U.S. Strategy*, ed. Frank R. Barnet, B. Hugh Tovar, and Richard H. Shultz (Washington, D.C.: National Defense University Press, 1984), p. 62.

53. Quoted by Lloyd N. Cutler, "The Right to Intervene," *Foreign Affairs* 64 (Fall 1985): 97.

54. Quoted by Paul Schroeder, *Metternich's Diplomacy at Its Zenith, 1820–1823* (Westport, Conn.: Greenwood Press, 1969), p. 126.

55. Richard N. Cooper and Joseph S. Nye, Jr., "Ethics and Foreign Policy," in *Global Dilemmas*, ed. Samuel P. Huntington and Joseph S. Nye, Jr. (Cambridge, Mass., and Langdon, Md.: Center for International Affairs, Harvard University, and University Press of America, 1985), pp. 30–34; and Eliot A. Cohen, "Constraints on America's Conduct of Small Wars," *International Security* 9 (Fall 1984): 154.

56. Manfred Halpern, for example, admitted that interventions undermine sovereignty, but he argued that sovereignty is even more undermined by international instability. Thus interventions are nevertheless justified by certain contingencies, to wit, the prior and adventurous interventions of the Soviet Union. To keep such adventures to a minimum, however, the United States should proclaim a clear policy of counterintervention and maintain a strong enough position globally not to tempt adversaries into prior interventions. In a similar vein, William V. O'Brien has acknowledged that because of the principle of sovereignty, the theory of a just war has to uphold the companion principle of nonintervention. Nevertheless, he asserted that there are four exceptions which allow intervention: counterintervention by invitation, intervention by treaty rights, intervention to protect lives and property, and humanitarian intervention to protect a people from its government. Specifically, for an American military intervention to be morally justifiable, Herbert Tillema has set forth three rules: there must be armed conflict posing a real threat to the host government, the host government (or supplicating insurgent group) must exercise some palpable de facto control in its country, and there must be demonstrable prior intervention by another country for the United States to condemn. See Manfred Halpern, "The Morality and Politics of Intervention," in *International Aspects of Civil Strife*, ed. James N. Rosenau (Princeton, N.J.: Princeton University Press, 1964), pp. 250, 280–85; William V. O'Brien, "Special Operations in the 1980s," pp. 62–64; and Herbert K. Tillema, *Appeal to Force: American Military Intervention in an Era of Containment* (New York: Thomas Y. Crowell, 1973), p. 36.

57. Hedley Bull, *The Anarchical Society: A Study of Order in World Politics* (New York: Columbia University Press, 1977), pp. 227–29.

58. Thomas H. Greene, *Comparative Revolutionary Movements: Search for Theory and Justice*, 2d ed. (Englewood Cliffs, N.J.: Prentice-Hall, 1984), pp. 90–92; and Race, *War Comes to Long An*, pp. 151–52.

59. These rough numbers, or benchmarks, have been influenced by several

studies. Chief among them is the "dumbbell hypothesis" of Ralph K. White in which he views an insurgency as a contest between an activist core of 20 to 30 percent of the adult population divided into two balanced or unbalanced weights at the ends of a bar of an indifferent mass of the remaining 70 to 80 percent. See White, "Attitudes of the South Vietnamese," *Papers of the Peace Research Society* 10 (June 1968): 53 55. Also, T. Robert Gurr contends that an insurgent challenge becomes a crisis when one-tenth of the adult population are numbered among its followers. Such a crisis becomes strategic, he further argues, when one-tenth of the elite in a society join the movement. See Gurr, "Vergleichende Analspe von Krisen und Rebellionen," in *Herschaft und Krise*, ed. Jäniche Martin (Opladen, W. Ger: Westdeutsche Verlag, 1973), p. 69, cited by Ekkart Zimmerman, ed., *Political Violence Crises and Revolutions: Theories and Research* (Cambridge, Mass.: Schenkman, 1983), p. 194. Ekkart Zimmerman himself, in concluding his own review of this topic, speculates that political stability can be maintained if basic consent to the regime does not drop below 50 percent and dissent from it does not rise above 30 to 35 percent. See ibid., p. 214.

60. William Howard Wriggins, *The Ruler's Imperative: Strategies for Political Survival in Asia and Africa* (New York: Columbia University Press, 1969), pp. 58–88.

61. U.S. Department of State, "Crisis in Asia—An Examination of U.S. Policy," by Dean Acheson, *Bulletin* 22, no. 55 (1950): 116–17.

Chapter Four

1. Joseph Buttinger, *Vietnam: A Political History* (New York: Frederick A. Praeger, 1968), pp. 21–22, 38–39.

2. Nguyen Khac Vien, "Traditional Vietnam: Some Historical Stages," *Vietnamese Studies* 21 (n.d. [1969?]): 35–36, 41–48, 78; Buttinger, *Vietnam*, pp. 15, 45–46, 50; and Truong Buu Lam, "Patterns of Vietnamese Response to Foreign Intervention: 1858–1900," *Southeast Asia Studies* 11 (1967): 55.

3. Alexander B. Woodside, *Vietnam and the Chinese Model: A Comparative Study of Nguyen and Ch'ing Civil Government in the First Half of the Nineteenth Century* (Cambridge, Mass.: Harvard University Press, 1971), p. 10; and Samuel L. Popkin, *The Rational Peasant: The Political Economy of Rural Society in Vietnam* (Berkeley: University of California Press, 1979), p. 112.

4. Bernard B. Fall, *The Two Viet-Nams: A Political and Military Analysis*, 2d rev. ed. (New York: Frederick A. Praeger, 1968), p. 18; Buttinger, *Vietnam*, pp. 48–49; Nguyen Khac Vien, "Traditional Vietnam," pp. 118–25; and Woodside, *Vietnam and the Chinese Model*, pp. 2–3. Interestingly, in the propaganda battle between North and South Vietnam, both sides claimed to be the true inheritors of the Tay Son legacy. The communists, for example, called the 1972 Easter invasion the Nguyen Hue Strategic Offensive.

5. Donald Lancaster, *The Emancipation of French Indochina* (London: Oxford University Press, 1961), pp. 27–30; David G. Marr, *Vietnamese Anticolonialism, 1885–1925* (Berkeley: University of California Press, 1971), pp. 22–25; and Woodside, *Vietnam and the Chinese Model*, p. 18.

6. Virginia Thompson, *French Indo-China* (New York: Macmillan, 1937), pp. 23–

25, 62–68; Truong Buu Lam, "Patterns of Vietnamese Response to Foreign Intervention," pp. 23–25, 87–89; and Lancaster, *Emancipation of French Indochina*, p. 44.

7. John T. McAlister, Jr., *Viet Nam: The Origins of Revolution* (New York: Knopf, 1969), p. 262; Alexander B. Woodside, *Community and Revolution in Modern Vietnam* (Boston: Houghton Mifflin, 1976), pp. 21, 139–41; and Jerry M. Silverman, "Local Government and National Integration in South Viet Nam," *Pacific Affairs* 47 (Fall 1974): 307.

8. William John Duiker, *The Rise of Nationalism in Vietnam, 1900–1941* (Ithaca, N.Y.: Cornell University Press, 1976), p. 290.

9. Marr, *Vietnamese Anticolonialism*, pp. 163–84, 194; and Duiker, *Rise of Nationalism*, pp. 135–49.

10. Marr, *Vietnamese Anticolonialism*, pp. 98–119, 185; Duiker, *Rise of Nationalism*, pp. 38–47, 69–76; and Thompson, *French Indo-China*, p. 90.

11. Duiker, *Rise of Nationalism*, pp. 156–65; McAlister, *Vietnam*, pp. 88–91; and Douglas Pike, *History of Vietnamese Communism, 1925–1976* (Stanford: Hoover Institution Press, 1978), pp. 25–27. Alexander Woodside provides a fascinating analysis of the contributions and weaknesses of the VNQDD in the making of revolution in Vietnam. See his *Community and Revolution in Modern Vietnam*, pp. 62–67.

12. Duiker, *The Rise of Nationalism*, p. 216; Jean Chesneaux, "The Historical Background of Vietnamese Communism," *Government and Opposition* 4 (Winter 1969): 118–41; and Pike, *History of Vietnamese Communism*, pp. 18–21.

13. Huynh Kim Khanh, *Vietnamese Communism, 1925–1945* (Ithaca, N.Y.: Cornell University Press, 1982), pp. 179–89. Woodside, *Community and Revolution in Modern Vietnam*, pp. 201–2, 214–15; and Buttinger, *Vietnam*, pp. 181–82.

14. Though vigorously denied by the communists, accusations of communist perfidy against other nationalist groups have cropped up repeatedly in the literature. Joseph Buttinger accused Ho Chi Minh of arranging a fake meeting of reconciliation with Phan Boi Chau in 1924 to set him up for an arrest by the French Sureté. See Buttinger, *Vietnam*, p. 159. Duiker's own account concedes to the setup but suggests that the responsibility lay with the intermediary, not Ho. See Duiker, *Rise of Nationalism*, pp. 85–88. One principal reason for the failure of the Trotskyites to resurface after 1939 may have been that the ICP turned in an entire list of the Trotskyite leadership to the Sureté. This, at least, is the charge levied by Douglas Pike and Vu Ngu Chieu. See Pike, *History of Vietnamese Communism*, p. 37; and Vu Ngu Chieu, "The Other Side of the 1945 Vietnamese Revolution: The Empire of Viet-Nam (March–August, 1945)," *Journal of Asian Studies* 45 (February 1986): 300. Huynh Kim Khanh, who is considerably more sympathetic to the ICP than Pike and Vu, has acknowledged that the party committed excesses against the Trotskyites and other nationalist groups. See his *Vietnamese Communism*, p. 255. From excesses, as John T. McAlister has related, the communists moved on to murder, assassinating forty top nationalist leaders in the south in 1945 and 1946. See his *Viet Nam*, pp. 206–8.

15. McAlister, *Viet Nam*, pp. 136–39; Pike, *History of Vietnamese Communism*, pp. 38–40; and Duiker, *Rise of Nationalism*, p. 292.

16. For an interesting "it did what it could under the circumstances" defense of the puppet regime of Tran Trong Kim under Emperor Bao Dai, see Vu Ngu Chieu, "The Other Side of the 1945 Vietnamese Revolution," pp. 294–328.

17. Woodside, *Community and Revolution in Modern Vietnam*, pp. 228–29; and McAlister, *Viet Nam*, pp. 192–206. The definitive communist account of the August Revolution is by Truong Chinh, who is also believed to be its principal architect. See Truong Chinh, *Primer for Revolt: The Communist Takeover in Viet Nam* (New York: Frederick A. Praeger, 1963), pp. 5 80.

18. McAlister, *Viet Nam*, pp. 298 301; and Fall, *Two Viet-Nams*, pp. 74–75.

19. Buttinger, *Vietnam*, pp. 265–66; McAlister, *Viet Nam*, pp. 307, 314–15; and Ronald H. Spector, *Advice and Support: The Early Years, 1941–1960* (Washington, D.C.: Center of Military History, United States Army, 1985), pp. 87–90.

20. Lancaster, *Emancipation of French Indochina*, pp. 418–28.

21. Buttinger, *Vietnam*, pp. 279, 297–311.

22. Dennis J. Duncanson, *Government and Revolution in Vietnam* (New York: Oxford University Press, 1968), p. 195; Popkin, *Rational Peasant*, pp. 230–32, 242; and Lancaster, *Emancipation of French Indochina*, pp. 247–50.

23. Commission for the Study of the History of the Viet Nam Workers' Party, *An Outline History of the Viet Nam Workers' Party (1930–1975)* (Hanoi: Foreign Languages Publishing House, 1976), pp. 55, 73; and Lancaster, *Emancipation of French Indochina*, pp. 216–17.

24. Lancaster, *Emancipation of French Indochina*, pp. 224–27; and Buttinger, *Vietnam*, p. 327.

25. See, for example, Robert F. Turner, *Vietnamese Communism: Its Origins and Development* (Stanford: Hoover Institution Press, 1975), p. 81; and Spector, *Advice and Support*, p. 125.

26. King C. Chen, *Vietnam and China, 1938–1954* (Princeton, N.J.: Princeton University Press, 1969), p. 273; Duncanson, *Government and Revolution in Vietnam*, p. 177; and Lancaster, *Emancipation of French Indochina*, pp. 254–55. Douglas Pike has estimated that the total value of Chinese military assistance from 1950 to 1954 at $500 million. See his *History of Vietnamese Communism*, p. 106.

27. George McTurnan Kahin and John W. Lewis, *The United States in Vietnam* (New York: Dial Press, 1967), p. 271; Hoang Van Chi, *From Colonialism to Communism: A Case History of North Vietnam* (New York: Frederick A. Praeger, 1964), p. 65; Duncanson, *Government and Revolution in Vietnam*, p. 177; and Stanley Karnow, *Vietnam: A History* (New York: Viking Press, 1983), pp. 195–96.

28. Ralph B. Smith, *An International History of the Vietnam War*, vol. 1: *Revolution versus Containment, 1955–1961* (London: Macmillan, 1983), p. 60.

29. Quoted in Turner, *Vietnamese Communism*, p. 86.

30. Jean Lacouture, *Vietnam: Between Two Truces*, trans. Konrad Kellen and Joel Carmichael (New York: Random House, 1965), p. 9; and Russell H. Fifield, "The Thirty Years War in Indochina: A Conceptual Framework," *Asian Survey* 17 (September 1977): 862. For a full account of America's near intervention in Dienbienphu in the form of massive air strikes, see John Prados, *The Sky Would Fall: Operation Vulture — The U.S. Bombing Mission in Indochina, 1954* (New York: Dial Press, 1983).

31. Lancaster, *Emancipation of French Indochina*, pp. 254–58, 264–65; and Kahin and Lewis, *The United States in Vietnam*, p. 102.

32. Commission for the Study of the History of the Viet Nam Workers' Party, *Outline History of the Viet Nam Workers' Party*, pp. 70–71; Duncanson, *Government*

and Revolution in Vietnam, p. 201; and Buttinger, *Vietnam*, p. 356. The most gripping full account of the siege is that of Bernard B. Fall, *Hell in a Very Small Place* (Philadelphia: J. B. Lippincott, 1967).

33. Pike, *History of Vietnamese Communism*, p. 159; and Fall, *Two Viet-Nams*, p. 129.

34. Buttinger, *Vietnam*, pp. 362–63.

35. Ibid., pp. 371, 375; and Philippe Devillers and Jean Lacouture, *End of a War: Indochina, 1954*, trans. Alexander Lieven and Adam Roberts (New York: Frederick A. Praeger, 1969), pp. 46, 198–99, 226–27, 230–31.

36. Guenter Lewy, *America in Vietnam* (New York: Oxford University Press, 1978), pp. 7–9; Fall, *Two Viet-Nams*, pp. 232–33; and Buttinger, *Vietnam*, pp. 378–79. The fullest account of the accords is by Robert F. Randle, *Geneva 1954: The Settlement of the Indochina War* (Princeton, N.J.: Princeton University Press, 1969).

37. Quoted in Smith, *International History of the Vietnam War*, 1:60.

38. Secret party documents reveal that Hanoi never expected the elections to take place. See Jeffrey Race, *War Comes to Long An: Revolutionary Conflict in a Vietnamese Province* (Berkeley: University of California Press, 1972), p. 34.

39. For an account of Diem's rise to and consolidation of power, see Buttinger, *Vietnam*, pp. 377–415.

40. Lewy, *America in Vietnam*, pp. 19, 26; and Kahin and Lewis, *The United States in Vietnam*, p. 131.

41. Joseph J. Zasloff, "Rural Resettlement in South Viet Nam: The Agroville Program," *Pacific Affairs* 35 (Winter 1962–63): 327–40; and Bernard B. Fall, "The Agonizing Reappraisal," *Current History* 48 (February 1965): 95.

42. Lewy, *America in Vietnam*, p. 24.

43. Frances FitzGerald, *Fire in the Lake: The Vietnamese and the Americans in Vietnam* (New York: Bantam House, 1972), pp. 173–82.

44. A full account of the cable affair in particular and of the development of a general consensus in Washington over the necessity of Diem's departure can be found in William J. Rust, *Kennedy in Vietnam* (New York: Charles Scribner's Sons, 1985), pp. 116–75. Rust has provided a facsimile of the first page of the cable, which includes the words: "U.S. Government cannot tolerate situation in which power lies in Nhu's hands. Diem must be given chance to rid himself of Nhu. . . . If . . . Diem remains obdurate and refuses, then we must face the possibility that Diem himself cannot be preserved." See ibid., p. 113.

45. Henry T. Graff, *The Tuesday Cabinet: Deliberation and Decision on Peace and War under Lyndon B. Johnson* (Englewood Cliffs, N.J.: Prentice-Hall, 1970), p. 53. The Diem coup and the man himself was, and remains, one of the sharpest controversies of the Vietnam War. Opinions on Diem, by both Americans and Vietnamese, are passionately divided. A hostile picture has been penned by Denis Warner, *The Last Confucian* (Baltimore: Penguin Books, 1964). Sympathetic portrayals have come from Marguerite Higgins, *Our Vietnam Nightmare* (New York: Harper & Row, 1965); and Ellen J. Hammer, *A Death in November* (New York: E. P. Dutton, 1987).

46. Buttinger, *Vietnam*, pp. 477–78.

47. Joint United States Public Affairs Office (hereafter JUSPAO), "The Viet-Nam Workers' Party's 1963 Decision to Escalate the War in the South," *Viet-Nam Documents and Research Notes* (hereafter VNDRN), no. 96 (Saigon: U.S. Mission in Viet-

nam, July 1971): 25; Lewy, *America in Vietnam*, pp. 38–40; and Race, *War Comes to Long An*, p. 136.

48. Neil Sheehan et al., eds., *The Pentagon Papers as Published by the New York Times* (New York: Bantam Books, 1971), p. 235; and Lewy, *America in Vietnam*, pp. 32, 35 36. Two useful accounts of the Tonkin Gulf attacks are Joseph C. Goulden, *Truth Is the First Casualty: The Gulf of Tonkin Affair—Illusion and Reality* (Chicago: Rand-McNally, 1969); and Eugene G. Windchey, *Tonkin Gulf* (Garden City, N.Y.: Doubleday, 1971).

49. William P. Bundy, "Path to Viet Nam: Ten Decisions," *Orbis* 11 (Fall 1967): 657–62. The fullest account of these July troop deployment decisions is that of George McTurnan Kahin, *Intervention: How America Became Involved in Vietnam* (New York: Knopf, 1986), pp. 347–97.

50. Lacouture, *Vietnam*, p. 182; David Hunt, "Organizing for Revolution in Vietnam: Study of a Mekong Delta Province," *Radical America* 8 (January–April 1974): 70, 98–99; Kahin and Lewis, *The United States in Vietnam*, pp. 187–88; and Lewy, *America in Vietnam*, p. 66.

51. Kahin and Lewis, *The United States in Vietnam*, pp. 184–86; Raphael Littauer and Norman Uphoff, eds., *The Air War in Indochina*, rev. ed. (Boston: Beacon Press, 1972), p. 172; and Lewy, *America in Vietnam*, pp. 42–51, 56, 64–66.

52. In his thorough discussion of this controversy, James Wirtz has found that Westmoreland's figure was far closer to the truth than that of CIA analyst Sam Adams. See his "'The Uncounted Enemy Revisited': Were Estimates of Viet Cong Strength Manipulated for Political Purposes?," paper presented at the New England Political Science Association Annual Conference, April 7, 1989. Two published works on the Westmoreland trial are Renata Adler, *Reckless Disregard: Westmoreland vs. CBS et al., Sharon vs. Time* (New York: Knopf, 1986); and Bob Brewin and Sydney Shaw, *Vietnam on Trial: Westmoreland vs. CBS* (New York: Atheneum, 1987).

53. I have discussed both the problems and utilities of these numbers in my *The War Everyone Lost—and Won: America's Intervention in Viet Nam's Twin Struggles*, rev. ed. (Washington, D.C.: Congressional Quarterly Press, 1993), pp. 70–73. The fullest reporting of the statistics of the war is that of Thomas C. Thayer, *War without Fronts: The American Experience in Vietnam* (Boulder, Colo.: Westview Press, 1988).

54. Hunt, "Organizing for Revolution," pp. 54–57. Samuel Huntington reported that between 1965 and 1967 the urban population of South Vietnam doubled. See his "Political Stability and Security in South Vietnam," a study prepared for the Policy Planning Council, Department of State, December 1967, pp. 13–21.

55. Robert Shaplen, *The Road from War: Vietnam 1965–1971*, rev. ed. (New York: Harper & Row, 1971), p. 29; and Allan E. Goodman, *The Lost Peace: America's Search for a Negotiated Settlement of the Vietnam War* (Stanford: Hoover Institution Press, 1978), p. 37.

56. Shaplen, *Road from War*, pp. 78–83; and Buttinger, *Vietnam*, p. 480. The best analysis of these electoral politics is by Allan E. Goodman, *Politics in War: The Bases of Political Community in South Vietnam* (Cambridge, Mass.: Harvard University Press, 1973), esp. pp. 45–63.

57. Wirtz, "The Uncounted Enemy Revisited," pp. 7–8; Karnow, *Vietnam*, pp. 512, 514.

58. Goodman, *Politics in War*, pp. 97–98; and Don Oberdorfer, *Tet!* (New York:

Doubleday, 1971), p. 330. A more recent scholarly account of the offensive is by James J. Wirtz, *The Tet Offensive: Intelligence Failure in War* (Ithaca, N.Y.: Cornell University Press, 1991).

59. Robert L. Sansom, *The Economics of Insurgency in the Mekong Delta of Vietnam* (Cambridge, Mass.: MIT Press, 1970), p. 241.

60. JUSPAO, "COSVN's Preliminary Report on the 1969 Autumn Campaign," VNDRN, no. 82 (August 1970): 5–11.

61. Lewy, *America in Vietnam*, p. 146. A concession of this support comes even from such a sharp critic of Nixon as Frances FitzGerald. See her *Fire in the Lake*, p. 539.

62. Race, *War Comes to Long An*, pp. 272–73; FitzGerald, *Fire in the Lake*, p. 540; and Harry H. Kendall, "Land-to-the-Tiller — Backgrounder" (Saigon: U.S. Mission JUSPAO, March 21, 1971), pp. 7–8. Theoretically, the land reform was explicitly based on the thesis that insurgency came from propertyless farmers. See Roy L. Prosterman and Jeffrey M. Riedinger, *Land Reform and Democratic Development* (Baltimore: Johns Hopkins University Press, 1987), pp. 113–41. A statistical profile of the impressive results of this program can be found in Thayer, *War without Fronts*, pp. 237–44.

63. Lewy, *America in Vietnam*, p. 192. In reciting these statistics, Lewy cautioned: "HES measured control and the suppression of opposition; it could not measure popular allegiance and the strength of commitment to the GVN." See ibid., p. 193. Nevertheless, a clear demonstration of the correlation between rural security and the implementation of land reform measures can be seen in McDonald Salter, "The Broadening Base of Land Reform in South Vietnam," *Asian Survey* 10 (August 1970): 724–37.

64. FitzGerald, *Fire in the Lake*, pp. 552–53.

65. For a full-length account of this unsuccessful South Vietnamese operation, see Keith William Nolan, *Into Laos: The Story of Dewey Canyon II/Lam Son 719; Vietnam 1971* (Novato, Calif.: Presidio Press, 1986).

66. Donald Kirk, "The Thieu Presidential Campaign: Background and Consequences of the Single-Candidacy Phenomenon," *Asian Survey* 12 (July 1972): 616; and Allan E. Goodman, "South Vietnam: Neither War Nor Peace," *Asian Survey* 10 (February, 1970): 113. For a discussion of the importance of the "institutional" creation of political parties for the establishment of a viable political community, see Goodman, *Politics in War*, pp. 2–10.

67. Kirk, "The Thieu Presidential Campaign," pp. 611, 624.

68. Lewy, *America in Vietnam*, p. 196; and Goodman, *Lost Peace*, p. 124.

69. Lewy, *America in Vietnam*, pp. 196–98. The official air force account of both Linebacker I and II is that of Carl Berger, ed., *The United States Air Force in Southeast Asia, 1961–1973* (Washington, D.C.: U.S. Air Force, Office of Air Force History, 1983). A more specific look at the Easter invasion is that of Major A. J. C. Lavalle, ed., *Air Power and the 1972 Spring Invasion*, U.S. Air Force Southeast Asia Monograph Series, vol. 2, monograph 3 (Washington, D.C.: U.S. Government Printing Office, 1976). A comprehensive account of the Easter invasion has still not been published. G. H. Turley's book confines itself to the fighting around the DMZ. See his *The Easter Offensive: Vietnam, 1972* (Novato, Calif.: Presidio Press, 1985). A useful monograph

is that of Ngo Quang Truong, *The Easter Offensive of 1972* (Washington, D.C.: U.S. Army Center of Military History, 1980).

70. Goodman, *Lost Peace*, pp. 91–122; and D. Gareth Porter, *A Peace Denied: The United States, Vietnam and the Paris Agreement* (Bloomington: Indiana University Press, 1975), pp. 121–22, 126, 132.

71. Goodman, *Lost Peace*, p. 146; Porter, *Peace Denied*, pp. 154–56; and Lewy, *America in Vietnam*, pp. 202–3.

72. Porter, *Peace Denied*, pp. 154–56. For a listing of this damage, see Robert M. Ginsburgh, "Strategy and Air Power: The Lessons of Southeast Asia," *Strategic Review* 2 (Summer 1973): 23. A discussion of the range of casualty figures can be found in Timothy J. Lomperis, "A Conceptual Framework for Deriving the 'Lessons of History': The U.S. Involvement in Viet Nam as a Case Study" (Ph.D. dissertation, Duke University, 1981), p. 283.

73. Porter, *Peace Denied*, pp. 136–37, 156–65; Thompson's statement is cited by Ulysses S. Grant Sharp, *Strategy for Defeat: Vietnam in Retrospect* (San Rafael, Calif.: Presidio Press, 1978), p. 255; and Goodman, *Lost Peace*, pp. 160–64.

74. Goodman, *Lost Peace*, pp. 188–97 (Appendix C).

75. JUSPAO, "COSVN's Directive 02/73 'On Policies Related to the Political Settlement and Cease-Fire,' " *VNDRN*, no. 113 (June 1973): iii.

76. For an inventory of Hanoi's huge resupply effort far in excess of a one-for-one replacement ratio, see Pike, *History of Vietnamese Communism*, p. 164.

77. Lewy, *America in Vietnam*, pp. 203–4.

78. Goodman, *Lost Peace*, p. 169.

79. Richard A. Falk, "Vietnam: The Final Deceptions," *Nation* 220 (May 17, 1975): 583; James P. Sterba, " 'Friendship Pass' No Longer Links Peking to Hanoi," *New York Times*, January 5, 1979, sec. 1, p. A3; David Remnick, "Soviets Had Combat Role in Vietnam, Paper Shows," *Washington Post*, April 14, 1989, p. A24; "China Admits Combat in Vietnam War," *Washington Post*, May 17, 1989, p. A31; and Kahin, *Intervention*; pp. 338–41.

80. Lewy, *America in Vietnam*, pp. 208–10.

81. Van Tien Dung, *Our Great Spring Victory*, trans. John Spragens, Jr. (New York: Monthly Review Press, 1977), pp. 13, 16–20; and Lewy, *America in Vietnam*, pp. 210–13.

82. Lewy, *America in Vietnam*, p. 453. These figures are mostly corroborated by Thayer, through he puts communist military deaths at a third higher. See his *War without Fronts*, pp. 125–36.

Chapter Five

1. Jerry Mark Silverman, "Local Government and National Integration in South VietNam," *Pacific Affairs* 47 (Fall 1974): 307–8.

2. Leonard Binder et al., *Crises and Sequences of Political Development* (Princeton, N.J.: Princeton University Press, 1971), p. 53.

3. For a discussion of the Vietnamese concepts of *chinh nghia* and *phuc duc*, see the following articles by Stephen B. Young: "Vietnamese Marxism: Transition in

Elite Ideology," *Asian Survey* 19 (August 1979): 775–77; and "Unpopular Socialism in United Vietnam," *Orbis* 21 (Summer 1977): 229.

4. Alexander B. Woodside, *Community and Revolution in Modern Vietnam* (Boston: Houghton Mifflin, 1976), p. 291.

5. Allan Goodman, "South Vietnam: Neither War Nor Peace," *Asian Survey* 10 (February 1970): 113; and Douglas Pike, *History of Vietnamese Communism, 1925–1976* (Stanford: Hoover Institution Press, 1978), p. 147.

6. Jeffrey Race, *War Comes to Long An: Revolutionary Conflict in a Vietnamese Province* (Berkeley: University of California Press, 1972), p. 147.

7. For a discussion of *uy tin*, see Young, "Unpopular Socialism in Vietnam," pp. 228–29.

8. Thomas C. Thayer, *War without Fronts: The American Experience in Vietnam* (Boulder, Colo.: Westview Press, 1985), p. 166.

9. For a listing of the accomplishments of the pacification effort during this period, see Robert W. Komer, *Bureaucracy at War: Performance in the Vietnam Conflict* (Boulder, Colo.: Westview Press, 1986), pp. 115–22; and William Colby and Peter Forbath, *Honorable Men: My Life in the CIA* (New York: Simon and Schuster, 1978), pp. 250–65.

10. By assigning responsibility for civilian casualties in the war as split among the categories of bombing (US/GVN), artillery (US/GVN), gunshot and mines (both sides), and mortaring (VC/NVA), Thomas Thayer has shown that the proportion of civilian casualties changed from more of a US/GVN responsibility at the beginning to more of a VC/NVA one at the end. See his *War without Fronts*, pp. 129–32.

11. In a brief pamphlet, Douglas Pike made the observation that people's war, in its requirement that liberated base areas had to be established to point out the possibility of a revolutionary future, had no answer to long-range bombing. See his *Vietnam War: Views from the Other Side* (Saigon: U.S. Mission, 1967) pp. 8, 21.

12. Bernard B. Fall, "The Agonizing Reappraisal," *Current History* 48 (February 1965): 98.

13. Nguyen Van Thieu (an NLF leader of no relation to the South Vietnamese president), "Our Strategy for Guerrilla War," in *Guerrilla Strategies: An Historical Anthology from the Long March to Afghanistan*, ed. Gerard Chaliand (Berkeley: University of California Press, 1982), p. 311.

14. An excellent discussion of this traditional/modern distinction between "patriotism" and "nationalism" in Vietnam can be found in Huynh Kim Kanh, *Vietnamese Communism, 1925–1945* (Ithaca, N.Y.: Cornell University Press, 1982), pp. 2–34.

15. In fairness, a land reform program carried out in the north in the same year was an even greater disaster. It prompted a rebellion in central North Vietnam that had to be crushed by the army. For details, see Bernard B. Fall, *The Two Viet-Nams: A Political and Military Analysis*, 2d rev. ed. (New York: Frederick A. Praeger, 1968), pp. 154–57.

16. James R. Bullington and James D. Rosenthal, "The South Vietnamese Countryside: Non-Communist Political Perceptions," *Asian Survey* 10 (August 1970): 652–54.

17. John C. Donnell, "Expanding Political Participation: The Long Haul from Villagism to Nationalism," *Asian Survey* 10 (August 1970): 700.

18. Thayer, *War without Fronts*, p. 60.

19. Woodside, *Community and Revolution in Modern Vietnam*, pp. 286–87.

20. Gerald C. Hickey, "Notes on the South Vietnamese Peasant of the Mekong Delta" (Santa Monica, Calif.: Rand Corp., Memorandum 4116-ISA, May 1964), pp. viii–ix.

21. For testimony of this resentment, see Truong Nhu Tang, *A Vietcong Memoir* (San Diego, Calif.: Harcourt Brace Jovanovich, 1985), pp. 186–200.

22. Thayer, *War without Fronts*, p. 185. This survey was one of a series of surveys conducted between 1969 and 1972 under the auspices of the joint U.S. and GVN pacification effort and analyzed under the rubric of the Pacification Attitude Analysis System (PAAS). Because government representatives were in the field conducting the surveys, complete candor in the responses could not be guaranteed. Not surprisingly, the surveys did show general support for the GVN and its policies. When the questions turned to elicitations of deeper commitment, answers became inconsistent and evasive. The clearest of all is the one cited above. For a discussion of the methodology of these surveys and a partial but interesting reporting of their results, see ibid., pp. 173–93.

23. Ky's portrayal of this corruption is one of the most graphic in the literature. See his *Twenty Years and Twenty Days* (New York: Stein and Day, 1976), pp. 101–16.

24. Alexander Woodside has reported the figures for both at three hundred thousand. See his *Community and Revolution in Modern Vietnam*, pp. 289, 301.

25. For a prescient recognition of this unwavering will, see Brian M. Jenkins, "Why the North Vietnamese Keep Fighting" (Santa Monica, Calif.: Rand Corporation, P-4395, August 1970), p. iii.

26. William J. Duiker, review of *The War Everyone Lost—and Won*, by Timothy J. Lomperis, in *Pacific Affairs* 59 (Spring 1986): 158.

27. For a description of this boomerang effect of communist legitimacy—from legitimacy on the road to power back to illegitimacy after power by the same terms, see Young, "Unpopular Socialism in Vietnam," pp. 227–40.

28. Thayer, *War without Fronts*, p. 24.

29. Douglas Pike has asserted that $8 billion from the Soviets alone poured into Hanoi from 1960 to 1975. See his *Vietnam and the Soviet Union: Anatomy of an Alliance* (Boulder, Colo.: Westview Press, 1987), p. 122.

30. Thayer, *War without Fronts*, pp. 85–87.

31. Allan Goodman has pointed out that 80 percent of Hanoi's oil and 100 percent of its sophisticated military equipment came from Moscow. See his *The Lost Peace: America's Search for a Negotiated Settlement of the Vietnam War* (Stanford: Hoover Institution Press, 1978), p. 79. For the Easter invasion in particular, all the freshly introduced tanks and long-range artillery pieces came from the Soviet Union. See Timothy J. Lomperis, *The War Everyone Lost—and Won: America's Intervention in Viet Nam's Twin Struggles*, rev. ed. (Washington, D.C.: Congressional Quarterly Press, 1993), pp. 87–88.

32. Pike, *Vietnam and the Soviet Union*, p. 101.

33. Quoted by Arnold R. Isaacs, *Without Honor: Defeat in Vietnam and Cambodia* (New York: Vintage Books, 1984), p. 496.

34. George C. Herring, *America's Longest War: The United States and Vietnam, 1950–1975*, 2d ed. (New York: Knopf, 1986), p. 202.

35. Michael Mandelbaum, "Vietnam: The Television War," *Daedalus* 111 (Fall 1982): 165–66.

36. Pike, *Vietnam and the Soviet Union*, pp. 86–97.

37. For an account of the enormous boost to agricultural productivity touched off by these water pumps, see Robert F. Sansom, *The Economics of Insurgency in the Mekong Delta of Vietnam* (Cambridge, Mass.: MIT Press, 1970), pp. 164–79.

38. William Darryl Henderson, *Why the Vietcong Fought: A Study of Motivation and Control in a Modern Army in Combat* (Westport, Conn.: Greenwood Press, 1979), p. xv.

39. This was especially true in the cities. See Thayer, *War without Fronts*, p. 187.

40. For an account of the depth of U.S. defeatism in the Korean War after both the shock of the Chinese intervention and the disgraceful performance of entire American divisions, see Max Hastings, *The Korean War* (New York: Simon and Schuster, 1987), pp. 165–77.

41. The Korean War was also the precedent for the much maligned one-year rotation policy. As Kurt Lang has pointed out, it was an eminently successful policy for MACV in that, in a long, drawn-out war, it individualized the war for the GIS and all but precluded any collectivization of discontent. Lang's one recommendation on this score is that for continuity of effort officers and noncommissioned officers should have drawn longer tours. See Kurt Lang, "American Military Performance in Vietnam: Background and Analysis," *Journal of Political and Military Sociology* 8 (Fall 1980): 274–81.

Parenthetically, it should be noted that the Korean War had a deleterious effect on the North Vietnamese as well. When they moved up to organizing large-scale conventional assaults, their copying of Chinese-style attacks was disastrous. This was particularly true during the Easter invasion, when they hurled futile human-wave charges against entrenched ARVN positions in Kontum and An Loc. See Lomperis, *The War Everyone Lost—and Won*, p. 90.

42. Samuel P. Huntington, "Political Stability and Security in South Vietnam" (study prepared for the Policy Planning Council, U.S. Department of State, December 1967), pp. 77–80.

43. Allan E. Goodman, *Politics in War: The Bases of Political Community in South Vietnam* (Cambridge, Mass.: Harvard University Press, 1973), pp. 2–10.

44. Colby felt that the only way to end the fighting was to bring the communists into the political process, and, once in, they could be undercut by meaningful reform. See Colby and Forbath, *Honorable Men*, pp. 280–81. Colby also cites the bizarre coalition proposal of Edward Lansdale to divide South Vietnam into a communist north, neutralist center, and nationalist south achieved by letting everyone vote with their feet. See ibid., pp. 95–96.

45. Thayer, *War without Fronts*, p. 24.

46. Jerry Silverman, for example, has reported that the range of collaborators with the French of cabinet ministers in five South Vietnamese regimes was 60, 86, 71, 82, and 100 percent; the 60 percent, interestingly, was that of Ngo Dinh Diem. See his "Political Elites in South Vietnam: A National and Provincial Comparison," *Asian Survey* 10 (April 1970): 298.

47. John T. McAllister, Jr., *VietNam: The Origins of Revolution* (New York: 1969), p. 132; and Lomperis, *The War Everyone Lost—and Won*, p. 54.

48. The most vociferous in this criticism is George McTurnan Kahin, *Intervention: How America Became Involved in Vietnam* (New York: Knopf, 1986), pp. 427–32.

49. Lomperis, *The War Everyone Lost—and Won*, p. 167.

50. Harry G. Summers, Jr., *On Strategy: A Critical Analysis of the Vietnam War* (New York: Dell, 1984), pp. 126–32.

Chapter Six

1. For a listing of these reforms, see Theda Skocpol, *States and Social Revolutions* (Cambridge, U.K.: Cambridge University Press, 1979), p. 78.

2. Mary C. Wright, ed., *China in Revolution: The First Phase, 1900–1913* (New Haven, Conn.: Yale University Press, 1968), p. 50.

3. The rate of industrial growth in the 1930s, for example, averaged 8.4 percent per year. See George F. Botjer, *A Short History of Nationalist China, 1919–1949* (New York: G. P. Putnam's Sons, 1979), p. 166. For a full account of this expansion, see Thomas G. Rawski, *Economic Growth in Prewar China* (Berkeley: University of California Press, 1989).

4. Lucien Bianco, *Origins of the Chinese Revolution, 1915–1949*, trans. Muriel Bell (Stanford: Stanford University Press, 1971), p. 37.

5. The most influential of these groups was the new intellectuals which Chow Tse-tung estimates at ten million, or 3 percent of the population. In the other groups were two hundred thousand modern businessmen (members of eleven hundred Chambers of Commerce) and 1.8 million industrial workers. Chow also mentions the 60 million roaming landless and calamity-stricken peasants who provided the human material for the huge armies and disturbances of the day. See Chow Tse-tung, *The May Fourth Movement: Intellectual Revolution in Modern China* (Stanford: Stanford University Press, 1960), pp. 380–83.

6. Bianco, *Origins of the Chinese Revolution*, pp. 32–52.

7. Botjer, *Short History of Nationalist China*, p. 92.

8. Although the Guomindang came to represent primarily mercantile interests—half of its Central Executive Committee members in 1933 were the sons of merchants—fully one-third of its membership was taken from the intellectual class. See ibid., p. 93; and James Pinckney Harrison, *The Long March to Power: A History of the Chinese Communist Party, 1921–1972* (New York: Praeger, 1972), pp. 9–10. Similarly, the communists, eventually forced to rely on a peasant base, relied on intellectuals for 22 percent of their membership in 1927. See ibid., p. 70.

9. In 1920 the urban population was only 6 percent of China's total. In this urban sector Harrison estimates that there were only one million factory workers, which was a mere half percent of the total population. That they were concentrated, however, presented the communists with organizational opportunities. In Shanghai three hundred thousand factory workers made up 20 percent of the local work force. Another two hundred thousand were in the Guangzhou–Hong Kong corridor. See Harrison, *Long March to Power*, p. 9.

10. Ibid., pp. 36–37. Nevertheless, Arif Dirlik has argued that anarchism played a seminal role in the foundations of Chinese revolutionary thought and was a particularly strong influence on Mao. See his "Vision and Revolution: Anarchism in

Chinese Revolutionary Thought on the Eve of the 1911 Revolution," *Modern China* 12 (April 1986): 123–65.

11. Lucian W. Pye, *China, an Introduction*, 3d ed. (Boston: Little, Brown, 1984), p. 136. For a full account of Soviet activities during this period, see C. Martin Wilbur and Julie Lien-ying How, *Missionaries of Revolution: Soviet Advisors and Nationalist China, 1920–1937* (Cambridge, Mass.: Harvard University Press, 1989), esp. pp. 55–63.

12. Harrison, *Long March to Power*, pp. 76–77.

13. Pye, *China*, p. 158.

14. Barbara W. Tuchman, *Stilwell and the American Experience in China, 1911–1945* (New York: Macmillan, 1970), p. 94.

15. Bianco, *Origins of the Chinese Revolution*, p. 56. For a book-length treatment of this expedition, see Donald A. Jordan, *The Northern Expedition: China's National Revolution of 1926–1928* (Honolulu: University of Hawaii Press, 1976).

16. Edgar Snow, *Red Star over China*, 1st rev. and enl. ed. (New York: Grove Press, 1973), p. 420.

17. Harrison, *Long March to Power*, p. 7.

18. Pye, *China*, pp. 139–40, 160–61.

19. Tuchman, *Stilwell*, p. 121; and Botjer, *Short History of Nationalist China*, p. 104.

20. Benjamin I. Schwartz, *Chinese Communism and the Rise of Mao*, 2d ed. (Cambridge, Mass.: Harvard University Press, 1979), p. 78.

21. Ibid., pp. 175–78.

22. Bianco, *Origins of the Chinese Revolution*, pp. 64–65; and Harrison, *Long March to Power*, p. 201.

23. Snow, *Red Star over China*, pp. 186–87. For a fuller account of these campaigns, see William Wei, *Counterrevolution in China: The Nationalists in Jiangxi during the Soviet Period* (Ann Arbor: University of Michigan Press, 1985).

24. The Long March was not just one but four, all converging in Yanan. Of course, Mao Zedong's out of Jiangxi was the most famous. For a delineation of these four routes, see Bianco, *Origins of the Chinese Revolution*, p. 66.

25. Dick Wilson, *The Long March, 1935: The Epic of Chinese Communism's Survival* (New York: Viking Press, 1971), pp. 91–109, 192–203, 254–77. Harrison and other scholars have argued that Mao emerged from the Long March only as a first among equals and that his paramountcy in the CCP as a whole was not firmly established until the Rectification period in 1942–43. See Harrison, *Long March to Power*, p. 246.

26. Bianco, *Origins of the Chinese Revolution*, p. 68.

27. Wilson, *Long March*, p. 233.

28. Among those dispatched to Xian to exert pressure on Zhang was the communist Zhou Enlai. This was reportedly at the behest of the Russians, who feared the ensuing chaos would make too easy a gift of China to the Japanese. See Tuchman, *Stilwell*, p. 160.

29. These statistics are derived from the following sources: party membership in 1945, Bianco *Origins of the Chinese Revolution*, p. 150; party membership in 1937, Winberg Chai, ed., *Essential Works of Chinese Communism*, rev. ed. (New York: Bantam Books, 1972), pp. 94–95; the 1945 CCP base areas population and the size of the Guomindang forces in 1945, Lionel Max Chassin, *The Communist Conquest of China: A History of the Civil War, 1945–1949*, trans. Timothy Osato and Louis Gelas (London: Donald Moore Books, 1966), pp. 19, 177; and the rest, Harrison *Long March to*

Power, pp. 294–95, 314. These numbers, of course, can vary from source to source. For a summary comparison of figures from four sources, see Jerome Ch 'en, *Mao and the Chinese Revolution* (New York: Oxford University Press, 1967), p. 374.

30. Tuchman, *Stilwell*, pp. 169–71. For fuller treatment of the Guomindang's war record, see Hsi-sheng Ch'i, *Nationalist China at War: Military Defeats and Political Collapse, 1937–1945* (Ann Arbor: University of Michigan Press, 1982).

31. Thus, in my view, both Mark Selden, who stressed the reformist proposition, and Chalmers Johnson, the nationalist, are correct. See Chalmers A. Johnson, *Peasant Nationalism and Communist Power* (Stanford: Stanford University Press, 1962), p. viii; and Mark Selden, *The Yenan Way in Revolutionary China* (Cambridge, Mass.: Harvard University Press, 1971), p. 277.

32. Bianco, *Origins of the Chinese Revolution*, pp. 168, 174–79, 194. On these campaigns, see also William Whitson, *The Chinese High Command: A History of Communist Military Politics, 1927–1971* (New York: Praeger, 1973), pp. 178–86, 312–19.

33. Chassin, *Communist Conquest of China*, p. 52.

34. Ibid., pp. 209–12, 228.

35. Quoted by Lloyd Eastman, "Who Lost China? Chiang Kaishek Testifies," *China Quarterly* 88 (December 1981): 666.

36. Chassin, *Communist Conquest of China*, pp. 207–8.

37. For an account of the determined but futile efforts of the communists in the cities, see Lawrence R. Sullivan, "Reconstruction and Rectification of the Communist Party in the Shanghai Underground, 1931–1934," *China Quarterly* 101 (March 1985): 78–97.

38. Ralph Thaxton, *China Turned Rightside Up: Revolutionary Legitimacy in the Peasant World* (New Haven, Conn.: Yale University Press, 1983), pp. 32–51.

39. The three authority systems that Mao insisted on abolishing were those of the state, the clan, and the supernatural. See his *Report on an Investigation of the Peasant Movement in Hunan* (1927; rpr. Peking: Foreign Language Press, 1967), p. 30.

40. The critical communist success in attracting the middle peasantry to its ranks is stressed by Suzanne Pepper, *Civil War in China: The Political Struggle, 1945–1949* (Berkeley: University of California Press, 1978), p. 433.

41. Both the strengths and weaknesses of the prominence of Shanghai to Chiang Kai-shek are explored by Joseph Fewsmith, "In Search of the Shanghai Connection," *Modern China* 11 (January 1985): 111–44.

42. George M. Beckman, *The Modernization of China and Japan* (New York: Harper & Row, 1962), pp. 461–62; and Stephen C. Averill, "The New Life in Action: The Nationalist Government in South Jiangxi, 1934–1973," *China Quarterly* 88 (December 1981): 594–628.

43. Ralph Thaxton, "On Peasant Revolution and National Resistance: Toward a Theory of Peasant Mobilization and Revolutionary War with Special Reference to Modern China," *World Politics* 30 (October 1977): 45.

44. Thaxton, *China Turned Rightside Up*, pp. 94–116.

45. For an analysis of Sun Yat-sen's ideological vision and his pragmatic decision to accept reorganization of the Guomindang under Soviet direction, see F. Gilbert Chan, "Sun Yat-sen and the Origins of the Guomindang Reorganization," in *China in the 1920s: Nationalism and Revolution*, ed. F. Gilbert Chan and Thomas H. Etzold (New York: New Viewpoints, 1976), pp. 15–37.

46. As factors to this nationalism, Mary Wright has mentioned the reassertion of Chinese power at the periphery, anti-imperialism, anti-Manchuism, and modernization. See her *China in Revolution*, p. 50.

47. Pepper, *Civil War in China*, pp. 181–219; and Raymond F. Wylie, *The Emergence of Maoism: Mao Tse-tung, Ch'en Po-ta, and the Search for Chinese Theory, 1935–1945* (Stanford: Stanford University Press, 1980), pp. 282–83.

48. Though Chiang himself professed his support for Marshall's arrangements, cliques within the Guomindang, to which the generalissimo was beholden, were adamant in keeping the communists out of the government. See Lloyd E. Eastman, *Seeds of Destruction: Nationalist China in War and Revolution* (Stanford: Stanford University Press, 1984), pp. 108–18.

49. Beckman, *Modernization of China and Japan*, pp. 431, 454–55, 499, 509–10.

50. Tuchman, *Stillwell*, p. 154.

51. Mao proclaimed this faith of "men over weapons" in his vehement argument against "weapons decide everything." See his *On Protracted War* (1938; rpr. Peking: Foreign Language Press, 1967), pp. 44–46.

52. Pepper, *Civil War in China*, pp. 95–132, 423–25.

53. Bianco, *Origins of the Chinese Revolution*, p. 186.

54. The material on Soviet aid is derived from Botjer, *A Short History of Nationalist China*, pp. 155, 204–5; Chassin, *Communist Conquest of China*, p. 9; and Tuchman, *Stilwell*, p. 154.

55. For an account of the value of German assistance, see Donald S. Sutton, "German Advice and Residual Warlordism in the Nanking Decade: Influences on Nationalist Military Training and Strategy," *China Quarterly* 91 (September 1982): 386–410. For a book-length treatment, see William Kirby, *Germany and Republican China* (Stanford: Stanford University Press, 1984).

56. Tuchman, *Stilwell*, pp. 214–15, 414, 529–30.

57. Chassin, *Communist Conquest of China*, p. 96.

58. Botjer, *Short History of Nationalist China*, p. 91.

59. Chassin, *Communist Conquest of China*, pp. 44–48; and Tuchman, *Stilwell*, pp. 192, 311, 337, 387.

60. Chassin, *Communist Conquest of China*, p. 203.

61. John Spanier, *American Foreign Policy since World War II*, 10th ed. (New York: Holt, Rinehart and Winston, 1985), p. 58.

62. No one was more publicly vociferous on this issue than General Stilwell. See, for example, Chassin, *Communist Conquest of China*, pp. 27–28.

63. Quoted by Chai, *Essential Works of Chinese Communism*, p. 61.

64. Harrison, *Long March to Power*, p. 222.

65. Selden, *Yenan Way*, pp. 138–39, 180–87.

66. Botjer, *Short History of Nationalist China*, p. 221.

67. Snow, *Red Star over China*, p. 430.

68. Wilson, *Long March*, p. 267.

69. The program targeted against the communists of "burn all, kill all, destroy all" reduced the size of the PLA from 400,000 to 300,000 and base area populations from 44 million to 25 million. See Walter Laqueur, *Guerrilla: A History and Critical Study* (London: Weidenfeld and Nicolson, 1977), p. 257.

70. The size of this booty has been variously reported. The Russians claimed they

provided the PLA with 740,000 rifles, 18,000 machine guns, 800 aircraft, 800 tanks, and 4,000 artillery pieces. See Harrison, *Long March to Power*, p. 379. Other sources have called these figures exaggerated. Chassin, for example, has contended that at the start of the civil war in 1947, the PLA had no tanks and only 600 artillery pieces. See his *Communist Conquest of China*, p. 49. For a discussion of both the critical value of a Manchurian industrial base to the communists and its strategic loss to the nationalists, see Eastman, *Seeds of Destruction*, pp. 223–25.

71. The Guomindang retreats to Nanjing and Chongqing, away from its urban revenue base, occasioned a 63 percent drop in national government revenues. See Eastman, *Seeds of Destruction*, p. 219.

72. Ibid., p. 218.

73. Pepper, *Civil War in China*, pp. 8–14.

74. For all their errors in Jiangxi, it was there that the communists developed their basic skills in peasant mobilization and guerrilla warfare. See Marcia R. Ristaino, "Communist Strategy by 1928: The Mobilization of Discontent," *China Quarterly* 84 (December 1980): 694–719.

75. Eastman, "Who Lost China?," p. 658.

76. Pepper, *Civil War in China*, p. 435.

Chapter Seven

1. Richard J. Barnet, *Intervention and Revolution: The United States in the Third World* (New York: World, 1968), p. 97. It is a central contention of such revisionists as Lawrence Wittner and D. Michael Shafer that the assumption that American assistance was critical to the Greek government's victory was unwarranted. See Lawrence S. Wittner, *American Intervention in Greece, 1943–1949* (New York: Columbia University Press, 1982), p. 253; and D. Michael Shafer, *Deadly Paradigms: The Failure of U.S. Counterinsurgency Policy* (Princeton, N.J.: Princeton University Press, 1988), p. 166.

2. Edgar O'Ballance, *The Greek Civil War, 1944–1949* (New York: Frederick A. Praeger, 1966), p. 122. Although the Greek civil war is the only analogy in this book taken from a European setting, the Greece of the civil war period had many of the features of a contemporary underdeveloped country. Forty percent of the population, for example, was illiterate. Roughly comparable in size to England, Greece had only 10,000 miles of paved roads and 2,000 miles of railway track as opposed to 180,000 miles and 32,000 miles, respectively, for Britain. Similar to other lesser developed countries, agriculture, employing 55 percent of the work force, was its economic mainstay. The principal cities of Athens, Piraeus, and Salonika held 25 percent of the population of eight million, and 40 percent of the population lived in the interior as peasants. See ibid., pp. 20–22; and Christopher Montague Woodhouse, *The Struggle for Greece, 1941–1949* (London: Hart-Davis and MacGibbon, 1976), p. 235.

3. Bruce Robellet Kuniholm, *The Origins of the Cold War in the Near East* (Princeton, N.J.: Princeton University Press, 1980), pp. 74–75; and O'Ballance, *Greek Civil War*, pp. 25–28.

4. Kuniholm, *Origins of the Cold War*, p. 74; and O'Ballance, *Greek Civil War*, p. 27.

5. Constantine Tsoucalis, *The Greek Tragedy* (Baltimore, Md.: Penguin Books, 1969), p. 19. For these figures, see also Richard Clogg, *A Short History of Modern Greece* (Cambridge, U.K.: Cambridge University Press, 1979), p. 70.

6. Kuniholm, *Origins of the Cold War*, p. 77; and Clogg, *Short History of Modern Greece*, p. 121.

7. Kuniholm, *Origins of the Cold War*, pp. 75–79; and Harry Cliadakis, "The Political and Diplomatic Background to the Metaxis Dictatorship, 1935–1936," *Journal of Contemporary History* 14 (January 1979): 127.

8. Dimitrios George Kousoulas, *Revolution and Defeat: The Story of the Greek Communist Party* (London: Oxford University Press, 1965), pp. 41–42, 82–83; and Dominique Eudes, *The Kapetanios: Partisans and Civil War in Greece, 1943–1949*, trans. John Howe (New York: Monthly Review Press, 1972), pp. 66–67.

9. For an account of Greece's economic "takeoff" during the interwar years, see Nicolas Svoronos, "Greek History, 1940–1950: The Main Problems," in *Greece in the 1940s: A Nation in Crisis*, ed. John O. Iatrides (Hanover, N.H.: University Press of New England, 1981), pp. 1–16.

10. A classic statement of the Megali Idea is cited by Richard Clogg quoting a nineteenth century orator: "The Kingdom of Greece is not Greece. . . . A Greek is not only a man who lives within this kingdom but also one who lives . . . in any land associated with Greek history or the Greek race." See Clogg, *Short History of Modern Greece*, p. 76.

11. Cliadakis, "The Political and Diplomatic Background to the Metaxis Dictatorship," p. 135.

12. The vote in parliament to transfer power was 214 for, 16 against, and 4 abstentions. See Svoronos, "Greek History," p. 8.

13. O'Ballance, *Greek Civil War*, pp. 35–39, 41–45, 47; and Martin Van Creveld, "Prelude to Disaster: The British Decision to Aid Greece, 1940–1941," *Journal of Contemporary History* 9 (July 1974): 65–92.

14. Kuniholm, *Origins of the Cold War*, p. 86; and Eudes, *The Kapetanios*, p. 16.

15. O'Ballance, *Greek Civil War*, pp. 52, 57, 67, 88; and Woodhouse, *Struggle for Greece*, p. 57.

16. In effecting this armistice, an American major served as mediator because the United States was perceived by both sides to be more neutral than the British. See Woodhouse, *Struggle for Greece*, pp. 65–66.

17. According to communist sources, 1.8 million Greeks voted to elect 220 council representatives. See John C. Loulis, *The Greek Communist Party, 1940–1944* (London: Croom Helm, 1982), p. 126.

18. Woodhouse, *Struggle for Greece*, p. 77.

19. The latter was in reference to a communist campaign of assassination and intimidation directed against its political enemies by the newly formed National Civil Guard (EP). See O'Ballance, *Greek Civil War*, p. 92.

20. Woodhouse, *Struggle for Greece*, pp. 75, 77, 87–88, 95; and R. V. Burks, "Hellenic Time of Troubles," *Problems of Communism* 33 (November–December 1984): 46–47. For a full discussion of the percentages agreement, see Kuniholm, *Origins of the Cold War*, pp. 109–25.

21. Martin F. Hertz, *Beginnings of the Cold War* (New York: McGraw-Hill, 1966),

p. 127; John O. Iatrides, *Revolt in Athens: The Greek Communist "Second Round,"* *1944–1945* (Princeton, N.J.: Princeton University Press, 1972), p. 132; and O'Ballance, *Greek Civil War*, pp. 77, 79.

22. The variations in figures can be attributed to discrepancies between the statistics of German occupation versus Greek resistance sources. See Woodhouse, *Struggle for Greece*, p. 105.

23. For these figures, see Burks, "Hellenic Time of Troubles," p. 49; Loulis, *Greek Communist Party*, p. xiv; Woodhouse, *Struggle for Greece*, pp. 88, 112; and Iatrides, *Revolt in Athens*, p. 176.

24. Woodhouse, *Struggle for Greece*, pp. 127–29.

25. Kuniholm, *Origins of the Cold War*, pp. 225–26; and O'Ballance, *Greek Civil War*, pp. 95–96, 104–5, 108.

26. O'Ballance, *Greek Civil War* pp. 107–10; and Woodhouse, *Struggle for Greece*, pp. 63, 133, 135.

27. Hertz, *Beginnings of the Cold War*, p. 130.

28. These terms and figures can be found in O'Ballance, *Greek Civil War*, pp. 105–8, 110–13; and Woodhouse, *Struggle for Greece*, pp. 137–38, 161.

29. Woodhouse, *Struggle for Greece*, p. 135.

30. O'Ballance, *Greek Civil War*, p. 115.

31. Though both these elections have stirred up considerable controversy, modern scholarship has come to accept their essential legitimacy. See Kuniholm, *Origins of the Cold War*, pp. 252, 351–53, 367–68; and Evangelos Averoff-Tossizza, *By Fire and Axe: The Communist Party and Civil War in Greece, 1944–1949*, trans. Sarah Arnold Rigos (New Rochelle, N.Y.: Caratzas Brothers, 1978), pp. 166–69, 183–84. The latter argued that the communists had, in any case, squandered any hope of winning these elections.

32. Kuniholm, *Origins of the Cold War*, p. 401.

33. Averoff-Tossizza, *By Fire and Axe*, pp. 179, 199.

34. Averoff-Tossizza referred to this government as the Grand Alliance because it was a coalition crafted by the new monarch, King Paul, and "represented the nation." See ibid., p. 232.

35. O'Ballance, *Greek Civil War*, pp. 136, 145–48; and Woodhouse, *Struggle for Greece*, pp. 186, 209.

36. O'Ballance, *Greek Civil War*, pp. 162–78.

37. Ibid., pp. 179–80, 195, 200; and Alexander Papagos, "Guerrilla Warfare," *Modern Guerrilla Warfare*, ed. Franklin Mark Osanka (New York: Free Press, 1962), p. 239; and Edward R. Wainhouse, "Guerrilla War in Greece, 1946–1949: A Case Study," ibid., pp. 224–26.

38. Woodhouse, *Struggle for Greece*, pp. 237, 261, 278–84; and O'Ballance, *Greek Civil War*, pp. 196–97.

39. O'Ballance, *Greek Civil War*, p. 202; Woodhouse, *Struggle for Greece*, p. 286. A more detailed and slightly different listing of casualties is provided by Howard Jones, *"A New Kind of War": America's Global Strategy and the Truman Doctrine in Greece* (New York: Oxford University Press, 1989), p. 221.

40. The harshness of a wartime life is grimly portrayed in Nicholas Gage, *Eleni* (New York: Random House, 1983), pp. 30–37.

41. For an account of this terror in the Peloponnese, see Lars Baerentzen, "The Liberation of the Peloponnese, September, 1944," in *Greece in the 1940s*, ed. Iatrides, pp. 131–41.

42. John O. Iatrides, "Civil War, 1945–1949: National and International Aspects," in *Greece in the 1940s*, ed. Iatrides, p. 213.

43. Indeed, the Metaxis regime had infiltrated the KKE to such an extent that, to sow confusion, it was able to set up its own faction within the party. See Loulis, *Greek Communist Party*, pp. 4–6.

44. Ibid., pp. 14–20.

45. Ibid., pp. xiv, 40, 49–56; Averoff-Tossizza, *By Fire and Axe*, pp. 33–35; and Burks, "Hellenic Time of Troubles," p. 48.

46. On the markedly right-wing character of this para-state, the *parakratos*, see Burks, "Hellenic Time of Troubles," p. 50.

47. A good overview of the political troubles in Athens is that of Keith Legg, "Musical Chairs in Athens: Analyzing Political Instability, 1946-1952," in *Studies in the History of the Greek Civil War 1945–1949*, ed. Lars Baerentzen, John O. Iatrides, and Ole L. Smith (Copenhagen: Museum Tusculanum Press, 1987), pp. 9–24.

48. Jones, "*A New Kind of War*," p. 152.

49. Kenneth Matthews found the morale among women fighters to be high. One of them told him: "None of us is married. Our guns are our husbands." See his *Memories of a Mountain War: Greece, 1944–1949* (London: Longman Press, 1972), p. 149. Women were not allowed to vote in national elections until 1956.

50. Averoff-Tossizza, *By Fire and Axe*, p. 24.

51. Ibid., p. 66.

52. R. V. Burks has speculated that at the time of these elections, support for the KKE had shrunk to no more than a third of the electorate from a wartime high of two-thirds. See his "Hellenic Time of Troubles," p. 49.

53. Jones, "*A New Kind of War*," p. 65; and Averoff-Tossizza, *By Fire and Axe*, p. 231.

54. Constantine Tsoucalas, "The Ideological Impact of the Civil War," in *Greece in the 1940s*, ed. Iatrides, pp. 330-32. Tscoucalis noted a flocking of intellectuals into the civil bureaucracy. Thus there was little criticism of the government from intellectuals, who saw themselves as "servants of the state." This co-optation is best illustrated by the career of Greece's leading intellectual, Nikos Kazantzakis, who ultimately rejected communism and stood Hegel back on his feet by returning to a special destiny for the nation of Greece. See ibid., pp. 332–34.

55. Jones, "*A New Kind of War*," pp. 89, 198–201.

56. Loulis, *Greek Communist Party*, pp. xvi-xvii, 34, 41–43; and Averoff-Tossizza, *By Fire and Axe*, p. 75.

57. On this debate, see Loulis, *Greek Communist Party*, pp. 174–79; Burks, "Hellenic Time of Troubles," pp. 49–50; and Averoff-Tossizza, *By Fire and Axe*, pp. 130–33.

58. The only justification the KKE gave for the executions was that the British held thousands of mutineers in concentration camps. The British rejoinder was that none of them was killed. See Woodhouse, *Struggle for Greece*, p. 133.

59. Christopher Woodhouse has discounted any Maoist influence on the Greeks. Among those who are more convinced of a Maoist stamp are Edgar O'Ballance and

Dimitrios Kousoulas. See Woodhouse, *Struggle for Greece*, pp. 217–18; O'Ballance, *Greek Civil War*, p. 181; and Kousoulas, *Revolution and Defeat*, pp. 240–41.

60. Averoff-Tossizza, *By Fire and Axe*, pp. 285–90.

61. Burks, "Hellenic Time of Troubles," pp. 54–55.

62. Svoronos, "Greek History," p. 5.

63. During World War II anyway, 70 percent of the communist guerrillas were peasants. Their officers, however, were overwhelmingly urban. See Loulis, *Greek Communist Party*, p. 54.

64. Svoronos, "Greek History," p. 7.

65. Ibid., pp. 5–7. In similarly describing this process, Kostas Vergopoulos called this rural class the "peripheral bourgeoisie." See his "The Emergence of the New Bourgeoisie, 1944–1952," in *Greece in the 1940's*, ed. Iatrides, pp. 300–304.

66. Peter J. Stavrakis, *Moscow and Greek Communism, 1941–1949* (Ithaca, N.Y.: Cornell University Press, 1989), p. 3.

67. For a discussion of this split, see ibid., pp. 189–97; and Burks, "Hellenic Time of Troubles," p. 57.

68. Loulis, *Greek Communist Party*, p. 82; and Michael Macrakis, "Russian Mission on the Mountains of Greece, Summer, 1944," *Journal of Contemporary History* 23 (July 1988): 387–408. Interestingly, British advisers held ELAS fighters in a similar low regard. See Matthews, *Memories of a Mountain War*, p. 81.

69. Macrakis, "Russian Mission on the Mountains," p. 398; and Loulis, *Greek Communist Party*, pp. 141–42.

70. For Stalin, of course, this was the ultimate insult. See Matthews, *Memories of a Mountain War*, p. 88.

71. As late as August 1948, three Soviet ships offloaded military supplies at Tirana, Albania, for the DA. Although the aid was sufficient for guerrilla operations, it was not enough for a conventional stand at Vitsi and Grammos. See Stavrakis, *Moscow and Greek Communism*, pp. 162–64, 176–77; and Jones, "A New Kind of War," p. 253.

72. Elisabeth Barker, "The Yugoslavs and the Greek Civil War," in *Studies in the History of the Greek Civil War*, ed. Baerentzen, Iatrides and Smith, pp. 305–08.

73. Matthews, *Memories of a Mountain War*, pp. 73–82. The heavy hand of the Greek communists in these mutinies, however, was not helpful to their nationalist credentials either. See Loulis, *Greek Communist Party*, pp. 115–23.

74. This, of course, was by way of popular historical recollection of the famous British poet's involvement in the war of independence. Gage also noted the popularity of British agents in Greece's northern mountains during the war. See Gage, *Eleni*, pp. 31, 89. Matthews reported on enthusiastic receptions given to British forces in the Peloponnese in 1944. See his *Memories of a Mountain War*, pp. 111–12.

75. Wittner, *American Intervention in Greece*, p. 189.

76. Lincoln P. Bloomfield and Amelia C. Leiss, *Controlling Small Wars: A Strategy for the 1970s* (New York: Knopf, 1969), p. 181. Under the British, the Greek army grew to 100,000 men. The English maintained a sizable military presence in Greece. From the 75,000 sent to Athens in Round 2, British soldiers still numbered 14,000 in 1947, including a 1,300-man training mission. A brigade-sized force remained until the end that was stationed mainly around Salonika. Their presence precluded any

possibility of the DA seizing the port and cutting the country in two. See Wittner, *American Intervention in Greece*, p. 228.

77. Bloomfield and Leiss, *Controlling Small Wars*, p. 181; and Vergopoulos, "Emergence of the New Bourgeoisie," p. 304.

78. Tsoucalis, "Ideological Impact of the Civil War," p. 322.

79. Vergopoulos, "Emergence of the New Bourgeoisie," pp. 302-3, 311; and Wittner, *American Intervention in Greece*, p. 189.

80. In his account of this less than savory tale of American penetration, Wittner cited U.S. Embassy reports of a 70 percent communist following in the urban labor force in 1945. Thus, the distance traveled in this effort was considerable. See Wittner, *American Intervention in Greece*, pp. 192-222 (figure on p. 193). For confirmation of this penetration, see also Adamantia Pollis, "U.S. Intervention in Greek Trade Unions," in *Greece in the 1940s*, ed. Iatrides, pp. 259-74.

81. For the scale and impact of this assistance, see Jones, *"A New Kind of War,"* pp. 124, 160, 219.

82. The strategy was one of concentrated military sweeps across the country south to north. Soldiers would enter an area and detain civilian sympathizers of the guerrillas for sufficient time to force the guerrillas to move out of the area if they were to find continued support. This had the dual effect of driving the guerrillas toward the intended destination and depriving the DA of its life-sustaining intelligence network along the way. See ibid., pp. 201-2. It was precisely this strategy that General Palmer advocated for Vietnam. See Bruce Palmer, *The 25-Year War* (Lexington: University Press of Kentucky, 1984), pp. 59-62.

83. The contention that U.S. restraint in Greece imposed a wider European restraint on the Soviets is advanced by Jones, *"A New Kind of War,"* pp. 224-26.

84. For evidence that the Truman administration was well aware of the classic balance-of-power and economic lifeline implications of its more publicized moral crusade against communism in Greece, see Wittner, *American Intervention in Greece*, pp. 17-22.

85. Recently, such revisionist scholars as Lawrence Wittner and D. Michael Shafer have argued that this "victory" in Greece was a defeat for the United States because it gave rise to an interventionist foreign policy of "contentless universalism" that set Washington up for its debacle in Vietnam. See Wittner, *American Intervention in Greece*, pp. 253, 312; and Shafer, *Deadly Paradigms*, pp. 203-04.

Chapter Eight

1. For the numbers, see Lawrence M. Greenberg, *The Hukbalahap Insurrection: A Case Study of a Successful Anti-Insurgency Operation in the Philippines—1946–1955* (Washington, D.C.: U.S. Army Center of Military History, 1987), p. 142; and Kenneth M. Hammer, "Huks in the Philippines," in *Modern Guerrilla Warfare*, ed. Franklin Mark Osanka (New York: Free Press, 1962), p. 181.

2. Eduardo Lachicha, *The Huks: Philippine Agrarian Society in Revolt* (New York: Praeger, 1971), pp. 5, 123-24; José V. Abueva, *Ramon Magsaysay: A Political Biography* (Manila: Solidaridad Publishing House, 1971), p. 155; and Stanley Karnow, *In Our*

Image: America's Empire in the Philippines (New York: Random House, 1989), p. 344.

3. José Maria Sison with Ranier Werning, *The Philippine Revolution: The Leader's View* (New York: Crane Russack, 1989), pp. xxiv–xxv.

4. Gregorio F. Zaide, *The Republic of the Philippines* (Manila: Rex Book Store, 1963), p. 3; and Fred Poole and Max Vanzi, *Revolution in the Philippines: The United States in a Hall of Cracked Mirrors* (New York: McGraw-Hill, 1984), p. 34.

5. Republic of the Philippines, Department of Commerce and Industry, *Philippine Statistics, 1960: Handbook* (Manila: Bureau of the Census and Statistics, 1960), p. 14.

6. Zaide, *Republic of the Philippines*, p. 14. Only a portion of this 25 percent could be counted as a modern middle class.

7. Republic of the Philippines, Department of Commerce and Industry, *Census of the Philippines, 1948* (Manila: Bureau of the Census and Statistics, 1951), pp. 9–10.

8. Renato Constantino, *A History of the Philippines: From the Spanish Colonization to the Second World War* (New York: Monthly Review Press, 1975), p. 27.

9. David R. Sturtevant, *Popular Uprisings in the Philippines, 1840–1940* (Ithaca, N.Y.: Cornell University Press, 1976), pp. 21–24; and David Joel Steinberg, *Philippine Collaboration in World War II* (Ann Arbor: University of Michigan Press, 1967), pp. 1–4. For an insightful discussion of Spanish Catholicism's integration of *utang na loob* and *hiya*, see Vicente L. Rafael, *Contracting Colonialism: Translation and Christian Conversion in Tagalog Society under Early Spanish Rule* (Ithaca, N.Y.: Cornell University Press, 1988), pp. 121–35.

10. By the 1850s Tagalog and the Visayan languages had become so varied that the speakers could not understand each other. See Peter W. Stanley, *A Nation in the Making: The Philippines and the United States, 1899–1922* (Cambridge, Mass.: Harvard University Press, 1974), p. 14.

11. Sturtevant, *Popular Uprisings*, pp. 32–33.

12. Steinberg, *Philippine Collaboration*, pp. 178–79.

13. John Morgan Gates, *Schoolbooks and Krags: The United States Army in the Philippines, 1898–1902* (Westport, Conn.: Greenwood Press, 1973), p. 9. For a social portrait of this rising Inquilino class, see Soledad Borromeo-Buehler, "The Inquilinos of Cavite: A Social Class in Nineteenth Century Philippines," *Journal of Southeast Asian Studies* 16 (March 1985):69–98. For the Chinese more generally, see Edgar Wickberg, *The Chinese in Philippine Life, 1850–1898* (New Haven, Conn.: Yale University Press, 1965).

14. Sturtevant, *Popular Uprisings*, p. 41.

15. Thus began a family tradition of attacking the enemy's rear at critical moments. His son Douglas struck the Japanese from behind in 1944 at Ormoc when he was bottled up in trench warfare on Leyte Island at the start of his reconquest of the Philippines. In Korea, his great masterstroke of the Inchon landings, therefore, should not have come as a surprise.

16. For a vivid account of Funston's exploit, see David Howard Bain, *Sitting in Darkness: Americans in the Philippines* (Boston: Houghton Mifflin, 1984), pp. 344–74.

17. Karnow, *In Our Image*, p. 194. For three scholarly accounts of the Philippine-American War, see Gates, *Schoolbooks and Krags*; Brian McAlister Linn, *The U.S. Army and Counterinsurgency in the Philippine War, 1899–1902* (Chapel Hill: University of North Carolina Press, 1980); and Stuart C. Miller, *"Benevolent Assimilation":*

The American Conquest of the Philippines, 1899–1903 (New Haven, Conn.: Yale University Press, 1983).

18. Glenn Anthony May, *Social Engineering in the Philippines: The Aims, Expectations, and Impact of American Colonial Policy, 1900–1913* (Westport, Conn.: Greenwood Press, 1980), p. 29.

19. David Wurfel, *Filipino Politics: Development and Decay* (Ithaca, N.Y.: Cornell University Press, 1988), pp. 9, 44.

20. May, *Social Engineering*, pp. 28–32.

21. Karnow, *In Our Image*, p. 329.

22. Stanley, *Nation in the Making*, pp. 187, 203–7.

23. Sturtevant, *Popular Uprisings*, p. 61.

24. Lachicha, *The Huks*, pp. 54–59; and Benedict J. Kerkvliet, *The Huk Rebellion: A Study of Peasant Revolt in the Philippines* (Berkeley: University of California Press, 1977), p. 27.

25. Sturtevant, *Popular Uprisings*, pp. 145, 221–226; and Lachicha, *The Huks*, pp. 71–73. The Philippine communists had opposed the revolt as suicidal. See William J. Pomeroy, ed., *Guerrilla Warfare and Marxism* (London: Lawrence and Wishart, 1969), p. 28. The Sakdalist revolt played a similar role to the 1930 Yen Bay mutiny in Vietnam. In both cases the communists profited from the elimination of political competitors through these premature and suicidal eruptions.

26. Kerkvliet, *Huk Rebellion*, pp. 27–36, 46, 55–56.

27. Lachicha, *The Huks*, pp. 91, 97, 99–102; Kerkvliet, *Huk Rebellion*, pp. 51–53; and Tomas C. Tirona, "The Philippine Anti-Communist Campaign," in *Modern Guerrilla Warfare*, ed. Osanka, pp. 203–4. Brief portraits of Pedro Santos can be found in Karnow, *In Our Image*, pp. 338–39; and Sturtevant, *Popular Uprisings*, pp. 251–54.

28. Kerkvliet, *Huk Rebellion*, pp. 79–80.

29. Lachicha, *The Huks*, pp. 111–14; and William Manchester, *American Caesar: Douglas MacArthur, 1880–1964* (Boston: Little, Brown, 1978), pp. 374–75, 381.

30. Manchester, *American Caesar*, pp. 406, 413; and David Bergami, *Japan's Imperial Conspiracy* (New York: William Morrow, 1971), p. 1033.

31. Zaide, *Republic of the Philippines*, p. 293.

32. Manchester, *American Caesar*, p. 429; Karnow, *In Our Image*, p. 316; and Lucian W. Pye, *Asian Power and Politics: The Cultural Dimensions of Authority* (Cambridge, Mass.: Harvard University Press, 1985), quote from p. 126.

33. For an account of the Malolos massacre, see Karnow, *In Our Image*, p. 340; and Kerkvliet, *Huk Rebellion*, p. 113.

34. Kerkvliet, *Huk Rebellion*, pp. 110–16; and Tirona, "Philippine Anti-Communist Campaign," p. 205. The MacArthur quote is in Manchester, *American Caesar*, p. 420.

35. Abueva, *Magsaysay*, p. 77.

36. Douglas MacArthur, *Reminiscences* (New York: McGraw-Hill, 1964), pp. 236–37.

37. Kerkvliet, *Huk Rebellion*, p. 19; and *Census of the Philippines*, p. 7.

38. Frances Lucille Starner, *Magsaysay and the Philippine Peasantry: The Agrarian Impact on Philippine Politics, 1953–1956*, University of California Publications in

Political Science, vol. 10 (Berkeley: University of California Press, 1961), p. 14

39. Lachica, *The Huks*, p. 119.

40. Kerkvliet, *Huk Rebellion*, pp. 121, 128.

41. Lachica, *The Huks*, pp. 119–20; and Kerkvliet, *Huk Rebellion*, p. 140.

42. Kerkvliet, *Huk Rebellion*, pp. 52, 153; and Lachica, *The Huks*, p. 123.

43. Douglas S. Blaufarb, *The Counterinsurgency Era: U.S. Doctrine and Performance* (New York: Free Press, 1977), p. 26.

44. Kerkvliet, *Huk Rebellion*, pp. 200–202; and Lachicha, *The Huks*, pp. 121–22.

45. Lachica, *The Huks*, pp. 123–24, 127–28. The plans were discovered in documents seized in the October 1950 politburo raid. See Boyd T. Bashore, "Dual Strategy for Limited War," in *Modern Guerrilla Warfare*, ed. Osanka, p. 194. On the explicit Maoist cast to the plan, see Blaufarb, *Counterinsurgency Era*, p. 25.

46. Bashore, "Dual Strategy for Limited War," pp. 196–97; Blaufarb, *Counterinsurgency Era*, p. 28; and Greenberg, *Hukbalahap Insurrection*, pp. 88, 110, 131. Eventually, thirty-one BCTs and one independent artillery battalion were organized. See Abueva, *Magsaysay*, p. 178.

47. For an account of the politburo raid, see Abueva, *Magsaysay*, pp. 166–69. The leader of the subsequent communist New People's Army, José Maria Sison, has conceded that this raid thwarted the military offensives planned for November 1951. See Sison, *Philippine Revolution*, p. 43.

48. Abueva, *Magsaysay*, p. 178. All told in 1951 the Huks lost thirteen thousand men to either combat or defection, nearly half their total losses. See Greenberg, *Hukbalahap Insurrection*, p. 136.

49. This brief military account has been culled from Hammer, "Huks in the Philippines," p. 183; Abueva, *Magsaysay*, p. 178; Lachicha, *The Huks*, pp. 128–32; Kerkvliet, *Huk Rebellion*, pp. 234–36; and Greenberg, *Hukbalahap Insurrection*, pp. 136–40. The official casualty figures are taken from Bashore, "Dual Strategy for Limited War," p. 198.

50. Kerkvliet, *Huk Rebellion*, p. 239. Even such a critic as D. Michael Shafer has conceded that EDCOR worked in stealing the Huk's thunder. See his *Deadly Paradigms: The Failure of U.S. Counterinsurgency Policy* (Princeton, N.J.: Princeton University Press, 1988), p. 237. Douglas Blaufarb has further argued that much of the credit for the high defection rate of the Huks should go to EDCOR. See his *Counterinsurgency Era*, p. 33.

51. David Wurfel, "Foreign Aid and Social Reform in Political Development: A Philippine Case Study," *American Political Science Review* 53 (June 1959): 421; and "Philippine Agrarian Reform under Magsaysay," *Far Eastern Survey* 27 (January 1958): 10, 12.

52. Starner, *Magsaysay and the Philippine Peasantry*, pp. 6, 60–62, 127, 138.

53. Jorge Maravilla, "The Postwar Huk in the Philippines," in *Guerrilla Warfare and Marxism*, ed. Pomeroy, p. 240.

54. The *compadrazgo* networks are explained well by Steinberg, *Philippine Collaboration*, pp. 5–8; and Karnow, *In Our Image*, pp. 21–22.

55. Zaide, *Republic of the Philippines*, p. 298.

56. Manchester, *American Caesar*, p. 413.

57. *Census of the Philippines, 1948*, p. 9.

58. Amando Doronilo, "The Transformation of Patron-Client Relations and Its Political Consequences in Postwar Philippines," *Journal of Southeast Asian Studies* 16 (March 1985): 103.

59. Wurfel, "Foreign Aid and Social Reform in Political Development," pp. 466–68; and Abueva, *Magsaysay*, p. 355.

60. On the successful military operations that thwarted these Huk expansions, see Abueva, *Magsaysay*, p. 166; and Greenberg, *Hukbalahap Insurrection*, p. 125.

61. Robert P. Stephens, "The Prospect for Social Progress in the Philippines," *Pacific Affairs* 23 (June 1950): 139–52.

62. In his first thirty days in office, Magsaysay removed thirteen senior officers from the ten BCTs that had then been organized. See Abueva, *Magsaysay*, pp. 162–63.

63. Cecil B. Currey, *Edward Lansdale: The Unquiet American* (Boston: Houghton Mifflin, 1988), p. 119.

64. Karnow, *In Our Image*, p. 342.

65. Wurfel, "Foreign Aid and Social Reform in Political Development," p. 471.

66. Ibid., pp. 469–71.

67. Abueva, *Magsaysay*, pp. 102–6.

68. Doronilo, "Transformation of Patron-Client Relations," pp. 108–9.

69. Karnow, *In Our Image*, p. 347.

70. Pye, *Asian Power and Politics*, p. 127. A sophisticated set of essays has traced this weakness of modern Filipino democracy to the way the American imperium extended an electoral system throughout the islands that paradoxically "provided a mechanism for elaborating and deepening factional rivalries." See Ruby R. Paredes, ed., *Philippine Colonial Democracy*, Monograph Series 32 (New Haven, Conn.: Yale University Southeast Asia Studies, 1988), quote on p. 7.

71. Lee Young Leng, "Race, Language, and National Cohesion in Southeast Asia," *Journal of Southeast Asian Studies* 11 (March 1980): 138.

72. It is difficult to assess the importance of this ethnic split both between Huk fighters and between the two parallel politburos. Edward Mitchell has argued that it was only in areas with large Pampagueno populations that the Huks had strong local support, whereas Harvey Averich and John Koehler, in an examination of the same demographic data, have countered that the degree of Huk control depended more on their efforts of coercion and terror irrespective of the ethnic population of particular localities. See Edward J. Mitchell, "Some Econometrics of the Huk Rebellion," *American Political Science Review* 63 (December 1969): 1165; and Harvey Averich and John Koehler, "Explaining Dissident Success: The Huks in Central Luzon" (Santa Monica, Calif.: Rand Corp., P-4753, January 1972), pp. 1, 12, 20.

73. On these group patterns and traditions, see Zaide, *Republic of the Philippines*, pp. 20–21; Constantino, *History of the Philippines*, p. 94; Sturtevant, *Popular Uprisings*, p. 90; and Stanley, *Nation in the Making*, pp. 14–15.

74. Karnow, *In Our Image*, pp. 46–47.

75. Ibid., pp. 67–70.

76. Gregorio F. Zaide, *Philippine History and Civilization* (Manila: Philippine Education Co., 1939), p. 485.

77. For a brief discussion of this debate, see Glenn Anthony May, "Resistance and Collaboration in the Philippine-American War: The Case of Batangas," *Journal of Southeast Asian Studies* 15 (March 1984): 70.

78. Bain, *Sitting in Darkness*, p. 57.

79. Two such works are Teodoro Agoncillo, *Malalos: The Crisis of the Republic* (Quezon City: University of the Philippines, 1960), esp. pp. viii–ix, 621–78; and Renato Constantino, *The Philippines: A Past Revisited* (Manila: Tala Publishing, 1979), pp. 233–44.

80. Glenn Anthony May, "Private Presher and Sergeant Vergara: The Underside of the Philippine-American War," in *Reappraising an Empire: New Perspectives on Philippine-American History*, ed. Peter W. Stanley (Cambridge, Mass.: Harvard University Press, 1974), p. 57.

81. Wong Kwok Chu, "The Jones Bill, 1912–1916: A Reappraisal of Filipino Views on Independence," *Journal of Southeast Asian Studies* 13 (September 1982): 252–69.

82. Stephen Rosskamm Shalom, *The United States and the Philippines: A Study of Neocolonialism* (Philadelphia: Institute for the Study of Human Issues, 1981), p. 1.

83. Donald Blackburn, "War within a War: The Philippines, 1942–1945," *Conflict* 7 (March 1987): 144.

84. Steinberg, *Philippine Collaboration*, pp. 165–67, 175.

85. Kerkvliet, *Huk Rebellion*, pp. xv, 67.

86. Starner, *Magsaysay and the Philippine Peasantry*, pp. 4, 6.

87. Karnow, *In Our Image*, pp. 338–39; and Lachicha, *The Huks*, pp. 88–89.

88. Lachicha, *The Huks*, pp. 123–26.

89. The government informer was a great-great nephew of José Rizal whom the communists, like Aguinaldo with his forebear, recruited for his *ilustrado* luster. He was also a protégé of President Quirino. See Abueva, *Magsaysay*, pp. 166–68.

90. Ibid., pp. 249–68.

91. William J. Pomeroy, "The Philippine Peasantry and the Huk Revival," *Journal of Peasant Studies* 5 (July 1978): 499.

92. Quoted by Stuart R. Schram, *The Political Thought of Mao Tse-tung* (New York: Praeger, 1969), p. 172.

93. Kerkvliet, *Huk rebellion*, pp. 188, 193, 244.

94. Currey, *Edward Lansdale*, pp. 106, 131.

95. Greenberg, *Hukbalahap Insurrection*, p. 108.

96. Maravilla, "The Postwar Huk," p. 240.

97. Kerkvliet, *Huk Rebellion*, p. 245.

98. Lachicha, *The Huks*, p. 131.

99. Kerkvliet, *Huk Rebellion*, p. 191. For an account of the involvement of the American Communist party with the Huks, including its role in establishing the PKP and then in brokering the alliance with the socialists in 1938, see Karnow, *In Our Image*, pp. 337–38.

100. Blaufarb, *Counterinsurgency Era*, p. 25; and Karnow, *In Our Image*, pp. 310–11.

101. Maravilla, "The Postwar Huk," p. 241.

102. Edward Geary Lansdale, *In the Midst of Wars* (New York: Harper & Row, 1972), p. 26.

103. For this disproportionate desertion of the Tagalog Huks to Magsaysay, see Mitchell, "Some Econometrics of the Huk Rebellion," p. 1167.

104. Gregg R. Jones, *Red Revolution: Inside the Philippine Guerrilla Movement* (Boulder, Colo.: Westview Press, 1989), pp. 25–27, 33, 59–72, 131.

105. William Chapman, *Inside the Philippine Revolution* (New York: Norton, 1987), p. 14.

106. Jones, *Red Revolution*, p. 297.

Chapter Nine

1. Victor Purcell, *Malaysia* (London: Thames and Hudson, 1965), p. 39; Lucian W. Pye, *Guerrilla Communism in Malaya* (Princeton, N.J.: Princeton University Press, 1956), p. 99; and John Gullick, *Malaysia: Economic Expansion and National Unity* (Boulder, Colo., Westview Press, 1981), p. 2.

2. Edgar O'Ballance, *Malaya: The Communist Insurgent War, 1948–1960* (Hamden, Conn.: Archon Books, 1966), p. 37.

3. Paul H. Kratoska, "Rice Cultivation and the Ethnic Division of Labor in British Malaya," *Comparative Studies in Society and History* 24 (April 1982): 282.

4. These and subsequent figures do *not* include Singapore, with its one million inhabitants, 80 percent of whom were Chinese. See Pye, *Guerrilla Communism*, p. 12.

5. Twenty-five percent of the total labor force worked in rice fields and another 27 percent on rubber plantations. See Charles Hirschman, "Industrial and Occupational Change in Peninsular Malaysia, 1947–1970," *Journal of Southeast Asian Studies* 13 (March 1982): 16.

6. Karl von Vorys, *Democracy without Consensus: Communalism and Political Stability in Malaysia* (Princeton, N.J.: Princeton University Press, 1975), p. 142.

7. Hirschman, "Industrial and Occupational Change," pp. 18–19.

8. Forty-two percent of the 50 percent rural Indian population worked on the rubber plantations, while, in 1937, only 10 percent of the rubber workers were Malays. In 1931, of twenty-five thousand miners, a mere five hundred were Malays. Officially, all but 3 percent of the land under rice cultivation was owned by Malays. Unofficially, after the war, with a half million Chinese squatters without titles, the percentage of Chinese rice farmers was considerably higher. See ibid.; P. P. Courtenay, "The Plantation in Malaysian Economic Development," *Journal of Southeast Asian Studies* 12 (September 1981): 334; Hua Wu Yin, *Class and Communalism in Malaysia: Politics in a Dependent Capitalist State* (London: Zed Books, 1983), p. 54; and Kratoska, "Rice Cultivation," p. 283.

9. K. J. Ratnam, *Communalism and the Political Process in Malaya* (Kuala Lumpur: University of Malaya Press, 1965), p. 2; and Peter J. Rimmer and George C. H. Cho, "Urbanization of the Malays since Independence: Evidence from West Malaysia, 1957 and 1970," *Journal of Southeast Asian Studies* 12 (September 1981): 352.

10. Richard L. Clutterbuck, *Conflict and Violence in Singapore and Malaysia, 1945–1983* (Boulder, Colo.: Westview Press, 1985), p. 35.

11. Though these ingredients provided the basis for a powerful group identity as Malays, such a mix should make clear that they were not all of a piece. The several sultanates were products of widely separated waves of migrations with different principles of rule. Negri Sembilan, for example, was matriarchal in property rights and succession. All the sultanates had their own founding myth for dynastic legitimation, most having to do with various missions, matings, and bathings in the sacred river Melayu. Some even traced their roots to encounters with Alexander the

Great and the emperor of Constantinople. For good discussions of these sources of rule, see John M. Gullick, *Indigenous Political Systems of Western Malaya* (London: Athlone Press, 1958), pp. 3–22.; Virginia Matheson, "Concepts of Malay Ethos in Indigenous Malay Writings," *Journal of Southeast Asian Studies* 10 (September 1979). 351–71; and Horace Stone, *From Malacca to Malaysia, 1400–1965* (London. George G. Harrap, 1966), pp. 11–35.

12. J. H. Drabble and P. J. Drake, "The British Agency Houses in Malaysia: Survival in a Changing World," *Journal of Southeast Asian Studies* 10 (September 1981): 298.

13. Stone, *From Malacca to Malaysia*, p. 124; C. D. Cowan, *Nineteenth Century Malaya: The Origins of British Political Control*, London Oriental Series, no. 11 (London: Oxford University Press, 1961), p. 82; and Rupert Emerson, *Malaysia: A Study in Direct and Indirect Rule* (New York: Macmillan, 1937), p. 156. The U.S. dollar figures were derived by dividing by three the Malay dollar figures in the texts.

14. Ong Chit Chung, "Major General William Dobbie and the Defense of Malaya, 1935–38," *Journal of Southeast Asian Studies* 17 (September 1986): 290. As an illustration of this value, in 1948 the net surplus earned by Malaya was $172 million. This was more than double the total amount earned by the next three British Empire dollar earners of the Gold Coast, Gambia, and Ceylon. See Hua Wu Yin, *Class and Communalism in Malaysia*, p. 91.

15. Leon F. Comber, *Chinese Secret Societies in Malaya: A Survey of the Triad Society from 1800 to 1900* ((Locust Valley, N.Y.: J. J. Augustin, 1959), p. 50; and Victor Purcell, *The Chinese in Malaya* (London: Oxford University Press, 1948), pp. 114, 117.

16. John M. Gullick, *Malay Society in the Late Nineteenth Century* (Singapore: Oxford University Press, 1987), pp. 51–54.

17. Malacca with a large Malay population and Johore with a huge Chinese community are near exceptions to these generalizations. See von Vorys, *Democracy without Consensus*, pp. 22, 142.

18. Purcell, *Chinese in Malaya*, Appendix III.

19. Ratnam, *Communalism and the Political Process*, pp. 9–10. All told, from 1909 to 1940, 16 million Chinese and Indians passed in and out of Malaya. During the same period, interestingly, 19 million immigrants came to the United States to stay. See Collin E. R. Abraham, "Racial and Ethnic Manipulation in Colonial Malaya," *Ethnic and Racial Studies* 6 (January 1983): 22.

20. For a full account of the British campaign against the secret societies, see Comber, *Chinese Secret Societies in Malaya*, pp. 255–72.

21. Pye, *Guerrilla Communism*, pp. 56–57. Though the Indians were predominantly from the south, there was great variety in this community. For a full specification, see A. Arasaratnam, "Indian Society of Malaysia and Its Leaders: Trends in Leadership and Ideology among Malaysian Indians, 1945–1960," *Journal of Southeast Asian Studies* 13 (September 1982): 236–51.

22. The Malay Reservations Law was enacted in 1913. By 1930, of 669,000 acres under rice cultivation, only 3 percent was cultivated by Indians and Chinese. A survey conducted the same year revealed, nevertheless, that some 13 percent of reservation land was "held" by non-Malays. The pressures of Chinese squatters during the Emergency certainly produced further encroachments, but it is noteworthy that in 1970, a decade after the end of the Emergency, non-Malay rice growers amounted

to the same 3 percent. That the British were in the unique position of being able to please everyone is demonstrated by Rupert Emerson's report in 1937 that though 6 million acres had been alienated for agriculture, only 5 million were under cultivation, including 3.2 million in rubber. For the Emergency after the war, this "slack" of a million acres was critical for the political and economic accommodation of the Chinese squatters. See Paul H. Kratoska, " 'Ends that we cannot foresee': Malay Reservations in British Malaya," *Journal of Southeast Asian Studies* 14 (March 1983): 149, 157; Kratoska, "Rice Cultivation and Ethnic Division," pp. 283, 314; and Emerson, *Malaysia*, p. 37.

23. Pye, *Guerrilla Communism*, pp. 47–50; and William R. Roff, *The Origins of Malay Nationalism*, Yale Southeast Asia Studies, no. 2 (New Haven, Conn.: Yale University Press, 1967), p. 109. For a full, if hagiographic, account of the MCS, see Robert Heussler's two-volume work, *British Rule in Malaya: The Malayan Civil Service and Its Predecessors, 1867–1942*, and *Completing a Stewardship: The Malayan Civil Service, 1942–1957*, Contributions in Comparative Colonial Studies, nos. 6 and 15 (Westport, Conn.: Greenwood Press, 1981 and 1983).

24. The Hindu principle of the *devaraja* (divine king), which was part of the regal rituals of all the sultanates, was utter blasphemy in any pure renaissant Islam. See Kenneth Perry Landon, *Southeast Asia: Crossroad of Religions* (Chicago: University of Chicago Press, 1949), pp. 83–85.

25. Roff, *Origins of Malay Nationalism*, pp. 254–56.

26. Richard L. Clutterbuck, *The Long Long War: Counterinsurgency in Malaya and Vietnam* (New York: Frederick A. Praeger, 1966), pp. 13–14; and von Vorys, *Democracy without Consensus*, p. 21.

27. The Hailams were the fifth largest dialect/regional grouping among the Chinese. (Hainan became one of the strongholds of communism in China.) In 1931 they numbered 98,000 of the 1.7 million Chinese. The rival Guomindang derived its support from the larger communities originally from the cities of Canton and Hong Kong as well as from the surrounding rural provinces of Southeast China, which was the heartland of Guomindang strength. See Purcell, *Chinese in Malaya*, Appendix V; and Justus M. Van der Kroef, *Communism in Malaysia and Singapore: A Contemporary Survey* (The Hague, Netherlands: Martinus Nijhoff, 1967), p. 23.

28. Pye, *Guerrilla Communism*, p. 47; O'Ballance, *Malaya*, pp. 24, 30–31; Michael R. Stenson, *Industrial Conflict in Malaya: Prelude to the Communist Revolt of 1948* (London: Oxford University Press, 1970), p. 22; and Robert W. Komer, *The Malayan Emergency in Retrospect: Organization of a Successful Counterinsurgency Effort* (Santa Monica, Calif.: Rand Corporation R-957-ARPA, 1972), p. 2.

29. Winston S. Churchill, *Second World War*, vol. 4: *Hinge of Fate* (Boston: Houghton Mifflin, 1950), p. 92.

30. O'Ballance, *Malaya*, pp. 55–57.

31. Indeed, the postwar Malay leader Tunku Abdul Rahman spirited away his father (the sultan of Kedah) from the British officials who sought his evacuation. See Cheah Boon Kheng, "The Social Impact of the Japanese Occupation of Malaya (1942–1945)," in *Southeast Asia Under Japanese Occupation*, ed. Alfred W. McCoy Monograph Series 22 (New Haven, Conn.: Yale University Southeast Asia Studies, 1980), p. 95.

32. Yoji Akashi, "The Japanese Occupation of Malaya: Interruption or Transformation?", ibid., pp. 78, 80.

33. These four sultanates (Kelantan, Trengganu, Kedah, and Perlis) had been acquired by the British from Thailand in 1909.

34. Cheah Boon Kheng, "The Social Impact of the Japanese Occupation," pp. 98–99.

35. Von Vorys, *Democracy without Consensus*, pp. 55, 58–59; Akashi, "Japanese Occupation," p. 76; and Gullick, *Malaysia*, p. 81.

36. Purcell, *Chinese in Malaya*, pp. 245–46; von Vorys, *Democracy without Consensus*, pp. 57–58; Clutterbuck, *Long Long War*, pp. 14–18; and Major Daniel S. Challis, "Counterinsurgency Success in Malaya," *Military Review* 67 (February 1987): 57.

37. O'Ballance, *Malaya*, p. 58. Lucian Pye has contended that this figure represented total Japanese casualties in Malaya during World War II, including those inflicted by the British, and that MPAJA itself accounted for just a few hundred. See Pye, *Guerrilla Communism*, p. 69.

38. Thus, in 1947, 64 percent of the Chinese population was locally born, as was 52 percent of the Indian. See Ratnam, *Communalism and the Political Process*, pp. 9–10.

39. O'Ballance, *Malaya*, pp. 65–66.

40. Donald L. Horowitz, *Ethnic Groups in Conflict* (Berkeley: University of California Press, 1985), p. 398.

41. O'Ballance, *Malaya*, p. 59; and Cheah Boon Kheng, "Sino-Malay Conflicts in Malaya, 1945–1946: Communist Vendetta and Islamic Resistance," *Journal of Southeast Asian Studies* 12 (March 1980): 108–10, 113–14.

42. Clutterbuck, *Long Long War*, pp. 22–24.

43. Ibid., pp. 26–28, 30; and Stenson, *Industrial Conflict in Malaya*, p. 124.

44. He fled to Thailand, where he was assassinated by an MCP "Traitor Killing Squad." See O'Ballance, *Malaya*, p. 72.

45. Clutterbuck, *Long Long War*, p. 28.

46. For details of the Federation plan, see James P. Ongkili, *Nation-Building in Malaysia, 1946–1974* (Singapore: Oxford University Press, 1985), pp. 53–74.

47. James E. Dougherty, "The Guerrilla War in Malaya," in *Modern Guerrilla Warfare*, ed. Franklin Mark Osanka (New York: Free Press, 1962), p. 304; and Pye, *Guerrilla Communism*, p. 61.

48. Robert O. Tilman, "Non-Lessons of the Malayan Emergency," *Asian Survey* 6 (August 1966): 409; Pye, *Guerrilla Communism*, pp. 91, 98; and Clutterbuck, *Long Long War*, pp. 44, 87–88.

49. Clutterbuck, *Long Long War*, pp. 42–44; and O'Ballance, *Malaya*, p. 83.

50. For details, see Anthony Short, *The Communist Insurrection in Malaya, 1948–1960* (New York: Crane, Russak, 1975), pp. 119–20, 286–90. These squabbles are reminiscent of the clashes in Vietnam among the State Department, the military, and the CIA.

51. Komer, *Malayan Emergency in Retrospect*, p. 6.

52. Clutterbuck, *Conflict and Violence*, pp. 170–74.

53. Noel Barber, *The War of the Running Dogs: The Malayan Emergency, 1948–1960* (New York: Weybright and Talley, 1971), pp. 83–87; and Riley Sunderland, *Army*

Operations in Malaya, 1947–1960 (Santa Monica, Calif.: Rand Corporation, RM-4170-ISA, 1964), pp. 75–76.

54. Clutterbuck, *Long Long War*, p. 86; and Tilman, "Non-Lessons of the Malayan Emergency," p. 410.

55. Tilman, "Non-Lessons of the Malay Emergency," pp. 410, 416; Clutterbuck, *Long Long War*, p. 62; Short, *Communist Insurrection*, p. 395; and Lucian Pye, letter to author, March 26, 1991. The final total of the number resettled reached 563,000 in March 1953. See Paul H. Kratoska, "The Peripatetic Peasant and Land Tenure in British Malaya," *Journal of Southeast Asian Studies* 16 (March 1985): 37.

56. Clutterbuck, *Long Long War*, pp. 55–58.

57. In these numbers, the 350,000 Home Guardsmen reported by Tilman are put at only 100,000 by Pye because this lower figure (whom he calls "auxiliary police") represents those who were armed. See Tilman, "Non-Lessons of the Malayan Emergency," p. 418; and Pye, *Guerrilla Communism*, pp. 96–97.

58. Major J. B. Oldfield, *The Green Howards in Malaya (1949–1952)* (Aldershot, U.K.: Gale and Polden, 1953), p. xv.

59. Short, *Communist Insurrection*, pp. 339–59; and Challis, "Counterinsurgency Success," pp. 64–66.

60. Clutterbuck, *Conflict and Violence*, p. 195.

61. Clutterbuck, *Long Long War*, pp. 137–39, 142; Lucian W. Pye, *Asian Power and Politics: The Cultural Dimensions of Authority* (Cambridge, Mass.: Harvard University Press, 1985), p. 252; and O'Ballance, *Malaya*, p. 119.

62. Horowitz, *Ethnic Groups in Conflict*, pp. 401–3.

63. Ongkili, *Nation-Building*, p. 81; and O'Ballance, *Malaya*, p. 157.

64. Challis, "Counterinsurgency Success," p. 66; and Sunderland, *Army Operations*, pp. 212–16.

65. Sunderland, *Army Operations*, p. 198. For the exploits of Special Branch inspector Irene Lee's destruction of this network, see Barber, *War of the Running Dogs*, pp. 162–77.

66. Challis, "Counterinsurgency Success," pp. 68–69; and Sunderland, *Army Operations*, p. 254. For details of Hor Lung's surrender, see Barber, *War of the Running Dogs*, pp. 216–27. As a historical footnote, Chin Peng did not surrender to Malayan authorities until December 2, 1989. See "Malaysia Communists Agree to Cease-Fire After 41 Years," *New York Times*, December 3, 1989, sec. 1, p. A3.

67. Tilman, "Non-Lessons of the Malayan Emergency," p. 408. A more complete listing of other casualties can be found in O'Ballance, *Malaya*, p. 177.

68. Tilman, "Non-Lessons of the Malayan Emergency," p. 418; Stenson, *Industrial Conflict in Malaya*, p. 88; and Clutterbuck, *Long Long War*, p. 67.

69. Komer, *Malayan Emergency in Retrospect*, p. 7.

70. Rimmer and Cho, "Urbanization of the Malays since Independence," p. 350.

71. Oldfield, *Green Howards*, p. xvi.

72. Ibid., p. 119.

73. Ongkili, *Nation-Building*, p. 84. Renewed attempts at attracting Chinese were somewhat more successful. In 1952, 2,488 Chinese were among the 28,000 Police Force, and in 1953, 50,000 were in the Home Guard force of 150,000. This was still far below their proportionate share, and the Home Guards served almost exclusively

in Chinese settlements. See Komer, *Malayan Emergency in Retrospect*, pp. 38, 41. It is important to acknowledge that Chinese *were* recruited into the Special Branch and were pivotal to its numerous successes.

74. Ratnam, *Communalism and the Political Process*, pp. 221–23; Barber, *War of the Running Dogs*, p. 228; and Clutterbuck, *Long Long War*, p. 24.

75. Stenson, *Industrial Conflict in Malaya*, p. 132; and Hua Wu Yin, *Class and Communalism in Malaysia*, p. 75.

76. Stenson, *Industrial Conflict in Malaya*, pp. 234–38.

77. Ratnam, *Communalism and the Political Process*, p. 105.

78. Von Vorys, *Democracy without Consensus*, p. 95. The British first officially recognized the special rights of Malays in 1927. The new constitution essentially re-certified this. See Ratnam, *Communalism and the Political Process*, pp. 62–63, 72–73.

79. Arasaratnam, "Indian Society of Malaysia," pp. 243–45.

80. Heng Pek Koon, "The Social and Ideological Origins of the Malayan Chinese Association," *Journal of Southeast Asian Studies* 14 (September 1983): 291–92, 301, 309.

81. For fuller portraits of these two men, see Tunku Abdul Rahman, *Viewpoints* (Kuala Lumpur: Heinemann Educational Books [Asia], 1978); and K. J. Tregonning, "Tan Cheng Lock: A Malayan Nationalist," *Journal of Southeast Asian Studies* 10 (March 1979): 25–76.

82. Koon, "The Social and Ideological Origins of the Malayan Chinese Association," p. 309; and Richard Stubbs, "The United Malays National Organization, the Malayan Chinese Association, and the Early Years of the Malayan Emergency, 1948–1955," *Journal of Southeast Asian Studies* 10 (March 1979): 82–84.

83. A. J. Stockwell, "Insurgency and Decolonization during the Malayan Emergency," *Journal of Commonwealth and Comparative Politics* 25 (March 1987): 78.

84. Rahman, *Viewpoints*, p. 117.

85. Roff, *Origins of Malay Nationalism*, p. 209.

86. Von Vorys, *Democracy without Consensus*, pp. 80, 143.

87. Ratnam, *Communalism and the Political Process*, p. 62.

88. O'Ballance, *Malaya*, p. 90.

89. Clutterbuck, *Long Long War*, p. 44. For a discussion of the party directives that orchestrated this campaign, see Ongkili, *Nation-Building*, pp. 78–80; and Clutterbuck, *Conflict and Violence*, pp. 170–74, 195–200.

90. Clutterbuck, *Conflict and Violence*, p. 32.

91. This "education" function of the MCA was a constant theme of Tan Cheng Lock. See Tregonning, "Tan Cheng Lock," pp. 60–61.

92. The rest were American, Belgian, Dutch, and Japanese. See Sunderland, *Army Operations*, p. 67.

93. O'Ballance, *Malaya*, pp. 58–59, 135; and Pye, *Guerrilla Communism*, pp. 11, 84.

94. Short, *Communist Insurrection*, p. 14; and, Lucian W. Pye, "Five Years to Freedom: Sir Gerald Templer's Part in Building a Nation," *Round Table* 70 (April 1980): 149–53.

95. Indeed, it can be said that the British only added to the legitimacy of the Triple Alliance by making the "mistake" of favoring the more initially multiethnic party, the Independence of Malaya Party (IMP) under Dato Onn. This cleared the *tunku*

and the Alliance of the charge of being British puppets. Templer himself thought the *tunku* to be a "slow-witted playboy" and Tan Cheng Lock an "old dodderer." See Stockwell, "Insurgency and Decolonization," p. 79.

96. Against the Japanese, they learned quickly to stay off the roads, to break up into small units, and, after the costly attempt to keep the "Chindits" going deep in Burma, never to commit themselves to provisioning large interior bases far from ready logistical support (like Dienbienphu). These were lessons the French had to learn the hard way. See Komer, *Malayan Emergency in Retrospect*, p. 50; Arthur Campbell, *Jungle Green* (Boston: Little, Brown, 1953), p. 14; and Sunderland, *Army Operations*, pp. 27, 102–3, 165–69.

97. Von Vorys, *Democracy without Consensus*, p. 64; and Ratnam, *Communalism and the Political Process*, p. 44.

98. Horowitz, *Ethnic Groups in Conflict*, pp. 400–401.

99. Tilman, "Non-Lessons of the Malayan Emergency," p. 416. For a full comparison of the two programs, see Milton E. Osborne, *Strategic Hamlets in South Viet-Nam: A Survey and Comparison* (Ithaca, N.Y.: Cornell University Southeast Asia Program, 1965).

100. Barber, *War of the Running Dogs*, pp. 56–58; O'Ballance, *Malaya*, p. 85; and Sunderland, *Army Operations*, p. 66. For a flavor of the qualitative military differences between the respective communist guerrilla forces, compare on Vietnam the works of S. L. A. Marshall with military accounts of Malaya by M. C. A. Henniker and J. B. Oldfield. See Marshall, *Ambush* (New York: Cowles, 1969), *Bird* (New York: Cowles, 1968), *The Fields of Bamboo* (New York: Dial Press, 1971); Henniker, *Red Shadow over Malaya* (London: William Blackwood and Sons, 1955); and Oldfield, *Green Howards*.

101. Clutterbuck, *Long Long War*, p. 80.

Chapter Ten

1. Tambiah coined this phrase to describe this culture's *weltanschauung* of a political-religious society centered geographically on a temple-palace complex as the apex point surrounded by a square of four points for the four directions and branches of the royal bureaucracy. The King's Council of Ministers represented these five cosmopolitical points. The higher center point marked the cosmic axis between the temporal and transcendant spheres. See Stanley J. Tambiah, *World Conqueror and World Renouncer: A Study of Buddhism and Polity in Thailand against a Religious Background* (Cambridge, U.K.: Cambridge University Press, 1977), pp. 102–31.

2. Wilfred G. Burchett, *The Second Indochina War: Cambodia and Laos* (New York: International Publishers, 1970), p. 15. For the level of cultivation, see Craig Etcheson, *The Rise and Demise of Democratic Kampuchea* (Boulder, Colo.: Westview Press, 1984), p. 14; and Frank M. LeBar and Adrienne Suddard, eds., *Laos: Its People, Its Society, Its Culture* (New Haven, Conn.: HRAF Press, 1960), pp. 26–29.

3. Nina S. Adams and Alfred W. McCoy, eds., *Laos: War and Revolution* (New York: Harper & Row, 1970), p. 10.

4. Martin Stuart-Fox, "Marxism and Theravada Buddhism: The Legitimation

of Political Authority in Laos," *Pacific Affairs* 56 (Fall 1983): 431–33. The historical model of the *chakravartin* is the great Indian emperor Asoka of the third century B.C. See Tambiah, *World Conqueror and World Renouncer*, pp. 54–72.

5. Southeast Asian scholars report this practice of dual kingship as originating in India. Though principles of royal administration in Indic Southeast Asia were clearly of Indian origin, monarchy in ancient India was never formally set up as a dual kingship. Instead, kings traced their ancestry back to the mythical *Manu* through either a solar or a lunar line. See A. L. Basham, *The Wonder That Was India* (New York: Grove Press, 1959), p. 86.

6. Arthur J. Dommen, *Laos: Keystone of Indochina* (Boulder, Colo.: Westview Press, 1985), pp. 4–7, 14–20.

7. David P. Chandler, *A History of Cambodia* (Boulder, Colo.: Westview Press, 1983), pp. 108–13; and Milton E. Osborne, *The French Presence in Cochinchina and Cambodia: Rule and Response (1859–1905)* (Ithaca, N.Y.: Cornell University Press, 1969), pp. 6–7.

8. Milton E. Osborne, *Politics and Power in Cambodia: The Sihanouk Years* (Victoria: Longman Australia, 1973), pp. 19, 27–30.

9. Adams and McCoy, *Laos*, pp. 67, 82–84, 87–92.

10. This penetration of the global economy into the heart of Cambodian village life is the main argument of the doctoral dissertation of Khieu Samphan, a leading Cambodian communist politburo member. A more refined rendering of this argument came from his African friend Samir Amin. Samphan's solution was economic independence and mutual aid teams in the countryside, not a holocaust. See Etcheson, *Democratic Kampuchea*, pp. 51–52.

11. Norodom Sihanouk, *My War with the CIA: The Memoirs of Prince Norodom Sihanouk* (New York: Random House, 1973), pp. 144–45.

12. Osborne, *Politics and Power in Cambodia*, pp. 29–31.

13. Chandler, *History of Cambodia*, pp. 166–69; and Osborne, *Politics and Power in Cambodia*, p. 32.

14. Chandler, *History of Cambodia*, pp. 170–73; and Osborne, *Politics and Power in Cambodia*, pp. 40–42.

15. Chandler, *History of Cambodia*, pp. 185–91.

16. Elizabeth Becker, *When the War Was Over: The Voices of Cambodia's Revolution and Its People* (New York: Simon and Schuster, 1986), p. 99.

17. Adams and McCoy, *Laos*, p. 94; and Arthur J. Dommen, *Conflict in Laos: The Politics of Neutralization*, rev. ed. (New York: Praeger, 1971), p. 19.

18. Dommen, *Conflict in Laos*, pp. 22–24.

19. Ibid., pp. 24–25, 332.

20. Dommen, *Laos*, pp. 40–44.

21. Dommen, *Conflict in Laos*, pp. 32–34.

22. Ibid., pp. 40–42, 52–53; and Paul F. Langer and Joseph J. Zasloff, *North Vietnam and the Pathet Lao: Partners in the Struggle for Laos* (Cambridge, Mass: Harvard University Press, 1970), pp. 49–51, 93–94.

23. Becker, *When the War*, pp. 88, 92–94.

24. Ibid., pp. 70–71.

25. Etcheson, *Democratic Kampuchea*, pp. 50–55.

26. Ibid., p 51.

27. François Debré, *Cambodge: La Revolution de la forêt* (Paris: Flammarion, 1976), p. 86.

28. Osborne, *Politics and Power in Cambodia*, pp. 57–59.

29. Ibid., pp. 52–79.

30. Ibid., pp. 61, 67.

31. Indeed, the title he gave to his official memoirs was *My War with the CIA*, as cited in note 11.

32. Becker, *When the War*, pp. 111, 116–17; and Etcheson, *Democratic Kampuchea*, p. 60.

33. Osborne, *Politics and Power in Cambodia*, pp. 4–7.

34. Etcheson, *Democratic Kampuchea*, p. 65.

35. Osborne, *Politics and Power in Cambodia*, pp. 93–97.

36. Timothy Michael Carney, comp. and ed., *Communist Party Power in Kampuchea (Cambodia): Documents and Discussion*, Cornell University Southeast Asia Program Data Paper 106 (Ithaca, N.Y.: Cornell University, 1977), pp. 93–97.

37. Etcheson, *Democratic Kampuchea*, pp. 40–41.

38. Becker, *When the War*, pp. 105–7.

39. Etcheson, *Democratic Kampuchea*, pp. 60–61.

40. Carney, *Communist Party Power*, p. 3.

41. Becker, *When the War*, p. 118; Carney, *Communist Party Power*, pp. 17–18; and Etcheson, *Democratic Kampuchea*, pp. 66–71.

42. This is what made the initial U.S. reaction to him cool. See Martin E. Goldstein, *American Policy Toward Laos* (Rutherford, N.J.: Fairleigh Dickenson University Press, 1973), p. 119.

43. Arthur J. Dommen, "Lao Nationalism and American Policy, 1954–1959," in *Laos: Beyond the Revolution*, ed. Joseph J. Zasloff and Leonard Unger (London: Macmillan, 1991), p. 263; Goldstein, *American Policy toward Laos*, pp. 109, 117–18; and LeBar and Suddard, *Laos*, pp. 108–10.

44. Goldstein, *American Policy toward Laos*, pp. 152–57; and LeBar and Suddard, *Laos*, pp. 113–14.

45. Goldstein, *American Policy toward Laos*, p. 279; and Marek Thee, *Notes of a Witness: Laos and the Second Indochinese War* (New York: Random House, 1973), pp. 99–100.

46. The four members of his party elected in the 1958 elections sat with the NLHS in the National Assembly.

47. Thee, *Notes of a Witness*, pp. 132, 175.

48. Goldstein, *American Policy toward Laos*, pp. 256–59.

49. Langer and Zasloff, *North Vietnam and the Pathet Lao*, p. 205.

50. Dommen, *Conflict in Laos*, pp. 223–25.

51. Ibid., p. 240.

52. Goldstein, *American Policy toward Laos*, p. 293; and Langer and Zasloff, *North Vietnam and the Pathet Lao*, pp. 88–89.

53. Becker, *When the War*, pp. 123–26.

54. Osborne, *Politics and Power in Cambodia*, pp. 84, 104, 109–10. During these fourteen months, 3,630 B-52 bombing raids dropped about 100,000 tons of ordnance on fifteen base areas. See William Shawcross, *Sideshow: Kissinger, Nixon, and the Destruction of Cambodia* (New York: Simon and Schuster, 1979), pp. 23, 26–28.

55. Becker, *When the War*, p. 131.

56. On this question of CIA involvement, Prince Sihanouk has always assumed it. William Shawcross is convinced of it, though his evidence is circumstantial and, as he has admitted, not definitive. Catherine Becker has argued that the coup was the handiwork of Sirik Matak and "had the earmarks of American approval." Whatever its foreknowledge and even encouragement, Craig Etcheson and Milton Osborne have concluded that the CIA was not "operationally" involved in the coup itself. See Sihanouk, *My War with the CIA*, p. 122; Shawcross, *Sideshow*, pp. 116–22; Becker, *When the War*, pp. 127, 131; Etcheson, *Democratic Kampuchea*, pp. 87–88; and Osborne, *Politics and Power in Cambodia*, p. 112.

57. Becker, *When the War*, p. 132.

58. Etcheson, *Democratic Kampuchea*, pp. 110–15.

59. Ibid., pp. 103–8, 129–30.

60. Becker, *When the War*, p. 172. Two writers who make much of this agricultural revolution in the midst of political revolution are George Hildebrand and Gareth Porter, *Cambodia: Starvation and Revolution* (New York, Monthly Review Press, 1976), pp. 57–94.

61. Carney, *Communist Party Power*, p. 51.

62. Becker, *When the War*, pp. 137–47; and Etcheson, *Democratic Kampuchea*, p. 115.

63. Becker, *When the War*, p. 151; and Carney, *Communist Party Power*, pp. 7–8.

64. Carney, *Communist Party Power*, p. 51.

65. The intricacies of these internecine party struggles can be found in the works of Elizabeth Becker, Craig Etcheson, and Ben Kiernan and Chanthoua Boua. Though they differ on details, the general pattern to these accounts is similar. See Becker, *When the War*, pp. 187–95; Etcheson, *Democratic Kampuchea*, pp. 130–31, 164–77; and Ben Kiernan and Chanthoua Boua, eds., *Peasants and Politics in Kampuchea, 1942–1981* (London: Zed Press, 1982), pp. 252–85.

66. Becker, *When the War*, p. 180; and Joseph S. Zasloff and MacAlister Brown, "The Passion of Kampuchea," *Problems of Communism*, 28 (January–February 1979): 41.

67. Becker, *When the War*, p. 147.

68. Etcheson, *Democratic Kampuchea*, pp. 92–93.

69. Ibid., p. 118; and Arnold R. Isaacs, *Without Honor: Defeat in Vietnam and Cambodia* (New York: Vintage Books, 1984), pp. 221–30.

70. Becker, *When the War*, pp. 164–68.

71. Etcheson, *Democratic Kampuchea*, p. 123.

72. Kimmo Kiljunen, ed., *Kampuchea: Decade of the Genocide* (London: Zed Books, 1984), p. 30.

73. Arthur J. Dommen, "Neutralization Experiment in Laos," *Current History* 48 (February 1965): 93–94.

74. Dommen, *Laos*, p. 93.

75. Ibid., p. 90; and Goldstein, *American Policy toward Laos*, p. 308.

76. Isaacs, *Without Honor*, pp. 169–70; and Joseph S. Zasloff, "Laos 1972: The War, Politics and Peace Negotiations," *Asian Survey* 13 (January 1973): 61, 63–65.

77. Adams and McCoy, *Laos*, pp. 220–21; and Langer and Zasloff, *North Vietnam and the Pathet Lao*, pp. 90–91.

78. Norman B. Hannah, *The Key to Failure: Laos and the Vietnam War* (Lanham, Md.: Madison Books, 1987), pp. 64–73. The existence of such an understanding is sharply disputed by Douglas Blaufarb, another seasoned U.S. official in Laos. See his *The Counterinsurgency Era: U.S. Doctrine and Performance* (New York: Free Press, 1977), pp. 159–60.

79. As Roland Paul opined, "That they did not push on and seize this city is one of the curiosities of the war and may be of more than passing significance." See his "Laos: Anatomy of American Involvement," *Foreign Affairs* 49 (April 1971): 537.

80. Blaufarb, *Counterinsurgency Era*, p. 163.

81. "The Great Victory of the Lao Revolution," *Nhan Dan*, October 12, 1972, p. 1 (Joint Publication Research Service Reel No. 57,699, p. 16).

82. Dommen, *Laos*, p. 90.

83. Joseph J. Zasloff and MacAlister Brown, eds., *Communism in Indochina: New Perspectives* (Lexington, Mass.: Lexington Books, 1975), pp. 262–65.

84. MacAlister Brown and Joseph J. Zasloff, "Laos in 1975: Democratic Revolution—Lao Style," *Asian Survey* 16 (February 1976): 192–99.

85. Dommen, *Conflict in Laos*, p. 329.

86. Congressional hearings were held on the "secret" war in Laos in 1970 and marked one of the few "windows" in which specific information was made public. These figures came out of these hearings. See Blaufarb, *Counterinsurgency Era*, p. 165; Dommen, *Conflict in Laos*, p. 403; and Isaacs, *Without Honor*, pp. 162–169.

87. In 1968, for example, an FAO study showed 68 percent of rural households were below the national standard of 1,000 riels a month (about $30), while only 30 percent of urban households were. See Carney, *Communist Party Power*, pp. 15–17.

88. Isaacs, *Without Honor*, p. 209; and Kiljunen, *Kampuchea*, p. 33.

89. Becker, *When the War*, pp. 144, 162–64.

90. Osborne, *Politics and Power in Cambodia*, pp. 51, 91.

91. Ibid., pp. 57, 79.

92. To debunk fears of a postrevolutionary bloodbath, Prince Sihanouk had predicted that at liberation both sides would come together in a "village fête." See François Ponchaud, *Cambodia: Year Zero*, trans. Nancy Amphoux (New York: Holt, Rinehart and Winston, 1977), p. 6.

93. On the nationalist appeals of Cambodian communism, see Carney, *Communist Party Power*, pp. 3, 51.

94. Becker, *When the War*, p. 134.

95. Langer and Zasloff, *North Vietnam and the Pathet Lao*, p. 26.

96. Dommen, *Conflict in Laos*, p. 38.

97. Thomas H. Stanton, "Conflict in Laos: The Village Point of View," *Asian Survey* 8 (November 1968): 889; and Thee, *Notes of a Witness*, p. 8.

98. Joel M. Halpern, "Government, Politics, and Social Structure in Laos," *South-East Asia Studies* 4 (1964): 43–44; and Stanton, "Conflict in Laos," p. 892. By contrast, public name recognition of the president in the United States approaches 100 percent.

99. Stanton, "Conflict in Laos," p. 896.

100. Martin Stuart-Fox and Rod Bucknell, "Politicization of the Buddhist Sangha in Laos," *Journal of Southeast Asian Studies* 13 (March 1982): 63–64.

101. Ethnolinguistic maps of Laos show the Lao Theung to be widely scattered.

Further, they subdivide into fifteen major tribal groups. Consequently, they lack the cohesion of the Hmong who are concentrated in the Plain of Jars around their "capital city" of Xiengkhouang. See LeBar and Suddard, *Laos*, pp. 37, 42.

102. In his discussion of the Hmong, Martin Goldstein cites estimates that the war brought a 50 percent reduction of the men and a 25 percent drop in the population of women and children. See his *American Policy toward Laos*, pp. 317-30. A more recent and vivid account of the Hmong is Jane Hamilton-Merritt, *Tragic Mountains: The Hmong, the Americans, and the Secret Wars for Laos, 1942-1992* (Bloomington, Ind.: Indiana University Press, 1993).

103. Dommen, *Conflict in Laos*, pp. 74-75.

104. Zasloff and Brown, *Communism in Indochina*, pp. 276, 282; and Wendy Batson, "After the Revolution: Ethnic Minorities and the New Lao State," in *Laos*, ed. Zasloff and Unger, p. 144.

105. For details of the local elections, see Allen D. Kerr, "Municipal Government in Laos," *Asian Survey* 12 (June 1972): 510-17.

106. Goldstein, *American Policy toward Laos*, pp. 117-18; and Zasloff and Brown, *Communism in Indochina*, p. 268.

107. Dommen, *Conflict in Laos*, p. 289.

108. Stuart-Fox and Bucknell, "Politicization of the Buddhist Sangha," p. 63.

109. Leonard Unger, "The U.S. and Laos, 1962-1965," in *Laos*, ed. Zasloff and Unger, p. 284.

110. Stuart-Fox and Bucknell, "Politicization of the Buddhist Sangha," pp. 63-64, 67, 80.

111. Martin Stuart-Fox, "Marxism and Theravada Buddhism: The Legitimation of Political Authority in Laos," *Pacific Affairs* 56 (Fall 1983): 442-44.

112. Geoffrey Gunn, "Resistance Coalition in Laos," *Asian Survey* 23 (March 1983): 317.

113. Stuart-Fox and Bucknell, "Politicization of the Buddhist Sangha," pp. 72-78.

114. C. J. Christie, "Marxism and the History of the Nationalist Movement in Laos," *Journal of Southeast Asian Studies* 10 (March 1979): 146-58.

115. Don Fletcher and Geoffrey Gunn, "Revolution in Laos: The 'Fourth Generation' of Peoples's War?" South East Asia Monograph Series No. 8 (Townsville, Aus.: James Cook University of North Queensland, 1981), p. 2.

116. Etcheson, *Democratic Kampuchea*, pp. 28-30.

117. Ibid., p. 134.

118. Becker, *When the War*, p. 180.

119. Pol Pot could only bring himself to acknowledge this assistance as "not to be forgotten," even if it was only of "secondary significance." See Etcheson, *Democratic Kampuchea*, p. 124.

120. John Barron and Paul Anthony, *Murder of a Gentle Land* (New York: Reader's Digest Press, 1977), pp. 36, 39. Frank Snepp has conceded that the chaos of the evacuations destroyed the stay-behind spy networks set up by the CIA. He also said that the purpose of these networks was to provide intelligence, not to organize a coup. See his *Decent Interval: An Insider's Account of Saigon's Indecent End* (New York: Random House, 1977), pp. 339-40.

121. Etcheson, *Democratic Kampuchea*, p. 132.

122. Becker, *When the War*, pp. 252, 260-64, 281.

123. Kiernan and Boua, *Peasants and Politics*, pp. 286–87.

124. Stephen Heder, "Kampuchea 1980: Anatomy of a Crisis," *Southeast Asia Chronicle* 77 (February 1981): 3–11.

125. Except for notes 123 and 124, this account of the cycle of killing is taken from Becker, *When the War*, pp. 271–98; and Etcheson, *Democratic Kampuchea*, pp. 170–80.

126. After examining several sources on casualties and comparing census data before and after the war, a Finnish commission concluded that, including the loss of refugees, two million people were lost to Cambodia from 1970 to 1979. They conceded that between 75,000 and 150,000 were executed outright. Craig Etcheson reported a range of reports. Though there was some consensus on 600,000 killed from 1970 to 1975, from 1975 to 1979 there was a range of one million to over two million. See Kiljunen, *Kampuchea*, pp. 30–34; and Etcheson, *Democratic Kampuchea*, p. 148.

127. Not to overdo this point, it must be conceded that the flexible Ho Chi Minh and diplomatic Zhou Enlai were also educated in France.

128. Quoted by Christie, "Nationalism and the History," p. 154.

129. Becker, *When the War*, p. 122.

130. Sihanouk, *War and Hope*, p. 86.

131. Becker, *When the War*, p. 168.

132. Dommen, *Conflict in Laos*, p. xiv.

133. Langer and Zasloff, *North Vietnam and the Pathet Lao*, pp. 93–94.

134. MacAlister Brown and Joseph J. Zasloff, *Apprentice Revolutionaries: The Communist Movement in Laos, 1930–1985* (Stanford: Hoover Institution Press, 1986), pp. 123–27.

135. Paul, "Laos," pp. 533–36.

136. Brown and Zasloff, *Apprentice Revolutionaries*, pp. 270–71.

137. Zasloff and Unger, *Laos*, p. 6.

138. Etcheson, *Democratic Kampuchea*, p. 124.

139. Barron and Paul, *Murder of a Gentle Land*, p. 51.

140. Goldstein, *American Policy toward Laos*, p. 303; and Thee, *Notes of a Witness*, p. 383. The cost of the bombing has been estimated at $2 billion per year. See Adams and McCoy, *Laos*, p. 231.

141. For documentation and details of these activities, see William Colby and Peter Forbath, *Honorable Men: My Life in the CIA* (New York: Simon and Schuster, 1978), pp. 197–98; Dommen, *Conflict in Laos*, pp. 280–84; Goldstein, *American Policy toward Laos*, pp. 196–98, 312–13, 317–18; and Neil Sheehan et al., eds., *The Pentagon Papers as Published by the New York Times* (New York: Bantam Books, 1971), pp. 130–38.

142. Dommen, *Laos*, pp. 94–96.

143. Goldstein, *American Policy toward Laos*, pp. 230, 236; and Langer and Zasloff, *North Vietnam and the Pathet Lao*, pp. 70–72.

144. The fullest account of these Chinese activities is by G. McMurtrie Godley and Jimmy St. Goar, "The Chinese Road in Northwest Laos, 1961–1973: An American Perspective," in *Laos*, ed. Zasloff and Unger, pp. 285–314.

145. Goldstein, *American Policy toward Laos*, p. 107. For additional confirmation, see Thee, *Notes of a Witness*, pp. 128–29.

146. Langer and Zasloff, *North Vietnam and the Pathet Lao*, pp. 63, 106–16.

147. Ibid., pp. 67, 78; and Thee, *Notes of a Witness*, p. 129.

148. MacAlister Brown and Joseph J. Zasloff, "Laos 1974. Coalition Government Shoots the Rapids," *Asian Survey* 15 (February 1975): 179; and Colby and Forbath, *Honorable Men*, p. 195.

149. Thee, *Notes of a Witness*, p. 109.

150. Dommen, *Laos*, p. 112.

151. For an account of Le Duan's ideological imprint on Laos, see Amphay Doré, "The Three Revolutions in Laos," in *Contemporary Laos: Studies in the Politics and Society of the Lao People's Democratic Republic*, ed. Martin Stuart-Fox (New York: St. Martin's Press, 1982), pp. 101–15.

152. Isaacs, *Without Honor*, p. 224. In the Cambodian incursion, thirty thousand American troops and forty-eight thousand ARVN soldiers poured into the Cambodian "sanctuaries" of the Ho Chi Minh trail complex. The South Vietnamese stayed on for about a year. See ibid., p. 203.

153. Roy Godson, ed., *Intelligence Requirements for the 1980's: Covert Action* (Washington, D.C.: National Strategy Information Center, 1981), p. 199.

154. Becker, *When the War*, p. 131.

155. Despite the incursion's less than complete success as a military victory in that COSVN headquarters was not captured, the U.S. command in Saigon insisted that the incursion gave the Vietnamization program a breathing spell of a year. See Shelby L. Stanton, *The Rise and Fall of an American Army: U.S. Ground Forces in Vietnam, 1965–1973* (Novato, Calif.: Presidio Press, 1987), pp. 335–42.

156. Becker, *When the War*, p. 135. A condensed translation of the last half of the book can be found in Carney, *Communist Party Power*, pp. 42–55.

157. There is widespread evidence that the elections were rigged. One U.S. diplomat reported seeing CIA agents distributing bagfuls of money to village headmen for further distribution to voters. See Dommen, *Conflict in Laos*, pp. 133–34.

158. Nevertheless, Joseph Zasloff is certainly correct in his assertion that after the twin capitulations of Phnom Penh and Saigon in April 1975, there was then no alternative to collapse for Vientiane as well. Telephone interview with Joseph J. Zasloff, University of Pittsburgh, Pittsburgh, Pa., November 12, 1991.

159. Carney, *Communist Party Power*, p. 41.

160. Karl Marx and Friedrich Engels, *The Communist Manifesto*, trans. Samuel Moore (1848; New York: Washington Square Press, 1964), p. 116.

161. Etcheson, *Democratic Kampuchea*, p. 154.

162. Becker, *When the War*, p. 281.

163. Chalmers A. Johnson, *Autopsy on People's War* (Berkeley: University of California Press, 1973), p. 45.

164. "Sihanouk Returns as Symbol of Unity," *Raleigh* (N.C.) *News and Observer*, November 15, 1991, p. 10A.

165. Quoted by Ponchaud, *Cambodia*, p. xiv. Their argument can be found in Porter and Hildebrand, *Cambodia*, pp. 33–38.

166. Kiernan and Boua, *Peasants and Politics*, p. 280.

167. Becker, *When the War*, pp. 182–84; and Zasloff and Brown, "The Passion of Kampuchea," p. 37.

168. Richard Dean Burns and Milton Leitenberg, *The Wars in Vietnam, Cambodia and Laos, 1945–1982: A Bibliographic Guide* (Santa Barbara, Calif.: ABC-Clio Information Services, 1984), p. 177.

169. Becker, *When the War*, p. 170.

170. Thomas D. Boettcher, *Vietnam: The Valor and the Sorrow* (Boston: Little, Brown, 1985), p. 341. Folded into this figure is the more than one hundred thousand tons dropped around Khe Sanh during its seventy-seven-day siege. See Earl H. Tilford, Jr., *Setup: What the Air Force Did in Vietnam and Why* (Maxwell Air Force Base, Ala.: Air University Press, 1991), p. 169. This exceeded the eighty-eight thousand tons of ordnance expended during Desert Storm. See Trish Wilson, "Panel Accuses U.S. Officials of War Crimes," *Raleigh* (N.C.) *News and Observer*, November 24, 1991, p. 8c.

171. Isaacs, *Without Honor*, pp. 228–29. Isaacs cites Department of Defense target lists, as does William Shawcross, to back up their contentions of civilian casualties from the bombing. Isaacs more cautiously refers to these bombings as targets in support of Cambodian army activities overlapping civilian population areas which Shawcross more generally calls "civilian bombing." See ibid., p. 230; and Shawcross, *Sideshow*, pp. 264–72.

172. Sihanouk, *War and Hope*, p. 34.

173. Ponchaud, *Cambodia*, p. 37.

174. Quoted in *University Press of America Complete Catalog of Books* (Lanham, Md.: Fall 1991), p. 27.

Chapter Eleven

1. Some contemporary rational choice theorists have similarly tried to dismiss it by confining their analysis to those few neutral moments of history in which leadership made no difference. See Margaret Levy, *Of Rule and Revenue* (Berkeley: University of California Press, 1988), p. 22.

2. Thomas Kamm, "Historic Chance: Peru Strives to Turn Its Fortune Around with Terrorist's Arrest," *Wall Street Journal*, September 25, 1992, p. A1.

3. Nathaniel C. Nash, "Shining Path Still Strong, but Lima Ignores Strike Order," *Raleigh* (N.C.) *News and Observer*, November 20, 1992, p. 2A.

4. Ernest W. Ranly, "Letter from Peru: Shaky Reforms," *Christian Century*, March 3, 1993, p. 229.

5. A classic statement of the focalist strategy is by Régis Debray. Debray emphasizes the differences between Latin America and Asia. See his *Revolution in the Revolution? Armed Struggle and Political Struggle in Latin America*, trans. Bobbye Ortiz (New York: Grove Press, 1967), pp. 19–21. Abimael Guzman, on the other hand, devoted himself to the Chinese revolution as the supreme model for Peru.

6. Americas Watch, *Peru under Fire: Human Rights since the Return to Democracy* (New Haven, Conn.: Yale University Press, 1992), p. xxv; and Michael Reid, *Peru: Path to Poverty* (London: Latin American Bureau, 1985), p. 3.

7. Central Intelligence Agency, *The World Factbook, 1992* (Washington, D.C. Superintendent of Documents, 1993), p. 272. These are only estimates because the 1940 census was the last one to tabulate Peru's ethnic groups. See Richard F. Nyrop,

ed., *Peru: A Country Study* (Washington, D.C.: American University Foreign Area Studies, 1981), p. 72.

8. José Carlos Mariategui, *Seven Interpretive Essays on Peruvian Reality*, trans. Marjory Urquidi (Austin: University of Texas Press, 1971), pp. 3–6.

9. Reid, *Peru*, pp. 2, 109. Figures for 1990 show a Gross Domestic Product of $19 billion, which translates to a per capita GDP of $920. See Americas Watch, *Peru under Fire*, p. xxv; and Central Intelligence Agency, *World Factbook, 1992*, p. 273.

10. From 1970 to 1974, the growth rate averaged 6.3 percent a year. See Reid, *Peru*, p. 2.

11. Americas Watch, *Peru under Fire*, p. xxv; and Central Intelligence Agency, *World Factbook, 1992*, p. 273.

12. Reid, *Peru*, p. 2; and Americas Watch, *Peru under Fire*, p. 2.

13. Andrew Wheat, "Shining Path's 'Fourth Sword' Ideology," *Journal of Political and Military Sociology* 18 (Summer 1990): 47.

14. Americas Watch, *Peru under Fire*, p. 3.

15. David Scott Palmer, "Rebellion in Rural Peru: The Origins and Evolution of Sendero Luminoso," *Comparative Politics* 18 (January 1986): 137, 139.

16. Indeed, Sir Francis Drake commanded a fleet of sixty armed ships to prey upon bullion-laden Spanish vessels. See Millicent Todd, *Peru: A Land of Contrasts* (Boston: Little, Brown, 1918), pp. 81–82.

17. Reid, *Peru*, pp. 17, 19. In Peru itself, the estimated Inca population of nine million is believed to have been reduced to 600,000 by 1620. See Simon Strong, *Shining Path: The World's Deadliest Revolutionary Force* (London: HarperCollins, 1992), p. 49.

18. Strong, *Shining Path*, p. 60.

19. Todd, *Peru*, pp. 220–21.

20. Reid, *Peru*, pp. 20–21.

21. Ibid., pp. 24–25.

22. Ibid., pp. 8, 31.

23. Mariategui, *Essays on Peruvian Reality*, p. 29.

24. Reid, *Peru*, pp. 36–37. As late as the early 1960s, just 280 families owned over half of the country's best farm land. See Cynthia McClintock, "Why Peasants Rebel: The Case of Peru's Sendero Luminoso," *World Politics* 37 (October 1984): 64.

25. Reid, *Peru*, pp. 7–12, 43–44.

26. Ibid., pp. 40–43; and McClintock, "Why Peasants Rebel," p. 78.

27. Reid, *Peru*, pp. 44–45.

28. McClintock, "Why Peasants Rebel," pp. 64–65.

29. For details of this mismanagement, see Cristóbal Kay, "Achievements and Contradictions of the Peruvian Agrarian Reform," *Journal of Development Studies* 18 (January 1982): 149–50.

30. Palmer, "Rebellion in Rural Peru," p. 137.

31. Strong, *Shining Path*, pp. 27–30. Originally founded in 1677, it was shut down in the 1800s. See ibid., p. 30.

32. Deborah Poole and Gerardo Renique, "The New Chroniclers of Peru: U.S. Scholars and Their 'Shining Path' of Peasant Rebellion," *Bulletin of Latin American Research* 10 (1991): 147.

33. This focus on Huamanga as a revolutionary starting point is stressed by sev-

eral scholars and observers of Sendero Luminoso, among them David Palmer and Simon Strong. See Palmer, "Rebellion in Rural Peru," pp. 135–39; and Strong, *Shining Path*, pp. 27–39. Such a focus has been sharply attacked by Deborah Poole and Gerardo Renique, who contend that the movement's origins were far more widely based among Peruvian intellectuals in several universities. See Poole and Renique, "New Chroniclers of Peru," pp. 156–62. Whatever its broad base, the point remains that the armed struggle launched in Ayacucho was a direct outgrowth of cell-building conducted from the Huamanga University base.

34. It was on this same day in 1780 that Tupac Amaru II started his bloody revolt against the Spanish to restore the Inca Empire. See Orin Starn, "New Literature on Peru's Sendero Luminoso," *Latin American Research Review* 27 (1992): 217.

35. Gordon H. McCormick, *The Shining Path and Peruvian Terrorism* (Santa Monica, Calif.: Rand Corporation, P-7297, 1987), p. 15. One voice of protest against this mindless approach came from General Adrien Huaman, a former governor of the first Military Emergency Zone, who warned that "the solution for Ayacucho is not military, but the reversal of 160 years of abandonment." See Palmer, "Rebellion in Rural Peru," p. 146.

36. Reid, *Peru*, p. 110. This was later articulated as a more detailed strategy of five stages: first, political mobilization and armed propaganda; second, attacks on the state through sabotage and initial guerrilla war; third, more general guerrilla war that confronts the armed forces; fourth, expansion of the support base, establishing liberated zones, and spreading guerrilla activity country-wide to disperse the army; and, finally, conducting a general civil war that lays siege to the cities resulting in a collapse of state power. See Henry Dietz, "Peru's Sendero Luminoso as a Revolutionary Movement," *Journal of Political and Military Sociology* 18 (Summer 1990): 131; and Gordon H. McCormick, *From the Sierra to the Cities: The Urban Campaign of the Shining Path* (Santa Monica, Calif.: Rand Corporation, R-4150-USDP, 1992), p. 23.

37. McCormick, *From the Sierra to the Cities*, p. 14.

38. Ibid., p. 20.

39. Ibid., pp. 6, 37.

40. Strong, *Shining Path*, pp. 219–22.

41. McCormick, *From the Sierras to the Cities*, p. 20. In 1990 alone, Sendero Luminoso was responsible for 1,500 killings, only 200 of whom were members of the security forces. This is a civilian casualty rate of over 85 percent. "Disappearances," on the other hand, are almost exclusively a government activity conducted against civilians. From 1983 to 1989, there were 2,405 cases. The numbers have diminished since 1990. See Americas Watch, *Peru under Fire*, pp. 5,18, 19.

42. Wheat, "Shining Path's 'Fourth Sword' Ideology," p. 48; and McCormick, *From the Sierra to the Cities*, p. 38.

43. McCormick, *From the Sierra to the Cities*, pp. 59–67.

44. For details, see Phillip Smith, "Andean Armageddon: Peru on the Brink," *Peace and Democracy News* 6 (Winter 1992–93): 29–31.

45. James Brooke, "Dictatorial Rule Working, Peruvian Leader Says," *Raleigh* (N.C.) *News and Observer*, April 8, 1993, p. 10A. Indeed, his approval rating after the capture of Guzman climbed to 74 percent from 56 percent before the capture. See Kamm, "Historic Chance," p. 1A.

46. Kamm, "Historic Chance," p. 1A.

47. Edward N. Muller, Henry A. Dietz, and Steven E. Frinkel, "Discontent and the Expected Utility of Rebellion: The Case of Peru," *American Political Science Review* 85 (December 1991): 1279-80.

48. Starn, "New Literature on Peru's Sendero Luminoso," p. 223.

49. Reid, *Peru*, p. 4.

50. Americas Watch, *Peru under Fire*, p. 2. That same year, the GNP fell by 20 percent. See Dietz, "Peru's Sendero Luminoso," pp. 88-89.

51. The literature appears to be virtually unanimous on this point of Sendero Luminoso's failure among the urban proletariat. See Palmer, "Rebellion in Rural Peru," p. 131; McCormick, *From the Sierra to the Cities*, p. 31; and Wheat, "Shining Path's 'Fourth Sword' Ideology," p. 49.

52. Ronald H. Berg, "Explaining Sendero Luminoso," paper presented at the Area Studies Symposium, "The Legitimacy of Political Violence?", University of Massachusetts at Amherst, April 10-11, 1987, p. 10.

53. Ranly, "Letter from Peru," p. 230; and Smith, "Andean Armageddon," p. 32.

54. Reid, *Peru*, p. 80. The United Left's electoral share increased to 22 percent in 1985. In 1990, after losing in the first round, IU joined APRA in supporting Fujimori. See Palmer, "Rebellion in Rural Peru," p. 131; and Smith, "Andean Armageddon," p. 29.

55. This is a call very similar to the deliberately nonrevealing "New Democracy" promised by the Khmer Rouge. See Wheat, "Shining Path's 'Fourth Sword' Ideology," p. 48; and Ronald Berg, "Sendero Luminoso and the Peasantry of Andahuaylas," *Journal of Interamerican Studies and World Affairs* 28 (1986-87): 193.

56. For tables detailing these figures, see McClintock, "Why Peasants Rebel," pp. 56-57.

57. "Peruvian Elections Pit Voters against Violent Maoist Rebels," *Raleigh* (N.C.) *News and Observer*, January 29, 1993, p. 9A.

58. Gordon McCormick lists four: Movement of the Revolutionary Left (MIR), Puka Llacta (Red Flag), People's Revolutionary Commandos, and Revolutionary Movement of Tupac Amaru (MRTA). See his *Shining Path*, p. 2.

59. Reid, *Peru*, p. 108. In the eyes of Sendero Luminoso, Guzman became "the fourth sword of Marxism" when the Chinese revolution succumbed to the counter-revolution of Deng Xiaoping, leaving Sendero Luminoso as the "sole repository of revolutionary orthodoxy." See Wheat, "Shining Path's 'Fourth Sword' Ideology," p. 47.

60. Nyrop, *Peru*, p. 92; and Smith, "Andean Armageddon," p. 29.

61. J. Atlin and J. Nef, "Peru's 'Shining Path,'" *International Perspectives*, May-June 1985, p. 28.

62. In her account of the Senderistas' victory over rival guerrillas of the MRTA by 1987, Cynthia McClintock also noted that in the face of their harsh social policies (against homosexuals and prostitutes, for example), popular support among the peasants in the valley may be tapering off. See her "War on Drugs: Peruvian Case," *Journal of Interamerican Studies and World Affairs* 39 (Summer-Fall 1988): 137-39.

63. Wheat, "Shining Path's 'Fourth Sword' Ideology," pp. 42, 49.

64. McCormick, *From the Sierra to the Cities*, pp. 8, 37; and Reid, *Peru*, p. 4.

65. Smith, "Andean Armageddon," p. 32; and Wheat, "Shining Path's 'Fourth Sword' Ideology," p. 48.

66. Wheat, "Shining Path's 'Fourth Sword' Ideology," p. 48.

67. Since very few of Guzman's writings have appeared in public, the most explicit Maoist formulations of Sendero Luminoso are contained in the works of Antonio Diaz Martinez, who was one of Guzman's chief lieutenants and was killed in the prison riots of 1986. See Colin Harding, "Antonio Diaz Martinez and the Ideology of Sendero Luminoso," *Bulletin of Latin American Research* 7 (1988): 65–74.

68. Poole and Renique, "New Chroniclers of Peru," p. 144.

69. Reid, *Peru*, pp. 3, 25–27, 46.

70. Central Intelligence Agency, *World Factbook*, 1992, p. 273.

71. Nyrop, *Peru*, pp. 224, 239.

72. Donald J. Mabry, ed., *The Latin American Narcotics Trade and U.S. National Security* (New York: Greenwood Press, 1989), p. 64.

73. The United States maintained a large antidrug base in the valley called Santa Lucia, which had a complement of forty Americans and five hundred Peruvians. Another forty Americans served in Lima. See Strong, *Shining Path*, p. 127.

74. McCormick, *From the Sierra to the Cities*, p. 110.

75. McClintock, "War on Drugs," p. 137.

76. Lin Piao, *Long Live the Victory of People's War* (Peking: Foreign Languages Press, 1965), p. 18.

77. Atlin and Nef, "Peru's 'Shining Path,'" p. 26.

78. Kamm, "Historic Chance," p. A6.

79. Writing from Yanan in 1936 on handling the peasantry, even regarding "politically alien elements," Mao insisted that "the main point is to explain things to them politically and win their neutrality" and cautioned, "Only against the very few elements who are most dangerous should stern measures like arrest by taken," See Mao Tse-tung, *Problems of Strategy in China's Revolutionary War* (1936; rpr. Peking: Foreign Languages Press, 1967), p. 46.

80. *Chollos* is a derogatory term and suggests problems with a full social acceptance of these transitions of identity. See Nyrop, *Peru*, pp. 74, 81.

81. The very presence of Mariategui in its title makes explicit the Andean mysticism link with Sendero Luminoso. It was Mariategui who first identified the Andean Indians as the revolutionary proletariat of Peru. The insurgency began on the anniversary of the Tupac Amaru revolt. Its popular anthem is "The Broom Flower," an Indian *huayno* ballad, and most of its recruiting is done through Andean folklore clubs. See Starn, "New Literature on Peru's Sendero Luminoso," p. 217.

82. Strong, *Shining Path*, p. 118. *El Diario* was published in the early 1980s by the legal left, but by the late 1980s it had been taken over by Sendero Luminoso. See Starn, "New Literature on Peru's Sendero Luminoso," p. 213.

83. Strong, *Shining Path*, pp. 129–31.

84. McCormick, *From the Sierra to the Cities*, pp. 48–50, 62.

85. Central Intelligence Agency, *World Factbook*, 1992, p. 273.

86. Strong, *Shining Path*, p. 67.

87. Calvin Sims, "Fujimori Is Well Ahead in an Election Exit Poll in Peru," *New York Times*, April 10, 1995, sec. 1, p. A8; and Calvin Sims, "Shining Path Rebels Step Up Terror Campaign in Peru," *New York Times*, March 20, 1995, sec. 1, p. A5.

88. Along the curve of this arc, rational choice theory can provide some fine-grained detail that the more macro-level modernization theory lacks. This is

particularly true in accounting for interest- and opportunity-level calculations of choice. Rational choice theory, however, is less useful for explaining belief-level calculations because it is not willing to accept culturally specific definitions of rationality as this study does for legitimacy. Michael Taylor is a noteworthy exception. See Taylor, ed., *Rationally and Revolution* (Cambridge, U.K.: Cambridge University Press, 1988), pp. 63–97.

Conclusion

1. The first wave, having its roots in the American and French revolutions, was a long one, lasting from 1828 to 1926. The second wave went from 1943 to 1962, and the third one began in 1974 and is still continuing. See Samuel P. Huntington, *The Third Wave: Democratization in the Late Twentieth Century* (Norman: University of Oklahoma Press, 1991), pp. 14–16.

2. William H. Overholt, "The Moderation of Politics," in *The Pacific Basin: New Challenges for the United States*, ed. James W. Morley (New York: Academy of Political Science and Columbia University, 1986), pp. 36–37.

3. Quoted by Chalmers A. Johnson, *Autopsy on People's War* (Berkeley: University of California Press, 1973), pp. 30–31.

4. Ho Chi Minh, *Selected Writings (1920–1969)* (Hanoi: Foreign Languages Publishing House, 1973), p. 361.

5. Keith B. Richburg, "Bataan: Battleground for a New Kind of Warfare," *Washington Post*, February 27, 1989, p. A12. With some exaggeration, Ross H. Munro has made a similar comparison in his "The New Khmer Rouge," *Commentary* 80 (December 1985): 19–38.

6. Timothy Michael Carney, comp. and ed., *Communist Party Power in Kampuchea (Cambodia): Documents and Discussion*, Cornell University Southeast Asia Program Data Paper 106 (Ithaca, N.Y.: Cornell University, 1977), p. 41.

7. Reinhard Bendix, *Kings or People: Power and the Mandate to Rule* (Berkeley: University of California Press, 1978), p. 5.

8. Frances Farmer, comp. and ed., *The Wilson Reader* (New York: Oceana Publications, 1956), pp. 157–58.

9. Ibid., p. 177.

10. The "hyperrealist" case that in the post–Cold War era America's vital interests lie only in Europe is argued by Jerome Slater, "Dominos in Central America: Will They Fall? Does It Matter?" *International Security* 12 (Fall 1987): 105–34; and Stephen Van Evera, "The Case against Intervention," *Atlantic* 266 (July 1990): 72–80. A strong case against hyperrealism is made by Steven David, "Why the Third World Matters," *International Security* 14 (Spring 1989): 50–85.

11. Such a fear is voiced by Charles F. Andrain, *Political Change in the Third World* (Boston: Unwin Hyman, 1988), pp. 61–64.

12. Francis Fukuyama, "The End of History?" *National Interest* 16 (Summer 1989): 3–18.

13. Bill Adler, *The Generals: The New American Heroes* (New York: Avon Books, 1991), p. 72.

1. John Rawls, *A Theory of Justice* (Cambridge, Mass.: Harvard University Press, 1971), pp. 407–24. The earliest expression of this criterion of a life plan as being rationally exercised under a regime of liberty can be found in John Stuart Mill's *On Liberty*, ed., Currin V. Shields (Indianapolis: Bobbs-Merrill, 1956), pp. 100–104.

2. James De Nardo, *Power in Numbers: The Political Strategy of Protest and Rebellion* (Princeton, N.J.: Princeton University Press, 1985), pp. 61–67, 195.

3. Instead, she settled on the phlegmatic proxy for legitimacy of "quasi-voluntary compliance." See Margaret Levi, *Of Rule and Revenue* (Berkeley: University of California Press, 1988), pp. 1, 179–82.

4. For a good representative of this total questioning, see Denis Goulet, *The Cruel Choice: A New Concept in the Theory of Development* (New York: Atheneum, 1975). For the appropriateness of Western models, see Erich F. Schumacher, *Small Is Beautiful: Economics as If People Mattered* (New York: Harper & Row, 1973).

5. Perhaps the most persistent writer in this literature is Immanuel Wallerstein. His classic work is *The Modern World System* (New York: Academic Press, 1971). My book is based on the assumption that Western interventions in Third World insurgencies during the Era of People's War were explained by the dynamics of the Cold War rather than by deliberately contrived inequities between rich countries and poor countries. Hence I have not been informed by any writings of this school. One work on the Vietnam War that is written from this perspective is Gabriel Kolko, *Anatomy of a War: Vietnam, the United States, and the Modern Historical Experience* (New York: Pantheon Books, 1985).

6. The most frequently cited work in this regard is Mancur Olson, *The Logic of Collective Action: Public Goods and the Theory of Groups* (Cambridge, Mass.: Harvard University Press, 1971).

7. I refer here to the political economy associated with comparative politics in political science, not the political economy of international relations, which is based more on the theories of international trade and international "regimes."

8. Within this fifth wave, Robert Bates has criticized purely economic analyses of economic policies and behavior. His findings, such as the political manipulation of agricultural markets to achieve a demobilization of the peasantry in Africa, are based on a political analysis of economic policies. He calls this analysis collective choice. See Robert H. Bates, *Markets and States in Tropical Africa: The Political Basis of Agricultural Policies* (Berkeley: University of California Press, 1981), pp. 2–8, 108–13; and his "Some Skeptical Notes on the 'New Political Economy' of Development," Duke University Program in Political Economy, Papers in International Political Economy 93 (Durham, N.C.: Duke University, October 2, 1989), pp. 1–21.

9. Levi, *Of Rule and Revenue*, pp. 17–22.

10. De Nardo, *Power in Numbers*, pp. 90, 106–23, 154–55.

11. Michael Taylor, ed., *Rationality and Revolution* (Cambridge, U.K.: Cambridge University Press, 1988), pp. 66–68.

12. Plato found will and its attendant value of honor to be particularly frustrating. In the *Gorgias*, his inability to win over Callicles to philosophy and away from politics illuminates the power of this spirited element and of the limitations of any

purely rational theory of political behavior. See Plato, *Gorgias*, trans. and intro. Walter Hamilton (Harmondsworth, U.K.: Penguin Books, 1960), pp. 74–149.

13. David E. Apter, *Rethinking Development: Modernization, Dependency, and Post Modern Politics* (Newbury Park, Calif.: Sage, 1987), pp. 49–50.

14. It is precisely to such integrative work that Robert Bates has called future students of comparative politics to direct their efforts. See his *Markets and States*, pp. 177–85.

15. James N. Rosenau, ed., *International Aspects of Civil Strife* (Princeton, N.J.: Princeton University Press, 1964); and Harry Eckstein, ed., *Internal War* (New York: Free Press, 1964). A recent work that combines both levels is William E. Odom, *On Internal War: American and Soviet Approaches to Third World Clients and Insurgents* (Durham, N.C.: Duke University Press, 1992).

16. See, in order of discussion, James N. Rosenau, ed., *Linkage Politics: Essays on the Convergence of National and International Systems* (New York: Free Press, 1969), pp. 1–17, 44–63; Thomas C. Schelling, *Arms and Influence* (New Haven, Conn.: Yale University Press, 1966), pp. 69–78; Alexander L. George, David K. Hall, and William E. Simons, *The Limits of Coercive Diplomacy* (Boston: Little, Brown, 1971), p. 24; and Andrew J. Mack, "Why Big Nations Lose Small Wars: The Politics of Asymmetric Conflict," *World Politics* 27 (January 1975): 175–200.

Some recent thoughtful works on intervention are by D. Michael Shafer, Edward Rice, Colin Gray, Samuel Huntington, and Michael Desch. See Shafer, *Deadly Paradigms: The Failure of U.S. Counterinsurgency Policy* (Princeton, N.J.: Princeton University Press, 1988); Rice, *Wars of the Third Kind: Conflict in Underdeveloping Countries* (Berkeley.: University of California Press, 1988); and Gray, *Maritime Strategy, Geopolitics, and the Defense of the West* (New York: National Strategy Information Center, 1986); Samuel P. Huntington, "Patterns of Intervention: America and the Soviets in the Third World," *National Interest* 7 (Spring 1987): 39–47; and Desch, "The Keys That Lock Up the World: Identifying American Interests in the Periphery," *International Security* 14 (Spring 1989): 86–121. The continuation of this debate in the post–Cold War era is taken up in the conclusion.

17. Andrew M. Scott, *The Revolution in Statecraft: Intervention an Age of Interdependence* (Durham, N.C.: Duke University Press, 1982), pp. 177–207.

18. David Galula, *Counterinsurgency Warfare: Theory and Practice* (New York: Praeger, 1964), pp. 96–135. Other counterinsurgency theorists who used a Maoist framework were Lincoln P. Bloomfield and Ameila C. Leiss, *Controlling Small Wars: A Strategy for the 1970's* (New York: Knopf, 1969); Frank Kitson, *Low Intensity Operations: Subversion, Insurgency, Peace-Keeping* (Harrisburg, Pa.: Stackpole Books, 1971); Julian Paget, *Counter-Insurgency Operations: Techniques of Guerrilla Warfare* (New York: Walker, 1967); John S. Pustay, *Counterinsurgency Warfare* (New York: Free Press, 1965); and Thedore Shackley, *The Third Option: An American View of Counterinsurgency Operations* (New York: McGraw-Hill, 1981). One interesting exception to these political approaches was the work of Nathan Leites and Charles Wolf, Jr., who argued, symbolically, that it was not necessary to woo away villagers politically and dry up the human sea of protection. It was sufficient to leave the sea alone and develop military techniques to spear the guerrilla fish. See Leites and Wolf, *Rebellion and Authority: An Analytic Essay on Insurgent Conflicts* (Chicago: Markham, 1970), pp. 149–58.

19. These criteria are listed and briefly discussed by David T. Twining, "Vietnam and the Six Criteria for the Use of Military Force," *Parameters* 15 (Winter 1985): 10–18.

20. "Bush Shares Lessons Learned When Deciding Military Force," *Raleigh* (N.C.) *News and Observer*, January 6, 1993, p. 3A.

Appendix Two

1. Though Giap's dream of a Dienbienphu is clear enough, Westmoreland never fleshed out his nightmare as explicitly as I have above. Nevertheless, his obsession with a threat to Saigon emanating from a conventional overrunning of the north of South Vietnam is rife throughout his memoir, *A Soldier Reports* (New York: Double-day, 1976). His worries about the Central Highlands come out on pages 144, 150, 156–58, 171, 178–79, 238–39, and 406. On page 163 he forthrightly acknowledges his fear of the country being cut in two, and on page 406 he notes that Giap viewed the Central Highlands as the key to solving "the problem of South Vietnam." His concerns for the demilitarized zone emerge on pages 150, 164, 168, 196–201, and 350–51. His fears of a linkup are most clearly expressed when he talks of the coastal cities of Hue, Danang, and Qui Nhon, as on page 167.

2. Ho Chi Minh, *Selected Writings (1920–1969)* (Hanoi: Foreign Languages Publishing House, 1973), p. 361.

3. *Communist Party of Viet Nam Fourth National Congress: Documents* (Hanoi: Foreign Languages Publishing House, 1977), p. 185.

4. Ho Chi Minh, *Selected Writings*, p. 277.

5. Vo Nguyen Giap and Le Duan, *How We Won the War* (Ypsilanti, Mich.: RE-CON Publications, 1976), p. 40.

6. See, for example, his "The Party's Military Work among the Peasants: Revolutionary Guerrilla Methods" (1928), in *Armed Insurrection*, ed. A. Newberg (London: NLB, 1970), pp. 255–72.

7. Truong Chinh and Vo Nguyen Giap, "The Peasant Question (1937–1938)," trans. Christine Pelzer White, *Data Paper: Number 94 Southeast Asia Program* (Ithaca, N.Y.: Cornell University, 1974), pp. 20–21.

8. Truong Chinh, *Primer for Revolt: The Communist Takeover in Viet-Nam* (New York: Frederick A. Praeger, 1963); and Vo Nguyen Giap, *People's War, People's Army* (New York: Frederick A. Praeger, 1962), pp. 134–44.

9. For further discussion of the Vietnamese adaptation of people's war, see Timothy J. Lomperis, *The War Everyone Lost—and Won: America's Intervention in Viet Nam's Twin Struggles*, rev. ed. (Washington D.C.: Congressional Quarterly Press, 1993), pp. 120–32, 141–46.

10. JUSPAO, "World Situation and Our Party's International Mission," *VNDRN*, no. 98 (September 1971): 1.

11. *The Anti-U.S. Resistance War for National Salvation 1954–1975: Military Events* (Hanoi: People's Army Publishing House, 1980 [Joint Publication Research Service Reel No. 80968, June 3, 1982]), p. 30.

12. JUSPAO, "World Situation," p. 23.

13. Giap, *People's War, People's Army*, p. 123.

14. William S. Turley, *The Second Indochina War: A Short Political and Military History, 1954–1975* (Boulder, Colo · Westview Press, 1986), pp. 45–48. The most vivid account of the battle of Ap Bac can be found in Neil Sheehan, *A Bright Shining Lie: John Paul Vann and America in Vietnam* (New York: Random House, 1988), pp. 201–65.

15. JUSPAO, "The Viet-nam Workers' Party 1963 Decision to Escalate the War in the South," *VNDRN*, no. 96 (July 1971): 25.

16. Guenter Lewy, *America in Vietnam* (New York: Oxford University Press, 1978), pp. 38–40.

17. The best account of this debate is still Patrick J. McGarvey's Analytical Introduction to his edited *Visions of Victory: Selected Vietnamese Communist Military Writings, 1964–1968* (Stanford: Hoover Institution Publications, 1969), pp. 3–57.

18. Neil Sheehan et al., *The Pentagon Papers as Published by the New York Times* (New York: Bantam Books, 1971), p. 617. For a discussion and confirmation of this figure, see Don Oberdorfer, *Tet!* (New York: Doubleday, 1971), p. 262; and Turley, *Second Indochina War*, p. 106.

19. Oberdorfer, *Tet!*, dedication page. William Turley insists that U.S. estimates of communist casualties were inflated but concedes, nevertheless, that in the Tet offensive they were "cripplingly high." See his *Second Indochina War*, p. 108.

20. Oberdorfer, *Tet!*, p. 32. For all of 1968, fifty-eight Medals of Honor were awarded for action in Vietnam. By comparison, no single engagement in World War I or in the Korean War equaled Tet in this category. In World War II's Pacific theater, Guadalcanal yielded eleven Medal of Honor winners, Okinawa nineteen, and Iwo Jima twenty-two. See Gordon Hardy, Sr., ed., *Above and Beyond: A History of the Medal of Honor from the Civil War to Vietnam* (Boston: Boston Publishing Co., 1985), pp. 298, 334–37.

21. Robert S. Shaplen, *The Road from War: Vietnam, 1965–71*, rev. ed. (New York: Harper & Row, 1971), p. 219.

22. Sheehan, *Pentagon Papers*, p. 616.

23. Ibid., p. 620. General Westmoreland contends that this request was not his idea, but, in fact, was Wheeler's. See his *Soldier Reports*, pp. 352–58.

24. The Senator Gravel edition, *The Pentagon Papers* (Boston: Beacon Press, 1975), 4:549.

25. George C. Herring, *America's Longest War: The United States and Vietnam, 1950–1975*, 2d ed. (New York: Knopf, 1986), pp. 201–2.

26. JUSPAO, " 'The Decisive Hour': Two Directives for Tet," *VNDRN*, nos. 28–29 (April 1968): 4.

27. William Turley reports that the Lao Dong party had been led to believe that it had a popular support base of four million people in the south that would respond to its calls, if only the communist troops could get around American forces. See his *Second Indochina War*, p. 99.

28. Gabriel Kolko, *Anatomy of a War: Vietnam, the United States, and the Modern Historical Experience* (New York: Pantheon Books, 1985), p. 308.

29. Gravel ed., *Pentagon Papers*, 4:539.

30. Kolko, *Anatomy of a War*, p. 328; and Colonel Hoang Ngoc Lung, *The General Offensives of 1968–69* (Washington, D.C.: U.S. Army Center of Military History, 1981), pp. 103–4, 110.

31. JUSPAO, "North Vietnam's Role in the South," *VNDRN*, nos. 36–37 (June 1968): 1, 13. As the war progressed to its conclusion, these proportions became even more weighted with northerners.

32. Frances FitzGerald, *Fire in the Lake: The Vietnamese and the Americans in Vietnam* (New York: Random House, 1972), p. 527.

33. This "wondering" is noted by William Turley in his *Second Indochina War*, p. 113. In 1981 Stanley Karnow found persistent bitterness against northerners by southern communists over Tet. In an interview with Karnow, one female commando in the offensive denounced it as a "grievous miscalculation" by Hanoi that "wantonly squandered the southern insurgent movement." See his *Vietnam: A History* (New York: Viking Press, 1983), p. 545.

34. Oberdorfer, *Tet!*, p. 304.

35. The Inchon landings were Douglas MacArthur's masterstroke of the Korean War. Staged well behind enemy lines, they so disrupted the North Korean logistical system at the front that the Americans were able to break out of their perimeter in Pusan and drive the invading North Koreans back across the thirty-eighth parallel. Indeed, the Inchon landings would seem to offer a perfect example of Van Tien Dung's "blossoming lotus" tactics of "attacking on the rear to collapse the front," a supposed innovation that the communist general introduced in the 1975 campaign. See Hung P. Nguyen, "Communist Offensive Strategy and the Defense of South Vietnam," *Parameters* 14 (Winter 1984): 11.

36. Westmoreland, *Soldier Reports*, pp. 148, 153.

37. Gravel ed., *Pentagon Papers*, 4: 550–55; and Andrew Krepinevich, Jr., *The Army and Vietnam* (Baltimore: Johns Hopkins University Press, 1986), pp. 242, 244.

38. The article was reprinted in the *Pentagon Papers*. See the Gravel ed., *Pentagon Papers*, 4: 586.

39. JUSPAO, "Viet-nam Workers' Party 1963 Decision," p. 40.

40. Turley, *Second Indochina War*, p. 105. For a well-written account of the siege of Khe Sanh, see Robert Pisor, *The End of the Line: The Siege of Khe Sanh* (New York: Norton, 1982).

41. *Anti-U.S. Resistance War*, pp. 104–5.

42. JUSPAO "Let Us Be Grateful to Karl Marx and Follow the Path Traced by Him," *VNDRN*, no. 52 (February 1969): 1. For a brief account of these recriminations, see Lomperis, *The War Everyone Lost—and Won*, pp. 152–54.

43. Karnow, *Vietnam*, p. 537.

44. Ibid., p. 523.

45. Truong Nhu Tang, *A Vietcong Memoir* (San Diego, Calif.: Harcourt Brace Jovanovich, 1985), pp. 143–44.

46. Tran Van Tra, *Vietnam: History of the Bulwark B2 Theatre*, vol. 5: *Concluding the 30-Years War* (Ho Chi Minh City: Van Nghe Publishing House, 1982 [Joint Publication Research Service Reel No. 82783, February 2, 1983]), pp. 35–36.

47. Keith William Nolan, *Battle for Hue: Tet, 1968* (Novato, Calif.: Presidio Press, 1983), pp. xiii, 3–6, 28–29.

48. Moyers S. Shore II, *The Battle for Khe Sanh* (Washington, D.C.: Historical Branch, Headquarters, U.S. Marine Corps, 1969), p. 55.

49. Keith B. Richburg, "U.S., Vietnamese Historians Hold Seminar on War," *Washington Post*, December 11, 1988, p. A30.

50. Nolan, *Battle for Hue*, p. 29. Abrams was Westmoreland's successor as commander of MACV.

51. *Anti-U.S. Resistance War*, pp. 105–38.

52. Truong Nhu Tang, *Vietcong Memoir*, pp. 186–200, 213.

53. Kolko, *Anatomy of a War*, p. 334.

54. Alexander S. Cochran, Jr., "American Planning for Ground Combat in Vietnam, 1952–1965," *Parameters* 14 (Summer 1984): 63–65. Further confirmation of this planning is provided by Ronald H. Spector, *Advice and Support: The Early Years of the U.S. Army in Vietnam, 1941–1960* (New York: Free Press, 1985), pp. 268–74. It is nothing more than this plan that the provocative book of Harry Summers contends would have turned the war around. See Harry G. Summers, Jr., *On Strategy: A Critical Analysis of the Vietnam War* (New York: Dell, 1984), esp. pp. 126–32.

55. George McTurnan Kahin, *Intervention: How America Became Involved in Vietnam* (New York: Knopf, 1986), p. 473.

56. Michael L. Brown, "Vietnam: Learning from the Debate," *Military Review* 67 (February 1987): 49.

57. Cochran raises some legitimate questions as to whether there was a such a dichotomous debate. Rather, he argues, the so-called debate over an enclave versus a big unit war strategy was actually a discussion over refining preexisting plans. See his "American Planning for Ground Combat," p. 67.

58. On the military side alone, Jeffrey Clark catalogs a debate among conventional war advocates, enclave defenders, Vietnamization and guerrilla war enthusiasts, and proponents of a beefed-up advisory and training effort. See his "On Strategy and the Vietnam War," *Parameters* 16 (Winter 1986): 39–46.

59. Westmoreland, *Soldier Reports*, p. 142.

60. Krepinevich, *The Army and Vietnam*, pp. 180–82, 232–33.

61. Thomas C. Thayer has convincingly laid out the numbers, in terms of the casualty replacement capabilities of Hanoi, that show that even during the war's major offensives North Vietnam had the manpower to keep going. See his *War without Fronts: The American Experience in Vietnam* (Boulder, Colo.: Westview Press, 1985), pp. 90–92.

62. Truong Nhu Tang, *Vietcong Memoir*, pp. 212–13.

63. For an account of the failed offensive in the Mekong Delta, see Ngo Quang Truong, *The Easter Offensive of 1972* (Washington, D.C.: U.S. Army Center of Military History, 1980), pp. 137–56.

64. Lewy, *America in Vietnam*, p. 198.

65. For a litany of these mistakes, see ibid., p. 199, and Ngo Quang Truong, *Easter Offensive of 1972*, pp. 158–60.

66. The official communist account of the campaign is by General Van Tien Dung, *Our Great Spring Victory*, trans. John Spragens, Jr. (New York: Monthly Review Press, 1977). An American account that closely tracks Dung's narrative and adds the political and diplomatic maneuvering to the military drama is Frank Snepp's *Decent Interval: An Insider's Account of Saigon's Indecent End* (New York: Random House, 1977). Colonel William E. Le Gro provides a terse blow-by-blow account of the military action in his *Vietnam from Cease-Fire to Capitulation* (Washington, D.C.: U.S. Army Center for Military History, 1981).

67. An insightful analysis of communist strategy and tactics in their victorious

campaign can be found in Hung P. Nguyen's "Communist Offensive Strategy and the Defense of South Vietnam," *Parameters* 14 (Winter 1984): 3–19. I, however, remain to be convinced that the communist campaign exemplified Tran Van Tra's "war of syntheses."

68. Al Santoli, "Why Viet Cong Flee" *Parade*, July 11, 1982, p. 5.

69. This point has been made by Samuel P. Huntington among others, in Stanley Hoffman, Samuel P. Huntington, Richard N. Neustadt, and Thomas C. Schelling, "Vietnam Reappraised," *International Security* 6 (Summer 1981): 6–7.

70. Larry E. Cable, *Conflict of Myths: The Development of American Counterinsurgency Doctrine and the Vietnam War* (New York: New York University Press, 1986), pp. 177–78. The basic point of Cable's book, however—and it is a prescient one—is that the U.S. Army has failed to distinguish between *partisan* guerrillas (which are adjuncts to conventional forces) and *insurgent* guerrillas (which are internally supported forces in their own right). See ibid., pp. 5–7.

71. T. E. Lawrence, *Seven Pillars of Wisdom: A Triumph* (Garden City, N.Y.: Doubleday, Doran, 1935), p. 386.

72. Sun Tzu, *The Art of War*, trans. Samuel B. Griffith (London: Oxford University Press, 1963), p. 77.

INDEX

Abdul Rahman (Tunku), 213; coalition government of, 207; in Bailing talks, 208, 215, 217; and Tan Cheng Lock, 212; leadership of, 220, 283, 284; in World War II, 390 (n. 31); and British government, 393 (n. 95)

Abrams, Creighton, 339

Accelerated Pacification Program (South Vietnam), 117, 370 (n. 9)

Access: components of, 63, 360 (nn. 30–31); to education, 77. See also Political participation; Societal access

Acheson, Dean, 82

Achi Mean, 228

Adams, Sam, 367 (n. 52)

Adat (Malay customs), 200, 213

Advisers, American: in Vietnam, 99, 123; to Guomindang Party, 146; in Greece, 152, 160, 378 (n. 16). See also Intervention, American

Advisers, British: to Nixon, 218; in Greece, 381 (n. 68)

Afghanistan, military force in, 35, 81

Africa: liberation groups in, 15

Agency for International Development, in Peru, 299

Agrarian inequality. See Land reform

Aguinaldo, Emilio, 175, 176, 187, 195

Albania: in World War II, 155; Greek communists in, 159, 160, 166, 381 (n. 71)

Algeria, Muslim nationalists in, 15

Alliance for Progress, 42–43

Almond, Gabriel, 52, 360 (nn. 30–31)

American Revolution, aims of, 38, 355 (n. 30)

Anarchism, in China, 135, 373 (n. 10)

Angkor Wat (Cambodia), 223, 224; symbolism of, 316

Angola, people's war in, 14, 15

Annam: French protectorate of, 88; Viet Minh in, 93

Anticolonialism, 44

Antiwar movement (Vietnam War), 105, 122, 335–36, 338

Ap Bac, battle of, 333, 411 (n. 14)

Apter, David, 53, 326; on access, 63

Aquino, Benigno, 196

Aquino, Corazon, 81, 197; presidential campaign of, 196, 318

Arendt, Hannah, 38, 355 (n. 30)

Aristotelian middle, 38, 311

Armed Forces of the Philippines (AFP): basic combat teams of, 181, 184, 385 (n. 46), 386 (n. 62)

Army of the Republic of Vietnam (ARVN): losses by, 101; cohesiveness of, 103; in Cambodia, 105, 401 (n. 152); ground fighting by, 106; breakdowns in, 109; defeat of, 110; treatment of peasants, 114; political power in, 117, 118; under Nguyen Van Thieu, 119; in Laos, 128, 342; American support of, 333; in Easter invasion, 342, 372 (n. 41); in Ho Chi Minh campaign, 343; proselytizing of troops in, 344

Asia Minor: Greek intervention in, 153

Asoka (Indian emperor), 395 (n. 4)

Asymmetries. See Insurgency: dynamics of balance in (under individual country)

Athens: in civil war, 158, 172, 380 (n. 47); KKE withdrawal from, 165; population of, 377 (n. 2); British military in, 381 (n. 76)

Atomic bomb, Soviet detonation of, 41–42

August Revolution (Vietnam, 1945), 92, 112, 332, 334; communist accounts of, 365 (n. 17)

Authority: and political legitimacy, 5–6, 11, 32, 51, 55; justification for, 31, 32; in decolonization, 48; charismatic, 354

(n. 20); as variable in development, 357
(n. 53); Mao's treatment of, 375 (n. 39)
Ayacucho (Peru): social reform in, 289,
298; insurgency in, 292–93
Ayllus (Peru), 290

Bailing talks (1955), 208, 215, 217, 221
Balkan Communist Federation, 154, 164
Balkan Wars (1912–13), 153
Bandung Conference (1955), 44
Ban Me Thuot (Vietnam), 343
Bao Dai (emperor of Vietnam), 364
(n. 16); abdication of, 92, 112, 332;
American view of, 92; treaty with
French, 93–94; legitimacy of, 219
Barangays (Philippine communities), 174,
175
Bates, Robert, 358 (n. 9), 408 (n. 8), 409
(n. 14)
Batista, Fulgencio, 46
Batista regime (Cuba), 14–15; legitimacy
of, 32
Battambang (Cambodia), 247
Bayan (New Nationalist Alliance, Philip-
pines), 196
Beijing: fall to communists, 139
Belaunde Terry, Fernando, 292–93
Belief. *See* Legitimacy of belief
Bell Act (United States, 1946), 192
Benchmarks of insurgent success, 77, 79,
80, 266–88, 348, 362 (n. 59)
Binh Gia, battle of, 333
Biscayno, Bernabe, 195
Blum, Léon, 90
Bolivar, Simon, 290
Bombings, 150; of Hue, 88; Linebacker
campaigns, 106, 107, 368 (n. 69);
Christmas (1971), 107, 369 (n. 72); of
Cambodia, 236, 241, 251, 255, 260–61,
279, 396 (n. 54), 402 (n. 171); of Laos,
237, 239, 252, 400 (n. 140); Le Duc Tho
on, 260; effect on legitimacy, 279; and
revolutionary strategy, 370 (n. 14)
Bonapartism, xiii, 319
Bonifacio, Andrès, 175
Bose, Subhas Chandra, 203

Boun Oum, Prince, 233
Breakout, strategic (insurgency), 20, 79,
80–82, 266, 267, 348, 349; in Cambodia, 80, 247, 252; in Vietnam War,
118, 129; in China, 149; in Greek civil
wars, 162, 167; in the Philippines, 196;
in Malaya, 216; in Laos, 250; effect of
military action on, 269; importance of
belief-level legitimacy to, 282; in Peru,
294, 295, 297, 300–301, 305, 307
Briggs, Sir Harold, 206–7; leadership of,
220, 283
Briggs resettlement plan (Malaya), 207,
211, 217, 220
British Trade Union Council, 211
"Broom Flower, The" (Peruvian ballad),
406 (n. 81)
Buddhism: revivals in Vietnam, 90;
political culture of, 222; of Laos/
Cambodia, 224, 242, 243, 247, 254;
Thammayut, 244; politicization in
Laos, 245
Buddhists, South Vietnamese: martyrs,
64, 99; opposition to Ngo Dinh Diem,
99; in elections, 102, 105; and commu-
nists, 127; Struggle Force of, 128
Bulgaria: coup (1944), 157
Bumiputras (Malays), 200, 219; under
Malayan Union, 204; under Federation
of Malaya, 205, 211; and *merdeka*, 213.
See also Malays, indigenous
Burma: independence from Britain, 42;
nonlegitimacy in, 53; British campaign
in, 202, 203, 217, 394 (n. 96)
Bush, George, 328; on Vietnam War, 4
Byron, Lord, 167, 381 (n. 74)

Caciquism ("bossism"), 177
Cadres: legitimacy of opportunity for,
58, 61; Viet Cong, 100, 116; of Malayan
Communist party, 205
Cairo Conference (1943), 145
Camau peninsula, settlement of, 87
Cambodian incursion (1970), 105; effect
on North Vietnamese Army, 235, 251,
256; bombings in, 236, 241, 251, 255,

260–61, 279, 396 (n. 54), 402 (n. 171); effect on American intervention, 251, 255, 280; public reaction to, 342

Campesino Rondo (Peru), 296

Can Lao party (Vietnam), 99, 116

Can Vuong patriots (Vietnam), 89, 90

Cao Dai sect (Cambodia), 226

Cao Dai sect (Vietnam), 90; French treatment of, 93; and Nguyen Van Thieu, 119, 127

Case study: typological, xi, 22; fundamental questions of, 5, 10, 15; paradigmatic presupposition of, 5, 21–22; method of, 11–14; similarities and differences in, 14; spillover effects, 23; qualified prediction (Peru), 23, 294, 304; six thematic questions of, 24–29, 269–87, 348–49

Castro, Fidel, 32; "focalist" strategy of, 14, 33

Casualties: Viet Minh, 96; of Guomindang Party, 140; of Greek civil wars, 159, 160, 379 (n. 39); Huk, 181–82; in Malayan Emergency, 207, 209, 392 (n. 67); Cambodian, 248, 400 (nn. 125–26); in Tet offensive, 335, 411 (n. 19); among Meo people, 399 (n. 102); in Peruvian insurgency, 404 (n. 41)

— of Vietnam War, 107; Viet Cong, 101–2, 106, 110, 115, 369 (n. 82); American, 104, 110, 369 (n. 82); civilian, 370 (n. 10)

Catholic community, Vietnamese, 114, 118–19; opposition to communists, 127

Catholicism: in the Philippines, 174–75, 176, 186, 189, 383 (n. 9); in Peru, 296

Central America, intervention in, 328

Central Intelligence Agency (CIA): Vietnamese policies of, 99, 100, 391 (n. 50); in the Philippines, 190; and deposition of Sihanouk, 234, 397 (n. 56); in Laos, 250, 252–53, 300 (n. 141), 401 (n. 157); in Cambodia, 260, 399 (n. 120)

Central Office of South Vietnam (COSVN), 105, 333; in Cambodia, 251, 288, 401 (n. 155)

Chakravartin (universal emperor), 224, 395 (n. 4)

Champa (Indic kingdom), 87

Chams (Cambodia), 247

Chenla offensives (Cambodia), 234–35, 246, 252

Chennault, Claire, 146

Chiang Kai-shek: Northern Expedition of, 136; "White Terror" campaign, 136; war with Japan, 138, 270; defeat of, 139; rural support for, 140–41; use of New Life Movement, 141; importance of Shanghai to, 141, 375 (n. 41); legitimacy of, 142, 151; and Marshall Mission, 143, 376 (n. 48); rule by emergency decree, 144; fascism of, 145; American aid to, 146; and CCP, 148; and Guomindang, 149; and Chinese of Malaya, 203; errors of, 283, 309; as leader, 285–86

China Aid Act (1948), 146

Chinese: in the Philippines, 175; in Laos, 243, 244; in Cambodia, 247

— of Malaya, 199, 309; squatters among, 26, 203, 216, 274, 318, 388 (n. 8), 389 (n. 22); immigration of, 201, 389 (n. 19); secret societies of, 201, 389 (n. 20); during World War II, 203; in MPAJA, 204; support of MRLA, 205, 216, 303, 318; resettlement of, 206, 212, 220, 392 (n. 55); citizenship for, 208, 213; role in independence, 209; murder by MRLA, 210; participation in elections, 210, 212; in urban work force, 211; rejection of Triple Alliance, 218; nonimmigrant, 391 (n. 38); in Home Guard, 392 (n. 73)

Chinh nghia, 113, 118, 124, 369 (n. 3); communist commitment to, 120, 129, 371 (n. 25)

Chin Peng, 204, 206; defeat of, 207; in Bailing talks, 208, 215, 217, 221; strategy of, 214; and elections, 218; surrender of, 392 (n. 65)

Churchill, Winston: accord with Stalin, 157, 158, 166; support of Greek monarchy, 167; on fall of Singapore, 202

Civil wars: foreign intervention in, 34–35; Khrushchev on, 70; reversibility of outcome, 170

Civil wars, Greek. *See* Insurgency, Greek

Clausewitz, Karl von, 152, 330

"Clects" (organizations), 60

Cochinchina, 89, 225

Colby, William, 126, 130, 372 (n. 44)

Cold War, 25, 34, 314; end of, 43; belief systems of, 315; cost of, 321; and Era of People's War, 408 (n. 5)

Colonialism: Western, 10, 186–87; Portuguese, 14, 15; British, 26, 42, 65; French, 44, 65

Cominform forums, 44

Comintern agents: in China, 135, 147, 148; in the Philippines, 178; in Malaya, 202

Committee for the Defense of National Interests (CDNI, Laos), 232, 233

Committee of Labor Organizations (CLO, Philippines), 180, 185, 189

Communalism, 62

Communism, legitimacy of, 66, 67, 361 (n. 40), 371 (n. 27)

Communist party, Chinese, 69, 80; and Guomindang Party, 135–39, 145, 146–47, 149; in Northern Expedition, 136; urban policy of, 137, 140, 144, 149, 375 (n. 37); New Fourth Army of, 139, 147; Mandate of Heaven, 140, 278, 287; rural support for, 140–42; "three-thirds system" of, 142; national legitimacy of, 142–43; use of guerrillas, 144, 377 (n. 74); self-reliance of, 146; industrial base of, 148; reasons for victory, 149–50; errors of, 283; intellectuals in, 373 (n. 8)

Communist party, Peruvian, 290–91

Communist party, Philippines. *See* Partido Komunista Ng Pilipinas (PKP)

Communist Party of Greece (KKE), 80, 150; defeat of, 152, 161; in National Liberation Front, 156; British support for, 158; in civil war, 158–61; Tito's support of, 159; boycott of elections, 159, 165, 170; execution of collaborators, 161, 165; effect of World War II on, 161–62, 166, 168–69; organizations of, 162; postwar support for, 162; legitimacy of, 163, 164, 169; on Balkan Federation, 164; defections from, 164, 165; revolutionary strategy of, 164–65, 171–72, 281; destruction of EKKA, 165, 169; use of assassination, 165, 378 (n. 19), 380 (n. 58); and Egyptian mutinies, 167, 381 (n. 73); rural strategy of, 168; Maoist influence on, 380 (n. 59); in urban labor force, 382 (n. 80)

Communists, Cambodian, 229; factions among, 231; rural policy of, 241; national legitimacy of, 242, 309, 398 (n. 93)

Communists, Eastern European, 125, 126

Communists, Laotian. *See* Pathet Lao

Communists, Vietnamese: revolutionary strategy of, xi, 120, 128, 219, 273, 308, 317, 357 (n. 52); in 1930s, 90; collaboration with French, 91, 127, 364 (n. 14); body counts of, 101–2; in Mekong Delta, 127; goals of, 129; use of assassination, 364 (n. 14). *See also* North Vietnam; Viet Cong; Viet Minh

Compadrazgo (Peru), 292

Compadrazgo (Philippines), 182, 185, 303, 385 (n. 54); among ethnic groups, 186

Concepts, nominal and essential, 11

Confucianism, 87, 119; political concepts of, 40, 355 (n. 37); revivals of, 90; Chiang Kai-shek's use of, 141. *See also* Mandate of Heaven

Congress, U.S.: financial aid to Vietnam, 109–10, 122–23; and Ho Chi Minh campaign, 129; and bombing of Cambodia, 251, 255, 279; hearings on Laos, 398 (n. 86). *See also* Intervention, American

Constantine (king of Greece): military campaigns of, 153; alliance with kaiser, 154–55

Constituent Assembly (South Vietnam), 102, 113

Constitutionalist party (Vietnam), 89

Containment policy (United States), 18, 40–46, 315; two tracks of, 42; global,

42, 127; psychological and geopolitical, 44; goals of, 45–46, 319, 356 (nn.
49–50); in Vietnam, 126, 356 (n. 51);
justification for, 316; consensus for, 328
Contra rebels (Nicaragua), 4
Cooper-Church Amendment (1973), 122
COSVN. *See* Central Office of South
Vietnam
Counterinsurgency, 5, 25; role of leadership in, 28, 349; as police work, 35; of
1960s, 43; in China, 147; in the Philippines, 192, 277; Malayan, 216, 277; in
Greece, 277; in Peru, 294; against Maoist people's war, 327–28; in Vietnam,
340; theorists of, 409 (n. 18)
Critical mass (insurgency), 20, 79, 282,
300, 348, 349; level of support for, 80;
in Vietnam, 127; in Greek civil wars,
168; in Malaya, 214, 216; in Cambodia,
234, 268; in Laos, 249, 268; in China,
267; in Peru, 295, 297, 305, 307
Crossover points (insurgency), 20, 79–80,
266–67, 324, 348, 349; in Vietnam War,
103, 128, 130; in China, 149; in Greek
civil war, 162, 163, 167, 169; in the Philippines, 181, 184, 268; in Malaya, 214,
268; in Cambodia, 235, 246; in Laos,
249; volatility of, 268; in Peru, 294,
300, 305–6
Cuban Missile Crisis (1962), 122
Cultural Revolution (China, 1966–69),
249, 308; mobilization of peasants in,
297–98
Czechoslovakia, coup in (1948), 126

Danda (upholding of order), 40
Dato Onn, 393 (n. 95)
Datus (chiefs, Philippines), 174
David (king of Israel), 66; as insur-
gent, 38
Decolonization, 7, 47, 316; in Third
World, 10, 41; transfers of authority
in, 48
Decoux, Jean, 226
De Gaulle, Charles, 242
Democracy, 7–8, 319; in French Revo-
lution, 66; Guomindang Party's

advocacy of, 142, 148–49, Chinese, 143;
in Vietnam, 150; Greek, 154, 155, 169; in
the Philippines, 177, 185, 186–88, 309,
386 (n. 70); in Malaya, 216; Peruvian,
296; waves of, 314, 407 (n. 1); peasants'
participation in, 319; romance of, 319;
globalization of, 320; legitimacy in, 361
(n. 40)
Democratic Alliance (Philippines), 180,
189; unseating of, 192
Democratic Army (DA, Greece), 165, 382
(n. 76); strength of, 159, 162; defeat
of, 160; in split from Yugoslavia, 165;
tactics of, 169; Soviet support of, 381
(n. 71); intelligence network of, 382
(n. 82)
Democratic League (China), 143
De Nardo, James, 324, 325, 352 (nn. 9, 13)
Desert Storm, 4, 402 (n. 158)
Devaraja (Hindu monarch), 389 (n. 24)
Development: role of violence in, 50, 63,
358 (n. 5); stages of, 50, 357 (n. 3); nonlegitimacy in, 53; role of societal access
in, 63; importance of political participation in, 63, 64; role in national
legitimacy, 66; rural, 76; in Greece, 154,
377 (n. 2), 378 (n. 9); theories of, 324–
25, 358 (nn. 9, 14); effect of rational
choice on, 325; authority as variable in,
357 (n. 53)
Development Decade (1960s), 42
Dhammaraja (ruler) of *sangha*, 245–46
Dienbienphu, battle of, 94, 96; Vo
Nguyen Giap on, 329, 332; strategy of,
332; American interest in, 365 (n. 30)
Domino theory, 121
Drake, Sir Francis, 403 (n. 16)
Dulles, John Foster, 42

Easter offensive (1972), 106, 129, 363
(n. 4), 368 (n. 69); foreign aid to,
121; ARVN in, 124, 372 (n. 41); effect
on outcome of war, 268; strategy of,
342; Soviet support of, 371 (n. 31); in
Mekong Delta, 413 (n. 63)
Easton, David, 353 (n. 5)
East-West struggle: Vietnam War as,

6; balance of power in, 25; role of insurgency in, 34

Eckstein, Harry, 22, 352 (nn. 7–8); on intervention, 31; *Internal War,* 326; congruence theory of, 359 (n. 22)

Economic development. *See* Development

EDCOR, 184–85, 385 (n. 48)

Education, access to, 63, 77

Egypt, Islamic renaissance in, 201

Eisenhower, Dwight D., 320

ELAS. *See* National Liberation Army (ELAS, Greece)

El Diario (Senderista journal), 304, 406 (n. 82)

Elections, 7; role in insurgencies, 26, 77, 271, 317–18, 321; importance to legitimacy, 29, 63, 220; participation rates in, 63; intervention in, 72; Chinese, 134, 143, 144, 150; importance to incumbents, 310–11. *See also* Political participation
— Cambodian: of 1950s, 230; of 1960s, 231, 232, 233, 240; of 1970s, 236
— Greek, 170; of 1930s, 153–54; of 1944, 156, 378 (n. 17); of 1946, 158–59, 163, 165, 169, 170, 171, 380 (n. 52); legitimacy of, 309, 379 (n. 31); of 1960s, 318; support for KKE in, 380 (n. 52)
— Laotian, 244–45, 401 (n. 157); of 1950s, 232, 240, 396 (n. 46); of 1960s, 318
— Malayan, 210, 217–18, 272, 318; of 1950s, 212
— Peruvian: of 1970s, 292, 306, 307; of 1980s, 296
— Philippine, 196; of 1940s, 173, 178, 180, 181, 189, 192, 317, 318; of 1950s, 182, 184, 192; effect on insurgency, 185; effect of American intervention on, 190–91; effect on Huks, 281
— South Vietnamese, 102, 129, 150; of 1960s, 64, 102, 113, 317; of 1970s, 64, 105, 116–17, 124; Nguyen Van Thieu in, 220

Elites: societal access to, 69; Chinese, 141, 142; Filipino, 179, 187–88, 189, 190, 192, 195; of Malaya, 201, 212; Laotian, 227,

243, 257; Cambodian, 230; Peruvian, 290

Elitism: in nonlegitimacy, 52; landholding and, 62

Ellsberg, Daniel, 4

El Salvador, intervention in, 74

Elysée Agreement (France-Vietnam, 1949), 93

Emergency (Malaya, 1948–60), 11, 198, 205–9; terrorism in, 205, 214; British during, 205–8, 215–16; casualties of, 207, 209, 392 (n. 67); Home Guard in, 207, 392 (nn. 57, 73); end of, 209; effect on ethnic divisions, 216, 282. *See also* Insurgency, Malayan; Malayan Communist party

Era of People's Rule (1975–present), 8, 314–19

Era of People's War (1945–75), 7, 11, 312; containment during, 46; end of, 315; decolonization in, 316; revolutionary strategy in, 318; and Cold War, 408 (n. 5)

Errors. *See* Insurgency: dynamics of balance in (under individual country)

Europe: development of legitimacy in, 37–40; communist takeovers in, 125, 126

Europe First (foreign policy), 44, 320, 407 (n. 10)

Farabundo Marti Liberation Front (El Salvador), 74

Federalist party (Philippines), 176

Federated Malay States, 200

Federation of Malaya (1948), 205, 211, 217, 391 (n. 46)

Fifth Encirclement Campaign (China, 1935), 46

Filipinos: definition of, 175, 185; use of English, 176; elite, 179, 187–88, 189, 192, 195

FitzGerald, Frances, 337, 359 (n. 24), 368 (n. 61)

Focalist strategies, 14, 33, 288, 291, 306; in Asia, 402 (n. 5)

Ford, Gerald: on fall of Saigon, 3; Viet-

nam policy of, 110, 129; aid to Cambodia, 236

Foreign aid, 72; to Easter offensive, 121;
to Ho Chi Minh campaign, 121; to
Tet offensive, 121; to China, 145; to
Greece, 161; to Philippines, 190; effect
on insurgency, 276; to Peru, 299–300,
302

Foreign intervention. *See* Intervention

Foreign policy. *See* Containment policy

Foundation myths, 37–38; of Cambodia,
23; of Greece, 38; Vietnamese, 86; of
Malay sultanates, 388 (n. 11)

France: defeat in Algeria, 15; rule in Vietnam, 26, 88–89, 97; democratic front
in, 90–91; in battle of Dienbienphu,
96; intervention in Greece, 153; protectorate of Laos/Cambodia, 224–27

Franco–Viet Minh War (1946–54), 92–97,
116; United States' interest in, 95; land
reform in, 114; effect on Vietnam War,
127, 309; in Cambodia, 226; people's
war strategy in, 332

French Revolution, 38–39, 40; democracy
in, 66; influence in Cambodia, 246

Front of National and Social Liberation
(EKKA, Greece), 156; communists'
destruction of, 165, 169

Fujimori, Alberto: Peruvian economy
under, 289; election of, 294; antiguerrilla program of, 306, 307; land
reform by, 307; dictatorial powers of,
318; support of APRA for, 405 (n. 54)

Fulbright, William, 45

Funston, Frederick, 187; raid on Aguinaldo, 176, 195, 383 (n. 16)

Futian Incident (1920s), 69, 137

Gandhi, Mahatma, 36

Garcia, Alan, 293–94

General Confederation of Labor
(Greece), 167–68

Geneva Accords (1954), 96–97, 113, 126;
communists after, 127; Cambodia in,
229; Laos in, 229, 237, 398 (n. 78); effect
on nation-building, 240; Vietnam in,

332–33, 344; and American military
strategy, 340–42

Geneva Conference on Laos (1962),
44, 252, 253; collapse of, 250; North
Vietnamese defiance of, 255

Gent, Sir Edward, 206

George, Alexander L., 326–27, 352 (n. 7)

George II (king of Greece), 153, 154; mediation between parties, 155; exile of,
157; in plebiscite of 1946, 159, 167

Germany: aid to China, 145, 376 (n. 55);
occupation of Greece, 155–57, 161,
168–69, 379 (n. 22)

Glorious Revolution (1688–89), 38

Golden Emperor (China), 66

Gorbachev, Mikhail, 319

Gray, Colonel W. N., 206

Great Britain: colonialism of, 26, 42,
65; principles of government, 38, 355
(n. 30); rule of Malaya, 42, 199, 200–
209, 213, 315, 389 (n. 20), 390 (n. 22);
occupation of Vietnam, 92, conflict with China, 134; intervention in
Greece, 153, 157–58, 166–69, 381 (n. 76);
campaign against Japan, 202, 394
(n. 96); during Malayan Emergency,
205–8, 215–16; and Chinese Malayans,
210; and rights of ethnic Malays, 393
(n. 78)

Greater East Asia Co-Prosperity Sphere,
91, 226

"Great Idea" (Greece). *See* Megali Idea

Great Leap Forward (1958–62), 249, 308

Great Resistance War. *See* Franco–Viet
Minh War (1946–54)

Great Schism (Greece), 163, 168, 170

Great Tradition (anthropology), 62

Greek National Army, 161; leadership of,
162, 168

Ground combat troops: in interven-
tions, 27, 73, 74, 278–80, 312, 349; in
Vietnam War, 125, 219, 333–34, 342; in
Cambodia, 401 (n. 152)

Group interactions: in legitimacy
struggles, xii, 266

Guam Doctrine, 328

Guerrillas: in Zimbabwe, 15; Malayan,

37, 203, 206, 207, 208; role in Mao's strategy, 47; in Vietnam War, 121, 345; Chinese, 144; in Greece, 165, 172, 269, 381 (n. 63), 382 (n. 82); Filipino, 178–79, 184; Laotian, 250; Peruvian, 302, 404 (n. 36); romance of, 319; and partisans, 414 (n. 70)

Guevara, Ché: "focalist" strategy of, 14, 33, 288, 291, 306; defeat of, 15

Guinea-Bissau, people's war in, 14, 15

Gulf of Tonkin incident (1964), 100, 367 (n. 48)

Guomindang Party (GMD, China), 46; precursors to, 134; Second Congress (1926), 135; alliance with communists, 135–36, 145, 146–47, 149; left wing of, 136, 147, 149; conflict with communists, 136–39, 145; military strength of, 138; membership of, 138, 374 (n. 29); during World War II, 138–39; American support of, 139, 146; defeat of, 139, 152; casualties of, 140; legitimacy of, 140, 145, 147, 151; urban support for, 140–41; legitimacy of opportunity in, 141, 142; taxation by, 142, 146; advocacy of democracy, 142, 148–49; Fifth Congress (1935), 143; leadership of, 144; effect of Japanese intervention on, 148; in Malaya, 210, 212; encirclement campaigns of, 288; mercantile interests in, 373 (n. 8); retreats from urban bases, 377 (n. 71); sources of support, 390 (n. 27)

Gurney, Sir Henry, 206, 210

Gurr, T. Robert, 79, 363 (n. 56)

Guzman, Abimael: capture of, 287–88, 301, 306, 404 (n. 45); at Huamanga University, 292; strategy of, 293, 300–301, 302–3, 305; founding of Sendero Luminoso, 297; Marxism of, 297, 405 (n. 59); leadership of, 306; models for, 402 (n. 5)

Hailams (Malaya), 202, 390 (n. 27)

Hamlet Evaluation System (HES), 101–2; statistics of, 105, 115, 368 (n. 63)

Hankow railway workers strike (1923), 135

Hannibalism, xiii, 312, 349; in Magsaysay regime, 28, 194

Harriman, Averell, 238

Haya de la Torre, Raul, 290

Helicopter, role in military tactics, 35, 150

Heng Samrin regime (Cambodia), 259–60

Hierarchy, societal, 87

Hilsman, Roger, 70, 340

Hmong. See Meo people (Laos)

Hoa Hao sect (Vietnam), 69, 90; French treatment of, 93; and Nguyen Van Thieu, 119, 127

Ho Chi Minh: victory over France, 11; rise to prominence, 90; in Indochinese Communist party, 91; assumption of power, 92; accords with French, 96–97; death of, 104; in Malaya, 202; on imperialism, 315, 330–31; use of *khoi nghia*, 316; people's war strategy of, 332–33, 357 (n. 52); and Phan Boi Chau, 364 (n. 14); education of, 400 (n. 127)

Ho Chi Minh campaign (1975), 110, 124, 330, 413 (n. 66); foreign aid to, 121; Congress's attitude toward, 129; goals of, 330; strategy of, 343

Ho Chi Minh Trail, 105, 128; McNamara Line across, 130, 238; in Cambodia, 231; in Laos, 237, 238, 243, 254, 342; establishment of, 333; American disruption of, 337

Honda economy, 61; creation of, 72; insurgents' use of, 76; in Vietnam, 115; United States' aid to, 123

Hor Lung, 208, 392 (n. 66)

Hou Yuon, 229, 230, 231; on peasant dissatisfaction, 240

Huai-hai River campaign (1948), 139

Huamanga University, 403 (nn. 31, 33); reestablishment of, 292; revolutionaries at, 300

Hue: French bombing of, 88; siege of, 336, 339, 342

Huks (Philippines), 11, 37, 70, 309;

strength of, 173; in World War II, 178–79, 187; American opposition to, 179, 183, 315; outlawing of, 181; AFP attacks on, 181–82, 184; casualties of, 181–82, 385 (nn. 48–49); opportunity-level commitment to, 183, 184, 185, 190; strategy of, 183, 188; military defeat of, 184, 386 (n. 60); divisions within, 186, 188–89, 192–93, 194, 281, 386 (n. 72); belief-level commitment to, 187, 190, 191, 274, 311; Magsaysay's attacks on, 189, 194, 195, 283; external assistance to, 191; and land reform, 271, 274, 279, 281; use of terror, 386 (n. 72); American communists and, 387 (n. 99). *See also* Insurgency, Philippine

Hu Nim, 229, 230, 231; on peasant dissatisfaction, 240; political theory of, 248

Huntington, Samuel: on Third World, 33; on modernity, 38; on violence, 50, 63, 358 (n. 5); on nonlegitimacy, 52, 53; on societal access, 63; on Vietnam, 126, 130, 367 (n. 53), 414 (n. 69); on democracy, 314

Hussein, Saddam, 4; nonlegitimacy of, 52–53

Hyperrealism, 320, 407 (n. 10)

Ideology, legitimacy of. *See* Legitimacy of belief

Ieng Sary: in Paris, 229; on Phnom Penh, 229; revolutionary ideology of, 231, 232, 248

Illegitimacy locks, xiii; in South Vietnam, 73, 124–25, 219; of Chiang Kai-shek, 151; of Lon Nol, 251, 252, 278; effect on intervention, 278; avoidance of, 286, 312, 319. *See also* Nonlegitimacy

Ilocanos (Philippines), 186

Ilustrados (Philippines), 175, 176

Inca Empire: conquest of, 289–90; remnants of, 296; symbolism of, 298, 301; population of, 403 (n. 17); revolt against Spain, 404 (n. 34), 406 (n. 81)

Inchon campaign (Korean War), 383 (n. 15), 412 (n. 33)

Incumbents: competition with insurgents, 25–26; performance measures of, 76–77, 81, 311; foreign aid to, 278, 286; Peruvian, 301–2; importance of elections to, 310–11; legitimacy of, 348, 360 (n. 30); repressiveness of, 353 (n. 13)

Independence of Malaya party (IMP), 208, 218; British support of, 393 (n. 95)

Indian Independence League (IIL), 203

Indian National Army (INA), 203, 217

Indians of Malaya, 199, 389 (n. 21); role in society, 201, 388 (n. 8); in World War II, 203, 217; citizenship for, 208, 213; role in independence, 209; in urban work force, 211; in strikes, 214; immigration of, 389 (n. 19); non-immigrant, 391 (n. 38)

Indochina: French in, 44, 187, 224–27; Japanese domination of, 91; American intervention in, 238, 258; revolutionary legitimacy in, 257–58; legitimacy of opportunity in, 258; American bombing of, 261; transitional society in, 309

Indochinese Communist party (ICP), 11, 90–91; Laotians in, 228; and Nghe-Tin soviets, 232; in Cambodia, 252; and Trotskyites, 364 (n. 14)

Inquilinos (Philippines), 175, 383 (n. 13). *See also* Elites, Filipino

Insurgency: leadership in, xii–xiii, 28, 35–36, 64, 78, 81, 266, 280, 283–86; role of modernization in, 5, 50; as function of legitimacy crises, 5–6, 50–51, 58, 265, 286–87, 308, 312, 347, 352 (n. 9); in postwar era, 6, 11; effect of international environment on, 7–8, 270; historical context of, 9–10, 25, 270, 348; successful, 10, 19; effect on legitimacy crises, 10, 19–22, 74–76, 286–87; in Third World, 10, 35, 81, 265, 353 (n. 16); Western intervention in, 10–13, 16–24; Eastern intervention in, 13, 16; ethnic, 14; separatist, 14; role of land reform in, 26; effect of elections on, 26, 194, 271, 317–18, 321; importance of legitimacy of to, 27, 57–58, 74, 193, 270; reversibility of, 27, 282, 347, 348; contingencies to, 27–28; as challenge to authority, 32; as type of revolution, 33; military solutions to, 35; economic factors in, 36–37; political nature of, 36–37, 40; characteristics of, 51; during nonlegitimacy, 53–54; effect on societal transition, 54, 308, 318; cadre recruits to, 61–62; legitimacy of belief in, 74, 77, 78, 272–75, 281–82, 309–12; variables in, 75–78, 286–87; legitimacy of opportunity in, 76, 78, 265, 275, 312; legitimacy of interest in, 76, 78, 265, 312; benchmarks for, 77, 79, 80, 266–88, 348, 362 (n. 59); quantitative measures of, 79, 80, 363 (n. 56); motives for, 255–56; intersection with intervention, 276, 284, 287, 310–12, 326; effect of reform on, 282; errors in, 282–83, 318; middle ground in, 309–11; accountability of, 315–16, 317. *See also* Breakout, strategic; Critical mass; Crossover points; People's war, Marxist; Revolutionary strategy

—Cambodian, 222–23, 231–32, 234–36; breakouts in, 80, 252; critical mass in, 234, 267; reversibility of, 240, 256; legitimacy of belief in, 246, 274; revolutionary legitimacy in, 246–49; casualties in, 248, 400 (nn. 125–26); dynamics of balance in, 254–57; comparisons with Vietnam War, 257–70; effect of World War II on, 268, 270; American ground troops in, 401 (n. 152). *See also* Communists, Cambodian; Intervention, American

—Chinese: revolutionary legitimacy of, 144–45; asymmetries of power in, 148; dynamics of balance in, 148–50; reversibility of, 149; comparisons with Vietnam, 150–51; critical mass in, 267

—Greek (1941–49), 11, 44, 80, 156–60; legitimacy in, 155, 167, 171; casualties in, 159, 160, 379 (n. 39); crossover

points in, 162, 163, 167, 169; communist strategy in, 164–65, 171–72, 281; critical mass in, 168; dynamics of balance in, 168–71; comparisons with Vietnam, 171–72; effect of World War II on, 270; as people's war, 281; errors in, 283; leadership in, 284; women fighters in, 382 (n. 49). *See also* Communist Party of Greece; Intervention, American

—Laotian, 222, 232–33, 237–39; breakouts in, 80; casualties in, 239; reversibility of, 240, 256; dynamics of balance in, 255–57; comparisons with Vietnam War, 257–70; effect of World War II on, 268, 270. *See also* Intervention, American; Pathet Lao

—Malayan, 44, 198, 202–9; legitimacy of, 210–11; legitimacy of opportunity in, 211–12, 213, 214, 219, 274; legitimacy of belief in, 213, 216; critical mass in, 214, 216; crossover points in, 214, 268; revolutionary legitimacy of, 214–15; errors in, 216; effect of ethnic divisions on, 216, 282; dynamics of balance in, 216–18; comparisons with Vietnam, 218–21; effect of World War II on, 270; ground combat troops in, 278, 279. *See also* Emergency; Malayan Communist party

—Peruvian, xiii, 15, 23, 291–302; people's war in, 55, 292–94, 297–99, 300–306, 330; legitimacy of opportunity in, 295, 296, 297, 298, 301, 307; critical mass in, 295, 297, 305, 307; societal access in, 295, 298; political participation in, 296, 298; legitimacy of belief in, 300, 301, 307; dynamics of balance in, 300–302; errors in, 301; reversibility of, 302; prognosis for, 302, 304–5; casualties in, 404 (n. 41). *See also* Sendero Luminoso

—Philippine, 42, 80, 81, 177–82; strategy in, 70; crossover points in, 181, 184, 268; legitimacy of opportunity in, 183, 184, 185, 190, 197, 274; effect of elections on, 185; legitimacy of belief in, 187, 190, 191, 274; effect of World War II on, 191, 267, 270; dynamics of balance in, 191–93; comparisons with Vietnam, 193–95. *See also* Huks; Intervention, American; Partido Komunista Ng Pilipinas

—Vietnamese. *See* Vietnam War

Insurrections: volcanic, 33; strategies of, 34; and insurgencies, 51

Intellectuals: Chinese, 134, 373 (n. 5); Greek, 154, 380 (n. 54)

Interest. *See* Legitimacy of interest

International Commission of Control and Supervision, 108

International system: western bloc's role in, 31; role of foreign intervention in, 73; effect on Third World, 324

Intervention, xii–xiii, 70–74; in China, 6, 16, 134, 142, 143, 145–48; effect on legitimacy, 6, 16–17, 72, 73, 78, 275–80, 321, 327; Eastern, 13, 16; effectiveness of, 16; legitimacy of opportunity in, 26; legitimacy of belief in, 26, 82, 277–78, 349; critical level of, 27; in Marxist people's war, 30, 328, 347; in civil wars, 34–35; in revolutionary strategy, 70; effect on sovereignty, 70, 71, 362 (n. 56); justifications for, 70–72; for balance of power, 71–72; in elections, 72; in land reform, 72; in societal access, 73; rebound effect of, 73–74; constancy in, 78; scale of, 78, 82; in support of breakouts, 81; intersection with insurgency, 276, 284, 287, 310–12, 326; and rational choice, 323; theories of, 326–28; intrabloc/extrabloc, 327; effect on legitimacy crises, 348–49; scholarship on, 409 (n. 16)

Intervention, American: in Third World, 23, 307; in Indochina, 238, 258–59; in Peru, 306–7; justifications for, 362 (n. 56). *See also* Advisers, American; Containment policy

—in Cambodia, 78, 236, 251–52, 258–59, 276, 282; effect on North Vietnamese Army, 235, 251, 256; effect on legitimacy, 278; effect on incumbents, 279

—in Greece, 165–68, 269, 270; effect on legitimacy, 168, 171, 278; crossover points in, 268; effect on outcome, 377 (n. 1); Wittner on, 382 (n. 80); scale of, 382 (n. 81)

—in Laos, 78, 233–34, 237–39, 253, 258, 276; for Royalists, 243, 244, 245, 252, and Geneva agreement, 252, 253; effect on legitimacy, 278; effect on incumbents, 279; as secret war, 398 (n. 86)

—in the Philippines, 27, 175–77, 185–88, 190–91; effect on government, 186–88; effect on legitimacy, 188, 192, 193–94, 278; effect on international system, 191; effect on factions, 386 (n. 70)

—in Vietnam, 5, 16, 78, 99, 100, 120, 276; justifications for, 71, 121–22; role of cable affair in, 99, 366 (n. 44); scale of, 120–25; moral basis for, 121–22; effect on legitimacy, 121–24, 219; lessons of, 125–26; ground combat troops in, 333–34

Intervention, British: in Greece, 153, 157–58, 166–67, 168, 381 (n. 76); political receptivity to, 269; effect of ground combat troops on, 278, 279

—in Malaya, 205–8, 215–16, 219, 315; effect on legitimacy, 278; errors of, 283

Intervention, Metternichian, 123, 168, 327; in the Philippines, 191

Intervention, Soviet, 42; in Vietnam War, 371 (nn. 29, 31)

Intervention, Vattelian, 72, 123, 168, 327; in the Philippines, 191

Intervention, Western, 10–13; in Marxist people's war, 25, 312–13, 315; effect on political legitimacy, 26, 348–49; moral aspects of, 31; on behalf of incumbents, 286; as imperialism, 316; successes of, 317

Iran: insurrection in, 15; nonlegitimacy in, 55

Iraq, nonlegitimacy in, 52–53

Islamic renaissance, 390 (n. 24); in Egypt, 201

Italy: invasion of Greece, 155

Izquierda Unida, 292, 405 (n. 54)

Japan: as military power, 43, 59–60;

modernization in, 66, 361 (n. 39); Viet Minh opposition to, 91; dominance of Vietnam, 91, 92; collaborators with, 91, 149, 179, 180; intervention in China, 134, 138–39, 142, 143, 202, 267; invasion of Manchuria, 137, 139, 147–48; occupation of Philippines, 178–79, 180, 187–88, 193; invasion of Malaya, 202–3, 391 (n. 37); invasion of Cambodia, 226

Jervis, Robert, 302

Jesuits, in Philippines, 175

Jiangxi soviet (China): rural policies of, 69; Mao Zedong in, 137; land reform in, 149; errors of, 377 (n. 74)

Johnson, Chalmers, xii, 67, 196; on insurgency, 34, 352 (n. 9); on China, 142, 375 (n. 31); on Laos, 259

Johnson, Lyndon: and Ngo Dinh Diem, 98, 100; Vietnam policy of, 104, 122, 335–36

Johore (Unfederated Malay States), 201; Chinese in, 389 (n. 17)

Joint Chiefs of Staff (United States), 340–42

Joint U.S. Military Advisory Group (JUSMAG, Philippines), 190, 191

Katay Sasorith, 232

Kedah (Unfederated Malay States), 201, 391 (n. 33)

Kelantan (Unfederated Malay States), 201, 391 (n. 33)

Kennan, George F., 41, 43, 45, 355 (n. 40)

Kennedy, John F.: economic development policies of, 42; and Ngo Dinh Diem, 98; Vietnam policy of, 99, 100, 101, 340–41; assassination of, 100; Laotian policy of, 233

Kennedy, Robert F., 335

Kent State protests, 105

Kha people (Laos), 224, 225, 244; CIA recruitment of, 250

Khe Sanh, siege of, 336, 337, 402 (n. 170)

Khieu Samphan, 229, 230, 231; on peasant dissatisfaction, 240; political theory of, 248, 249, 395 (n. 10)

Khmer dynasty (Cambodia), 223

Khmer Isarrak (Free Khmer), 226

Khmer Krom (Cambodian people), 226

Khmer National United Front (FUNK), 235

Khmer People's National Liberation Armed Forces (PFLANK), 235, 236

Khmer People's Revolutionary party (KPRP), 228, 230

Khmer Resistance, First National Congress of, 228

Khmer Rouge, 11; siege of Phnom Penh, 236, 252, 260; beliefs of, 282; Vietnamese assistance to, 287; disunity in, 304; and elections, 317; "New Democracy" of, 405 (n. 55)

Khmer Serei (Free Khmer), 230

Khoi nghia (righteous revolt), 113, 316, 332

Khrushchev, Nikita, 43; "Three Wars" speech, 70

Killing Fields, The, (film), 316

Kingship. *See* Monarchy

Kissinger, Henry, 107, 340; on aid to Laos, 238, 253

KKE. *See* Communist Party of Greece

Klefths (Greece), 152–53

Kompongs (Malaya), 201, 212; failure of MRLA in, 217

Kong Le, Captain, 233, 246; coup (Laos, 1960), 245, 249, 253

Kongsis (Malaya), 200, 210

Korean War, 191; Soviet intervention in, 42; stalemate in, 46; impact on Vietnam War, 125–26, 372 (nn. 40–41); as conventional war, 345–46

Kossamak, Queen Mother (Cambodia), 234

Kurakas (Incas), 290

Labor unions, 63, 77, 78; of South Vietnam, 118; Philippine, 177–78, 180, 183

Lai Tek, 202, 203; flight to Thailand, 204, 391 (n. 44)

Land reform, 7; role in insurgency, 26; importance to legitimacy, 29, 62–63, 312; in Third World, 62; in China, 69, 248, 271; Philippine, 70, 184, 196, 271;

intervention in, 72; as variable in insurgency, 77, 78; in Mekong Delta, 104–5, 114; in South Vietnam, 116, 118, 120, 124, 130, 171, 368 (nn. 62–63); in Jiangxi soviet, 149; in Greece, 165, 303, 311; in Cambodia, 246, 258; effect on societal access, 271; and Huk insurgency, 271, 274, 279; in Malaya, 272; in Peru, 289, 292, 295, 296, 297, 303, 306–7, 403 (n. 29); in North Vietnam, 370 (n. 15). See also Societal access

Land Reform Acts (South Vietnam), 116

Lansdale, Edward, 191

Lan Xang, 243

Lao Dong party (Vietnam), 100, 333, 337; in Laos/Cambodia, 254; Fourth National Congress, 331; support base of, 411 (n. 27)

Lao Isarra (Free Laos), 227, 243, 250

Lao Loum (Laos), 224

Lao Seung people (Laos). See Meo people; Yao people

Lao Theung. See Kha people (Laos)

Lattre de Tassigny, Jean de, 94

Lava, Vicente, 178

Lava brothers (Philippines), 181, 189

Lawrence, T. E., 37, 346

Leadership: role in insurgency, xii–xiii, 28, 35–36, 64, 78, 81, 266, 280, 283–86, 349; bridge, xiii, 284–86, 310, 311, 319; personality structure components of, 36, 354 (n. 20); revolutionary, 69–70

Le Duan, 95, 106, 254, 317; on people's war, 331; on Tet offensive, 338; influence in Laos, 401 (n. 151)

Le Duc Tho, 107; on American bombings, 260

Le dynasty (Vietnam), 87

Legitimacy: levels of, xii, 25–26, 55, 79, 312, 353 (n. 5); definition of, 5; effect of intervention on, 6, 16–17, 72, 73, 78, 275–80, 321, 327; historical development of, 7; in postwar period, 10; bases for, 20, 25; effect of revolutionary strategy on, 26, 67–70; role of land reform in, 29, 62–63, 312; importance of elections to, 29, 63; exchange view

of, 30, 352 (n. 3); legal, 31; charismatic, 31, 52, 354 (n. 20); traditional, 31, 65, 316, levels of support for, 31–32; role of violence in, 32; role of societal norms in, 37–38, 67, 352 (n. 9); Eastern, 40; sources of, 52, 74; active support of, 56–58; passive support of, 56–58; processes of, 57–59; and modernization, 66; of communism, 66, 361 (n. 40), 371 (n. 27); effect of terrorism on, 69; domestic, 72, 114; transitions in, 74, 308; quantitative indicators of, 79; Greek definition of, 165; in Laos, 222, 223–24; in Cambodia, 222, 223–34, 242, 309; effect of people's war on, 280–81; Roman principles of, 355 (n. 32); congruence theory of, 359 (n. 22); performance goals for, 361 (n. 40); of Malay sultanates, 388 (n. 11)

—national, 59–66; sources of, 60; and transitional society, 66, 74; Vietnamese, 97, 111, 113, 273; in China, 140–44, 147, 151; in Greece, 161–65, 167, 171, 273–74; in the Philippines, 182–88; in Malaya, 209–13, 216; in Cambodia, 240–42, 309, 398 (n. 93); in Laos, 242–46, 254; of Pathet Lao, 245; in Peruvian insurgency, 294–97; effect of Marxist people's war on, 348

—revolutionary: in China, 144–45; in the Philippines, 188–89; in Malaya, 214–15; in Cambodia, 246–49; in Indochina, 257–58; in Laos, 258; in Peru, 297–99; effect of Marxist people's war on, 348

—Vietnamese, xi–xiii, 28, 257, 347; effect of intervention on, 27, 125; Mandate of Heaven as, 77, 85–86, 87, 97; communist claims to, 86, 111, 129; levels of, 114

Legitimacy crises, 82; insurgencies as function of, 5–6, 50–51, 58, 265, 286–87, 308, 312, 347, 352 (n. 9); effect of intervention on, 10, 348–49; effect of insurgency on, 19–22, 74–76, 286–87; outcomes of, 34; as basis for revolution, 34, 353 (n. 13); European, 38–39, 47; role of organization in, 58,

59; legitimacy of belief in, 58–59; in Greece, 154; effect of strategy on, 352 (n. 9)

Legitimacy of belief, xii, 57, 79, 348; effect of intervention on, 26, 82, 277–78, 349; importance to insurgency, 27, 74, 265–66, 274–75, 281–82, 309–12; economic factors in, 37; in legitimacy crises, 58–59; as measure of national legitimacy, 64–65; in revolutionary strategy, 69; as variable in insurgency, 74, 77, 78, 272–73; in South Vietnam GVN, 118, 258; in Thieu regime, 119; in Greece, 171; in Philippine insurgency, 187, 190, 191, 195, 274; in Malayan insurgency, 213, 216; in Laos, 245, 274; in Cambodia, 246, 274; importance to breakouts, 282; in Vietnam War, 282; in Peruvian insurgency, 300, 301, 307

Legitimacy of interest, xii, 26, 32, 348; economic factors in, 37; passivity in, 57; characteristics of, 58; role in insurgency, 74, 76, 78, 265, 312; in Vietnam War, 114, 115; of Greek nationalists, 161, 167, 169; in Cambodia, 240; in Laos, 243; critical mass in, 270; in China, 273; rational choice theory in, 323, 407 (n. 88)

Legitimacy of opportunity, xii, 32, 348; effect of intervention on, 26; economic factors in, 37; commitment in, 57, 61, 64; characteristics of, 58; in revolutionary strategy, 69; role in insurgency, 74, 76, 78, 265, 275, 312; in South Vietnam, 116, 123–24, 258; in Guomindang Party, 141, 142; in Greece, 165, 169, 171; in Philippine insurgency, 183, 184, 185, 190, 197, 274; in Malayan insurgency, 211–12, 213, 214, 219, 274; in Laos, 243; in Indochina, 258; effect of reforms on, 271; in China, 273; in Peruvian insurgency, 295, 296, 297, 298, 301, 307; rational choice in, 323, 407 (n. 88)

Le Loi, 87

Lenin, Vladimir, 8; revolutionary strategy of, 33, 46–47, 67, 68, 316–17, 320; on leadership, 36

Lessons of Vietnam. *See* Vietnam War: lessons of

Le Thanh Tong, 87

Liberation Struggle Command (AAA, Greece), 156

Lin Biao, 139, 357 (n. 52)

Linebacker bombing campaigns, 106, 107, 368 (n. 69)

Lippmann, Walter, 355 (n. 40)

Little Tradition (anthropology), 60–61

Long March (China), 11, 46, 137–38, 273, 308; route of, 137, 374 (n. 24); Comintern representatives on, 147; effect on Mao's strategy, 331–32

Lon Nol, 241, 255; rise of, 234; confrontation with North Vietnam, 235; American support of, 236, 242, 285; urban support for, 242; illegitimacy lock of, 251, 252, 278, 318; fall of, 257

Luang Prabang (Laos), 224, 237; monarchy of, 227

Luzon (Philippines), 174; Huks in, 173, 184; Spanish-American War in, 176; uprisings in, 177; rural unrest in, 180; Spanish rule of, 187

MacArthur, Arthur, 176

MacArthur, Douglas, 178–79, 188; reconquest of Philippines, 383 (n. 15), 412 (n. 35)

McCarthy, Eugene, 122

McCarthyism, 148

Macedonia: Greek control of, 153, 154, 274; communists in, 162–63; Soviet plan for, 164, 165, 281; separatism, 303, 317

McNamara, Robert, 130

McNamara Line (Vietnam War), 130, 238

McNaughton, John, 121

Magsaysay, Ramon, 27; reorganization of AFP, 181, 184, 386 (n. 62); raid on politburo, 181, 189, 385 (n. 47); peasant support for, 182; use of *utang na loob*, 185; legitimacy of, 188, 279; defeat of Huks, 189, 194, 195, 283, 318; American support of, 193; leadership of, 193, 194, 283, 284; death of, 194, 195, 283;

support of Tagalogs for, 386 (n. 103)

Mula ouphahat (Laotian viceroy), 224

Muharlikas (warriors, Philippines), 174, 175

Majapahit Dynasty (Java), 199

Malacca: British rule of, 200; Malays in, 389 (n. 17)

Malayan Alliance party (MAP), 207

Malayan Chinese Association (MCA), 207, 215; alliance with UMNO, 212, 218; educational function of, 393 (n. 91)

Malayan Civil Service (MCS), 201

Malayan Communist party (MCP), 11, 202; defeat of, 54, 80; as secret society, 202; during Emergency, 205–9; legalization of, 208, 211; and independence, 214; opportunity-level commitment to, 214; revolutionary strategy of, 214; Soviet support of, 215; urban strategy of, 217

Malayan Indian Congress (MIC), 207, 212, 217

Malayan People's Anti-Japanese Army (MPAJA), 203, 214, 391 (n. 37); execution of collaborators, 204; use of terror, 210, 217; British support for, 215

Malayan Races Liberation Army (MRLA), 205, 272; during Emergency, 206, 207, 208–9; defeat of, 208, 284; recruits of, 210; in Briggs plan, 211; British treatment of, 213, 215; use of terror, 214; sources of support for, 214, 393 (n. 95); Chinese in, 216, 303, 318; failure in *kompongs*, 217; leadership of, 220, 288; loss of legitimacy, 287

Malayan Trade Union Council, 211

Malayan Union (1946), 204, 209, 213; ethnic Malays under, 217; British abandonment of, 218

Malay Reservations Law (1913), 389 (n. 22)

Malays, indigenous, 303; status of, 199; religion of, 199–200; group identity of, 200, 388 (n. 11); during World War II, 203; under Malayan Union, 217; occupations of, 388 (n. 8); British treatment of, 393 (n. 78). See also *Bumiputras*

Malays, in the Philippines, 174

Malenkov, Georgi, 166

Malolos massacre (Philippines), 179

Manchu Dynasty, 133–34, 140

Manchuria, Japanese invasion of, 137, 139, 147–48

Mandate of Heaven: of Chinese emperors, 40, 133–34; xenophobia of, 64; and Vietnam legitimacy, 77, 85–86, 97, 171, 193, 219; in Vietnam, 87, 92, 112, 278; of Chinese communists, 140, 287

Manifest Destiny, 39

Manila, MacArthur's capture of, 179

Mao Zedong: revolutionary strategy of, 46–47, 77, 80, 144–45, 266, 282, 357 (n. 52); land reform of, 69; Hunan Report, 69, 141; in GMD, 134; on terror, 136, 301; mobilization of peasants, 137, 141–42, 297–98, 332, 357 (n. 53), 406 (n. 79); consolidation of power, 137, 374 (n. 25); *On New Democracy*, 143; geographical advantages of, 150; legitimacy of, 151; leadership of, 285–86; foreign assistance to, 311; anarchism of, 373 (n. 10); abolition of traditional authority, 375 (n. 39); "men over weapons" policy, 376 (n. 51). See also Long March

Marcos, Ferdinand, 46, 195; overthrow of, 81

Mariategui, José Carlos, 289, 290, 406 (n. 81)

Marshall, George C., 139, 151

Marshall Mission: and Chiang Kai-shek, 143, 376 (n. 48); failure of, 148, 151

Marshall Plan, 321

Marx, Karl: *Communist Manifesto*, 258

Marxism: and nationalism, 67, 361 (n. 44)

Marxist people's war. See People's war, Marxist

"Mass line" (strategy), 26, 77, 281; in Cambodia, 246; in Laos, 250; in Peru, 297

Mat nuoc (patriotism), 116

May Fourth Movement (China, 1919), 90, 134, 135, 144, 320

MCP. See Malayan Communist party

Medals of Honor (United States), 411
   (n. 20)
Megali Idea (Greece), 153, 168, 378 (n. 10);
   legitimacy of, 155, 171, 287; communists and, 163, 283; modernization of,
   163–64
Meiji Restoration (Japan, 1868), 66
Mekong Delta: Viet Minh in, 93; land
   reform in, 104–5, 114; United States aid
   to, 123, 372 (n. 37); uprising (1940), 127;
   in Easter invasion, 342
Mendès-France, Pierre, 96
Meo people (Laos), 224, 244; irregular
   army of, 237, 238, 239, 255; American aid to, 253; cohesion among, 399
   (n. 101); casualties among, 399 (n. 102)
Merdeka (Malayan independence), 207;
   legitimacy in, 209; British support of,
   213, 217; and MCP, 215
Metaxas, John, 154
Metaxas dictatorship (Greece), 154; in
   World War II, 155, 168; and KKE, 161,
   170, 382 (n. 43)
Metternich, Prince, 71, 72
Middle Tradition (anthropology), 62, 359
   (n. 27)
Military Advisory Group in Thailand, 252
Military Assistance Command in Viet-
   nam (MACV), 125–26, 321, 342, 372
   (n. 41); in Tet offensive, 335
Military Trade Agreement (Viet Minh–
   China, 1950), 94
Mill, John Stuart, 408 (n. 1)
Mindanao (Philippines), 174, 186
Ming dynasty: occupation of Viet-
   nam, 87
Minh Yuen (Malaya), 205, 206, 208;
   establishment of, 214
Mini-Tet, 335, 336
Mobilization, 7; strategies of, 14, 348; of
   peasants, 25, 47, 137, 141–42, 235, 247,
   297–98, 319, 357 (n. 53), 377 (n. 74);
   success in, 26; in legitimacy crises, 58;
   at village level, 361 (n. 45)
Modernization: role in insurgency, 5, 50,
   308; role in legitimacy, 25; in Third
   World, 49, 65; processes of, 49–50;

nonlegitimacy in, 52; access to, 63;
   role of industrialization in, 65; Japanese, 66, 361 (n. 39); resistance to, 67,
   316; Vietnamese, 86, 89, 97, 111, 347; in
   China, 140, 142, 376 (n. 46); and revolution, 320; dependency school of, 324;
   waves of, 324–25, 408 (n. 8); Western
   models of, 408 (n. 4)
Modernization theory, 324–25, 406
   (n. 88); "classic," 326
Monarchy: of Israel, 38; ideals of, 66;
   Vietnamese, 86–87; Hindu principles
   of, 200, 201–2, 224, 390 (n. 24), 395
   (n. 5); Laotian, 223–24, 229, 258; Cambodian, 224, 229; Buddhist principles
   of, 240
—European: legitimacy of, 38, 39
—Greek: divisiveness of, 153; legitimacy
   of, 154–55; as stabilizing force, 155,
   163, 169; plebiscite for, 158; in postwar
   period, 159; Churchill's support of, 167
Morales Bermuda, Francisco, 292
Movement of Leftist Revolutionaries
   (MIR, Peru), 291, 405 (n. 58)
Mozambique, people's war in, 14
Mujaheddin (Afghanistan), 35
Muslims: nationalist, 15; of Malaya, 200,
   201; of Cambodia, 247
Mysticism, Andean, 406 (n. 81)
Myth of the Cave (Plato), 36, 280
Myths, foundation, 23, 37–38, 86, 388
   (n. 11)

Nam Tien (march), 87, 110
National Civil Guard (EP, Greece), 378
   (n. 19)
National Council of Reconciliation and
   Concord (Vietnam), 108
National General Labor Union (China),
   135
Nationalism: role in insurgency, 37; importance in Third World, 43; political
   aspects of, 59; and Marxism, 67, 361
   (n. 44); effect of World War II on, 91;
   and coalitions with communism, 150–
   51; Greek, 163, 169; Philippine, 193;

Cambodian, 226; universality of, 351
(ch. 1, n. 3)
— Chinese, 134–35, 375 (n. 31); under
Chiang Kai-shek, 142; components of,
376 (n. 46)
— Vietnamese, xi, 90, 119, 370 (n. 14);
American opposition to, 44; origins
of, 89–90; communist mandate for, 98,
129; Western influence on, 112
Nationalist party (Philippines), 176
Nationalist party (VNQDD, Vietnam), 90;
weaknesses of, 364 (n. 11)
National liberation, wars of, 44
National Liberation Army (ELAS,
Greece): formation of, 156; strength
of, 157, 158, 169; in civil war, 158–59;
casualties of, 159; composition of, 162;
demobilization of, 162; Stalin on, 166,
381 (n. 70); and Macedonian sepa-
ratism, 317; British opinion of, 381
(n. 68)
National Liberation Front (EAM, Greece),
156; postwar strength of, 161; Socialist
Party in, 162; in World War II, 169
National Liberation Front (NLF, Viet-
nam), 333; intellectuals' view of, 113;
legitimacy of, 114; popular support for,
118
National Peasants Union (PKM, Philip-
pines), 180, 181; outlawing of, 185
National Republican Greek League
(EDES), 156, 158, 165; strength of, 157
National Revolutionary Movement
(South Vietnam), 116
National Society of Peasants in the Phil-
ippines (KPMP), 178, 188, 189
National Union of Plantation Workers
(Malaya), 211
Nation-building, xii, 7; in postwar
period, 10; nonlegitimacy in, 52; in the
Philippines, 184; in Malaya, 218, 219;
in Vietnam, 219–20; socialist image of,
319
Navarre, Henri, 95, 151, 332
Navarre Plan, 95–96
Negri Sembilan (Federated Malay States),
200, 388 (n. 11)

Neocolonialism, 43
Neo Lao Hak Sat. See Pathet Lao
New Life Movement (China, 1934), 141;
failure of, 142, 149
"New Life Villages" (Malaya), 206, 212,
215
New People's Army (NPA, Philippines),
81, 195, 284, 385 (n. 46); strength of,
196, 303–4; collapse of, 304; media
campaign against, 316
Nghe-Tin soviets (1930–31), 90, 232
Ngo Dinh Can, 99; unpopularity of, 119
Ngo Dinh Diem, xi; coup against, 45,
100, 333, 366 (n. 45); United States'
policy toward, 46, 99–100, 366 (n. 44);
consolidation of power, 98, 113, 126,
128, 366 (n. 39); entourage of, 99, 119;
as nationalist, 118; intellectual beliefs
of, 118–19; rural policy of, 220, 230;
leadership of, 286; collaboration with
French, 372 (n. 46)
Ngo Dinh Nhu, 99, 116; murder of, 100;
unpopularity of, 119
Ngo Dinh Thuc, 99
Ngo Quang Truong, 220
Ngo Quyen (Vietnamese ruler), 86
Nguyen Ai Quoc. See Ho Chi Minh
Nguyen Anh, 88
Nguyen Cao Ky, 100, 119–20, 124; factions
under, 102–3; on South Vietnamese
society, 119, 371 (n. 23)
Nguyen Chanh Thi, 102
Nguyen Chi Thanh, 334
Nguyen dynasty (Vietnam), 86, 88, 89
Nguyen Hue, 87–88
Nguyen Van Thieu (President of Viet-
nam), 104; under Nguyen Cao Ky, 102;
after Tet offensive, 103, 124; opposition
to, 105, 126; and Paris Peace Agree-
ment, 108, 109, 129; American support
of, 113; rural policy of, 114, 116, 119; and
ARVN, 117; illegitimacy of, 119, 278, 279,
317; role models of, 124; fall of, 127, 257;
and Chiang Kai-shek, 150; illegitimacy
lock of, 278; leadership of, 286
Nhu, Madame, 99; Women's Solidarity
Movement of, 116; unpopularity of, 119

Nicaragua, insurrection in, 4, 15

Nitze, Paul, 42, 45

Nixon, Richard M.: Vietnam policy of, 104, 105, 106, 107, 108–9, 122, 129; in China, 105; Cambodian policy of, 105, 236, 251, 256, 342; British advisers of, 218; Guam Doctrine of, 328

Nkomo, Joshua, 15

Nonlegitimacy, 32, 51–54; elitism in, 52; in Third World, 52–53; economic causes of, 53; insurgencies during, 53–54; stagnation in, 54; effect of intervention on, 73. *See also* Illegitimacy locks

Norodom Sihanouk, Prince, 398 (n. 87); ancestry of, 225; in World War II, 226; and independence for Cambodia, 227; abdication from monarchy, 229; as head of state, 229–31; peasants' support of, 230, 231; refusal of American aid, 230, 251; deposition (1970), 231, 234, 241, 247, 251, 255; American aid to, 234; alliance with communists, 235, 241, 246, 255, 268; suppression of communists, 240; "Buddhist socialism" of, 242; corruption of, 242; legitimacy of, 256, 260, 278; return from exile, 260; on American bombings, 261; leadership of, 283; *My War with the CIA*, 396 (n. 31)

Northern Expedition (China, 1926), 136, 143

North Vietnam: blockade of ports, 106; resupply efforts, 107, 369 (n. 76); in Paris peace negotiations, 107–8; legitimacy of, 112; modernization in, 112; governing of South Vietnam, 120; in Cambodia, 231, 246–47, 249, 251, 255, 256, 345; aid to Laos, 233, 237–38, 243, 249, 251, 253–54, 255, 282; support of Pathet Lao, 237–38, 245, 253–54, 257, 284, 309, 317; conventional strategy of, 330, 337–38, 343–46, 413 (n. 67); on victory in Vietnam War, 331; use of terror, 333; and Tet offensive, 336, 338–39; American strategy of, 340–44; errors of, 342–43, 413 (n. 65); abandonment

of people's war, 344–45; land reform in, 370 (n. 15); effect of Korean War on, 372 (n. 41)

North Vietnamese army (NVA), 101; effect of Cambodian incursion on, 235, 251, 256; in Laos, 237, 238, 239, 252, 254; invasion of south, 333; strength of, 334, 411 (n. 18), 412 (n. 61)

On New Democracy (Mao), 143

Operation Frequent Wind (Vietnam War), 3

Operation Lea (Vietnam, 1947), 93, 288

Operation Menu (Cambodia, 1969), 234

Operation Noah's Ark (Greece, 1944), 156

Operation Pegasus (Vietnam War), 337

Operation Summit (Greece, 1948), 160

Operation Zipper (Malaya), 202

Opportunity. *See* Legitimacy of opportunity

Organization: role in revolutions, 35–36; in legitimacy crises, 58, 59, 76, 266

Pacification Attitude Analysis System (PAAS), 371 (n. 22)

Pahang (Federated Malay States), 200

Pampaguenos (Philippines), 186, 192; support for Huks, 386 (n. 72)

Pan-Malayan Federation of Trade Unions (PMFTU), 204, 211; outlawing of, 205

Papagos, Alexander, 168, 284

Papandreou, George: government in exile, 156, 157, 161, 169; in civil war, 158

Paraguay, nonlegitimacy in, 53

Paris group (Cambodian communists), 229; in Cambodian politburo, 232; regions controlled by, 236; ideology of, 245, 248; mobilization of peasants, 247

Paris Peace Agreement (1973), 106, 107–8; North Vietnam's acceptance of, 123; Nguyen Van Thieu and, 129; effect on Laos, 253

Paris Peace Conference, 337

Parsons, Talcott, 49–50; pattern-variable scheme of, 50, 357 (n. 2); on legitimacy, 64

Partido Komunista Ng Pilipinas (PKP),
178, 189; defeat of, 182; support for, 183,
189; takeover of KPMP, 188; strategy of,
189, 192; boycott of elections, 193; and
Sakdalist revolt, 384 (n. 25)

Patenotre-Nguyen Van Tuong Treaty
(1884), 88

Pathet Lao, 44, 228; boycott of elections,
232; North Vietnamese support of,
237–38, 245, 253–54, 257, 284, 309, 317;
in Vientiane Peace Agreement, 238;
ethnic imbalance in, 244, 250; and
sangha, 244, 254, 258; national legitimacy of, 245; revolutionary strategy
of, 249–50; Soviet support of, 253, 256,
261. *See also* Insurgency, Laotian

Patron-client ties: in traditional society,
60, 76; Vietnamese, 111–12; in the
Philippines, 182–83, 185, 186, 190; in
Malaya, 210; in Laos, 243

Paul I (king of Greece), 163, 169

Paxa Sangkhom (PS, Laos), 233

Pax Britannica (Malaya), 199, 200

Peasants: mobilization of, 25, 47, 137, 247,
319, 377 (n. 74); effect of insurgency
on, 60–61, 62, 81; redistribution of
land to, 62; reaction to revolution, 68–
69; of North Vietnam, 112; Malayan,
201; participation in democracy, 319;
African, 359 (n. 14)
—Cambodian: support of Sihanouk,
230, 231; in Sumlaut uprising, 232; mobilization of, 235; Sihanouk's policy
toward, 240, 241; standard of living,
398 (n. 87)
—Chinese: Mao's mobilization of, 137,
141–42, 297–98, 332, 357 (n. 53), 406
(n. 79); landless, 373 (n. 5); attraction
to CCP, 375 (n. 40), 377 (n. 74)
—Greek, 165, 171, 377 (n. 2); as guerrillas,
381 (n. 63)
—Peruvian, 289, 405 (n. 62); coca-
growing by, 297, 299–300; Senderista
violence against, 301; stratification
among, 303
—Philippine: unions of, 177–78, 180;

support of Magsaysay, 182, 188; after
World War II, 183; economic reforms
for, 185
—Vietnamese: flight to cities, 102, 103,
115; ARVN treatment of, 114; patron-
client ties of, 114; communist membership among, 116; support for Viet
Cong, 361 (n. 48)

Peloponnese Peninsula: in civil war, 158,
160; terrorism in, 380 (n. 41); British
military in, 381 (n. 74)

Penang, British rule of, 200

Pentagon Papers, 121, 335, 337

People's Army (North Vietnamese journal), 337

People's Liberation Army (Philippines).
See Huks

People's Liberation Army (PLA, China):
size of, 139, 146, 376 (n. 69), 377 (n. 70);
Soviet advice to, 147; in Manchuria,
148

People's Party of Laos, 249, 250

People's Revolutionary Party (Vietnam),
164

People's Socialist Community (Sangkum
Reastr Niyum, Cambodia), 229, 230,
241, 242; in 1966 elections, 231

People's war: causes of, 14; role of geography in, 152

People's war, Marxist: Vietnam as, xi, 46,
120, 150, 219, 273, 344–46, 410 (n. 9);
elections as Achilles' heel to, 7, 194,
196, 218; as insurgent strategy, 10,
13–14, 26, 33, 280–81, 286, 313; intervention in, 12–13, 15–16, 30, 280, 328;
in Peru, 55, 292–94, 297–99, 300–306,
330; abandonment in Vietnam, 128,
150, 273, 281, 330, 331–32, 344–46; in
China, 139, 149, 277; in Greece, 165, 172;
in the Philippines, 181, 188, 191, 195,
330; in Malaya, 214–15, 218; in Cambodia, 235, 281; in Laos, 243, 246, 249–50,
281; effect on legitimacy, 280–81, 348;
political participation in, 281; societal
access in, 281; Western intervention in,
312–13, 315; in Third World, 315; effect

of democracy on, 319; North Vietnam's use of, 330. *See also* Revolutionary strategy

Perak (Federated Malay States), 200

Perlis (Unfederated Malay States), 201, 391 (n. 33)

Persian Gulf War, 4, 402 (n. 158)

Personalism, 52

Phan Boi Chau, 89–90; communist treatment of, 98; and Ho Chi Minh, 364 (n. 14)

Phan Chu Trinh, 89

Phan Dinh Phung, 89

Phetsareth, Prince, 243, 259

Phnom Penh (Cambodia), communist takeover of, 11, 231, 236, 247, 249, 250, 260, 261, 399 (n. 120)

Phoui Sananikone, 232

Phouma, Souvanna. *See* Souvanna Phouma, Prince

Phoumi Nosavan, 233

Phuc duc, 118, 369 (n. 3)

Pizarro, Francisco, 289

PKP. *See* Partido Komunista Ng Pilipinas

Plain of Jars (Laos): battle for, 237, 238, 250, 254; bombing in, 239

Plain of Jars Agreement (Laos, 1962), 233; Meo in, 244

Plaka Bridge Armistice (Greece, 1944), 156, 378 (n. 16)

Plato, 36, 280; *Gorgias,* 408 (n. 12)

Plaza Mirando bombing (Philippines), 195

Police activities, of incumbent regimes, 76

Political Committee for National Liberation (PEEA, Greece), 156, 162

Political economy, international, 325, 408 (n. 7)

Political legitimacy. *See* Legitimacy

Political participation, 348, 360 (n. 31); importance to development, 63–64; as variable in insurgency, 76, 271, 275, 308; in South Vietnam, 118; in the Philippines, 184; in Malaya, 212, 213; in Cambodia, 241, 258, 397 (n. 65); in people's war, 281; in Peruvian insur-

gency, 296, 298. *See also* Elections

Political parties: in South Vietnam, 126, 127; Philippine, 176; creation of, 368 (n. 66)

Pol Pot, 235; in Paris, 229; as party secretary, 231; organization of Cambodian communists, 231, 260; organization of army, 234, 247; revolutionary ideology of, 248; terrorism of, 248–49, 261, 281; victory of, 252; on North Vietnam, 399 (n. 119)

Pomeroy, William, 189

Popular Action (Peru), 292

Popular Christian party (Peru), 292

Popular Revolutionary Alliance of America (APRA, Peru), 288; founding of, 290; split of, 291; under Alan Garcia, 293; boycott of elections, 296; support of Fujimori, 405 (n. 54)

Populists (Greece), 153, 154; in 1946 elections, 159, 169; coalition with Republicans, 160, 169, 171

Post–World War II era: insurgency in, 6, 11; legitimacy in, 10; nation-building in, 10; intervention in, 71

Power: and political legitimacy, 5–6, 58

Pracheachon party (Cambodia), 229, 230; Paris group in, 231; in elections, 241

"Praetorianism," 52

Principales (Philippines), 174; American rule through, 177

Propaganda, in Vietnam War, 363 (n. 4)

Propaganda Movement (Spain), 175

Provisional Government of National Union (PGNU, Laos), 238, 239, 245

Provisional Revolutionary Government (Vietnam, 1969), 104

Pye, Lucian, 35, 355 (n. 38), 391 (n. 37); on legitimacy, 31, 65; on guerrilla warfare, 37; on Third World, 353 (n. 16)

Qing Dynasty (China): legitimacy of, 133–34; fall of, 140

Quang Tri, seizure of, 106

Quezon, Manuel, 178, 187

Quinim Pholsena, 233, 396 (n. 42); assassination of, 234

Quirino, Elpidio, 181, 184, 189, 386 (n. 77); on American intervention, 191

Race, Jeffrey, 79, 114, 220; on Middle Tradition, 360 (n. 29)
Rational choice, 408 (n. 1); at opportunity level, 323, 407 (n. 88); in Vietnam War, 324; effect on development, 325
Rational choice theory, 358 (nn. 8–9); and revolution, 323–26; limitations of, 325–26; on leadership, 402 (n. 1)
Red Bands of the Sabillah (Malaya), 204
Regroupees, Cambodian, 231, 235, 255
Reorganization War (China, 1928–30), 137
Republican Party (Greece), 153, 154; coalition with Populists, 160, 169, 171; acceptance of monarchy, 163
Resistance War. See Franco–Viet Minh War (1946–54)
Reversibilities. See Insurgency: dynamics of balance in (under individual country)
Revolutionary Alliance (China), 134
Revolutionary determinism, 126
Revolutionary Development Program (South Vietnam), 117
Revolutionary strategy, 348, 370 (n. 11); in Vietnam War, xi, 120, 128, 219, 273, 308, 317, 357 (n. 52); of Marxist people's wars, 10, 13–14, 26, 33, 46–47, 280–81, 313; of insurgents, 10, 33, 68; focalist, 14, 33; effect on legitimacy, 26, 67–70, 352 (n. 9); of Lenin, 33, 46–47, 67, 68; in Third World, 33, 358 (n. 8); of Mao Zedong, 46–47, 77, 80, 144–45, 266, 282, 317, 357 (n. 52); legitimacy of belief in, 69; intervention in, 70; of Viet Minh, 93; of Greek communists, 164–65, 171–72, 281; of Sendero Luminoso, 292–93; of North Vietnam, 330
Revolutions: types of, 33; European, 38–39; effect on social order, 68, 361 (n. 46)
Rice cultivation (Malaya), 198, 388 (n. 8), 389 (n. 22)
Rizal, José, 175, 176, 186, 387 (n. 89)
Rostow, Walt, 39, 340; on modernization, 43; on economic development, 50, 357 (n. 3)
Roxas, Manuel, 179; collaboration of, 188; American aid to, 190
Royal Laotian Army (RLA), 232, 237
Rubber plantations: of Malaya, 199, 388 (n. 8); of Cambodia, 225
Rural credit, 72; from incumbents, 76; in South Vietnam, 115, 123
Rural populations. See Peasants
Russia: intervention in Greece, 153
Russian Revolution, 361 (n. 46)

Saigon: fall of, 3, 11, 110, 315, 324; social relations in, 120; in Tet offensive, 334–35
Sakdalist insurrection (Philippines), 177, 384 (n. 25)
Saloth Sar. See Pol Pot
Sangha (Buddhist clergy), 224, 225; and Cao Daiism, 226; Norodom Sihanouk's cultivation of, 241; divisions within, 244, 245; and Pathet Lao, 244, 254, 258; Dhammaraja of, 245–46
Sangkum party. See People's Socialist Community (Sangkum Reastr Niyum, Cambodia)
San Martin, José de, 290
Santos, Pedro Abad, 178, 188–89, 384 (n. 27)
Saul (king of Israel), 38
Savang Vatthana (king of Laos), 239
Schwartzkopf, Norman, 321
Scipio Africanus, 194
SEATO treaty, 42
Security, personal, 60, 76; in Laos, 243
Selangor (Federated Malay States), 200
Sendero Luminoso (Peru), 15, 55; founding of, 289, 297, 403 (n. 33); revolutionary strategy of, 292–83, 404 (n. 36), 406 (n. 67); future of, 294, 304; urban policy of, 295, 300, 405 (n. 51); boycott of elections, 296, 318; drug dealings of, 297; rural policy of, 297–98; and legal left, 298; self-reliance of, 300, 304; crossover points of, 300, 305–6; terrorism by, 301, 303, 308, 404 (n. 41);

critical mass of, 305; breakout of, 305,
308; leadership of, 306; belief-level
appeal of, 307; victory over MRTA, 405
(n. 62). *See also* Insurgency, Peruvian
Shanghai: working-class uprising in,
136; massacres (1927), 140; importance
to Chiang Kai-shek, 141, 375 (n. 41);
nationalists in, 148; factory workers in,
373 (n. 9)
Shining Path. *See* Sendero Luminoso
Shultz, George, 328
Sian incident (China, 1936), 285
Sihanouk, Norodom. *See* Norodom
Sihanouk, Prince
Singapore: fall (1942), 199, 202, 216, 217;
British in, 200; strike (1930), 202;
population of, 388 (n. 4)
Sisowath Monireth (king of Cambodia),
226
Sisowaths (Democratic party), 230
Sisowath Sirik Matak, 234, 397 (n. 56)
Sison, José Maria, 195, 196, 318; on politburo raid, 385 (n. 47)
Societal access, 26, 348, 360 (n. 31); role
in development, 63, 65; to elites, 69;
intervention in, 73; as variable in
insurgency, 76, 272, 275; in South Vietnam, 118; in Greece, 162, 168; in the
Philippines, 184; importance in insurgencies, 194, 308; in Malaya, 212, 213; in
Cambodia, 241, 258; in Laos, 258; effect
of land reform on, 271; for labor force,
272; in people's war, 281; in Peruvian
insurgency, 295, 298. *See also* Land
reform
Societal norms: role in political legitimacy, 37–38, 67, 352 (n. 9); effect on
economic development, 50
Societies: "prismatic," 50; security in, 60,
76, 115; industrial, 65; effect of revolution on, 68, 361 (n. 46); Confucian, 87;
rationality in, 324; political-religious,
394 (n. 1)
— traditional, 60; "rational zone" in, 61;
in China, 134
— transitional, 50, 54–55, 59–66, 308, 318;
organization of, 60; effect of Western

ideas on, 65; "classic" modernization
theory of, 326; making of rules in, 358
(n. 8)
Society, Malayan: traditions of, 200–201;
effect of Japanese invasion on, 203–4
Society, Vietnamese: Confucian precepts
in, 87; traditionalists in, 89, 111; kinship
in, 112; of Saigon, 120; sociopolitical
aspects of, 126
Solomon (king of Israel), 66
Solon (lawgiver), 38
Somoza, Anastasio, 46
Son Ngoc Minh, 228
Son Ngoc Thanh, 226, 230
Souphanouvong, Prince, 227; aid from
Viet Minh, 228; in 1958 elections, 232;
in coalition government, 233; in Provisional Government, 239; in Lao Issara,
243; as president, 245
South Africa, nonlegitimacy in, 52
Southeast Asia: images of legitimacy in,
65; Golden Triangle of, 152; monarchy
in, 395 (n. 5)
South Vietnam: elections (1960s), 64,
102, 113, 317; elections (1970s), 64, 105,
116–17, 124; illegitimacy of government, 73, 81, 124–25, 219, 371 (n. 27);
military strength of, 81; National
Police of, 99; American military
strength in, 99, 150; Strategic Hamlet Program of, 99, 333; Constituent
Assembly, 102, 113; elections, 102, 129,
150, 220; urban population of, 102, 367
(n. 53); land reform in, 104–5, 116, 118,
120, 124, 130, 368 (nn. 62–63); in Paris
Peace Agreement, 108; resettlement
programs of, 114; legitimacy of government, 114–20, 124, 129; Land Reform
Act (1956), 116; legitimacy of opportunity in, 116, 123–24, 258; Revolutionary
Development Program, 117; societal
access in, 118; terrorism in, 118; corruption in, 120, 371 (n. 23); National
Assembly, 126; political parties in, 126,
127; collaboration with French, 127, 372
(n. 46); per capita income in, 222. *See
also* Intervention, American

—GVN: Regional Forces of, 114; rural policy of, 114–15, 116, 124; land reform of, 118; legitimacy of belief in, 118, 258; lack of commitment to, 119; constituencies of, 126; political legitimacy of, 219; commitment to, 368 (n. 61); pacification efforts of, 371 (n. 22)

Souvanna Phouma, Prince, 238; coalition government of, 232, 233, 234; relations with United States, 237, 253, 257, 396 (n. 42); resignation of, 239, 257; in Lao Issara, 243; death of, 245; legitimacy of, 259, 309; leadership of, 283, 284

Sovereignty: European conceptualization of, xiii; United Nations on, 70; effect of intervention on, 70, 71, 362 (n. 56); Vietnamese, 123

Soviet Union: nation-building by, 10; expansionism of, 41, 315; detonation of atomic bomb, 41–42; foreign policy of, 44; influence in Third World, 44, 356 (n. 47); aid to North Vietnam, 106, 109, 121, 123; aid to China, 135, 145, 147, 374 (n. 11), 376 (n. 54); influence on Sun Yat-Sen, 142, 375 (n. 45); in Manchuria, 147; intervention in Greece, 157, 166, 381 (n. 71); support of Malayan Communist party, 215; support of Pathet Lao, 253, 256; disintegration of, 320; support of North Vietnam, 371 (nn. 29, 31); aid to PLA, 376 (n. 69)

Spain: conquest of Philippines, 174–75, 190; conquest of Peru, 289–90

Spanish-American War, 175–76

Spirit of Camp David, 314

Sri Vijaya (Indonesia), 199

Stagnation: in nonlegitimacy, 54

Stalin, Joseph: influence with Chinese communists, 136, 147; accord with Churchill, 157, 158, 166; on ELAS, 166, 381 (n. 70); influence in Cambodia, 246

State: use of force by, 32–33; cohesive forces in, 38; bureaucratic, 39; Western concept of, 65; respect for sovereignty of, 70; "soft," 359 (n. 10); as predatory organization, 359 (n. 14); evolution of, 360 (n. 31)

Stilwell, Joseph, 146

Strategic breakout. See Breakout, strategic

Strategic Hamlet Program (South Vietnam), 99, 333

Structural dualism, 89

Student protesters, 105, 122

Sultanates, Malayan, 200–201, 388 (n. 11); of Perak, 200; under Japanese, 202, 390 (n. 31); dissolution of, 204; British acquisition of, 391 (n. 33)

Sumlaut uprising (Cambodia), 232, 233, 234, 241

Sun-Joffe Agreement (China–Soviet Union, 1923), 135, 145

Sun Yat-Sen, 134; "people's livelihood" of, 135, 144, 148; Three People's Principles of, 135, 290; and modernization, 140, 142; schools of, 141; and Soviet influence, 142, 375 (n. 45)

Taft, William Howard, 176

Tagalogs (Philippines), 174, 184, 186, 192; support of Magsaysay, 386 (n. 103)

Talleyrand-Perigord, Charles Maurice, 38, 355 (n. 32); on legitimacy, 39

Ta Mok, 248

Tan Cheng Lock, 209, 394 (n. 95); in Bailing talks, 208; and tunku Adbul Rahman, 212; implementation of Briggs plan, 217; leadership of, 220, 283; on education, 393 (n. 91); on the tunku, 394 (n. 95)

Tan Dai Viets (political party), 117, 215

Terrorism: role in legitimation, 69; in South Vietnam, 118; Chiang Kai-shek's use of, 136; by Greek communists, 157, 161, 378 (n. 19), 380 (n. 41); in Malayan Emergency, 205, 214; of MPAJA, 210, 217; of Pol Pot, 248–49, 261, 281; by Sendero Luminoso, 301, 303, 308; of North Vietnamese, 333; Huk use of, 386 (n. 72)

Tet offensive (1968), xi, 103, 334–40, 368 (n. 58); effect on legitimacy, 74, 279; effect on public opinion, 104, 122; effect on outcome of war, 127, 269,

270, 337, 344; as end of people's war, 128, 150, 273, 281, 330, 339–40, 341, 346; casualties in, 335, 411 (n. 19); American response to, 335–39; first wave of, 336; goals of, 336; and southern communists, 412 (n. 33)

Thailand: aggression against Laos/ Cambodia, 223, 225; alliance with Japanese, 227; mercenaries of, 237, 238, 253; Military Advisory Group in, 252; society of, 394 (n. 1)

Thang Long (Hanoi), 87

Thien Minh. *See* Mandate of Heaven

Thompson, Sir Robert, 107, 218, 369 (n. 73)

Thrace, Greek control of, 153, 154

Tien An Minh square incident, 308

Tito, Marshall, 159, 166

Tonkin, French control over, 88, 89

Touby Lyfang, 244

Touch Samouth, 231

Tran Ngoc Minh, 231

Tran Ngoc Thanh, 234–35

Tran Trong Kim, 364 (n. 16)

Tran Van Giau, 248

Tran Van Tra, 339

Treaty of Lausanne (1923), 153

Trengganu (Unfederated Malay States), 201, 391 (n. 33)

Triple Alliance (Malaya), 208, 215; Chinese rejection of, 218; use of *merdeka* issue, 219; legitimacy of, 393 (n. 95)

Trotsky, Leon, 36, 68

Trotskyites, Vietnamese, 91, 98; failure of, 364 (n. 14)

Truman administration, 82; Greek policy of, 382 (n. 84)

Truman doctrine, 164, 171

Truong Chinh, 332, 357 (n. 52), 365 (n. 17); on Tet offensive, 338, 339–40

Tu Duc (Vietnamese ruler), 88, 89, 112

Tunku (Malaya). *See* Abdul Rahman

Tupac Amaru II (Incan emperor), 404 (n. 34), 406 (n. 81)

Tupamaros (Uruguay), 14, 33

Unfederated Malay States, 201

United Front (China, 1937–41), 140, 147

United Front (Laos), 250

United Issarak Front (UIF, Cambodia), 228

United Left (IU, Peru), 292, 405 (n. 54)

United Malay National Organization (UMNO), 204, 207; Chinese in, 208; alliance with MCA, 212, 218

United Nations: United States' participation in, 41; view on sovereignty, 70; view on Vietnam War, 122; Peace Agreement on Cambodia, 259

Units for the Protection of the People's Struggle (OPLA, Greece), 158

Universal particularism, 11, 351 (ch. 1, n. 3)

University San Cristóbal de Huamanga. *See* Huamanga University

Upper Huallaga Valley (Peru), 293; Sendero Luminoso in, 297, 305–6; drug war in, 299, 306–7

Utang na loob (moral indebtedness), 182; Spanish Catholicism and, 174, 383 (n. 9); loss of, 177; of Magsaysay regime, 185; among ethnic groups, 186; communist view of, 189

Uy tin (virtue), 114, 118, 370 (n. 7)

Vafiades, Markos, 159, 165, 172

Vang Pao, 244, 250; American aid to, 253

Vann, John Paul, 220

Van Tien Dung, 109, 412 (n. 35), 413 (n. 66)

Vargas Llosa, Mario, 296, 299

Varkiza Agreement (1945), 158, 159, 164

Vattel, Emer de, 70–71, 72

Velasco Alvaredo, Juan, 291

Venizelos, Eleutherios, 153

Versailles treaty (1919), 320

Verstehen (empathy), 25, 352 (n. 8)

Vien Chang. *See* Vientiane

Vientiane (Laos), 225, 401 (n. 158); anti-American demonstrations in, 239

Vientiane Peace Agreement (1973), 259; American support of, 256, 257, 269

Viet Bac: Viet Minh in, 93, 94

Viet Cong: sappers, 35, 64; organization

of, 36; ralliers, 37; use of terror, 69; mobilization of, 100, 101; casualties of, 101–2, 106, 110, 115, 369 (n. 82); numerical strength of, 101–2, 367 (n. 52); legitimacy of, 114, 115, 287; peasant support for, 115–16, 361 (n. 48); exclusion from political process, 126; leadership of, 220; urban policy of, 298; in Tet offensive, 334–35. *See also* Communists, Vietnamese

Viet Minh, 340; in Indochina, 42, 44; formation of, 91; during World War II, 91; negotiations with French (1945), 92; war with France, 92–97; strategies of, 93; Chinese aid to, 94–95; control of rural areas, 95; casualties of, 96; at Dienbienphu, 96; victory of, 111; land reform by, 116; assassinations by, 127; errors of, 128; Cambodians in, 226; in Laos, 228, 229; in Cambodia, 228, 231

Vietnam I. *See* Franco–Viet Minh War

Vietnam II. *See* Vietnam War

Vietnamization: French policy of, 94, 95; Nixon's policy of, 104, 106, 129, 251, 401 (n. 155)

Vietnam War: lessons of, xi, 3–5, 7, 9–10, 15, 25, 28–29, 129, 286, 313, 321, 330, 349; character of, xi, 4; as Marxist people's war, xi, 46, 120, 150, 219, 273, 344–46, 410 (n. 9); revolutionary strategy in, xi, 120, 128, 219, 273, 308, 317, 357 (n. 52); as conventional war, xii, 103, 120, 334, 343–46; effect on American society, 3; as insurgency, 5, 120; international context of, 7, 40; historical context of, 10; before Tet, 97–104; escalation of, 100–101; American military strategy in, 101, 103, 130, 337, 340–42, 391 (n. 50), 413 (nn. 57–58); American airpower in, 101, 106, 107, 122, 125; casualties in, 101–2, 104, 107, 110, 115, 369 (n. 82); crossover points in, 103, 130; effect of Tet on, 103–4; after Tet, 104–10; opposition to, 105, 122–23; protest against, 105, 335–36; Linebacker bombing campaigns, 106, 107; peace negotiations in, 106–8; Christmas

bombing (1971), 107, 369 (n. 72); levels of legitimacy in, 114; break-out in, 118; scale of intervention in, 120–25; as guerrilla insurgency, 121, 345, United Nations' view of, 122; American naval forces in, 125; levels of intervention in, 125; ground combat troops in, 125, 219, 333–34, 342; reversibility of outcome, 126–28; comparisons with Chinese revolution, 150–51; comparisons with Greek civil wars, 171–72; effect on Laos/Cambodia, 240, 251, 255; effect of World War II on, 270; legitimacy of belief in, 282; leadership in, 284; comparison with Sendero Luminoso, 304; rational choice in, 324; propaganda in, 363 (n. 4); civilian casualties in, 370 (n. 10); rotation policy in, 372 (n. 41). *See also* Intervention, American; Tet offensive

Visayas (Philippines), 174

Vitsi and Grammos: communist defeat at, 160, 168, 172, 274, 284; Vafiades's defense of, 166

Vo Nguyen Giap, 91, 124, 150, 357 (n. 52); victories of, 94, 95; and Dienbienphu, 96, 329, 332; on American imperialism, 315; on people's war, 331, 333; mobilization of peasants, 332; and Tet offensive, 338, 344; errors of, 342–43; strategy of, 410 (n. 1)

Walang hiya (shamelessness), 174, 188, 383 (n. 9)

Wallace, George C., 122

Wang Jingwei, 147

Wang Ming, 248

War Powers Act (1973), 108–9, 123

Watergate affair, 108, 123, 129

Weber, Max: on insurgency, 25; on legitimacy, 31, 32, 39, 354 (n. 20); on leadership, 36; social theory of, 325–26

Weimar Republic, 321

Weinberger, Casper, 3, 328

Weltanschauung, 314–15; of Southeast Asia, 394 (n. 1)

Western bloc: role in international system, 31; military superiority of, 43

Westmoreland, William C., 411 (n. 23); strategy of, 101, 103, 130, 337, 341; on Viet Cong, 102, 367 (n. 52); and Korean War, 125; on North Vietnamese strategy, 329–30; *A Soldier Reports*, 410 (n. 1)

Westmoreland v. CBS trial, 102

Whampoa Military Academy (China), 145

Wheeler, Earle G., 335, 411 (n. 23)

White Man's Burden, 39

Wilson, Woodrow, 320, 321

Workers party of Kampuchea, 231

World War II: blitzkrieg in, 9; effect on insurgencies, 25, 191, 267, 270–71, 300, 319; effect on international politics, 43; nationalism during, 59–60; in Asia, 91; China-Burma-India theater in, 146; Greece during, 155–57, 161, 168–69, 171, 172; casualties in, 159; in the Philippines, 178–80, 183, 187–88, 191–92; in Malaya, 202–4; effect on Malayan economy, 209; Laos/Cambodia in, 226, 260, 268

Wuhan government (China), 136

"X" article (Kennan), 41, 43

Xian Incident (China, 1936), 140, 142, 151

"X" organization (Greece), 159, 160

Yalta Conference, 158

Yalta System, 41

Yao people (Laos), 244

Yen Bay mutiny (Vietnam, 1930), 90, 384 (n. 25)

Yugoslavia: surrender to Hitler, 155; Greek communists and, 159, 160, 166, 170; expulsion from Cominform, 160; partisan warfare in, 161

Zakhariadis, Nikos, 163, 165

Zervas, Napoleon, 156

Zhang Guotao, 138

Zhang Xueliang, 138, 328 (n. 28)

Zhdanov, Andrei, 166

Zhou Enlai, 136, 374 (n. 28); support of Mao, 137; education of, 400 (n. 127)

Zimbabwe, guerrilla war in, 15